YELLOW PAGES

VERENA ISSEL

INSTALLATIONS AND THEIR INDIVIDUAL COMPONENTS

M

+000 (7) .... *Preface*

INSTALLATIONS AND THEIR INDIVIDUAL COMPONENTS

+000 (21) .... *Traurige Tropen*
+000 (35) .... *Aset in Tadmor*
+000 (47) .... *Soft Ruins*
+000 (57) .... *Szenenwechsel/ Der fünfte Sockel*
+000 (69) .... *Backlash I*
+000 (91) .... *Backlash II*
+000 (105) .... *Petromania/Petromanus*
+000 (117) .... *Ethno Ethno & Trophy Delight*
+000 (133) .... *Modern Narcissus/ Temple Guardian*
+000 (139) .... *Grids and Flowers*
+000 (159) .... *Kunst-am-Bau-Projekt: Kindergarten „Am Krautgarten"*
+000 (167) .... *What I never thought (Umfragebasiertes Neonbett)*
+000 (179) .... *January Depression (Remedy)*
+000 (199) .... *January Depression*
+000 (207) .... *Klapp Klapp (January Depression)*
+000 (219) .... *Schnuckentempel*
+000 (227) .... *Antikensammlung*
+000 (235) .... *Die Brüste des Tiresias nach Apollinaire*
+000 (251) .... *Pandora Papers*
+000 (267) .... *Soundsoviele Thesen*
+000 (275) .... *Escaping the Mundane (Psychogeographies)*
+000 (287) .... *Autoscooter*
+000 (297) .... *Fitness. Kraft und Schönheit*
+000 (313) .... *Lob des Lernens*
+000 (325) .... *Silent Utopia (Murals of a Tourist)*
+000 (333) .... *Wurzelpost (Ecosystem M)*
+000 (341) .... *Argo (Wabi Sabi)*
+000 (349) .... *Hidden Agenda*
+000 (363) .... *WeChat*
+000 (377) .... *On Display (Aboriginality)*
+000 (385) .... *Strikes Back – Solar Radiation Management, Carbon Dioxide Removal, the Jungle and My Grandmother*
+000 (393) .... *Nugae*
+000 (409) .... *Dummheit von 1000 Töpfe (Das Moor: Überwachungsstaat)*

PAINTINGS AND OBJECTS

+000 (423) .... *Various works*

APPENDIX

+000 (451) .... *About the artist*
+000 (452) .... *Photo credits*
+000 (453) .... *Acknowledgements*
+000 (458) .... *Colophon*

M

YELLOW PAGES. INSTALLATIONS AND THEIR INDIVIDUAL COMPONENTS

EN There is a lot going on when you enter an installation by Verena Issel. Different textures, colors, and artistic practices collide, and it takes a moment to get an overview. Issel's works are microcosms, and not only in this respect. What happens on a large scale is revealed here on a (usually not quite so) small scale. Like a magnifying glass, they make various processes in the world visible, be it the shady corruption that holds governments together, the way we deal with nature and its exoticization, or the underlying processes that give the world the form it has.

In order to sort and understand these different components that come together in Verena Issel's installations and groups of works, we have this publication: *Yellow Pages*. Like the Yellow Pages that listed all the necessary contact information for businesses before the age of the Internet, all the groups and subgroups from 2004 to 2024 that together make up Verena Issel's oeuvre are collected here: on the one hand, a catalog in the classical sense and on the other hand, an opportunity to delve deeply into Verena Issel's archive and working methods. For every work of art always takes place in the context of the time in which it was created, as does the classification of this work. For this reason, the accompanying texts written at the time of the exhibition of the respective installation are included here. This is also to be understood as programmatic, for this is how Issel's practical approach works. In addition to her artistic training at the University of Fine Arts (HFBK) in Hamburg, the China Academy of Art in Hangzhou, and

M the Faculdade de Belas-Artes in Lisbon, Issel also studied Latin and Ancient Greek and holds a master's degree in classical philology.
"Delving deeply" and presenting an issue or phenomenon with archaeological thoroughness is part of the methodology of her artistic practice. This catalog thus organizes, sorts, and preserves an exuberant and complex body of work that is constantly evolving. It is a snapshot of a time in which Issel has continuously developed her artistic work over a span of twenty years.

The catalog itself can also be seen as part of Verena Issel's oeuvre. In addition to the works sorted and presented here, her oeuvre also includes artist's books and documentary films, which, for example, are devoted with surgical precision to a fish factory in Norway or a shooting club in Lower Saxony. The architecture of the space is also often a starting point for her artistic considerations. This is certainly one of the reasons why Verena Issel has been Professor of Fine Arts in the Department of Architecture at the Brandenburg University of Technology Cottbus-Senftenberg since 2023. The first localization of the human being always takes place in space, and it is from there that Issel conceives her comprehensive installations. When one speaks of "comprehensive installations," one could also speak of "world building," for Issel builds worlds that she fills with figures, works, issues, and questions that challenge the familiar view of what surrounds us. Issel's work is driven by a sincere curiosity to understand the world a little better, to sort it out, to break it down into its component parts. Her approach is always one of astonishment, but far from naïve.

M

Issel's interest in antiquity stems from classical philology, as can be seen in various works (e.g. *Nugae, Aset in Tadmor, Soft Ruins*). You can only know where you are going if you know where you have come from. This preoccupation with antiquity is central to her approach to the present.
In these works, Issel shows a colorful antiquity made of plastic: an allusion to the colorful design of antiquity that has not been preserved. Instead, today we see white marble, white temple columns and sculptures, that show only a seemingly smooth perfection. We would probably perceive this period differently today if we also took into account its colorfulness. Plastic antiquity is also an indication of the democratic and humane potential of plastic as a cheap and affordable material. Before it became clear what damage it was doing to the oceans, plastic was a beacon of hope, heralding a new age. One that was indeed full of hope. Soon, plastic will (hopefully) be as distant and remote to us as antiquity is to us today. Merely a strange greeting from a human presence that still believed it could conquer nature.

Issel repeatedly explores the intricate and complex relationship between humans and the planet (e.g., in works such as *Sad Tropics* and *Grids and Flowers*). She focuses on what is left behind when humans disappear. What is often pejoratively referred to as waste or detritus.
The small pieces of plastic, the inconspicuous objects that only attract attention when they disappear. Pipe cleaners, dividers to separate the sushi from the ginger, plastic straws, non-slip mats placed under carpets. In Issel's installations, these objects find an additional use—usually alienated and given new functions. This repurposing also

M challenges our understanding of value. A reputedly cheap material like plastic is expensive in the long run and should therefore be treated as a luxury item to be used only on special occasions. Issel's installation can certainly be seen as such a special occasion.

These groups of works are an anticipated interpretation of a present, of which one must be aware that it will soon also be the past and will then be treated as such. Namely, in a way that attempts to deduce from such human relics how we lived, what we surrounded ourselves with, and what was important to us. The fact that this story could also be told in a completely different way is inherent in all of Issel's works. Having grown up between Norway and Germany, she is aware of these small errors of interpretation in all their facets. This change of perspective is something that is also reflected in the fact that Issel presents her works as expansive installations that allow viewers to adopt different perspectives and to position themselves. Each visitor decides for him- or herself how to move through these spaces and how long to stay. The emancipation of the viewer from a predetermined line of approach is one of the most important sources of fascination in these colorful, exuberant universes, occupied by strangely friendly inhabitants that, thanks to Verena Issel, we can observe for a moment, as if under a microscope, and hopefully understand how many thousands of different perspectives there are in this wondrous world. For despite all her criticism, Issel's work always contains a reference to the beauty of the world, which is revealed not only in kitschy sunsets, but also in places and things where one would not expect it.

The past, the future, the beautiful, the ugly, the wondrous, and the cruel. Everything has a place here and can and must coexist in all its forms. Rarely has the persistence of these supposed opposites been more ethereal, friendly, and approachable. This catalog gathers and organizes all the inhabitants for the first time. It is worth getting to know them.

□ *Laura Helena Wurth*

M *YELLOW PAGES. INSTALLATIONS AND THEIR INDIVIDUAL COMPONENTS*

DE Es ist richtig viel los, wenn man eine Installation von Verena Issel betritt. Verschiedene Texturen, Farben und künstlerische Praktiken treffen aufeinander, und man braucht einen Augenblick, um sich einen Überblick zu verschaffen. Nicht nur in dieser Hinsicht sind Issels Arbeiten Mikrokosmen. Im (meistens nicht ganz so) Kleinen wird hier deutlich gemacht, was im Großen passiert. Wie eine Lupe vergrößern sie verschiedene Vorgänge in der Welt. Sei es der korrupte Filz, der Regierungen zusammenhält, der Umgang mit der Natur und ihre Exotisierung oder die unterliegenden Vorgänge, die der Welt die Form geben, die sie hat.

Um diese verschiedenen Komponenten, die in ihrem Aufeinandertreffen die Installationen und Werkgruppen von Verena Issel ergeben, zu sortieren und zu verstehen, gibt es diese Publikation: *Yellow Pages*.
Wie bei den Gelben Seiten, in denen vor den Zeiten des Internets alle Kontaktdaten verzeichnet waren, sind hier alle Gruppen und Untergruppen von 2004 bis 2024 versammelt, die gemeinsam das Werk Verena Issels ergeben. Es findet also einerseits eine Katalogisierung im klassischen Sinne statt; andererseits taucht man tief in das Archiv und die Arbeitsweise Verena Issels ein. Denn jede künstlerische Arbeit findet auch immer im Kontext des Zeitpunktes ihrer Entstehung statt und ebenso die Einordnung dieser Arbeit. Deswegen sind die Begleittexte, die zum Zeitpunkt der Ausstellung der jeweiligen Installation geschrieben wurden, mit abgedruckt.

Das ist auch deswegen geradezu programmatisch zu verstehen, weil so auch das praktische Vorgehen Issels funktioniert, die neben ihrer künstlerischen Ausbildung an der HFBK in Hamburg, der China Academy of Art Hangzhou (China) und der Faculdade de Belas-Artes Lisboa (Lissabon, Portugal) auch Latein und Altgriechisch studierte und einen Master in klassischer Philologie hat. Das In-die-Tiefe-Gehen und einen Sachverhalt oder ein Phänomen mit archäologischer Gründlichkeit darzustellen, liegt in der Methodik ihrer künstlerischen Praxis, und so ordnet, sortiert und bewahrt dieser Katalog ein überbordendes und komplexes Werk, das sich immerzu weiterentwickelt. Es ist eine Momentaufnahme zu einem Zeitpunkt, an dem Issel ihr künstlerisches Werk seit zwanzig Jahren kontinuierlich entwickelt.

Wobei auch der Katalog selbst als Teil des Werks Verena Issels zu verstehen ist. Zu ihrem Werk gehören neben den hier vorgestellten und geordneten Arbeiten auch Künstlerbücher und dokumentarische Filme, die sich mit sezierender Genauigkeit beispielsweise einer Fischfabrik in Norwegen oder einem Schützenverein in Niedersachsen widmen. Oft ist auch die Architektur des Raumes ein Ausgangspunkt ihrer künstlerischen Überlegung. Sicherlich auch ein Grund, warum Verena Issel seit 2023 die Professur für Bildende Kunst im Fachbereich Architektur an der BTU Cottbus-Senftenberg innehat. Die erste Verortung des Menschen findet immer im Raum statt, und von dort denkt Issel ihre umfassenden Installationen. Wenn man von „umfassender Installation“ spricht, dann könnte man auch von „Worldbuilding“ sprechen.

M Denn Issel baut Welten, die sie mit Figuren, Werken, Sachverhalten, Fragestellungen befüllt, die den eingeübten Blick auf das, was uns umgibt, herausfordern. Issels Arbeiten sind getrieben von einer aufrichtigen Neugier, die Welt ein bisschen besser zu verstehen, sie zu sortieren, aufzudröseln in Einzelteile. Ihr Vorgehen ist dabei immer staunend, aber weit davon entfernt, jemals naiv zu sein.

Aus der Altphilologie ergibt sich das Interesse Issels an der Antike, wie man in verschiedenen Arbeiten ablesen kann *(Nugae, Aset in Tadmor, Soft Ruins)*. Man kann nur wissen, wo man hingeht, wenn man weiß, wo man herkommt.
Und so ist gerade die Beschäftigung mit der Antike eine, die zentral ist für den Umgang mit der Gegenwart.
In diesen Werken zeigt Issel eine bunte Antike aus Plastik: eine Anspielung auf die farbenfrohe Gestaltung der Antike, die es nicht geschafft hat, bewahrt zu werden. Stattdessen sehen wir heute weißen Marmor, weiße Tempelsäulen und Skulpturen, die eine nur vermeintlich glatte Perfektion zeigen. Man würde diese Zeit heute wohl anders wahrnehmen, wenn man auch ihre Buntheit immer mitdächte.
Die Antike aus Plastik ist auch ein Hinweis auf das demokratische und menschenfreundliche Potenzial, das Plastik als günstigem und für alle erschwinglichem Wertstoff innewohnt. Bevor klar wurde, was es mit den Meeren macht, war Plastik ein Hoffnungsträger, der ein neues Zeitalter einläutete. Eines, das eigentlich hoffnungsvoll war. Bald wird Plastik (hoffentlich) so weit weg und entrückt für uns sein, wie die Antike es heute ist. Nur noch ein seltsamer Gruß aus einer menschlichen Gegenwart, die noch dachte, dass sie die Natur bezwingen könnte.

Das komplizierte und komplexe Verhältnis des Menschen zum Planeten untersucht Issel immer wieder (unter anderem in: *Traurige Tropen*, *Grids and Flowers*). Dabei konzentriert sie sich auf das, was übrig bleibt, wenn der Mensch wieder verschwindet. Das, was man gern abfällig Abfall oder Überbleibsel nennt. Die kleinen Plastikteile, die unauffälligen Gegenstände, die erst dann auffallen, wenn sie verschwinden. Pfeifenputzer, Trennscheiben, um das Sushi vom Ingwer zu trennen, Plastikstrohhalme, Antirutschmatten, die man unter Teppiche legt. Diese Gegenstände finden in Issels Installationen – zumeist verfremdet und neuen Funktionen zugeführt – einen weiterführenden Nutzen. Diese Umnutzung stellt auch das Verständnis von Wertigkeit infrage. Ein nur vermeintlich billiger Wertstoff wie Plastik muss auf lange Sicht teuer bezahlt werden, und genau deswegen sollte er wohl wie ein Luxusgut behandelt werden, das nur zu besonderen Anlässen hervorgeholt wird. Dabei kann man eine Installation Issels wohl gut und gern als einen solchen besonderen Anlass betrachten.

Diese Werkgruppen sind eine vorgegriffene Interpretation einer Gegenwart, von der man sich bewusst machen muss, dass sie schon bald ebenfalls Vergangenheit sein und dann auch als solche behandelt werden wird. Nämlich so, dass man versucht, aus den menschlichen Überbleibseln herauszulesen, wie wir gelebt haben, womit wir uns umgeben haben und was uns wichtig war. Dass diese Geschichte auch ganz anders erzählt werden könnte, dieses Potenzial wohnt allen Werken Issels inne. Aufgewachsen zwischen Norwegen und Deutschland, sind diese kleinen Interpretationsfehler ihr in allen Facetten bewusst.

M Dieser Perspektivwechsel ist etwas, das sich auch darin widerspiegelt, dass Issel ihre Arbeiten als raumgreifende Installationen präsentiert, die es dem Betrachtenden ermöglichen, verschiedene Standpunkte einzunehmen und sich selbst zu positionieren. Jeder Besuchende entscheidet selbst, wie er sich in diesen Räumen bewegt, wie lange er darin verweilt. Die Emanzipation des Betrachtenden von einer vorgegebenen Marschrichtung ist eine der wichtigsten Quellen der Faszination dieser bunten, überbordenden Universen, die bewohnt sind von seltsam-freundlichen Bewohnern, die wir dank Verena Issel für einen Moment, wie unter einem Mikroskop, betrachten können und dabei hoffentlich verstehen, wie viele Tausende verschiedene Perspektiven es auf dieser wundersamen Welt gibt. Denn trotz aller Kritik liegt in Issels Arbeit auch immer der Hinweis auf die Schönheit der Welt, die sich nicht nur in verkitschten Sonnenuntergängen zeigt, sondern auch an Orten und in Dingen, wo man sie nicht vermuten würde. Die Vergangenheit, die Zukunft, das Schöne, das Hässliche, das Wundersame und das Grausame. Alles hat hier Platz und kann und muss in all seinen Ausformungen nebeneinander existieren. Selten war das Aushalten dieser nur vermeintlichen Gegensätze ätherischer, freundlicher und zugewandter. In diesem Katalog sind erstmals alle Bewohner geordnet und versammelt. Es lohnt sich, sie kennenzulernen.

□ *Laura Helena Wurth*

INSTALLATIONS AND THEIR INDIVIDUAL COMPONENTS

M

TRAURIGE TROPEN

INGREDIENTS
Reisepalme ①
Sitzpalme ①
Instantpalme (Wegwerfpalme) ①
Zickenpalme ③
Sensenmannpalme ④
Tresenschlaupalme ⑤
Schlauchpalme (Eingeweidepalme) ⑥
Saufpalme ⑦
Raufpalme ⑧
Jesuspalme (mit dem Walther-Zögling) ⑨⑩
Beuyspalme ⑩
Reylepalme im Moseskörbchen ⑪
Franz-Erhard-Walther-Palme mit Zögling ⑫
Conceptual-Fuckers-Palme ⑬
Kuschelpalme ⑭
Weltpalme ⑮
Wegwerfpalme ②
Rothpalme ②
Militaryhasenpalme ②
Kindpalmen ②
Sauberpalmen ②
Artyfartypalme ②
Minimalpalme ②
Berghainpalmen ⑯
Erfurtpalmen ⑰⑱

EN The installation *Traurige Tropen (Tristes Tropiques)* is made up of numerous discrete objects, some green in color and each bearing the epithet "palm." Palm trees, those symbols of paradise, here manifest as arrangements of everyday objects bereft of their utilitarian functions. The mere attribution of palm-being, to which actually any random everyday object could be subjected, begets a gracefulness about the combinatorics of materials and formal similarity to real palms: a green travel bag attached to a stick turns into a Travel Palm, while several seat cushions on a staff form its counterpart, the Seat Palm; garden hoses, wine bottles and hammers make up a Drunken Brawl Palm. Other titles include the Techno Palm, the Block Palm, the Stone Palm, the Plinth Palm, Light Palms, Military Hare Palm, Mother-and-Child Palm, Clean Palm, World Palm, Arty-Farty Palm, Minimal Palm, Instant Palm, Disposable Palm, Beuys Palm, Franz Erhard Walter Palm, and Reyle Palm ... The palms become metaphors for more or less existential aspects of life: desire, travel, sitting (as well as in "being left on the shelf"), brawling (fight), stone (construction), also for fashionable necessities, assertions, and for successful growth in the forest of the arts. Their classification is not botanical but rather a comical inversion of some "scientific" taxonomy. The title *Traurige Tropen (Tristes Tropics)* refers to the eponymous book by ethnologist Claude Lévi-Strauss. In the final chapter, following a thorough analysis of Amazonian societies, he talks of the futility of attempts at one-dimensional explanation, and of that eternal question mark above and inside people's heads.

As symbols of fulfillment, the palms call paradise in question. Paradise, in fact, is slogging, brawling, traveling, sitting, boozing: a secular routine that may be—once recognized as pointless—met with humor if you yourself become a palm, traveling, boozing, sitting, in the state of highest fulfillment, and laughing at yourself.

☐ ***Uwe Carlson***

M

DE Die Installation *Traurige Tropen* besteht aus vielen einzelnen, teils grünen Gebilden, die jeweils den Beinamen ‚Palme' tragen. Palmen, Sinnbilder des Paradieses, erscheinen hier als Arrangements von Alltagsdingen, die ihrer zweckmäßigen Funktion beraubt werden. Die bloße Zuschreibung des Palmeseins, die eigentlich jeden beliebigen Alltagsgegenstand treffen könnte, erzeugt einen Liebreiz in der Kombinatorik der Materialien und der formalen Ähnlichkeit zu realen Palmen: eine an einem Stock befestigte grüne Reisetasche wird zur Reisepalme, mehrere Sitzkissen an einem Stab bilden das Gegenstück dazu, die Sitzpalme. Gartenschläuche, Weinflaschen und Hämmer sind Rauf- und Saufpalme.

Andere Titel sind Klotzpalme, Steinpalme, Sockelpalme und Leuchtpalmen, Militaryhasenpalme, Mutter mit Kindpalme, Sauberpalme, Weltpalme, Artyfartypalme, Minimalpalme, Instantpalme, Wegwerfpalme, Rothpalme und Reylepalme …

Die Palmen werden zu Metaphern für mehr oder weniger existenzielle Aspekte des Lebens: Sehnsucht, Reise, Sitzen (bleiben), Raufen (Kampf), Stein (Hausbauen) – auch für modische Notwendigkeiten, Behauptungen und erfolgreiches Wachstum im Wald der Kunst.

Ihre Klassifizierung ist keine botanische, eher eine komische Verkehrung einer „naturwissenschaftlichen" Taxonomie. Der Titel *Traurige Tropen* bezieht sich auf das gleichnamige Buch des Ethnologen Claude Lévi-Strauss. Er spricht im Schlusskapitel, nachdem er die Gesellschaften des Amazonas gründlich analysiert hatte, von der Sinnlosigkeit der Versuche eindimensionaler Erklärungen, von dem ewigen Fragezeichen über und in den Köpfen der Menschen.

Die Palmen als Symbol für Erfüllung stellen das Paradies infrage. Paradies, das ist Klotzen, Raufen, Reisen, Schlauchen, Sitzen, Saufen. Ein weltlicher Alltag, dem, wenn er selbst als sinnlos erkannt wird, mit Humor begegnet werden kann, indem man selbst zur Palme wird; reisend, saufend, sitzend, im Zustand höchster Erfüllung, über sich selber lacht.

□ ***Uwe Carlson***

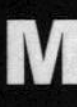

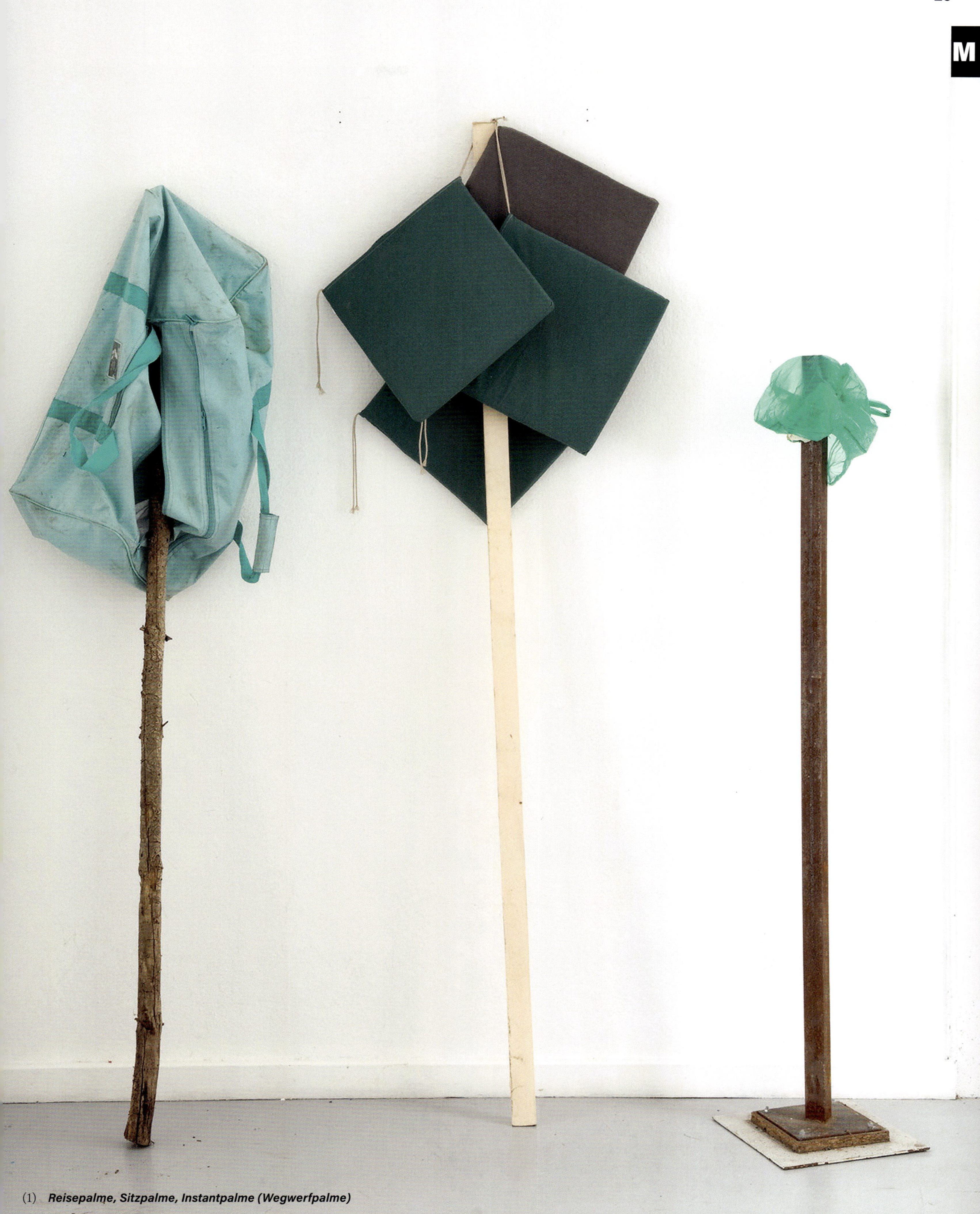

(1) ***Reisepalme, Sitzpalme, Instantpalme (Wegwerfpalme)***

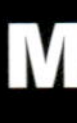

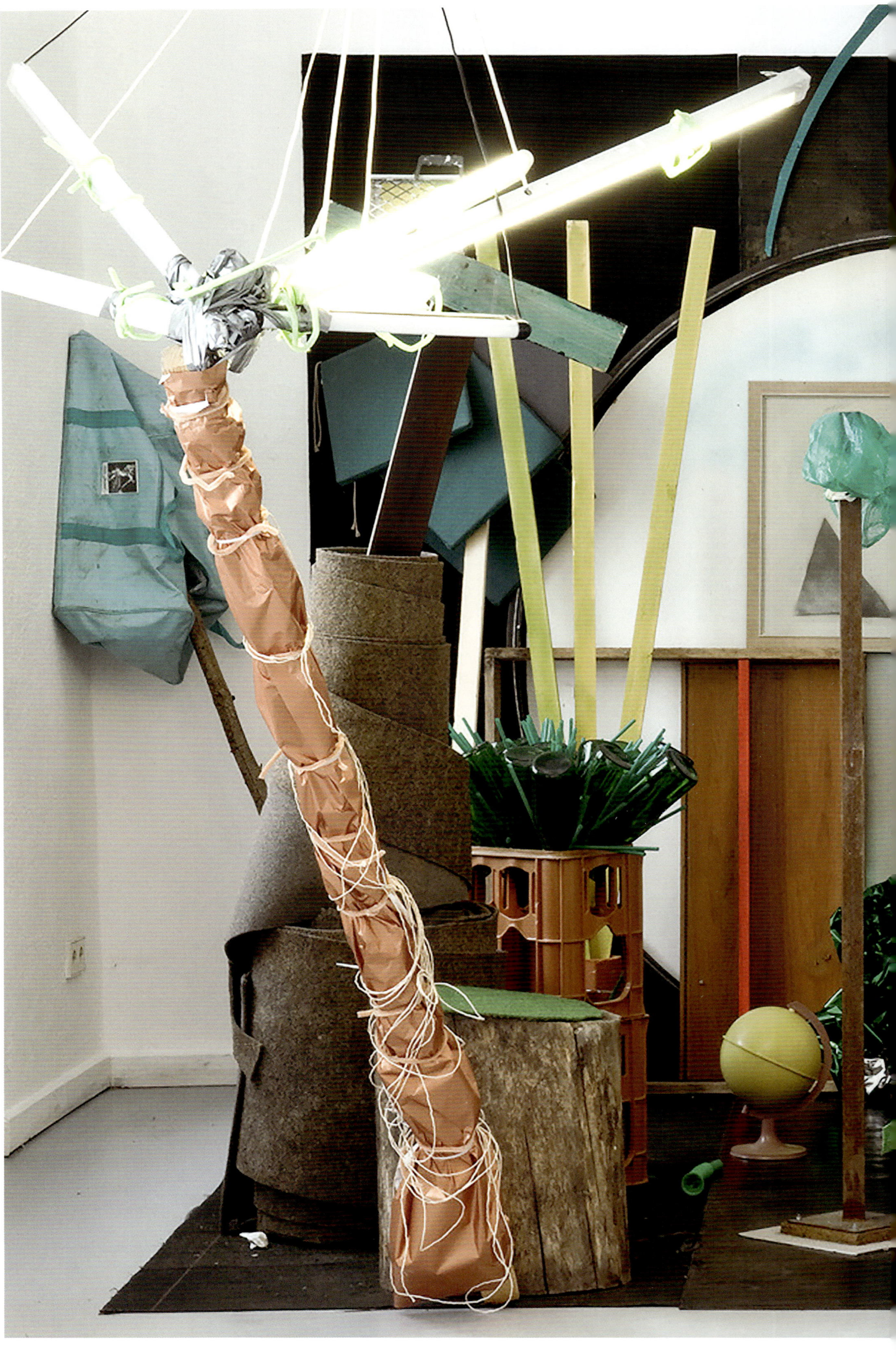

(2) ***Traurige Tropen***
2009, various materials, approx. 4 × 4 × 2.5 m, Installation view Kunstverein Ettlingen, 2010

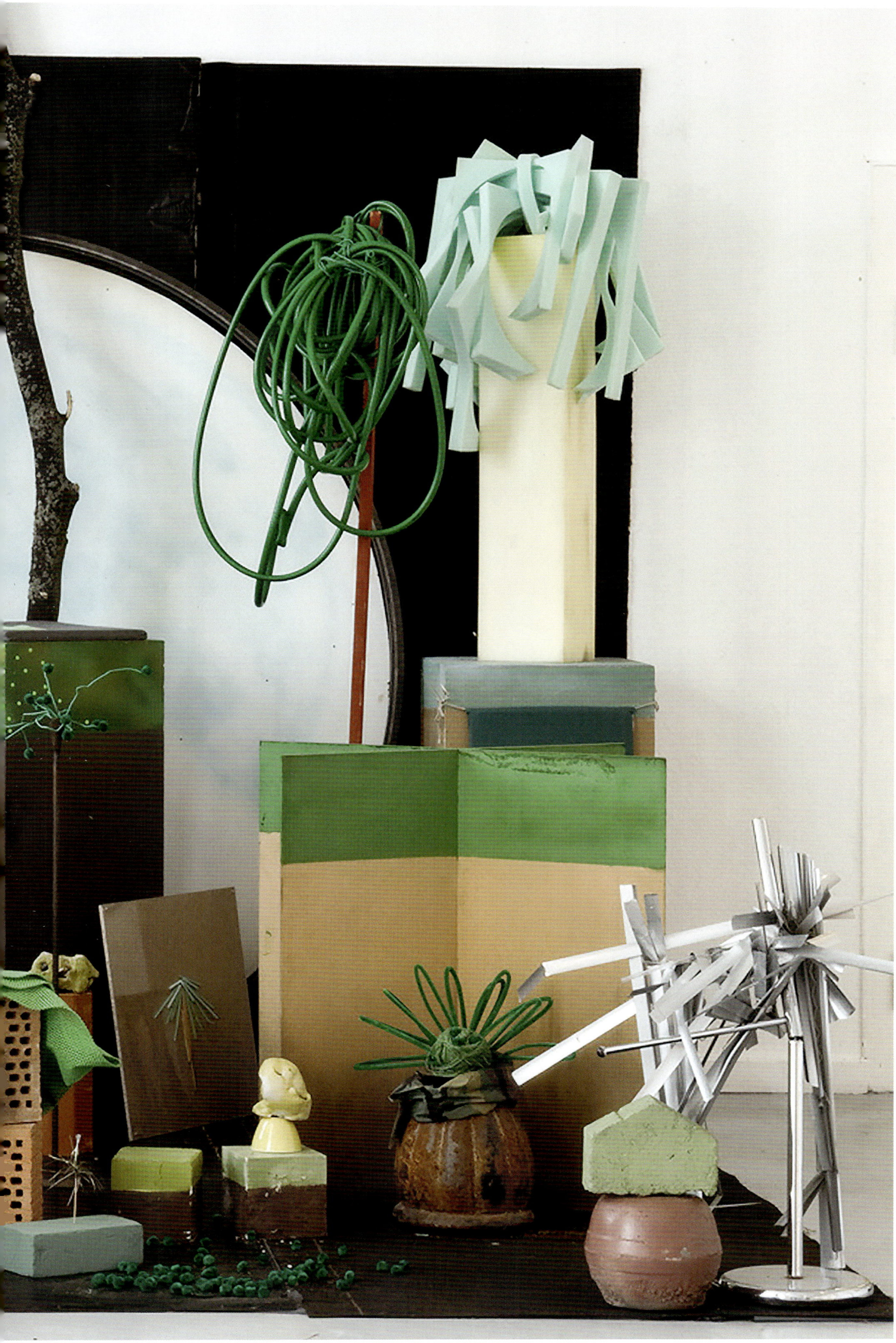

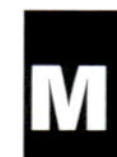

U

(3) ***Zickenpalme***
(4) ***Sensenmannpalme***
(5) ***Tresenschlaupalme***
(6) ***Schlauchpalme (Eingeweidepalme)***
(7) ***Saufpalme, Raufpalme***
(8) ***Jesuspalme (mit dem Walther-Zögling)***
(9) ***Beuyspalme***
(10) ***Reylepalme im Moseskörbchen***
(11) ***Franz-Erhard-Walther-Palme mit Zögling***
(12) ***Conceptual-Fuckers-Palme***
(13) ***Kuschelpalme***
(14) ***Weltpalme***

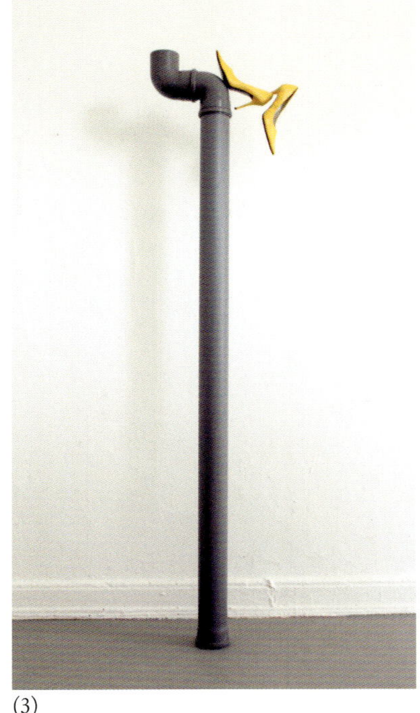
(3)

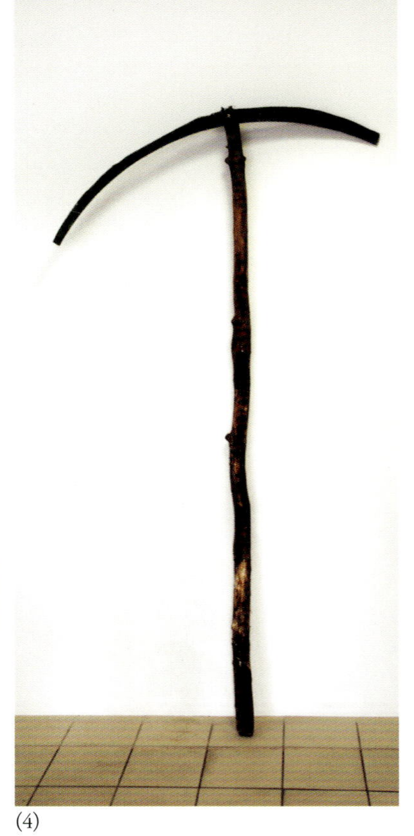
(4)

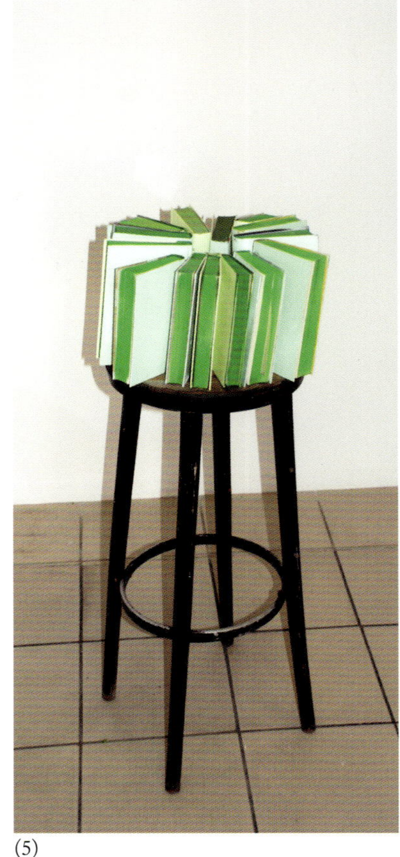
(5)

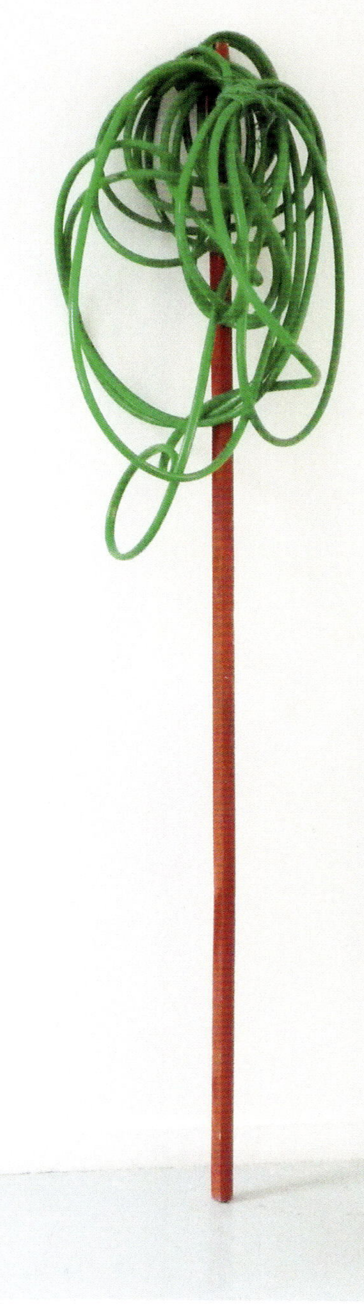
(6)

U

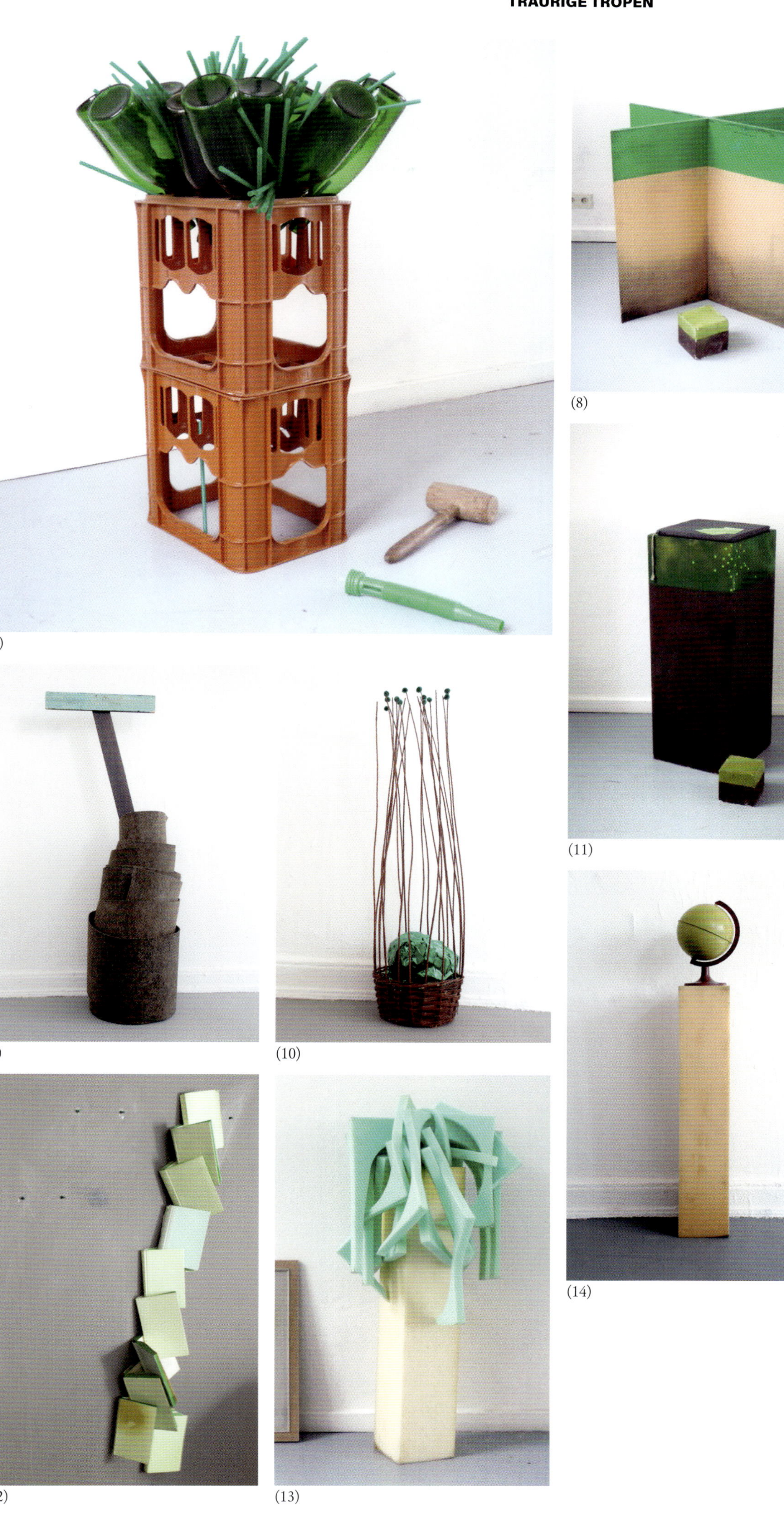

(7)

(8)

(9)

(10)

(11)

(12)

(13)

(14)

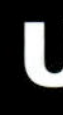

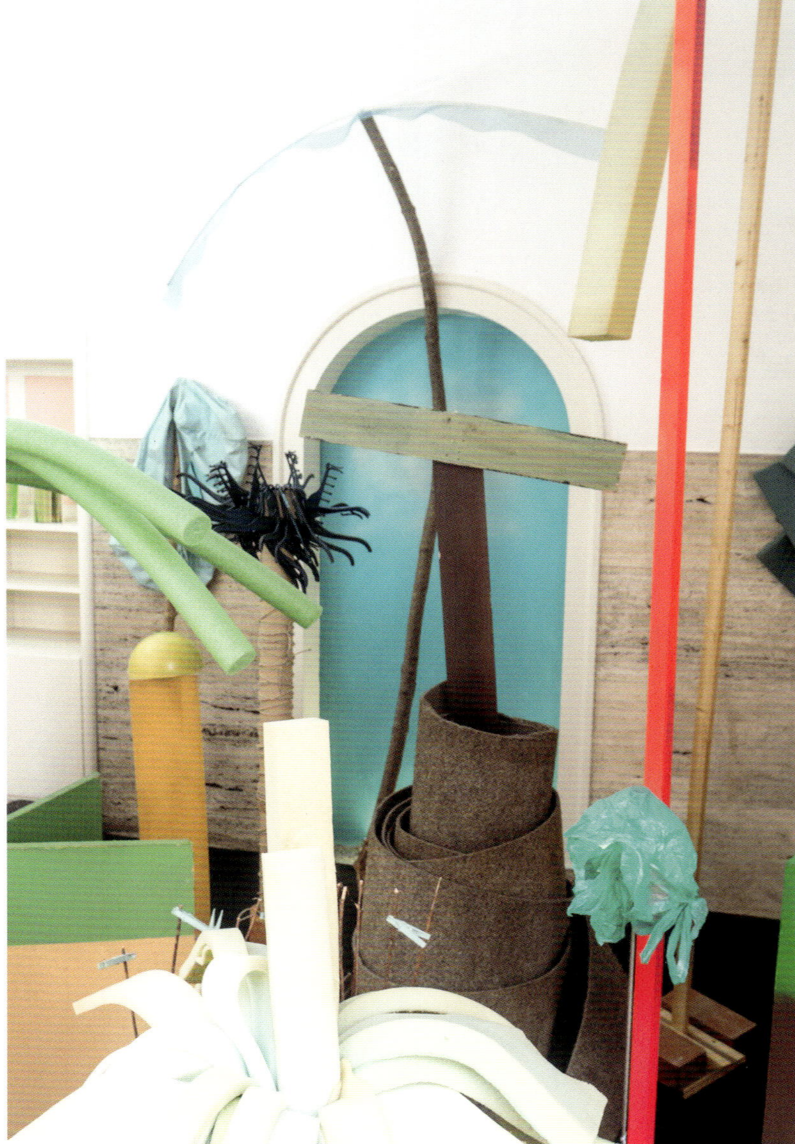

(15)

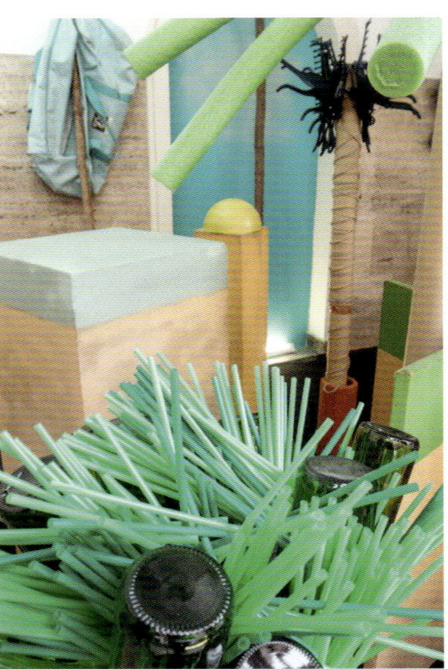

(16)

(15)
(16) ***Traurige Tropen***
2021, various materials, approx. 6 × 4 m, Installation view Hammerschmidt & Gladigau

U

ASET IN TADMOR

INGREDIENTS
Soft Column I (object) ②
Soft Wall (object) ②
Soft Column II (object) ②
Syrian Carpet Roll Column I (object) ①
Lazy Column (object) ②
Shards (object) ②
Friendly Buildings (assemblage) ②
Touch (painting) ②
Window (assemblage) ②
Syrian Carpet Roll Column II (object) ②
Window (assemblage) ①
Forbidden (assemblage) ①
Fashion (assemblage) ②

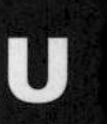

EN For the fourth exhibition of the *RADAR* series, the LWL Museum for Art and Culture and the Westfälischer Kunstverein invited Verena Issel from Hamburg. For the cooperatively used space between the two institutions, the artist arranged an installation titled *Aset in Tadmor*, which stages the large window as the display side. The glass pane acts as the fourth wall, turning the otherwise accessible exhibition space into a showcase only visible from the outside. Inside, the walls are dominated by the color pink. Various constructions and objects are distributed across the exhibition space, with one side facing the viewer. They formally reference window displays, stage designs, and set architectures. The supported surfaces inevitably evoke the added facades of Münster's Prinzipalmarkt. Verena Issel mounted architectural features made of foam and fragments from various materials, such as brown plastic flower pots, onto mainly light gray and pastel-colored wooden elements. With short lifespans, they stand in contrast to their referents: antique column forms, ceramic shards, arches, and massive walls. Everything is a backdrop. Bright spotlights additionally illuminate the scene, resembling both a tourist-prepared ancient site and, at the same time, a battlefield with wood elements resembling targets. Sarcasm finds its way through the pink space. Questions about the transience of historical buildings and relics of ancient cultures, the handling of destroyed sites, their possible reconstruction, and the preservation of objects in museums penetrate through the glass pane. The exhibition's title directly alludes to the unrest and civil wars in the Middle East and western Asia: 'Aset' is the Middle Egyptian name for the goddess Isis, the mother goddess in ancient Egyptian belief. Depending on the interpretation, she is associated with destruction or reconstruction. The term 'Tadmor,' derived from Old Arabic, still refers today to the ancient desert city of Palmyra in Syria. The dual meaning of Isis, the first self-proclaimed Islamic State (ISIS: Islamic State in Iraq and Syria), and its responsibility for the destruction of the ancient temple complex in Palmyra in the summer and fall of 2015 was the starting point for the artist's exploration. With her visual language and the chosen title, Verena Issel holds a bittersweet focus on the far-reaching consequences of the destruction of ancient sites. With European distance and a somewhat nonchalant lightness, she also questions the instrumentalization, displacement, and reconstruction of historical cultural monuments in other countries and thus the notion of societal identity. The exhibition is curated by Jenni Henke and Marijke Lukowicz.

☐ ***Marijke Lukowicz, exhibtion text***

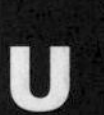

DE Für die vierte Ausstellung in der Reihe *RADAR* haben das LWL-Museum für Kunst und Kultur und der Westfälische Kunstverein die Hamburgerin Verena Issel eingeladen.
Eigens für den in Kooperation genutzten Raum zwischen den beiden Institutionen arrangierte die Künstlerin mit *Aset in Tadmor* eine Installation, welche das große Fenster als Schauseite inszeniert. Die Glasscheibe mimt dabei die vierte Wand. Sie macht aus dem sonst begehbaren Ausstellungsort einen lediglich von außen einsehbaren Schaukasten. Drinnen herrscht die Farbe Rosa an den Wänden. Auf der Ausstellungsfläche verteilt stehen verschiedenartige Konstruktionen und Objekte, die sich mit einer Schauseite dem Betrachter zuwenden. Sie nehmen formal Bezug zu Schaufensterdekorationen, Bühnenbildern und Kulissenarchitekturen. Die abgestützten Flächen vergegenwärtigen unweigerlich die aufgesetzten Fassaden des Münsteraner Prinzipalmarktes. Auf die hauptsächlich hellgrauen und pastellfarbenen Holzelemente montierte Verena Issel Scheinarchitekturen aus Schaumstoff sowie Fragmente aus verschiedenen Materialien wie beispielsweise braune Plastikblumenkübel. Mit ihrer kurzen Lebensdauer stehen sie im Gegensatz zu dem, was sie darstellen: antike Säulenformen, Keramikscherben, Torbögen und massive Mauern. Ding und Bedeutung sind nicht eins, alles ist Kulisse. Helle Scheinwerfer erleuchten zusätzlich die Szenerie, die einerseits einer für Touristen hergerichteten antiken Stätte ähnelt. Andererseits fliegen locker die Fetzen, die Holzelemente gleichen Zielscheiben, das Spielfeld ist zugleich Schlachtfeld. Der Sarkasmus bahnt sich seinen Weg durch den rosafarbenen Raum. Fragen nach der Vergänglichkeit historischer Bauwerke und von Relikten antiker Kulturen, nach dem Umgang mit zerstörten Stätten, ihrem möglichen Wiederaufbau sowie der Verwahrung von Objekten in Museen dringen durch die Glasscheibe.
Mit dem Titel der Ausstellung spielt Verena Issel konkret auf die Unruhen und Bürgerkriege im Nahen Osten und Vorderasien an: „Aset" ist der mittelägyptische Name der Göttin Isis, der Muttergöttin im altägyptischen Glauben. Je nach Interpretation wird sie mit Zerstörung oder Wiederaufbau in Verbindung gebracht. Die aus dem Altarabischen stammende Bezeichnung „Tadmor" hingegen bezeichnet noch heute die antike Wüstenstadt Palmyra in Syrien. Die doppelte Wortbedeutung von Isis, dem ersten selbst ernannten Islamischen Staat (ISIS: Islamischer Staat im Irak und Syrien) und dessen Verantwortlichkeit für die Zerstörung der antiken Tempelanlage in Palmyra im Sommer und Herbst 2015, war der Ausgangspunkt für die Auseinandersetzung der Künstlerin. Mit ihrer Bildsprache und dem gesetzten Titel richtet Verena Issel bittersüß ihren Fokus auf die weitgreifenden Folgen der Zerstörung antiker Stätten: Mit europäischer Distanz, einer durchaus nonchalanten Leichtigkeit befragt sie darüber hinaus auch die Instrumentalisierung, die Verschiebung und den Wiederaufbau historischer Kulturdenkmäler in anderen Ländern und damit die Vorstellung von gesellschaftlicher Identität.
Die Ausstellung wird kuratiert von Jenni Henke und Marijke Lukowicz.

☐ ***Marijke Lukowicz, Ausstellungstext***

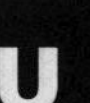

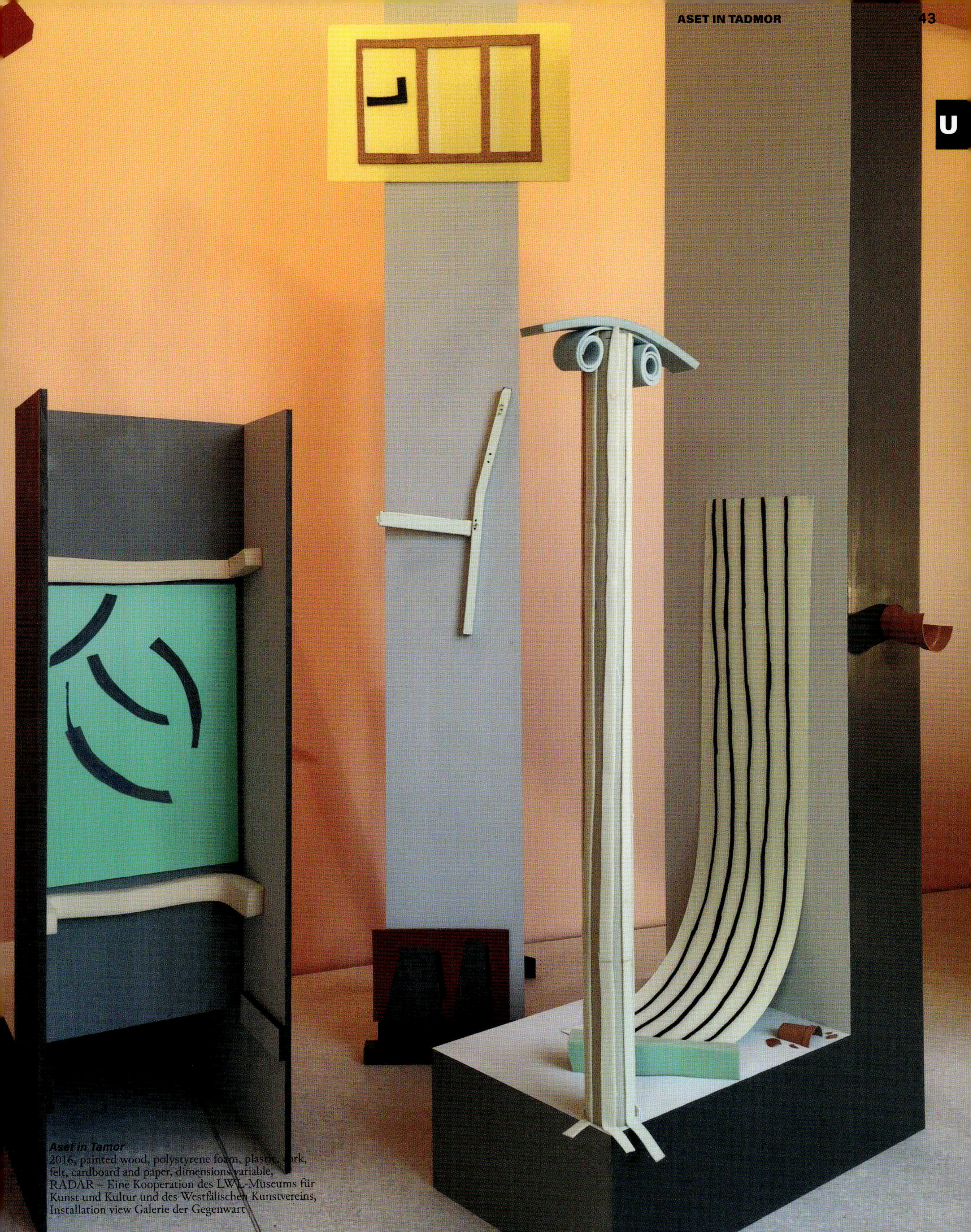

Aset in Tamor
2016, painted wood, polystyrene foam, plastic, cork, felt, cardboard and paper, dimensions variable, RADAR – Eine Kooperation des LWL-Museums für Kunst und Kultur und des Westfälischen Kunstvereins, Installation view Galerie der Gegenwart

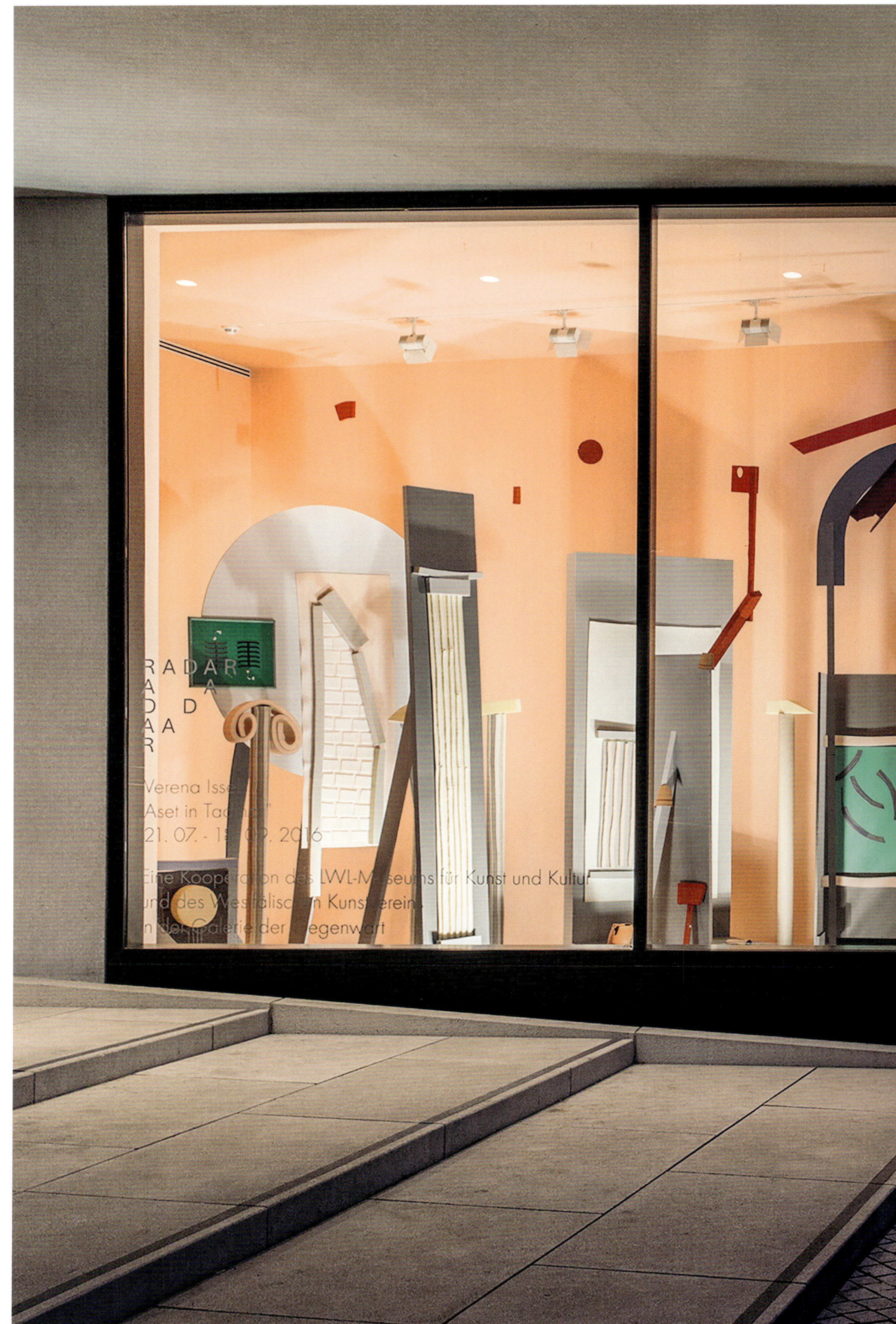

(2) ***Aset in Tamor***
2016, painted wood, polystyrene foam, plastic, cork, felt, cardboard and paper, dimensions variable, RADAR – Eine Kooperation des LWL-Museums für Kunst und Kultur und des Westfälischen Kunstvereins, Installation view Galerie der Gegenwart

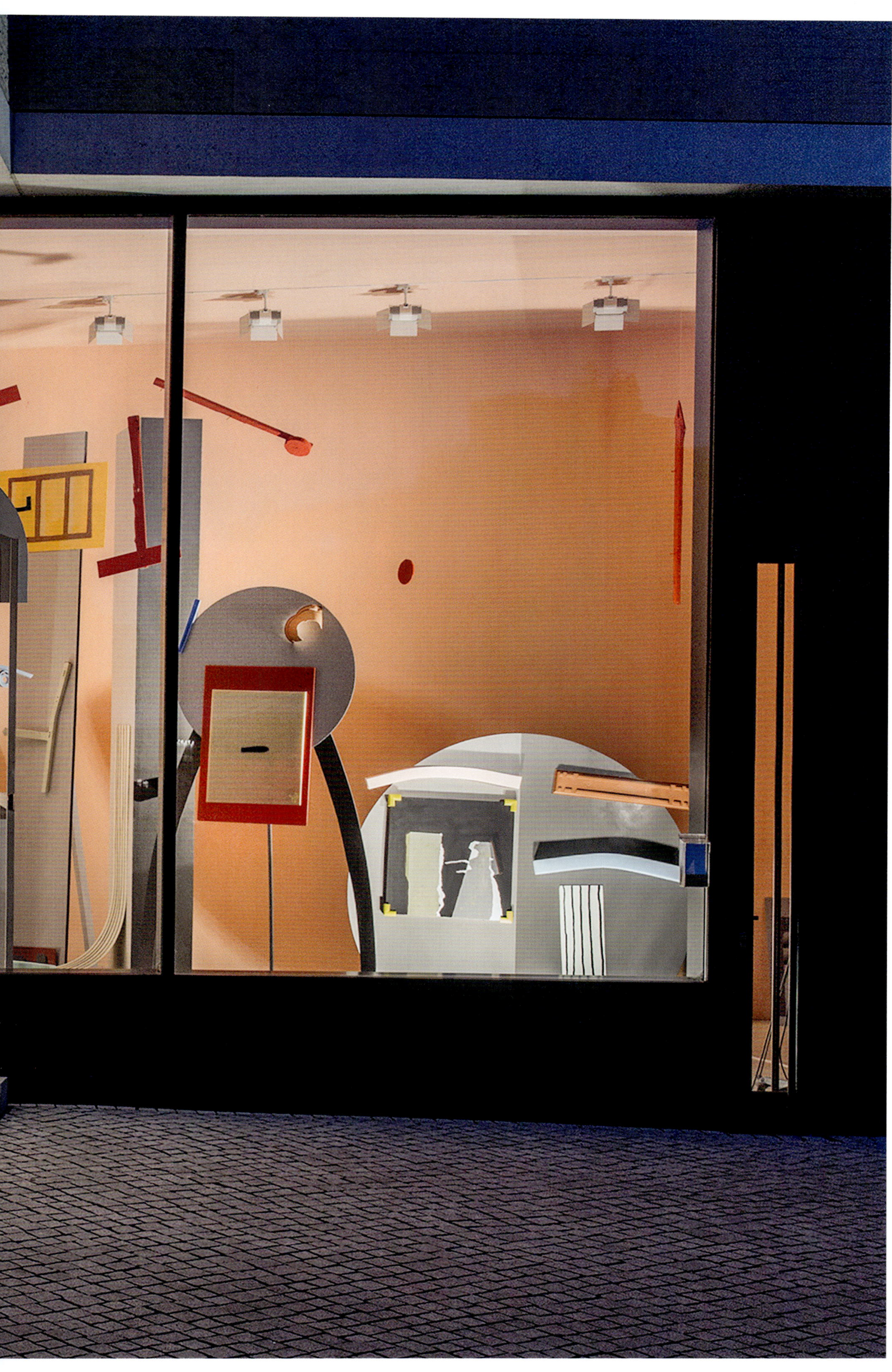

U

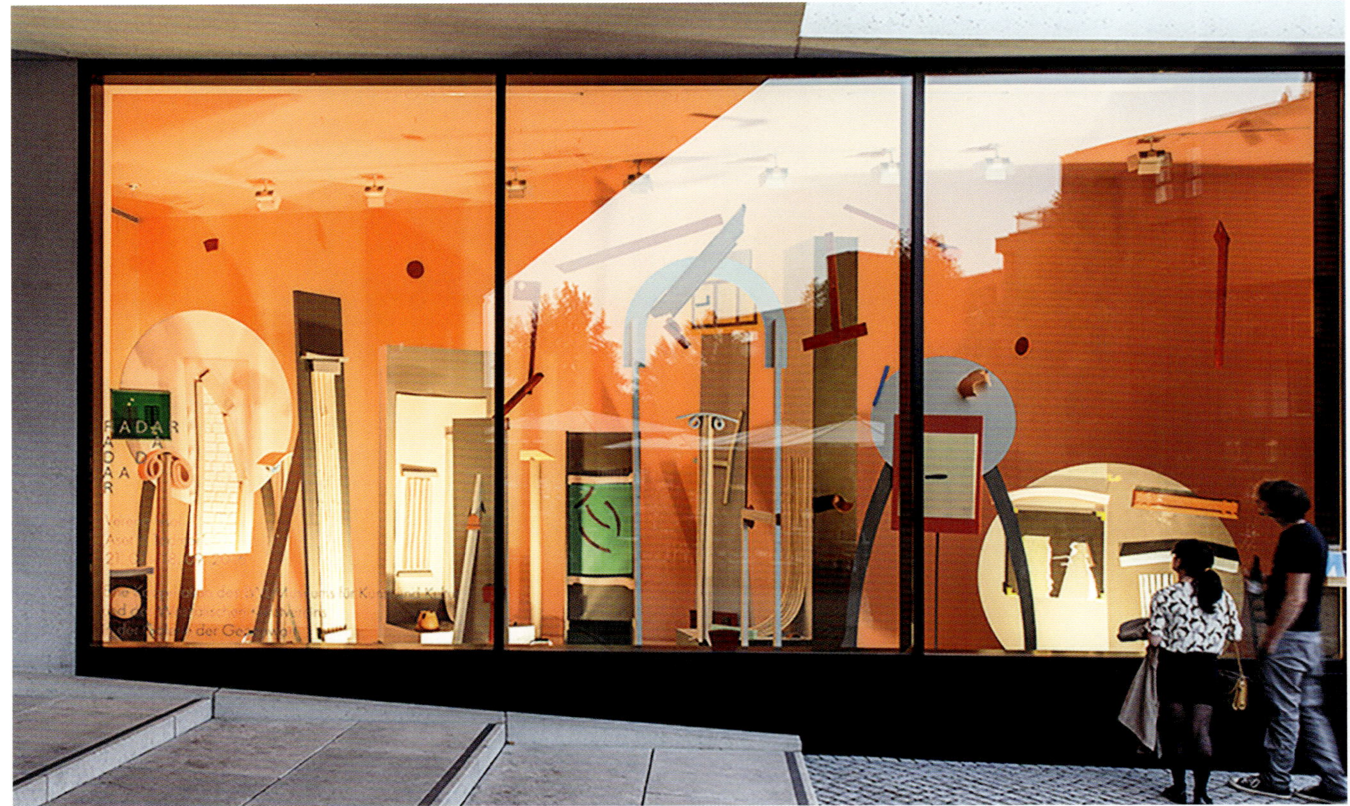

(3)

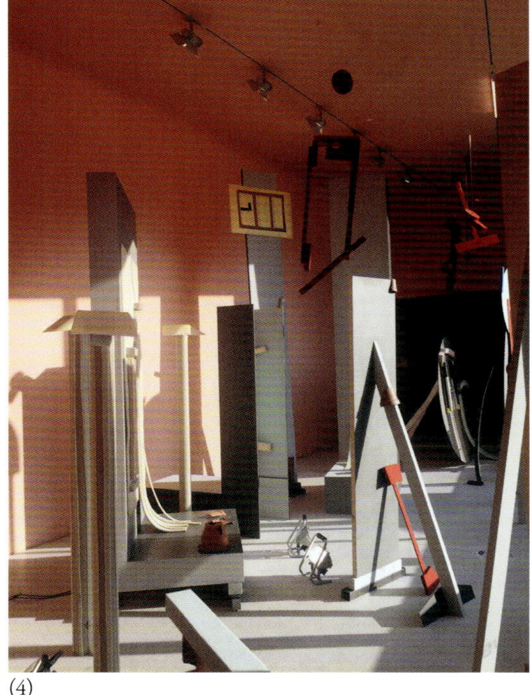

(4)

(3)
(4) ***Aset in Tadmor***
2016, painted wood, polystyrene foam, plastic, cork, felt, cardboard and paper, dimensions variable, RADAR – Eine Kooperation des LWL-Museums für Kunst und Kultur und des Westfälischen Kunstvereins, Installation view Galerie der Gegenwart

SOFT RUINS

L

INGREDIENTS
Soft Columns ①②③
Fake Vessels ①②③

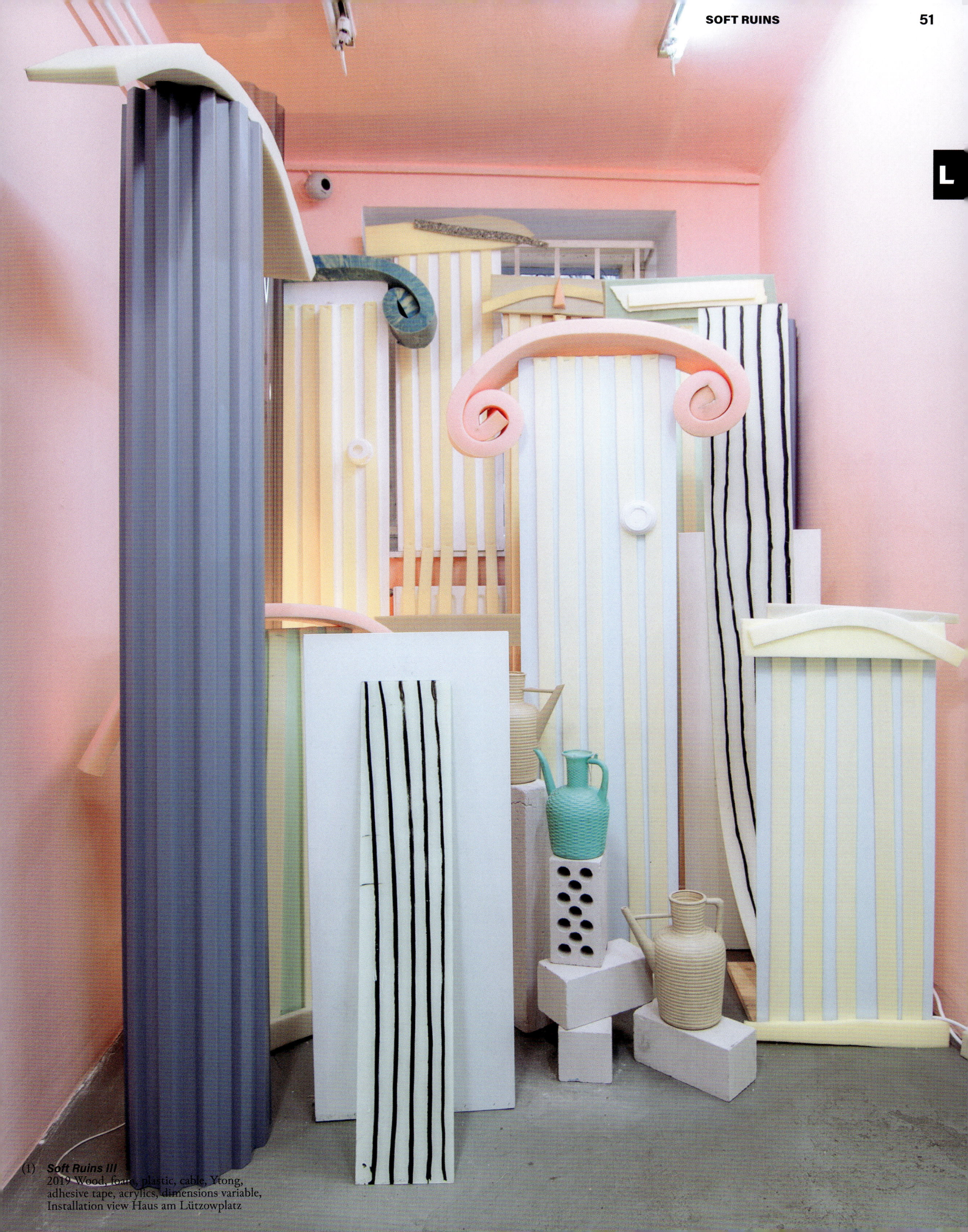

(1) ***Soft Ruins III***
2019 Wood, foam, plastic, cable, Ytong, adhesive tape, acrylics, dimensions variable, Installation view Haus am Lützowplatz

L

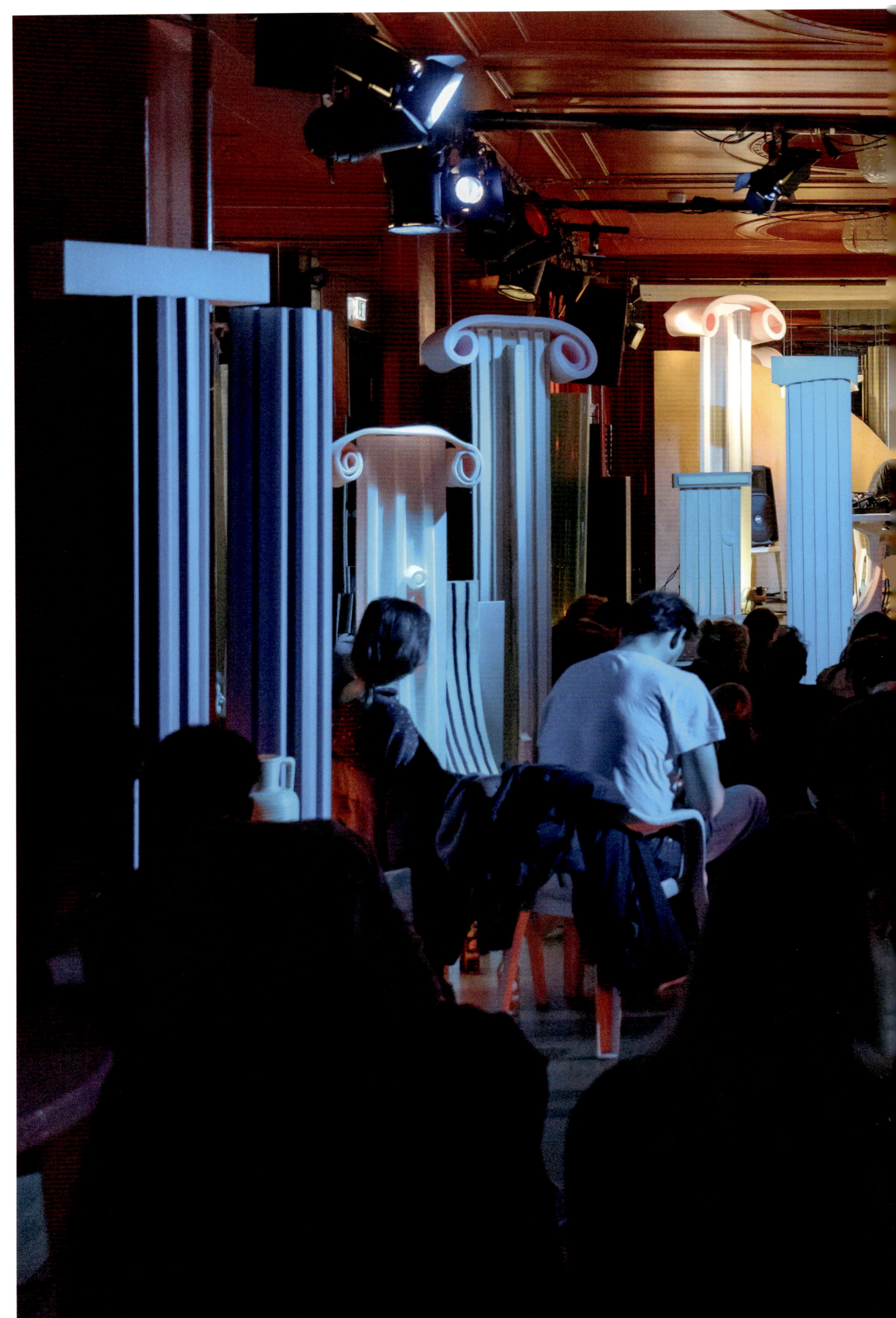

(2) ***Facetime – Soft Ruins***
2018, wood, foam, plastic, cable, Ytong, adhesive tape, acrylics, dimensions variable, Installation view of Volksbühne Berlin, Facetime with "Sky-walking" and "Schluss"

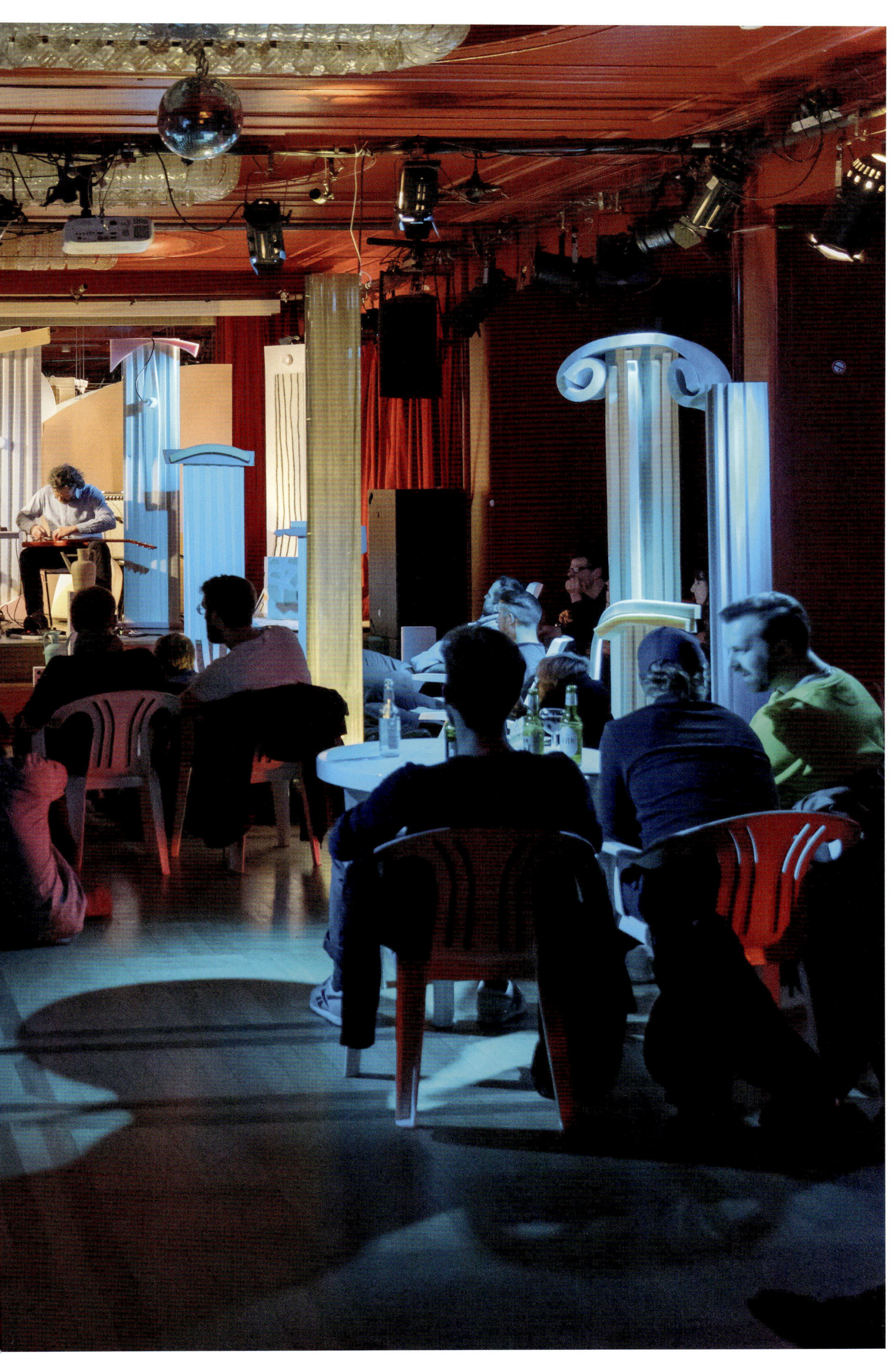

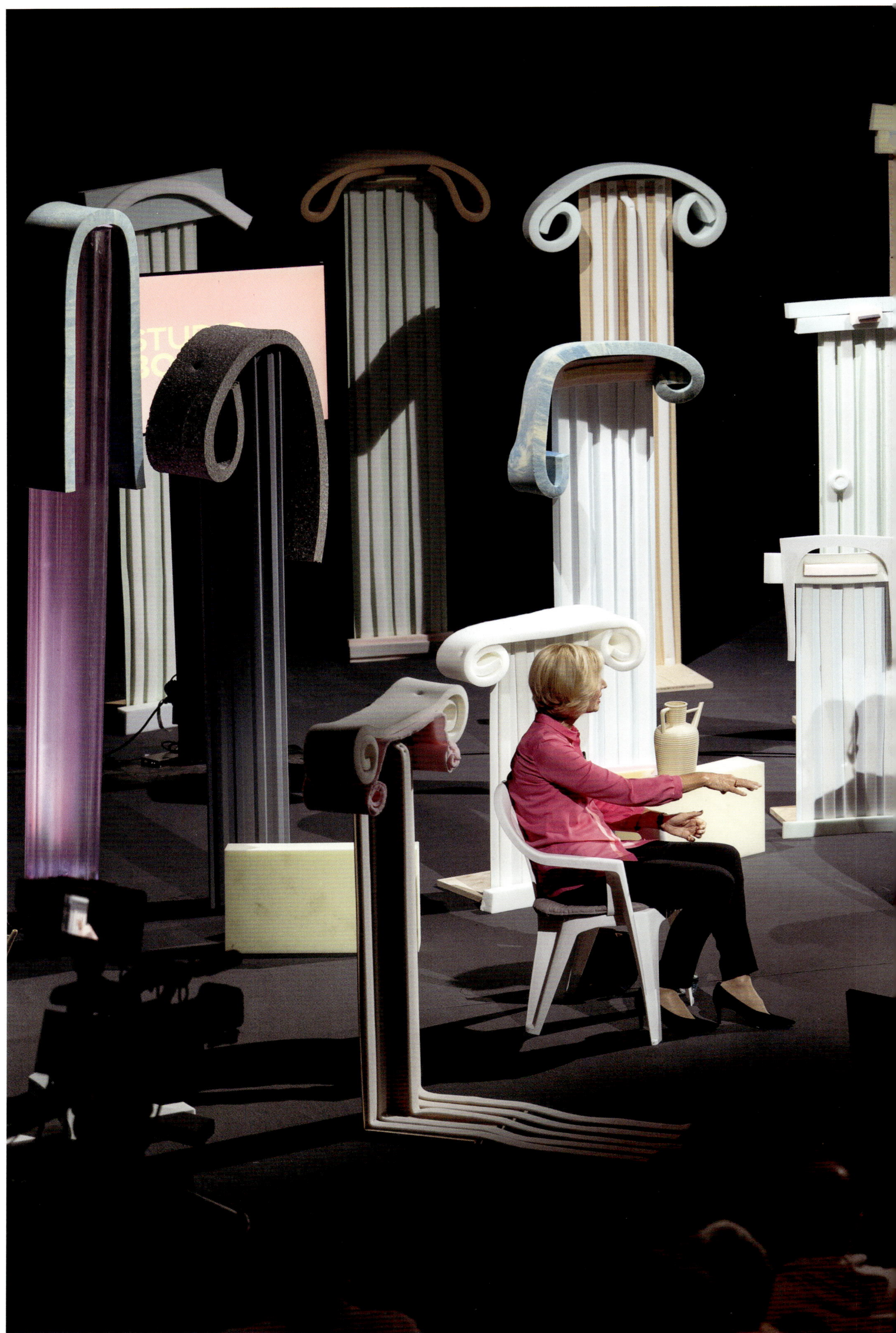

(3) ***Soft Ruins IV***
2021, wood, foam, plastic, cable, Ytong, adhesive tape, acrylics, dimensions variable, Installation view Studio Bonn/ Bundeskunsthalle, panel discussion with Mohamed Amjahid, Petra Gerster and Kolja Reichert

L

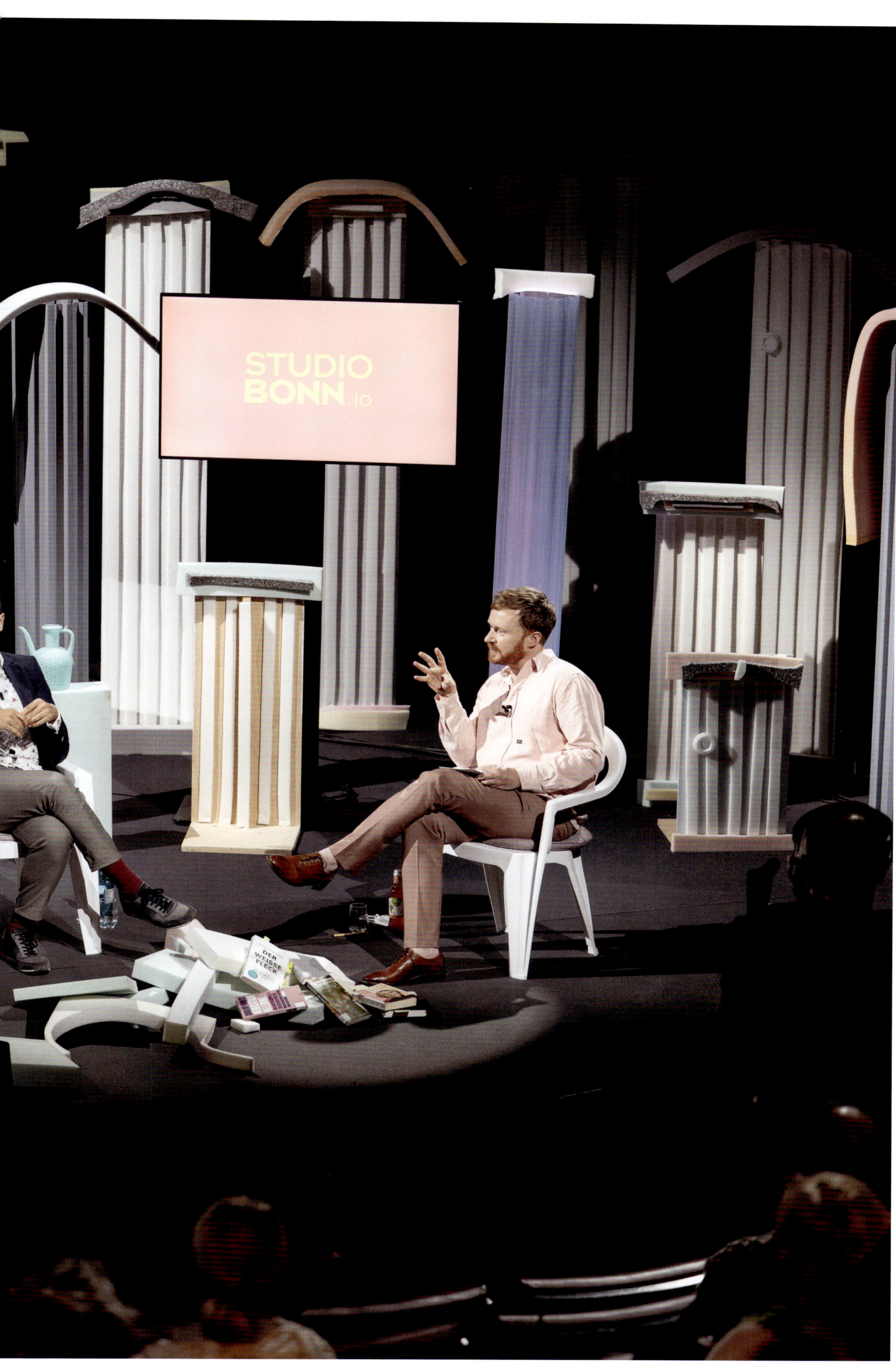

L

SZENEN-WECHSEL/ DER FÜNFTE SOCKEL

INGREDIENTS
Baroccoco vase with potatoes and felt ①②③

EN The Herrenhausen Gardens in Hanover are one of the most well-known Baroque gardens in Europe. Their garden stage was the first hedge theater in Germany and is also the only one that has been preserved. In 1690, a total of 27 lead figures were erected in Hanover, a part of the northern German county Niedersachsen, with bronze copies from 1974 on display in the embassy of Niedersachsen in Berlin. This historical ensemble in Berlin is occasionally interrupted by contemporary sculptures. The latest sculpture is by Verena Issel. Like the gilded figures, the artist copies historical models. In Issel's case, this is an ancient vase whose motifs simultaneously borrow from the Baroque. Upon closer inspection, Baroque ruffs, corsets, and hoop skirts can be found on the two-dimensional metal disc. But that's not all—in addition to references to antiquity and the Baroque, the artist combines typical materials from the area of Niedersachsen with universal high-tech materials. The signature staple of Niedersachsen, the Niedersachsen potatoes, meet industrial steel, and the likewise classical Niedersachsen sheep wool meets metal. A confusion in pink that playfully quotes and seems to wander through the centuries. An illusionistic drawing that pretends to be a vase but remains trapped in the second dimension.

☐ ***Stefanie Sembill***

L

DE Die Herrenhäuser Gärten in Hannover sind eine der bekanntesten Barockanlagen Europas. Deren Gartenbühne war das erste Heckentheater Deutschlands, und es ist auch das einzige, das erhalten geblieben ist. Bereits 1690 wurden insgesamt 27 Bleifiguren in Hannover aufgestellt, in Berlin sind Bronzekopien aus dem Jahr 1974 zu sehen. Dieser historische Reigen in Berlin wird in loser Folge durch zeitgenössische Skulpturen unterbrochen. Der sogenannte „Szenenwechsel" wird in Kooperation mit dem Netzwerk Niedersächsischer Kunstvereine veranstaltet. Die aktuelle Plastik stammt von Verena Issel.

Die Künstlerin kopiert, ebenso wie die vergoldeten Figuren, historische Vorbilder. In Issels Fall eine antike Vase, deren Motive zugleich Anleihen im Barock nehmen. Bei genauem Betrachten finden sich auf der zweidimensionalen Metallscheibe barocke Halskrausen, Korsagen und Reifröcke. Damit nicht genug: Die Künstlerin kombiniert neben den Bezügen zu Antike und Barock auch zutiefst niedersächsische Rohstoffe mit universellen Hightechmaterialien. Heidekartoffeln treffen auf Industriestahl und Schafswolle auf Metall. Ein Verwirrspiel in Pink, das lustvoll zitiert und durch die Jahrhunderte zu wandern scheint. Eine illusionistische Zeichnung, die vorgibt, eine Vase zu sein, und doch in der zweiten Dimension verhaftet bleibt.

☐ ***Stefanie Sembill***

L

L

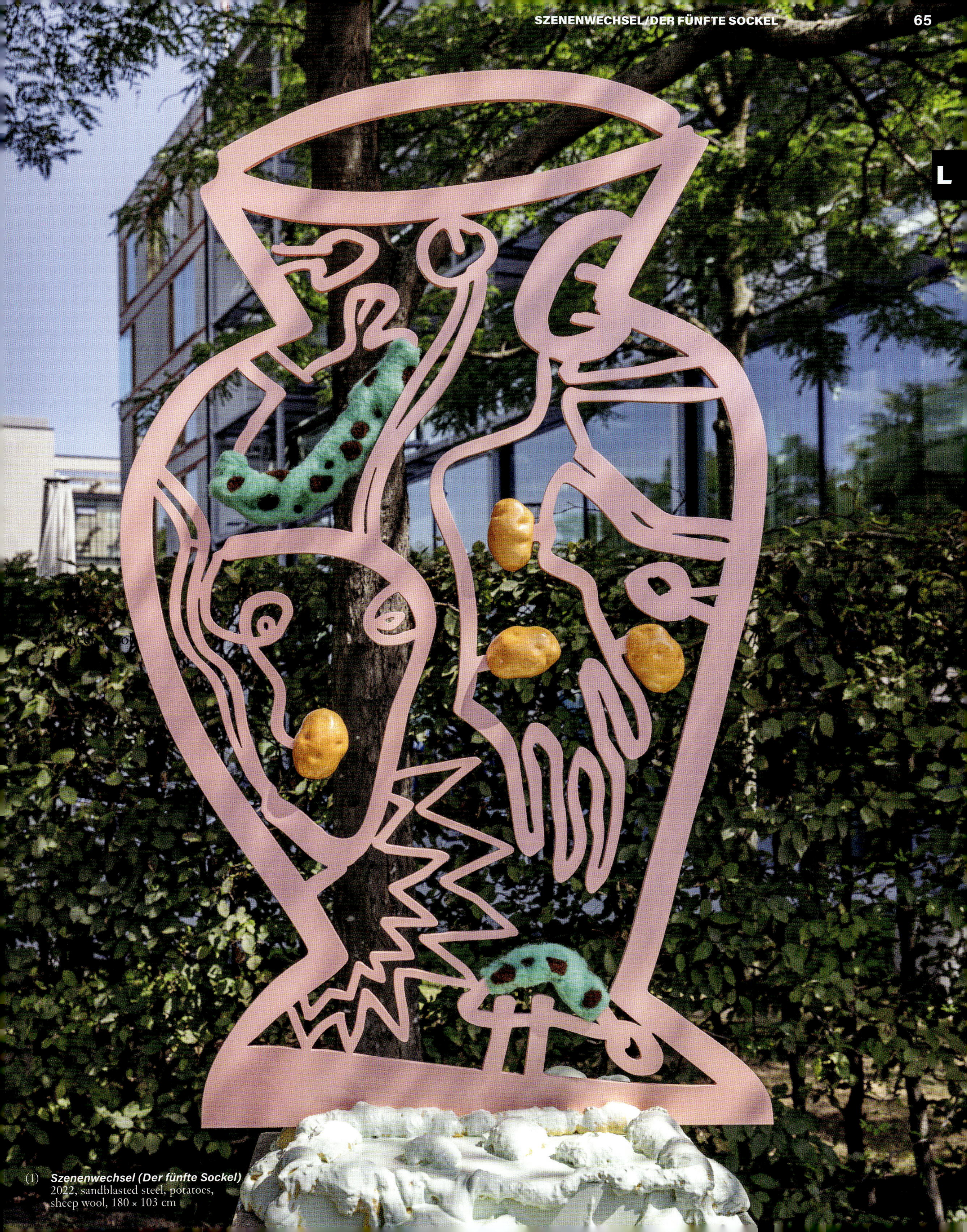

(1) ***Szenenwechsel (Der fünfte Sockel)***
2022, sandblasted steel, potatoes, sheep wool, 180 × 103 cm

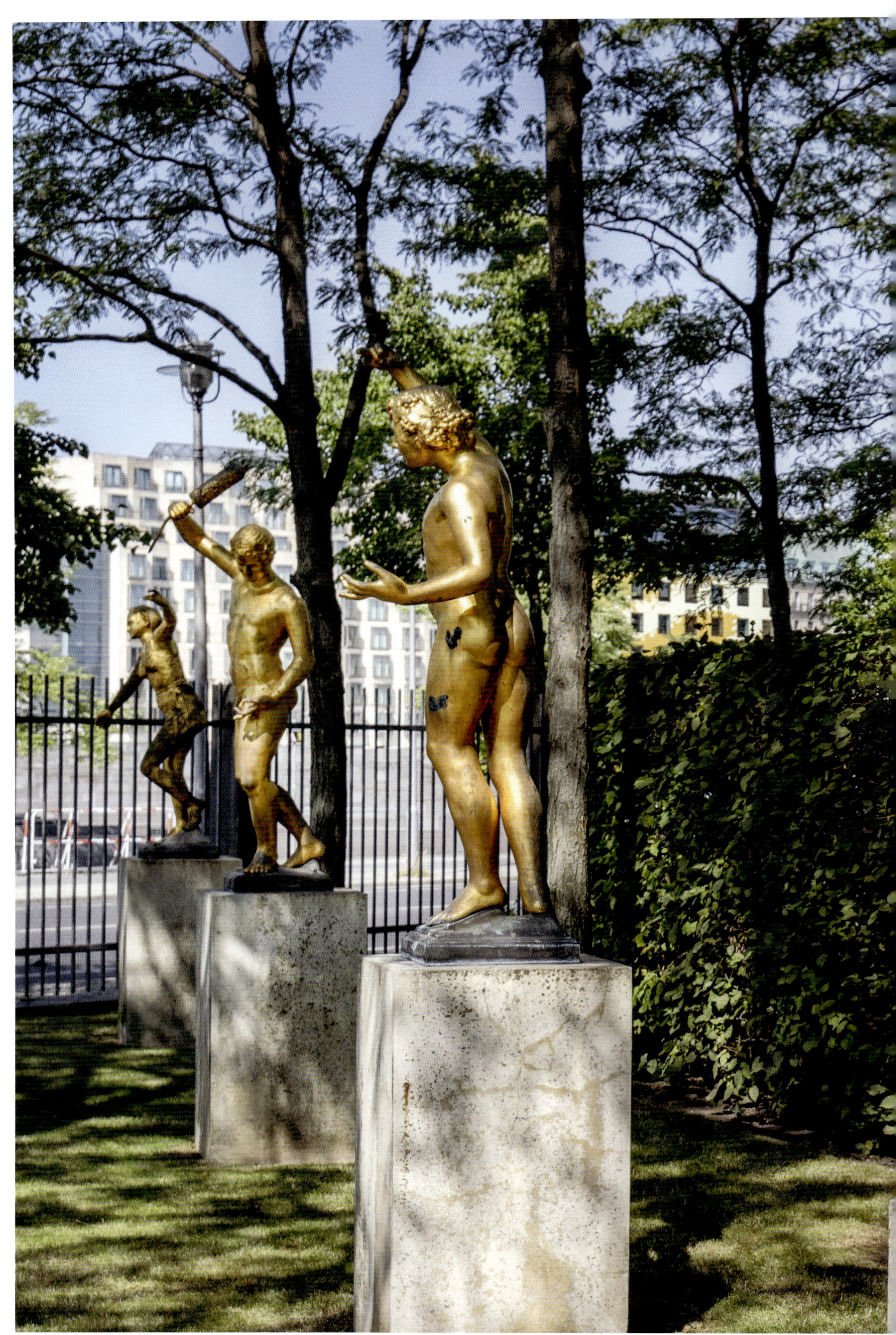

(2) ***Szenenwechsel (Der fünfte Sockel)***
2022, sandblasted steel, potatoes, sheep wool, 180 × 103 cm

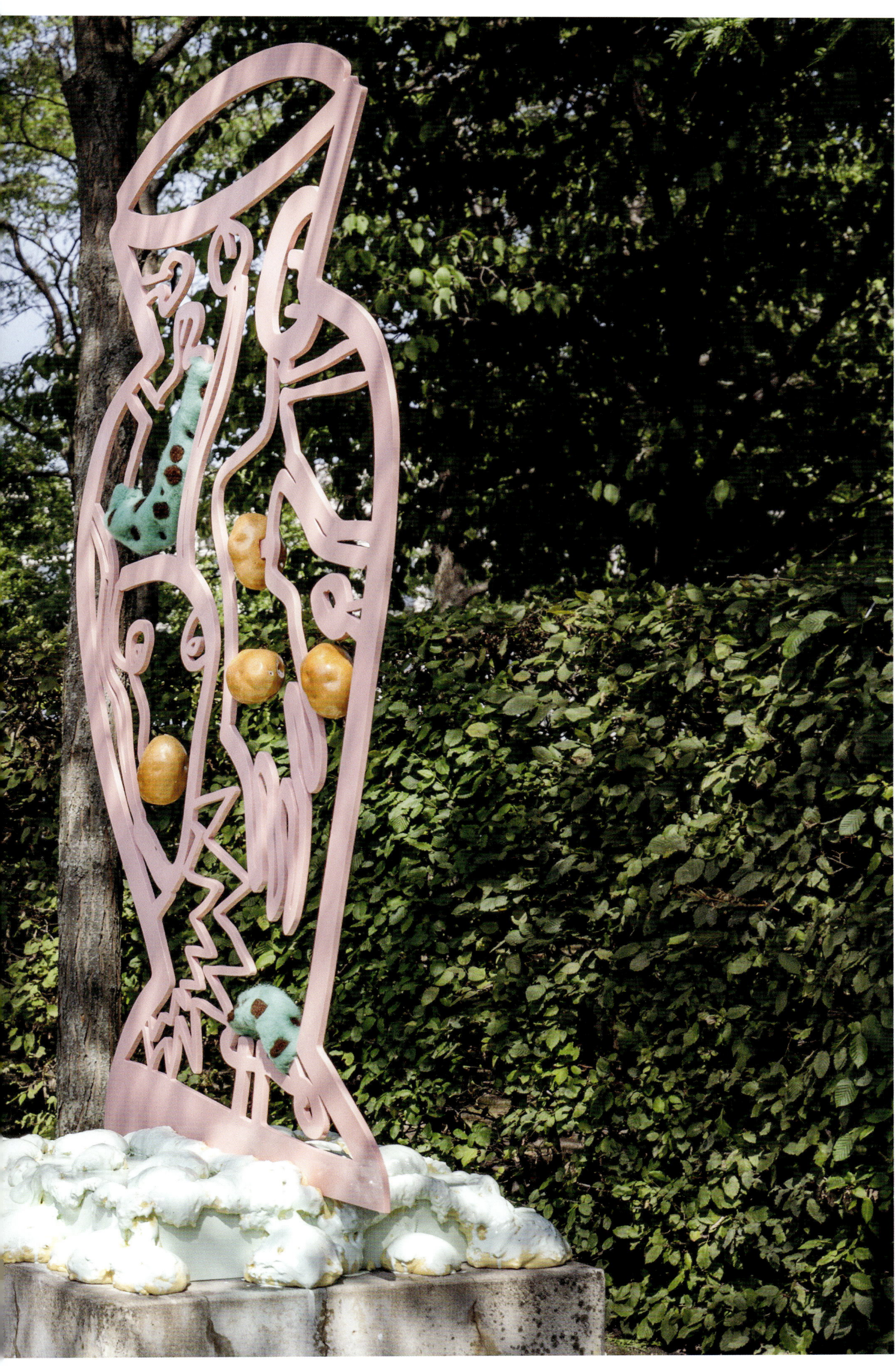

T

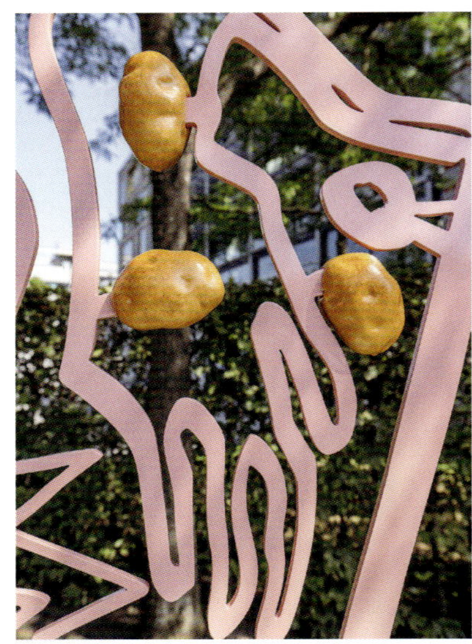
(3)

(3) ***Szenenwechsel (Der fünfte Sockel)***
2022, sandblasted steel, potatoes, sheep wool, 180 × 103 cm

BACKLASH I

T

INGREDIENTS
Backlash
(Female Ecosystem) I ②
Backlash
(Female Ecosystem) II ①
Backlash
(Female Ecosystem) III ③
Backlash
(Female Ecosystem) IV ②
Backlash
(Female Ecosystem) V ⑤
Backlash
(Female Ecosystem) VI ④
Backlash
(Female Ecosystem) VII ⑥
Backlash
(Female Ecosystem) VIII ②
Backlash
(Female Ecosystem) IX ②
Backlash
(Female Ecosystem) X
U my doormat? ⑨
Backlash
(Female Ecosystem:
Babyfeeding) ⑫
Backlash (Female
Ecosystem: Cleaning) ⑬
Backlash (Female
Ecosystem: Rollatoren) ⑭
Backlash (Female
Ecosystem: Rollatoren) ⑮
Messer (object) ⑯
Gabel (object) ⑯
Löffel (object) ⑪
Bigdick (object) ⑪
Bigdick II (object) ⑪
Carpet Mosaic ②⑪
Hanging Bottle (object) ②⑪
Hanging Shape (object) ②⑪
Hanging Bottle II (object) ⑦
Carpet Glass (object) ⑦
Carpet Shape (object) ⑪
Pool Noodles ②
Enlargement of society
problems (Big Bottle)
(object) ⑪

EN The space of the Museum Lother Fischer was designed specifically for sculptors to display their sculptures; however, Verena Issel plays with the shift between two- and three-dimensionality.
For her room installation, Verena Issel used household utensils and other everyday objects, mostly with so called feminine connotations. From baby diapers and walkers to kitchen appliances and sex toys, Verena Issel arranges these objects like still lifes on a black cardboard surface. Vibrant, cheerful, and flat. This flatness of the paintings is also transferred to her sculptures.
The freestanding objects each consist of two wooden panels that interlock and thus only seemingly create a three-dimensional figure.
For the first time, she has also conceived a floor installation. “It was important to me that something folds up into the room. But especially with this theme, I wanted it not to become truly spatial, even though it is sculptural, which is why they are sculptures that are flat,” says the artist.

Backlash is a criticism of the return to conservative value concepts. In the past pandemic years, Issel observed a resurgence of “modern housewifery.”
“I believe that during the pandemic, the last 30 years of feminist efforts were destroyed in many contexts. And that was also the central idea of this exhibition.”
Issel deliberately chose carpet as the working material for the installation as a symbol of the domestic-private environment. Since the installation is walkable, visitors inevitably become part of the work and cannot escape the social coding. The artist hopes that this provides a space for reflection.

□ ***Tanja Gorges, Bayerischer Rundfunk, June 27, 2022***

T

en. The space of the Museum Lothar Fischer was designed specifically for sculptors to display their sculptures; however, Verena Issel plays with the shift between two- and three-dimensionality. For her room installation, Verena Issel used household utensils and other everyday objects, mostly with so-called feminine connotations. From baby diapers and walkers to kitchen appliances and sex toys, Verena Issel arranges these objects like still lifes on a black cardboard surface. Vibrant, cheerful and flat. This flatness of her paintings is also transferred to her sculptures. The free-standing objects each consist of two wooden panels that interlock and thus only seemingly create a three-dimensional figure. For the first time, she has also conceived a floor installation. "It was important to me that something folds up into the room. But especially with this theme, I wanted it not to become truly spatial, even though it is sculptural, which is why they are sculptures that are flat," says the artist.

Verena Issel's criticism of the return to conservative value concepts in the past pandemic years, [illegible] observed the resurgence of "modern housewifery." "I believe that during the pandemic, the last 30 years of feminist efforts were destroyed in many contexts. And that was also the central idea of this exhibition." Issel deliberately chose carpet as the working material for the installation as a symbol of the domestic-private environment. Since the installation is walkable, visitors inevitably become part of the work and cannot escape the social coding. The artist hopes that this provides a space for reflection.

☐ Tanja Gergov, [illegible], June 27 2022

DE Das Museum Lothar Fischer wurde speziell für Bildhauer entwickelt, um ihre Skulpturen auszustellen. Verena Issel jedoch spielt hier mit dem Wechsel von Zwei- und Dreidimensionalität.

Für ihre Rauminstallation hat Verena Issel Haushaltsutensilien und andere Gebrauchsgegenstände, die meistens weiblich konnotiert sind, verwendet. Von Babywindeln, Rollatoren über Küchengeräte bis hin zu Sexspielzeug platziert Verena Issel diese Gegenstände wie Stillleben auf schwarzem Kartongrund. Bunt, fröhlich und flach. Diese Flachheit der Malereien überträgt sie auch auf ihre Skulpturen. Die freistehenden Objekte bestehen jeweils aus zwei Holzplatten, die ineinandergesteckt werden und so nur scheinbar eine dreidimensionale Figur ergeben.

Erstmals hat sie zudem eine Bodeninstallation konzipiert. „Mir war es wichtig, dass sich da etwas in den Raum hochklappt. Ich wollte aber gerade bei diesem Thema, dass es nicht wirklich räumlich wird, obwohl es skulptural ist, weshalb es Skulpturen sind […], die aber flach sind", sagt die Künstlerin.

Backlash – so der Titel der Installation – kritisiert die Rückkehr zu konservativen Wertevorstellungen. So hat Issel in den zurückliegenden Pandemiejahren einen Wiederaufstieg eines „modernen Hausfrauentums" beobachtet. „Ich glaube, in zwei Jahren wurden die letzten 30 Jahre feministischer Bestrebungen in vielen Kontexten vernichtet. Und das war auch Kerngedanke dieser Ausstellung."

Issel hat extra Teppich als Arbeitsmaterial für die Installation ausgewählt, als Sinnbild für das häuslich-private Umfeld. Da die Installation begehbar ist, werden Besucher unweigerlich Teil des Werkes und können sich der gesellschaftlichen Entwicklung nicht entziehen. Aber sie werden sich – so hofft die Künstlerin – der stereotypen Geschlechterrollen bewusst.

□ ***Tanja Gorges, Bayerischer Rundfunk, 27.06.2022***

T

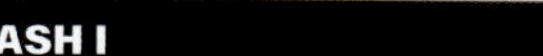

T

(1) ***Backlash (Female Ecosystem) II***
2022, car paint and acrylics on cardboard, each 70 × 50 cm

T

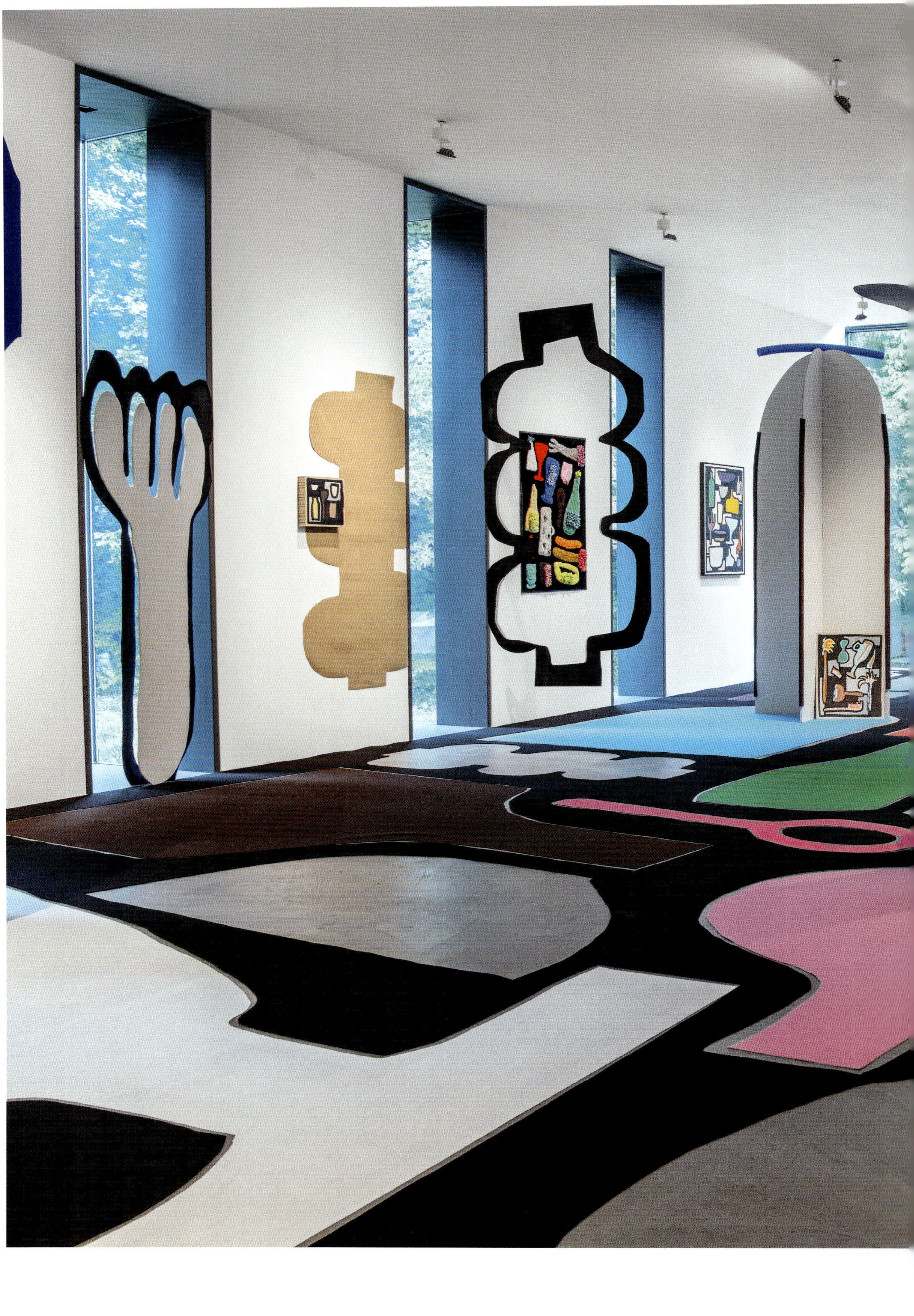

(2) ***Backlash***
2022, various materials, carpet, wood, varnish, edge protection, swimming noodles, drawings, dimensions variable,
Installation view
Museum Lothar Fischer

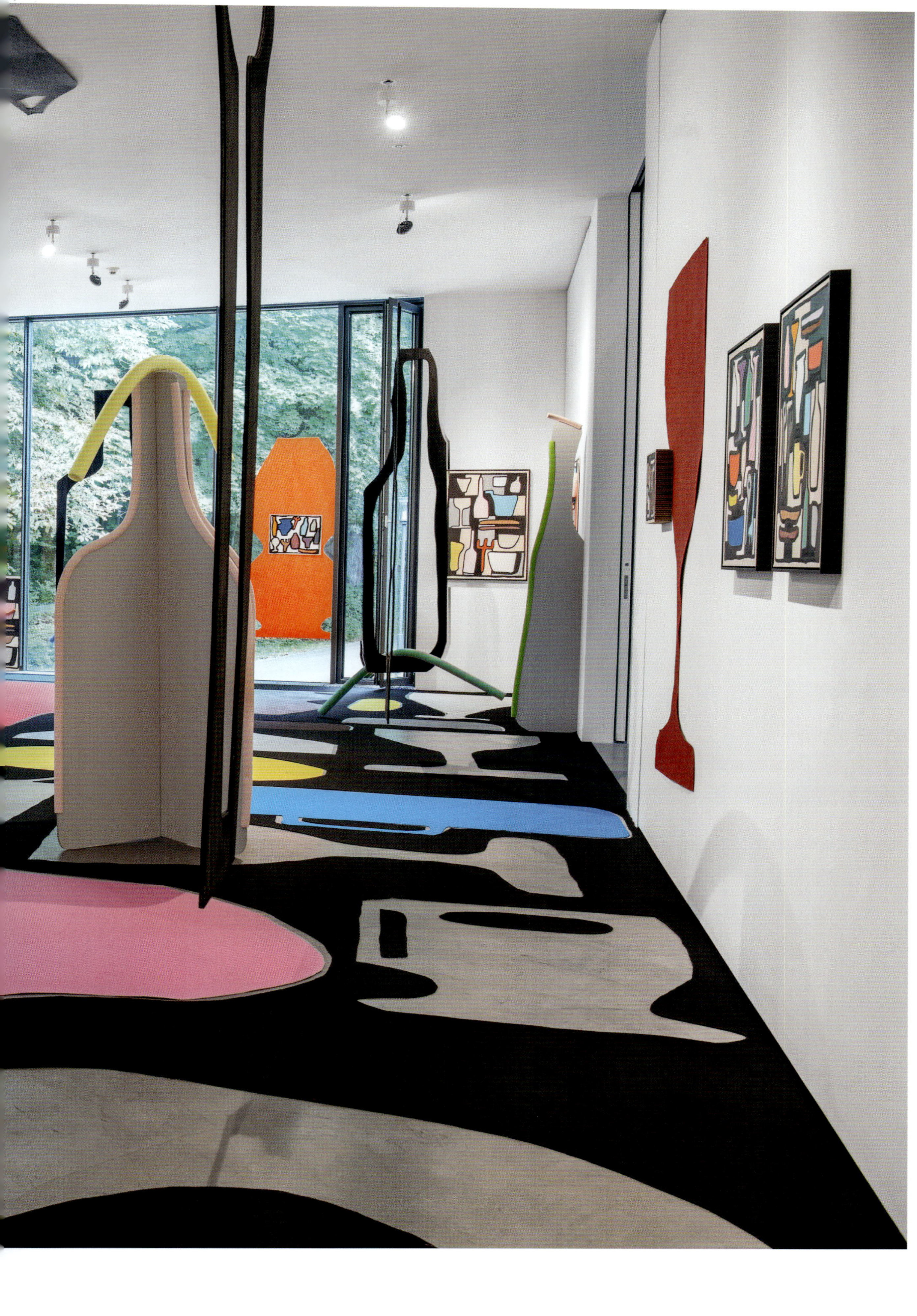

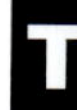

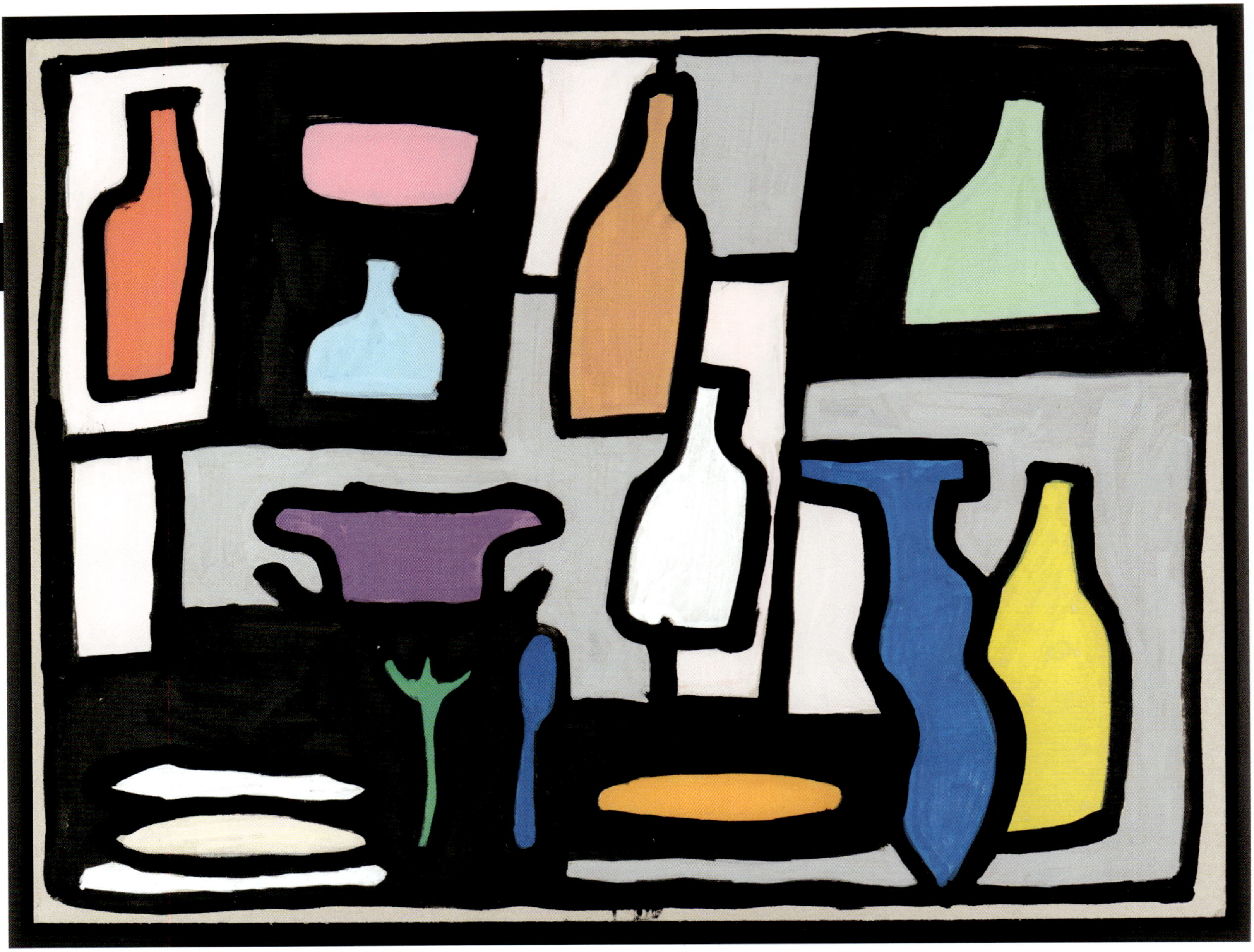

(3)

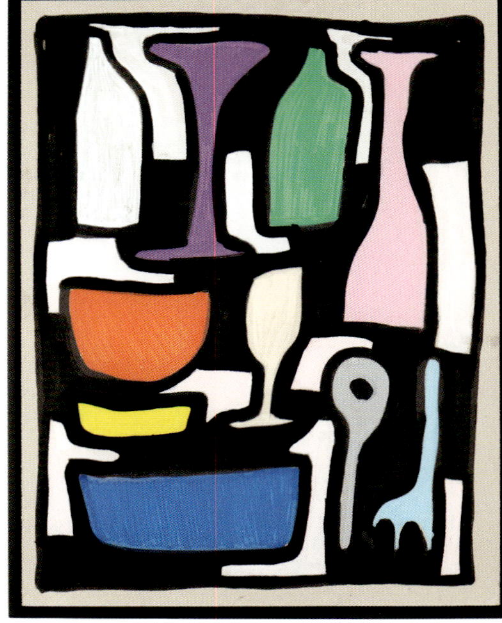

(4)

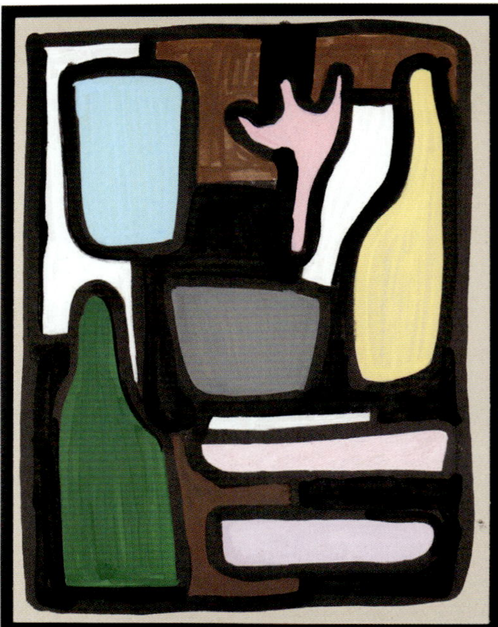

(5)

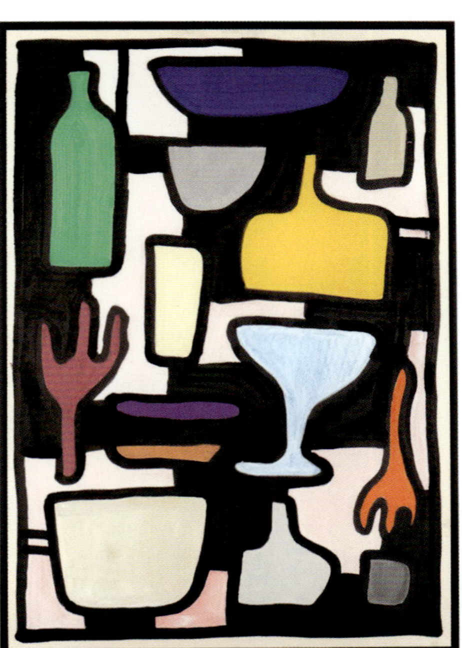

(6)

T

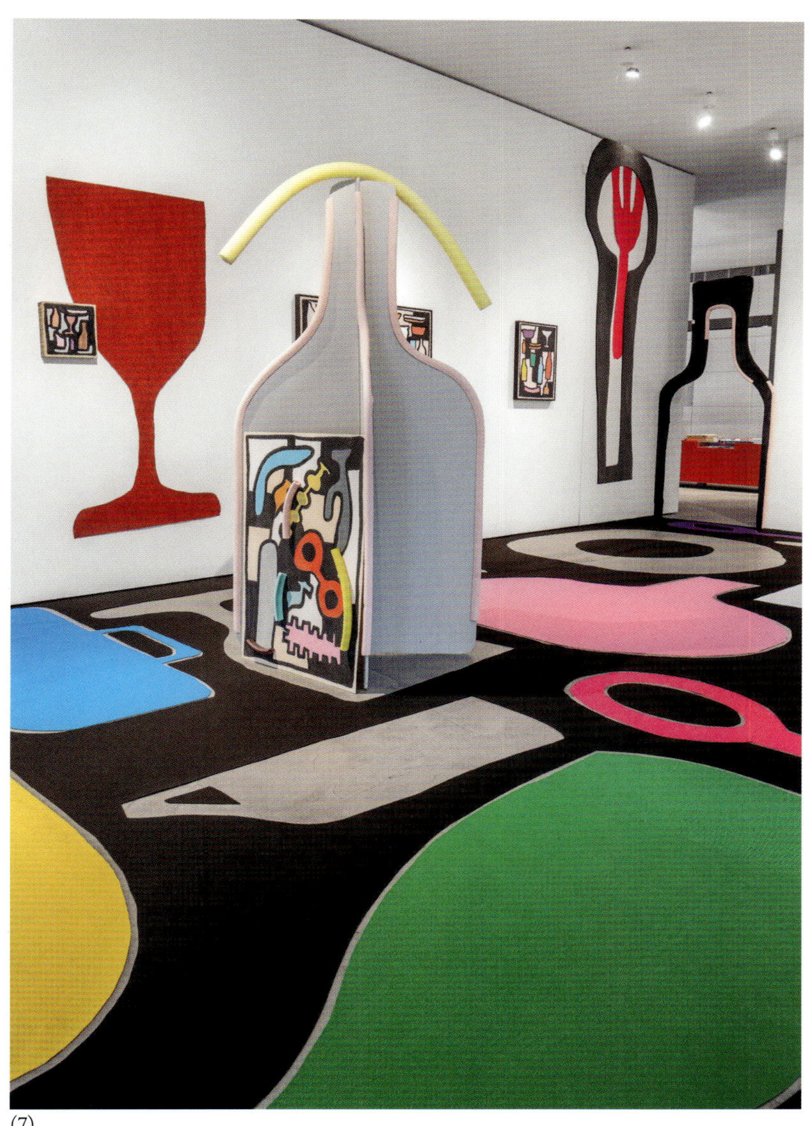

(7)

(3) ***Backlash (Female Ecosystem) III***
2022, car paint and acrylics on cardboard, 50 × 70 cm

(4) ***Backlash (Female Ecosystem) VI***
2022, car paint and acrylics on cardboard, 70 × 50 cm

(5) ***Backlash (Female Ecosystem) V***
2022, car paint and acrylics on cardboard, 70 × 50 cm

(6) ***Backlash (Female Ecosystem) VII***
2022, car paint and acrylics on cardboard, 70 × 50 cm

(7) ***Backlash***
2022, various materials, carpet, wood, varnish, edge protection, swimming noodles, drawings, dimensions variable, Installation view Museum Lothar Fischer

T

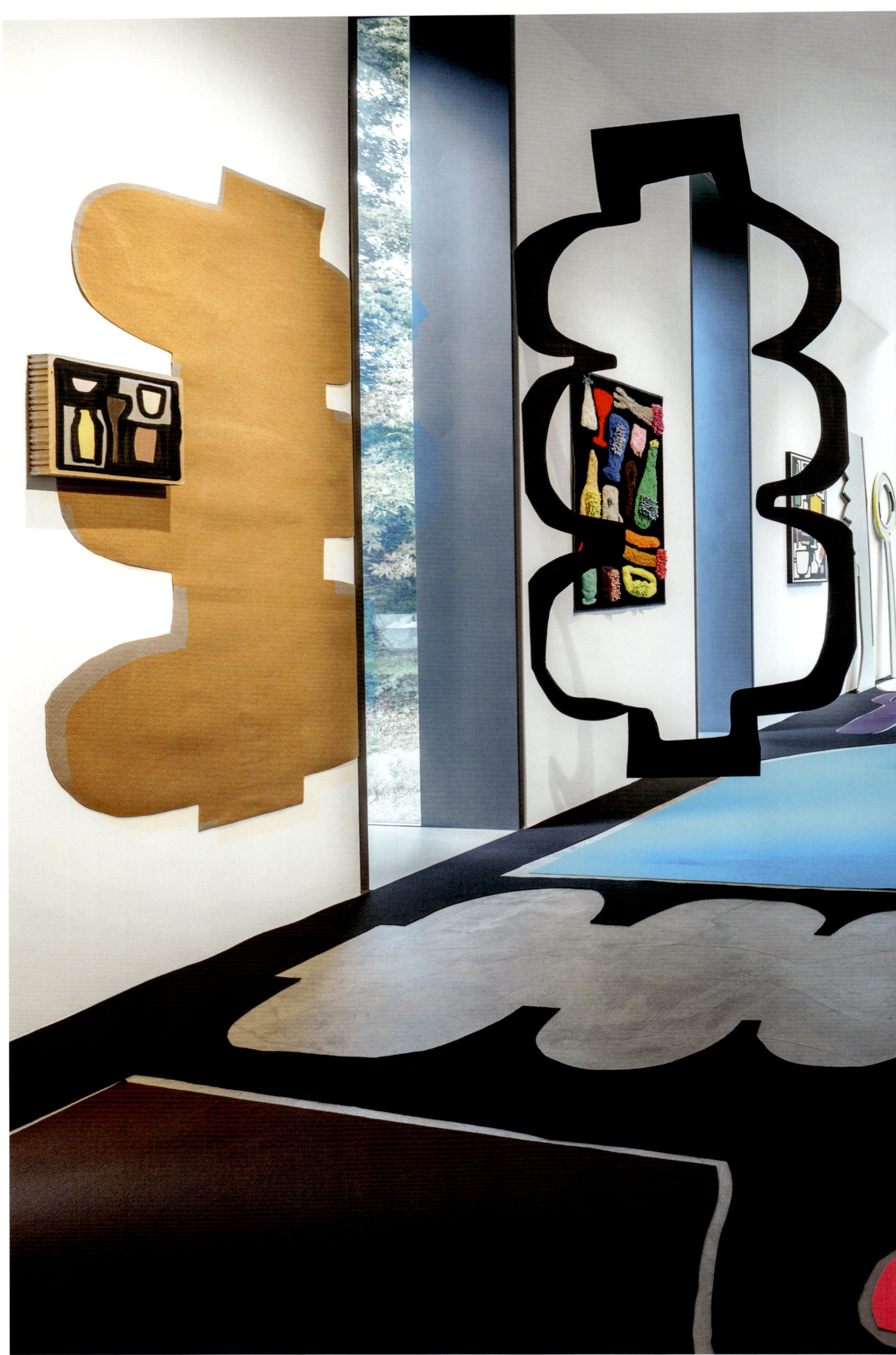

(8) ***Backlash***
2022, various materials, carpet, wood, varnish, edge protection, swimming noodles, drawings, dimensions variable, Installation view Museum Lothar Fischer

T

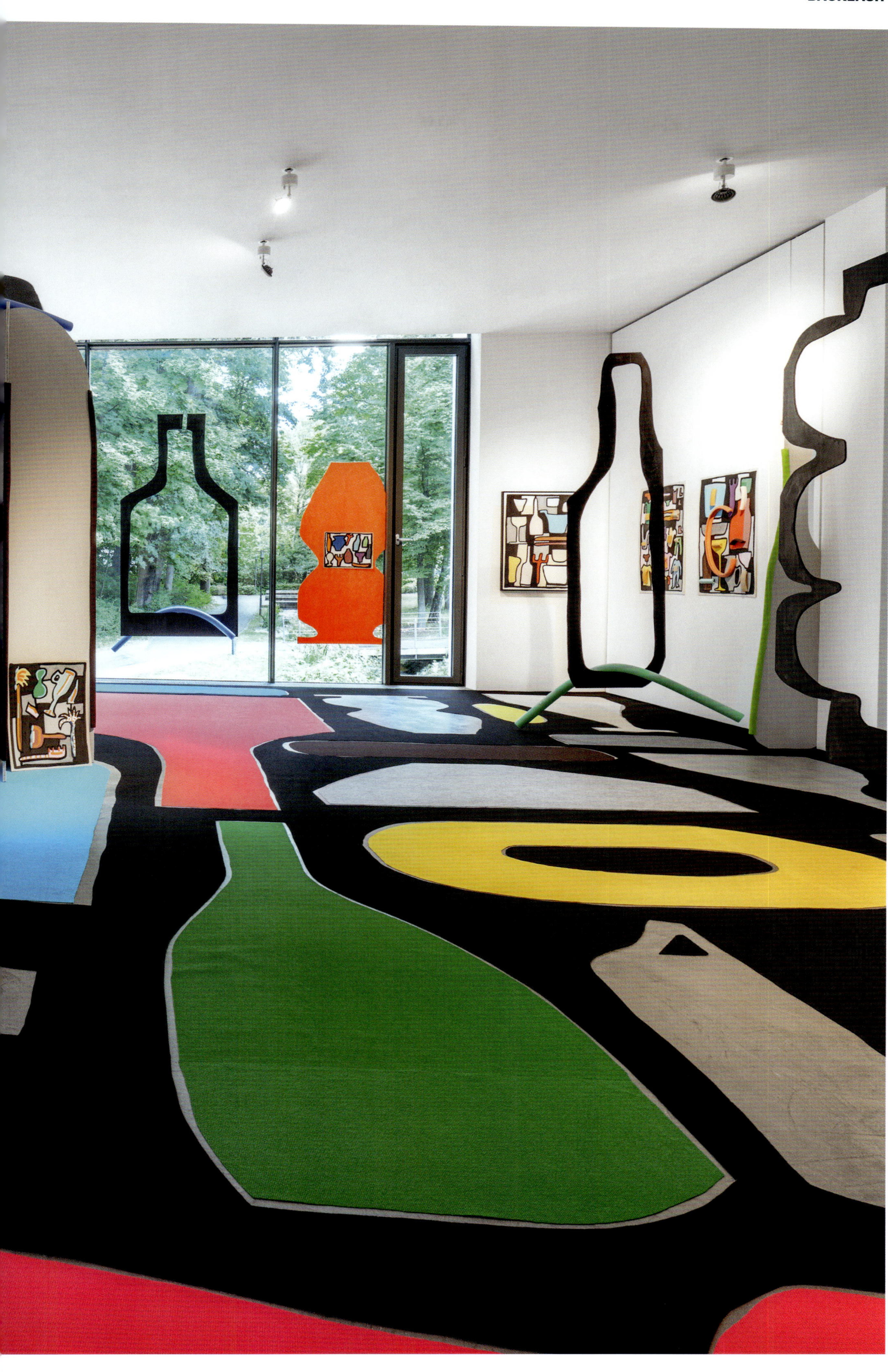

T

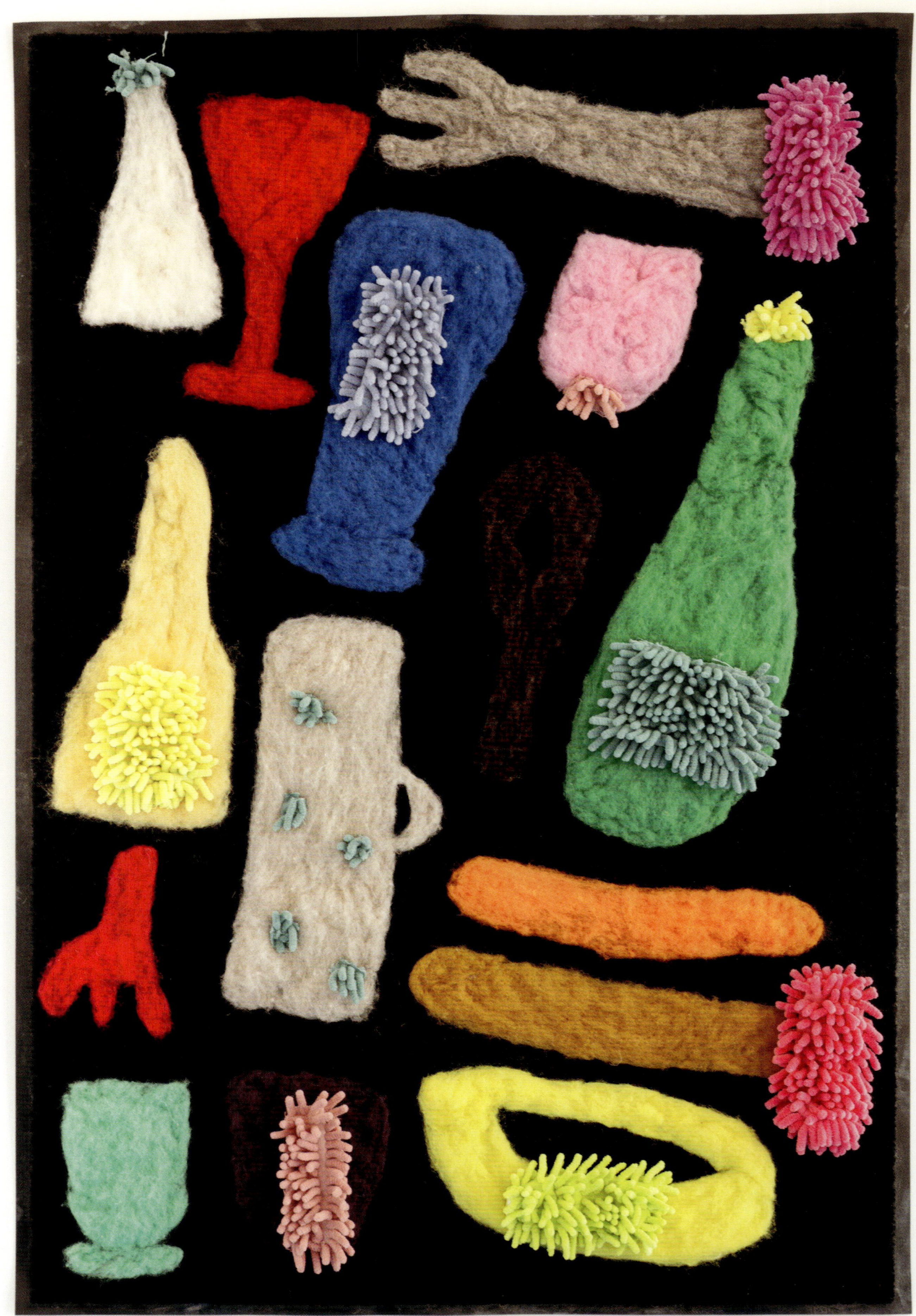

(9) ***U my doormat?***
2022, felt and cleaning rags on doormat, 100 × 70 cm

T

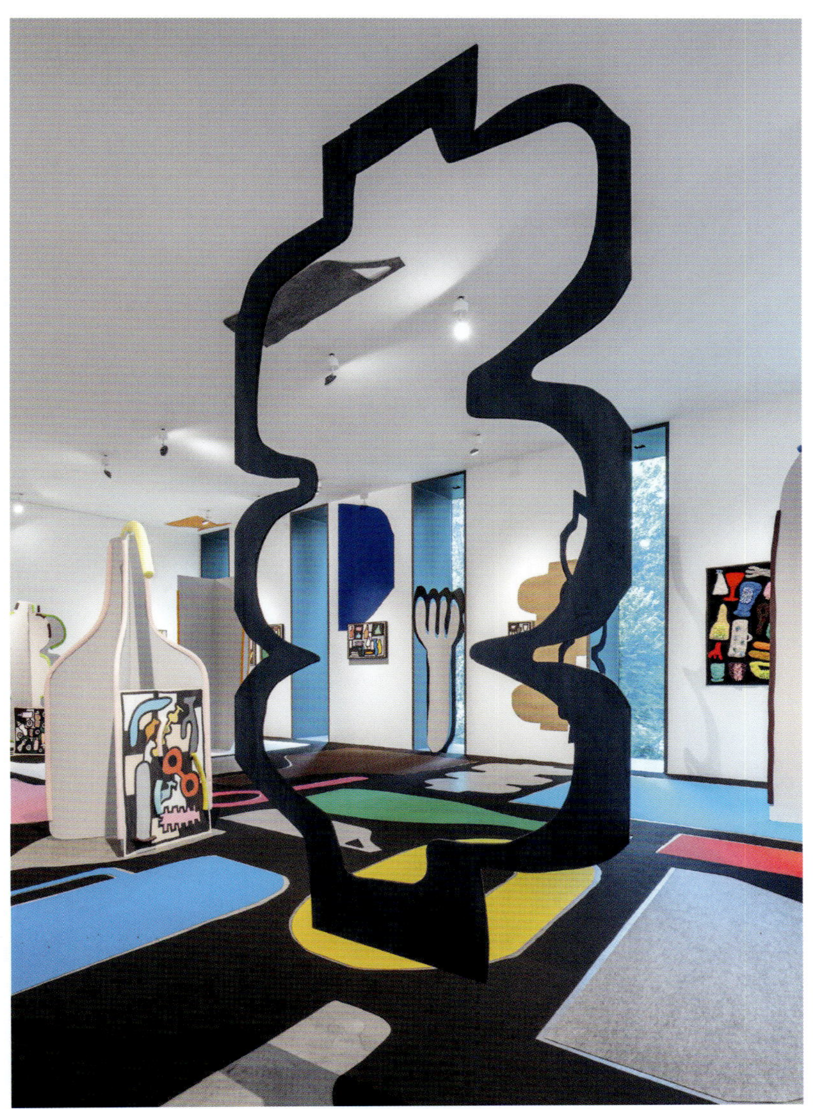
(10)

(10) ***Backlash***
2022, various materials, carpet, wood, varnish, edge protection, swimming noodles, drawings, dimensions variable, Installation view Museum Lothar Fischer

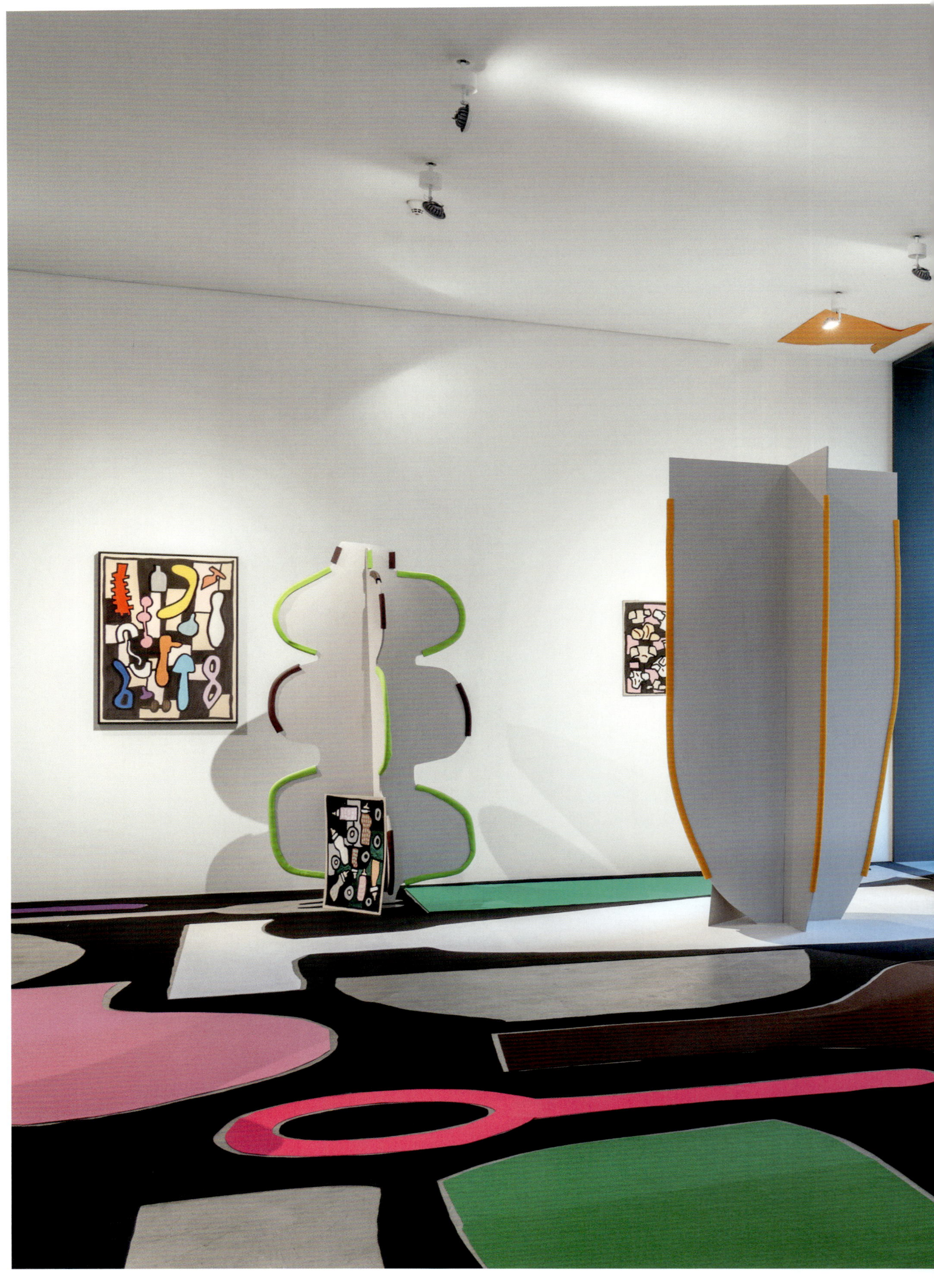

(11) ***Backlash***
2022, various materials, carpet, wood, varnish, edge protection, swimming noodles, drawings, dimensions variable, Installation view Museum Lothar Fischer

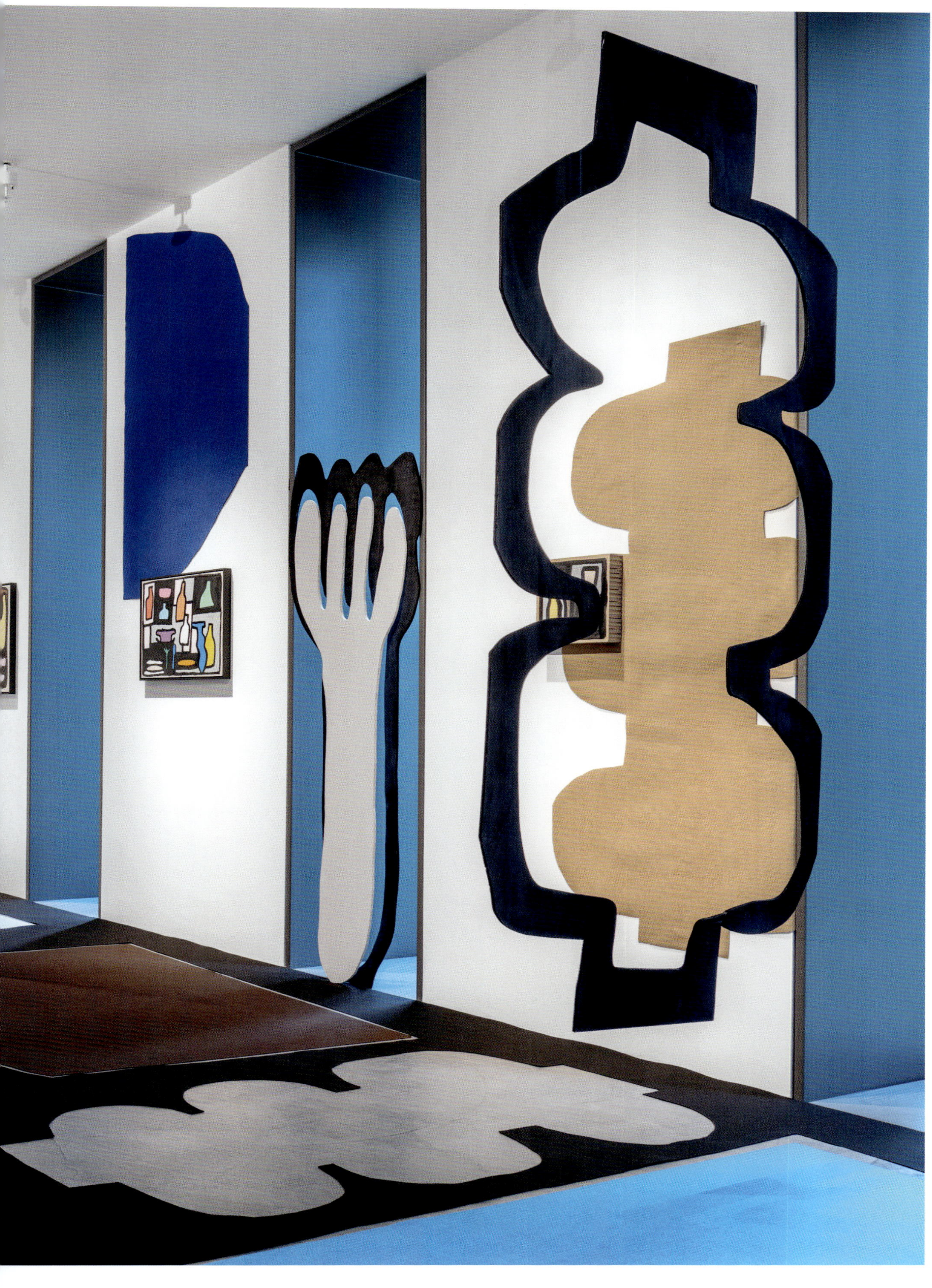

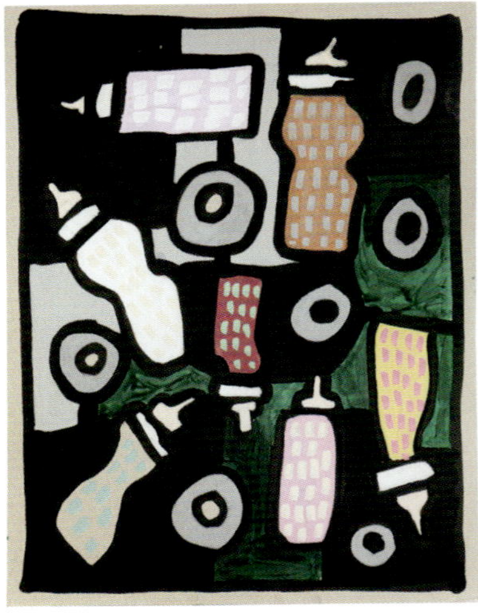
(12)

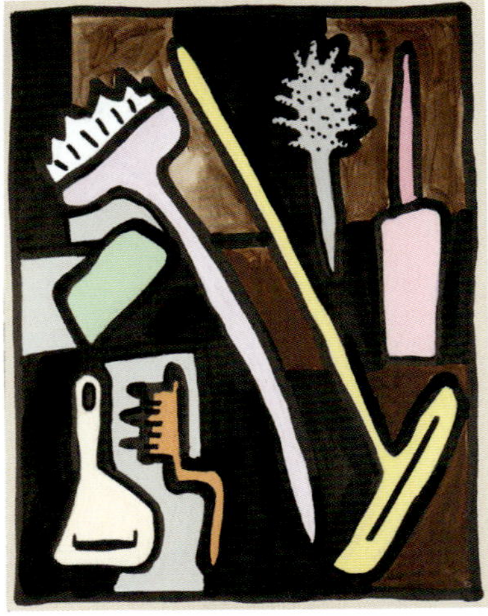
(13)

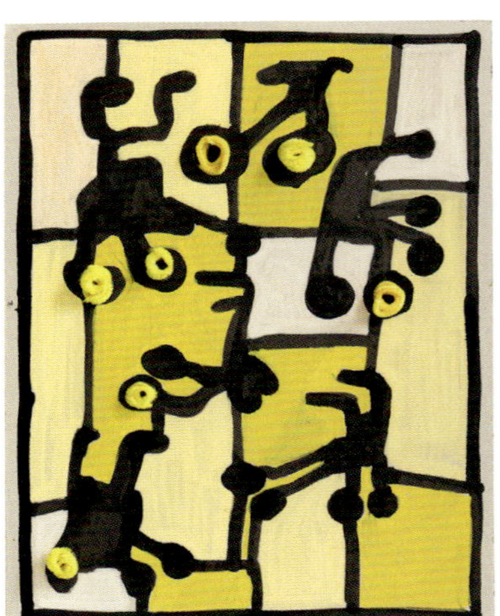
(14)

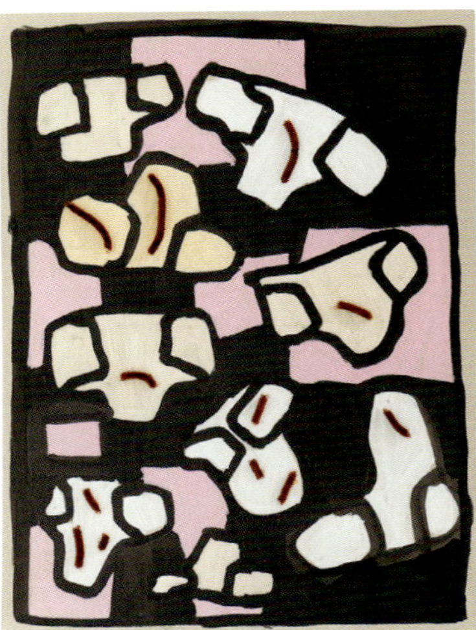
(15)

(12) ***Backlash (Female Ecosystem: Babyfeeding)*** 2022, car paint and acrylics on cardboard, 70 × 50 cm,
(13) ***Backlash (Female Ecosystem: Cleaning)*** 2022, car paint and acrylics on cardboard, 70 × 50 cm,
(14) ***Backlash (Female Ecosystem: Rollatoren)*** 2022, car paint and acrylics on cardboard, 70 × 50 cm,
(15) ***Backlash (Female Ecosystem: Pampers)*** 2022, car paint and acrylics on cardboard, 70 × 50 cm

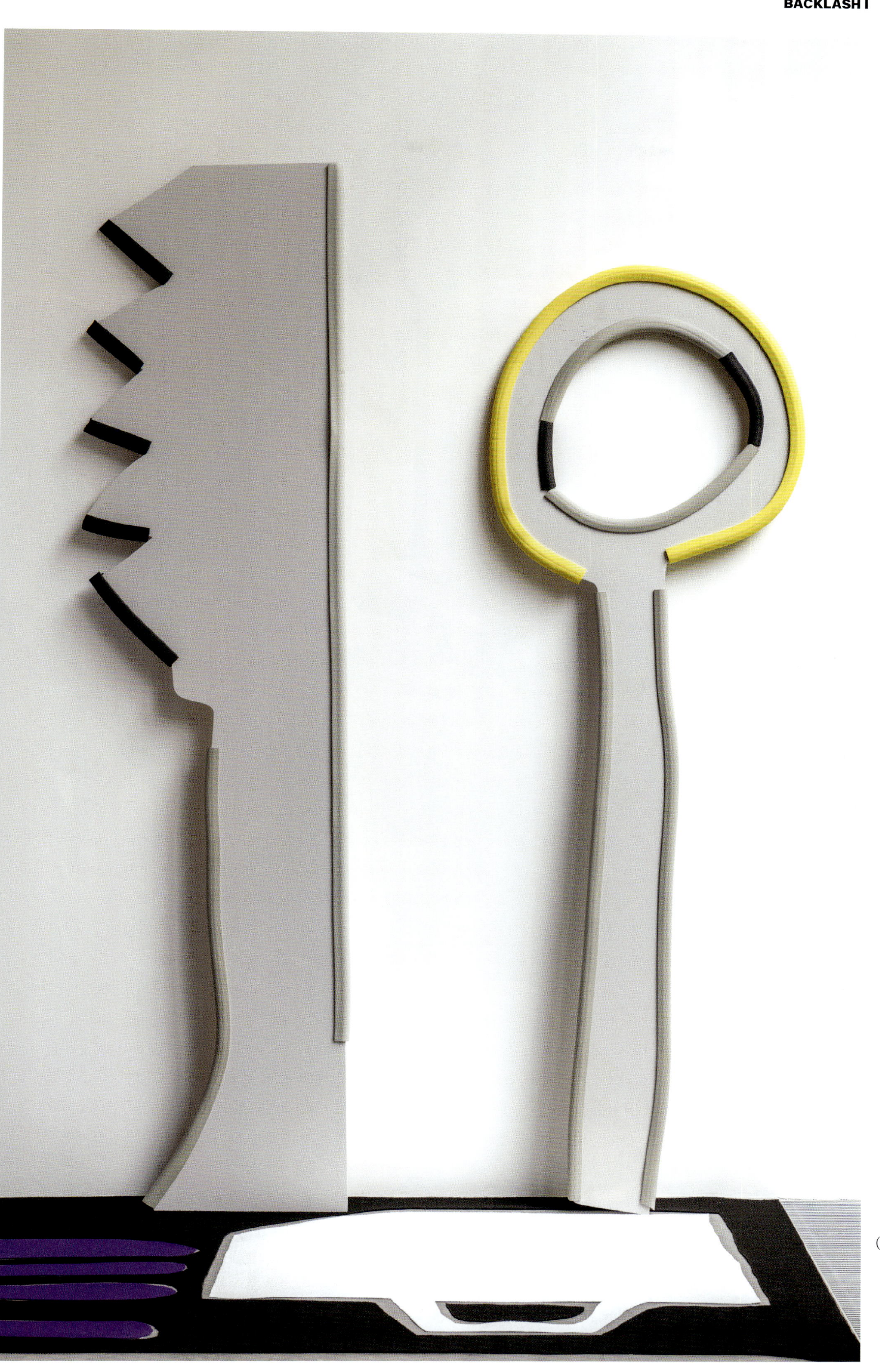

(16) ***Backlash***
2022, various materials, carpet, wood, varnish, edge protection, swimming noodles, drawings, dimensions variable,
Installation view
Museum Lothar Fischer

I

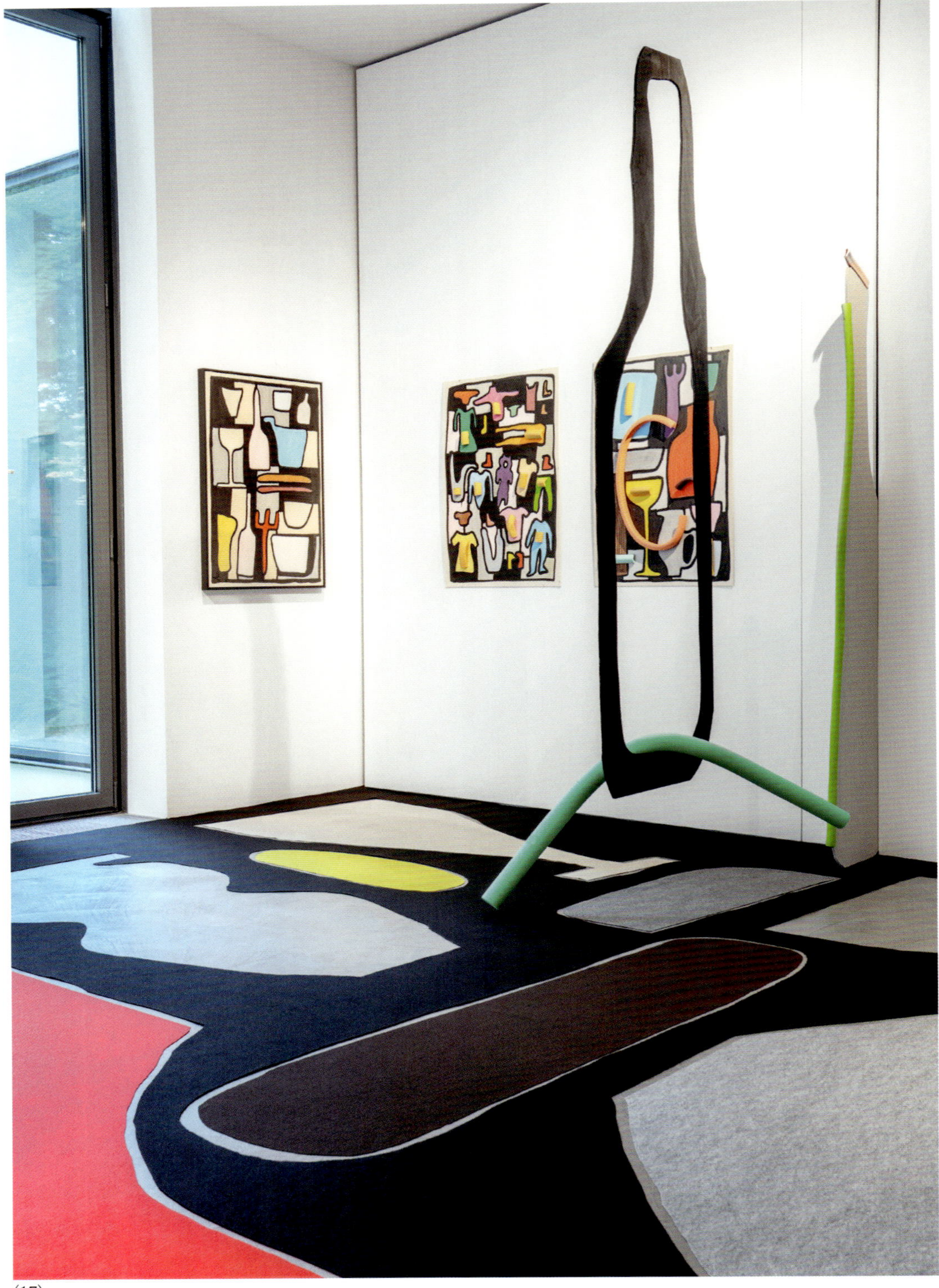

(17)

(17) ***Backlash***
2022, various materials, carpet, wood, varnish, edge protection, swimming noodles, drawings, dimensions variable, Installation view Museum Lothar Fischer

BACKLASH II

INGREDIENTS
Female Ecosystem ②
Backlash ③

EN An object transcends its physical existence, serving as more than just an object. It can become a symbol, evoke memories and fantasies, arouse desire or instil fear. It activates preconceived patterns of thought, scenarios of use and social roles. The work exhibited at the Kunsthalle Mannheim is part of a new series that juxtaposes everyday objects that still carry female connotations today.

[...] The small painting, which hangs on the large wall in the Kunsthalle's atrium near the entrance to the studio space, acts as a prologue to an expansive installation inside. Visitors encounter a curious doubling effect as the work is repeated in a monumental format on the central wall. It covers the entire surface, seems to want to expand indefinitely, and eventually spills out onto the floor of the room. From its initial obedient confinement within its frame, the installation seems to have developed a life of its own. The work not only takes on a new format, but also a new materiality. Through the use of cleaning rags, sponges and other more or less everyday objects, the acrylic painting is transformed into an expansive collage. [...]

Various processes of translation take place—from small to large format, from two-dimensional to three-dimensional, and from painting to collage or sculpture. As a viewer, one perceives their position in a new light. You are no longer standing in front of a small painting that you can easily take in at a glance, but in front of a larger-than-life, wall-sized work. [...] The representation of objects with female connotations and their transformation from small-scale painting into the monumental material collage become deliberate artistic statements, challenging prevailing gender stereotypes that persist in our everyday lives as well as in art.

☐ ***Anja Heitzer, catalog text for the exhibition STUDIO: Verena Issel at Kunsthalle Mannheim (excerpt)***

DE Ein Gegenstand ist mehr als nur ein physisches Objekt. Es kann als Symbol dienen, Erinnerungen und Fantasien provozieren, Begehren erwecken oder Angst einflößen. Es aktiviert vorgefertigte Denkmuster, Nutzungsszenarien und Rollenklischees. Die in der Kunsthalle Mannheim gezeigte Arbeit ist Teil einer neuen Werkserie, in der Alltagsgegenstände nebeneinandergestellt werden, die auch heute noch weiblich konnotiert sind.
[...] Die kleine Malerei, die an der großen Wand im Atrium der Kunsthalle neben dem Eingang zum Studioraum hängt, dient als Prolog zu einer raumgreifenden Installation im Inneren. Dort erwartet die Besucher*innen ein merkwürdiger Dopplungseffekt, denn an der zentralen Wand wiederholt sich die Arbeit in monumentalem Format.
Sie breitet sich über die gesamte Fläche aus, scheint sich unendlich ausdehnen zu wollen und ergießt sich schließlich über den Boden des Raumes. Ausgehend von dem gemalten Werk, das brav innerhalb seines Rahmens bleiben musste, scheint die Installation nun ein Eigenleben entwickelt zu haben. Das Werk erhält dabei nicht nur ein neues Format, sondern gleichsam eine neue Materialität. Aus dem Acrylgemälde wird durch den Einsatz von Putzlappen, Schwämmen und anderen mehr oder weniger alltäglichen Objekten eine raumgreifende Collage. [...]
So finden verschiedenste Übersetzungsprozesse statt – vom kleinen Format ins große, von der Zweidimensionalität zur Dreidimensionalität, von der Malerei zur Collage beziehungsweise zur Skulptur. Als Betrachterin nimmt man die eigene Position neu wahr. Wir stehen nicht mehr vor einem kleinen Gemälde, das auf einen Blick erfasst werden kann, sondern vor einer überlebensgroßen, wandfüllenden Arbeit. Die Collage breitet sich über den Raum aus und lässt uns plötzlich merkwürdig klein wirken.
[...] Die Darstellung weiblich konnotierter Gegenstände und ihre Übersetzung von der kleinformatigen Malerei in die monumentale Materialcollage werden zu bewussten künstlerischen Setzungen und hinterfragen gängige Rollenklischees, die sich in unserem Alltag ebenso hartnäckig halten wie in der Kunst.

☐ ***Anja Heitzer, Katalogtext zur Ausstellung STUDIO: Verena Issel in der Kunsthalle Mannheim (Auszug)***

I

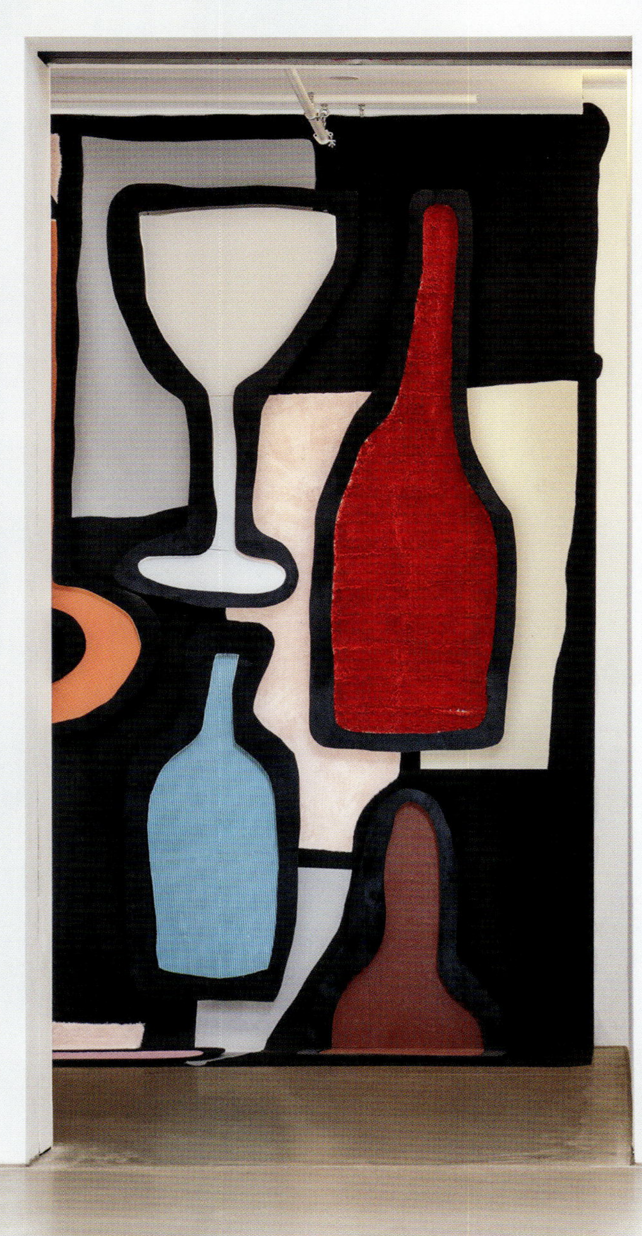

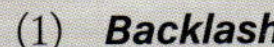

(1) ***Backlash***
2022, carpet, wood, cleaning utensils, framed painting, 600 × 600 cm, Installation view Kunsthalle Mannheim

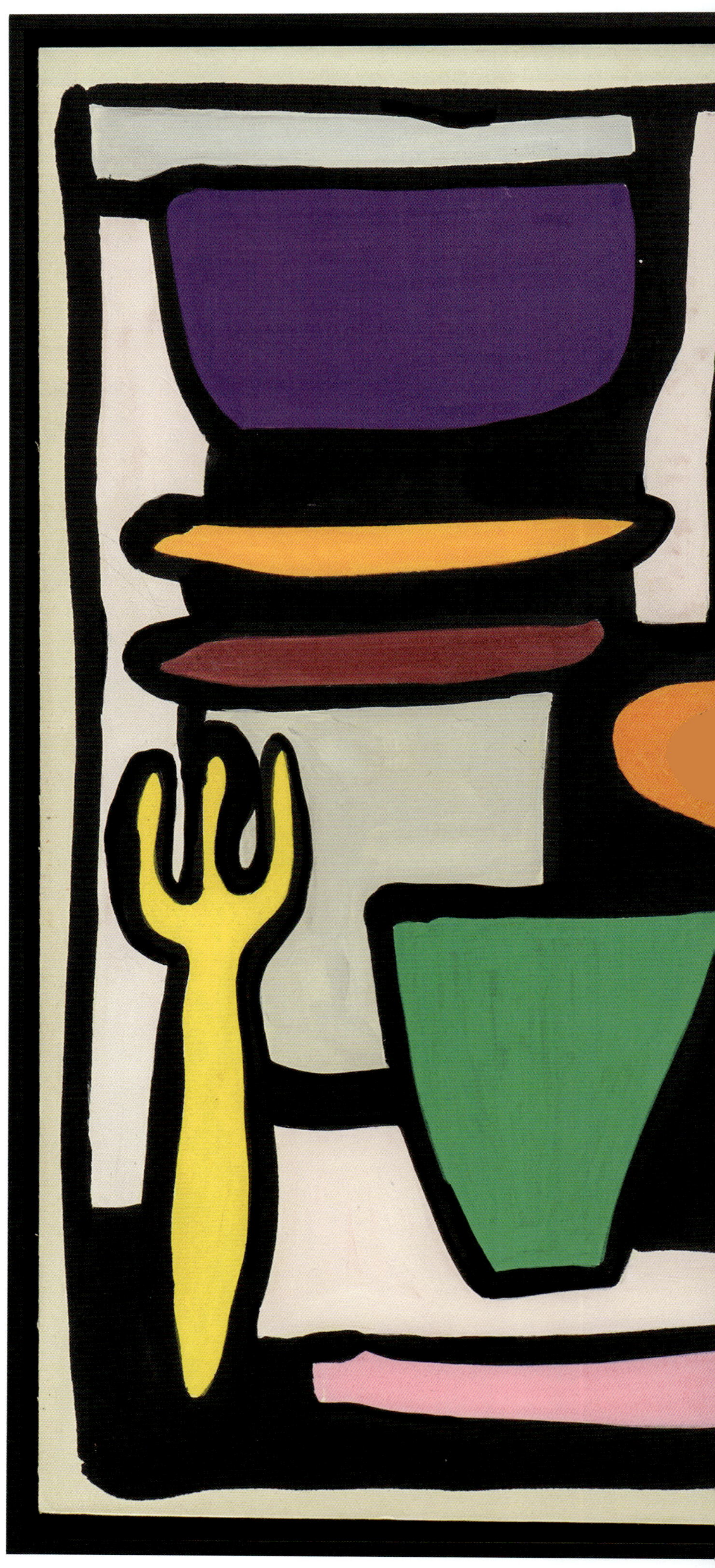

(2) ***Female Ecosystem***
2022, car paint and acrylics on cardboard, 60 × 60 cm

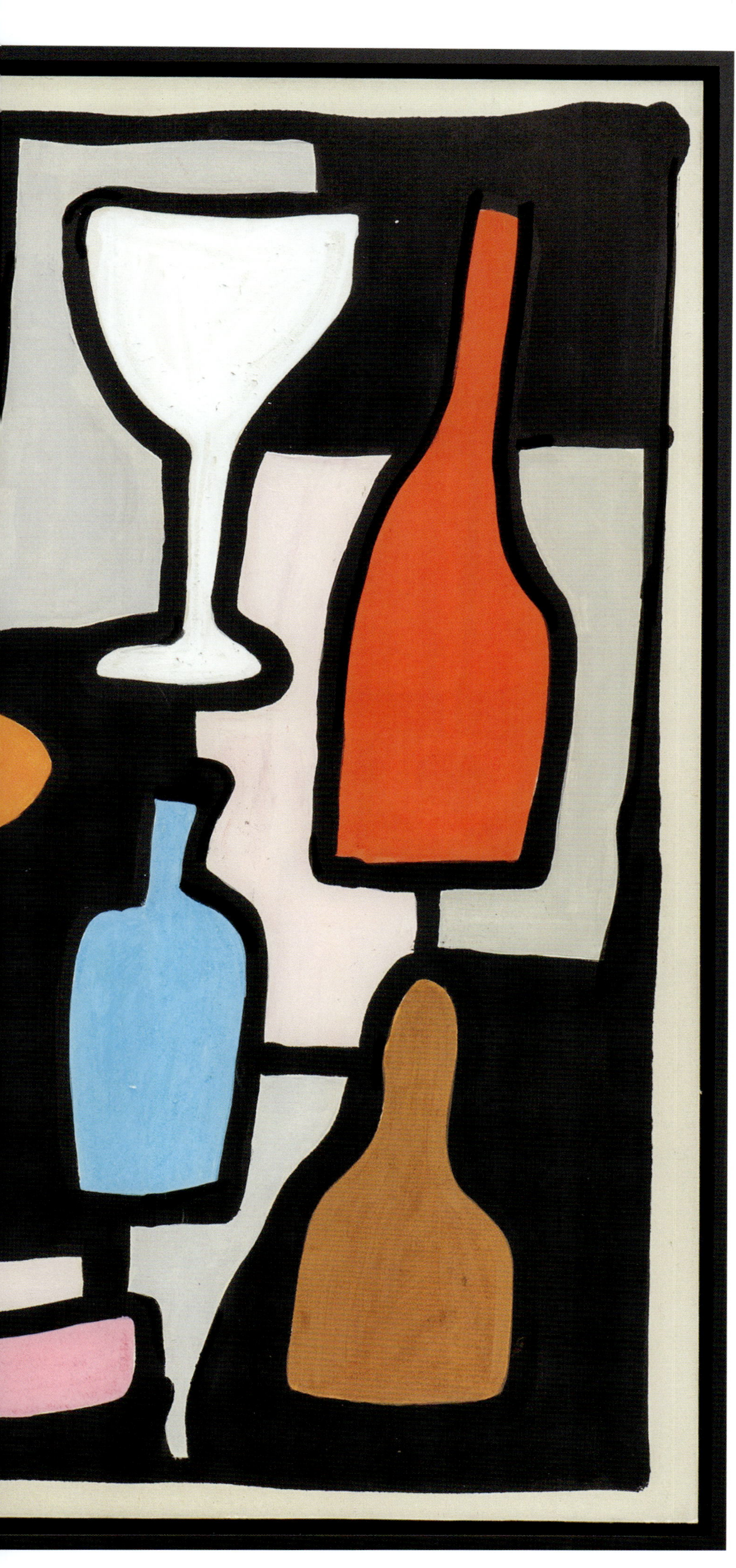

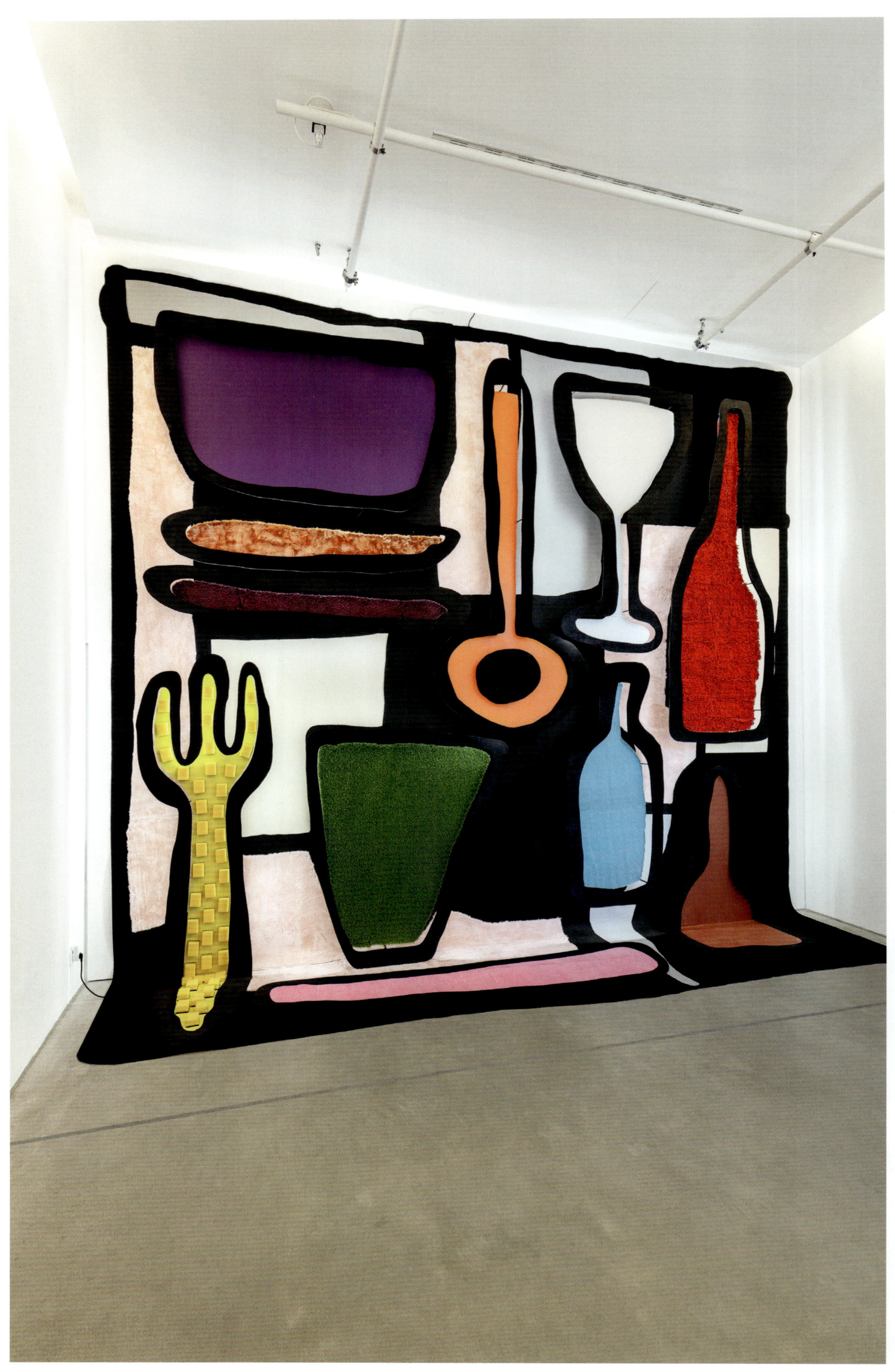

(3) ***Backlash***
2022, carpet, wood, cleaning utensils, framed painting, 600 × 600 cm, Exhibition view Kunsthalle Mannheim

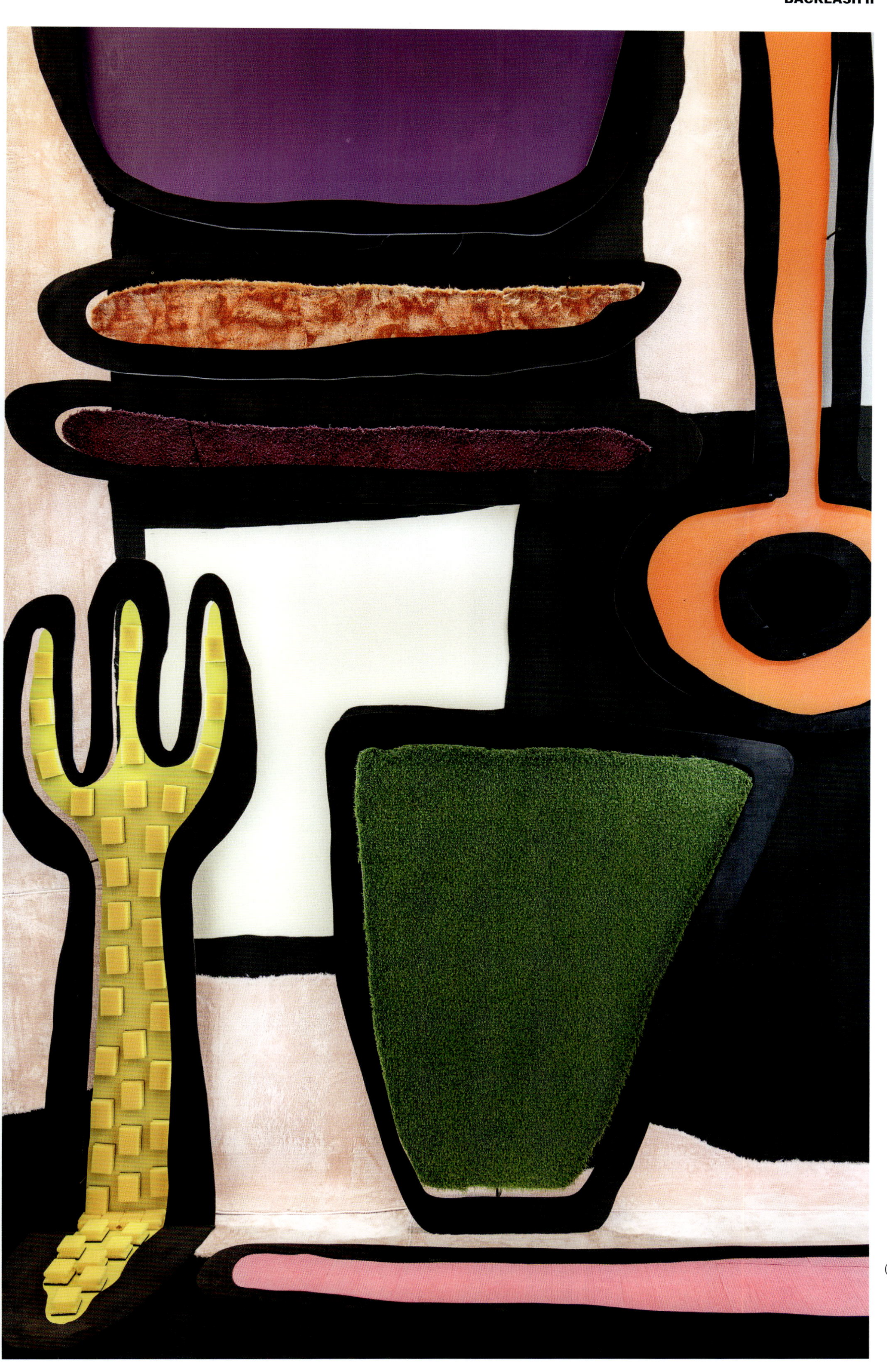

(4) ***Backlash***
2022, carpet, wood, cleaning utensils, framed painting, 600 × 600 cm, Installation view Kunsthalle Mannheim

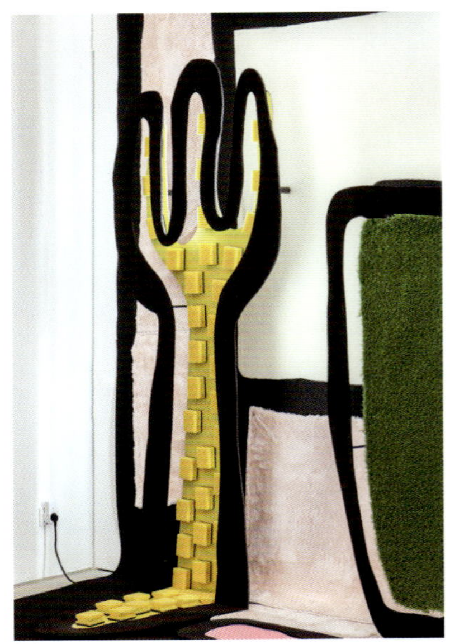
(5)

(5) ***Backlash***
2022, carpet, wood,
cleaning utensils,
framed painting,
600 × 600 cm,
Installation view
Kunsthalle Mannheim

PETRO-MANIA/ PETRO-MANUS

P

INGREDIENTS
Petromania/Petromanus ②

EN Verena Issel's work is a large carpet in honour of the great carpet tradition of Azerbaijan. But it's a different kind of carpet, made from very symbolic materials: plastic bags, rubber gloves, and yoga mats. The main elements are undoubtedly the black plastic bags. Woven into a thick black carpet, they can easily resemble an oil rug. And that's what they are, since plastic is essentially made from oil. Here and there, among the fluffy and wild pieces of plastic, a pink finger appears, pointing ... or is it something else? Oil arouses desires. And perhaps it is the desire for inner peace and well-being that wealth may or may not allow—we do yoga, they do war. Always the same thing. It doesn't stop, skin and skin for oil, until the very end.

□ ***Alfons Hug, exhibition text***

P

DE Verena Issel erschuf einen großen Teppich zu Ehren der bedeutenden Teppichtradition in Aserbaidschan. Aber es ist eine etwas andere Art von Teppich, hergestellt aus sehr symbolischen Materialien: Plastiktüten, Gummihandschuhe und Yogamatten. Die wichtigsten Elemente sind zweifellos die schwarzen Plastiktüten. Zu einem dicken schwarzen Teppich gewebt, können sie leicht an einen Ölteppich erinnern. Und genau das sind sie auch, denn Plastik wird im Wesentlichen aus Öl hergestellt. Hier und da taucht zwischen den flauschigen und wilden Plastikstücken ein rosafarbener Finger auf, der auf etwas zeigt ... oder ist es etwas anderes?
Öl weckt Begehrlichkeiten.
Und vielleicht ist es die Sehnsucht nach innerem Frieden und Wohlbefinden, die der Reichtum zulassen mag oder auch nicht – wir machen Yoga, die da machen Krieg. Immer das Gleiche.
Es hört nicht auf, Haut und Haut für Öl, immer weiter, bis zum Schluss.

☐ ***Alfons Hug, Ausstellungstext***

P

P

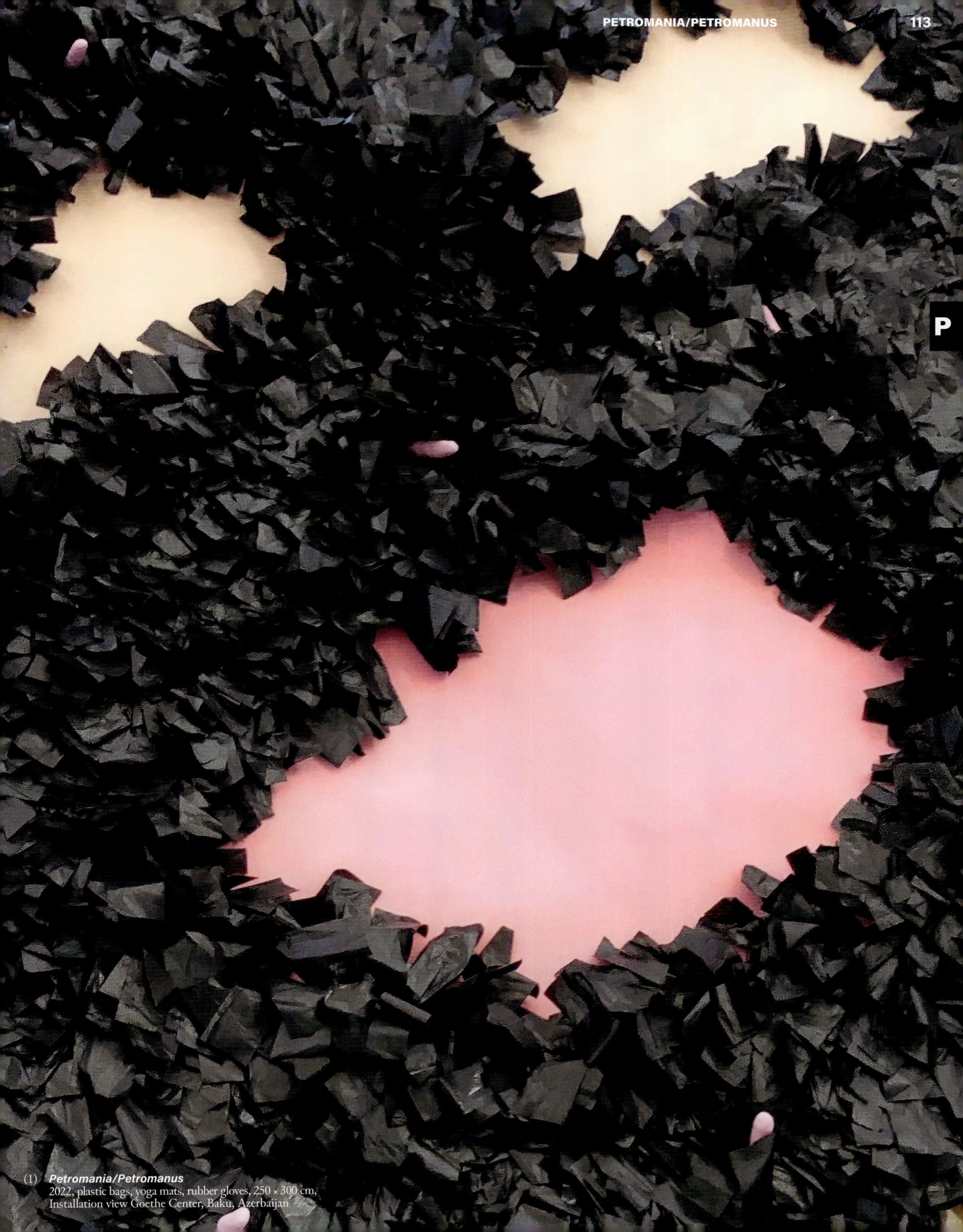

(1) ***Petromania/Petromanus***
2022, plastic bags, yoga mats, rubber gloves, 250 × 300 cm,
Installation view Goethe Center, Baku, Azerbaijan

P

P

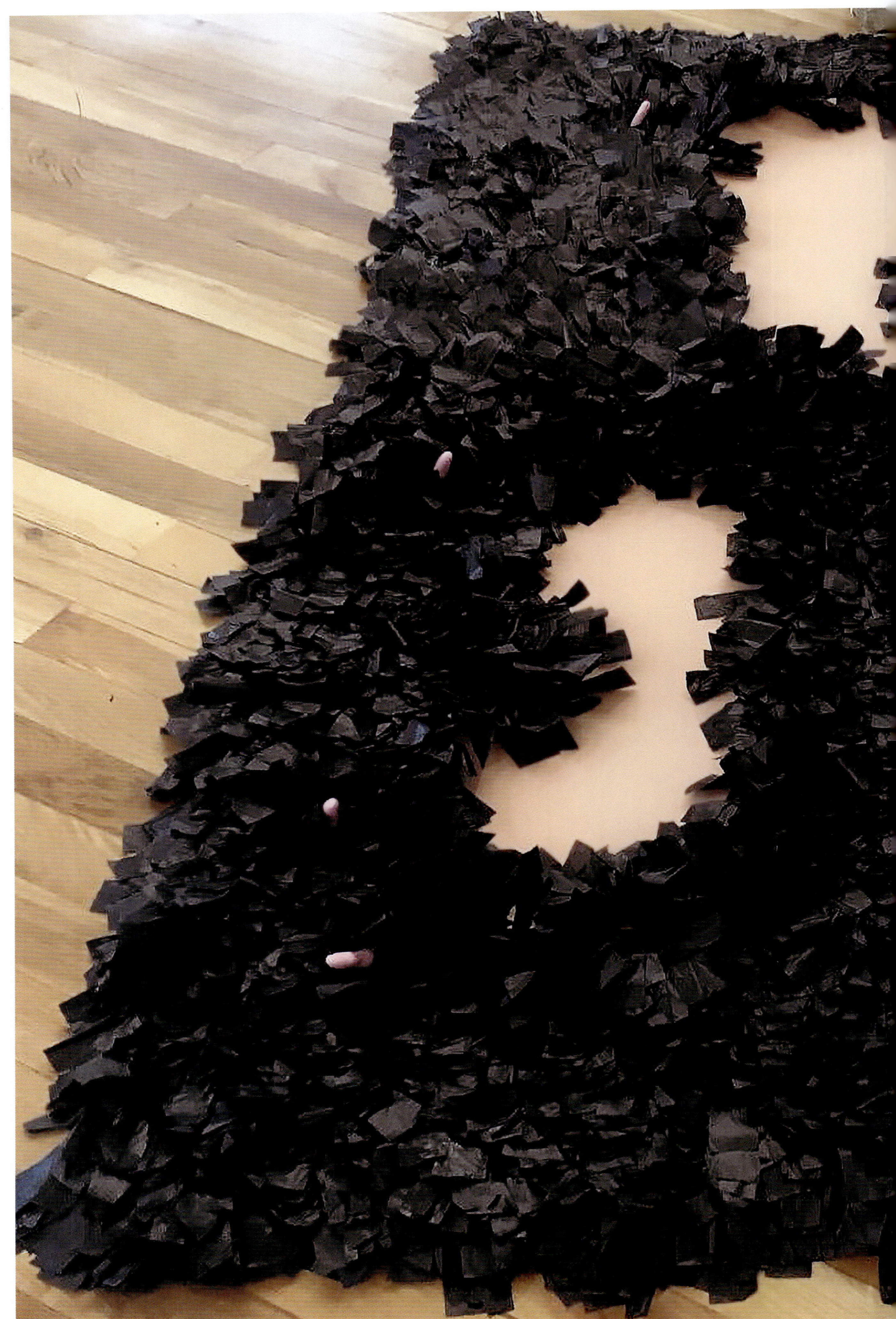

(2) ***Petromania/ Petromanus***
2022, plastic bags, yoga mats, rubber gloves, 250 × 300 cm, Installation view Goethe Center, Baku, Azerbaijan

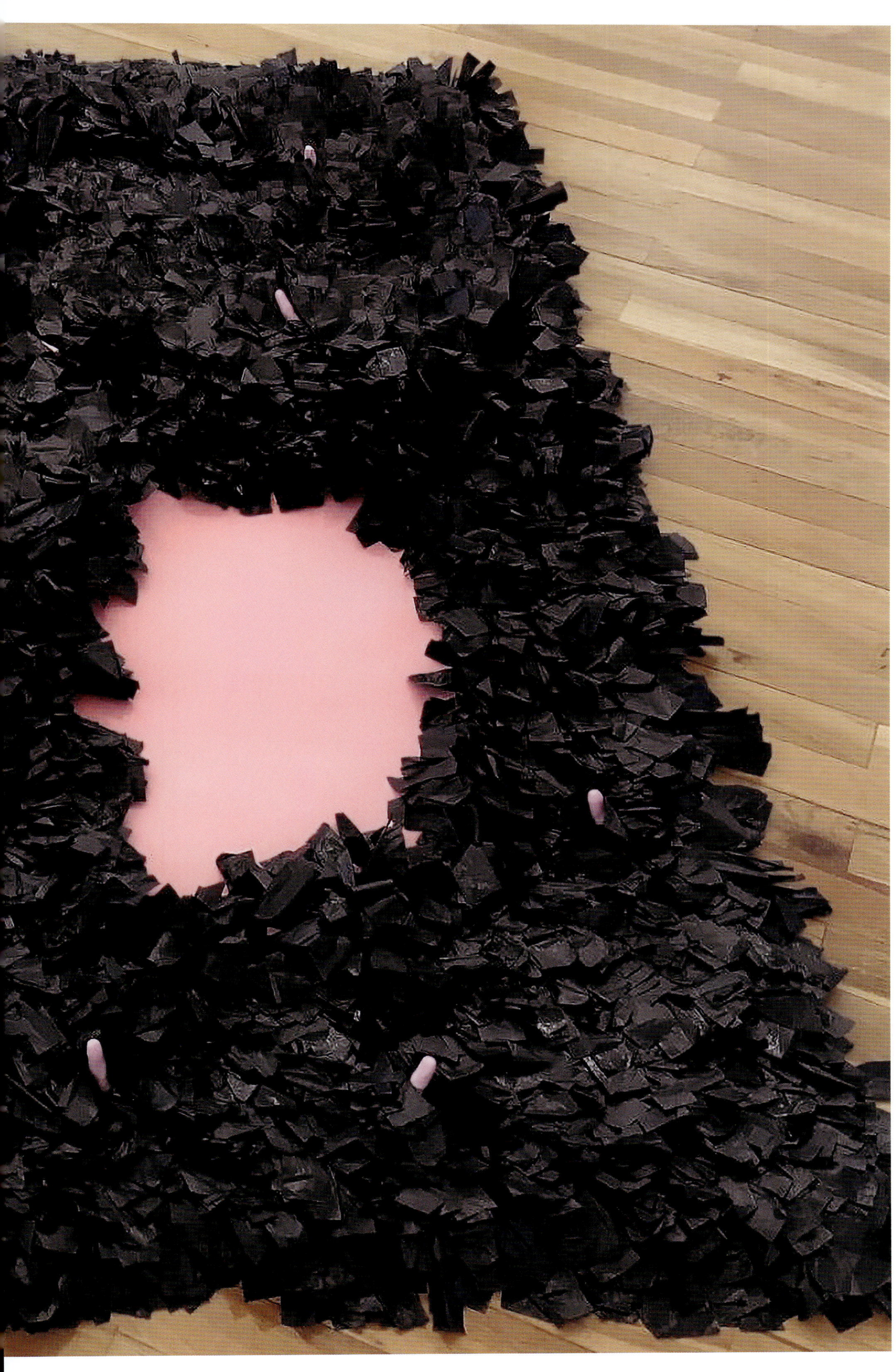

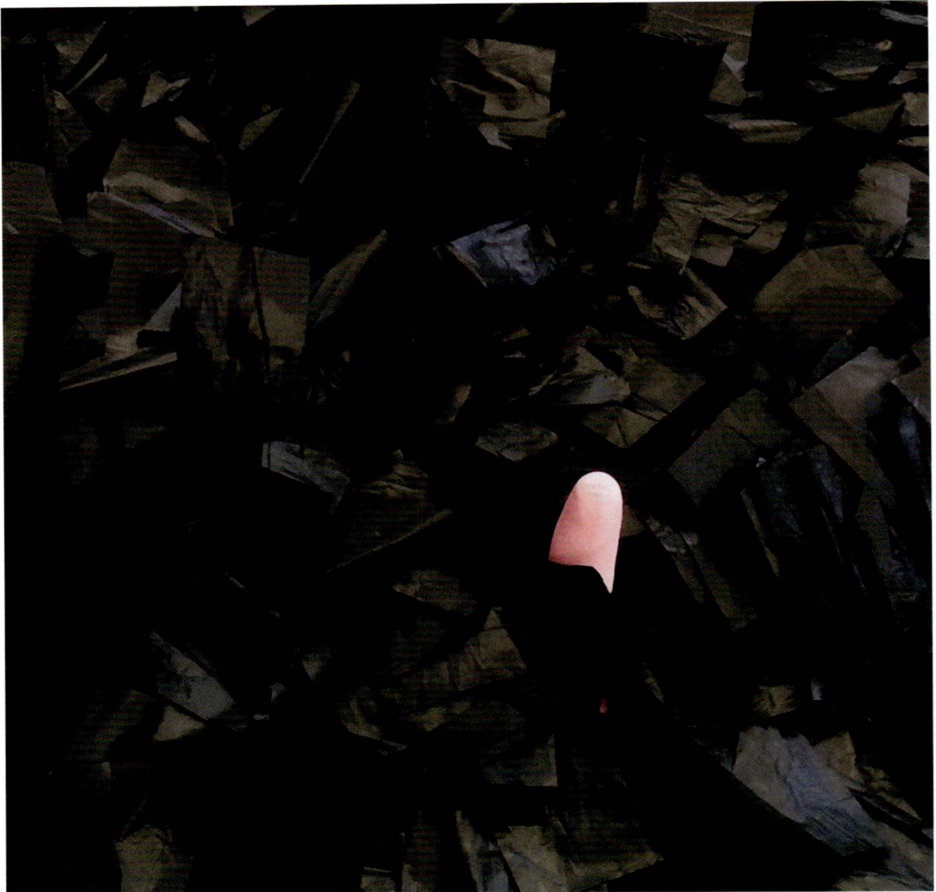

(3)

(4)

(3)
(4) ***Petromania/ Petromanus*** (detail)
2022, plastic bags, yoga mats, rubber gloves, 250 × 300 cm, Installation view Goethe Center, Baku, Azerbaijan

ETHNO ETHNO & TROPHY DELIGHT

P

INGREDIENTS
Meet Rose ②③④⑤
Meet Anthony ①④⑤
Backpackers Delight ⑦
Tropical Delight (precious wood ice cream) ⑧
Ohne Titel (Pantoffeltierchen) ⑨
Banane II ⑩
American Flag ⑪
Migränegurke mit Abwehr (Cultural Resistance) ⑫
Cargo: Wooden Radio ⑬
Cargo: Remote Control ⑭
Palme ⑮
Landkarte (Papua-Neuguinea) ⑯
Ohne Titel (Gelb) ⑰
Banana ⑱
Obstkorb ⑲
Flugzeug ⑳
Modern Apples ㉑
Tomate ㉒
Traube ㉓
Nippel und Agave ㉔
Apple No ㉕
Ohne Titel (Von der Rolle) ㉖
Manierismus heute: Da Sermoneta (Südseeschönheit) ㉗
Ohne Titel (kleine Teile und Erdnüsse) ㉘
Fresse, Mädchen! ㉙

EN Two room installations in an exhibition following a travel grant to Papua New Guinea.

The installation *Trophy Delight* deals with various aspects of cargo cults.
A cargo cult is a political, religious movement from Melanesia. The believers live in expectation of the return of their ancestors through symbolic acts of substitution, which are supposed to bring Western goods with them. There were and are various cargo cults. The cult has its roots in the encounter between Melanesians and Europeans, who brought new and supposedly miraculous cargo to previously isolated Melanesian cultures, and can be seen as a reaction to the sometimes radical social changes caused by missionization and colonial rule.
The occurrence was first observed and documented at the end of the 19th century. This phenomenon became particularly widespread in New Guinea during and after the Second World War. After initially mistaking the Europeans for the ancestors themselves, the indigenous population quickly realized that they were normal people, but much richer than themselves. They concluded that this wealth (the cargo) that had come from the Europeans was stolen from the land of the ancestors, who would come back to take revenge and hand over the cargo (firearms, cars, planes, etc.) to the indigenous people. In preparation for this event, they built replicas of port facilities, airfields or radio masts and partially destroyed their houses and plantations.
Verena Issel is rebuilding the replicas found in Papua New Guinea for *Trophy Delight*.
Issel created these replicas in various villages in Papua New Guinea while travelling there.
This public activity was an opportunity to talk to the local people. In a next step, these discussions resulted in the installation *Ethno Ethno*.

The technical devices—televisions and DVD players—are disguised to appear "exotic" and alien. Interviews could be heard through the telephone receivers attached to the televisions.
In these interviews, two women's rights activists from Papua New Guinea and Solomon Islands talk about the problems in their society, mostly caused by Western influence.

The two women's rights activists interviewed here have different motives for their commitment to women. While Rose calls on the matrilineal women in her village to adopt a more traditional way of life in order to be able to stand up to the economically invading Chinese through a local trade boycott, Anthony indirectly attacks the Catholic Church and the missionaries. "The machismo and the mistreatment of women, all of this came to us in the matriarchy through the Western church." Through their feminist commitment, both of them oppose influence from the West.

DE Zwei Rauminstallationen in einer Ausstellung nach einem Reisestipendium nach Papua-Neuguinea.

Die Installation *Trophy Delight* beschäftigt sich mit verschiedenen Aspekten von Cargo-Kulten. Ein Cargo-Kult (auch Cargokult) ist eine politische, religiöse Bewegung aus Melanesien. Die Gläubigen leben in der Erwartung der durch symbolische Ersatzhandlungen herbeigeführten Wiederkehr der Ahnen, die westliche Waren mit sich bringen sollen. Es gab und gibt verschiedene Cargo-Kulte.
Der Kult hat seine Wurzeln in der Begegnung von Melanesiern mit Europäern, die neuartiges und vermeintlich wundertätiges Frachtgut (englisch *cargo*) in ehemals isolierte melanesische Kulturen brachten, und ist als Reaktion auf die teilweise radikalen sozialen Veränderungen durch Missionierung und Kolonialherrschaft zu betrachten.
Beobachtet und dokumentiert wurde das Auftreten erstmals Ende des 19. Jahrhunderts. Besonders während des Zweiten Weltkriegs und danach erfuhr dieses Phänomen eine starke Verbreitung in Neuguinea. Nachdem die Europäer anfänglich für die Ahnen selbst gehalten wurden, erkannte die indigene Bevölkerung rasch, dass es normale Menschen waren, die aber viel reicher waren als sie selbst. Sie schlossen, dass dieser Reichtum (der Cargo) von den Europäern aus dem Land der Ahnen gestohlen wurde, die aber zurückkommen würden, um sich zu rächen und den Cargo (Feuerwaffen, Autos, Flugzeuge usw.) den Indigenen zu übergeben. Zur Vorbereitung dieses Ereignisses errichteten sie Nachbauten von Hafenanlagen, Flugplätzen oder Funkmasten und zerstörten teilweise ihre Häuser und Pflanzungen.
Verena Issel baut für *Trophy Delight* die in Papua-Neuguinea vorgefundenen Nachbauten wieder nach.
Diese Nachbauten erstellte Issel während der Reise vor Ort in verschiedenen Dörfern Papua-Neuguineas. Diese öffentliche Tätigkeit war Gesprächsanlass mit den Menschen vor Ort.
Aus diesen Gesprächen entstand dann in einem weiteren Schritt die Installation *Ethno Ethno*.

Die technischen Geräte – Fernseher und DVD-Player – werden getarnt, um „exotisch" und fremdartig zu wirken. Durch die Telefonhörer an den Fernsehern waren Interviews zu hören. In diesen Interviews sprechen Frauenrechtsaktivist*innen aus Papua-Neuguinea und Solomon Islands über die meist durch westlichen Einfluss produzierten Probleme in ihrer Gesellschaft. Die beiden hier interviewten Frauenrechtsaktivist*innen haben unterschiedliche Motive für ihr Engagement für Frauen. Während Rose die matrilinear lebenden Frauen in ihrem Dorf zu einer traditionelleren Lebensweise aufruft, um den hier wirtschaftlich einfallenden Chinesen durch einen lokalen Handelsboykott die Stirn bieten zu können, greift Anthony die katholische Kirche und die Missionare indirekt an. „Der Machismo und die Misshandlung der Frauen, all das kam durch die westliche Kirche zu uns ins Matriarchat." Beide stellen sich so durch das feministische Engagement gegen den Einfluss aus dem Westen.

P

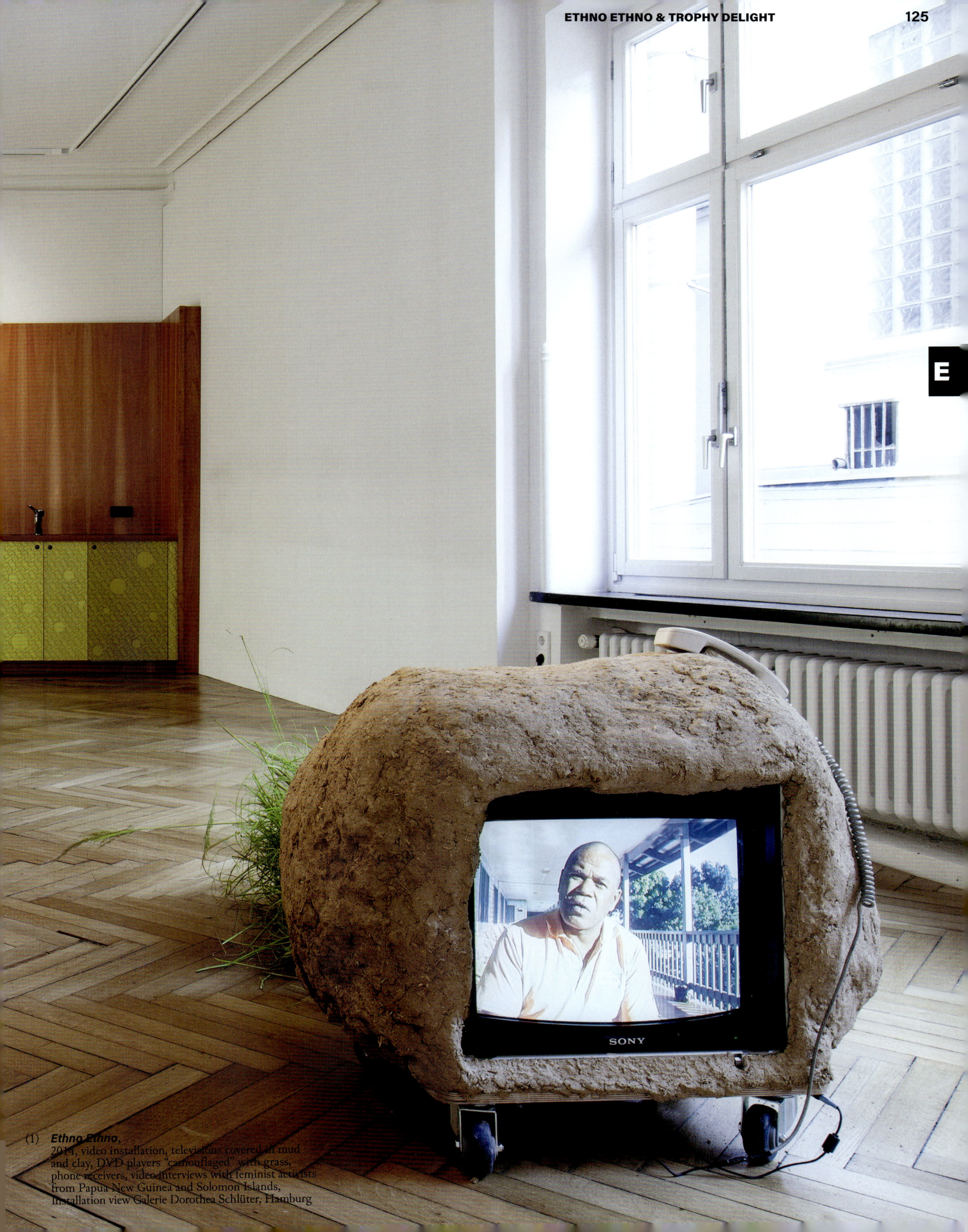

(1) ***Ethno Ethno***,
2014, video installation, televisions covered in mud and clay, DVD players "camouflaged" with grass, phone receivers, video interviews with feminist activists from Papua New Guinea and Solomon Islands, Installation view Galerie Dorothea Schlüter, Hamburg

E

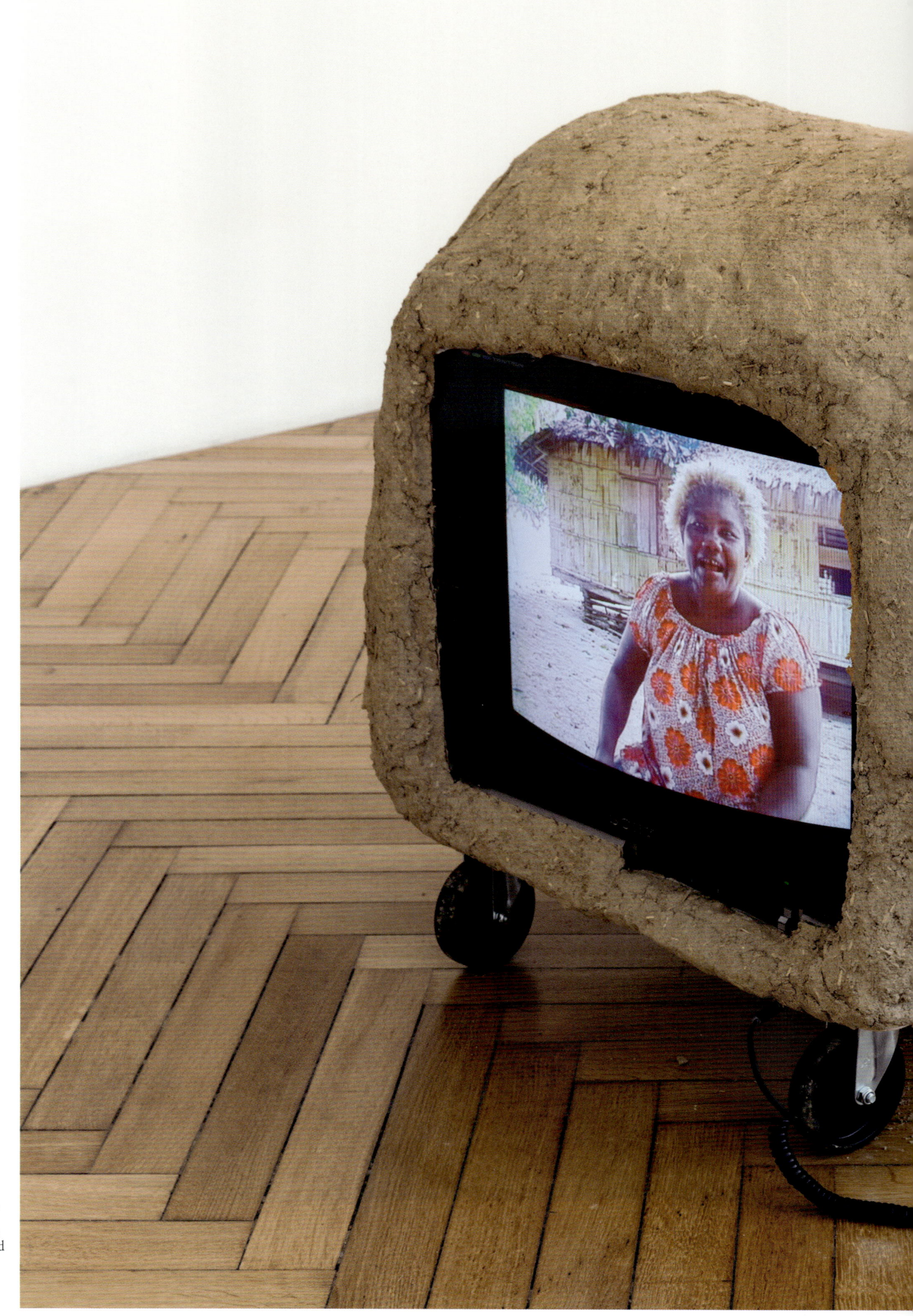

(2) ***Ethno Ethno***
2014, video installation, televisions covered in mud and clay, DVD players "camouflaged" with grass, phone receivers, video interviews with feminist activists from Papua New Guinea and Solomon Islands, Installation view Galerie Dorothea Schlüter, Hamburg

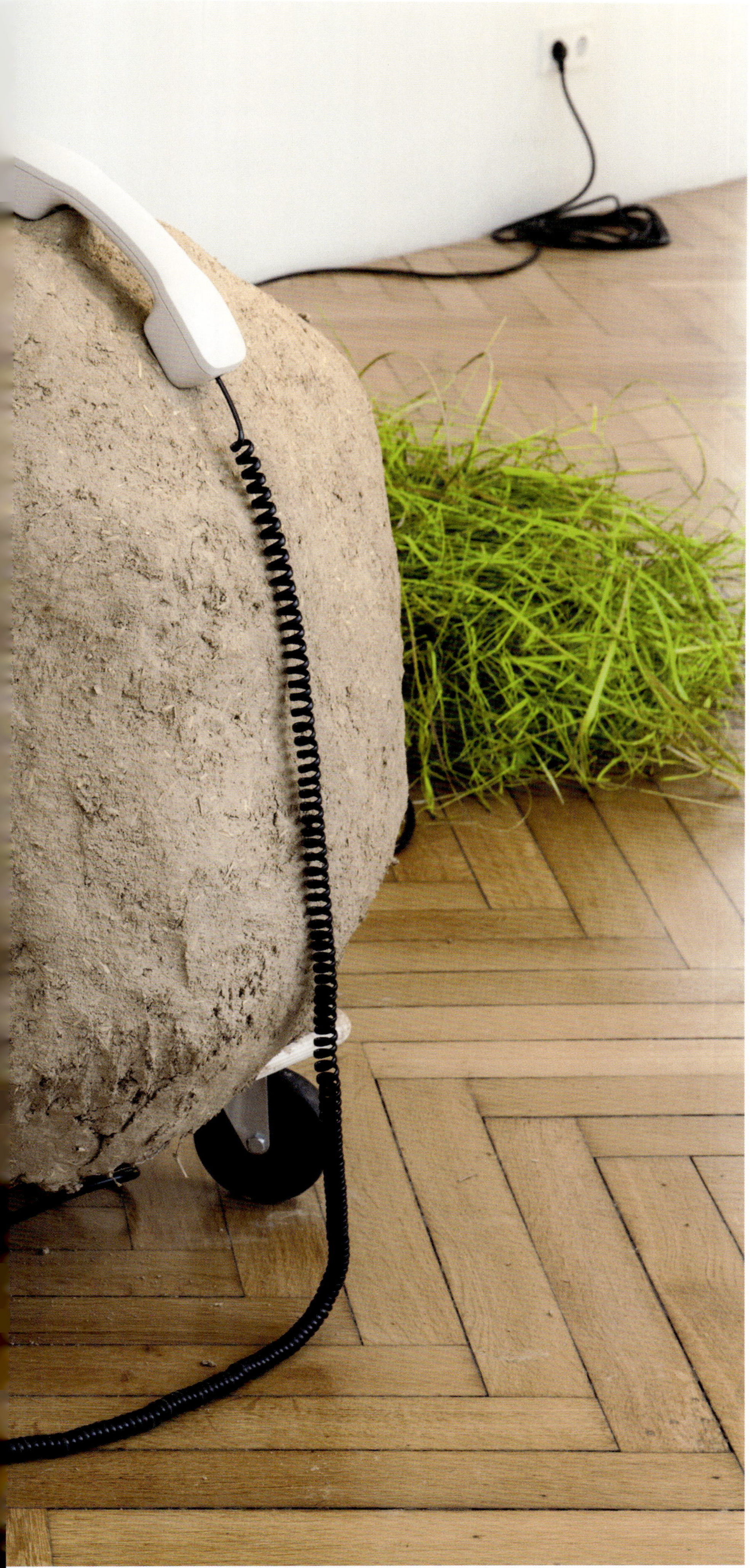

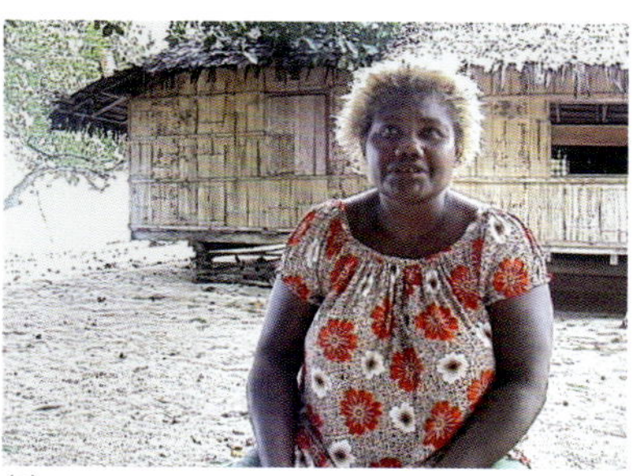

(3)

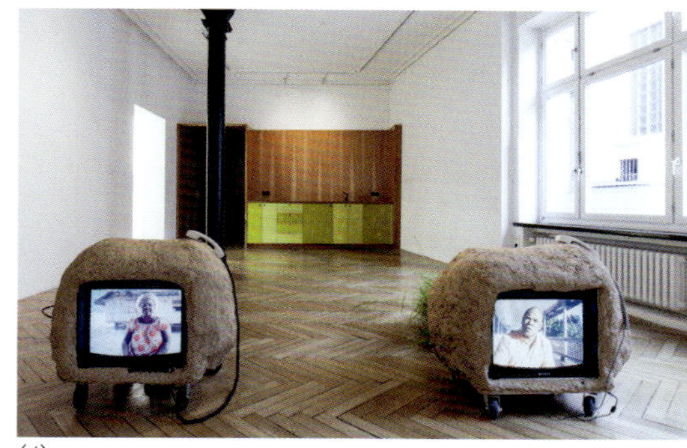

(4)

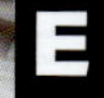

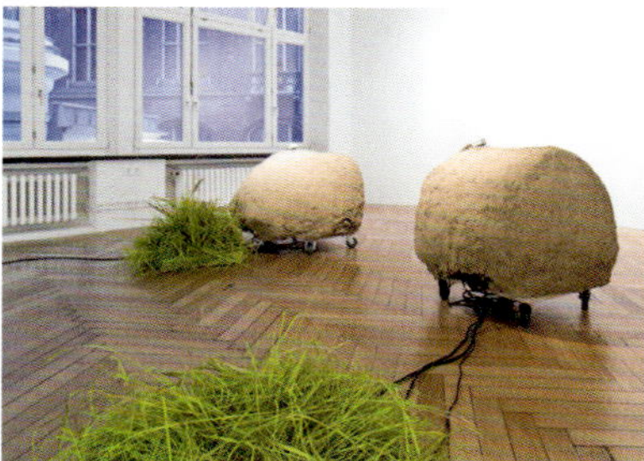

(5)

(3) ***Trophy Delight***, videostill of ***MEET ROSE (empowering women)***, 18 min., Mini-DV, interview with a women's rights activist from New Ireland (Papua New Guinea), Installation view Galerie Dorothea Schlüter, Hamburg

(4) ***Trophy Delight***, videostills of ***MEET ROSE (empowering women)***, 18 min., Mini-DV, interview with a women's rights activist from New Ireland (Papua New Guinea) and ***MEET ANTHONY (empowering women)***, 15 min., Mini-DV, interview with a women's rights activist from Choiseul (Solomon Islands), Installation view Galerie Dorothea Schlüter, Hamburg

(5) ***Trophy Delight***, here: Ethno-Ethno, 2014, video installation, televisions covered in mud and clay, DVD players "camouflaged" with grass, phone receivers, Installation view Galerie Dorothea Schlüter, Hamburg

E

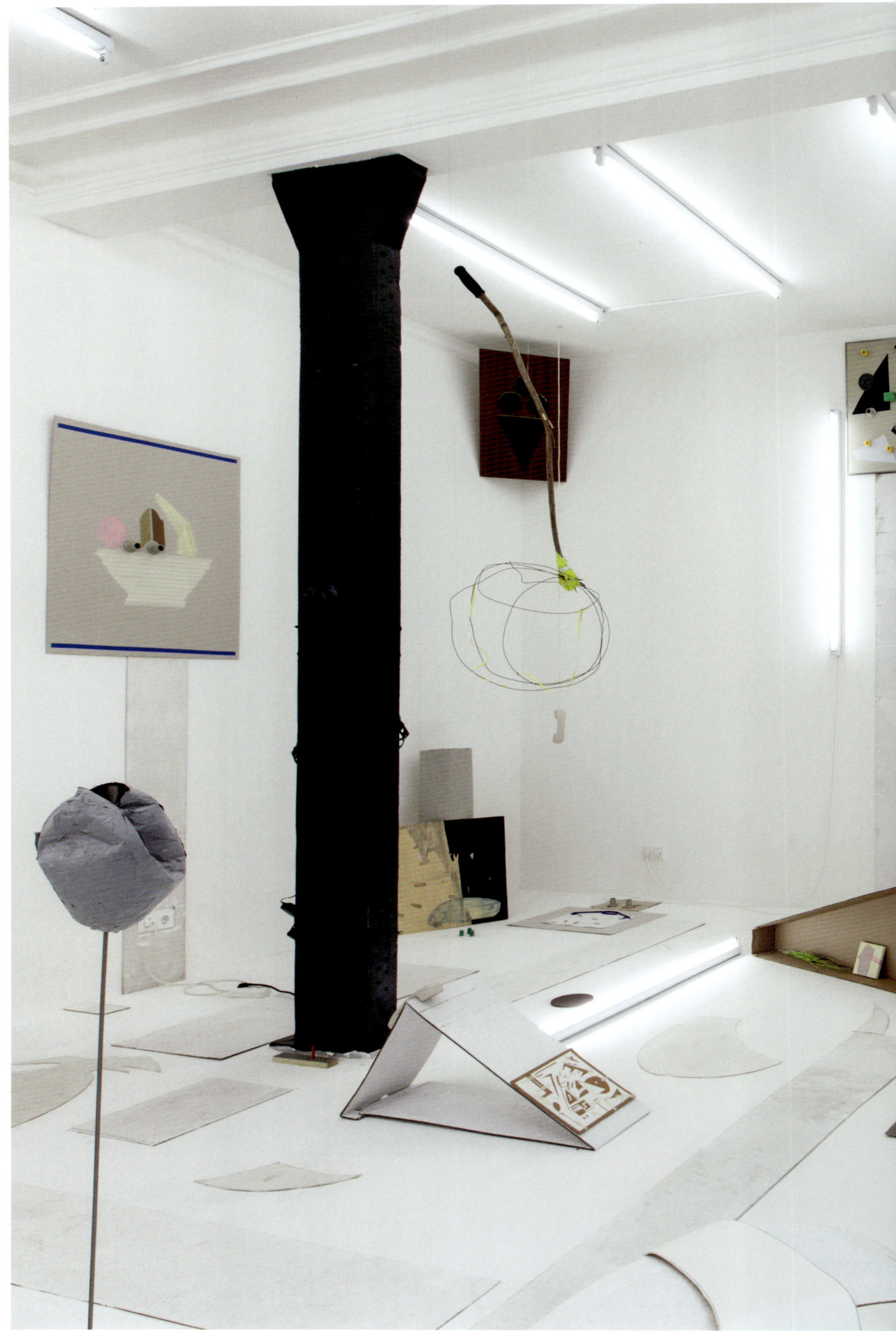

(6) ***TROPHY DELIGHT***
2014, various works and materials, dimensions of the room approx. 8 × 8 m, Installation view Galerie Dorothea Schlüter, Hamburg

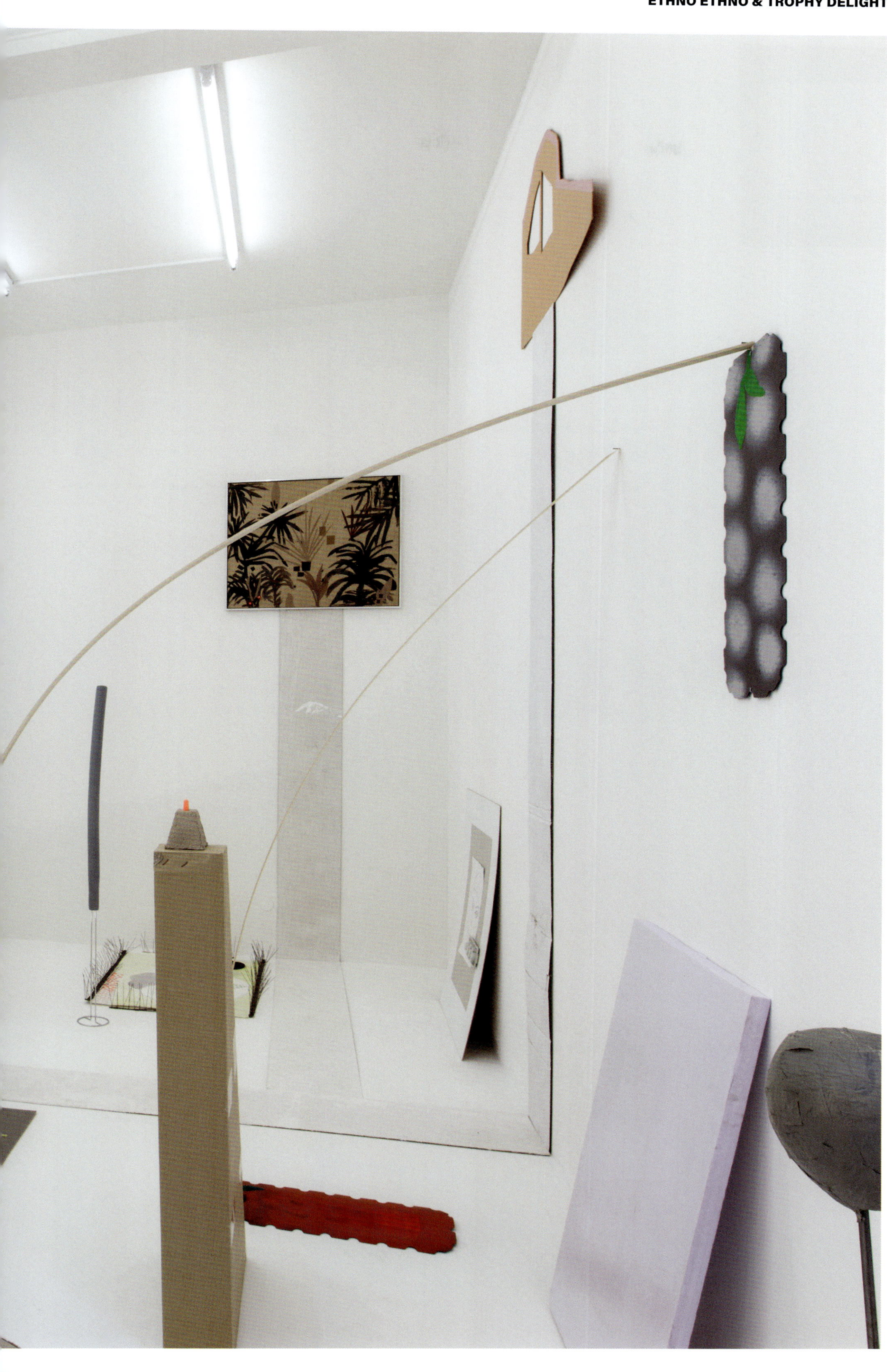

E

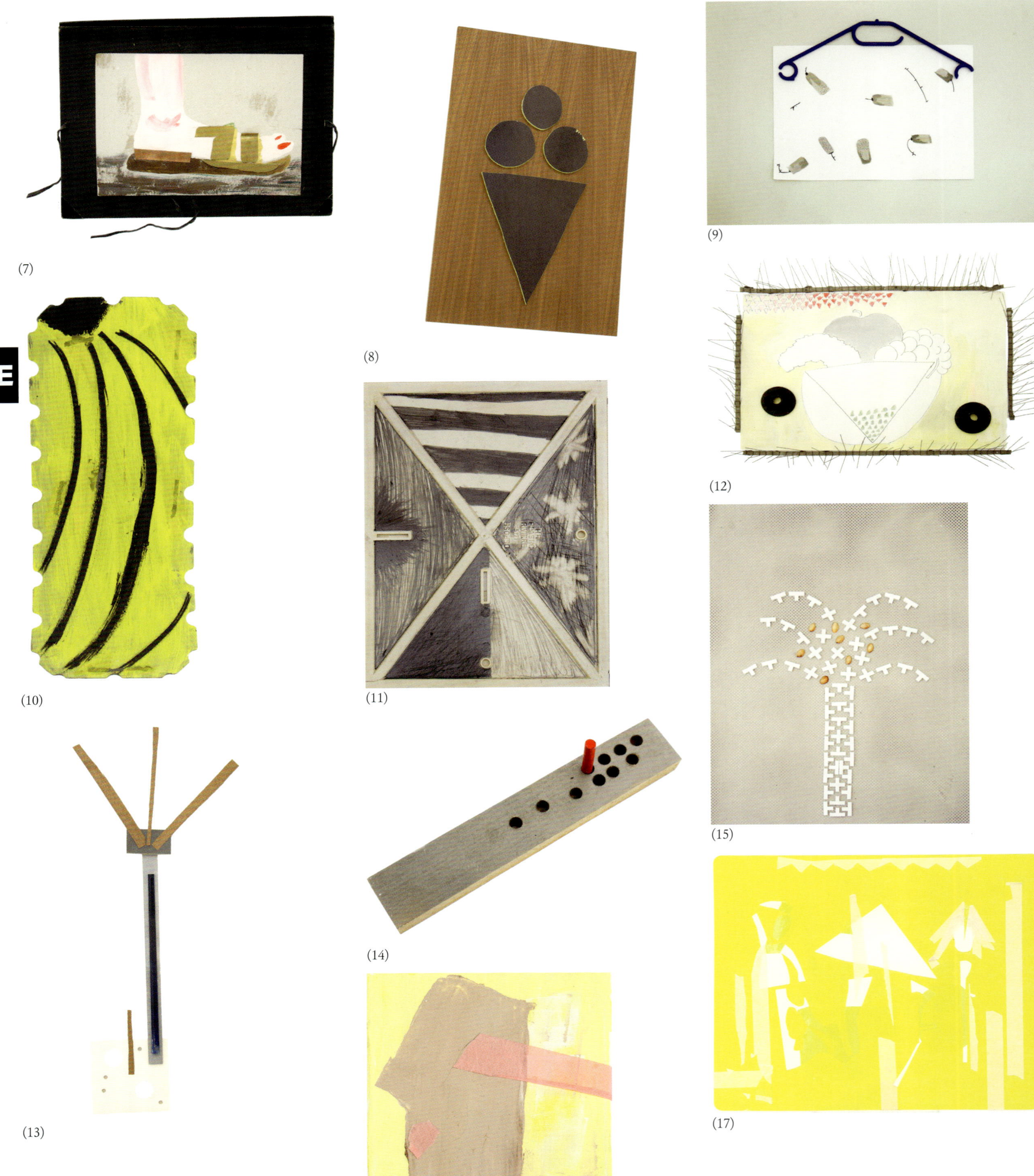

(7)

(8)

(9)

(10)

(11)

(12)

(13)

(14)

(15)

(16)

(17)

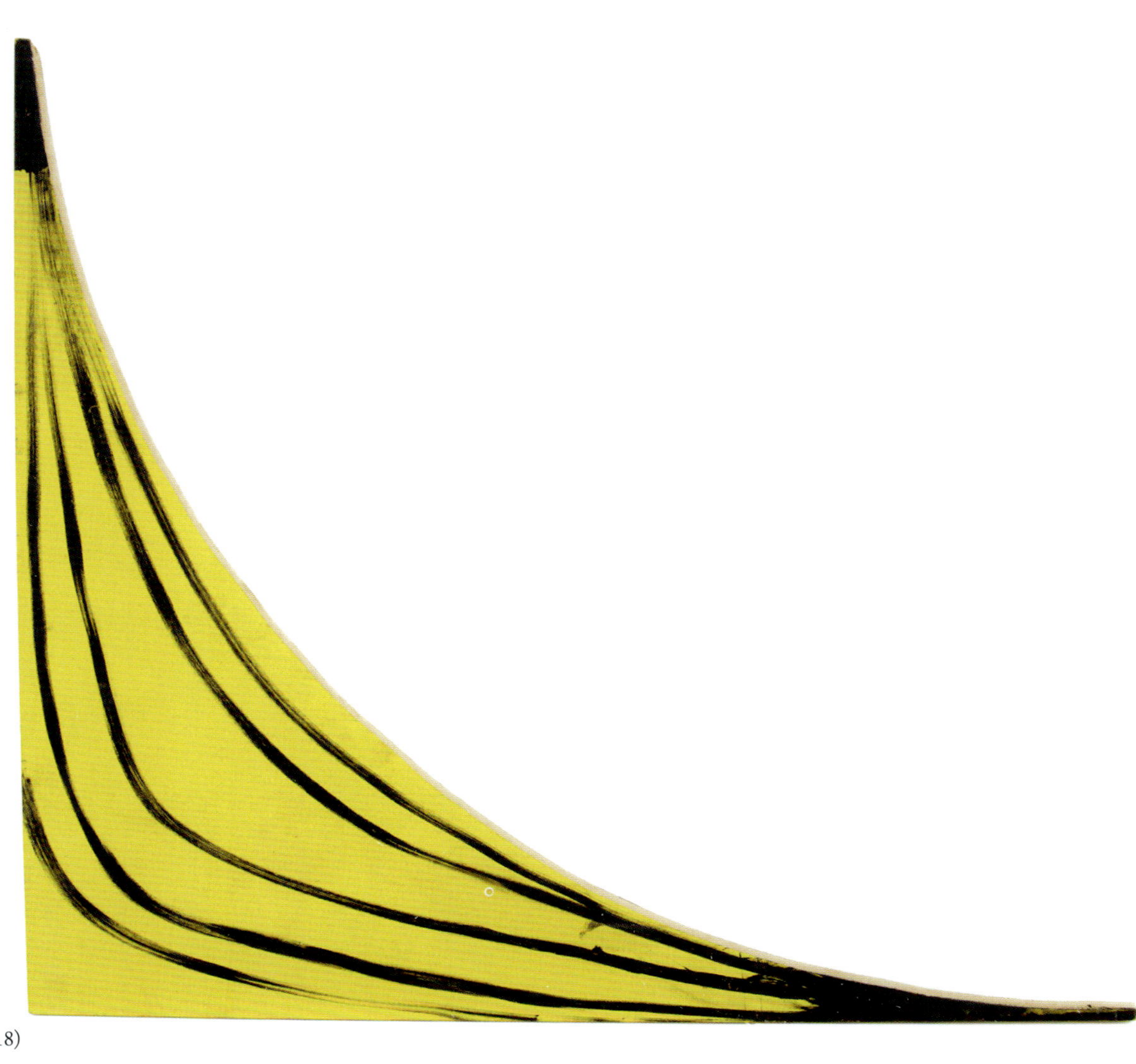

(18)

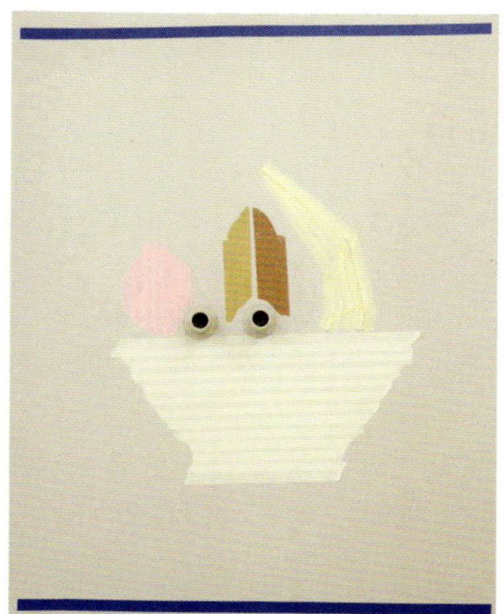

(19)

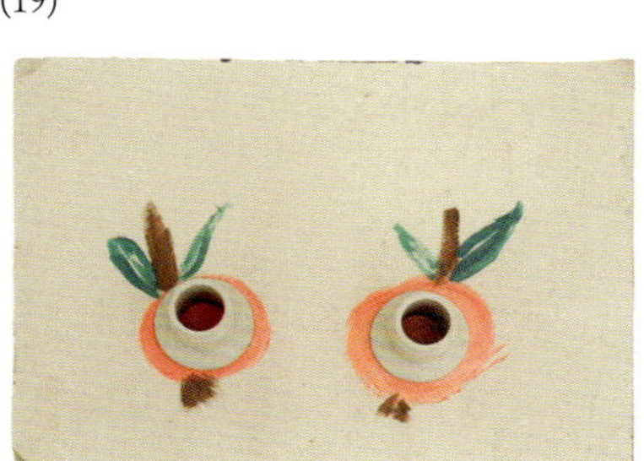

(21)

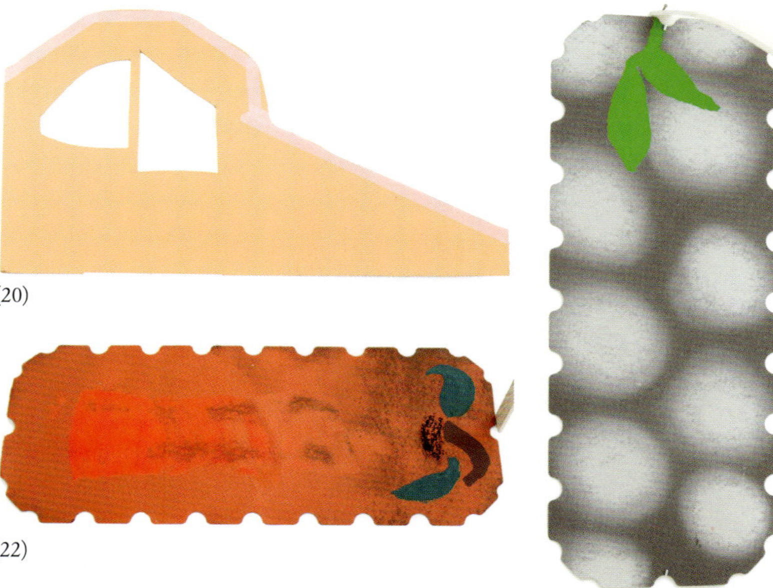

(20)

(22)

(23)

(7) **Backpackers Delight**
2010/2014, acrylic paint and metal on paper on cardboard, 34 × 45 cm

(8) ***Tropical Delight (precious wood ice cream)***
2014, oak on mahogany with text marker, 80 × 50 cm

(9) ***Ohne Titel (Pantoffeltierchen)***
2013, acrylic paint on paper with plastic, 50 × 70 cm

(10) ***Banane II***
2013, acrylic paint on cardboard, 62 × 24.5 cm

(11) ***American Flag*** 2013, graphite on plastic, 21 × 16 cm

(12) ***Migränegurke mit Abwehr (Cultural Resistance)***
2013, acrylic paint and plastic on paper, 70 × 100 cm

(13) ***Cargo: Wooden Radio***,
2014, acrylic paint on wood, 96 × 40 cm

(14) ***Cargo: Remote Control***
2014, acrylic paint on wood, 20 × 4 cm

(15) ***Palme***
2013, plastic and peanuts on plastic, 70 × 50 cm

(16) ***Landkarte (Papua-Neuguinea)***
2014, acrylic paint and adhesive tape on canvas, 15 × 15 cm

(17) ***Ohne Titel (Gelb)***
2013, paper and foil on plastic, 30.5 × 38 cm

(18) ***Banana***
2013, acrylic paint on wood, 110 × 48 cm

(19) ***Obstkorb***
2013, adhesive tape and plastic on cardboard, 100 × 80 cm

(20) ***Flugzeug***
2013, adhesive tape on cardboard, 60 × 110 cm

(21) ***Modern Apples***
2010/2013, acrylic paint and plastic on paper, 24 × 34 cm

(22) **Tomate**
2013, acrylic paint on cardboard, 62 × 24.5 cm

(23) **Traube**
2013, acrylic paint and spray paint on cardboard, 62 × 24.5 cm

(24) **Nippel und Agave**
2014, Stain and adhesive tape on wood, 68.5 × 86 cm

(25) ***Apple No***
2013, adhesive foil and wood on glass with plastic, 100 × 70 cm

(26) ***Ohne Titel (Von der Rolle)***
2013, pencil and foam rubber on paper, 25 × 25 cm

(27) ***Manierismus heute: Da Sermoneta (Südseeschönheit)***
2013, Styrofoam and cardboard on wood, 120 × 60 cm

(28) ***Ohne Titel (kleine Teile und Erdnüsse)***
2014, plastic, paper, peanuts on metal, 28 × 26.5 cm

(29) ***Fresse, Mädchen!***
2013, felt-tip pen on paper with plastic and wood, 100 × 80 cm

E

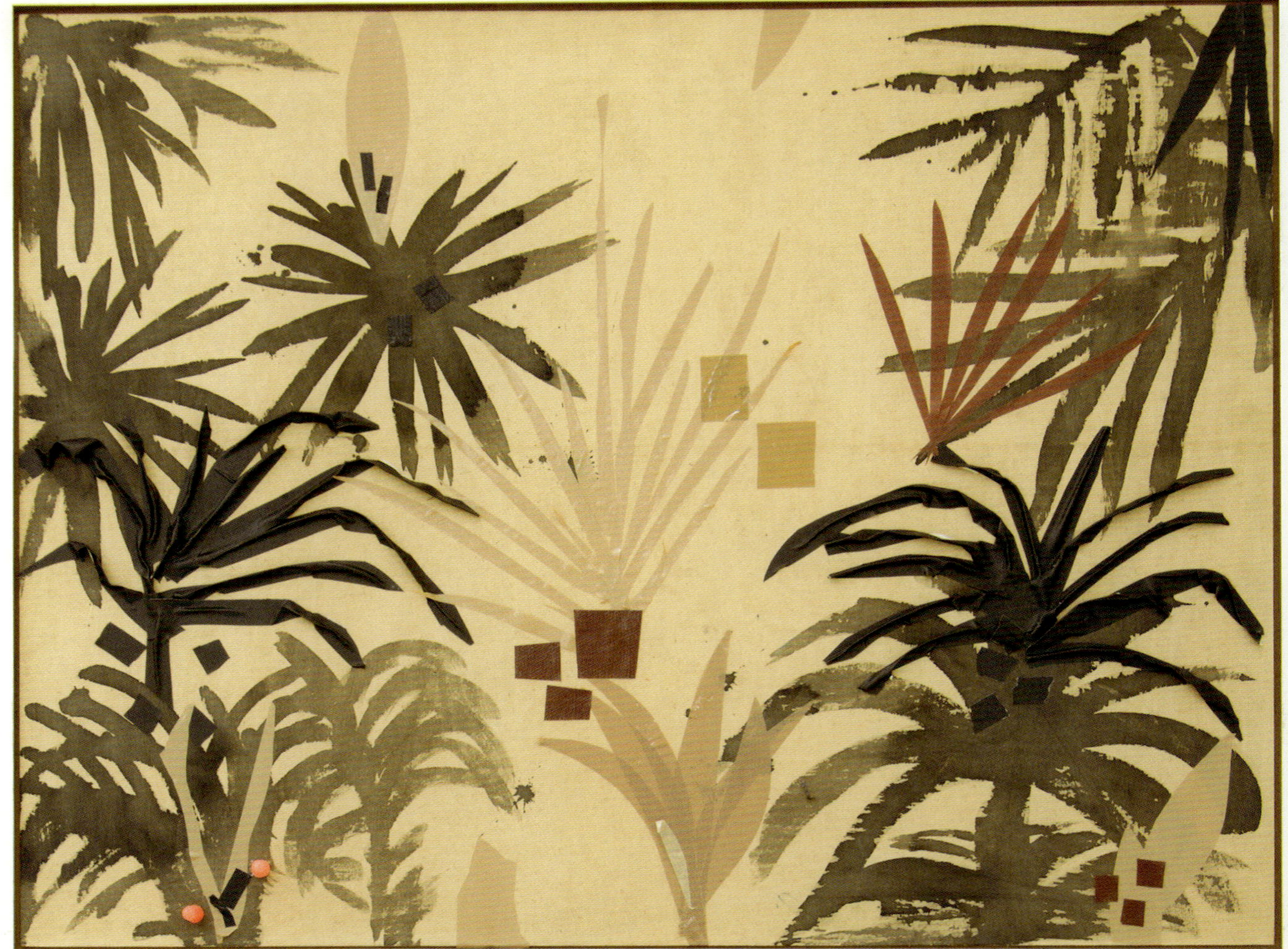
(24)

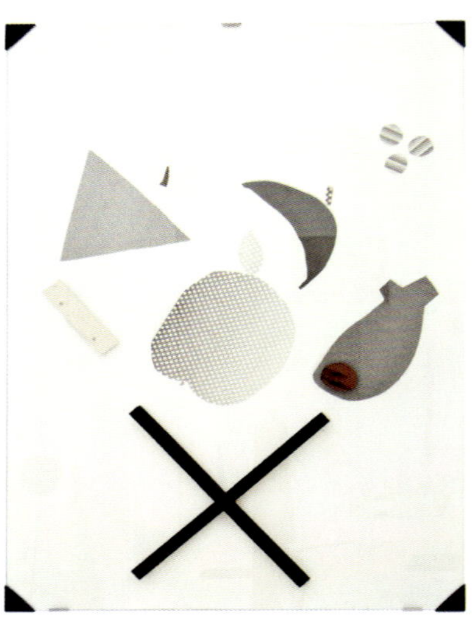
(25)

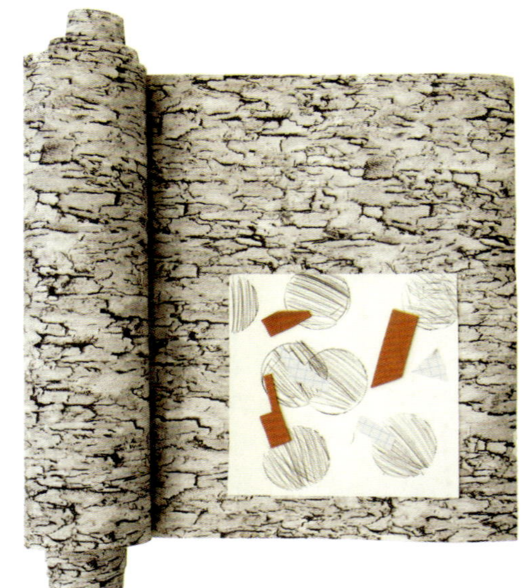
(26)

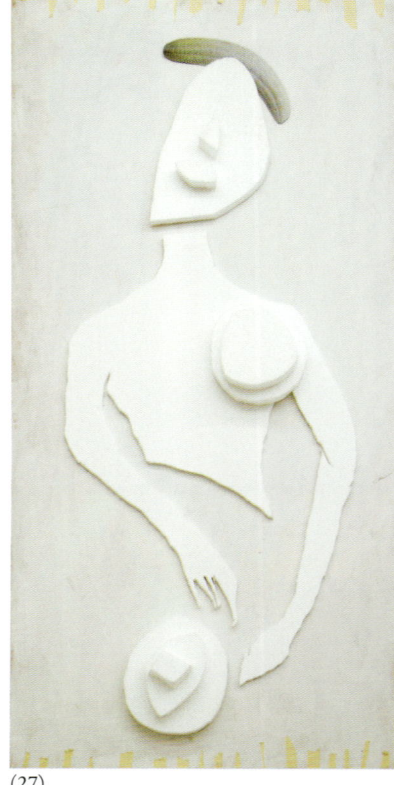
(27)

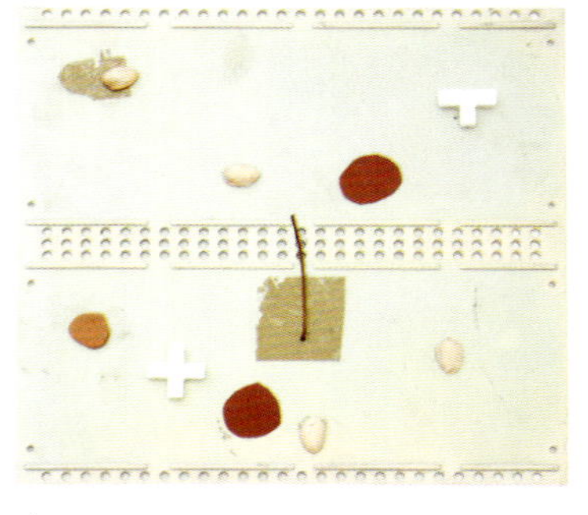
(28)

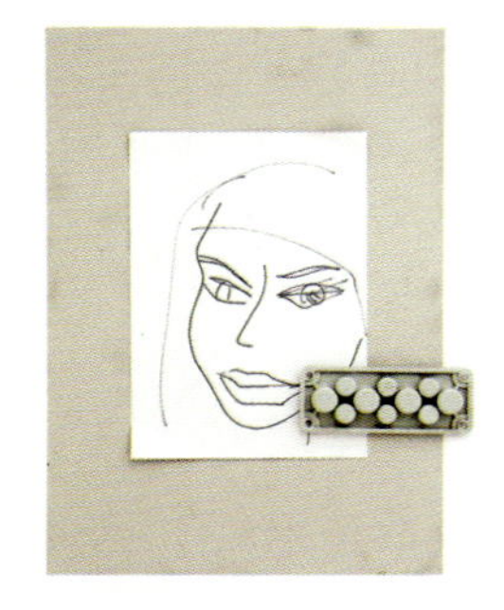
(29)

MODERN NARCISSUS/ TEMPLE GUARDIAN

E

INGREDIENTS
Modern Narcissus ①
Tempelhüter ①
Negative Narcissus ②

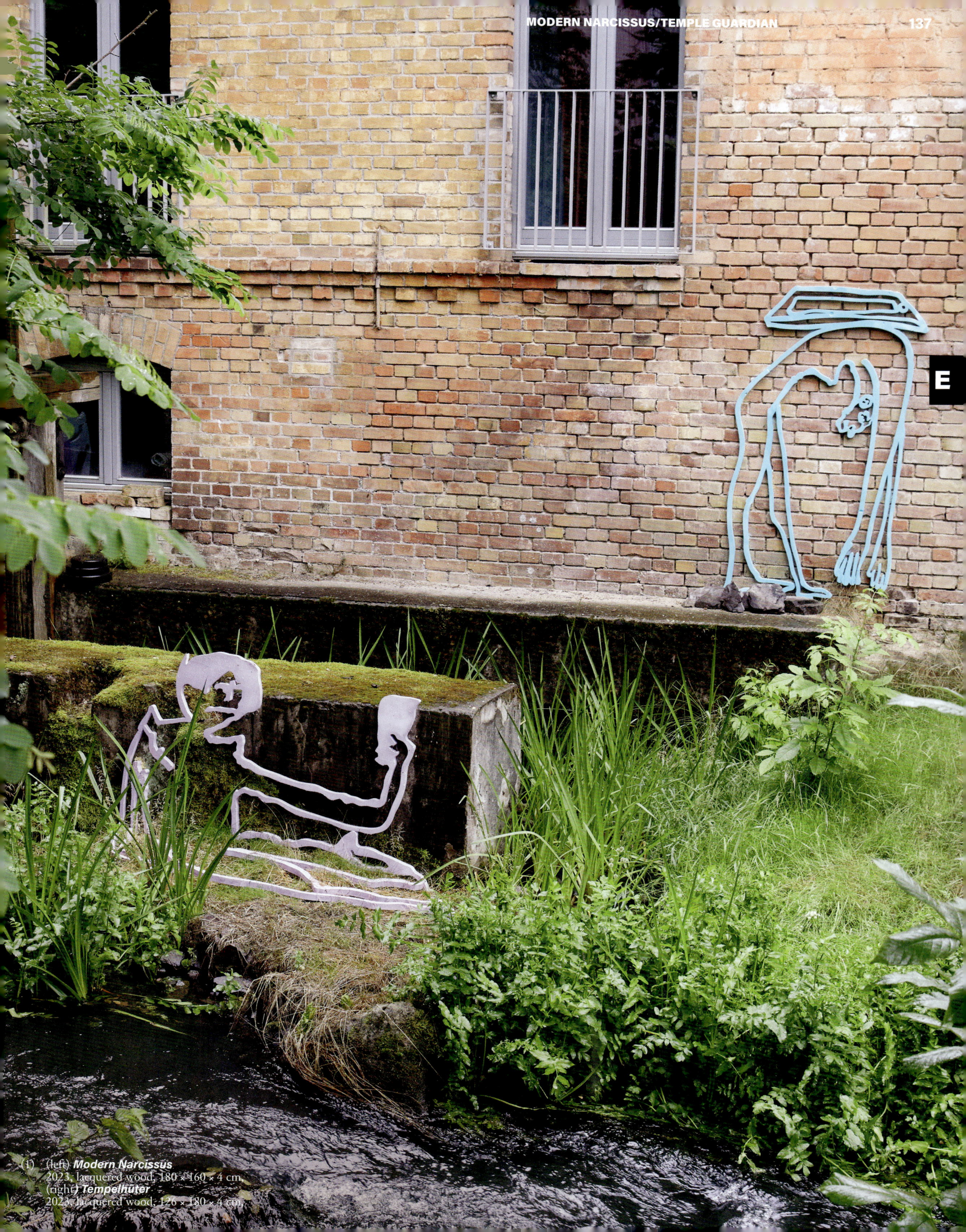

(1) (left) ***Modern Narcissus***
2023, lacquered wood, 180 × 160 × 4 cm,
(right) ***Tempelhüter***
2023, lacquered wood, 126 × 180 × 4 cm,

E

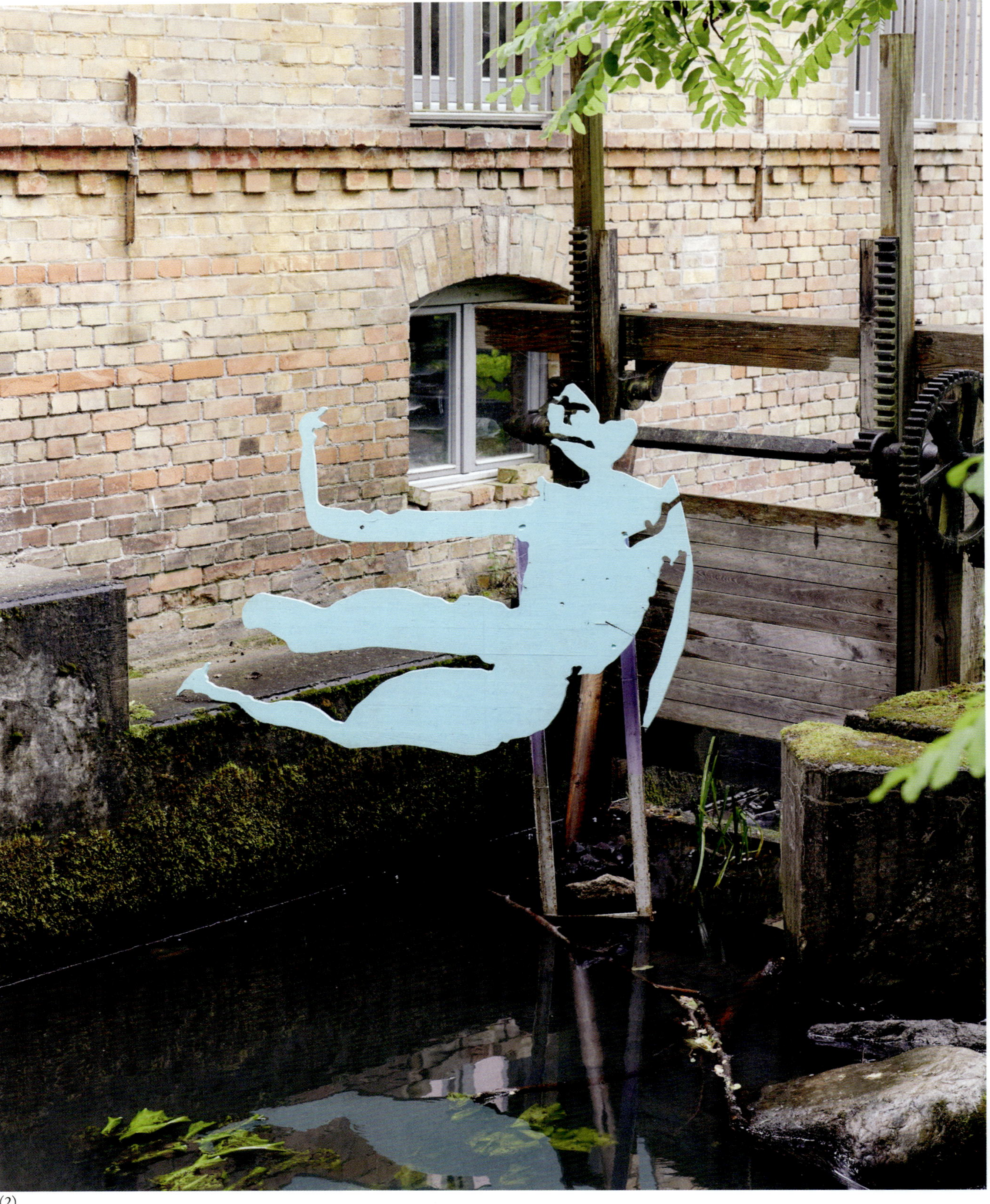

(2)

(2) ***Negative Narcissus***
2023, lacquered wood,
178 × 158 × 4 cm

GRIDS AND FLOWERS

E

INGREDIENTS
Grids and flowers 4 ③
Grids and flowers 2 ④
Grids and flowers 37 ⑤
Grids and Flowers 3 ⑥
Grids and flowers 5 ⑦
Grids and flowers 6 ⑧
Grids and flowers 8 ⑨
Grids and flowers 13 ⑩
Grids and flowers 12 ⑪
Grids and flowers 42 ①⑫
Grids and flowers 44 ⑬
Grids and flowers 17 ①⑭
Grids and flowers 23 ⑮
Grids and flowers 36 ⑯
Grids and flowers 1 ⑰
Grids and flowers 16 ⑱
Grids and flowers 26 ⑲
Grids and flowers 38 ⑳
Grids and flowers 30 ㉑
Grids and flowers 21 ㉒
Grids and flowers 24 ㉓
Grids and flowers 34 ㉔
Grids and flowers 29 ㉕
Grids and flowers 41 ㉖
Grids and flowers 9 ㉗
Grids and flowers 43 ㉘
Grids and flowers 33 ㉙
Grids and flowers 35 ㉚
Preserved Beauties 8 ㉛
Preserved Beauties 9 ㉜
Preserved Beauties 6 ㉝
Preserved Beauties 7 ㉞
Preserved Beauties 1 ㉟
Preserved Beauties 3 ㊱
Preserved Beauties 4 ①㊲
Preserved Beauties 15 ㊳
Preserved Beauties 11 ㊴
Preserved Beauties 16 ㊵
Worms II (51)
Palmtree (52)
Forest (53)
Flowers ②(54)
Worms ㊾
Landscape ②,(55)
Minigrids 1 (57)
Minigrids 2 (59)
Minigrids 3 (62)
Minigrids 4 ①(65)
Minigrids 5 (58)
Minigrids 6 (60)
Minigrids 7 (63)
Minigrids 8 (66)
Minigrids 10 (61)
Minigrids 11 (64)

EN *"Yet we humans are actually earthworms."*

Things sprout, blossom, fly, and crawl around the exhibition space. The walls teem with images of various inhabitants. We see garden arches that, instead of being neatly entwined with roses, are scattered throughout the space in a wide variety of shapes.
Verena Issel explores the tense relationship between nature and culture—an apparent contradiction that has become increasingly pronounced in recent years.
In the face of climate change, this is slowly calling into question humanity's continued existence and unrestricted dominance over the planet. Only ten percent of the Earth is still wild, i.e., not manipulated by humans. Every other corner has been shaped according to a specific idea.
But to think that order has now given way to chaos would be the next fallacy. Issel's work shows that this order is as ramified and rhizomatically interconnected as nature itself. Human beings are also part of nature, no matter how much they resist the fact that they are just one of many small cogs in the wheel of the world.

The exhibition that has now landed at Sexauer Gallery has several layers. One consists of found objects and set pieces that we use to shape this world, including pipe cleaners, earplugs, sushi bento dividers, and small polystyrene rolls. From these, Issel has created a microcosm that, if you allow yourself to follow its winding paths, proliferates and reveals the most surprising connections.
The small-format pictures sometimes show the same motif, increasingly abstracted, so that it is not clear who is referring to whom. Only one thing is certain: Everything is connected to everything else. The pictures were made in parallel. Therefore, if you take a step back and look at the big picture, you can also read them as a single fragmented image. You see flowers, blossoms, pits, beans, seeds—everything that makes nature bloom and flourish. The images describe a proliferating, growing, and ever-changing state of nature.

Another layer consists of pictures made of anti-slip mats. These mats are used to prevent carpets from slipping, so that everything stays where it belongs. Landscapes made of acrylic thread, curtain fringes, and ribbons are threaded and sewn into these titular grids. In this way, Issel brings to life dreamlike landscapes, lost palm trees, images of a paradise that probably never existed. Palm trees, beaches, coconuts, sea cucumbers, and other exotic-looking plants tell of the fact that the paradise conjured up in advertising is nothing more than the constructed idea of a tourist industry whose success is always destroying the very basis of this success. "Come visit unspoiled nature. Enjoy the peace and quiet!" screams the advertising, luring you in with photos that have been manipulated beyond recognition and resemble Issel's plastic replicas more than what nature actually produces.

The earthworm-like figures, which can also be seen on the large grid carpets, seem to look at each other, somewhat perplexed and lost in this world of their own making, and ask themselves: "What now?" The answer is probably a shrug of the shoulders.
Yet another layer of sediment can be found in the exhibition, consisting of what man produces, declares as a victory over nature, and calls culture. These artifacts, Greek temples and pickled vegetables (the cultural techniques of preservation) are painted on glass. Pickled and preserved for eternity. So that the history of mankind can continue to be told as a story of progress, even if we are currently feeling the full force of the fact that this progress is destroying the very basis of our existence. The garden arches also tell of this constant struggle of man against nature—and thus also against himself. Normally, these arches force plants to grow in certain shapes, either to look nicer or to be useful. Issel has imposed other shapes on these arches, and now they meander along the floor, too large or too small to fulfill their task properly.

The walls of the gallery space are covered with a grid in which the pictures find their place. The various layers hang in a wild jumble. It is like looking out of the window of an airplane on approach. One sees patches of nature, of the city, of man-made exoticism in close proximity and deceptive tranquility.

But one should not be deceived by the cheerful colors and friendly figures in this cosmos, for Issel's choice of materials is by no means arbitrary.
The cheap, mass-produced plastic objects that have found a new, more beautiful use in Issel's work are at the same time responsible for the fact that nature, the basis of all life, hardly exists anymore. It is precisely this plastic that covers the oceans in huge carpets and brings the lives of sea creatures to an agonizing end. But that is not all: Through the oceans, plastic finds its way back into the human organism in the form of microplastics. There could hardly be a more appropriate material to describe the paradoxical relationship between humans and the destruction of the very basis of their existence. How easily we are seduced by the friendly figures, the accessible and familiar material, is shown by the vicious circle in which we find ourselves, all singing the swan song of our existence together.
Rarely has this swan song been more friendly, cheerful, and seductive than in the work of Verena Issel.

☐ ***Laura Helena Wurth, exhibition text***

DE *„Dabei sind wir Menschen doch eigentlich Regenwürmer"*

Es sprießt, blüht, fleucht und kreucht im Ausstellungsraum. An den Wänden wimmelt es von Bildern mit verschiedensten Bewohnern. Im Raum sehen wir Blumenbögen, die sich, anstatt ordentlich mit Rosen berankt zu sein, in unterschiedlichsten Formen verteilen.
Verena Issel begibt sich in das Spannungsverhältnis zwischen Natur und Kultur. Ein nur vermeintlicher Widerspruch, der sich in den letzten Jahren zunehmend verstärkt hat. Langsam macht er der Menschheit angesichts des Klimawandels einen Strich durch die Rechnung der Weiterexistenz und der uneingeschränkten Dominanz über den Planeten. Nur noch zehn Prozent der Erde sind wild, also nicht vom Menschen manipuliert. Jeder andere Winkel wurde nach einer bestimmten Vorstellung gestaltet. Doch zu denken, dass man nun Ordnung ins Chaos gebracht hätte, wäre direkt der nächste Trugschluss. Issel zeigt in ihrer Arbeit, dass diese Ordnung genauso verzweigt und rhizomatisch verbunden ist wie die Natur selbst. Weil der Mensch eben auch Teil der Natur ist; sosehr er sich auch gegen die Tatsache sträubt, nur eines von vielen kleinen Rädchen im Getriebe der Welt zu sein.

Die Installation hat mehrere Schichten. Eine besteht aus Fund- und Versatzstücken, mit denen wir diese Welt gestalten. Das sind Pfeifenreiniger, Ohrstöpsel, Sushi-Bento-Trennblätter und kleine Styroporrollen. Daraus hat Issel einen Mikrokosmos geschaffen, der vor sich hinwuchert und die überraschendsten Verbindungen aufzeigt, wenn man sich darauf einlässt, seinen verschlungenen Wegen zu folgen.
Die kleinformatigen Bilder zeigen manchmal, immer weiter abstrahiert, das gleiche Motiv, sodass man nicht weiß, wer sich hier auf wen bezieht; nur eines ist sicher: Alles hängt mit allem zusammen. Die Bilder sind parallel zueinander entstanden. Deswegen kann man sie, wenn man einen Schritt zurücktritt und das große Ganze betrachtet, auch als ein einziges fragmentiertes Bild lesen. Man sieht Blumen, Blüten, Kerne, Bohnen, Samen – alles, was die Natur zum Blühen und Gedeihen bringt. Die Bilder beschreiben einen wuchernden, wachsenden und sich immerzu verändernden Zustand der Natur.

Eine weitere Schicht besteht aus Bildern, die aus Antirutschteppichen gefertigt sind. Man benutzt solche Matten, um das Rutschen von Teppichen zu verhindern; damit schön alles da bleibt, wo es hingehört. In diese Raster, die titelgebenden Grids, sind Landschaftsbilder aus Acrylfäden, Gardinenfransen und Bändern eingefädelt und genäht. So lässt Issel traumhafte Landschaften, verlorene Palmen, Bilder eines Paradieses, das es vermutlich nie gab, auferstehen. Palmen, Strände, Kokosnüssen, Seegurken und andere exotisch anmutende Gewächse erzählen davon, dass das in der Werbung beschworene Paradies nichts anderes ist als die konstruierte Idee einer Tourismusindustrie, die durch ihren Erfolg immer auch die Grundlage dieses Erfolges zerstört. „Kommen Sie in die unberührte Natur. Genießen Sie die Ruhe!", schreit die Werbung und lockt mit bis zur Unkenntlichkeit bearbeiteten Fotos, die eher Issels Plastiknachbildungen ähneln denn dem, was die Natur tatsächlich hervorbringt.

Die regenwurmähnlichen Figuren, die man auch auf den großen Rasterteppichen sieht, scheinen sich gegenseitig etwas ratlos und verloren anzusehen in dieser Welt, die sie doch selbst geschaffen haben, und sich zu fragen: „Was nun?" Achselzucken ist wohl die Antwort.
Man kann noch eine weitere Sedimentschicht innerhalb der Ausstellung finden. Bestehend aus dem, was der Mensch produziert, als Sieg über die Natur deklariert und Kultur nennt. Diese Artefakte, griechische Tempel, eingelegte Gemüsesorten (die Kulturtechniken des Konservierens), sind auf Glas gemalt. Eingelegt und konserviert für die Ewigkeit. Damit die Geschichte der Menschheit weiterhin als eine Geschichte des Fortschritts erzählt werden kann, auch wenn wir gerade mit voller Härte spüren, dass dieser Fortschritt die Zerstörung unserer Lebensgrundlagen mit sich bringt. Von diesem konstanten Kampf des Menschen gegen die Natur – also auch gegen sich selbst – erzählen auch die Blumenbögen. Normalerweise zwingen diese Bögen Pflanzen, in bestimmten Formen zu wachsen, um so entweder hübscher auszusehen oder nützlich zu sein. Issel hat diesen Bögen andere Formen aufgezwungen, und jetzt schlängeln sie sich am Boden entlang, sind zu groß oder zu klein, um ihre Aufgabe noch vernünftig erfüllen zu können.

Die Wände des Galerieraumes sind mit einem Plan, einem Raster überzogen, in dem die Bilder ihren Platz finden. Dort hängen die verschiedenen Schichten wild durcheinander. Es sieht aus, als würde man beim Landeanflug aus dem Flugzeugfenster gucken. Man sieht Flecken von Natur, von Stadt, von menschengemachter Exotik in unmittelbarer Nachbarschaft und trügerischem Frieden.

Doch man sollte sich nicht täuschen lassen von den fröhlichen Farben und den freundlichen Figuren in diesem Kosmos. Denn die Wahl von Issels Arbeitsmaterial ist keineswegs zufällig. Die Gegenstände aus Plastik, die günstig auf Masse produziert sind und die in Issels Werk einen neuen, einen schöneren Nutzen gefunden haben, sind gleichzeitig verantwortlich dafür, dass die Natur, die Lebensgrundlage von allem, mittlerweile kaum noch existiert. Es ist genau dieses Plastik, das sich in großen Teppichen über die Meere legt und das Leben der Meeresbewohner qualvoll beendet. Doch nicht nur das: Durch die Meere gelangt das Plastik in Form von Mikroplastik wieder zurück in den menschlichen Organismus. Und so kann kaum ein Material passender sein, um das paradoxe Verhältnis des Menschen, der seine eigene Existenzgrundlage zerstört, zu beschreiben. Wie leicht wir uns von den freundlichen Figuren, dem zugänglichen und vertrauten Material verführen lassen, zeigt den Teufelskreis, in dem wir uns befinden und dabei alle gemeinsam den Abgesang auf unsere Existenz singen.
Selten kam dieser Abgesang freundlicher, fröhlicher und verführerischer daher als bei Verena Issel.

☐ ***Laura Helena Wurth, Ausstellungstext***

E

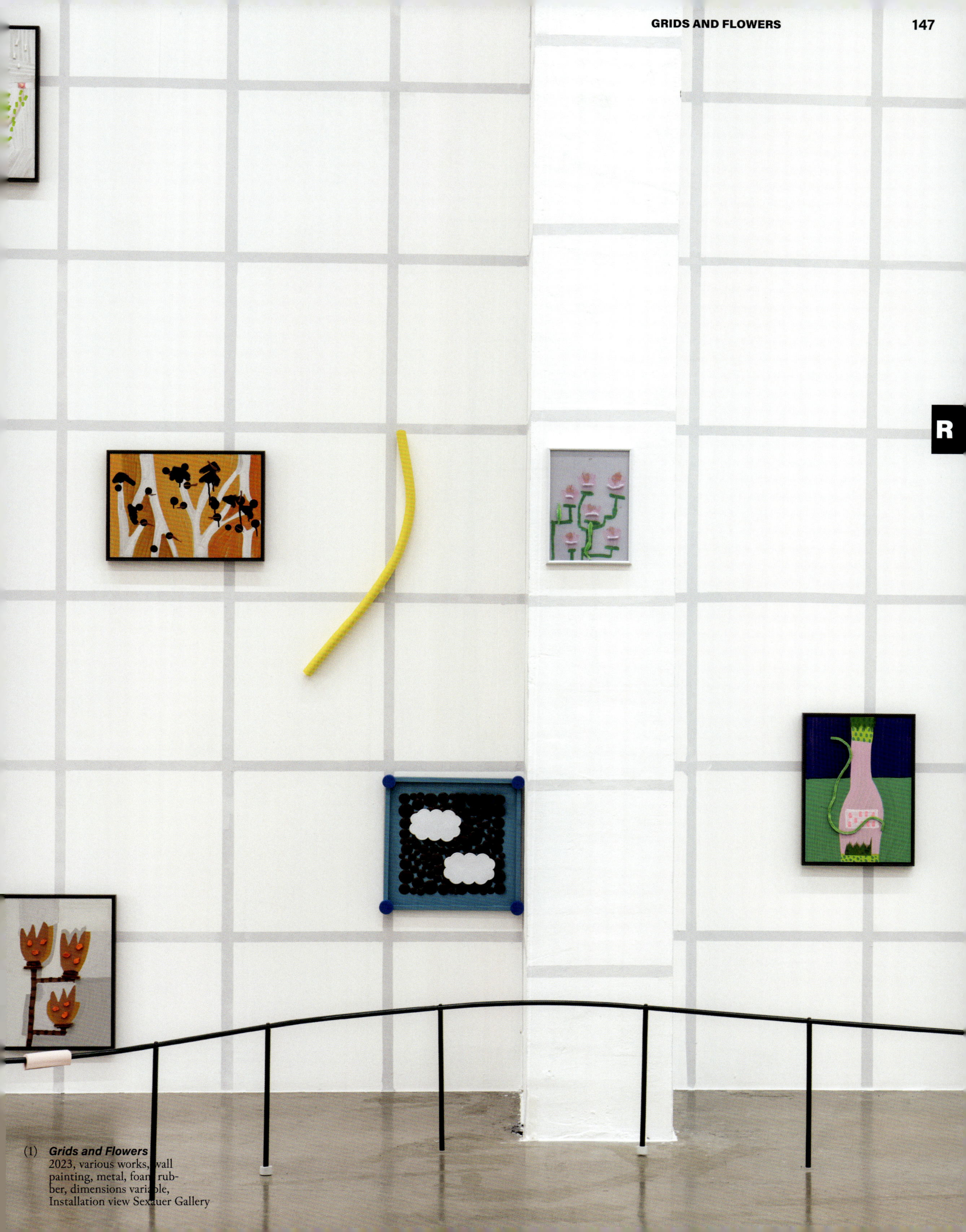

(1) ***Grids and Flowers***
2023, various works, wall painting, metal, foam rubber, dimensions variable, Installation view Sexauer Gallery

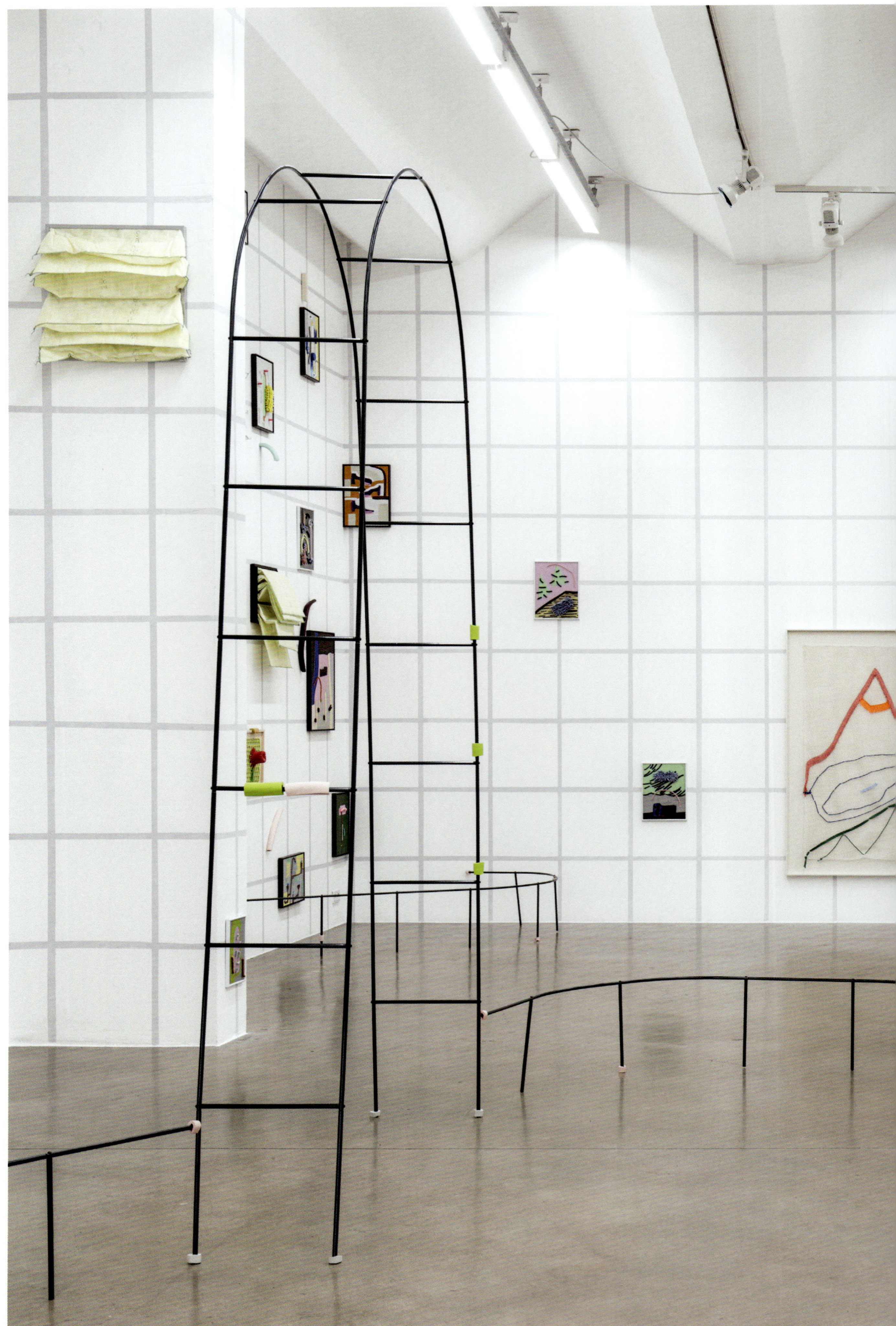

(2) ***Grids and Flowers***
2023, various works, wall painting, metal, foam rubber, dimensions variable, Installation view Sexauer Gallery

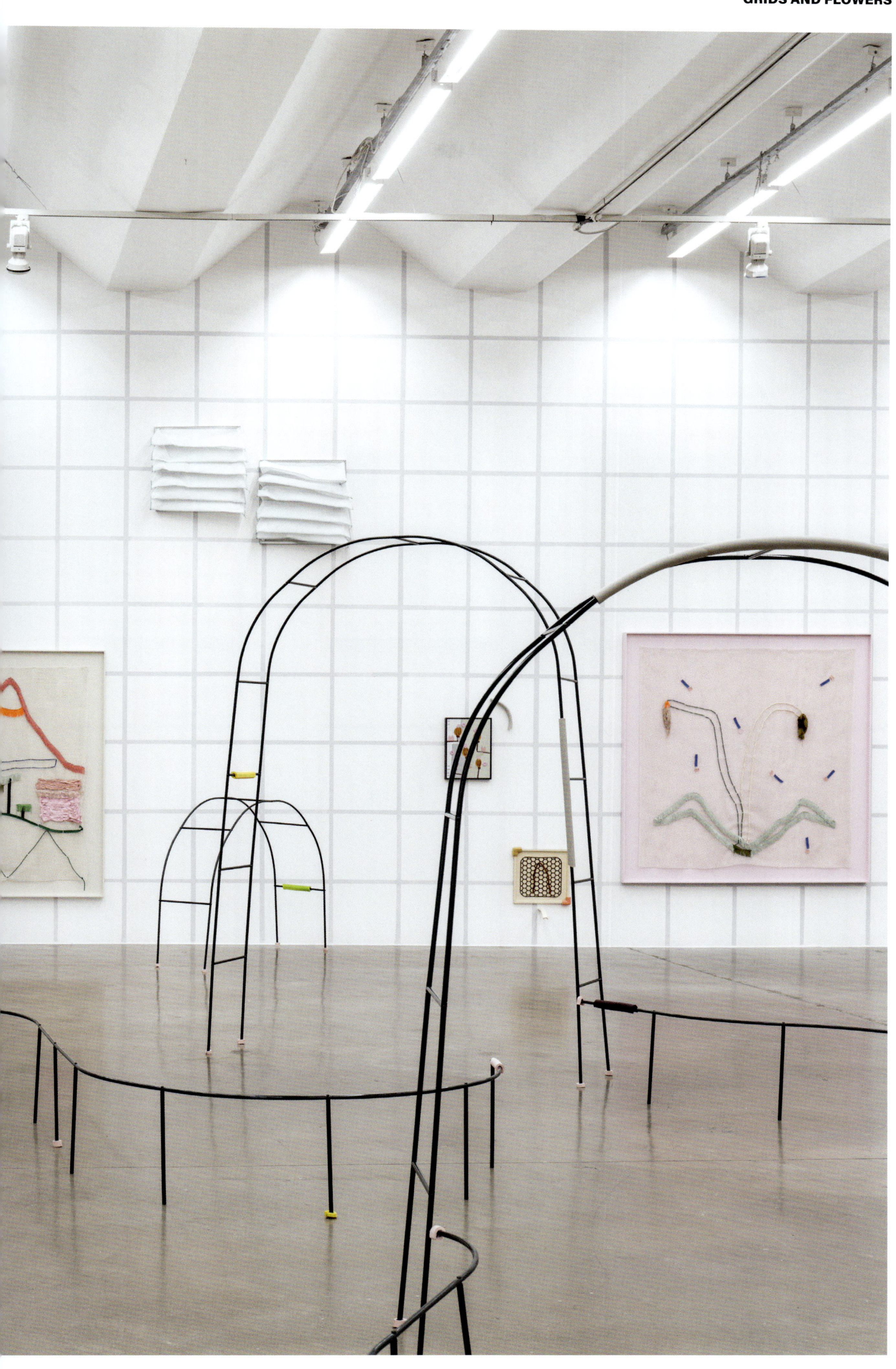

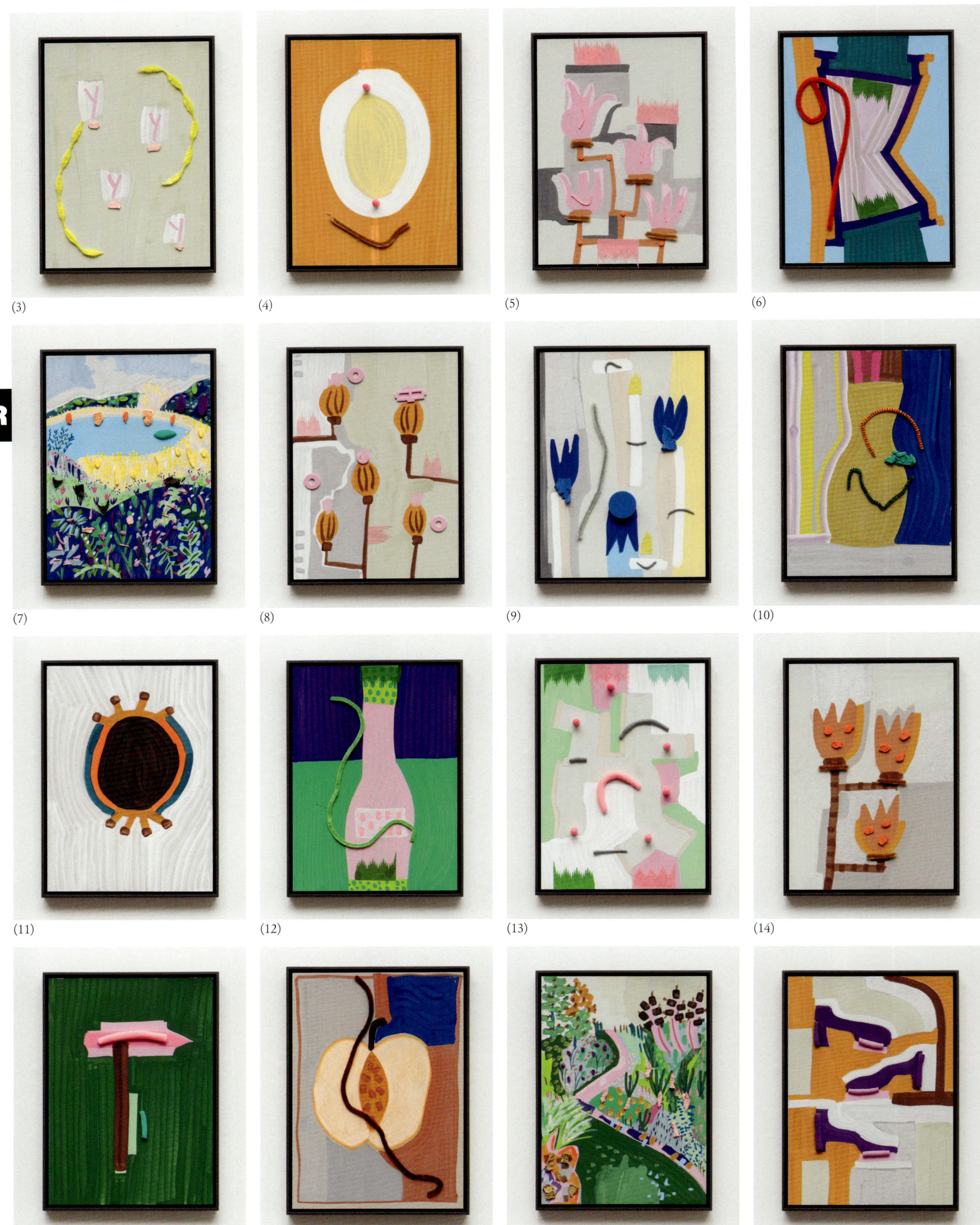

(3) (4) (5) (6)

(7) (8) (9) (10)

(11) (12) (13) (14)

(15) (16) (17) (18)

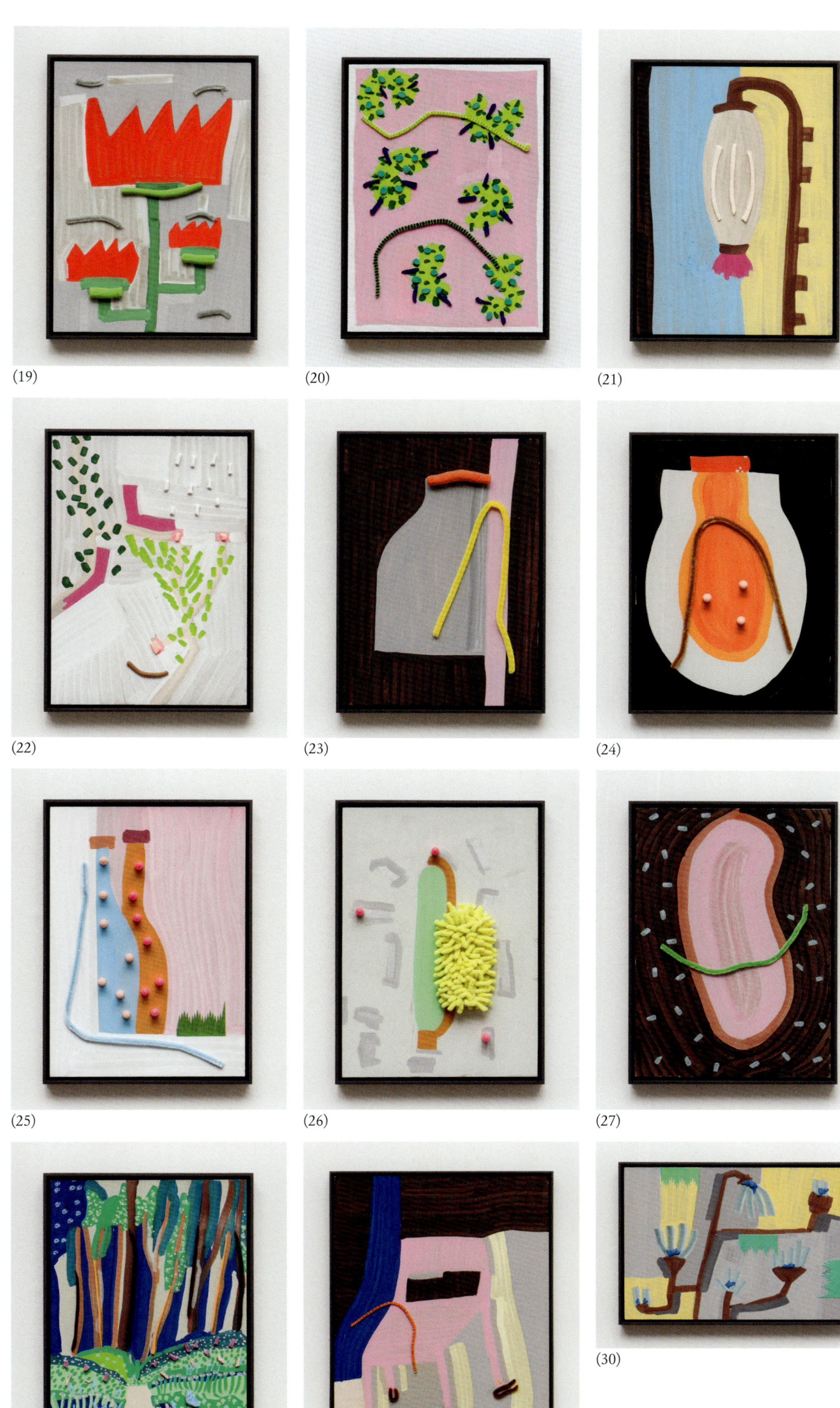

(19) (20) (21) (22) (23) (24) (25) (26) (27) (28) (29) (30)

(3) ***Grids and flowers 4***
(4) ***Grids and flowers 2***
(5) ***Grids and flowers 37***
(6) ***Grids and flowers 3***
(7) ***Grids and flowers 5***
(8) ***Grids and flowers 6***
(9) ***Grids and flowers 8***
(10) ***Grids and flowers 13***
(11) ***Grids and flowers 12***
(12) ***Grids and flowers 42***
(13) ***Grids and flowers 44***
(14) ***Grids and flowers 17***
(15) ***Grids and flowers 23***
(16) ***Grids and flowers 36***
(17) ***Grids and flowers 1***
(18) ***Grids and flowers 16***
(19) ***Grids and flowers 26***
(20) ***Grids and flowers 38***
(21) ***Grids and flowers 30***
(22) ***Grids and flowers 21***
(23) ***Grids and flowers 24***
(24) ***Grids and flowers 34***
(25) ***Grids and flowers 29***
(26) ***Grids and flowers 41***
(27) ***Grids and flowers 9***
(28) ***Grids and flowers 43***
(29) ***Grids and flowers 33***
(30) ***Grids and flowers 35***
all: 2023, acrylics on cardboard with household objects, 44 × 31.7 cm

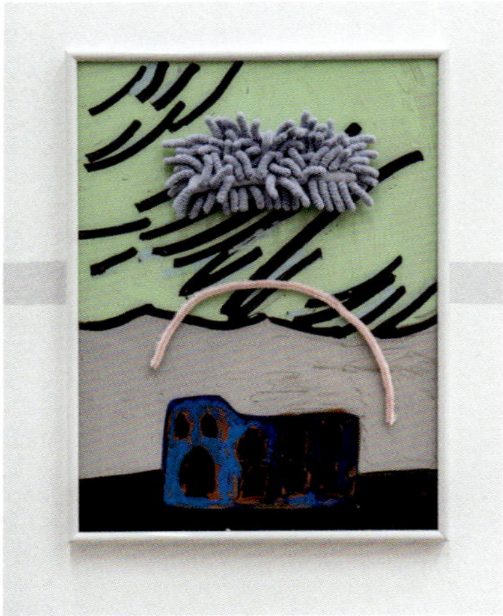

(31)

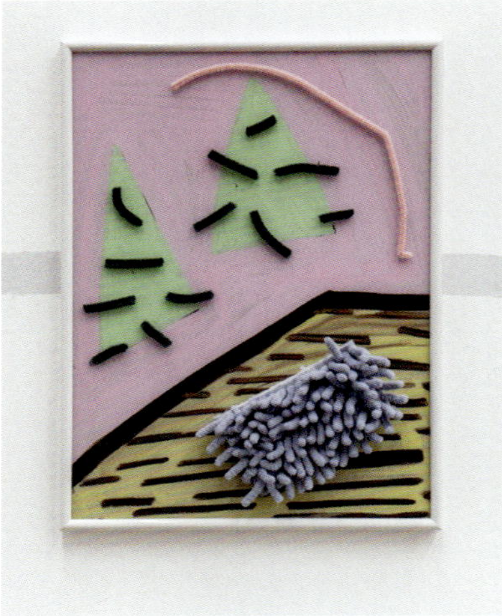

(32)

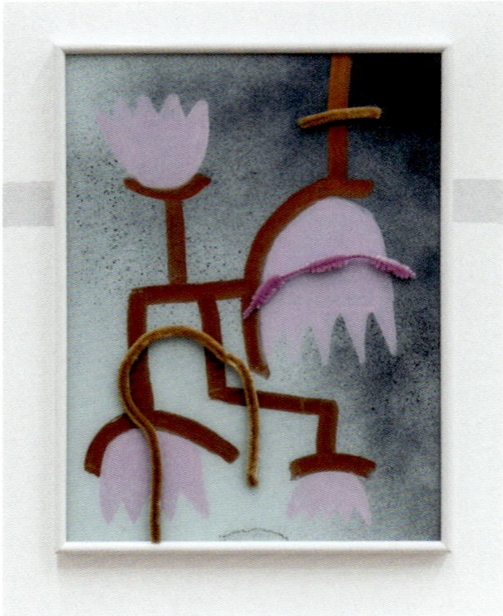

(33)

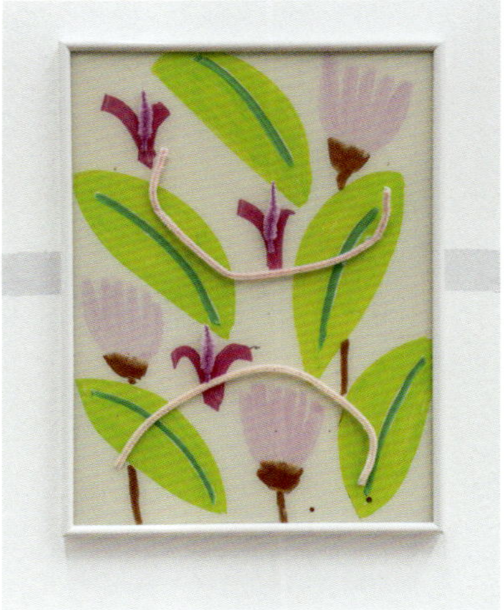

(34)

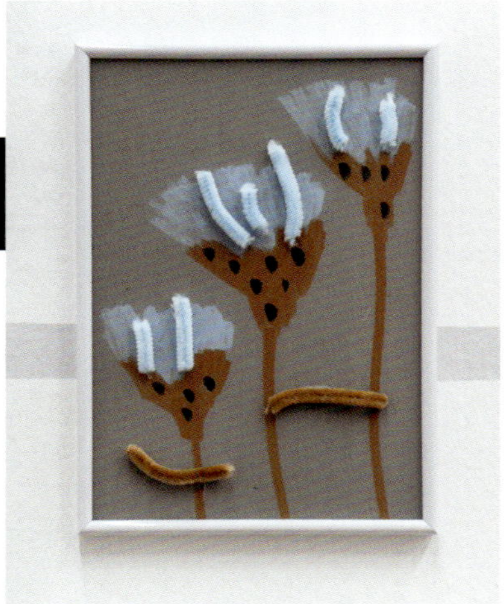

(35)

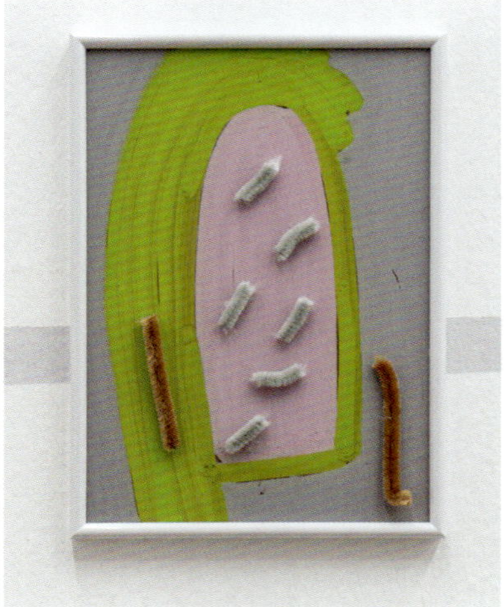

(36)

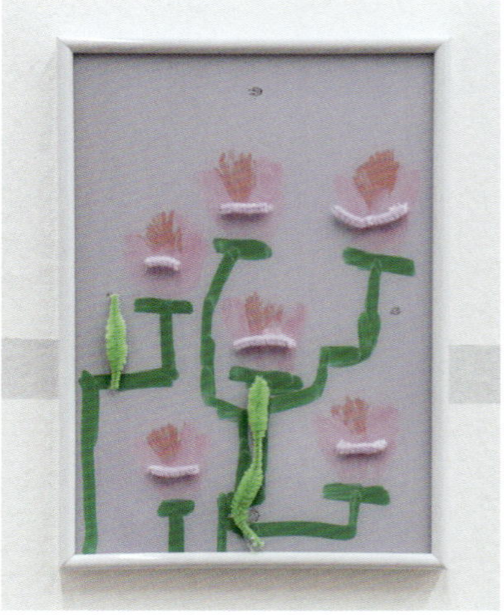

(37)

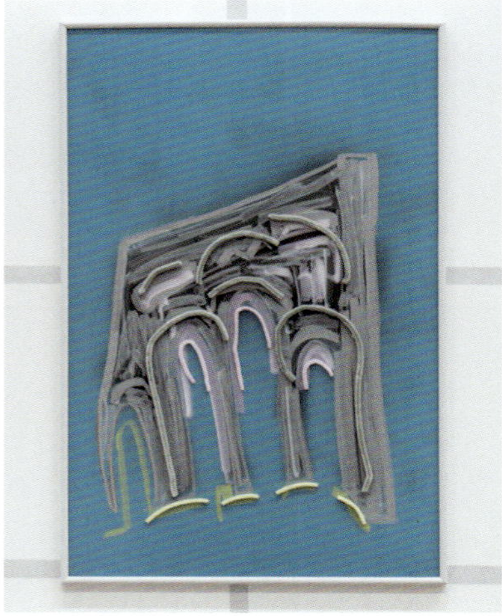

(38)

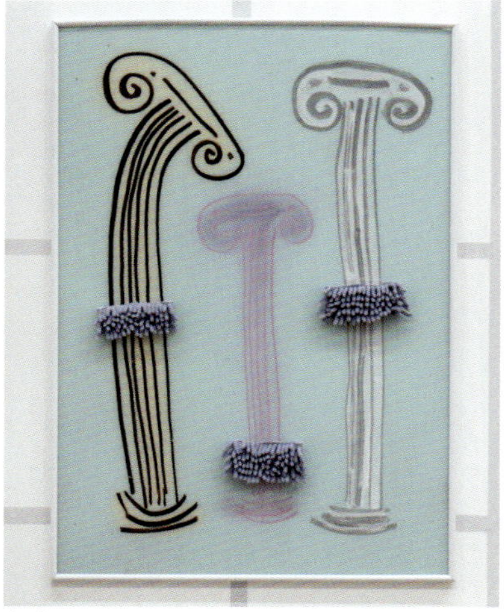

(39)

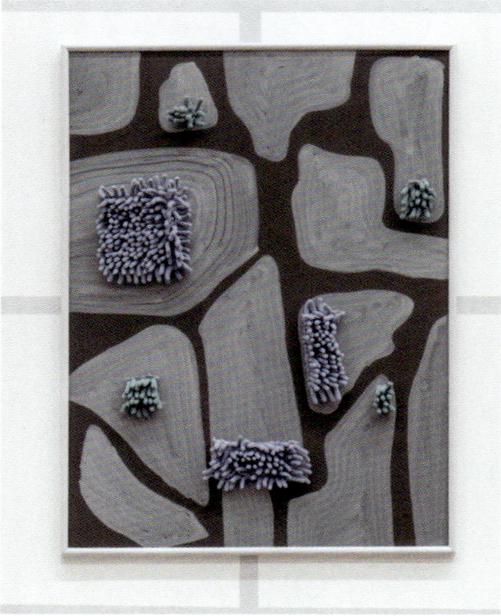

(40)

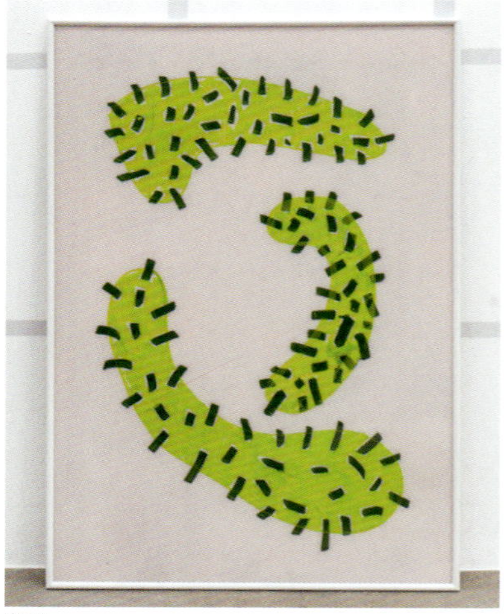

(41)

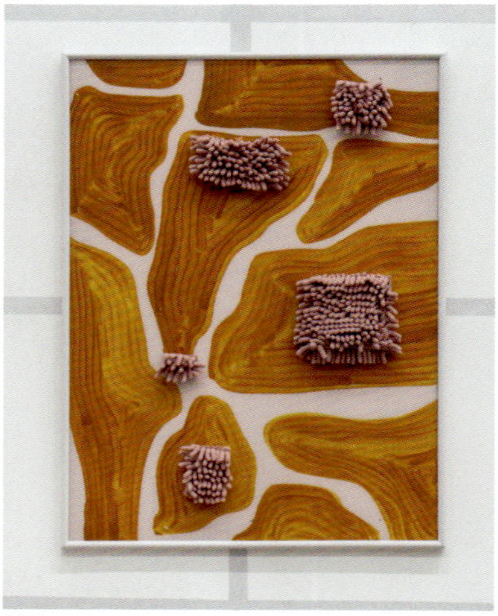

(42)

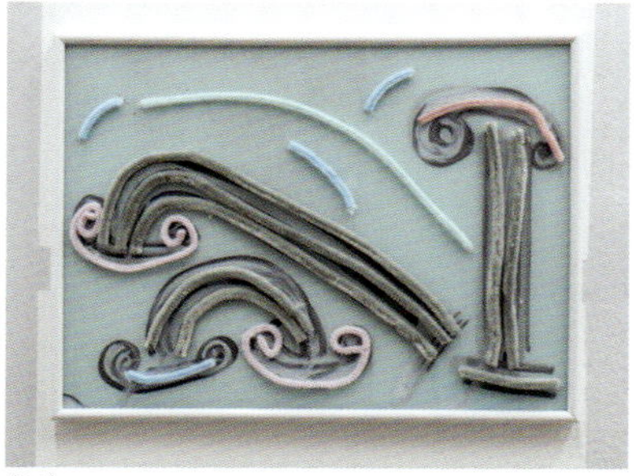

(43)

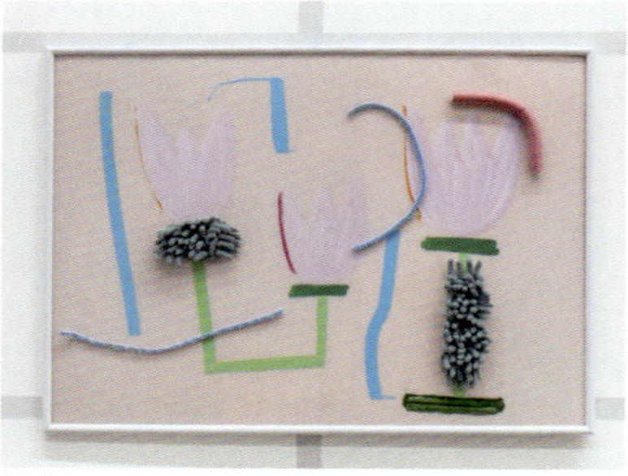

(44)

(31) ***Preserved beauties 8*** 2023, Acrylic behind glass with mop and pipe cleaner, 40 × 30 cm
(32) ***Preserved beauties 9*** 2023, Acrylic behind glass with mop and pipe cleaner, 40 × 30 cm
(33) ***Preserved beauties 6*** 2023, Acrylic behind glass with pipe cleaner, 40 × 30 cm
(34) ***Preserved beauties 7*** 2023, Acrylic behind glass with pipe cleaner, 40 × 30 cm
(35) ***Preserved beauties 1*** 2023, Acrylic behind glass with pipe cleaner, 30 × 22 cm
(36) ***Preserved beauties 3*** 2023, Acrylic behind glass with pipe cleaner, 30 × 22 cm
(37) ***Preserved beauties 4*** 2023, Acrylic behind glass with pipe cleaner, 30 × 22 cm
(38) ***Preserved beauties 15*** 2023, Acrylic behind glass with pipe cleaner, 90 × 60 cm
(39) ***Preserved beauties 11*** 2023, Acrylic behind glass with mop and pipe cleaner, 100 × 70 cm
(40) ***Preserved beauties 16*** 2023, Acrylic behind glass with mop, 80 × 60 cm
(41) ***Preserved beauties 12*** 2023, Acrylic behind glass, 100 × 70 cm
(42) ***Preserved beauties 14*** 2023, Acrylic behind glass with mop, 80 × 60 cm
(43) ***Preserved beauties 5*** 2023,Acrylic behind glass with pipe cleaner, 40 × 30 cm
(44) ***Preserved beauties 17*** 2023, Acrylic behind glass with mop and pipe cleaner, 51 × 71 cm

(45) ***Grids and flowers***
2023, various works,
wall painting,
metal, foam rubber,
dimensions variable,
Installation view
Sexauer Gallery

(46) ***Grids and flowers***
2023, various works,
wall painting,
metal, foam rubber,
dimensions variable,
Installation view
Sexauer Gallery

(47) ***Grids and flowers***
2023, various works,
wall painting, metal,
foam rubber, dimen-
sions variable,
Installation view
Sexauer Gallery

(48) ***Worms I***
2023, textiles and nylon
cords on anti-slip net
and painted wood,
242 × 172 cm

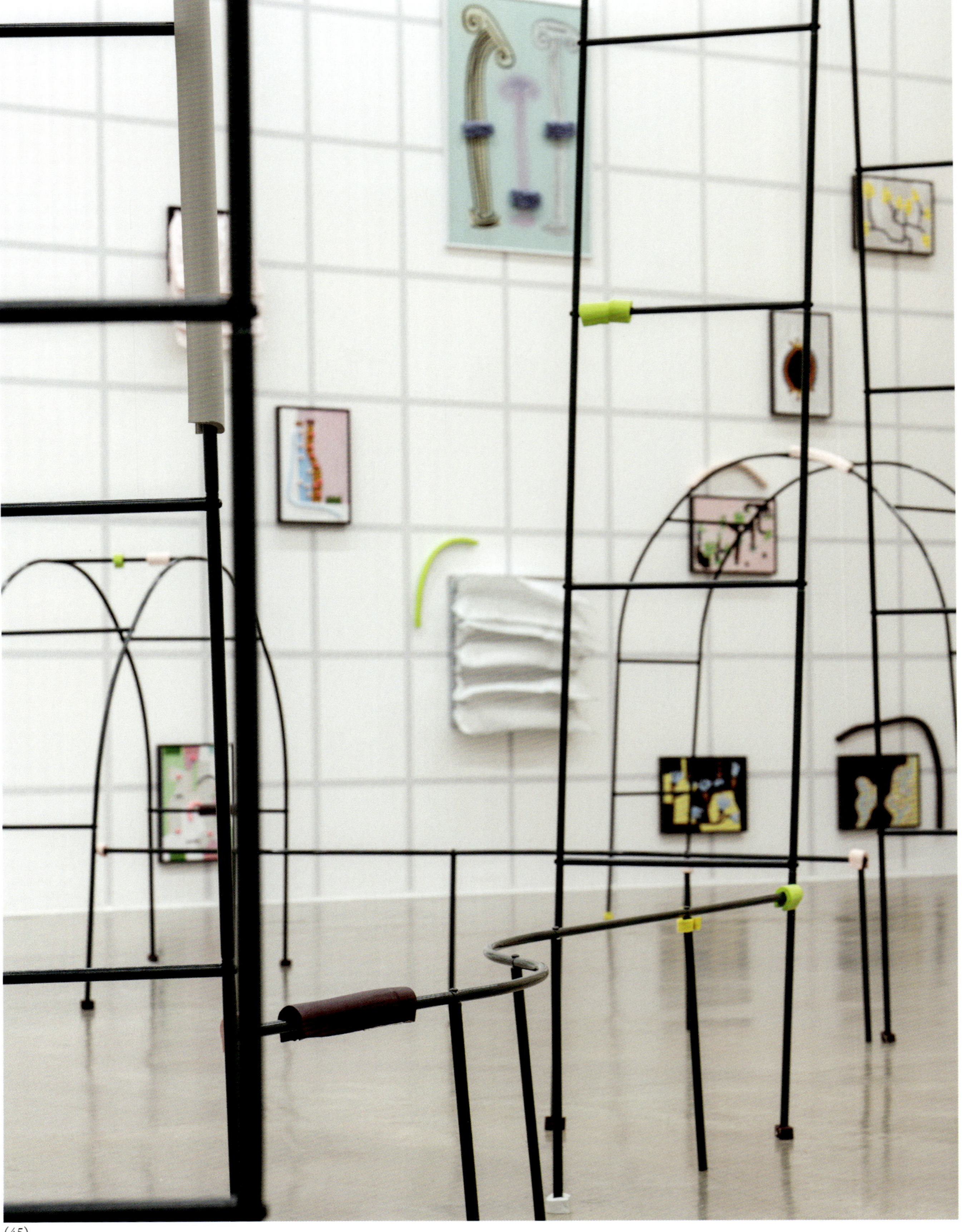

(45)

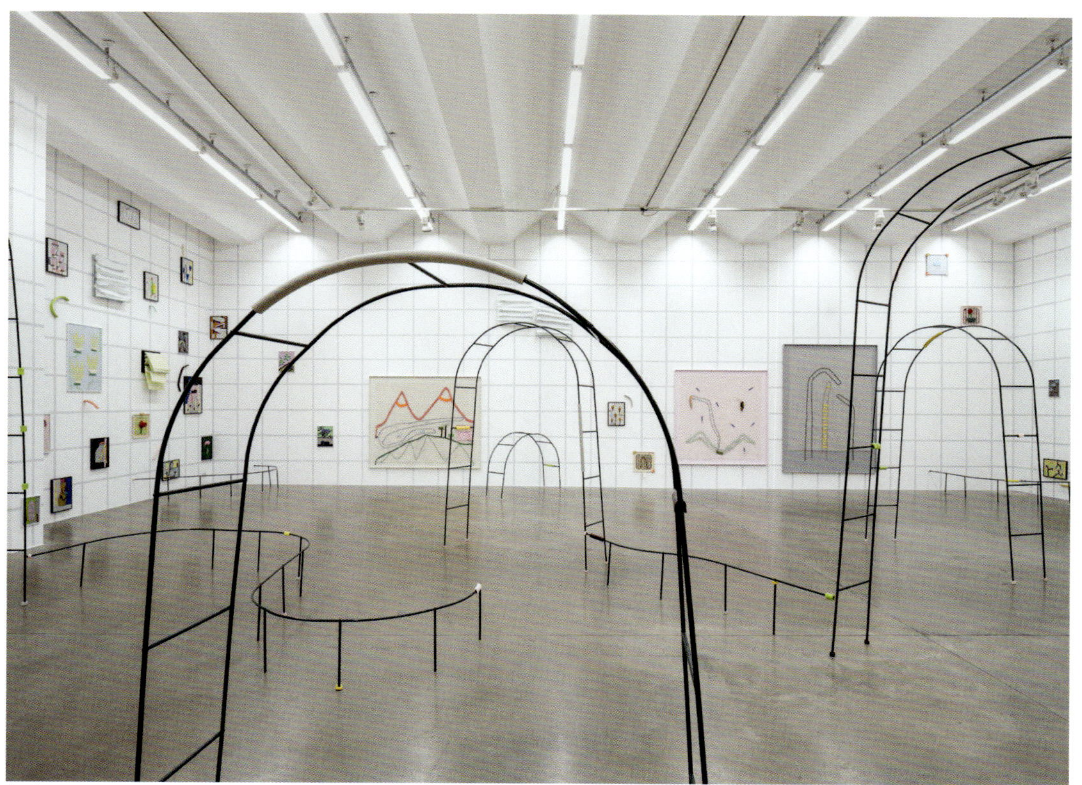
(46)

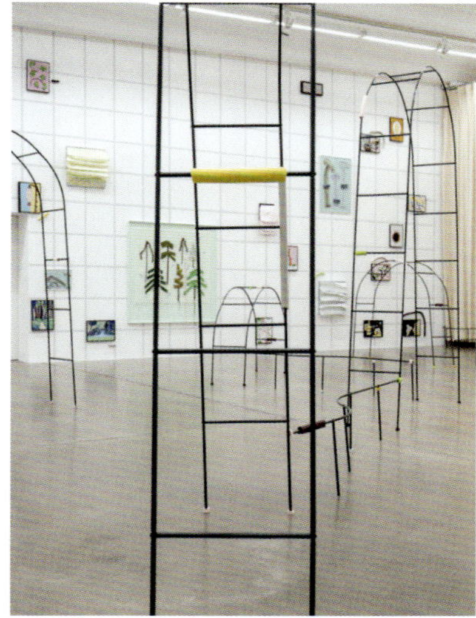
(47)

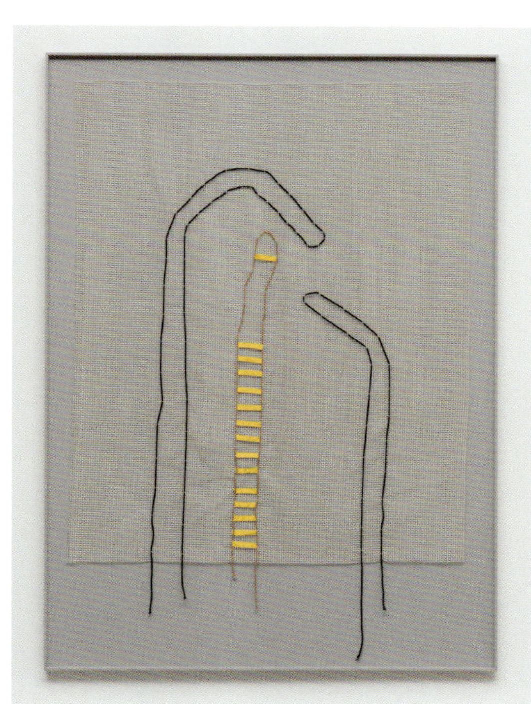
(48)

(49) ***Grids and flowers***
2023, various works, wall painting, metal, foam rubber, dimensions variable, Installation view Sexauer Gallery

(50) ***Worms II***
2023, textiles and nylon cords on anti-slip net and painted wood, 162 × 150 cm

(51) ***Palmtree***
2023, textiles and nylon cords on anti-slip net and painted wood, 242 × 172 cm

(52) ***Forest***
2023, textiles and nylon cords on anti-slip net and painted wood, 162 × 152 cm

(53) ***Flowers***
2023, textiles and nylon cords on anti-slip net and painted wood, 162 × 150 cm

(54) ***Landscape***
2023, textiles and nylon cords on anti-slip net and lacquered wood, 174 × 208 cm

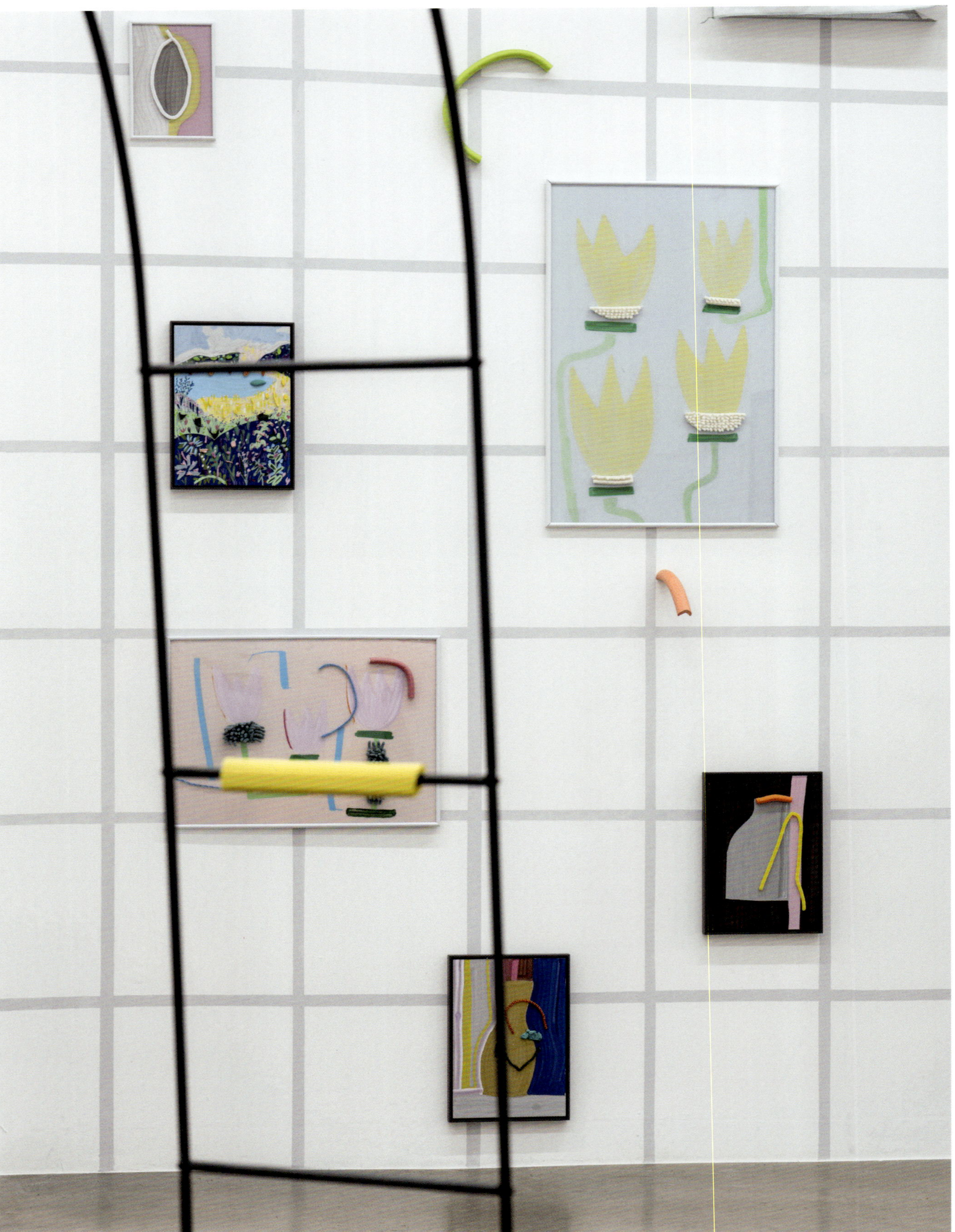

(49)

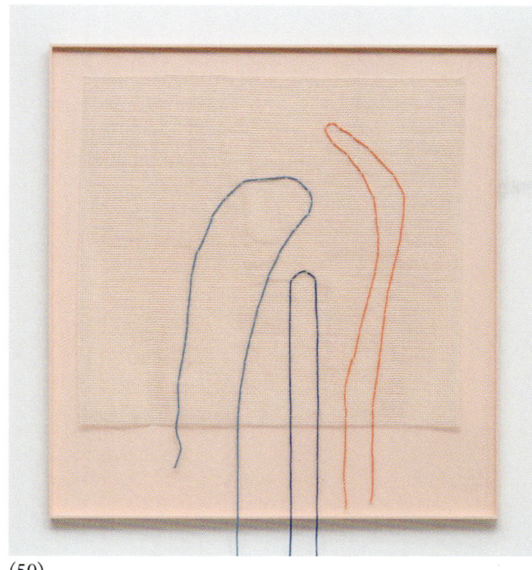

(50)

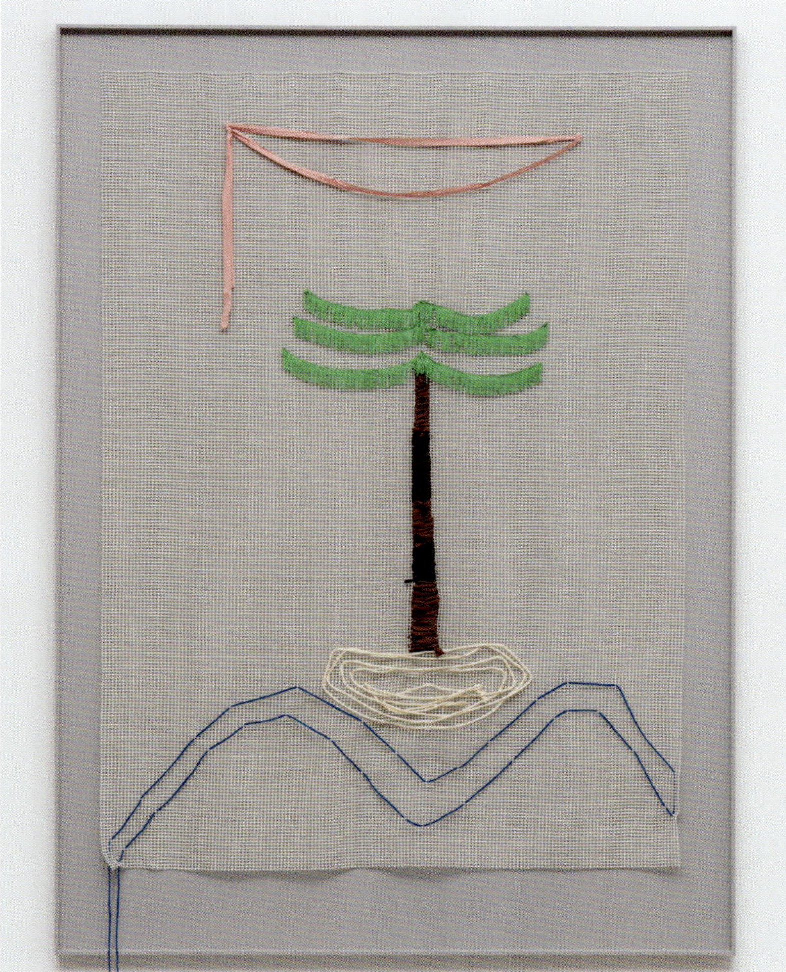
(51)

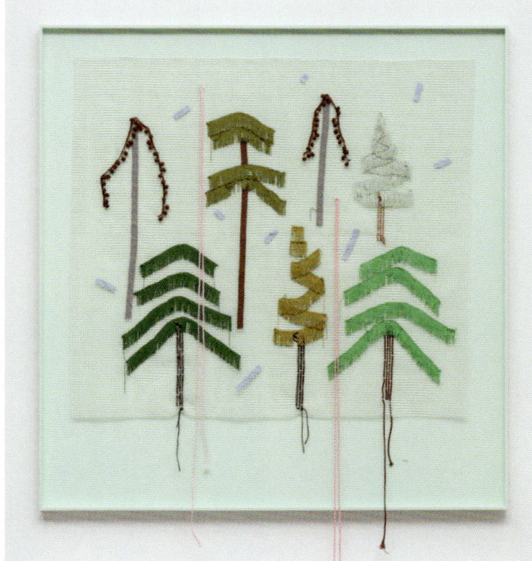

(52)

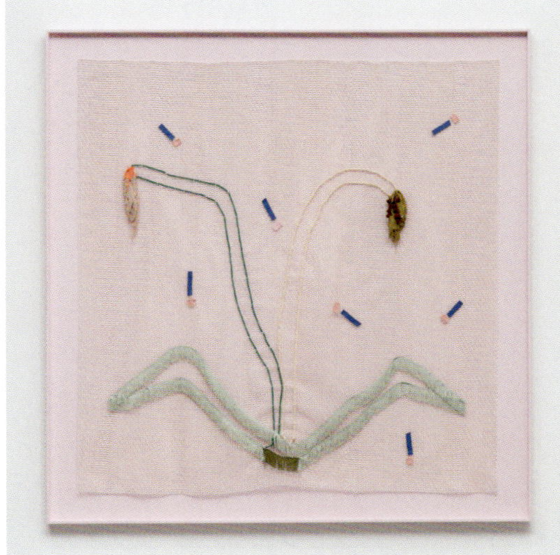
(53)

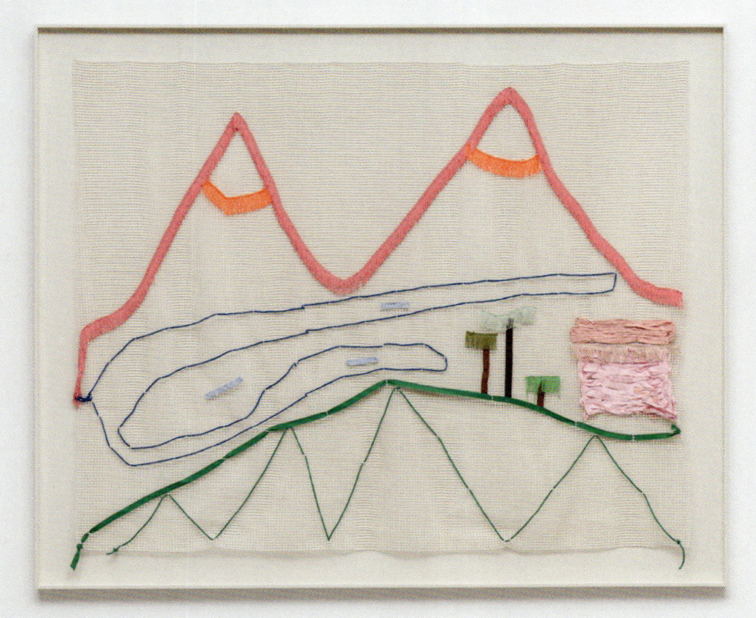
(54)

(55) ***Grids and flowers*** 2023, various works, wall painting, metal, foam rubber, dimensions variable, Exhibition view Sexauer Gallery
(56) ***Minigrids 1***
(57) ***Minigrids 5***
(58) ***Minigrids 2***
(59) ***Minigrids 6***
(60) ***Minigrids 10***
(61) ***Minigrids 3***
(62) ***Minigrids 7***
(63) ***Minigrids 11***
(64) ***Minigrids 4***
(65) ***Minigrids 8***
all Minigrids: 2023, collage and plastic on wood with foam, each 32 × 32 cm

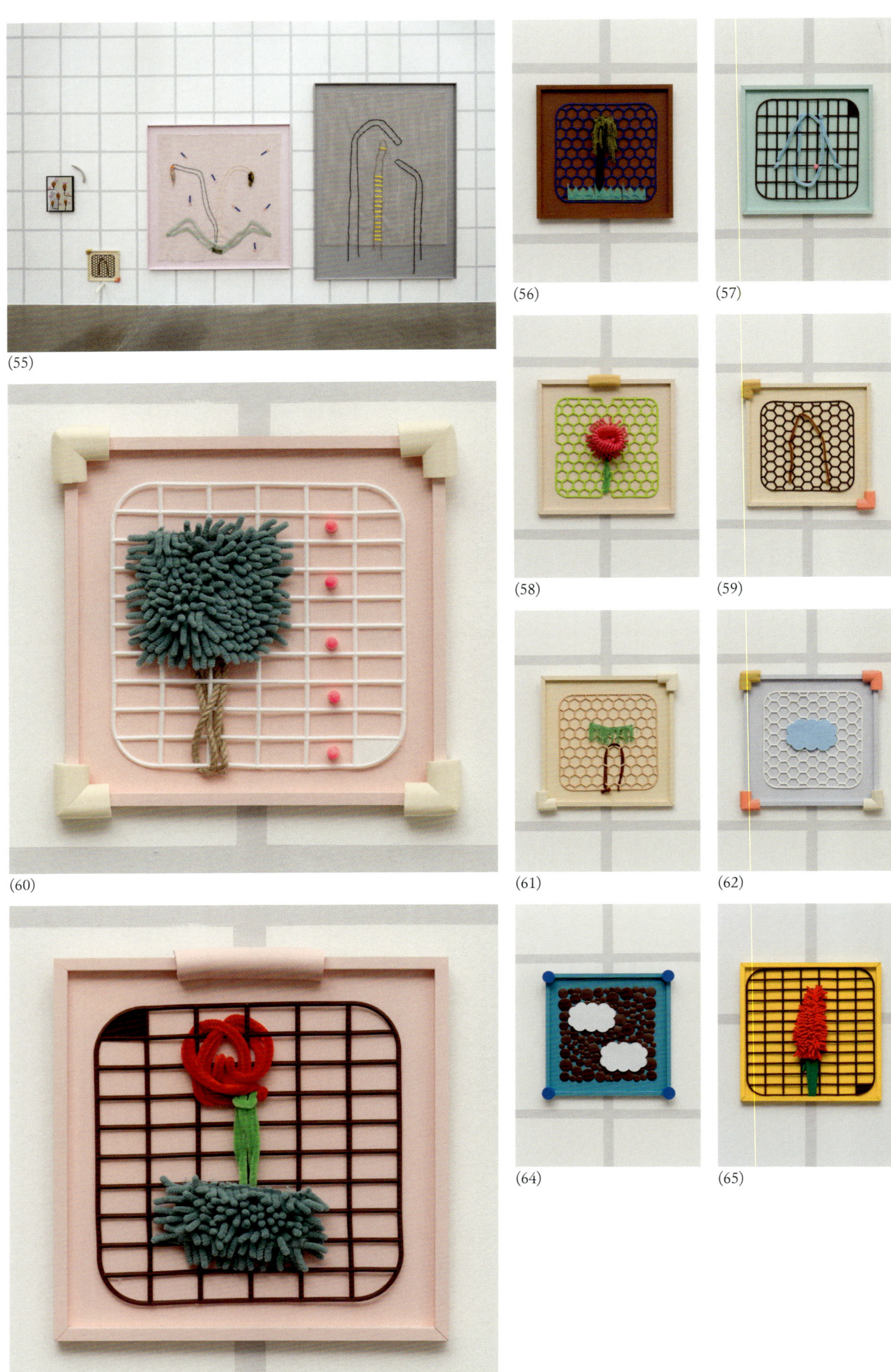

(55) (56) (57) (58) (59) (60) (61) (62) (63) (64) (65)

R

KUNST-AM-BAU-PROJEKT: KINDERGARTEN „AM KRAUTGARTEN“

R

INGREDIENTS
Eyes ①②③④⑤
Plants ①②③④⑤
Mountains ①②③④⑤
Tree ①②③④⑤
Vampire Mouth ①②③④⑤

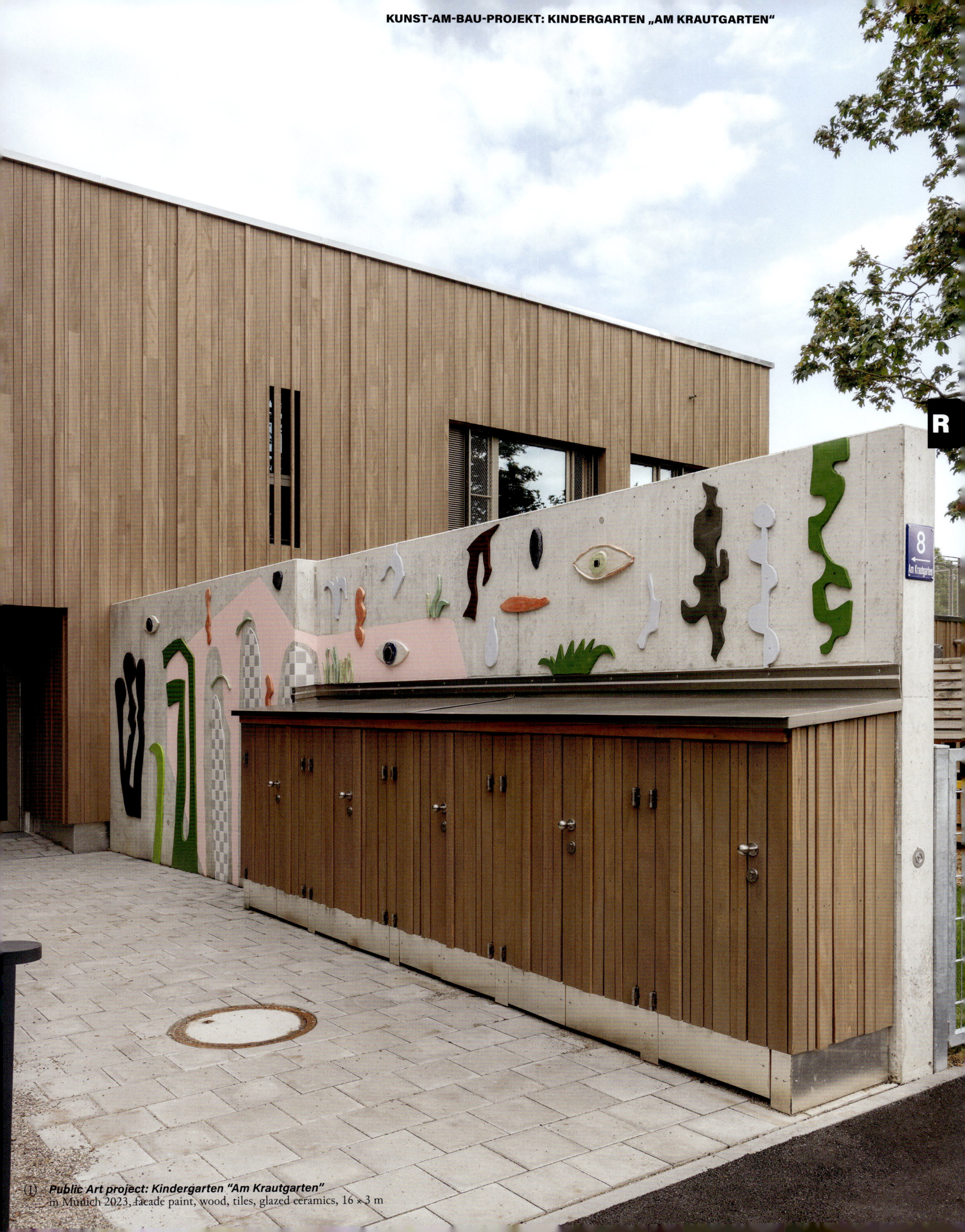

(1) ***Public Art project: Kindergarten "Am Krautgarten"***
in Munich 2023, facade paint, wood, tiles, glazed ceramics, 16 × 3 m

R

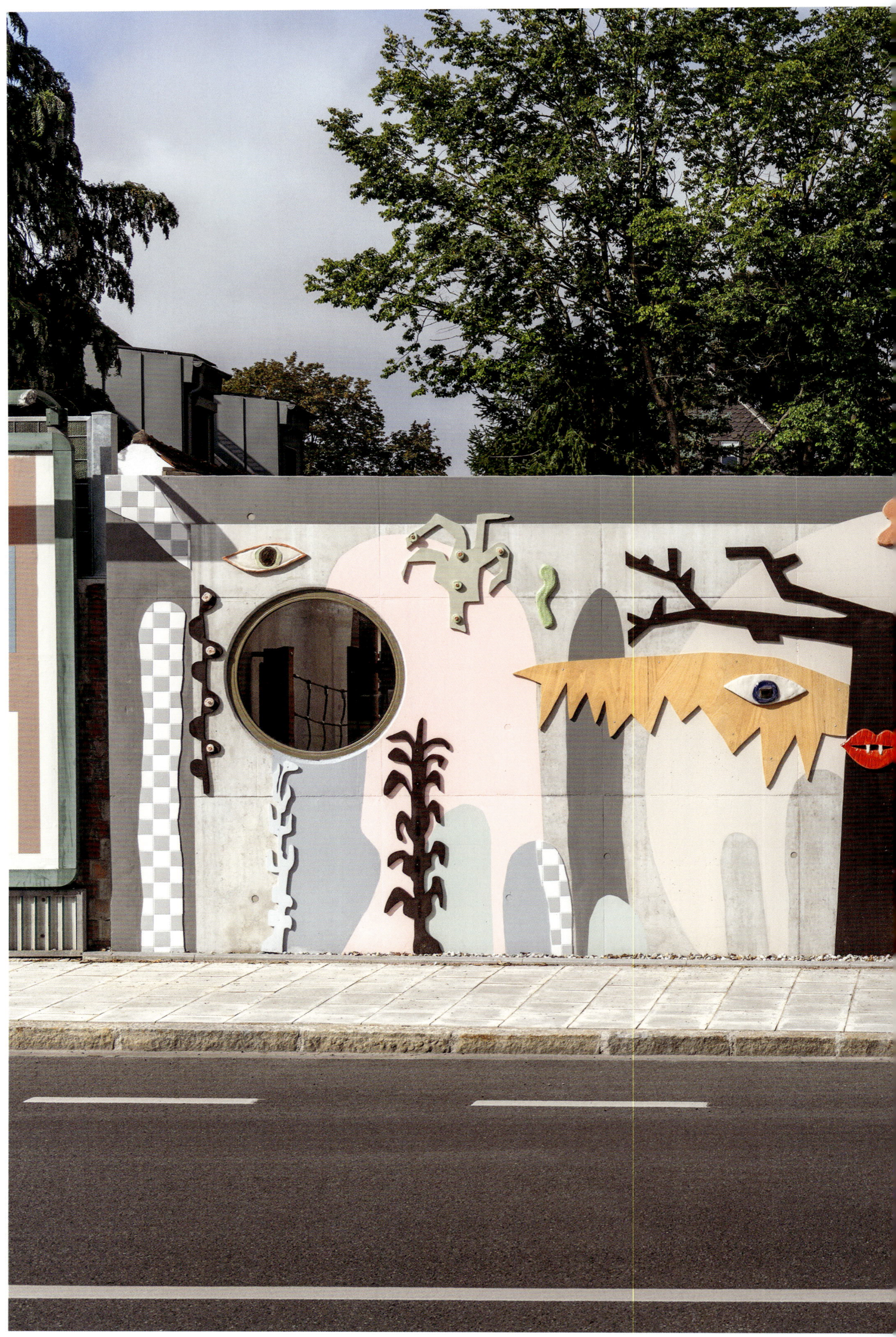

(2) ***Public Art project: Kindergarten "Am Krautgarten"***
2023, in Munich, facade paint, wood, tiles, glazed ceramics, 16 × 3 m

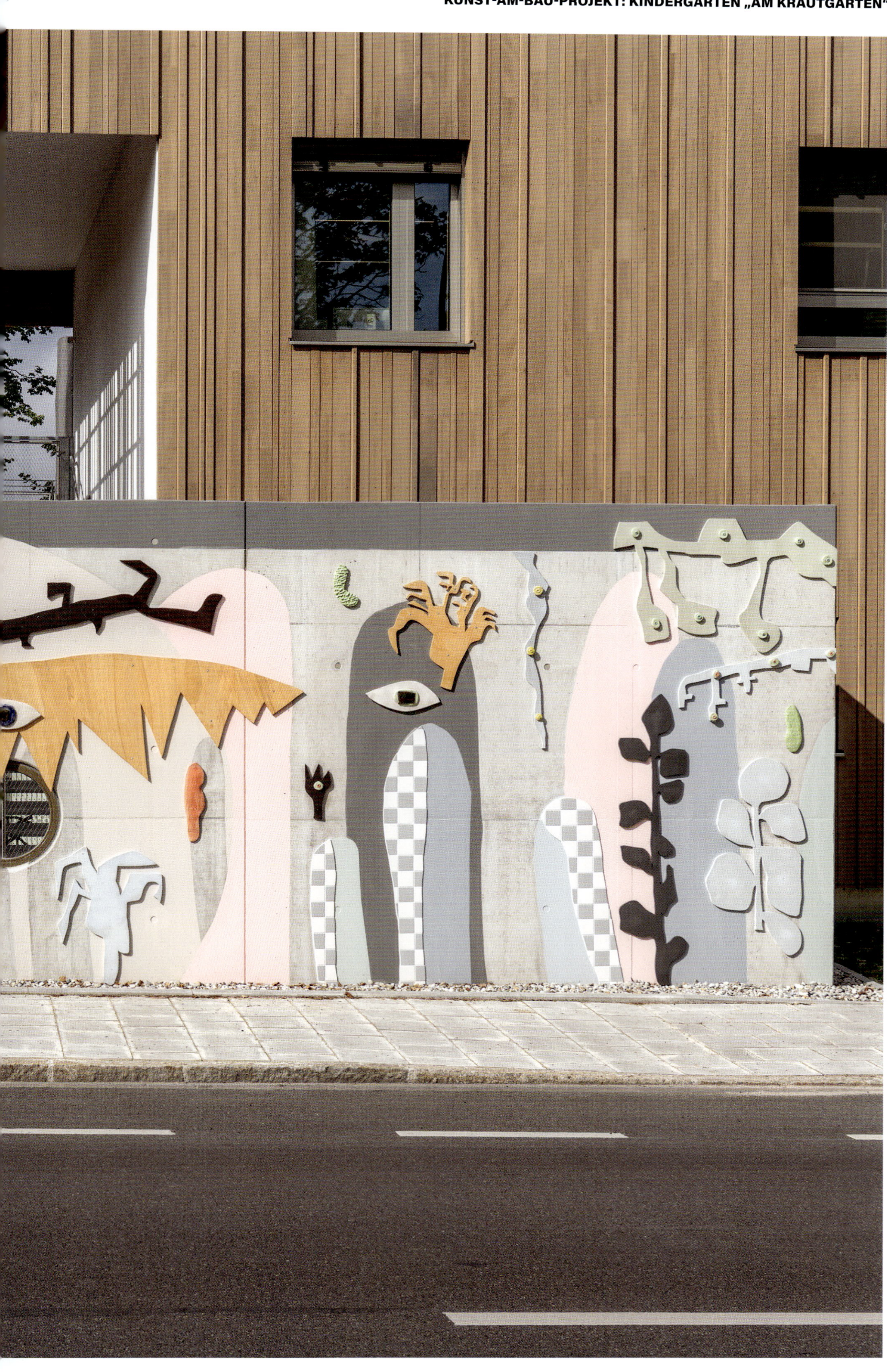

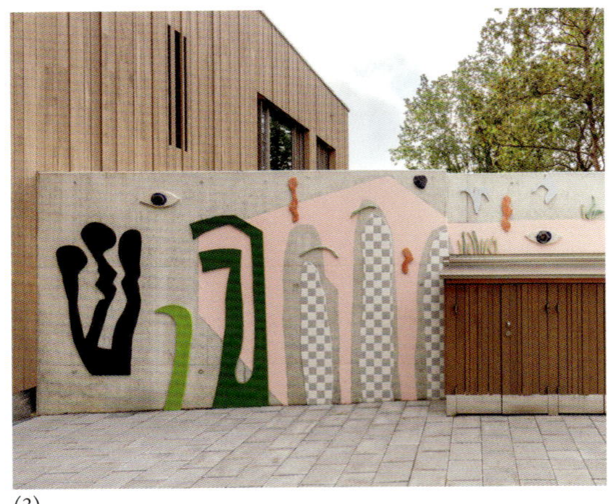
(3)

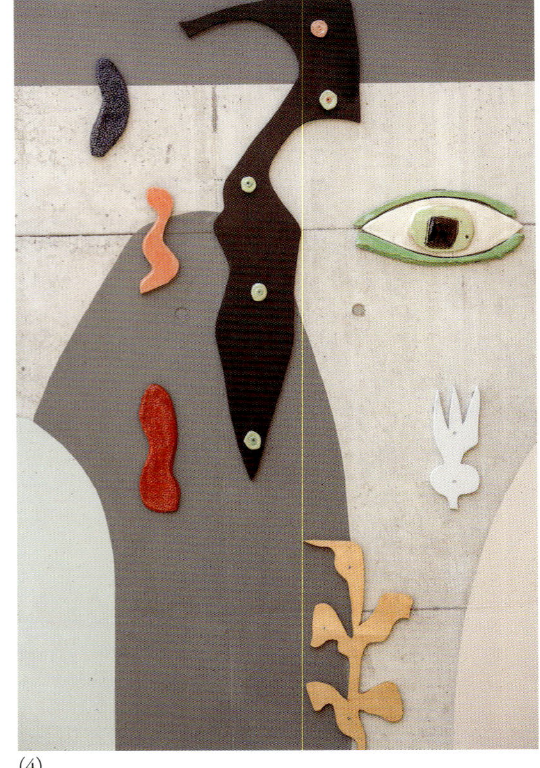
(4)

S

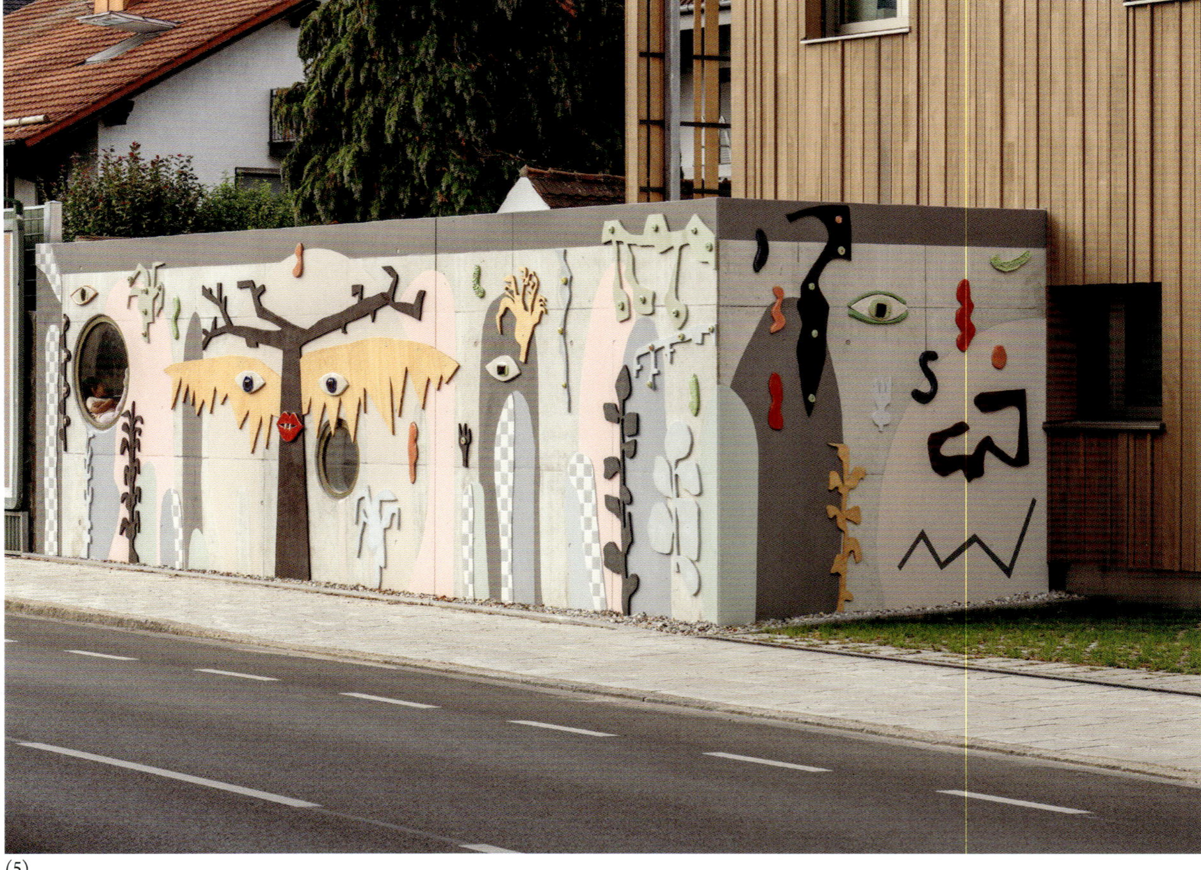
(5)

(3)
(4)
(5) ***Public Art project: Kindergarten "Am Krautgarten"***
2023, in Munich,
facade paint, wood,
tiles, glazed ceramics,
16 × 3 m

WHAT I NEVER THOUGHT

(UMFRAGE-BASIERTES NEONBETT)

S

INGREDIENTS
Umfragebasiertes
Neonbett ①②④
Book ②③

EN The outlines of a glowing, bright pink pillow and duvet swing vividly across the barn wall of Kunstverein Springhornhof. On the front door of the institution is a huge reverse glass painting of an open book. Verena Issel's installation *What I Never Thought (Survey-Based Neon Bed)* is based on a survey of the residents of the village where the institution is located. Some of the answers, such as "my son's smelly little friends," "fruitless meetings," "grandchildren who suck the air out of you," can now be read on the door of the institution. The former village priest misses "washing the bed linen after the visitors have gone, after spending the nights talking instead of sleeping." This provided the motif for the neon bed linen, which is best experienced during a stroll at dusk. "Of course, during a lockdown you long for parties with lots of people, going out to restaurants, travelling long distances—but you also miss a lot of things that you never thought you would miss," Verena Issel writes about her installation. "… maybe it's a nice idea to take these thoughts with us, as an appreciation of the small and big things that we have always taken for granted, that were a normal part of everyday life and now seem so special, distant and exotic."

☐ ***Bettina von Dziembowski, exhibition text (excerpt)***

DE Leuchtend schwingen sich die Umrisse eines rosa Kopfkissens und einer Bettdecke über die Scheunenwand des Kunstvereins Springhornhof, daneben auf den Doppelflügeln der Eingangstür ein aufgeschlagenes Buch in Hinterglasmalerei.
Die Installation *What I Never Thought (Umfragebasiertes Neonbett)* von Verena Issel geht auf eine Umfrage unter den Bewohnern des Heidedorfs und den Mitgliedern des ländlichen Kunstvereins zurück. Die Künstlerin erkundigte sich per Mailing, Facebook und Zeitungsaufruf nach nervigen Situationen, die man in Zeiten der Pandemie unverhofft vermisse.
Einige der Antworten wie „die stinkenden kleinen Freunde meines Sohnes", „ergebnislose Besprechungen", „Enkel, die einem die Luft abdrücken" kann man nun außen am Kunstverein nachlesen. Die ehemalige Pastorin des Ortes vermisst „Das Waschen der Bettbezüge, nachdem Besuch da war und man eigentlich eher die Nächte durchgeredet anstatt geschlafen hat." Damit lieferte sie das Motiv der Neonbettwäsche, die am schönsten bei einem Spaziergang in der Dämmerung zu erleben ist.
„Selbstverständlich sehnt man sich während eines Lockdowns nach Feiern mit vielen Menschen, nach Restaurantbesuchen, nach Fernreisen – man vermisst aber auch viele Dinge, von denen man selber nie gedacht hätte, dass man sie jemals vermissen würde", schreibt Verena Issel über ihre Installation. „… vielleicht ist es eine schöne Idee, sich diese Gedanken mitzunehmen, als eine Aufwertung und Wertschätzung der kleinen und großen Dinge, die wir immer für selbstverständlich gehalten haben, die ein normaler Teil des Alltags waren und die uns jetzt so besonders und weit entfernt und exotisch erscheinen."

☐ ***Bettina von Dziembowski, Ausstellungstext (Auszug)***

S

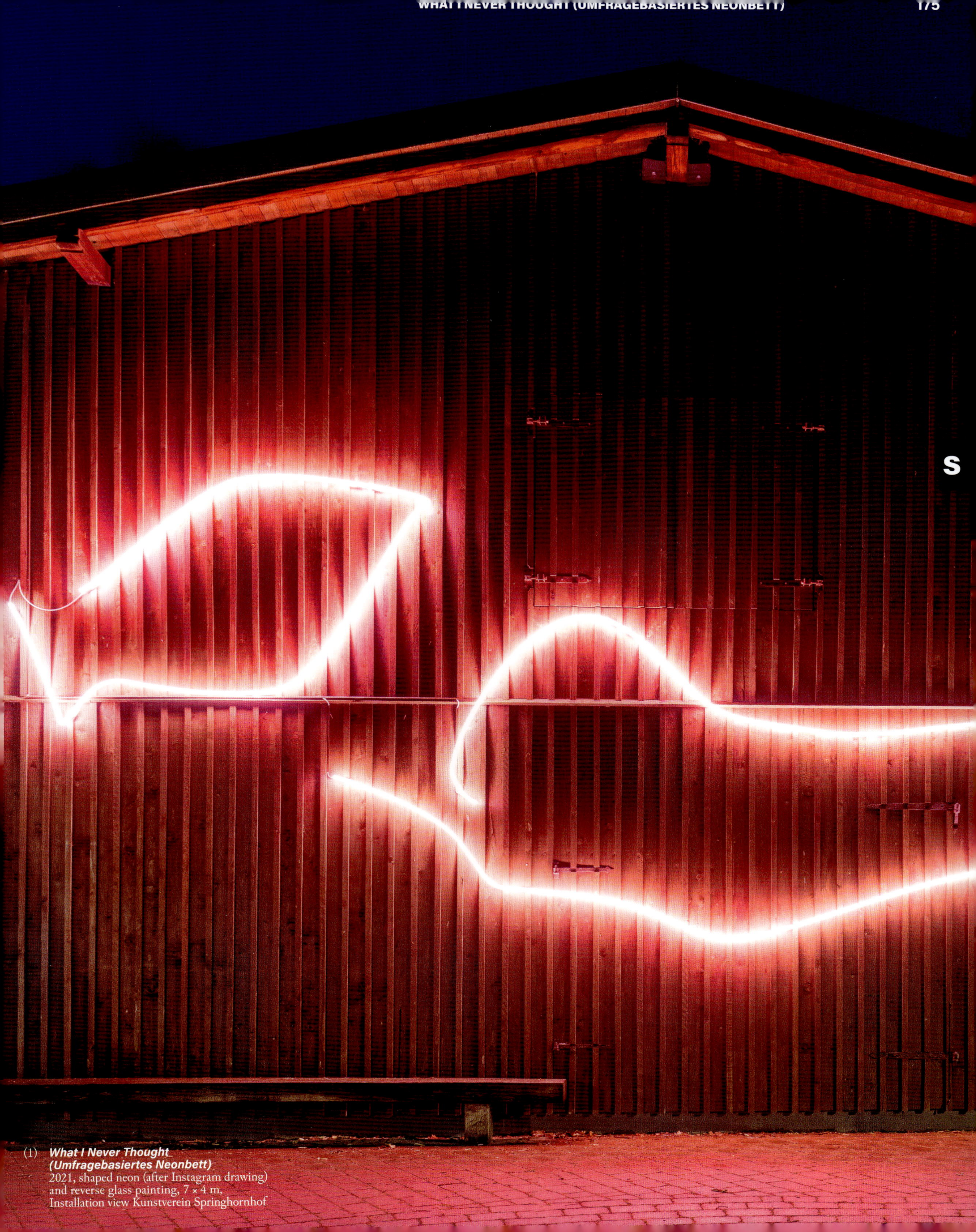

(1) ***What I Never Thought (Umfragebasiertes Neonbett)***
2021, shaped neon (after Instagram drawing) and reverse glass painting, 7 × 4 m, Installation view Kunstverein Springhornhof

S

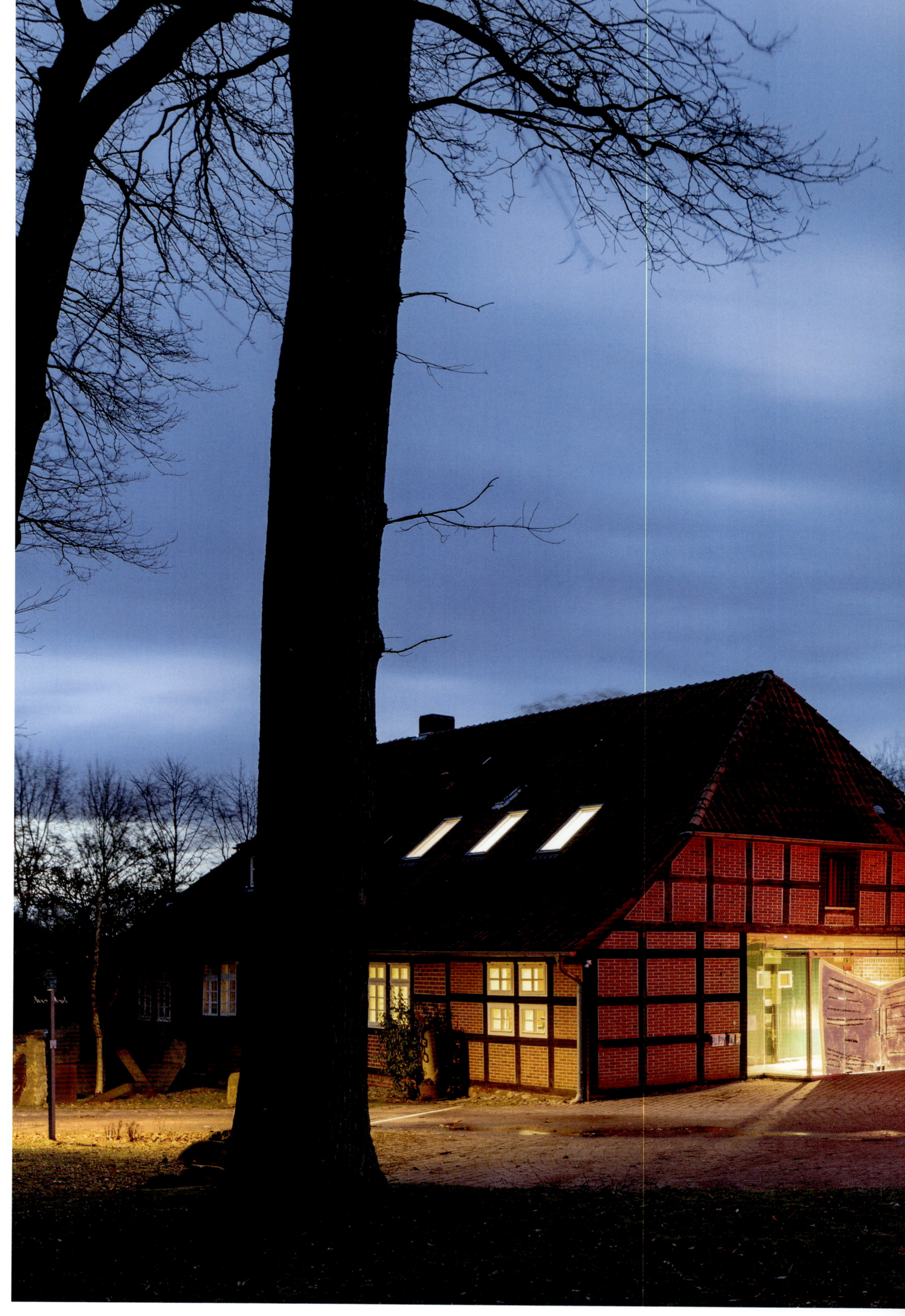

(2) ***What I Never Thought (Umfragebasiertes Neonbett)***
2021, shaped neon (after Instagram drawing) and reverse glass painting, 7 × 4 m, Installation view Kunstverein Springhornhof

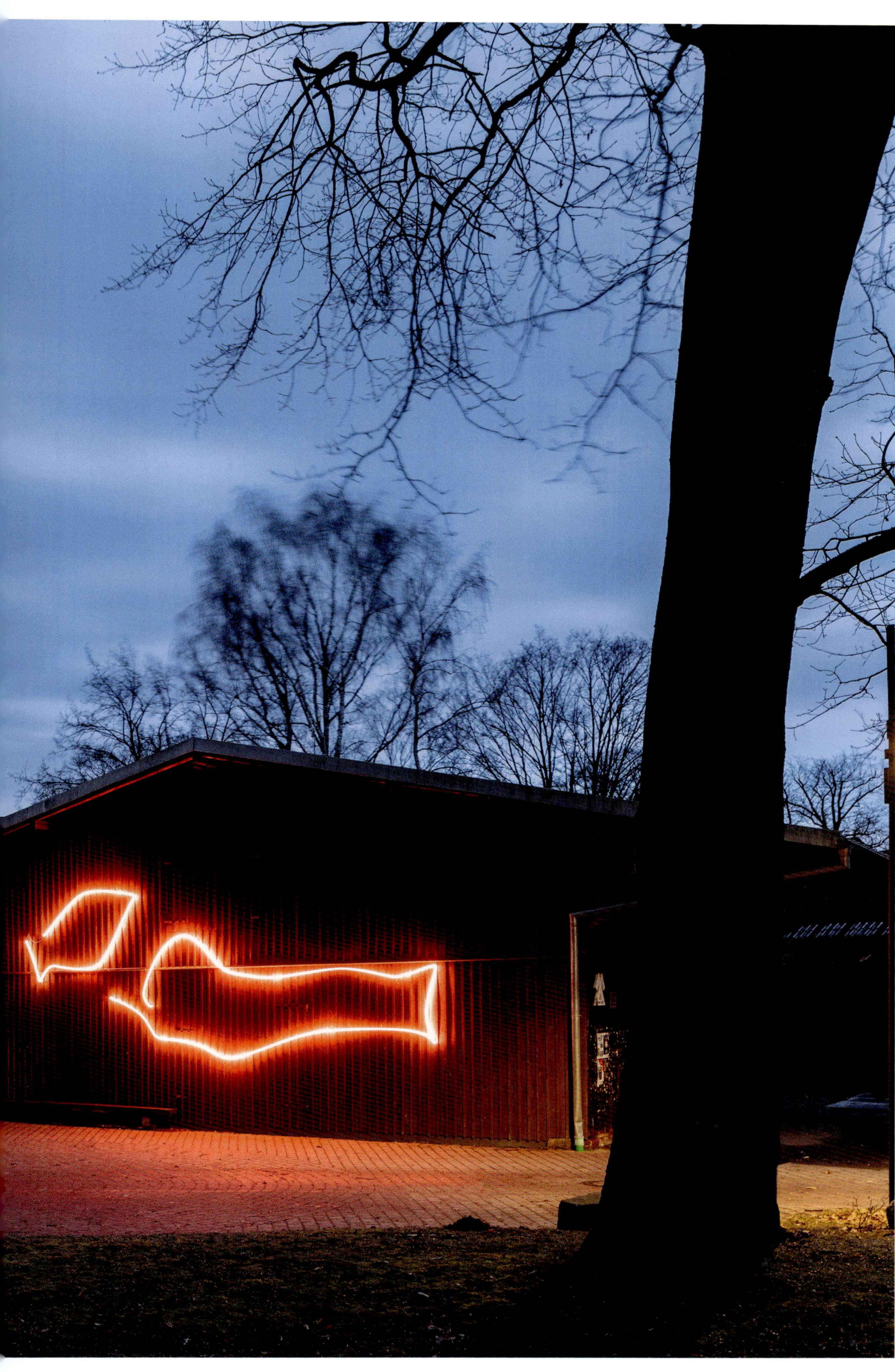

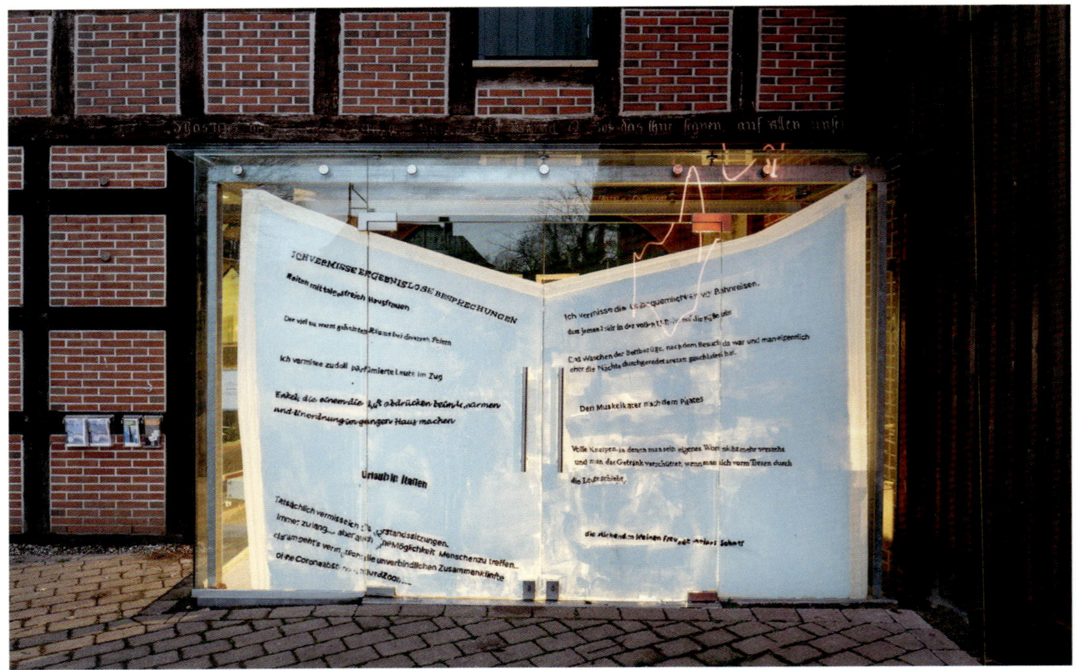

(3)

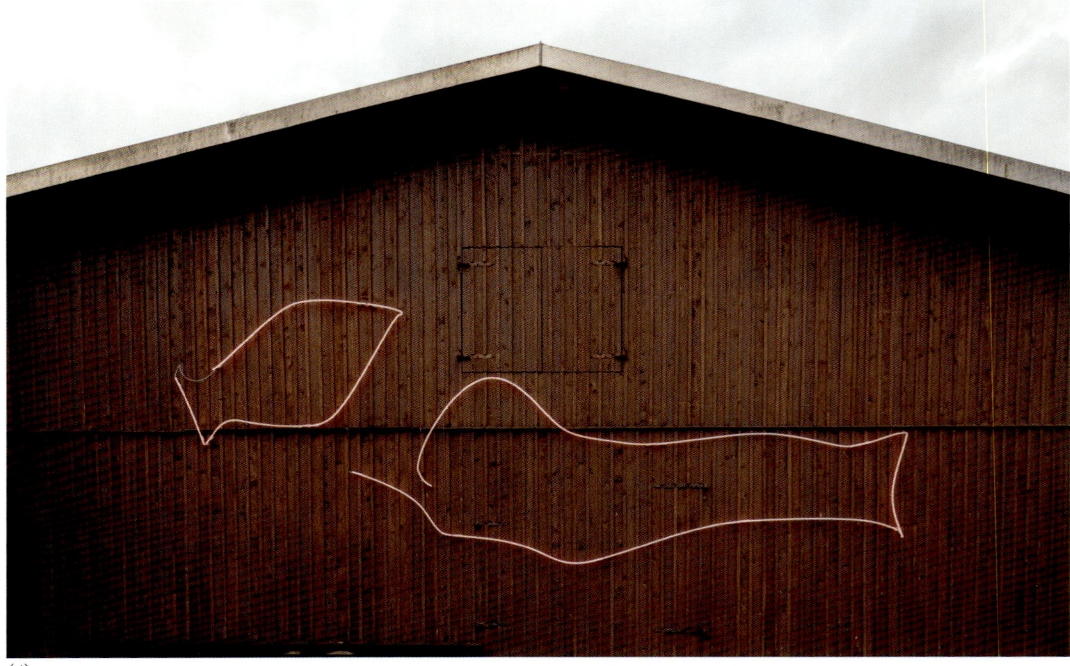

(4)

S

(3) ***What I Never Thought (Umfragebasiertes Neonbett)*** (detail) reverse glass painting on the institution's door with the village people's comments on the initial question

(4) ***What I Never Thought (Umfragebasiertes Neonbett)*** 2021, shaped neon (after Instagram drawing) and reverse glass painting, 7 × 4 m, Installation view Kunstverein Springhornhof

JANUARY DEPRESSION (REMEDY)

S

INGREDIENTS

January Depression 1 ⑧
January Depression 2 ⑨
January Depression 3 ⑩
January Depression 4 ⑪
January Depression 5 ⑫
January Depression 6 ⑬
January Depression 7 ⑭
January Depression 8 ⑮
January Depression 9 ⑯
January Depression 10 ⑰
January Depression 11 ⑱
January Depression 12 ⑲
January Depression 13 ⑳
January Depression 14 ㉑
January Depression 15 ㉒
January Depression 16 ㉓
January Depression 17 ㉔
January Depression 18 ㉕
January Depression 19 ㉖
January Depression 20 ㉗
January Depression 21 ㉘
January Depression 22 ㉙
January Depression 23 ㉚
January Depression 24 ㉛
January Depression 25 ㉝
January Depression 26 ㉟
January Depression 27 ㊲
January Depression 29
January Depression 30
January Depression 32
January Depression 33
January Depression 34
January Depression 35
January Depression 38
January Depression 39
Shoe ㊱
Chinese Cabbage ㊳
Cigarette ①
Flower ㉝
Flower II ㉝
Flower III ㉝
Untitled ㉜
Untitled II ㉜
Untitled III ㉜
Bottle Opener ②③
Mountains ③
Peanut ⑥

EN With the exhibition *KLAPP KLAPP*, Kunstverein Springhornhof presents a spectacular course of interconnected and colorful images and spaces by Verena Issel. [...] The starting point of Issel's installation, which covers the entire ground floor of the institution, is a series of drawings entitled *January Depression (Remedy)*. Some forty images were created in 2020, when the artist had to spend three weeks in strict quarantine in her Berlin apartment due to the COVID-19 pandemic. [...] In an attempt to accept spatial and social limitations rather than fight them, Issel imposed a set of strict rules on herself. She decided to restrict herself to the medium of painting, to paint only on grey cardboard in a format of 42 × 30 cm, to use only unmixed primarycolors from a very limited palette, to fill them into broad highlighter pens and to apply them to the paper. She only allowed herself to paint things that were in the house. This set of rules sounds simple enough, but for Issel, whose art usually explores the boundaries of entire spaces, rooms or walls, it was a severe restriction. Nevertheless, she forced herself to paint at least two pictures a day. The therapy was successful. Resisting the temptations of Netflix and the threat of pandemic depression, Verena Issel developed an unexpected joy in combining colors and forms on a small scale—sometimes abstract, sometimes figurative, sometimes clearly defined, sometimes playful. The only extra she allowed herself was to incorporate household objects—colored earplugs, plastic fringes or pieces of foam—into the game. In the exhibition at Springhornhof, the small pictures, originally intended as a private exercise, regain their freedom. The colorful motifs become the space, leap onto walls and floors, mutate into free-standing outlines, repeat themselves, change colors and proportions and flirt with each other.

☐ ***Bettina von Dziembowski, exhibition text, 2021***

DE Der Kunstverein Springhornhof zeigt mit der Ausstellung *KLAPP KLAPP* einen fulminanten Parcours bunt ineinander übergreifender Bilder und Räume von Verena Issel.
[...] Ausgangspunkt von Issels Installation, die sich über das gesamte Erdgeschoss des Kunstvereins erstreckt, ist eine Serie von Zeichnungen unter dem Titel *January Depression (Remedy)*. Die etwa vierzig Bilder entstanden im Frühling 2020, als die Künstlerin aufgrund der Coronapandemie drei Wochen in strikter Quarantäne in ihrer Berliner Wohnung verbringen musste. [...]
In dem Versuch, die räumlichen und sozialen Einschränkungen zu akzeptieren, statt sich daran aufzureiben, erlegte sich Issel eine Reihe strenger Regeln auf. Sie beschloss, sich nur auf das Medium Malerei zu beschränken, nur auf grauem Karton im Format 42 × 30 cm zu malen und nur ungemischte Grundfarben aus einer sehr begrenzten Farbskala zu verwenden, die sie in breite Textmarker einfüllte und damit auf das Papier auftrug und mit denen sie nur Dinge malte, die im Haus waren.

Das Regelwerk klingt recht simpel, bedeutete jedoch für Issel, die mit ihrer Kunst normalerweise über ganze Räume oder Wände verfügt, eine harte Einschränkung. Dennoch zwang sie sich, jeden Tag mindestens zwei Bilder zu malen.
Die Therapie gelang. Verena Issel entging den Verlockungen von Netflix und der drohenden Coronadepression und entwickelte ungeahnte Freude daran, Farben und Formen auf kleinem Format zu kombinieren – mal abstrakt, mal gegenständlich, mal klar umrissen, mal verspielt. Das Einzige, was sie sich zusätzlich erlaubte, war es, Gegenstände aus dem Haushalt – bunte Ohrstöpsel, Plastikfransen oder Schaumstoffteile – mit ins Spiel zu bringen.
In der Ausstellung im Springhornhof eroberten sich die kleinen Bilder, die zunächst als private Übung gedacht waren, nun die Freiheit zurück. Die bunten Motive werden zum Raum, springen über auf Wände und Böden, mutieren zu freistehenden Umrissen, wiederholen sich, wechseln Farben und Proportionen und flirten heftig miteinander.

☐ ***Bettina von Dziembowski, Ausstellungstext, 2021***

S

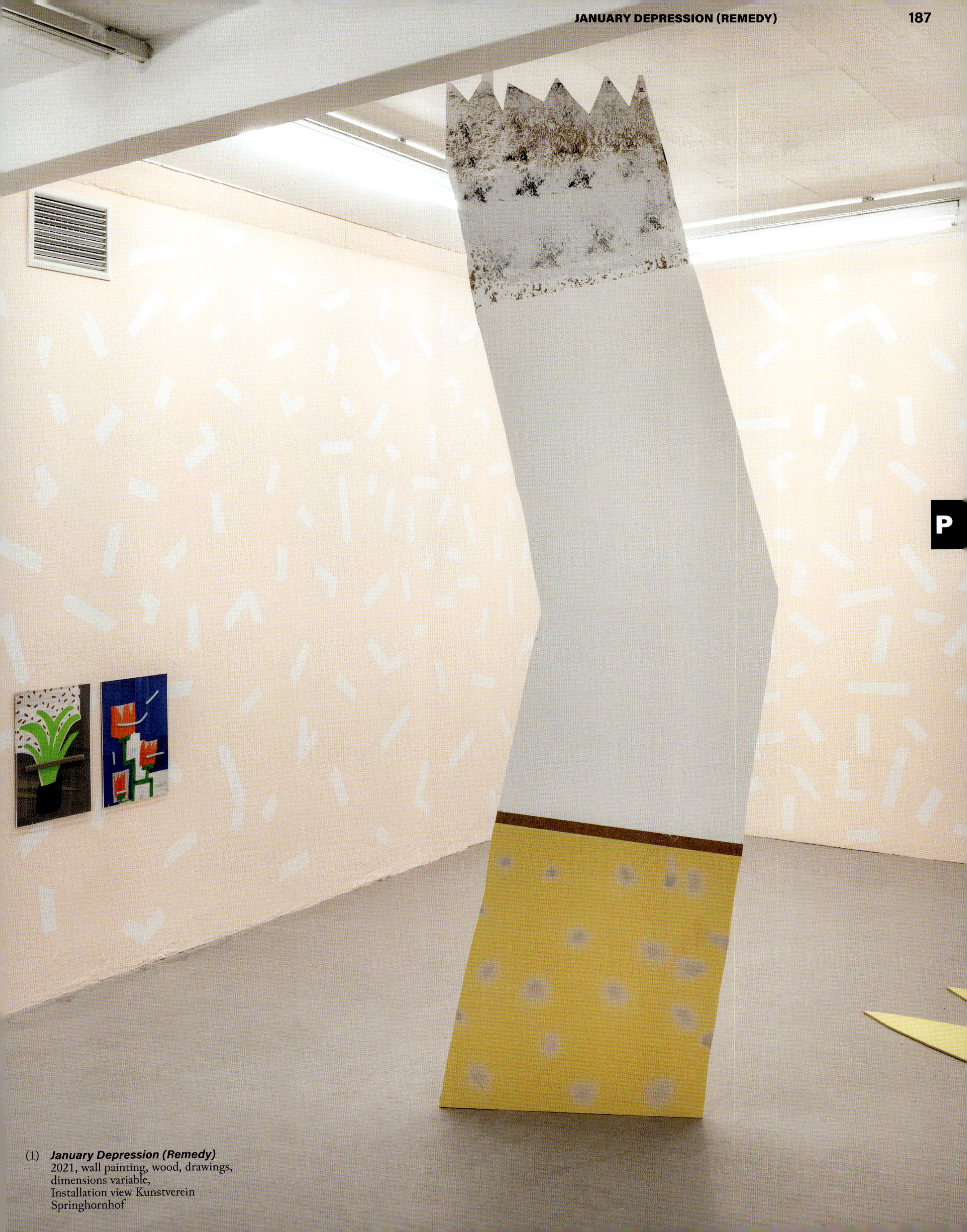

P

(1) ***January Depression (Remedy)***
2021, wall painting, wood, drawings, dimensions variable, Installation view Kunstverein Springhornhof

P

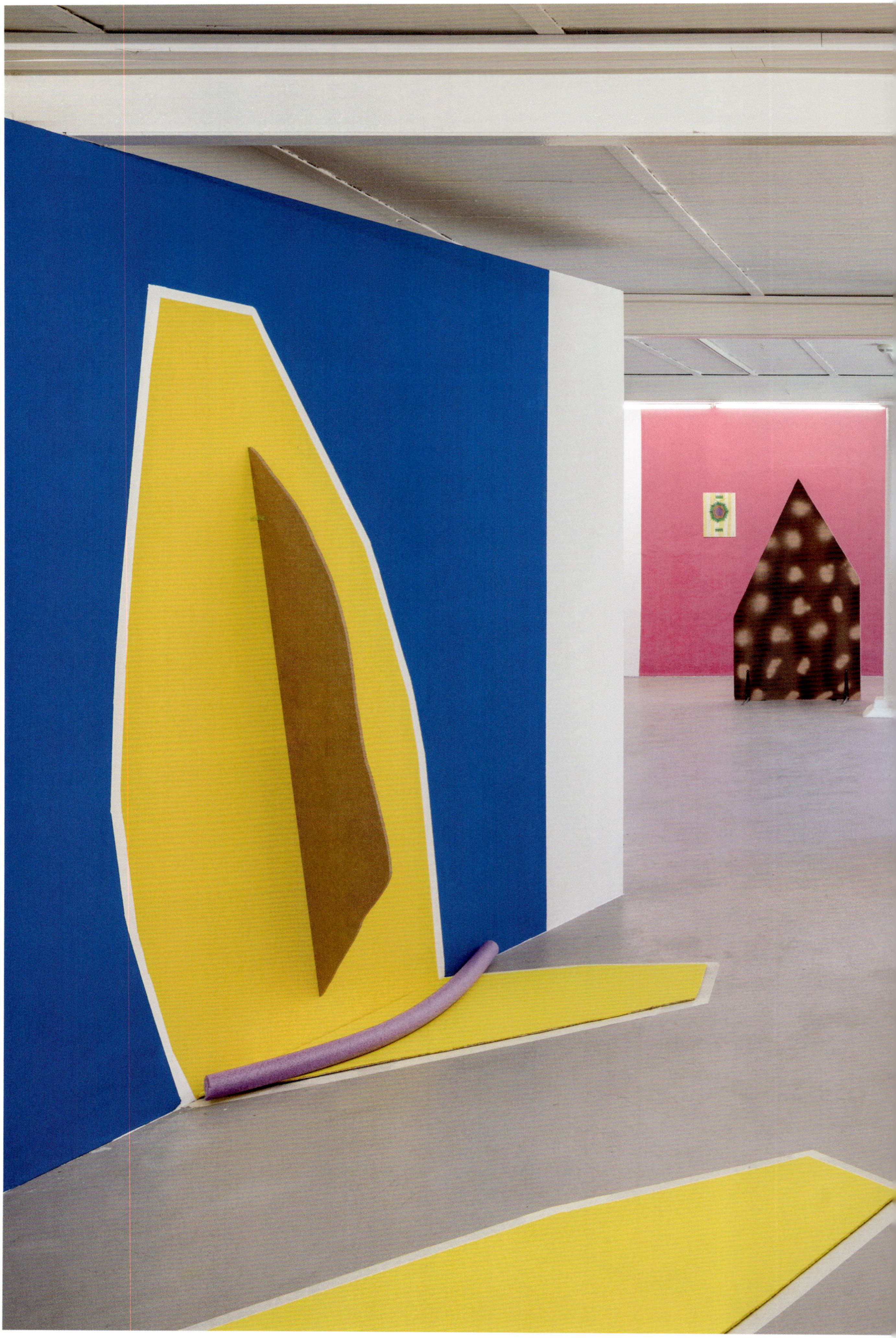

(2) ***January Depression (Remedy)***
2021, wall painting, wood, drawings, dimensions variable, Installation view Kunstverein Springhornhof

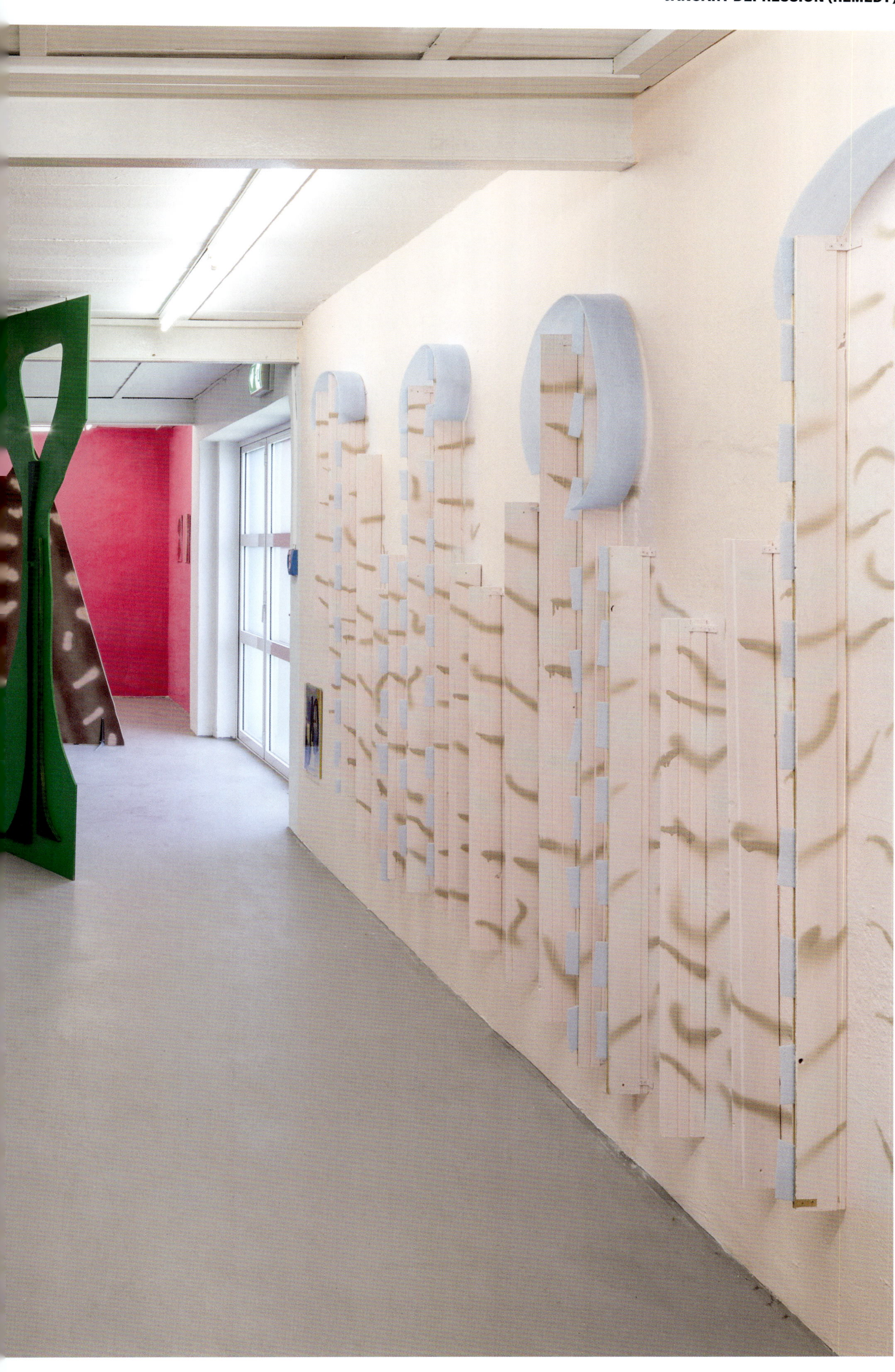

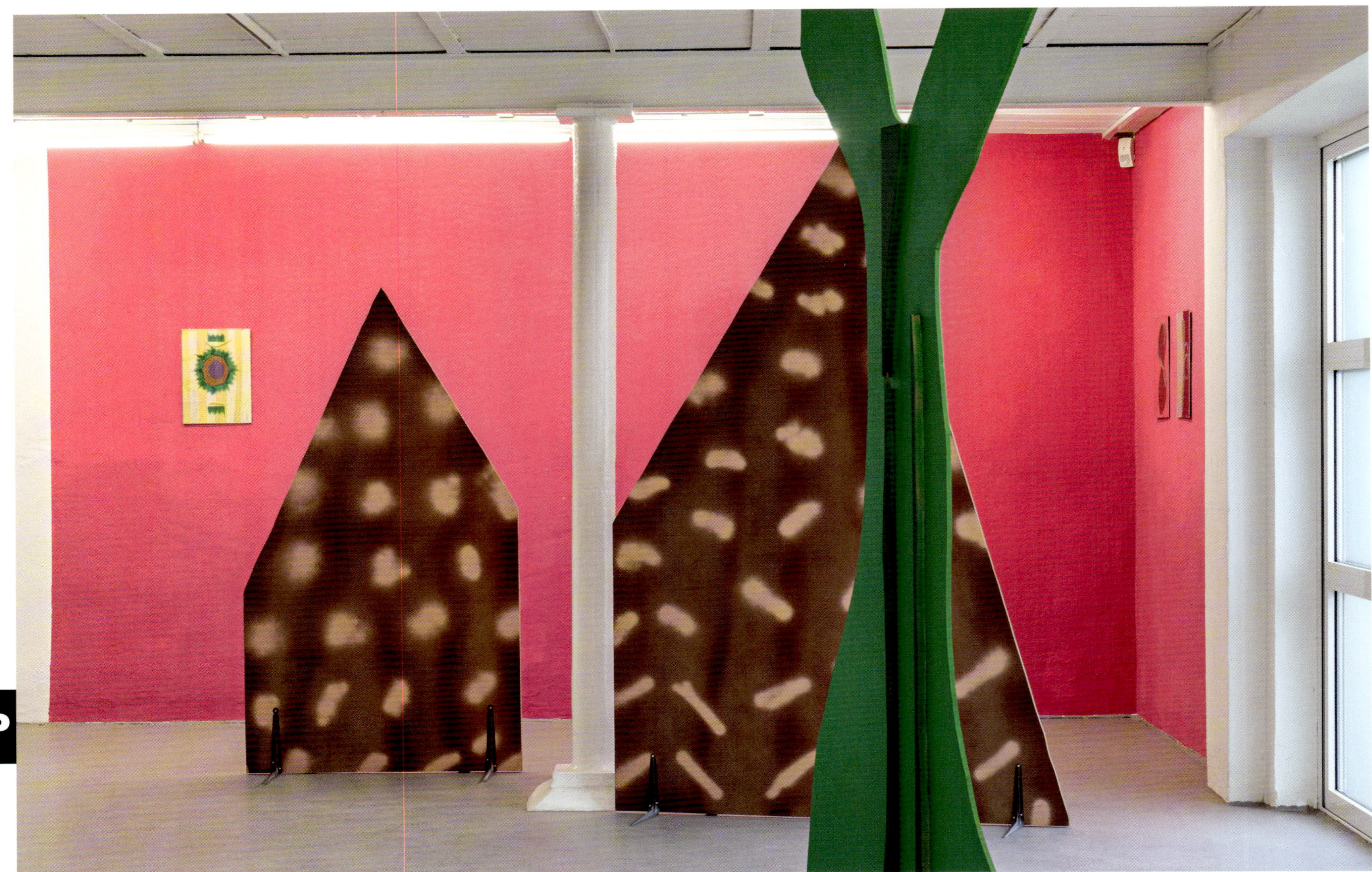

(3)

P

(3) ***January Depression (Remedy)***
2021, wall painting, wood, drawings, dimensions variable, Installation view Kunstverein Springhornhof

(4) ***January Depression 36***
2021, acrylics on cardboard with household objects, 42 × 30 cm

(5) ***January Depression 37***
2021, acrylics on cardboard with household objects, 42 × 30 cm

(6) ***January Depression (Remedy)***
2021, wall painting, wood, drawings, dimensions variable, Installation view Kunstverein Springhornhof

(7) ***January Depression 31***
2021, acrylics on cardboard with household objects, 42 × 30 cm

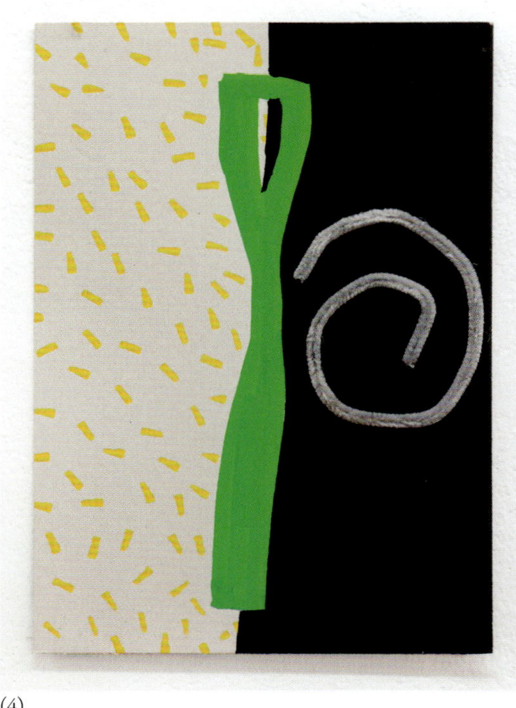

(4)

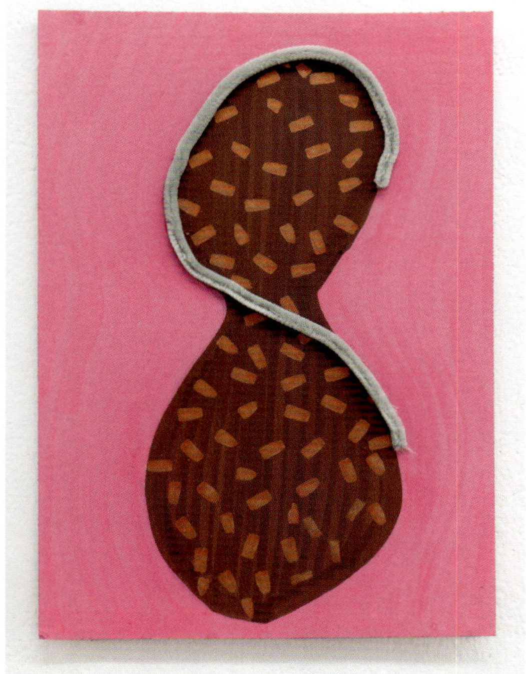

(5)

(6)

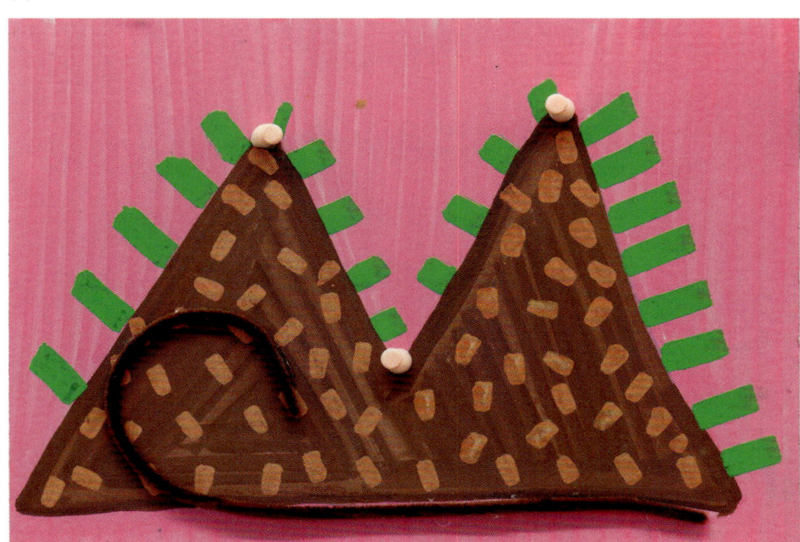

(7)

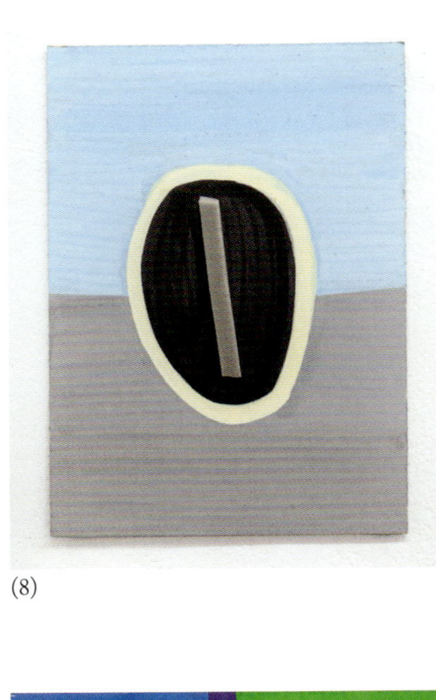
(8)

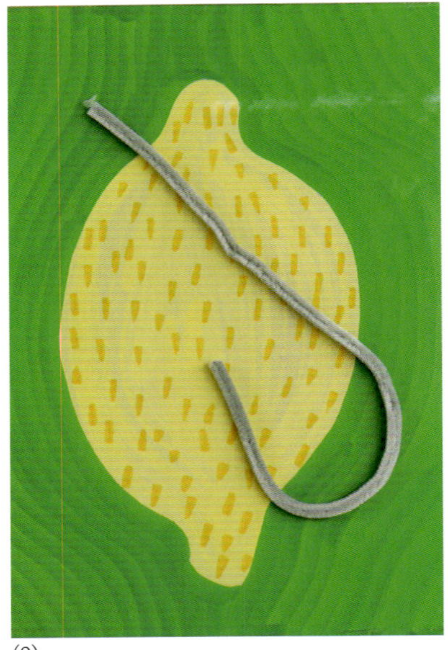
(9)

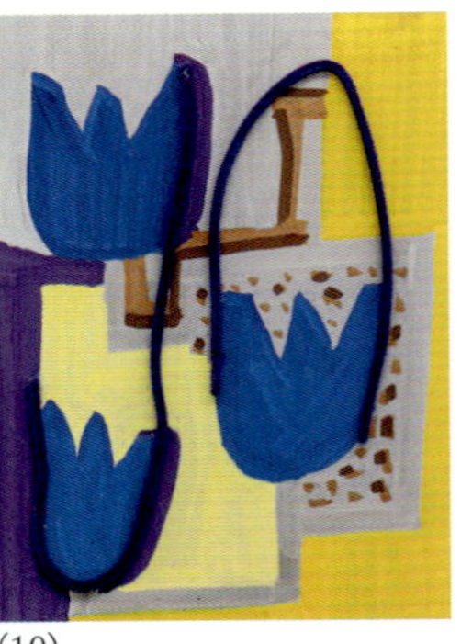
(10)

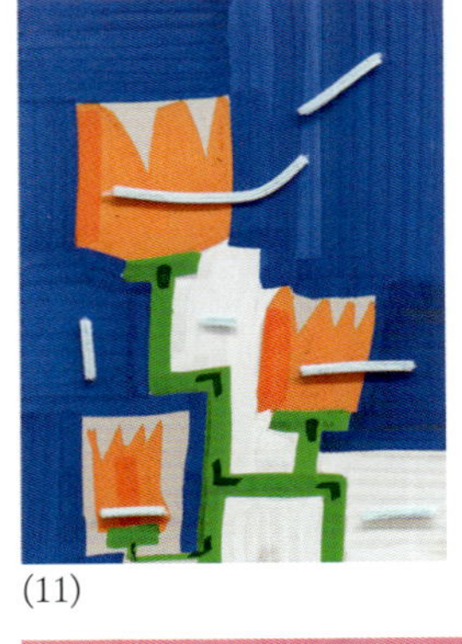
(11)

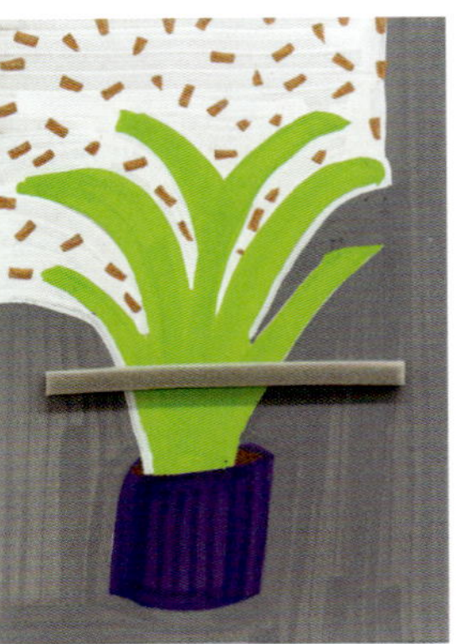
(13)

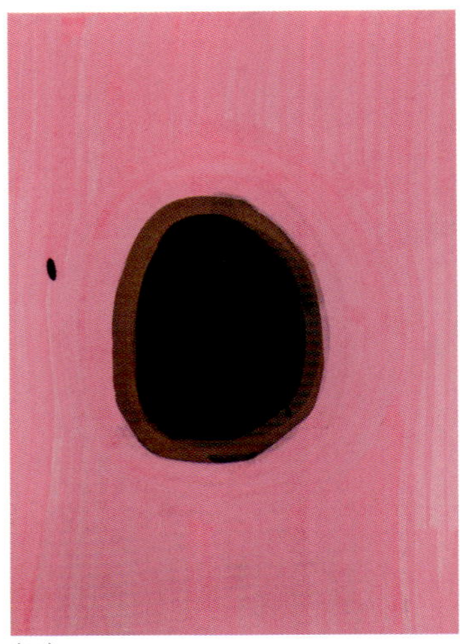
(14)

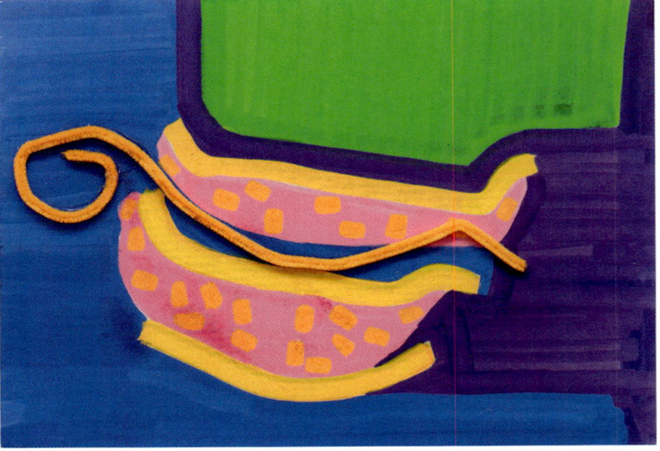
(12)

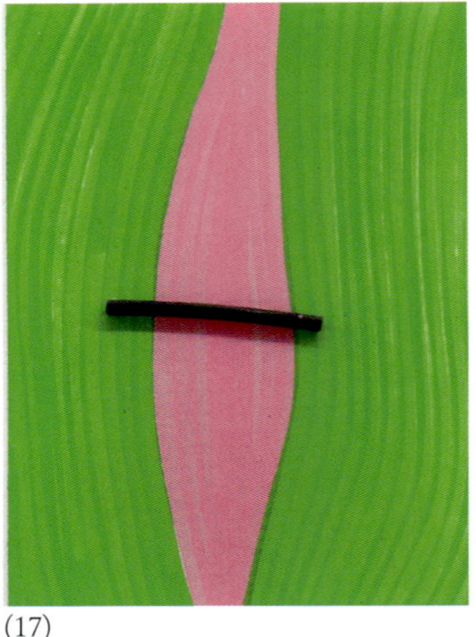
(17)

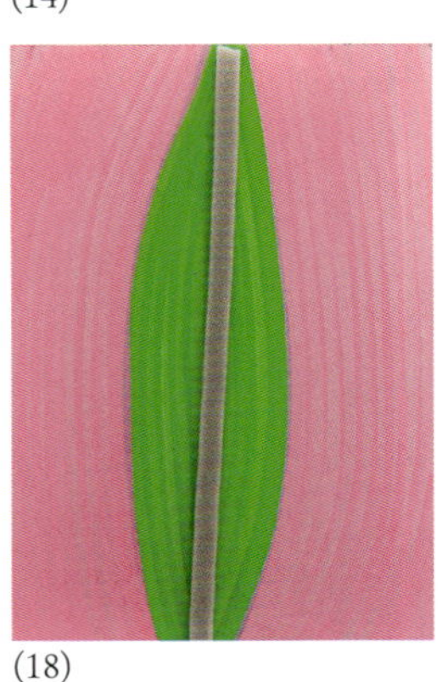
(18)

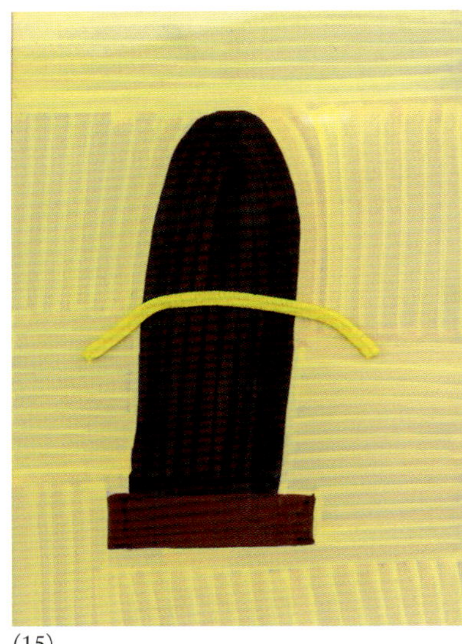
(15)

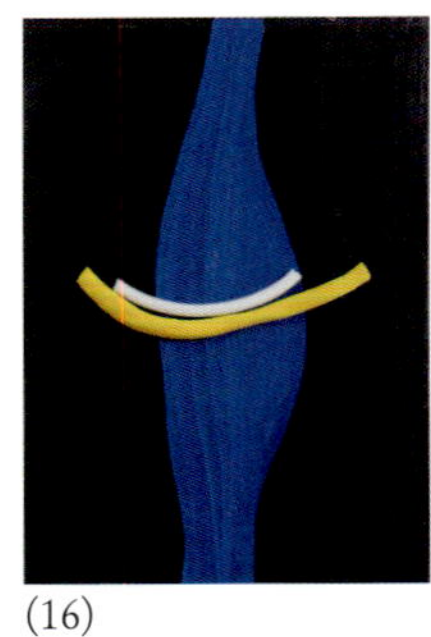
(16)

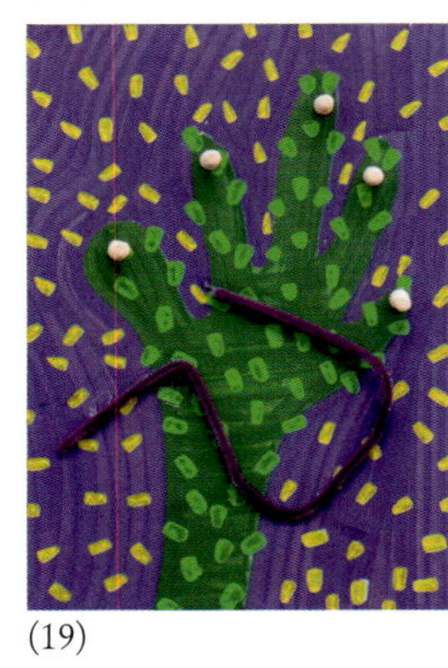
(19)

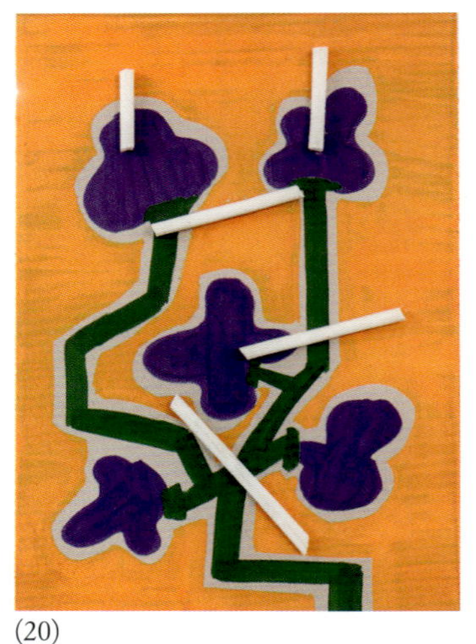
(20)

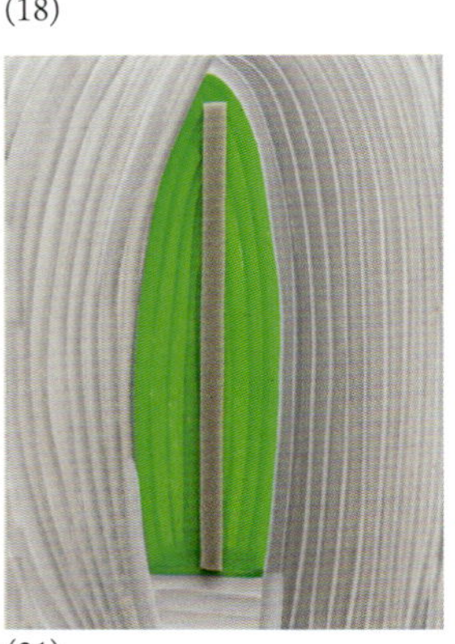
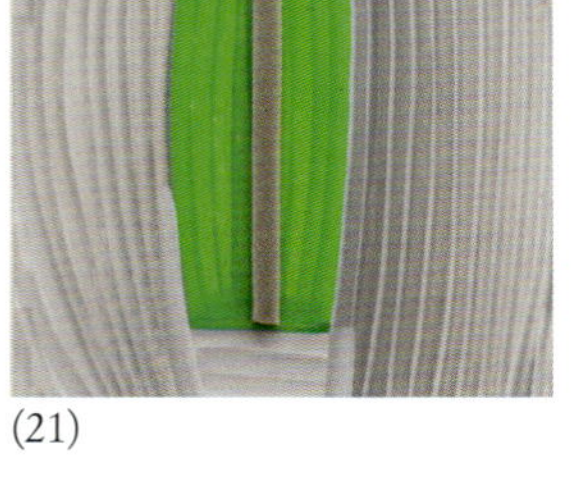
(21)

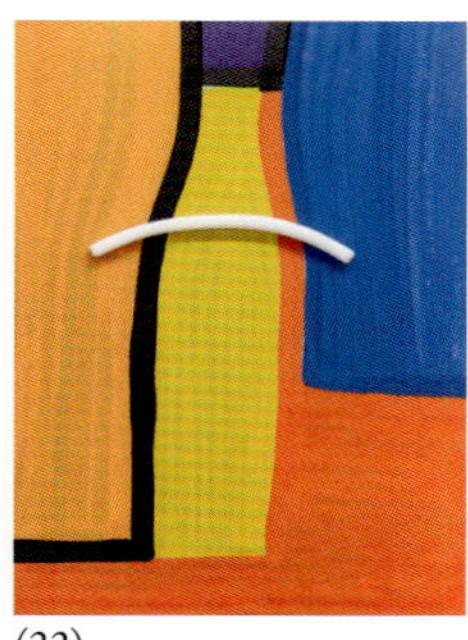
(22)

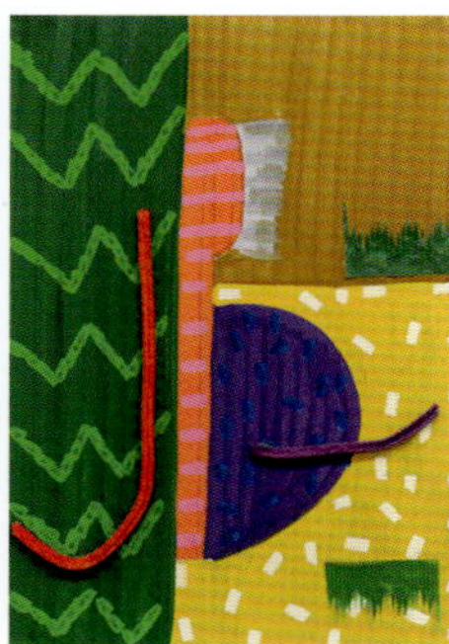
(25)

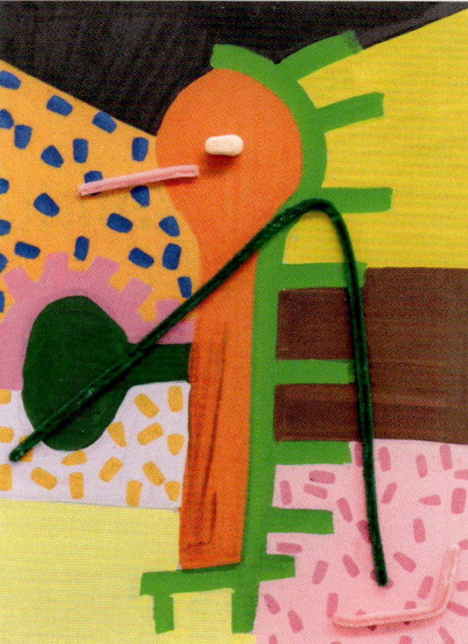

(23)

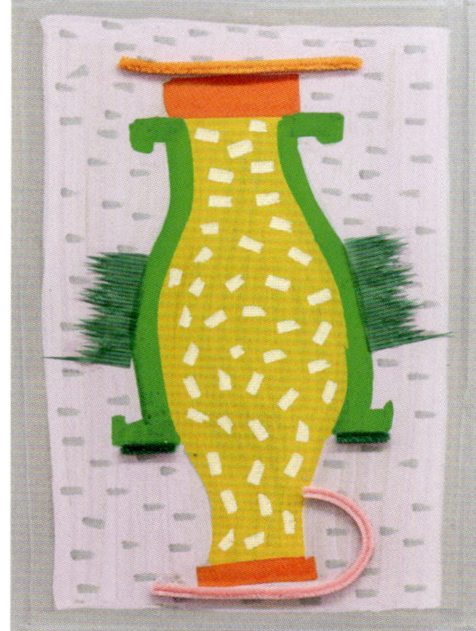
(24)

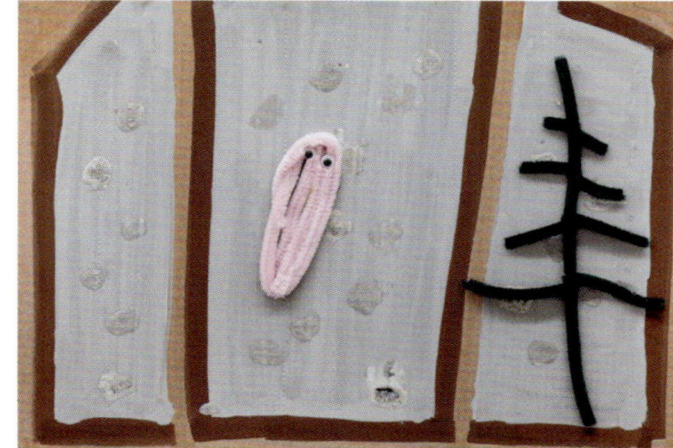
(26)

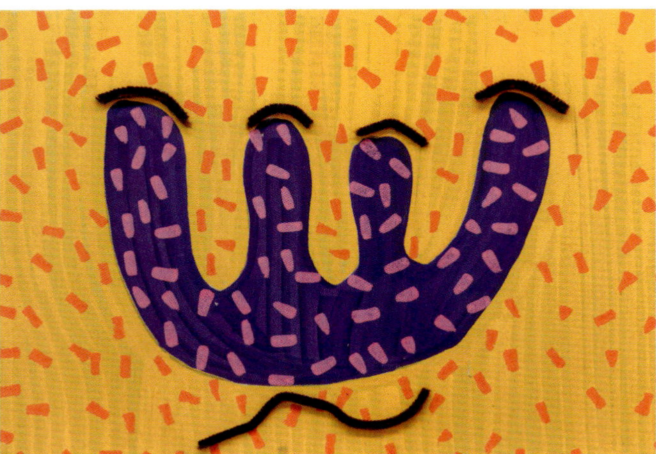
(27)

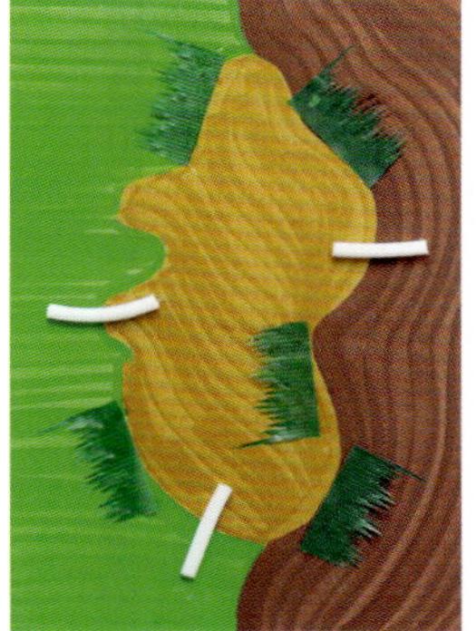
(28)

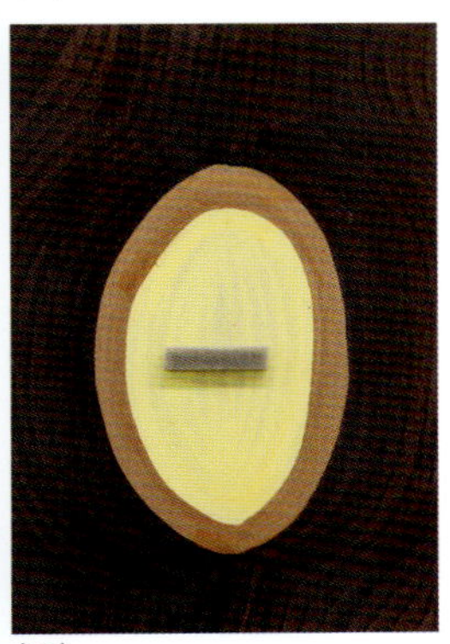
(29)

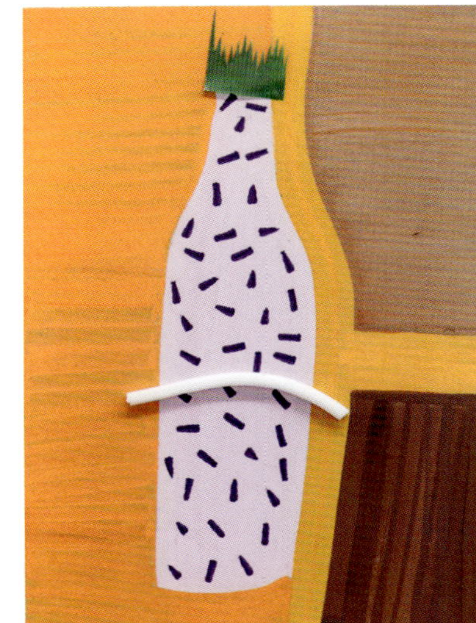

(30)

(31)

(8) ***January Depression 1***
(9) ***January Depression 2***
(10) ***January Depression 3***
(11) ***January Depression 4***
(12) ***January Depression 5***
(13) ***January Depression 6***
(14) ***January Depression 7***
(15) ***January Depression 8***
(16) ***January Depression 9***
(17) ***January Depression 10***
(18) ***January Depression 11***
(19) ***January Depression 12***
(20) ***January Depression 13***
(21) ***January Depression 14***
(22) ***January Depression 15***
(23) ***January Depression 16***
(24) ***January Depression 17***
(25) ***January Depression 18***
(26) ***January Depression 19***
(27) ***January Depression 20***
(28) ***January Depression 21***
(29) ***January Depression 22***
(30) ***January Depression 23***
(31) ***January Depression 24***
all: 2021, acrylics on cardboard with household objects, 42 × 30 cm

P

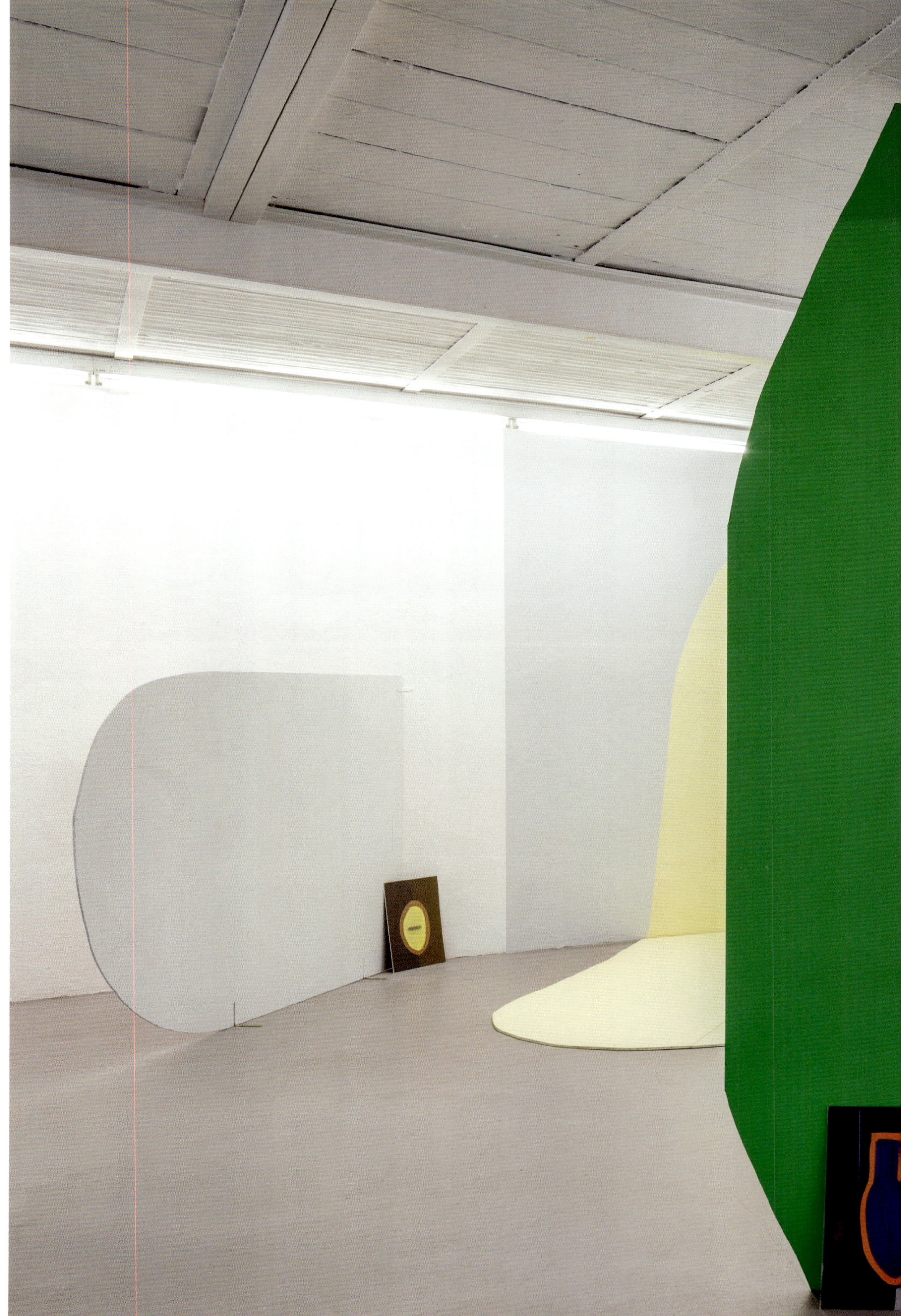

(32) ***January Depression (Remedy)***
2021, wall painting, wood, drawings, dimensions variable, Installation view Kunstverein Springhornhof

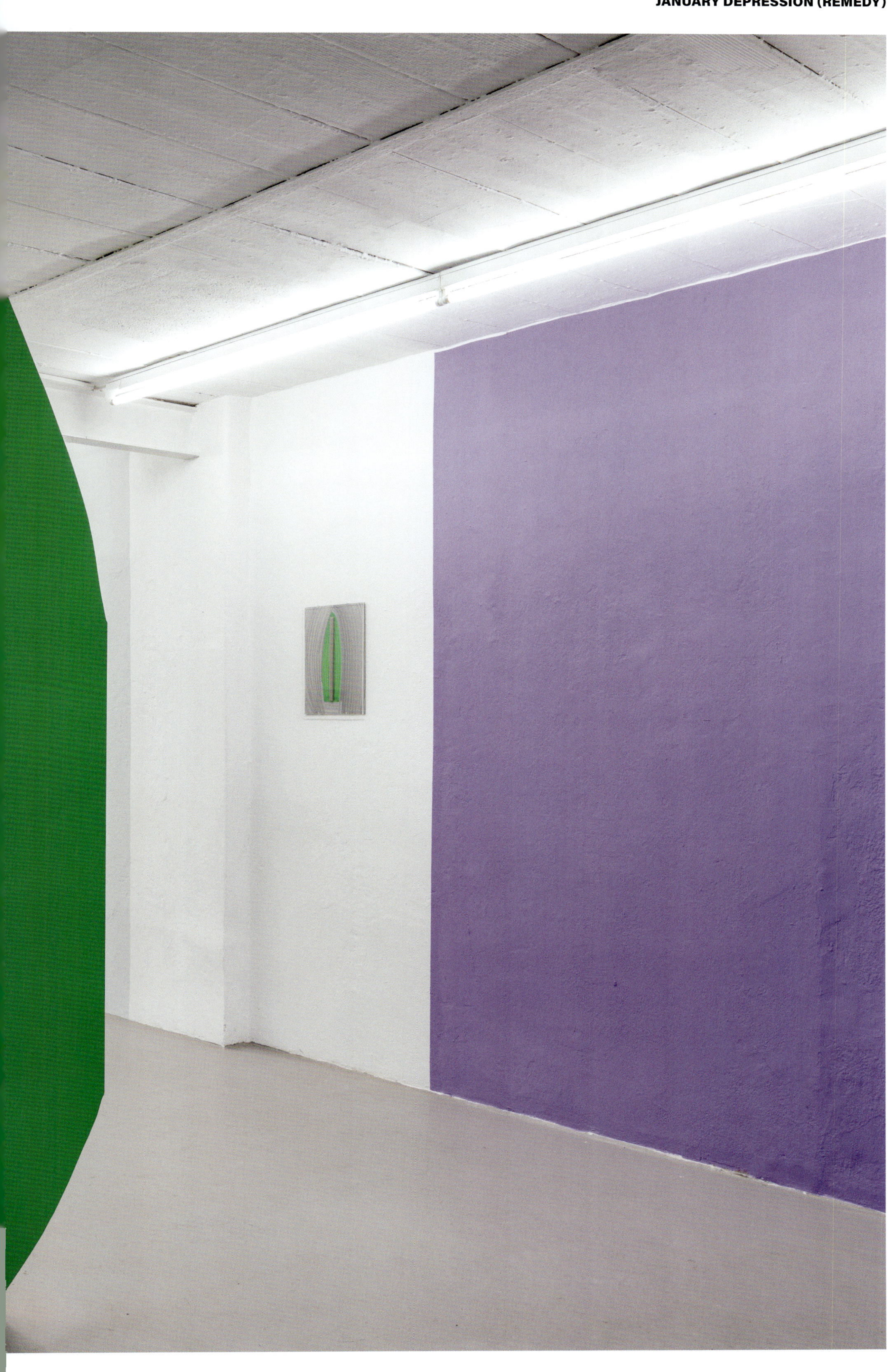

P

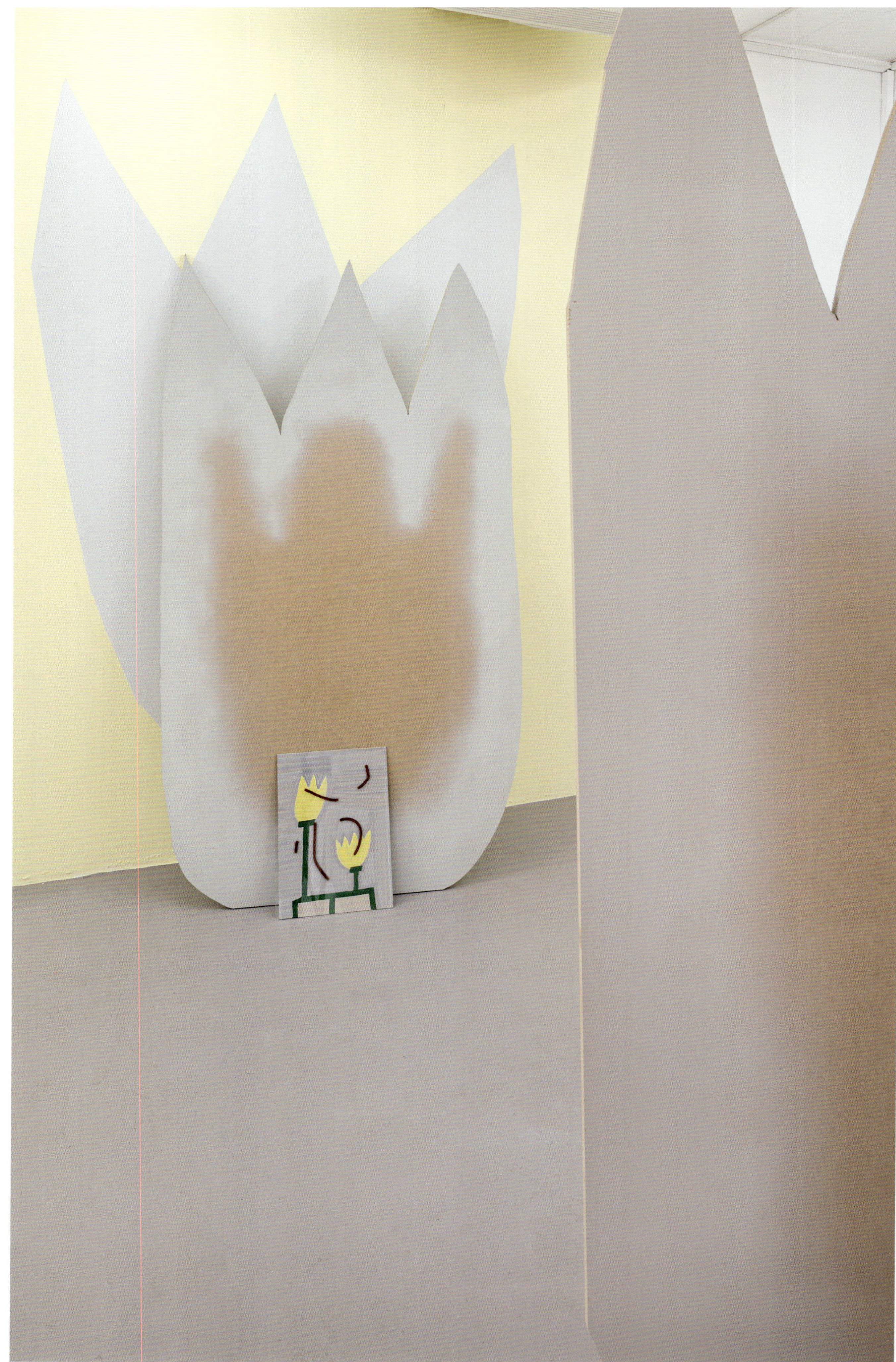

(33) ***January Depression (Remedy)***
2021, wall painting, wood, drawings, dimensions variable, Installation view Kunstverein Springhornhof

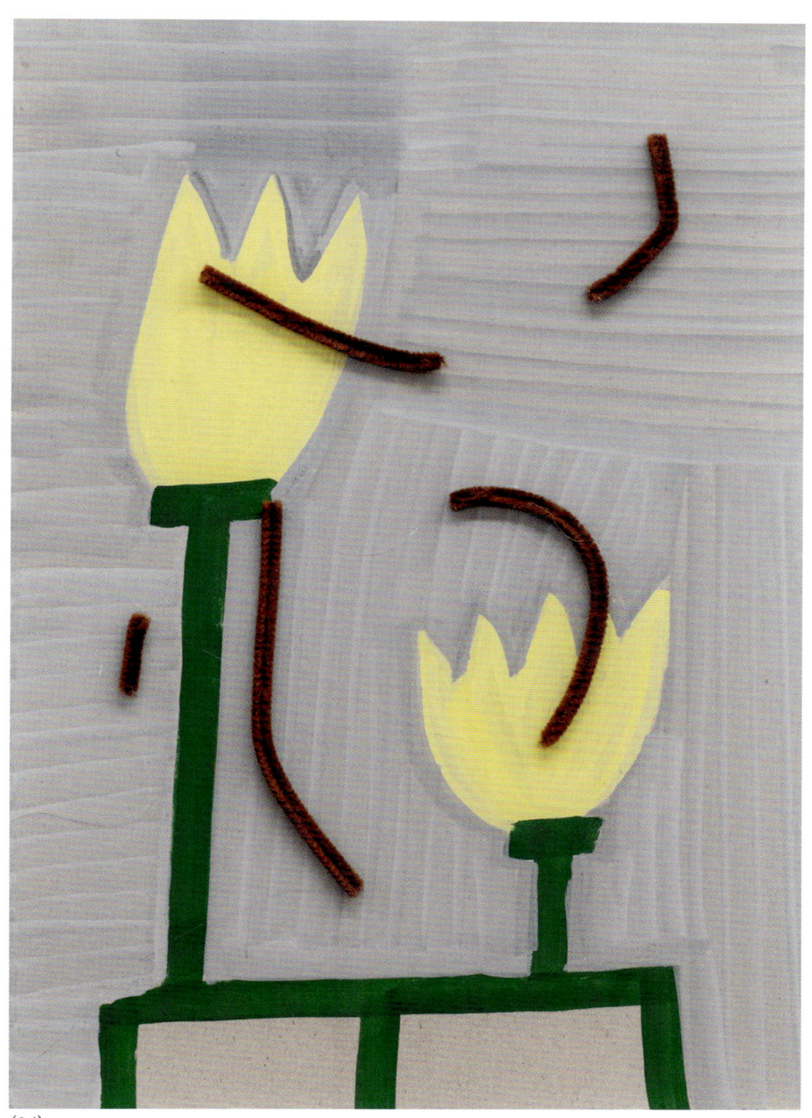
(34)

P

(34) ***January Depression 25***
2021, acrylics on cardboard with household objects, 42 × 30 cm

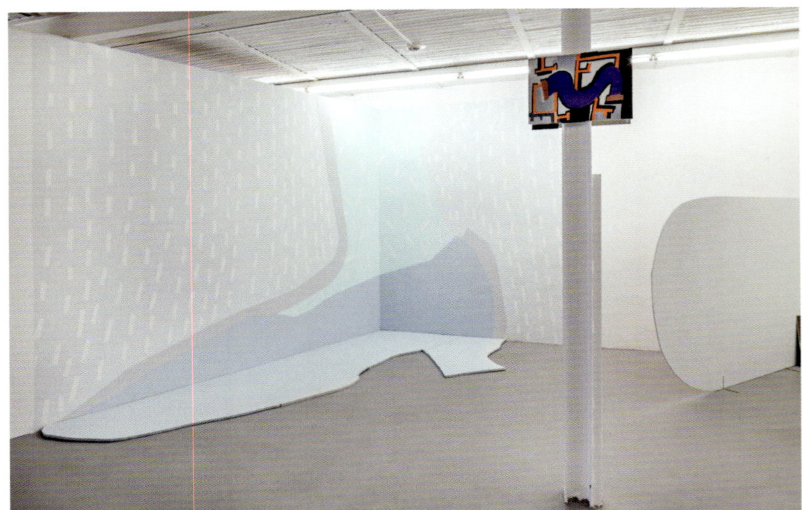
(35)

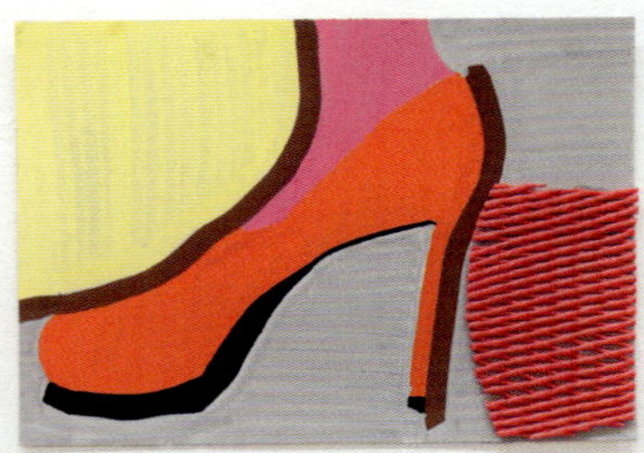
(36)

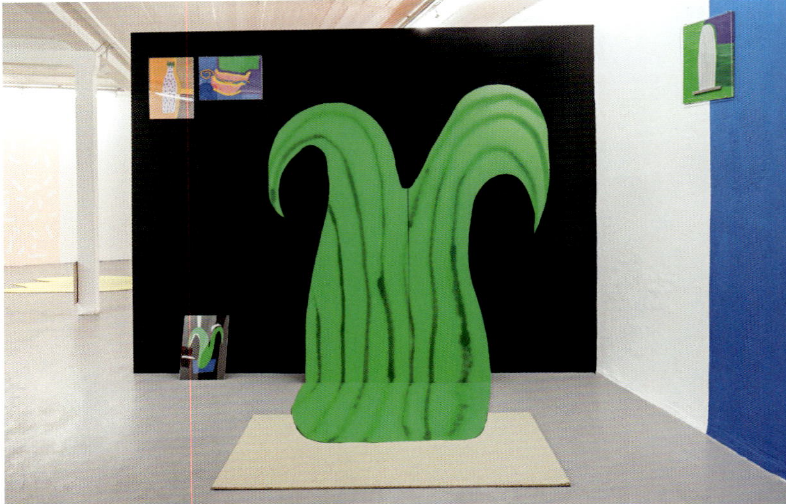
(37)

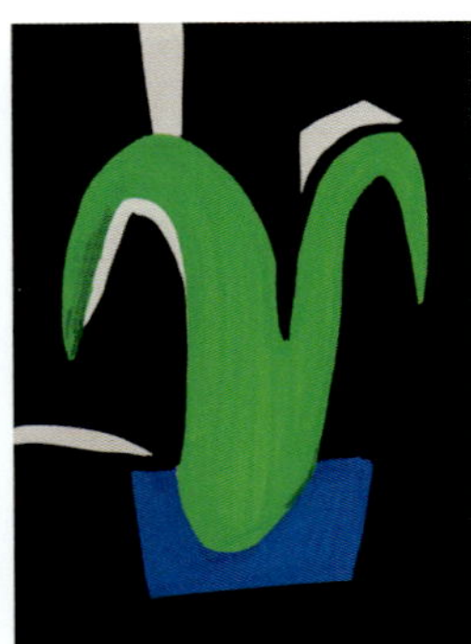
(38)

P

(35) ***January Depression 26***
2023, acrylics on cardboard with household objects, 44 × 31.7 cm

(36) ***January Depression (Remedy)***
2021, wall painting, wood, drawings, dimensions variable, Installation view Kunstverein Springhornhof

(37) ***January Depression 27***
2023, acrylics on cardboard with household objects, 44 × 31.7 cm

(38) ***January Depression (Remedy)***
2021, wall painting, wood, drawings, dimensions variable, Installation view Kunstverein Springhornhof

JANUARY DEPRESSION

P

INGREDIENTS
January Depression 50 ①
January Depression 51 ①
January Depression 52 ②
January Depression 53 ②
January Depression 54 ②
January Depression 55 ②
January Depression 56 ②
January Depression 57 ②
January Depression 58 ②
January Depression 59 ②
January Depression 60 ②
January Depression 61 ②
January Depression 62 ②
January Depression 63 ②
January Depression 64 ②
January Depression 65 ②
January Depression 66 ②
January Depression 67 ②

P

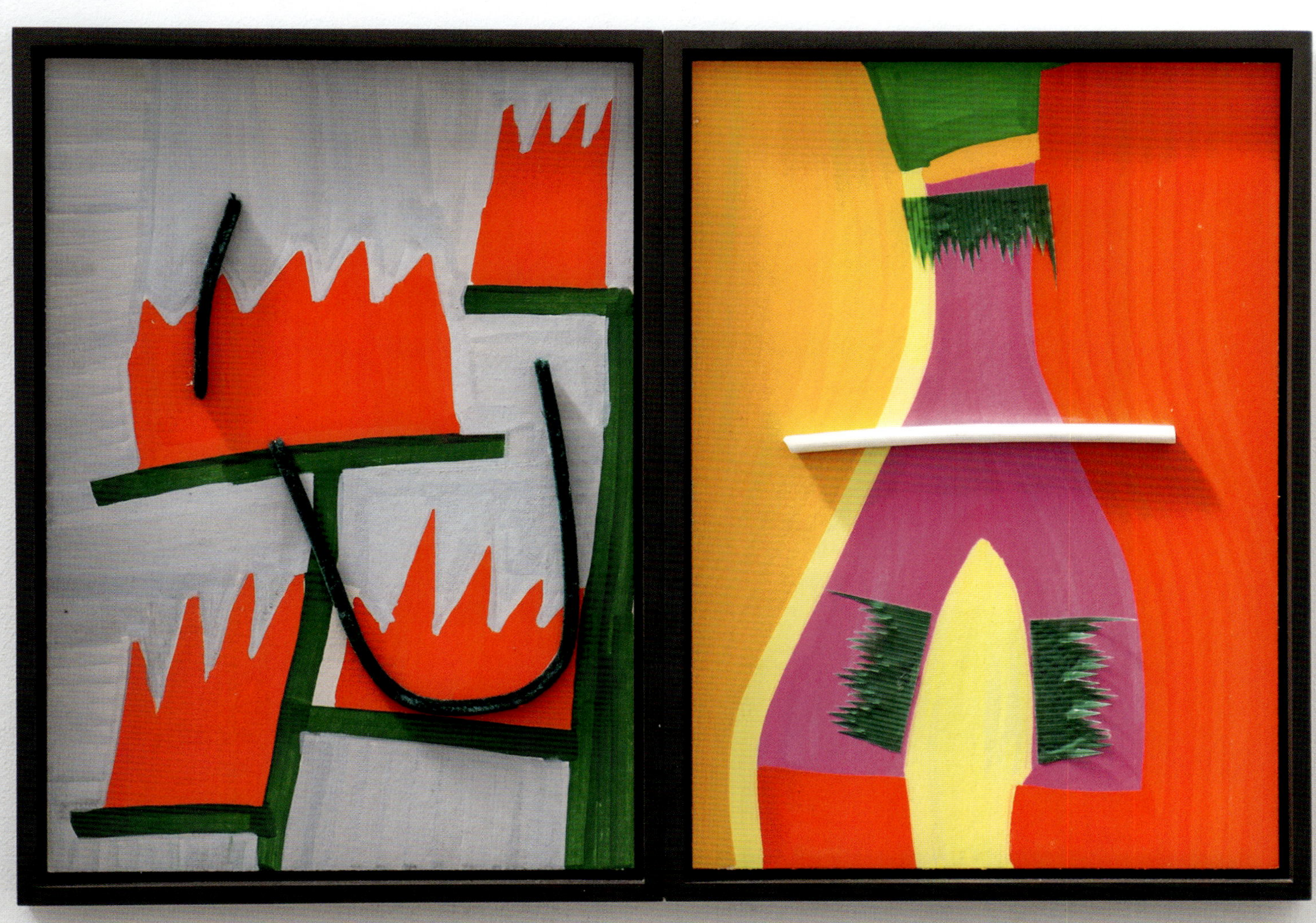

(1) ***January Depression 50 and 51***
2021, acrylics on cardboard with household objects, each 42 × 30 cm

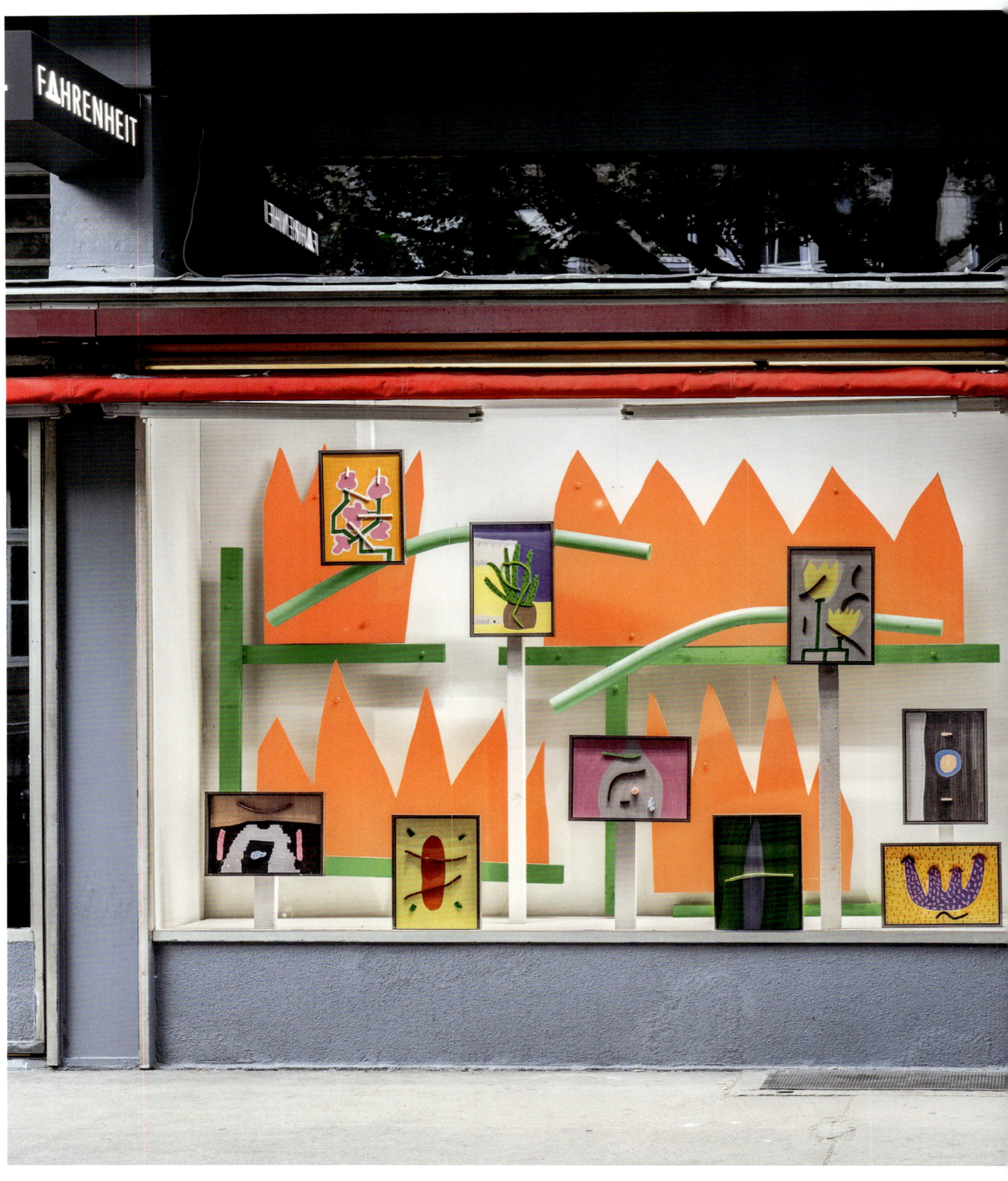

P

(2) ***January Depression***
2021, wood, varnish, pool noodles, individual pictures, dimensions of the shop window: 13.60 × 2.80 m
Installation view AKKURAT/ Fahrenheit, Berlin

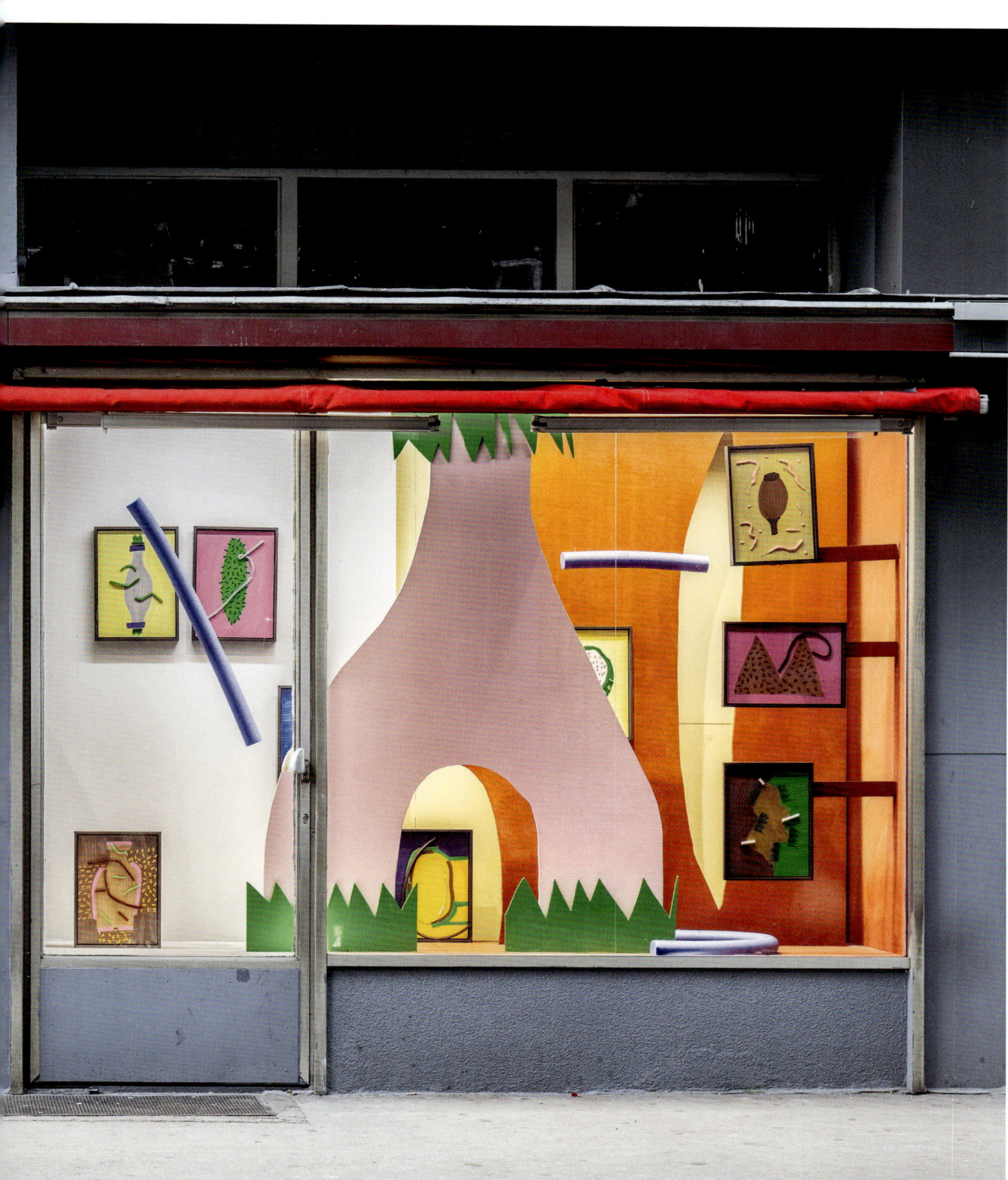

KLAPP KLAPP (JANUARY DEPRESSION II)

E

INGREDIENTS
January Depression 6 ②④
January Depression 12 ②④
January Depression 29 ②④
January Depression 20 ⑤⑦
January Depression 39 ⑤⑦
January Depression 23 ⑥⑨⑪
January Depression ⑤⑥⑨⑪
January Depression 25 ① ③
January Depression 21 ⑨
January Depression 17 ① ⑤
January Depression 35 ⑨
January Depression 2 ②④
January Depression 26 ②④
January Depression 31 ⑨
January Depression 36 ②④

E

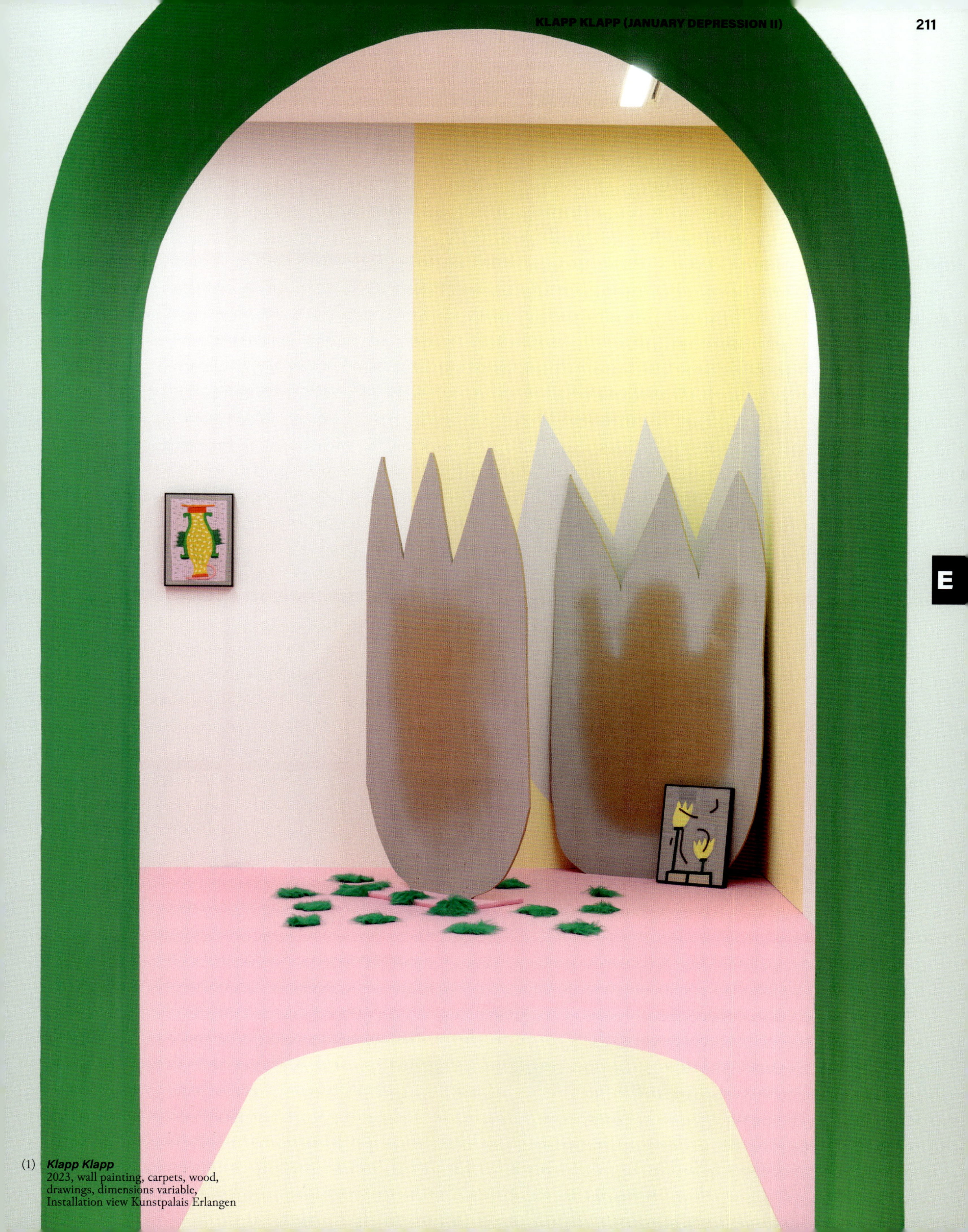

E

(1) ***Klapp Klapp***
2023, wall painting, carpets, wood, drawings, dimensions variable, Installation view Kunstpalais Erlangen

E

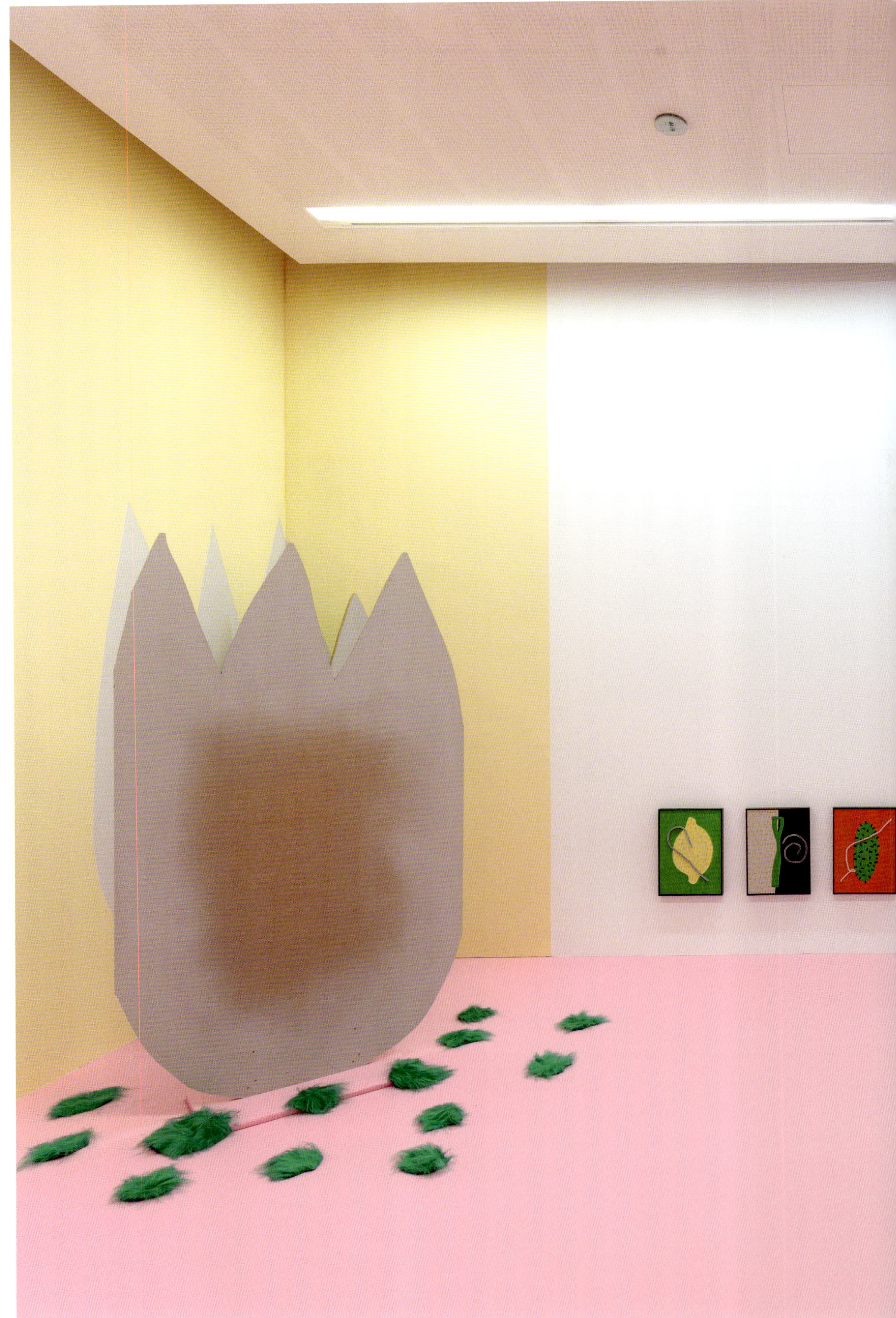

(2) ***Klapp Klapp***
2023, wall painting, carpets, wood, drawings, dimensions variable, Installation view Kunstpalais Erlangen

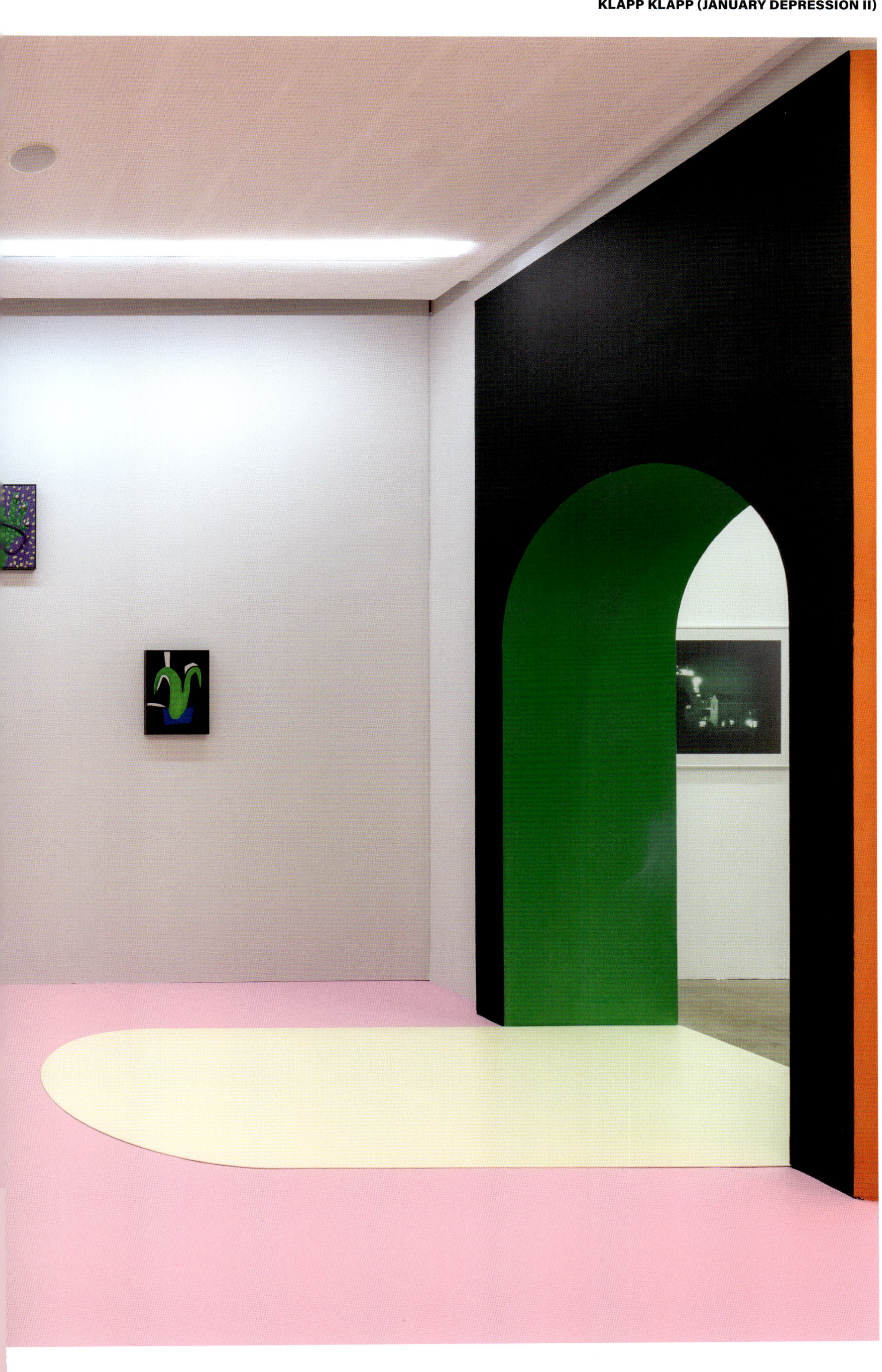

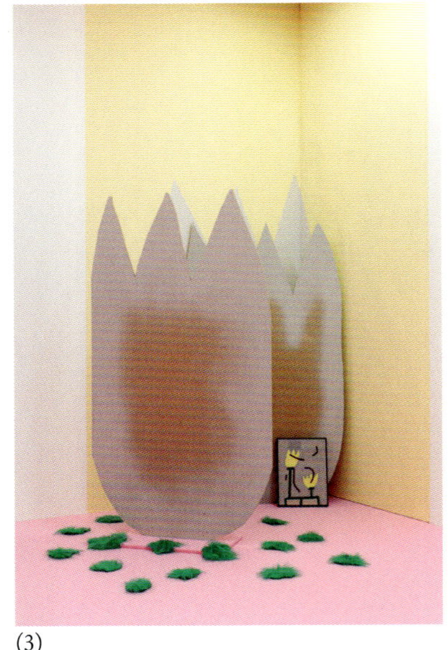

(3)

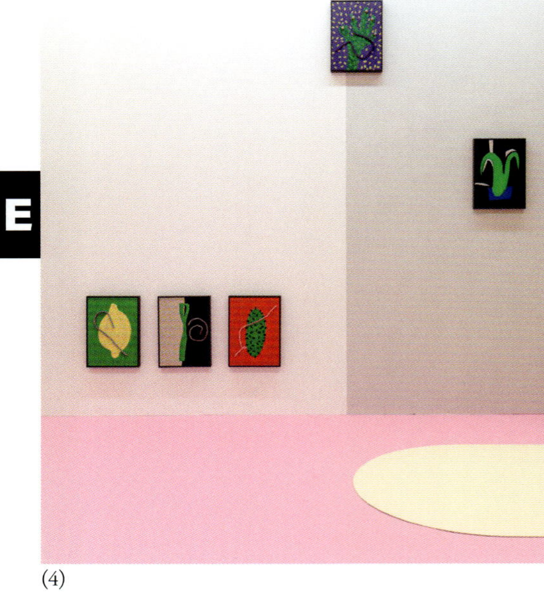

(4)

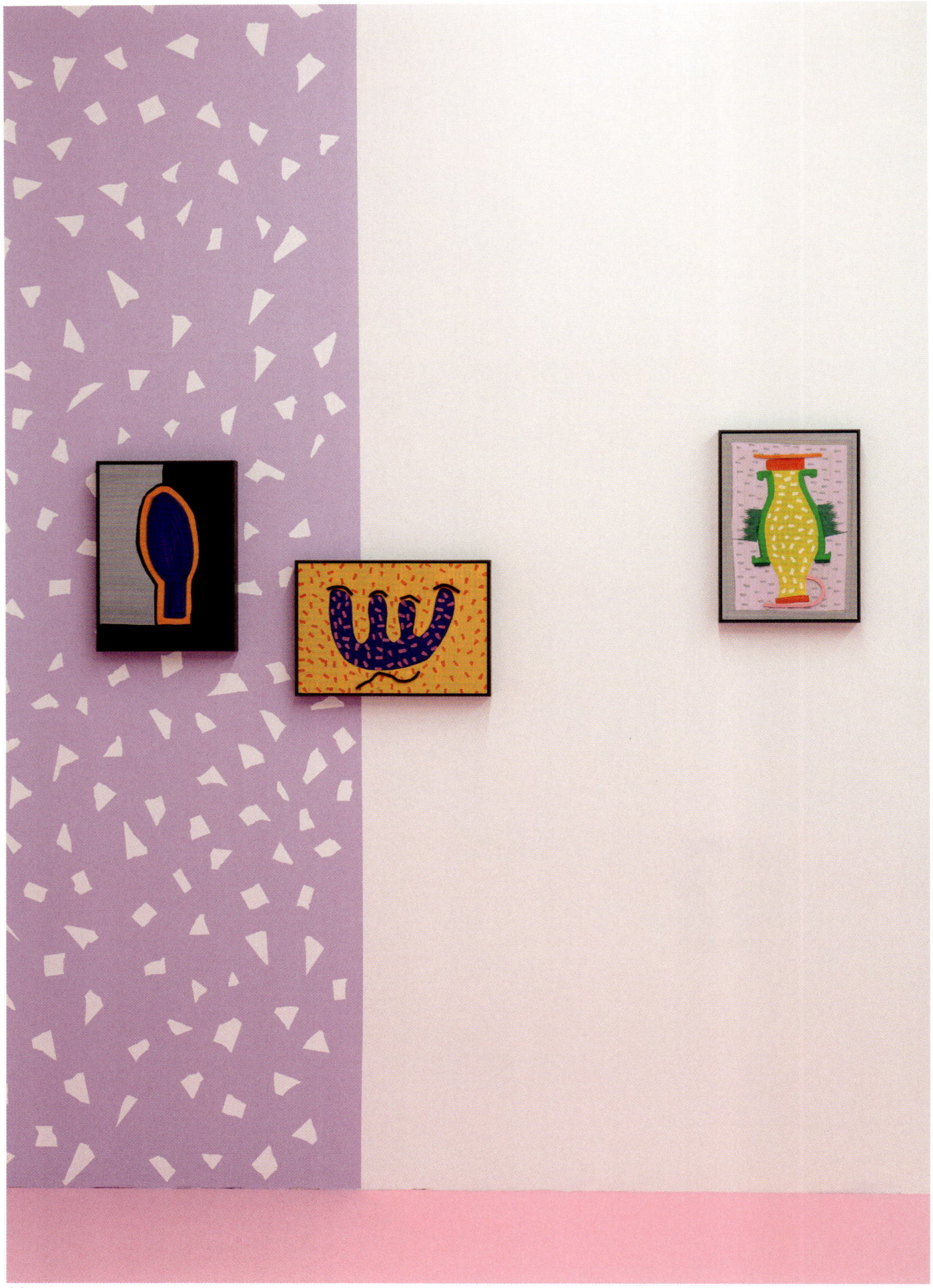

(5)

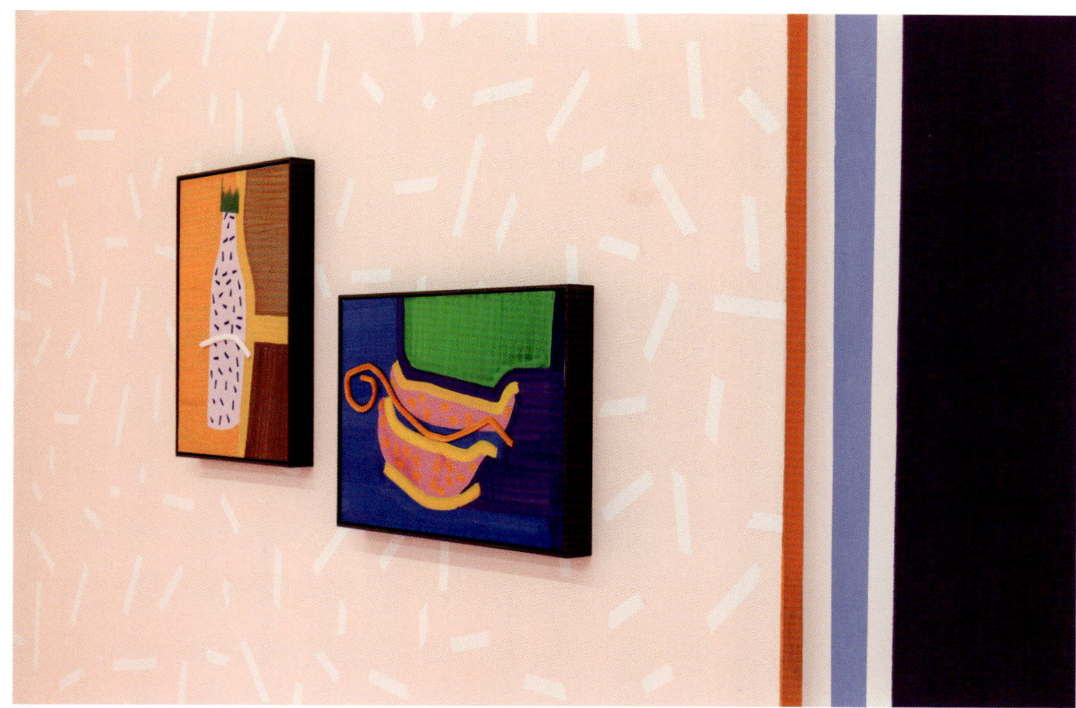
(6)

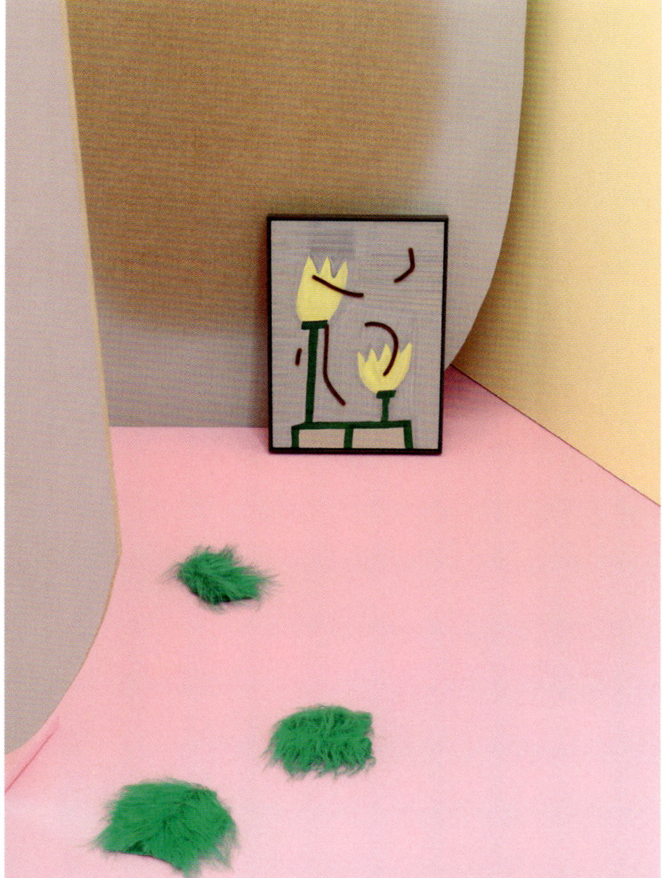
(8)

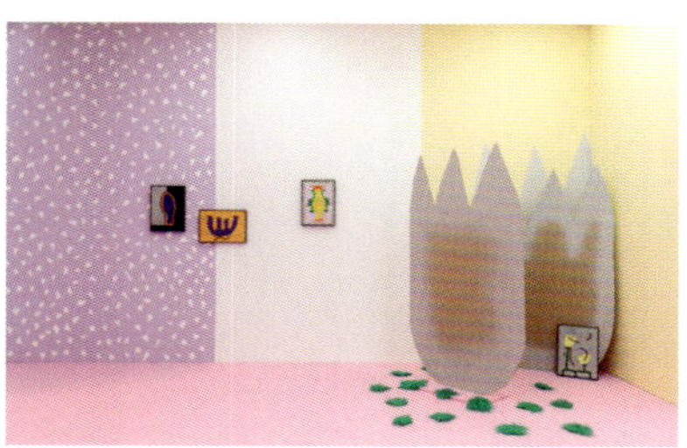
(7)

E

(3)
(4)
(5)
(6)
(7)
(8) ***Klapp Klapp***
2023, wall painting, carpets, wood, drawings, dimensions variable, Installation view Kunstpalais Erlangen

E

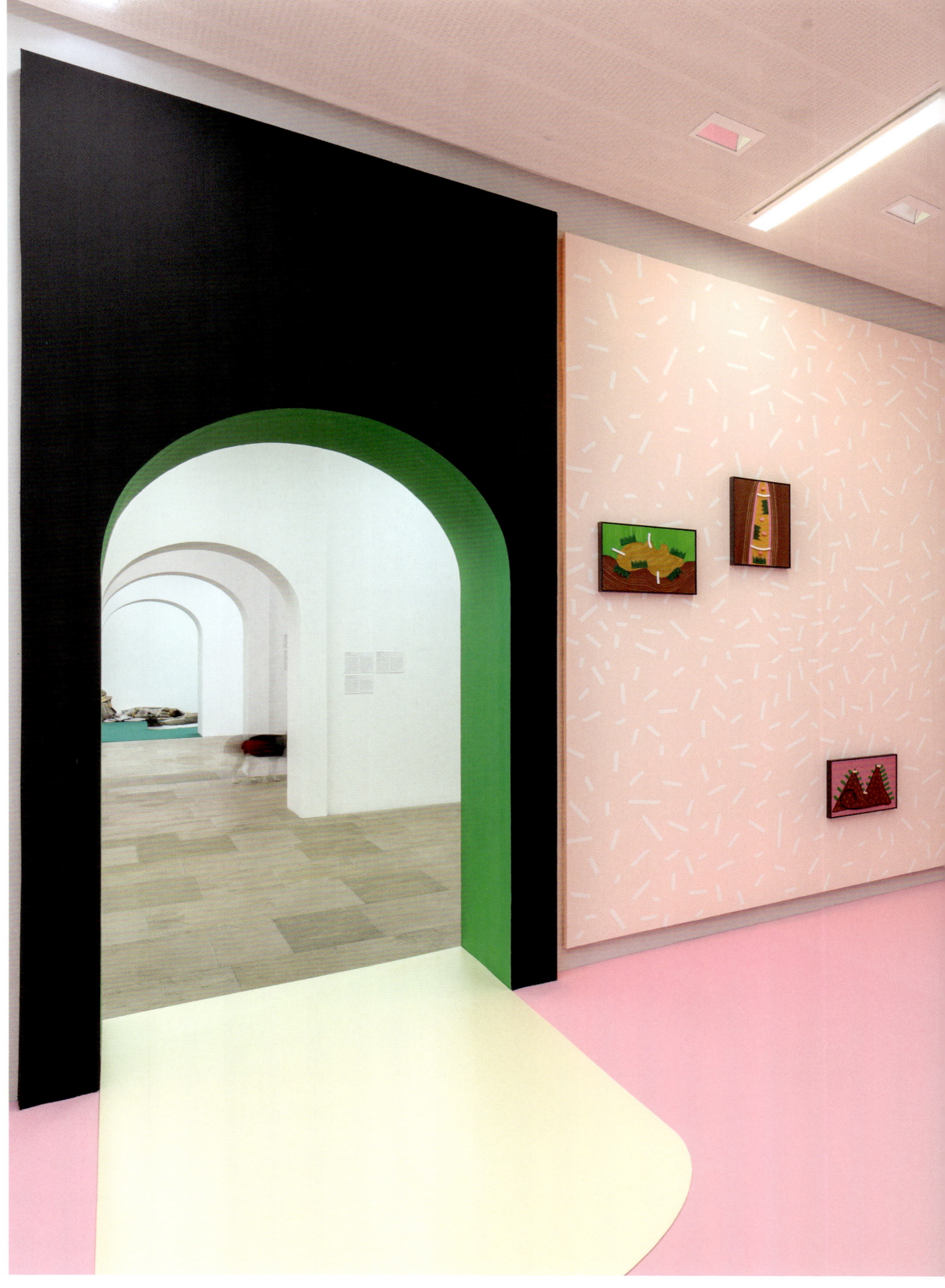

(9) ***Klapp Klapp***
2023, wall painting,
carpets, wood,
drawings,
dimensions variable,
Installation view
Kunstpalais Erlangen

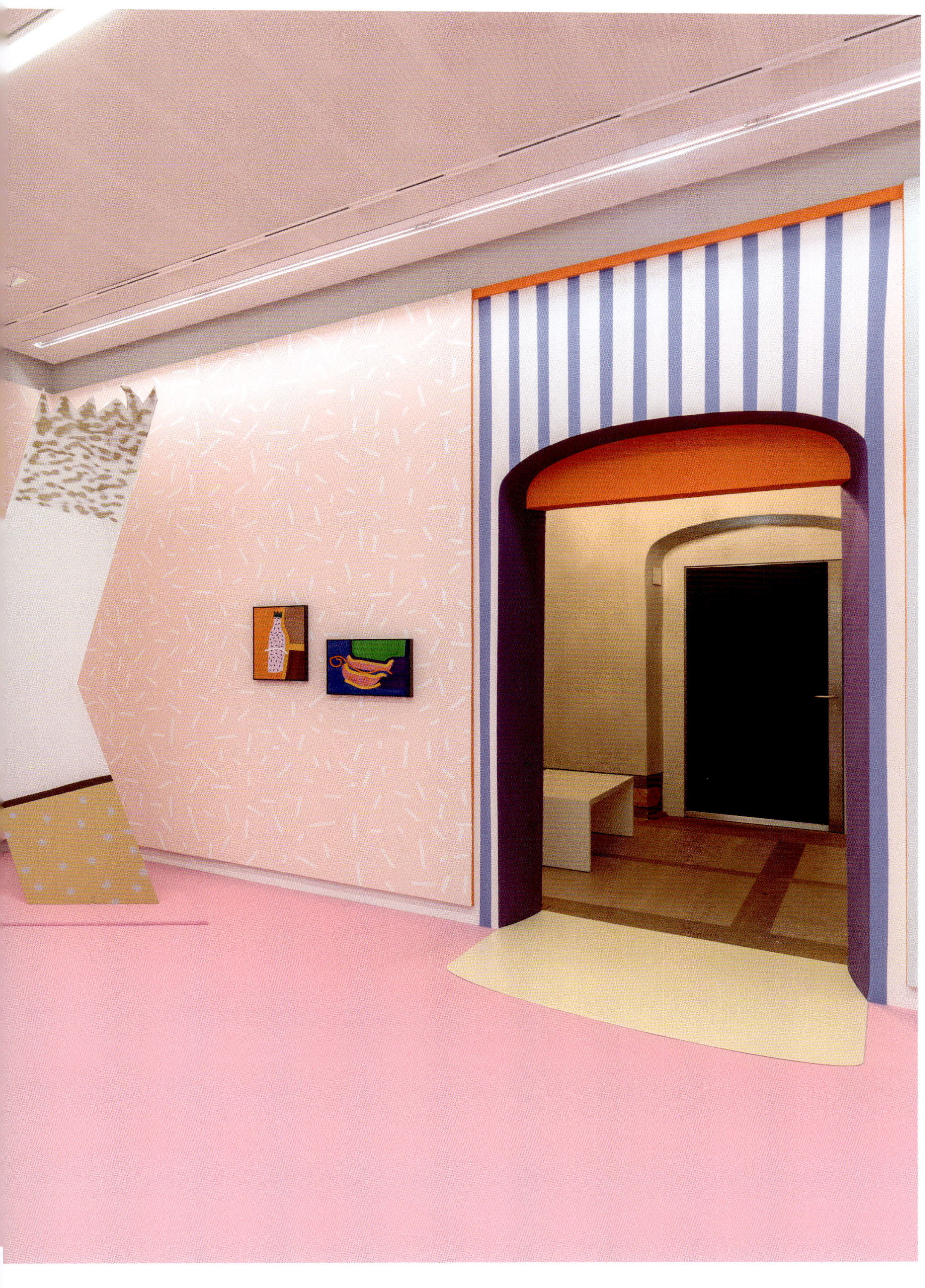

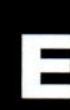

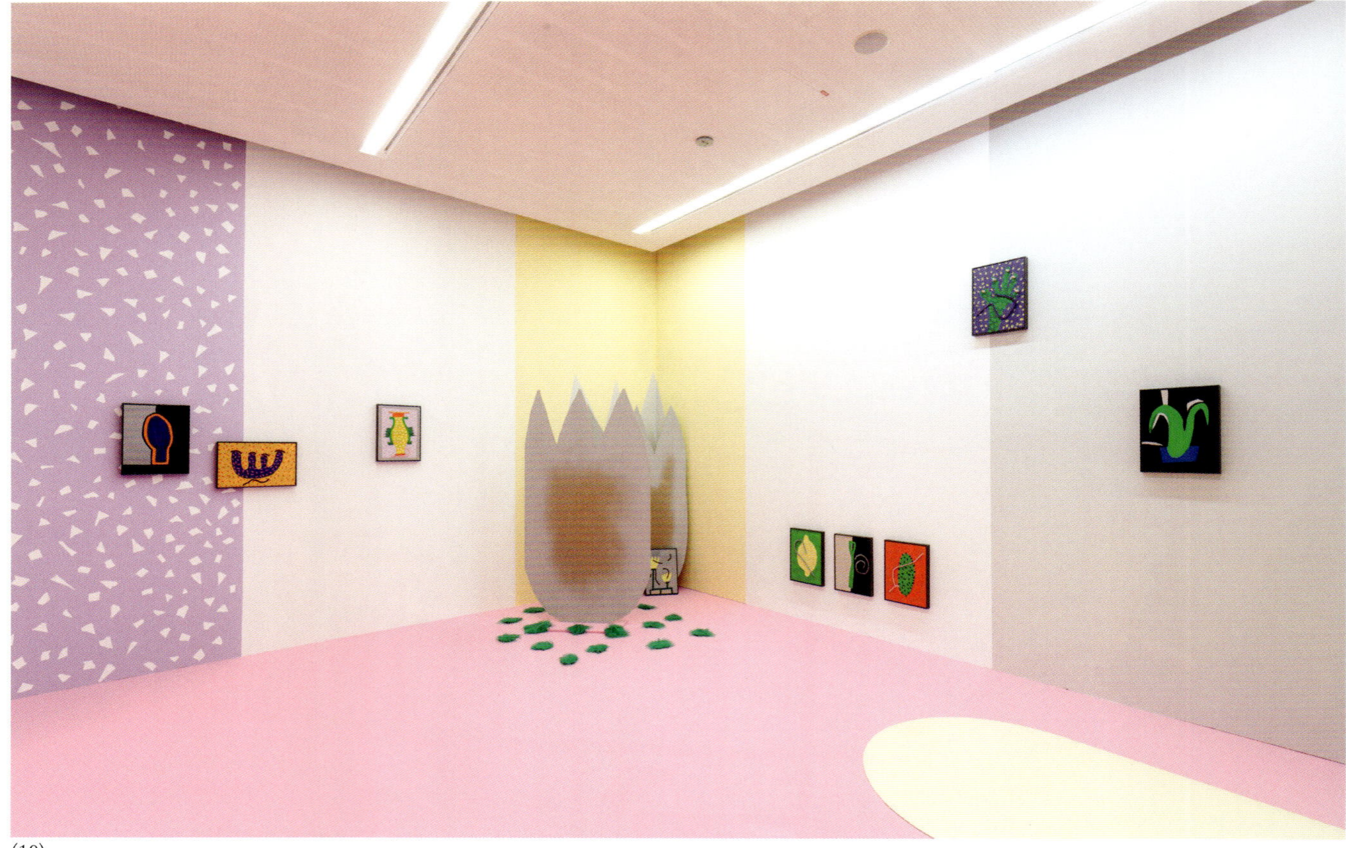

(10)

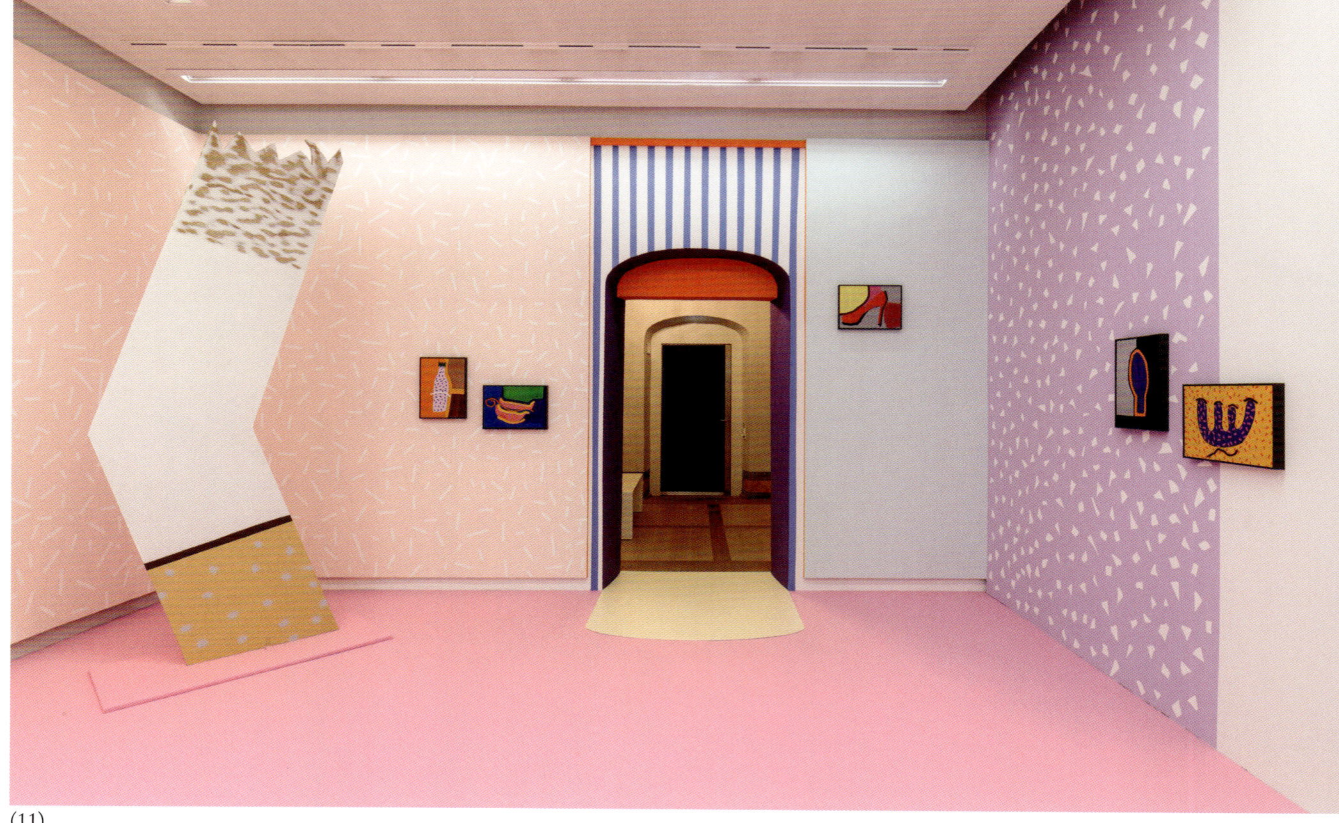

(11)

(10)
(11) ***Klapp Klapp***
2023, wall painting, carpets, wood, drawings, dimensions variable, Installation view Kunstpalais Erlangen

SCHNUCKEN-TEMPEL

INGREDIENTS
Schnuckenkapitelle ①②
Pergamonfries Schnucken
Version ①②③④

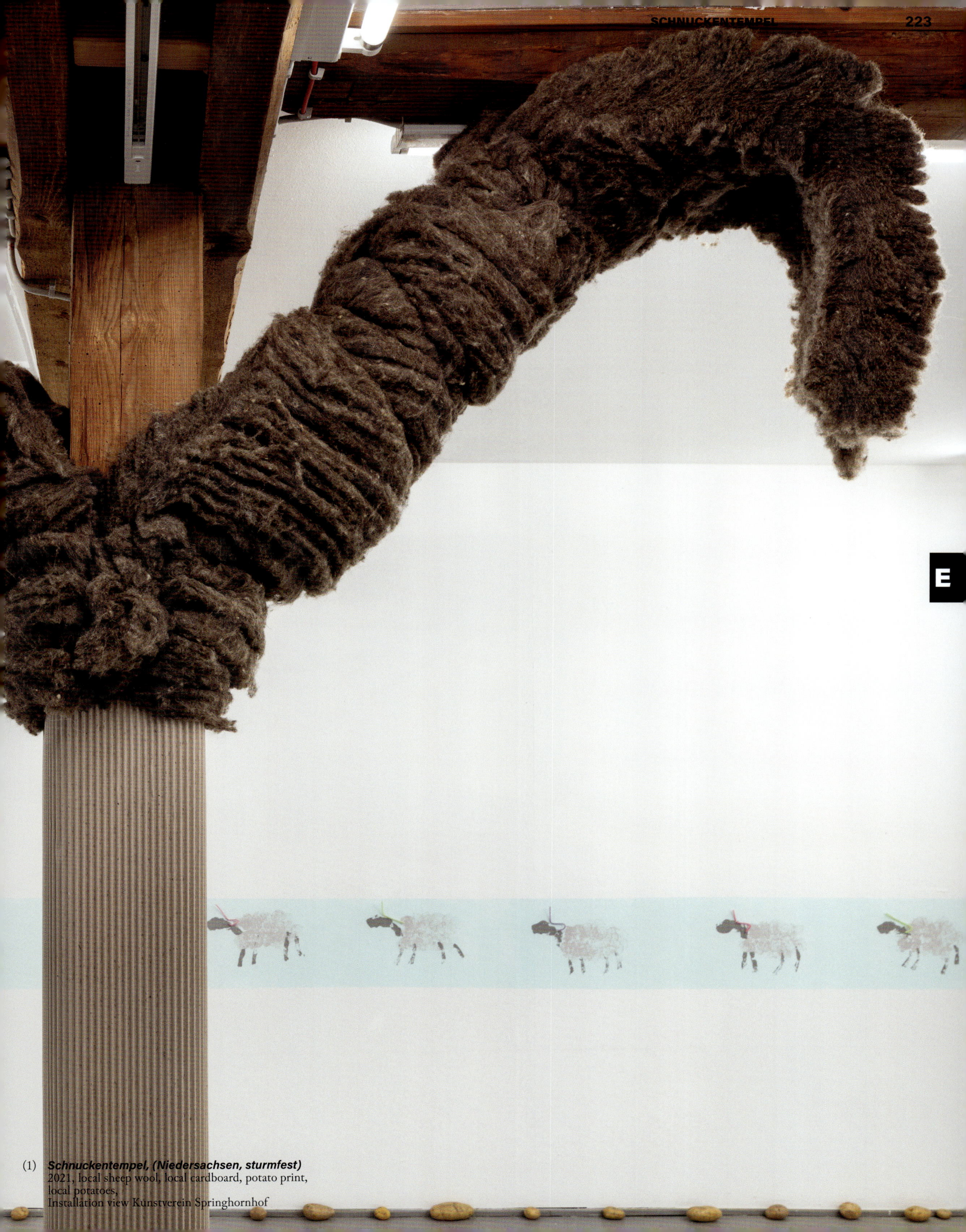

E

(1) ***Schnuckentempel, (Niedersachsen, sturmfest)***
2021, local sheep wool, local cardboard, potato print, local potatoes,
Installation view Kunstverein Springhornhof

E

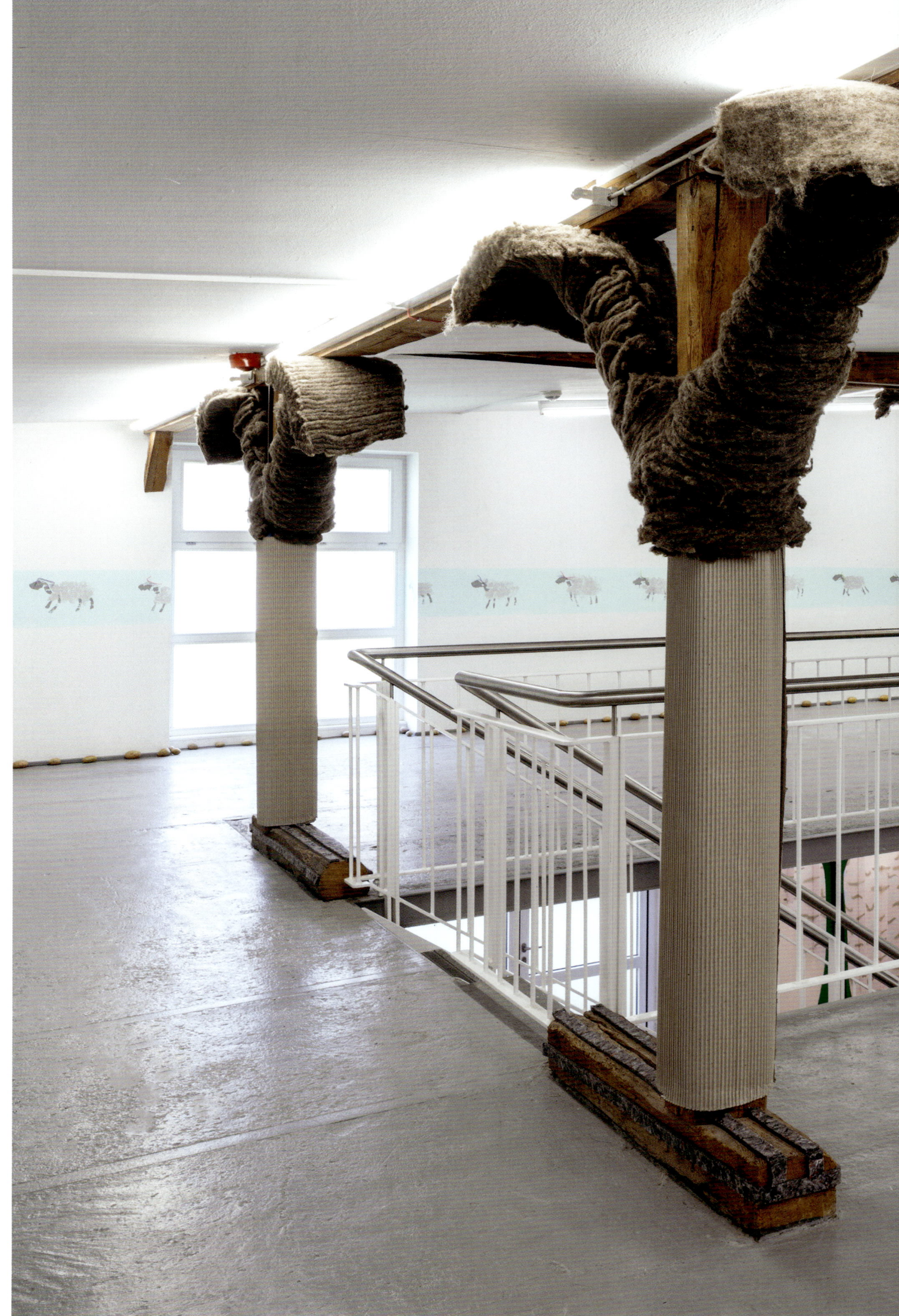

(2) ***Schnuckentempel, (Niedersachsen, sturmfest)***
2021, local sheep wool, local cardboard, potato print, local potatoes, Installation view Kunstverein Springhornhof

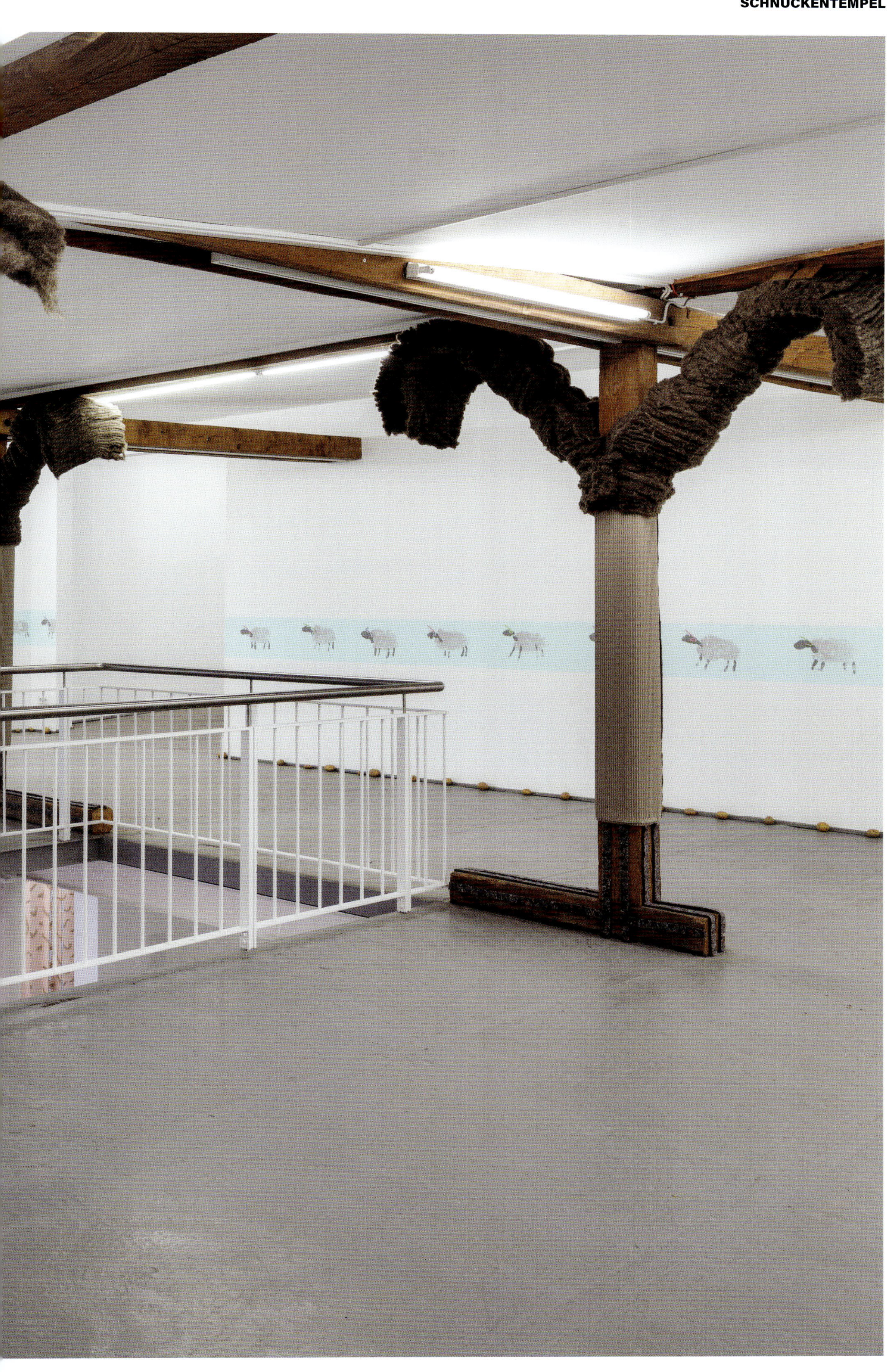

E

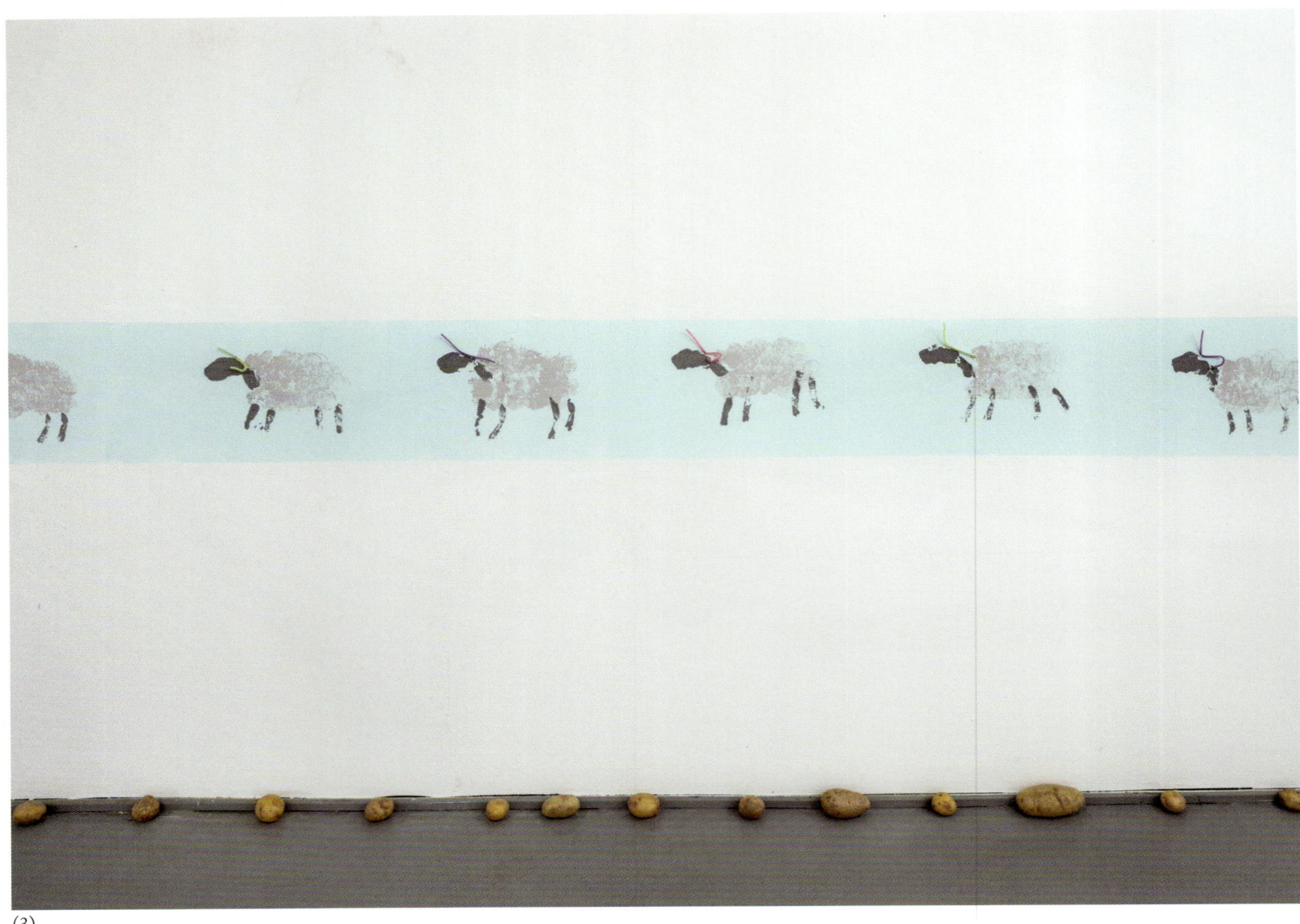

(3)

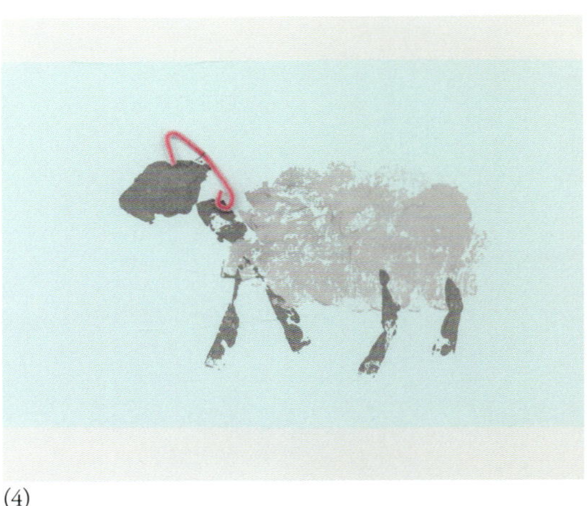

(4)

(3) ***Schnuckentempel, (Niedersachsen, sturmfest)*** 2021, local sheep wool, local cardboard, potato print, local potatoes, Installation view Kunstverein Springhornhof

(4) ***Schnuckentempel, (Niedersachsen, sturmfest)*** (detail) 2021, potato print

ANTIKEN-SAMMLUNG

INGREDIENTS
Vessel I ③
Vessel II ③
Vessel III ③
Vessel ④
Bottle ⑤
Bottle II ⑤
Tiger Vessels ⑥
Vessel IV ⑤
Untitled ①
Untitled ②
Tennisschläger ②
Shapenet ②
Kunstraub ②
Untitled ②

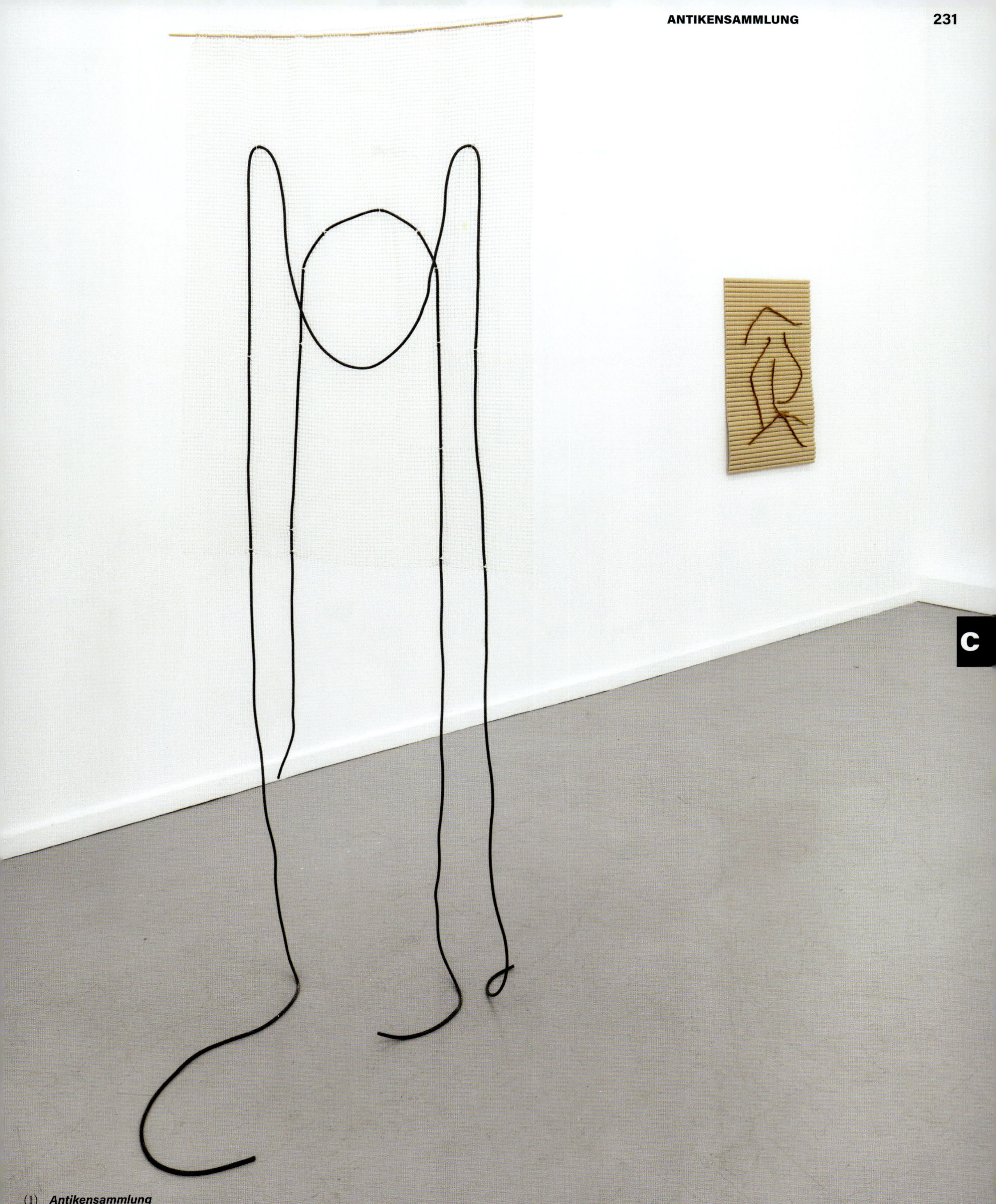

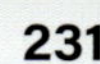

C

(1) ***Antikensammlung***
2021, (left) ***Shapenet***, 2021, rope and net, 45 × 190 cm,
(right) ***Untitled***, 2021, pipe cleanser and plastic, 60 × 90 cm,
Installation view Kunstverein Springhornhof

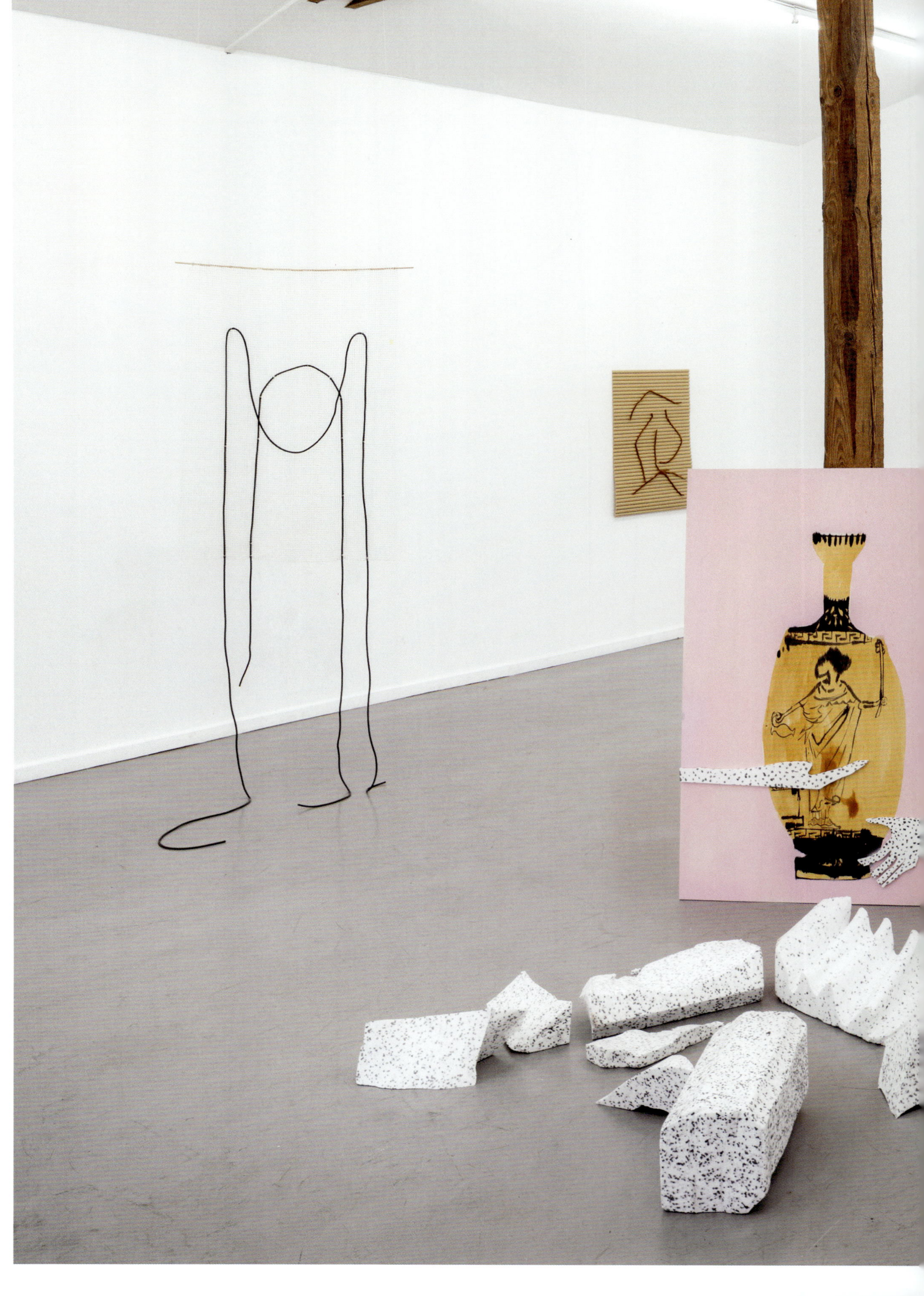

C

(2) ***Antikensammlung***
2021, various works, dimensions variable, object in the middle:
Kunstraub
2021, wood stain and Styrofoam on wood, 100 × 140 cm, Installation view Kunstverein Springhornhof

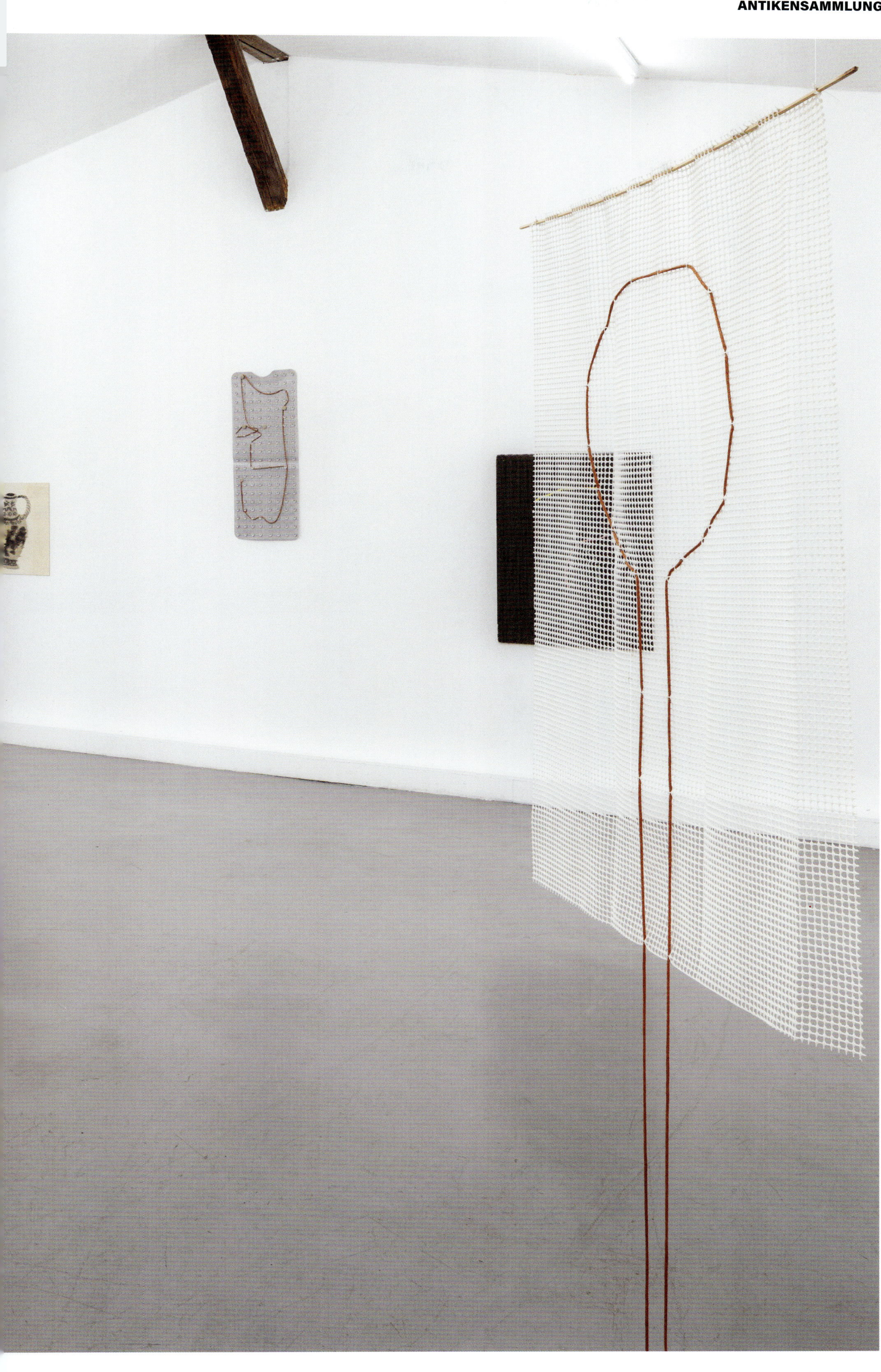

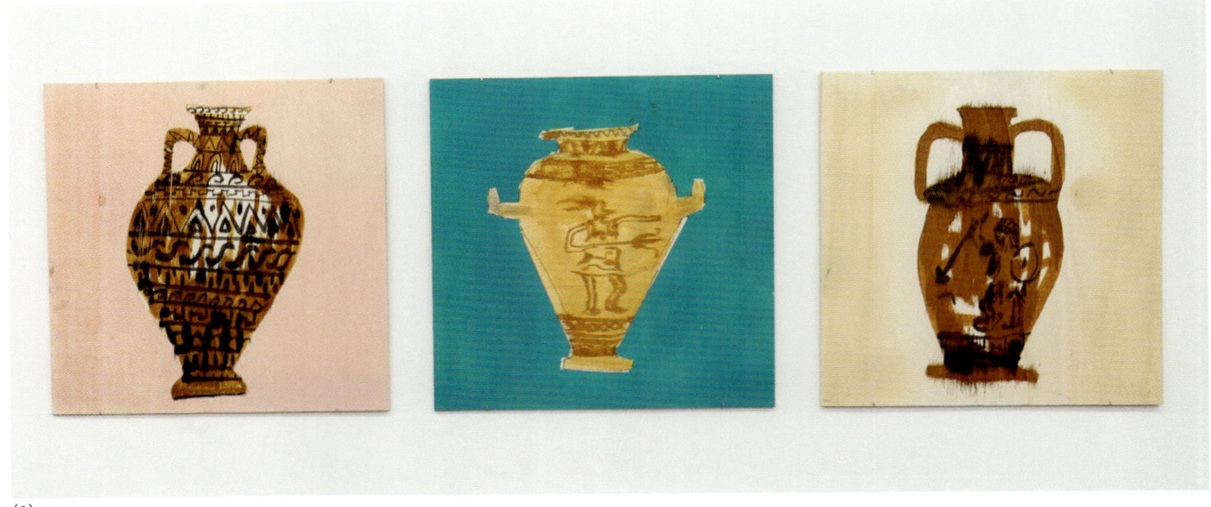

(3)

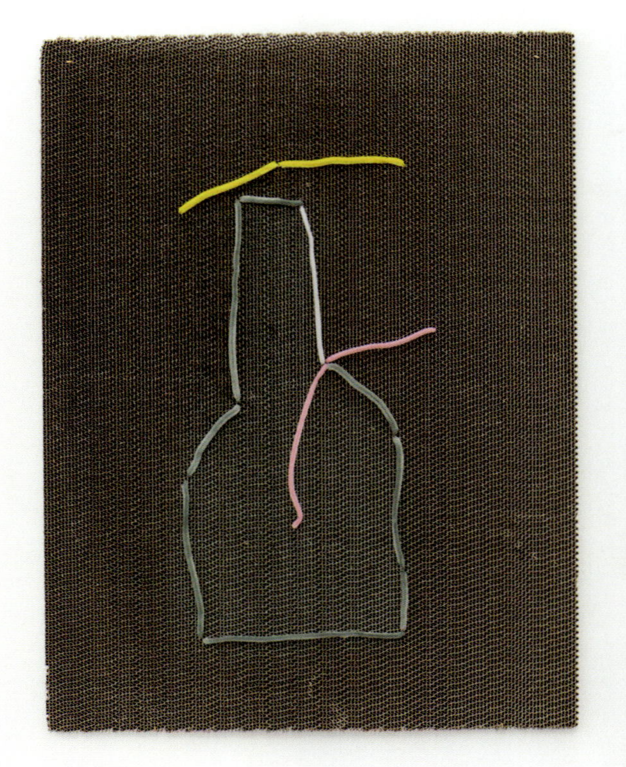

(4)

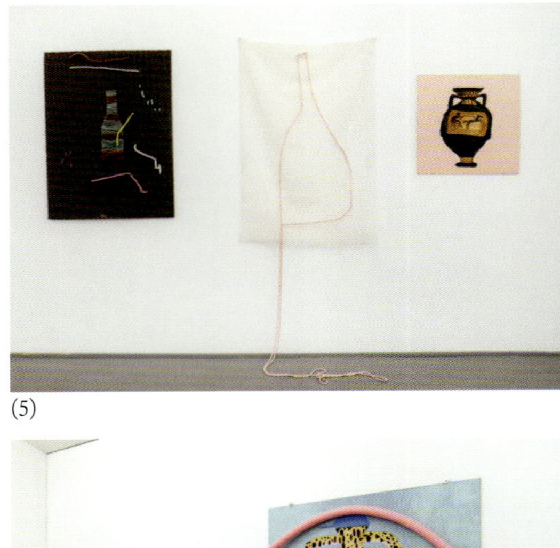

(5)

(6)

(3) ***Vessel I-III***
2021, wood stain and acrylics on wood, each 60 × 60 cm

(4) ***Vessel***
2021, pipe cleaners and laquer on cardboard, 70 × 50 cm

(5) (left to right) **Bottle**
2021, pipe cleaners on cardboard, 70 × 50 cm,
Bottle II
2021, 80 × 60 cm, mesh and yarn
Vessel IV
wood stain and acrylics on wood, 60 × 60 cm

(6) **Tiger Vessels**
wood stain and acrylics on wood with pool noodles, 140 × 140 cm

DIE BRÜSTE DES TIRESIAS NACH APOLLINAIRE

C

INGREDIENTS
Hände ①
SZENE VII:
Bin ein herrlicher Frau-Herr/Meine Frau ist eine dämliche Mann-Dame ③
SZENE VII:
Bau dir eine neue Brust/Dazu hab ich keine Lust ④
SZENE VI:
Ihr habt's geschafft/Ihr habt's vollbracht/40.500 Kinder an einem Tag ⑤
Ich lasse dich gehen ⑥
SZENE IX:
Nicht nur mein Bart wächst famos/Auch mein Schnauz wird groß ⑦
SZENE VIII:
Da die Frau nicht kann/Muss der Mann nun ran ⑧
SZENE I:
Blaues Gesicht ⑨
SZENE VIII:
Bin ich einmal hübsch und fein/Fallen die Mädchen auf mich rein ⑩
Szene VIII:
Bin ich einmal hübsch und fein/Fallen die Mädchen auf mich rein ⑫
SZENE IX:
Ja kommt nur abends, um zu sehen/Wie ganz ohne Frauen Kinder entstehen ⑭

EN Some of the literally multi-layered images in Verena Issel's work *The Breasts of Tiresias* (2021) are illustrations of scenes from the surrealist drama of the same name by Guillaume Apollinaire (orig. title: *Les Mamelles de Tirésias*), published in 1917. Inspired by the Greek myth of the blind soothsayer Tiresias, who spends seven years of his existence as a woman after divine transformation, the absurd drama tells the story of a couple who swap gender roles so that she can become a general while he counteracts the problems of demographic change by bearing children (over 40,000 in a single day). In its time, it represented a deeply offensive debate on prevailing images of femininity and masculinity. Apollinaire's play not only served as the libretto for an opera by the openly homosexual composer Francis Poulenc, which was highly provocative in the outgoing nationalist-influenced Vichy regime in 1944, but also as Verena Issel's point of departure for a challenging look at contemporary norms and stigmas. The partly amorphous visual formal language expresses—in a contemporary as well as humorous way—the dynamics and ambiguity that already characterised gender and the body beyond social stereotypes in ancient myths.

☐ ***Silvan Wilms, exhibition text for Kunsthalle Nürnberg***

DE Die im wahrsten Sinne des Wortes mehrschichtigen Bilder in Verena Issels Werk *Die Brüste des Tiresias* sind zum Teil Szenenillustrationen des gleichnamigen surrealistischen Dramas von Guillaume Apollinaire (orig. Titel: *Les Mamelles de Tirésias*), veröffentlicht im Jahre 1917. Inspiriert durch den griechischen Mythos um den blinden Wahrsager Tiresias, der durch göttliche Verwandlung sieben Jahre seines Daseins als Frau verbringt, erzählt das absurde Drama die Geschichte eines Paares, welches seine Geschlechterrollen tauscht, sodass sie zum General wird, er hingegen den Problemen des demografischen Wandels entgegenwirkt, indem er Kinder gebärt (über 40.500 an einem einzigen Tag). Zu ihrer Zeit eine zutiefst anstößige Auseinandersetzung mit vorherrschenden Stereotypen von Weiblichkeit und Männlichkeit, diente Apollinaires Stück nicht nur als Libretto für eine unverhohlen homosexuelle Komposition von Francis Poulenc, die 1944 im ausgehenden nationalistisch geprägten Vichy-Regime für Provokation sorgte, sondern auch als Anknüpfungspunkt Issels, ihrerseits heutige Normative und Stigmata herauszufordern. Die teils amorphe Formsprache bringt die Dynamik und Ambiguität, die Geschlecht und Körper jenseits gesellschaftlicher Stereotypen bereits in antiken Mythen auszeichnete, zeitgenössisch und auf humoristische Weise zum Ausdruck.

☐ ***Silvan Wilms, Ausstellungstext für die Kunsthalle Nürnberg***

C

C

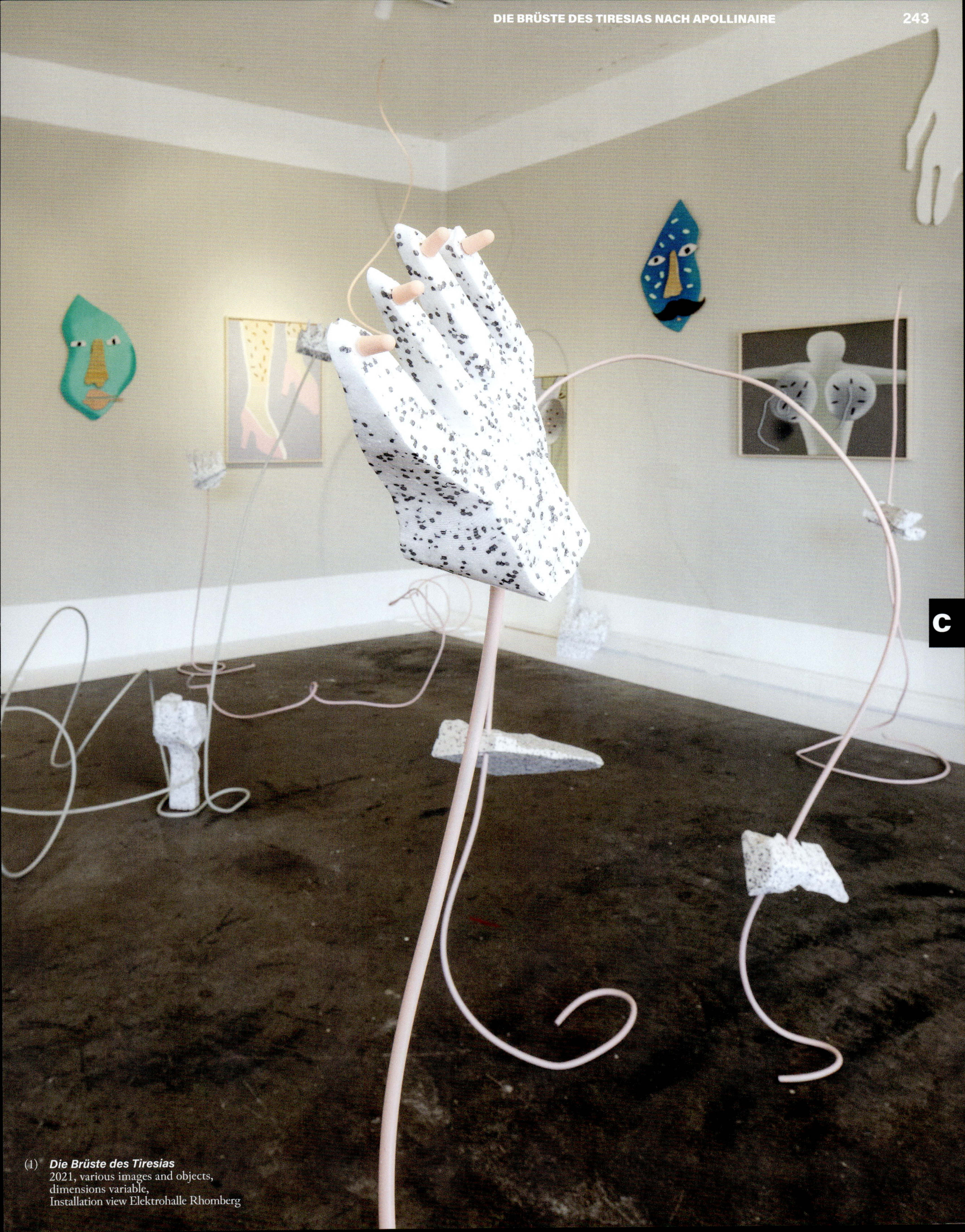

C

(1) ***Die Brüste des Tiresias***
2021, various images and objects,
dimensions variable,
Installation view Elektrohalle Rhomberg

C

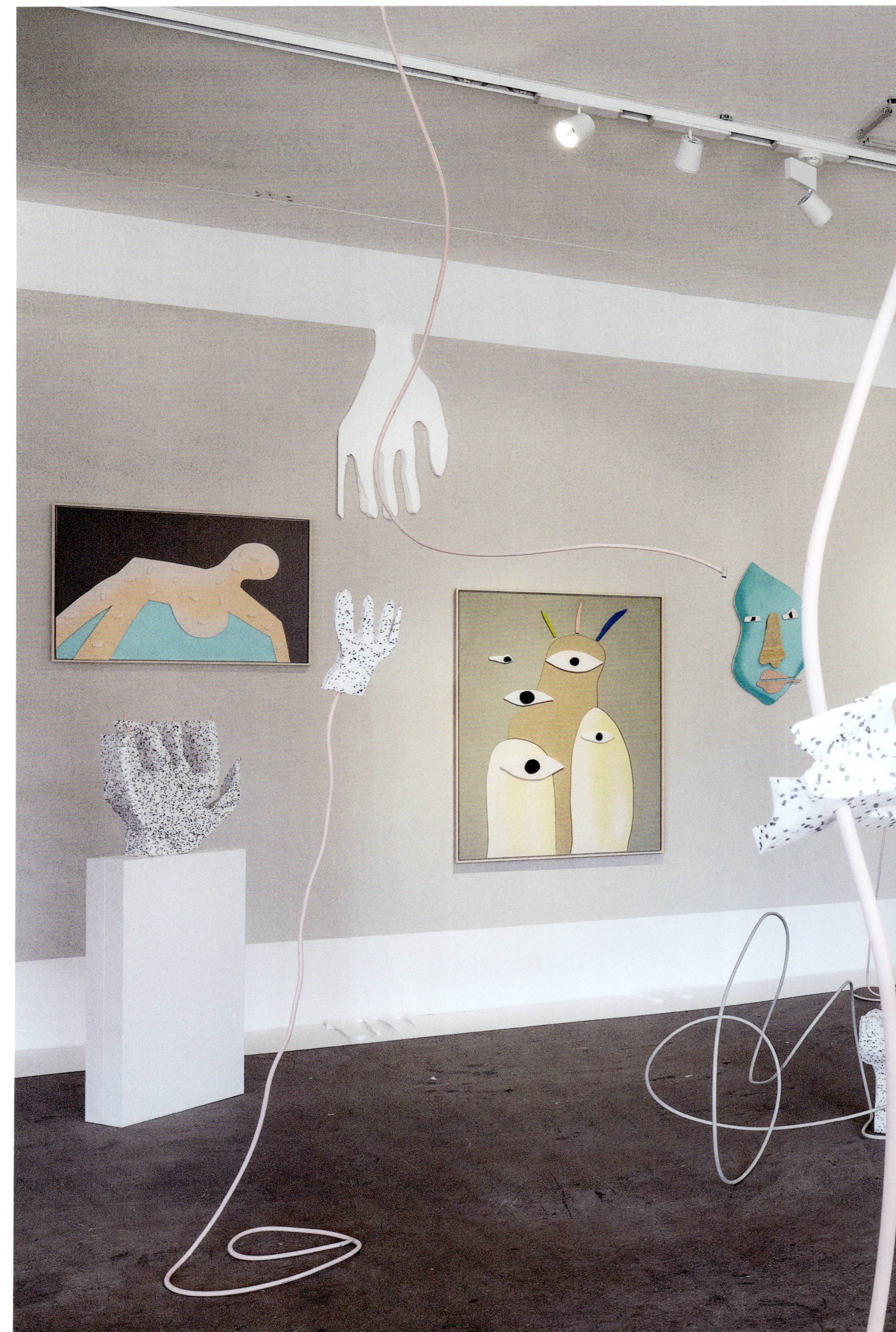

(2) ***Die Brüste des Tiresias***
2021, various images and objects, dimensions variable, Installation view Elektrohalle Rhomberg

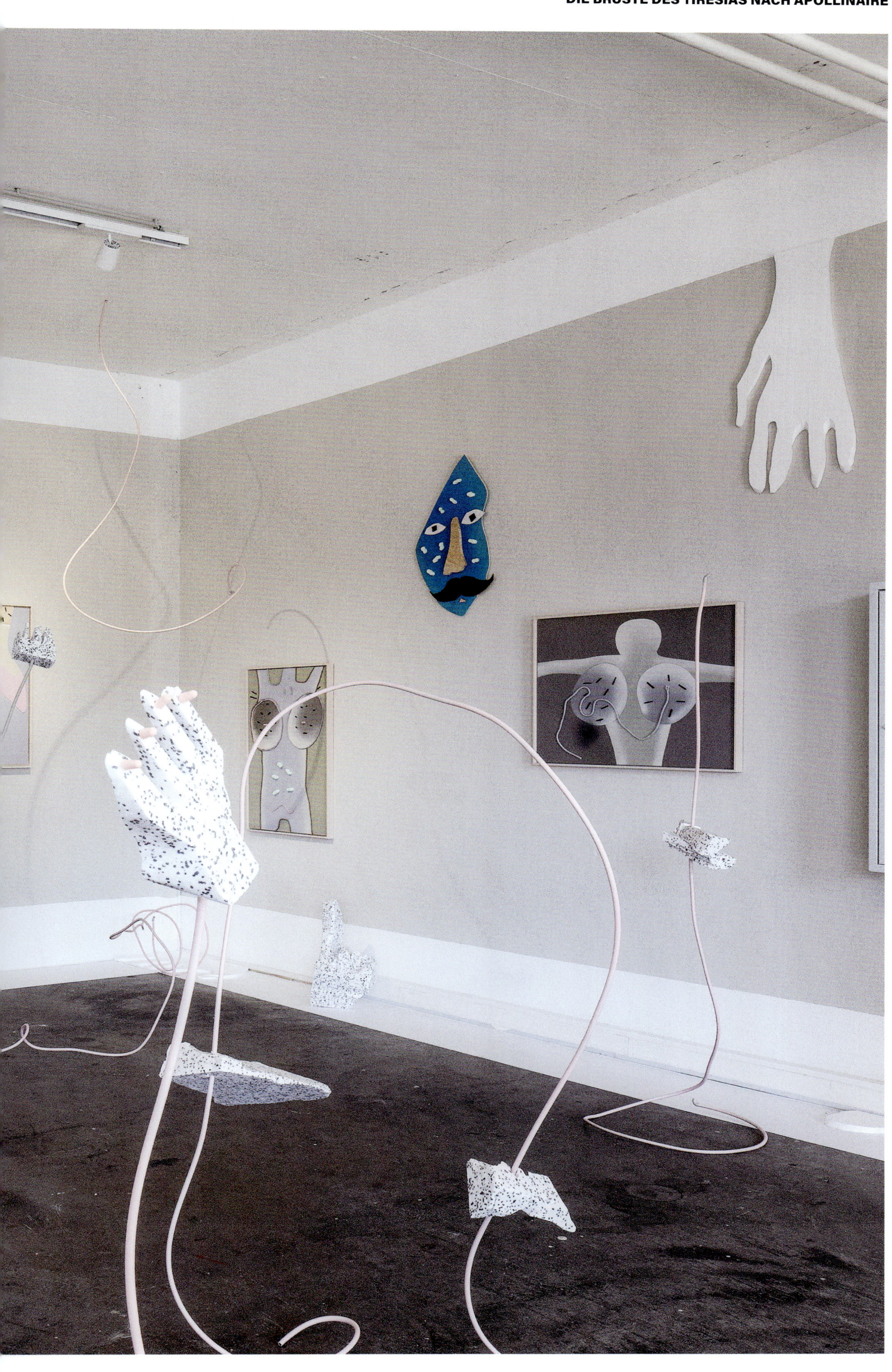

C

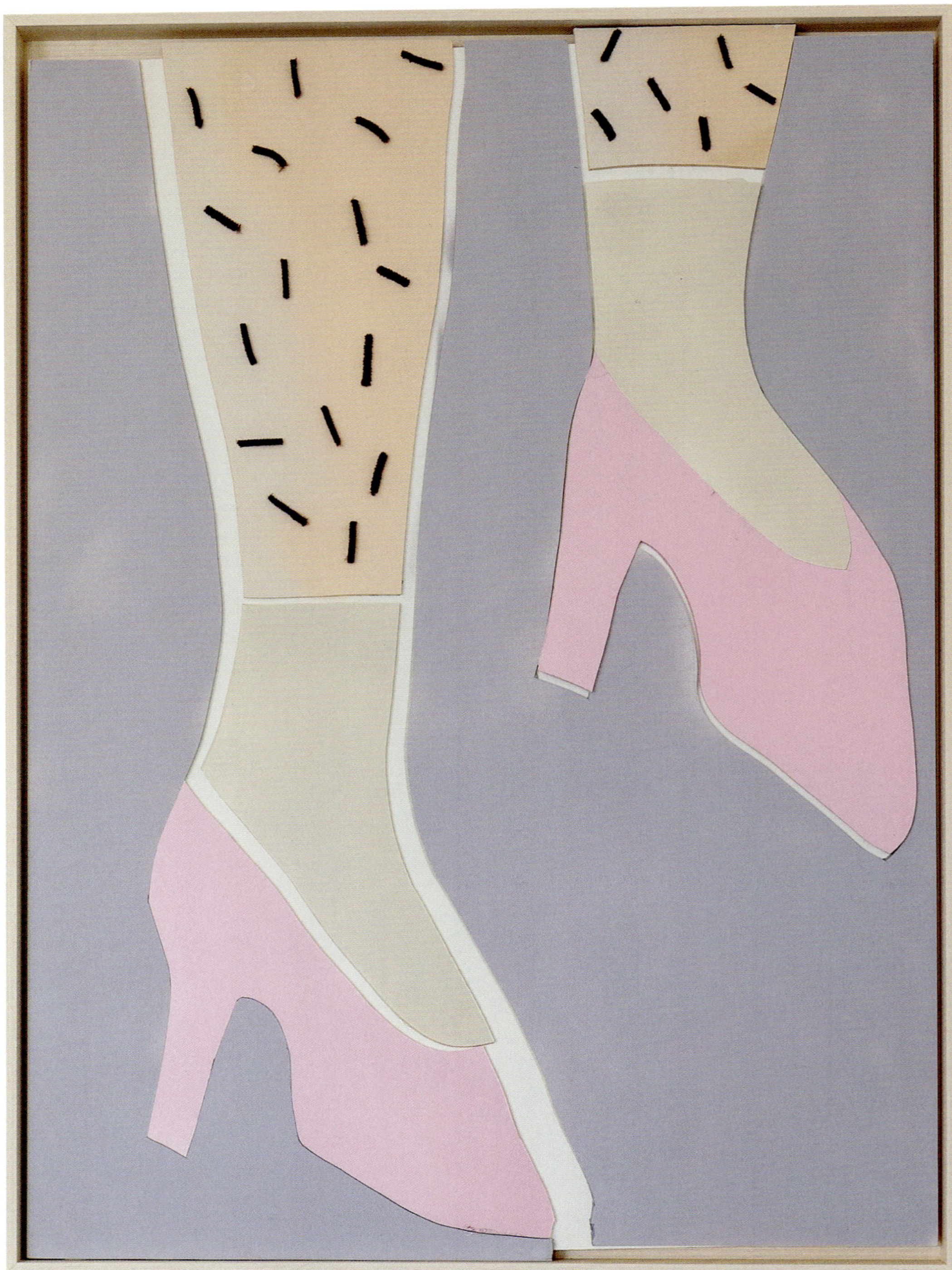

(3)

C

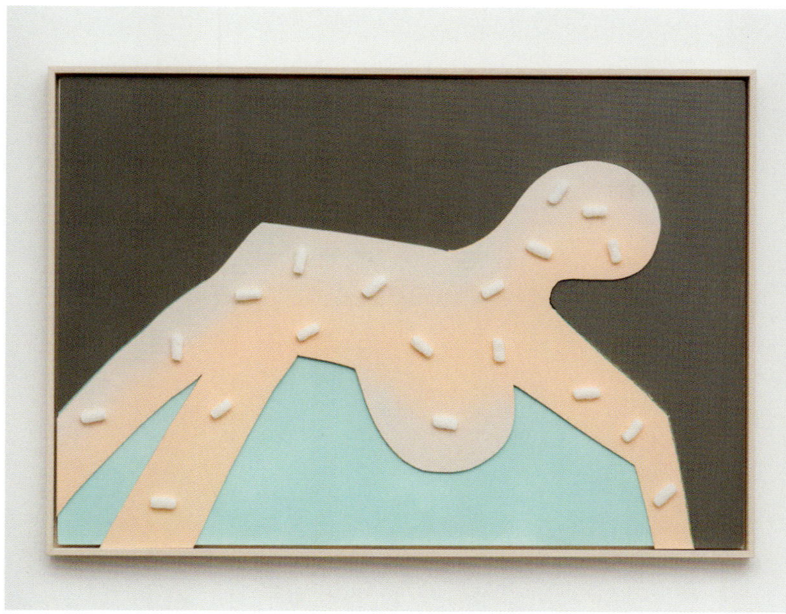
(4)

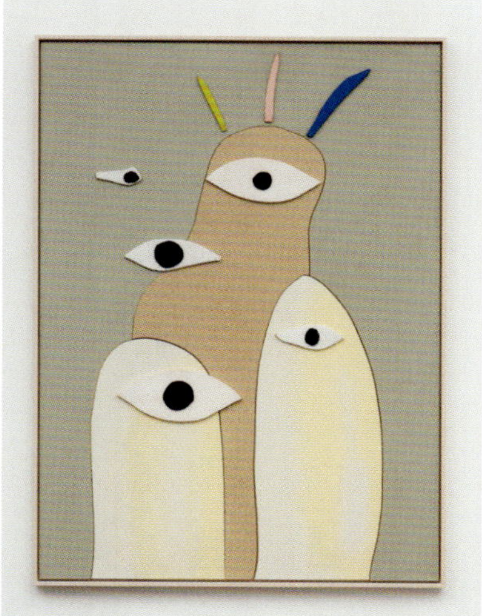
(5)

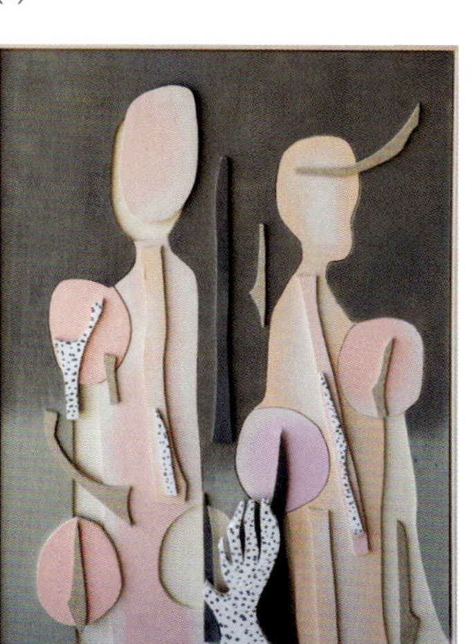
(6)

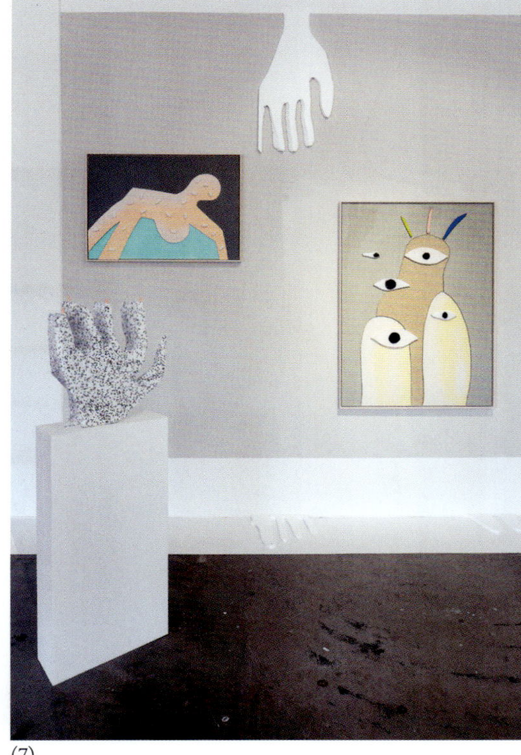
(7)

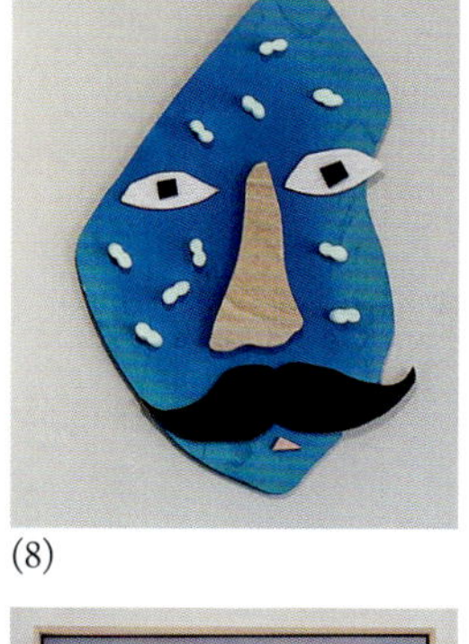
(8)

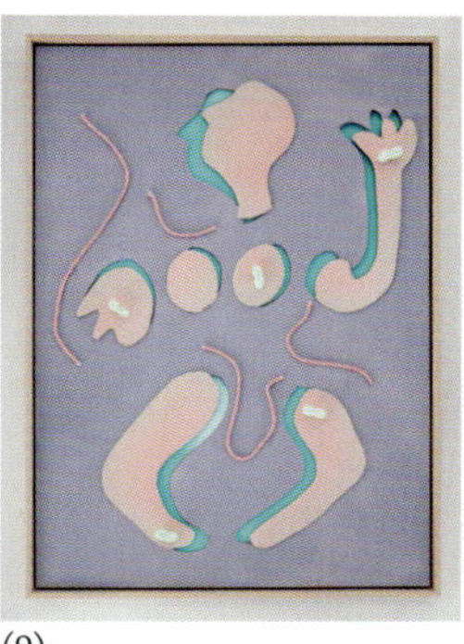
(9)

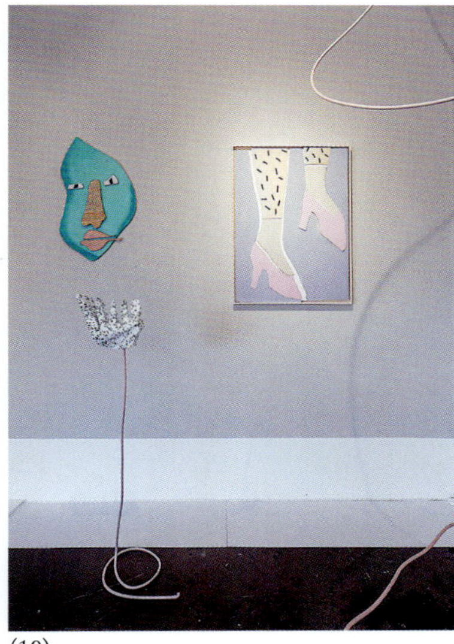
(10)

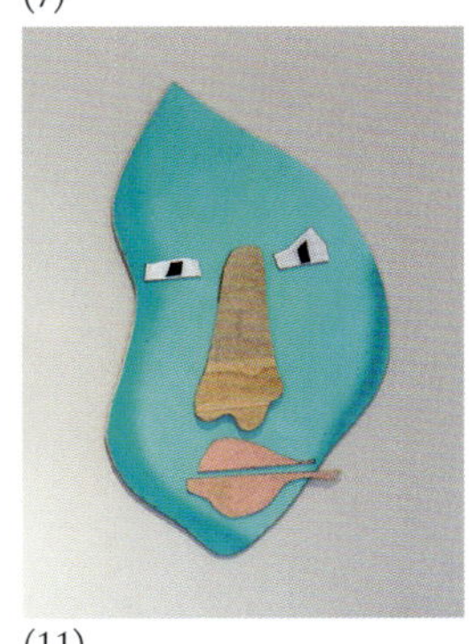
(11)

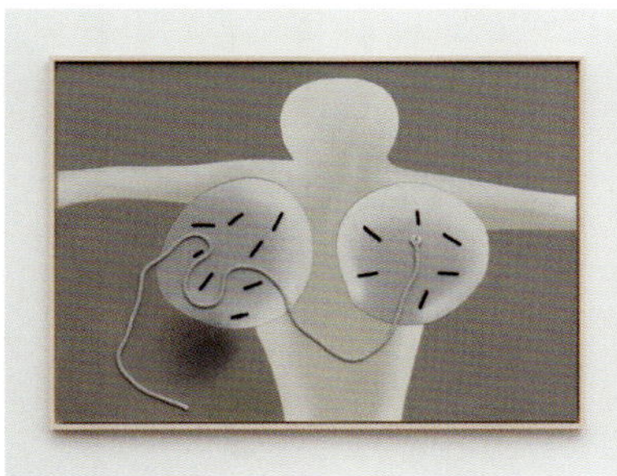
(12)

(3) ***SZENE VII: Bin ein herrlicher Frau-Herr/ Meine Frau ist eine dämliche Mann-Dame***
2021, foam board, varnish and pipe cleaner, 105 × 76 × 4 cm

(4) ***SZENE VII: Bau dir eine neue Brust/ Dazu hab ich keine Lust***
2021, foam board, paint, pipe cleaner, rope, 74 × 104 × 4 cm

(5) ***SZENE VI: Ihr habt's geschafft/Ihr habt's vollbracht/40.500 Kinder an einem Tag***
2021, Pressboard, oil paint, rubber, 144 × 104 × 4 cm

(6) ***Ich lasse dich gehen***
2021, wood and varnish, 144 × 104 × 4 cm

(7) ***Die Brüste des Tiresias***
2021, various images and objects, dimensions variable, Installation view Elektrohalle Rhomberg

(8) ***SZENE IX: Nicht nur mein Bart wächst famos/Auch mein Schnauz wird groß***
2021, wood and acrylics, 84 × 55 × 3 cm

(9) ***SZENE VIII: Da die Frau nicht kann/Muss der Mann nun ran***
2021, foam board, varnish, foam, cord, 105 × 76 × 4 cm

(10) ***Die Brüste des Tiresias***
2021, various images and objects, dimensions variable, Installation view Elektrohalle Rhomberg

(11) ***Szene I: Blaues Gesicht***
2021, wood, lacquer, 84 × 55 × 3 cm

(12) ***SZENE VIII: Bin ich einmal hübsch und fein/Fallen die Mädchen auf mich rein***
2021, foam board, lacquer, pipe cleaner, cord, 74 × 104 × 4 cm

T

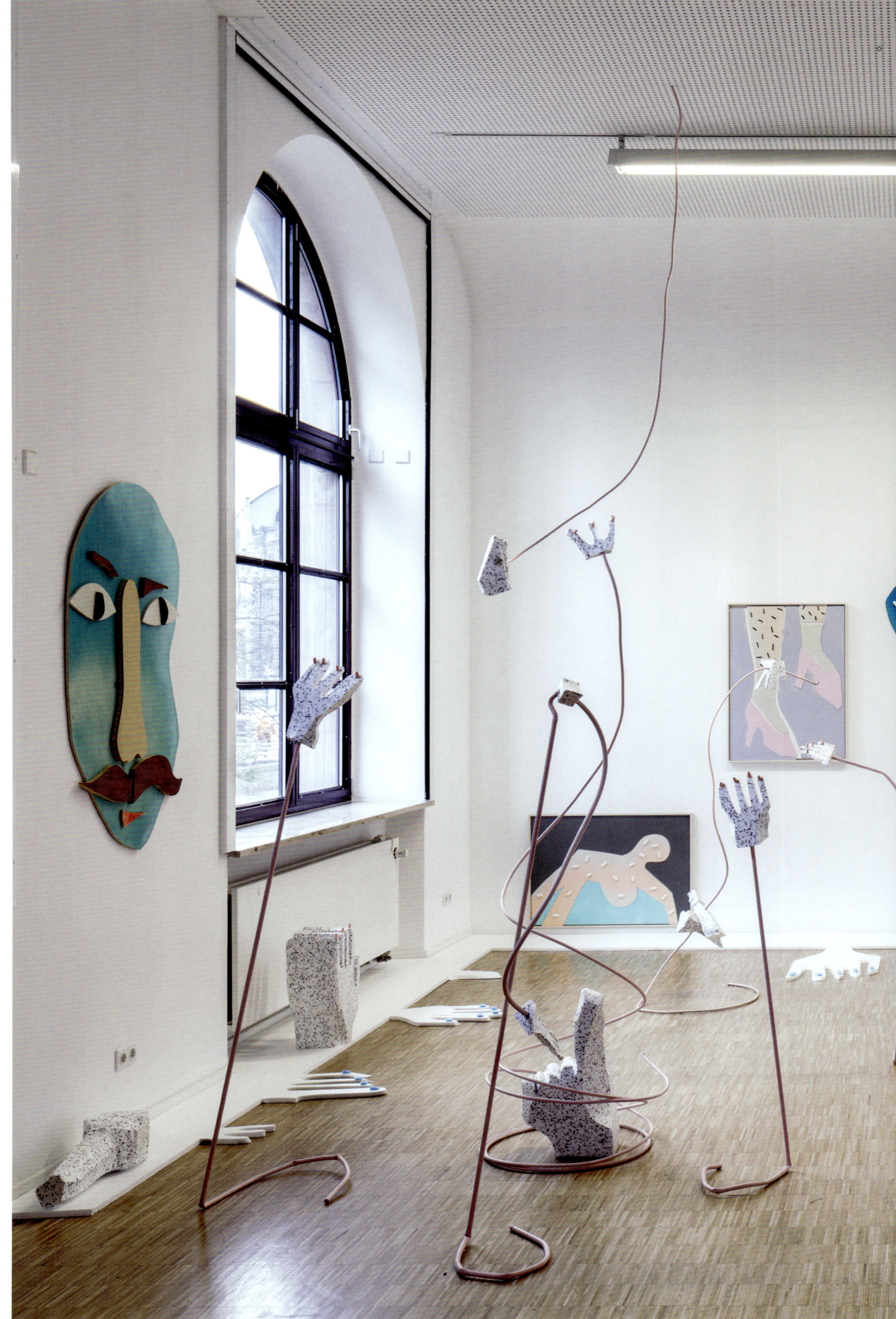

(13) ***Die Brüste des Tiresias***
2021, various images and objects, dimensions variable, Installation view Kunsthalle Nürnberg

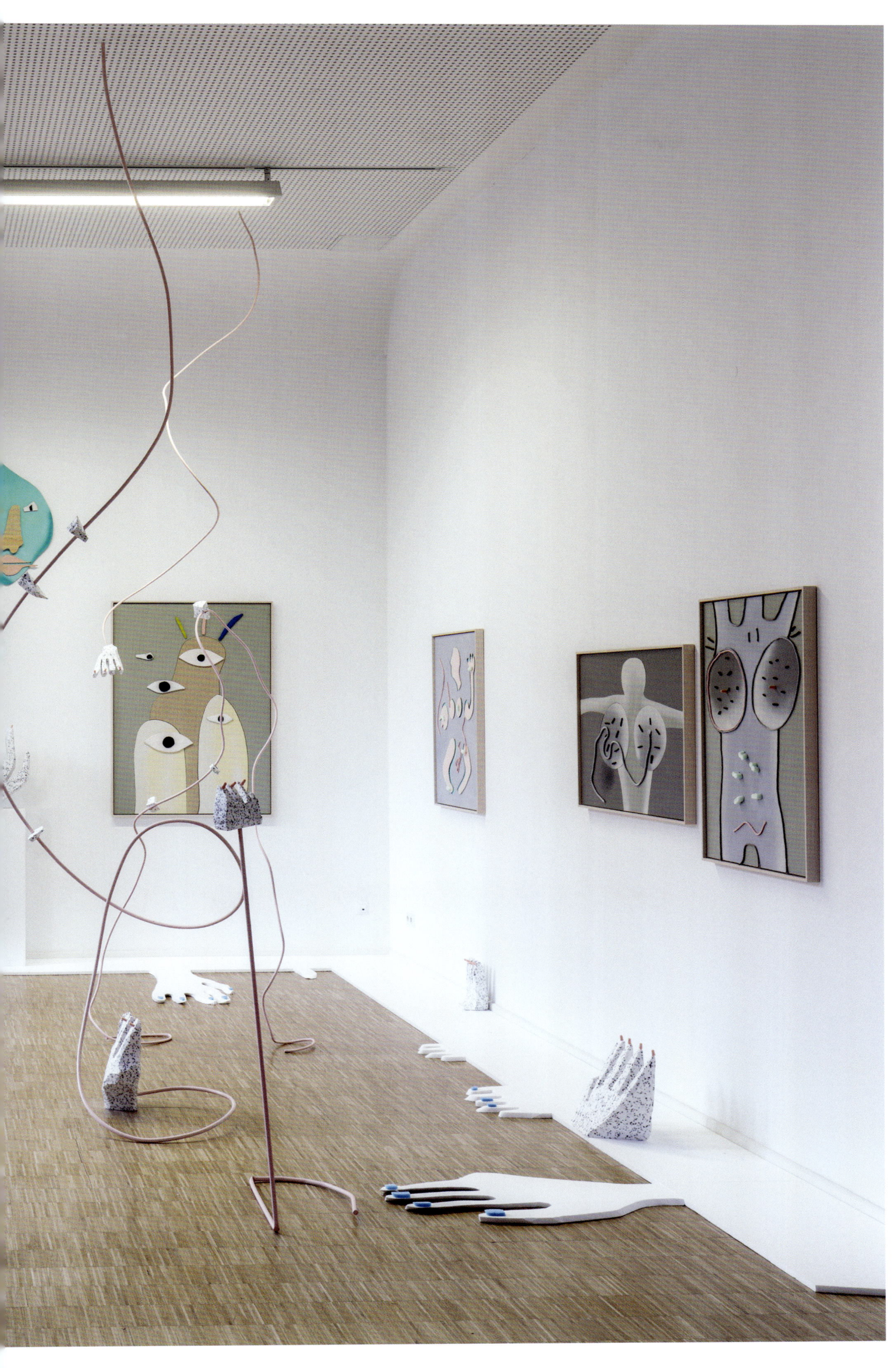

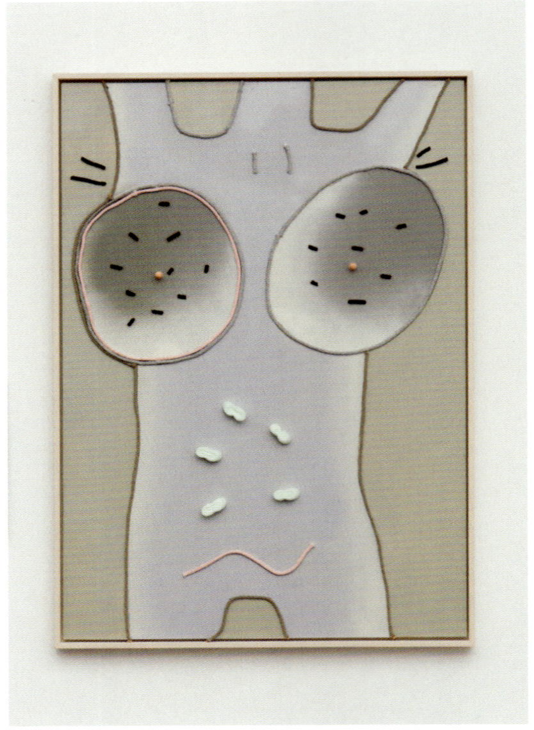

(14)

T

(14) ***SZENE IX: Ja kommt nur abends, um zu sehen/Wie ganz ohne Frauen Kinder entstehen***
2021, foam board, paint, Styrofoam, 104 × 74 × 4 cm

PANDORA PAPERS

T

INGREDIENTS
Bromance und Verrat ①
Seilschaft VII ③
Eine Hand wäscht
die andere ④
Vettern ersten Grades
(Win Win) ⑤
Saufbrüder ⑥
Coole Boys ⑦
Bestechendes Ergebnis ⑧
Allsehend ⑨
Auf dem Boden hoher
Stellungen
Verstrickungens
Filzokratie II

EN For her exhibition *Pandora Papers* Issel worked for the first time with a material that is very rarely found in contemporary art: felt. It is created by rubbing combed virgin wool. The fibers are formed into a durable bond by the microscopic platelets on the surface of the animal hair getting caught together. Issel forms colorful, comic-like images with the self-rolled felt, which are then fixed on a solid support material, either directly on the wall or on canvases stretched over stretcher frames.
The total of thirteen felt pictures in the exhibition have titles such as "First Cousins," "One Hand Washes the Other," "Drinking Brothers," and "Seilschaft VII" and have been related to each other by the artist in a complex spatial installation. The supporting motifs are shadowy, black shapes on the walls and floor of the exhibition room as well as rope or tube-shaped structures, which also partially respond to elements of the picture frames. At first glance, the arrangement appears playful and colorful. It operates on a material-iconographic level with childlike associations as felt pictures are mostly found in kindergartens, schools and craft courses. This is largely due to their haptic qualities. Felt pictures want to be touched and caressed. But that's not possible with Verena Issel's work. In addition, there are serious topics hidden behind the fluffy surface of the pictures.
For Verena Issel, art is a method to see and understand the world differently. Her humor, which is effective on all levels, is ultimately subversive. For Issel, the matting process necessary to produce the image material is a metaphor for social connections. The legendary "Berlin felt" (an expression for corrupt businesses) between the construction industry and politics in times of high subsidies was her starting point for thinking about all kinds of "unclean" human entanglements. On this simultaneously abstract and very concrete level, she is concerned with interweaving society with structures of power.
The title of the exhibition refers to the largest leak to date about so-called tax havens and names the most effective means against corruption and the shadow economy, namely an independent judiciary and journalism.
☐ ***Marc Wellman***

T

DE Issel hat für ihre Ausstellung *Pandora Papers* erstmals mit einem Material gearbeitet, das sehr selten in der zeitgenössischen Kunst anzutreffen ist: Filz. Es entsteht durch das Walken von gekämmter Schurwolle. Die Fasern werden dabei zu einem haltbaren Verbund gebracht, indem sich die mikroskopisch kleinen Plättchen auf der Oberfläche der Tierhaare ineinander verhaken. Issel formt mit dem selbstgewalkten Filz bunte, comichafte Bilder, die dann auf einem festen Trägermaterial fixiert werden; entweder direkt auf der Wand oder auf Leinwänden, die über Keilrahmen gespannt sind.

Die insgesamt dreizehn Filzbilder in der Ausstellung tragen Titel wie *Vettern ersten Grades*, *Eine Hand wäscht die andere*, *Saufbrüder* oder *Seilschaft VII* und sind von der Künstlerin in einer komplexen Rauminstallation miteinander in Beziehung gesetzt worden. Tragende Motive sind schattenhafte, schwarze Formen auf den Wänden und dem Boden des Ausstellungsraums sowie seil- oder röhrenförmige Gebilde, die auch teilweise auf Elemente der Bilderrahmen antworten.

Das Arrangement wirkt auf den ersten Blick spielerisch und farbenfroh und operiert auf der materialikonografischen Ebene mit kindlichen Assoziationen. Filzbilder sind tatsächlich größtenteils in Kindergärten, Schulen und Bastelkursen anzutreffen. Das liegt zu großen Teilen an ihren haptischen Qualitäten. Filzbilder wollen angefasst und gestreichelt werden. Doch das geht bei Verena Issels Arbeiten natürlich nicht. Zudem verbergen sich hinter der flauschig-fluffigen Oberfläche der Bilder durchaus ernste Themen.

Für Verena Issel ist Kunst eine Methode, um die Welt anders zu sehen und zu begreifen. Ihr auf allen Ebenen wirksamer Humor ist letztlich subversiv. Und so hat sie auf sehr spezielle Weise auf den Ausstellungsraum der IG Metall reagiert. Der zur Herstellung des Bildmaterials notwendige Vorgang der Verfilzung ist bei Issel eine Metapher gesellschaftlicher Zusammenhänge. Den legendären „Berliner Filz“ zwischen Bauwirtschaft und Politik in Zeiten der Hochsubvention war ihr Ausgangspunkt, um über alle Arten „unsauberer“ (Issel) menschlicher Verstrickungen nachzudenken. Auf dieser gleichzeitig abstrakten und sehr konkreten Ebene geht es ihr um die Durchwebung der Gesellschaft mit Strukturen der Macht. Der Titel der Ausstellung verweist auf das bis dato größte Leak über sogenannte Steueroasen und benennt die wirksamsten Mittel gegen Korruption und Schattenwirtschaft, nämlich eine unabhängige Justiz und einen ebensolchen Journalismus.

□ ***Marc Wellmann***

T

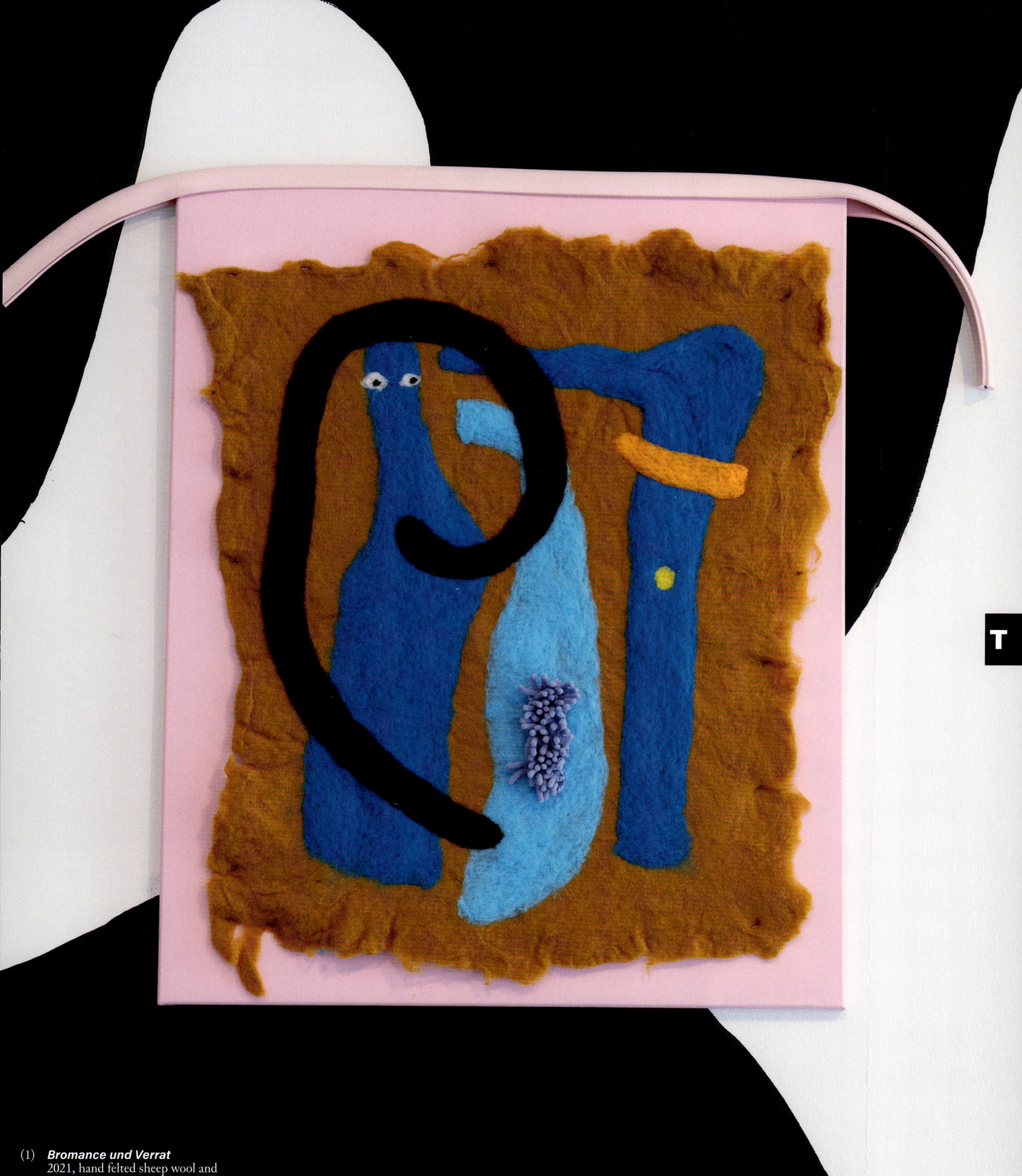

(1) ***Bromance und Verrat***
2021, hand felted sheep wool and wiping cloth on canvas with foam rubber, 80 × 100 cm

T

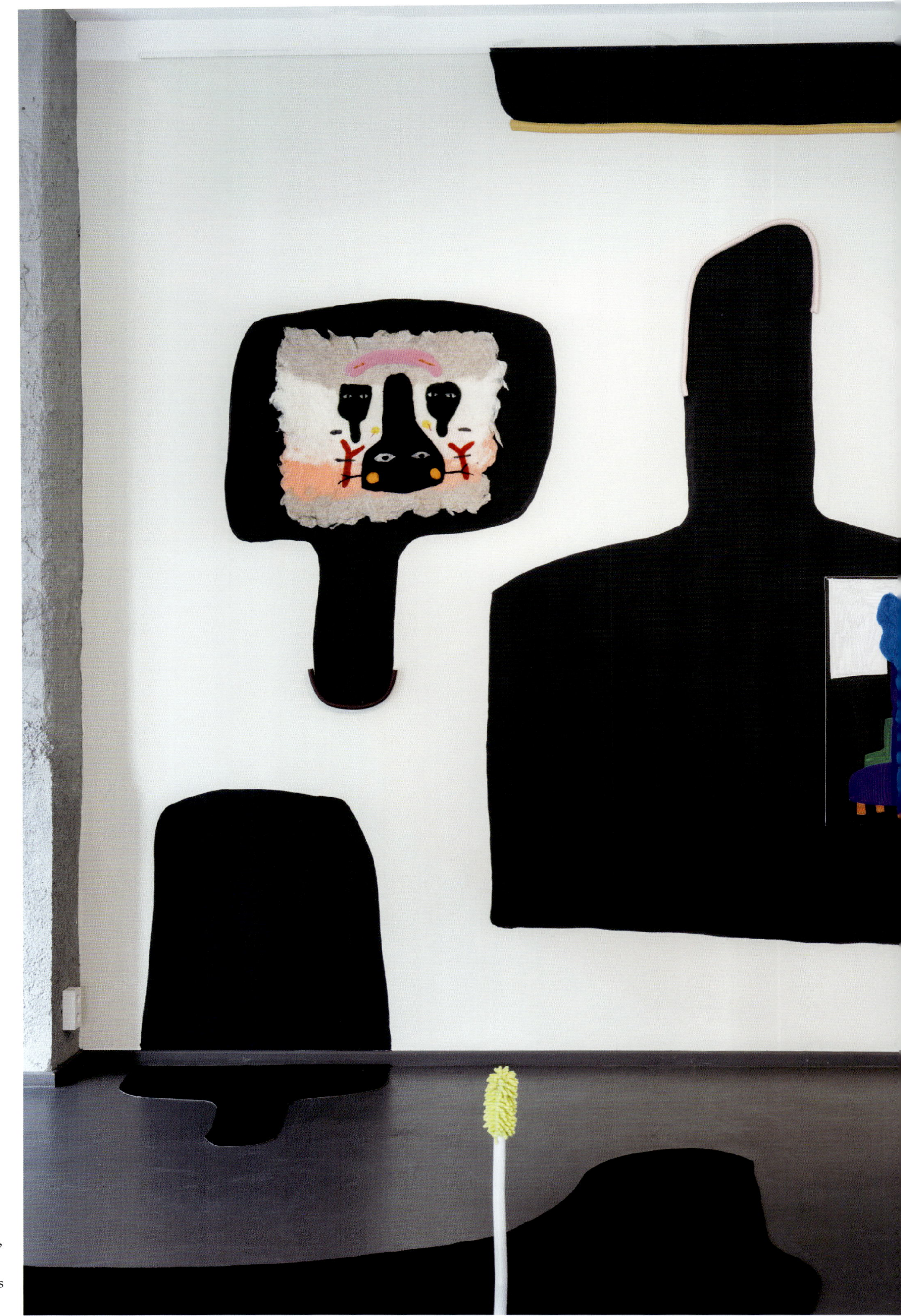

(2) ***Pandora Papers***
2021, wall painting, felt carpets, hand felted sheep wool, paintings, drain pipes, shock absorbers, dimensions variable, Installation view Haus am Lützowplatz/IG Metall, Berlin

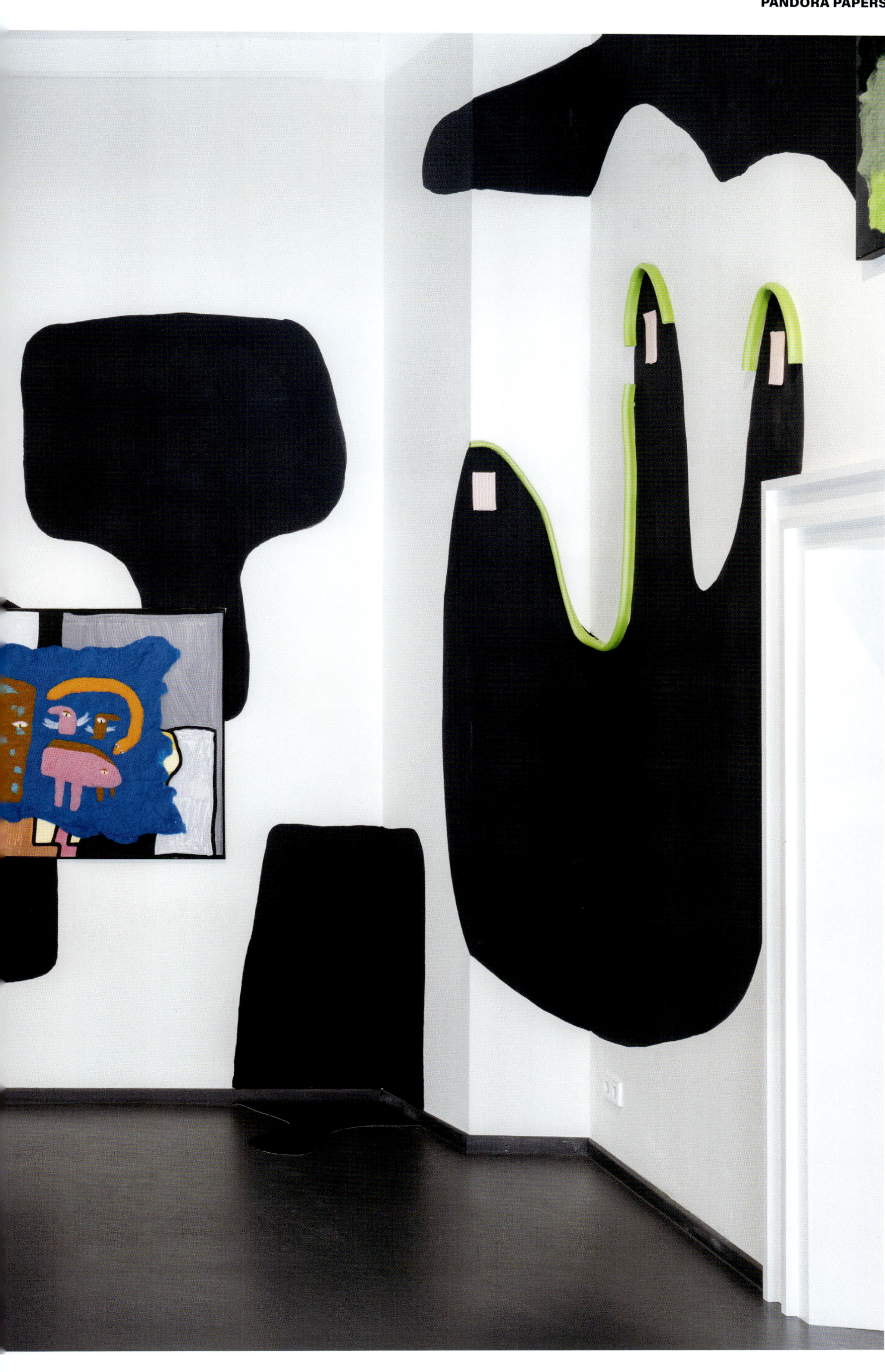

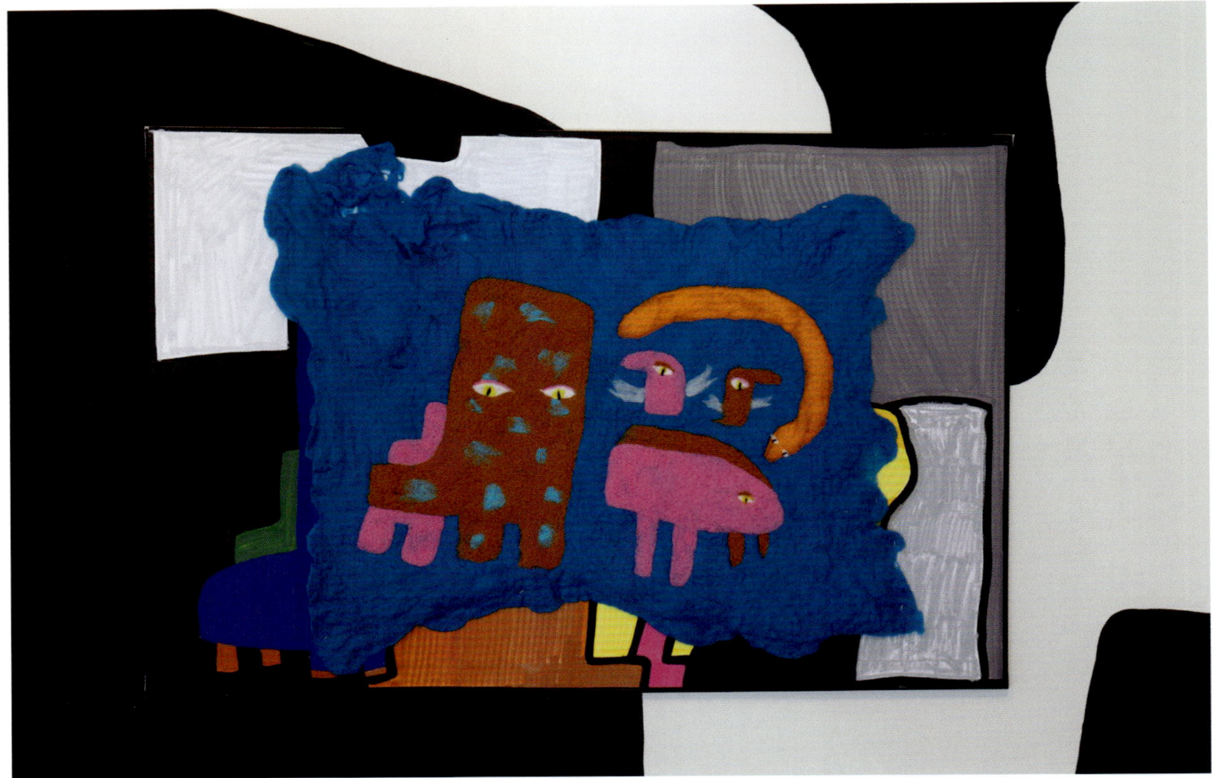

(3)

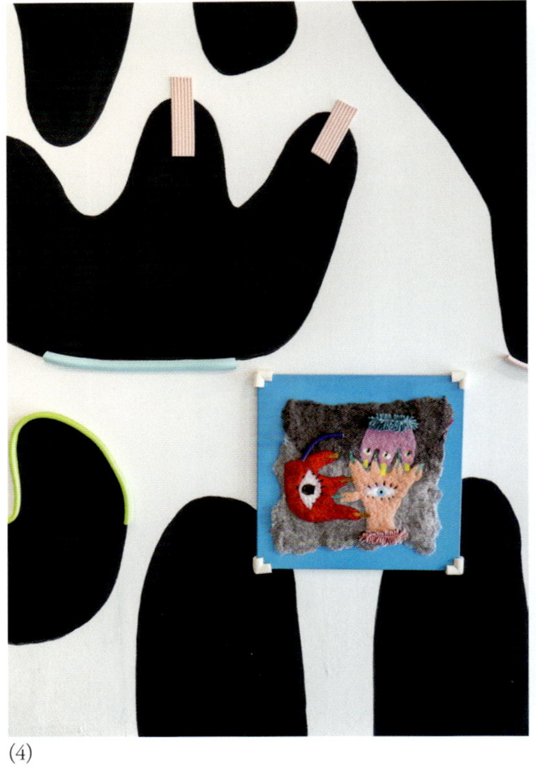

(4)

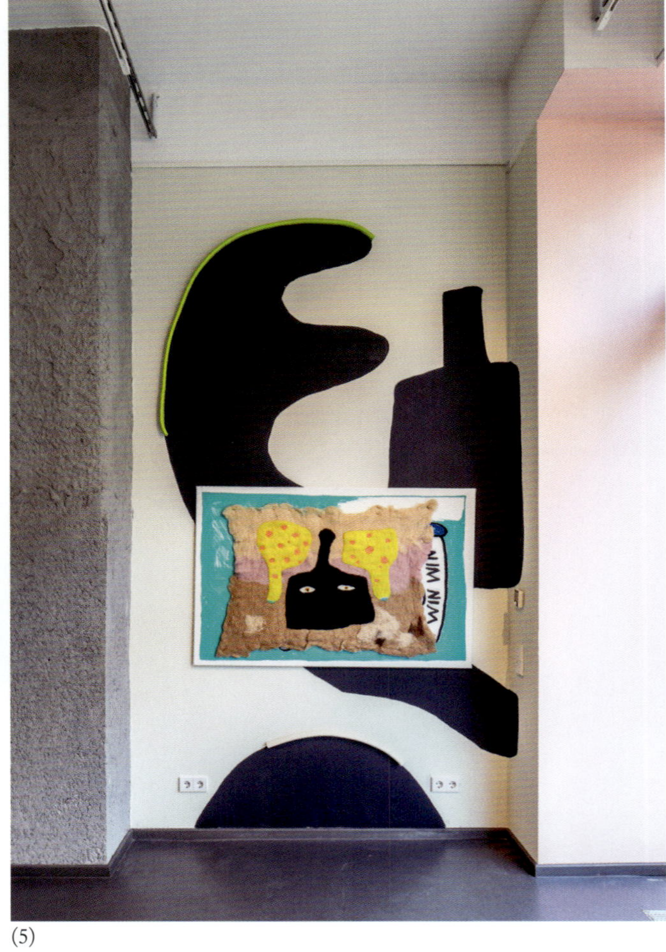

(5)

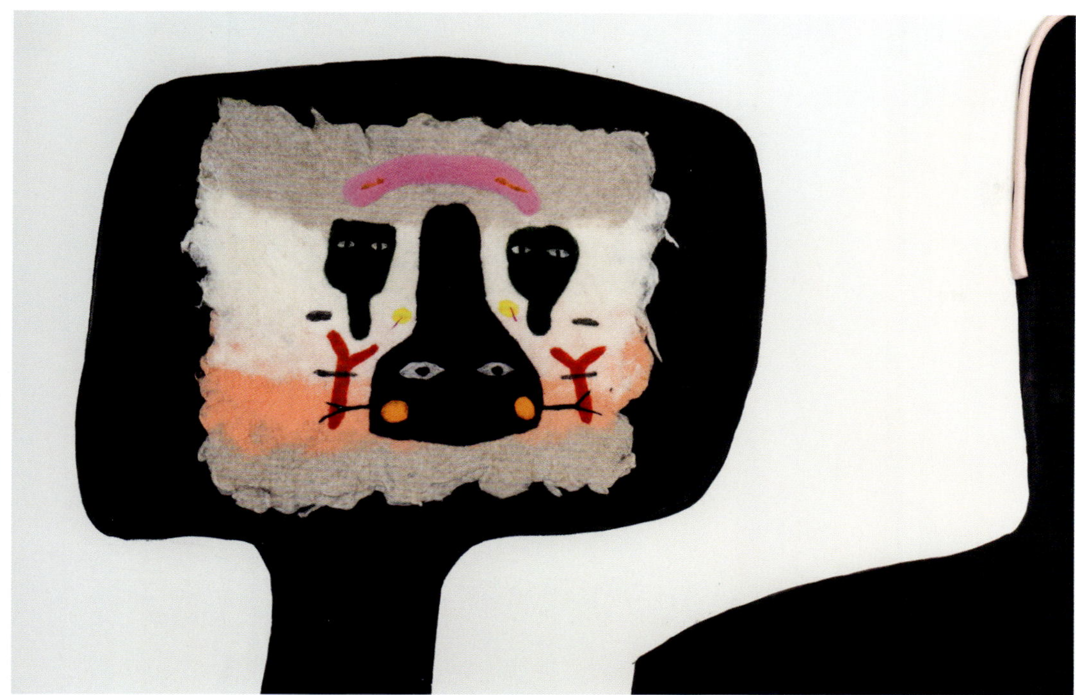

(6)

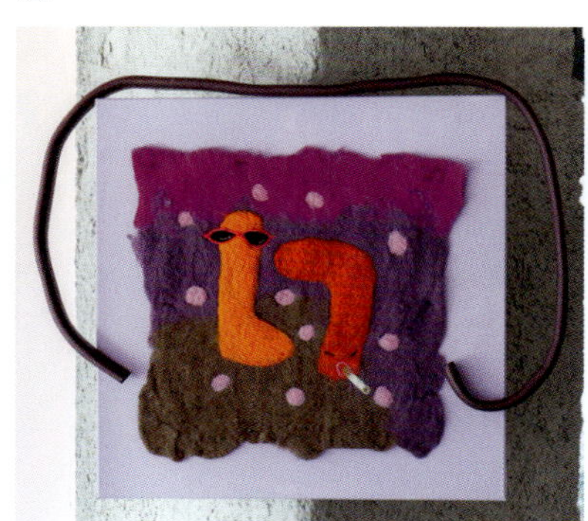

(7)

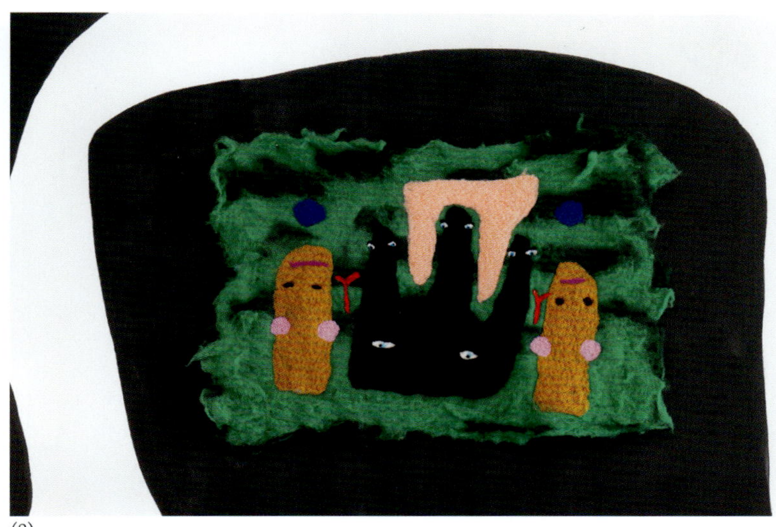

(8)

(3) ***Seilschaft VII***
2021, hand felted sheep wool, acrylics and oil on canvas, 100 × 140 cm

(4) ***Eine Hand wäscht die andere***
2021, hand felted sheep wool on canvas with curlers and cleaning rags, Installation view Haus am Lützowplatz/ IG Metall, Berlin

(5) ***Vettern ersten Grades (Win Win)***
2021, hand felted sheep wool and oil on canvas, 100 × 140 cm, Installation view Haus am Lützowplatz/ IG Metall, Berlin

(6) ***Saufbrüder***
2021, hand felted sheep wool, 80 × 80 cm, Exhibition view Haus am Lützoplatz/ IG Metall, Berlin

(7) **Coole Boys**
2021, hand felted sheep wool on canvas, 70 × 70 cm

(8) **Bestechendes Ergebnis**
2021, hand felted sheep wool, 50 × 70 cm

T

T

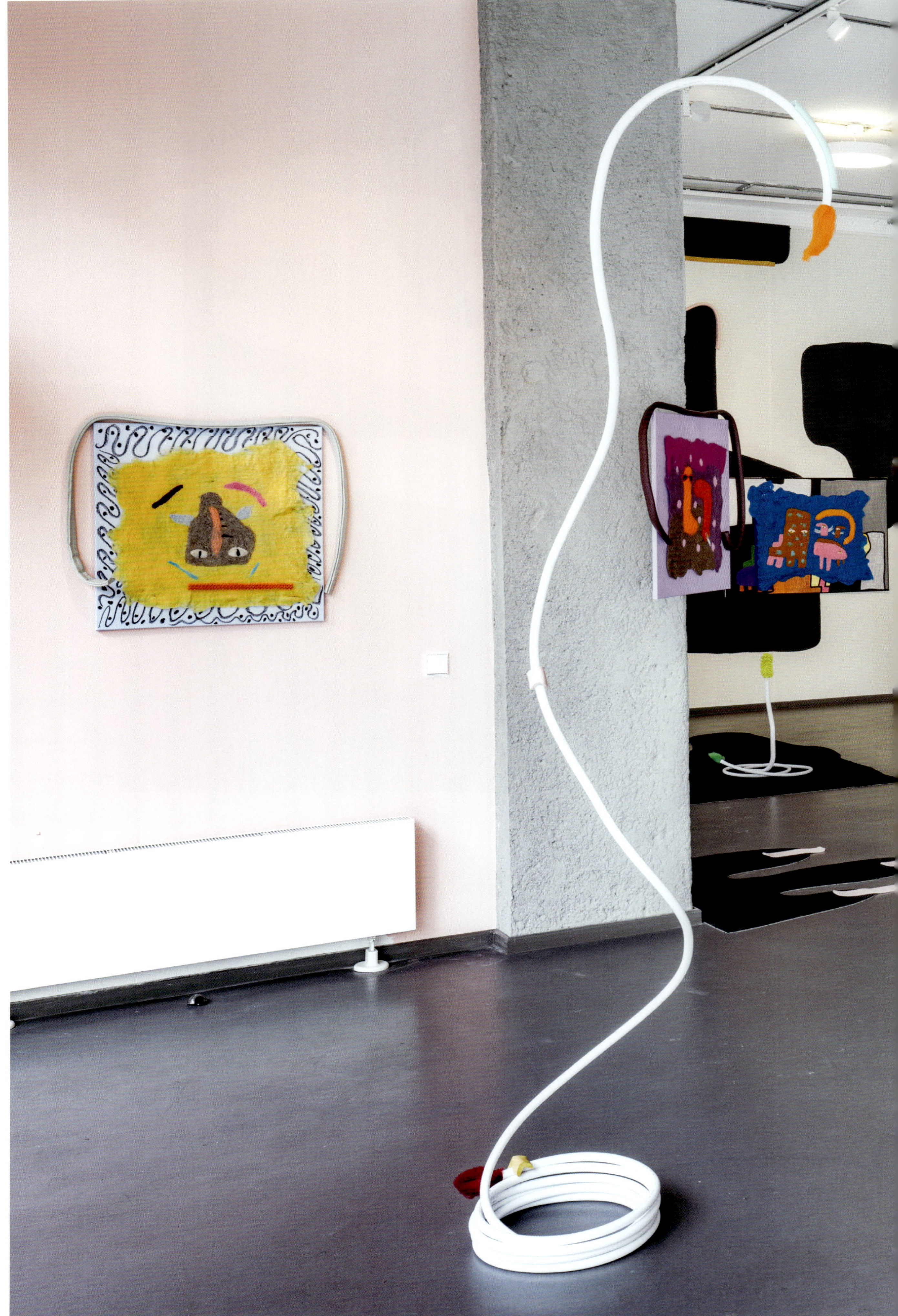

(9) ***Pandora Papers***
2021, wall painting, felt carpets, hand felted sheep wool, paintings, drain pipes, shock absorbers, dimensions variable, Installation view Haus am Lützowplatz/ IG Metall, Berlin

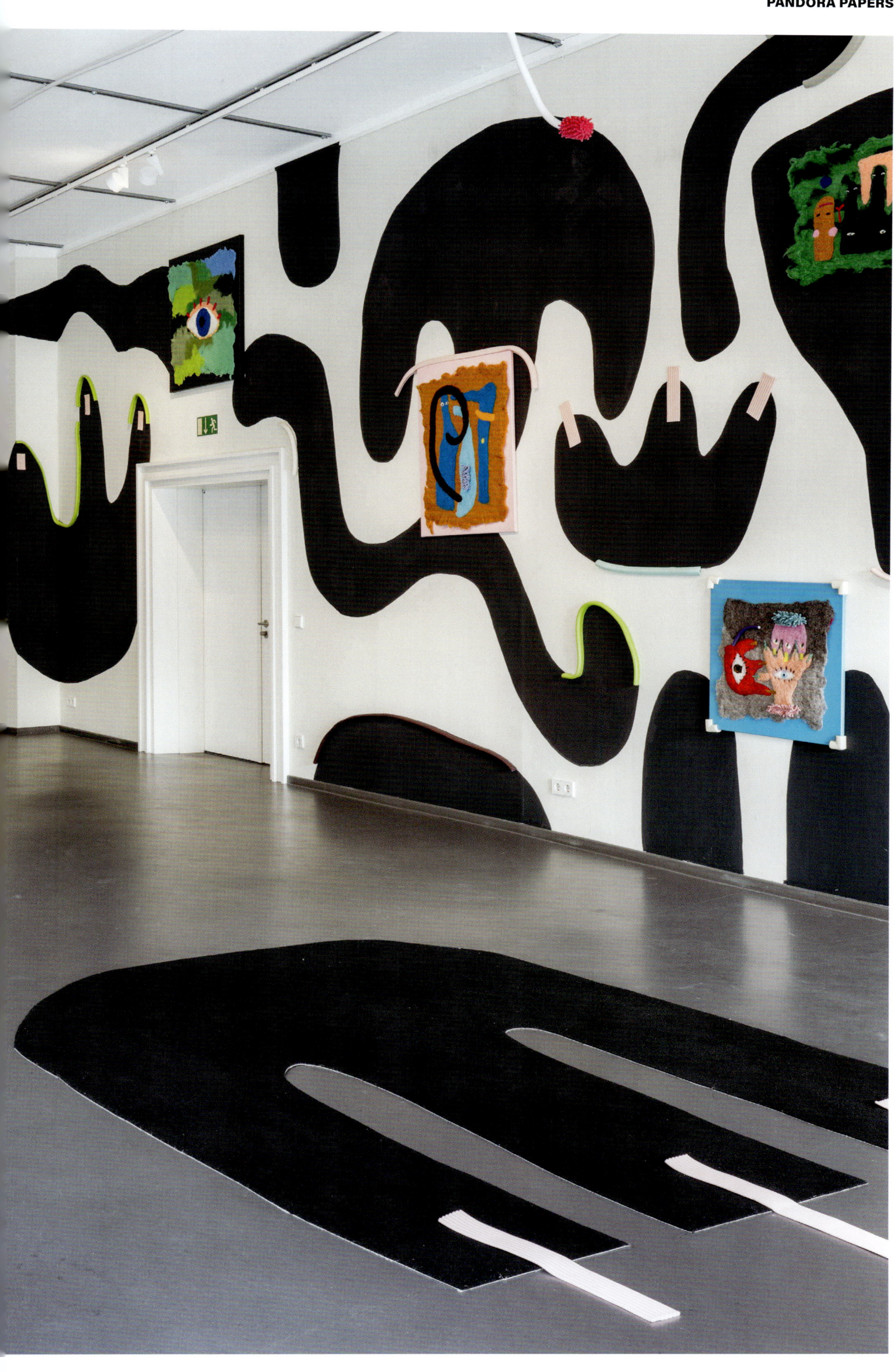

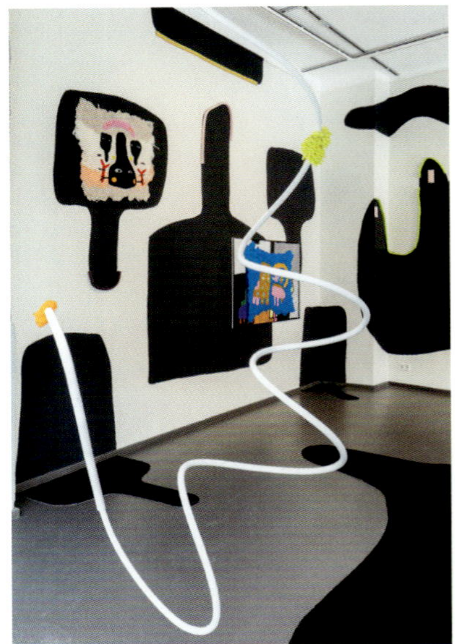
(10)

(10) ***Pandora Papers***
2021, wall painting, felt carpets, hand felted sheep wool, paintings, drain pipes, shock absorbers, dimensions variable, Installation view Haus am Lützowplatz/ IG Metall, Berlin

SOUNDSO VIELE THESEN

I

INGREDIENTS
Martins Bar ①
Untitled 1 ②
Untitled 2 ②
Untitled 3 ②
Untitled 4
Fake Raufaser ②
Lemon
Untitled 5
Taking Trees
Y
Crazy Horst II
Untitled 6 ③
Untitled 7 ④
Untitled 8 ⑤
Untitled 9 ⑥

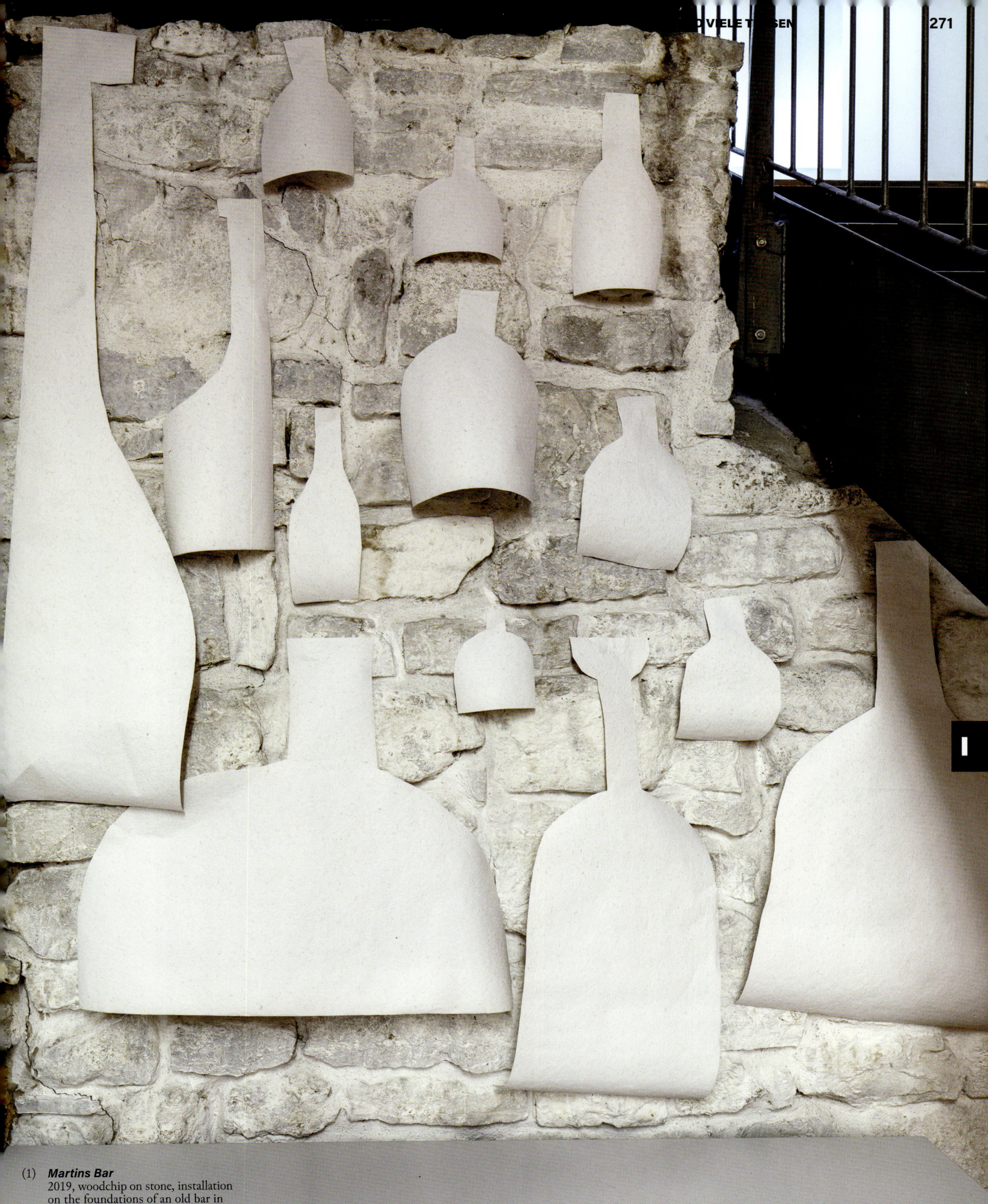

(1) ***Martins Bar***
2019, woodchip on stone, installation on the foundations of an old bar in which Martin Luther is said to have hung out as a student, Installation view Kunsthaus Erfurt

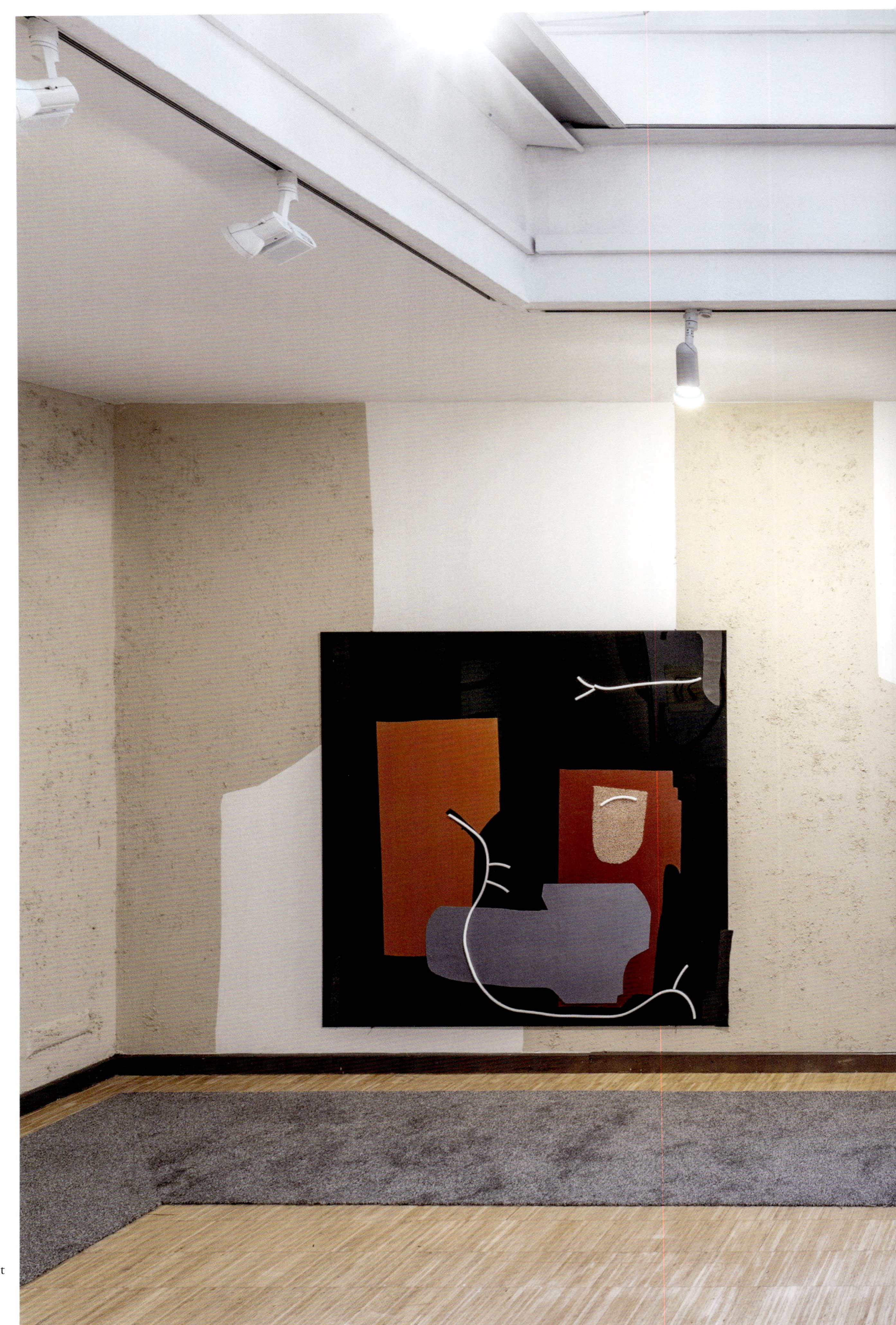

(2) ***Soundso viele Thesen***
2019, various works, carpet and fake Erfurt woodchip wallpaper made according to the GDR recipe with rabbit litter and wall paint, dimensions variable, Installation view Kunsthaus Erfurt

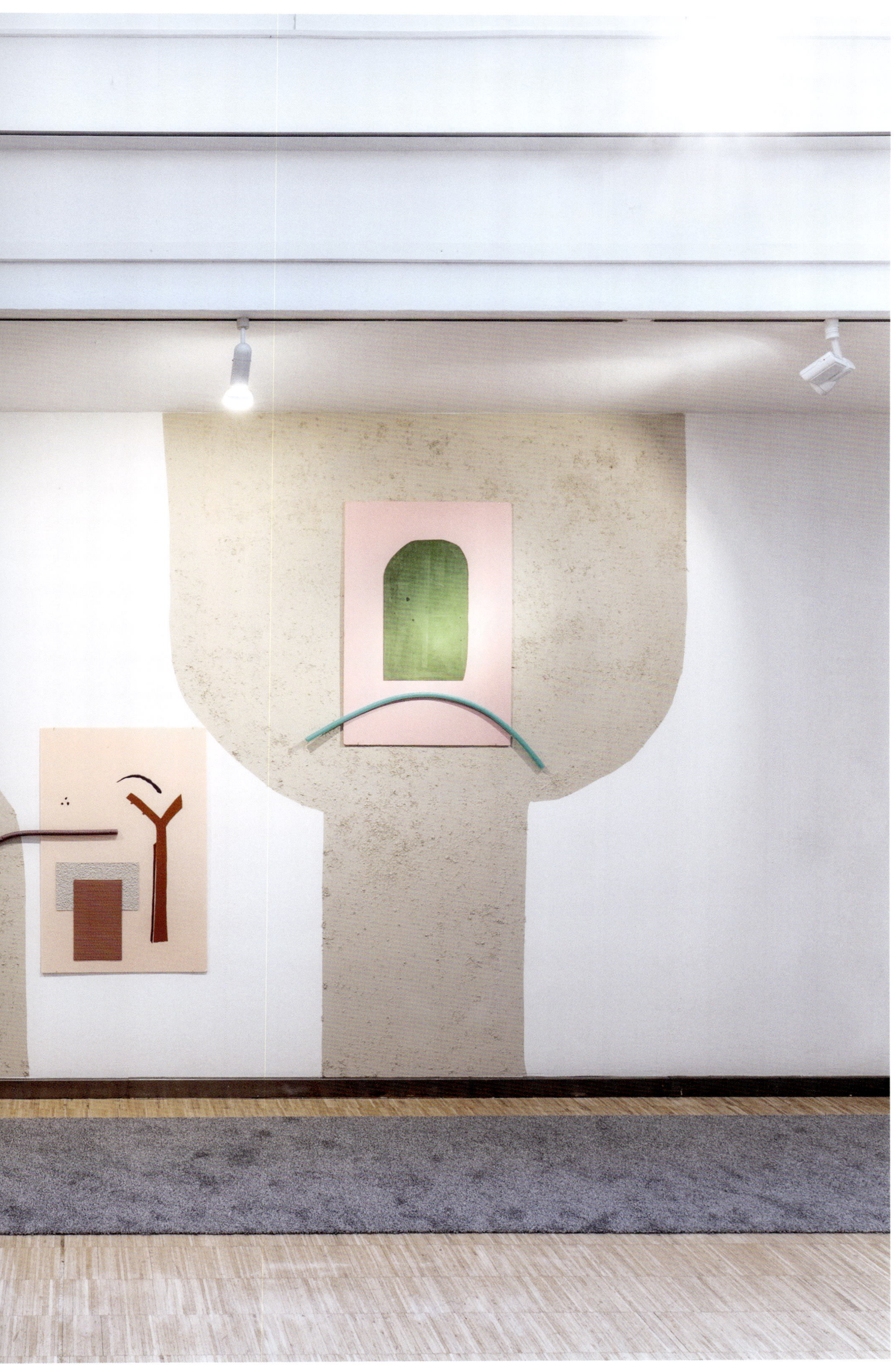

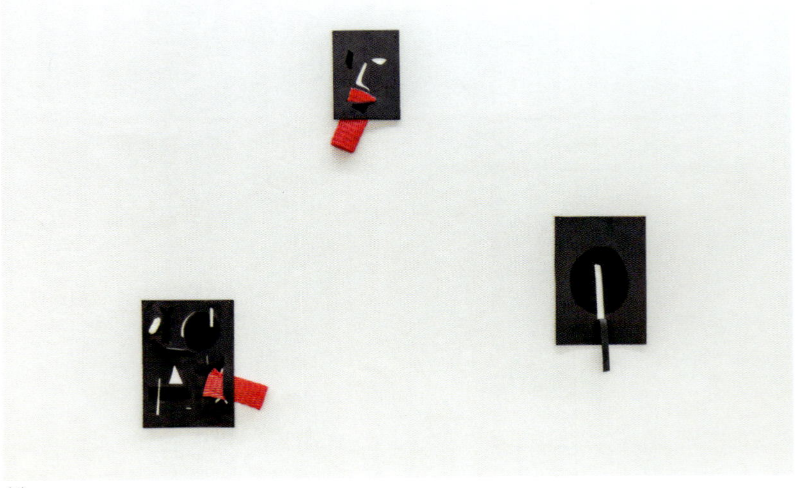
(3)

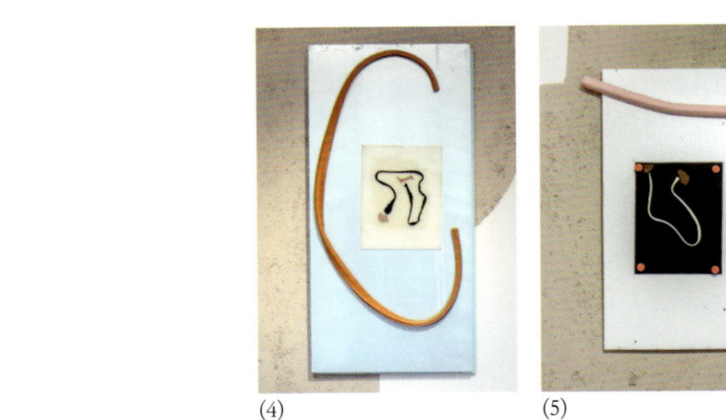
(4) (5)

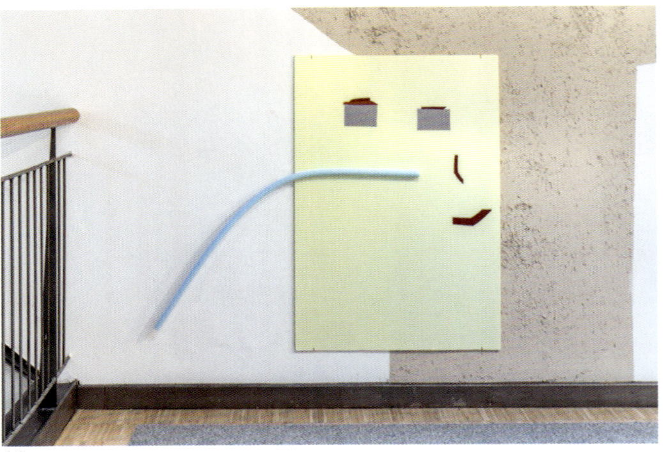
(6)

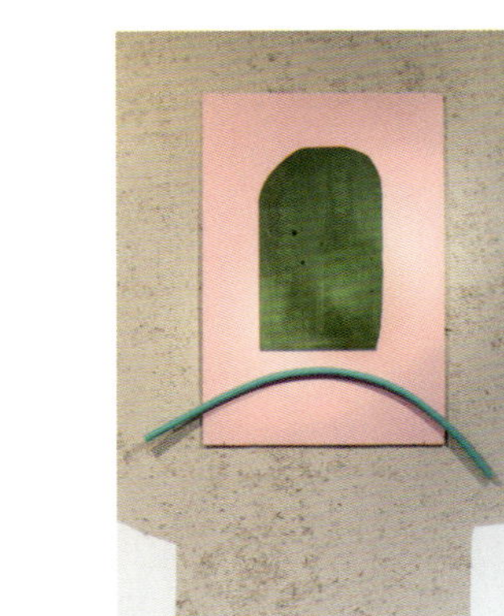
(7)

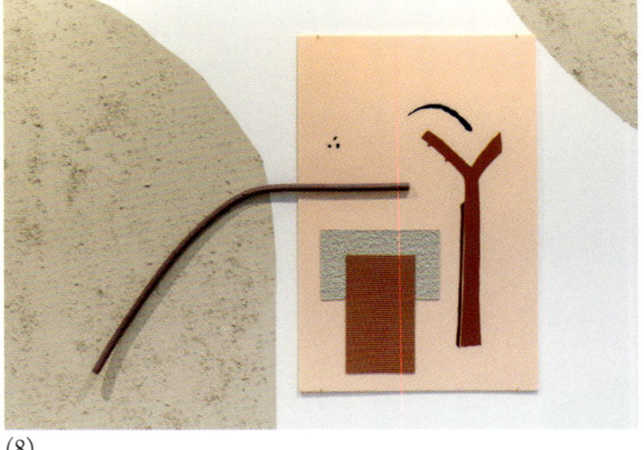
(8)

(3) ***Untitled***
each 2018, felt on tar with plastic, 39 × 27 cm

(4) ***Untitled***
2019, plastic, rubber, Styrofoam-silicone and adhesive tape on Styrofoam, 100 × 50 cm, Installation view Kunsthaus Erfurt

(5) ***Untitled***
2019, plastic, foam, rubber, Styrofoam-silicone and adhesive tape on Styrofoam, 100 × 50 cm, Installation view Kunsthaus Erfurt

(6) ***Untitled***
2019, plastic, rubber, Styrofoam-silicone and adhesive tape on Styrofoam, 100 × 50 cm, Installation view Kunsthaus Erfurt

(7) ***Untitled***
2019, leather and Styrofoam on Styrofoam, 90 × 60 cm, Installation view Kunsthaus Erfurt

(8) ***Untitled***
2019, plastic, rubber, Styrofoam-silicone and adhesive tape on Styrofoam, 100 × 50 cm

ESCAPING THE MUNDANE (PSYCHO-GEOGRAPHIES)

INGREDIENTS
Hi ④
Fight ⑤
Touch ⑥
Loving Buildings ②
Make out houses ②
Friendo houses ②
Wardrobe ②
Kiss ③
Dead House ②
Wardrobe ③
Shadows ①

EN Our urban environment is undergoing rapid changes: modern city architecture is fragmented in function, conditioning and predetermining the ways in which citizens move. Dictated by advanced capitalism, more and more public spaces are privatized and become purposive. 'Psychogeography', a coin termed by Guy Debord (1931-1994), describes the mode of moving through the urban environment in a playful, explorative way, allowing pedestrians to wander away from predictable paths.
Psychogeographies—Escaping the Mundane is a mixed media exhibition revolving around the rediscovery of our very own cities. Through painting, installation and sculpture, the artist reminds us to experience pedestrianism and to find new ways to interact with our built environment and cultural habitat.

☐ ***Lee Dong-Uk, exhibition text Gallery Unofficial Preview***

DE Unsere städtische Umwelt ist einem raschen Wandel unterworfen: Die Architektur moderner Städte ist in ihren Funktionen fragmentiert und bestimmt die Art und Weise, wie sich die Menschen bewegen. Unter dem Diktat des hoch entwickelten Kapitalismus werden immer mehr öffentliche Räume privatisiert und zweckgebunden. Der von Guy Debord (1931–1994) geprägte Begriff „Psychogeographie" beschreibt die Art und Weise, sich spielerisch und explorativ durch die städtische Umwelt zu bewegen, und ermöglicht es dem Fußgänger, sich von vorhersehbaren Wegen zu entfernen. *Escaping the Mundane (Psychogeographies)* ist eine Mixed-Media-Ausstellung über die Wiederentdeckung unserer eigenen Städte. Durch Malerei, Installation und Skulptur erinnert uns die Künstlerin daran, Fußgängerfreundlichkeit zu erleben und neue Wege der Interaktion mit unserer gebauten Umwelt und unserem kulturellen Lebensraum zu finden.

☐ ***Lee Dong-Uk, Ausstellungstext Gallery Unofficial Preview***

I

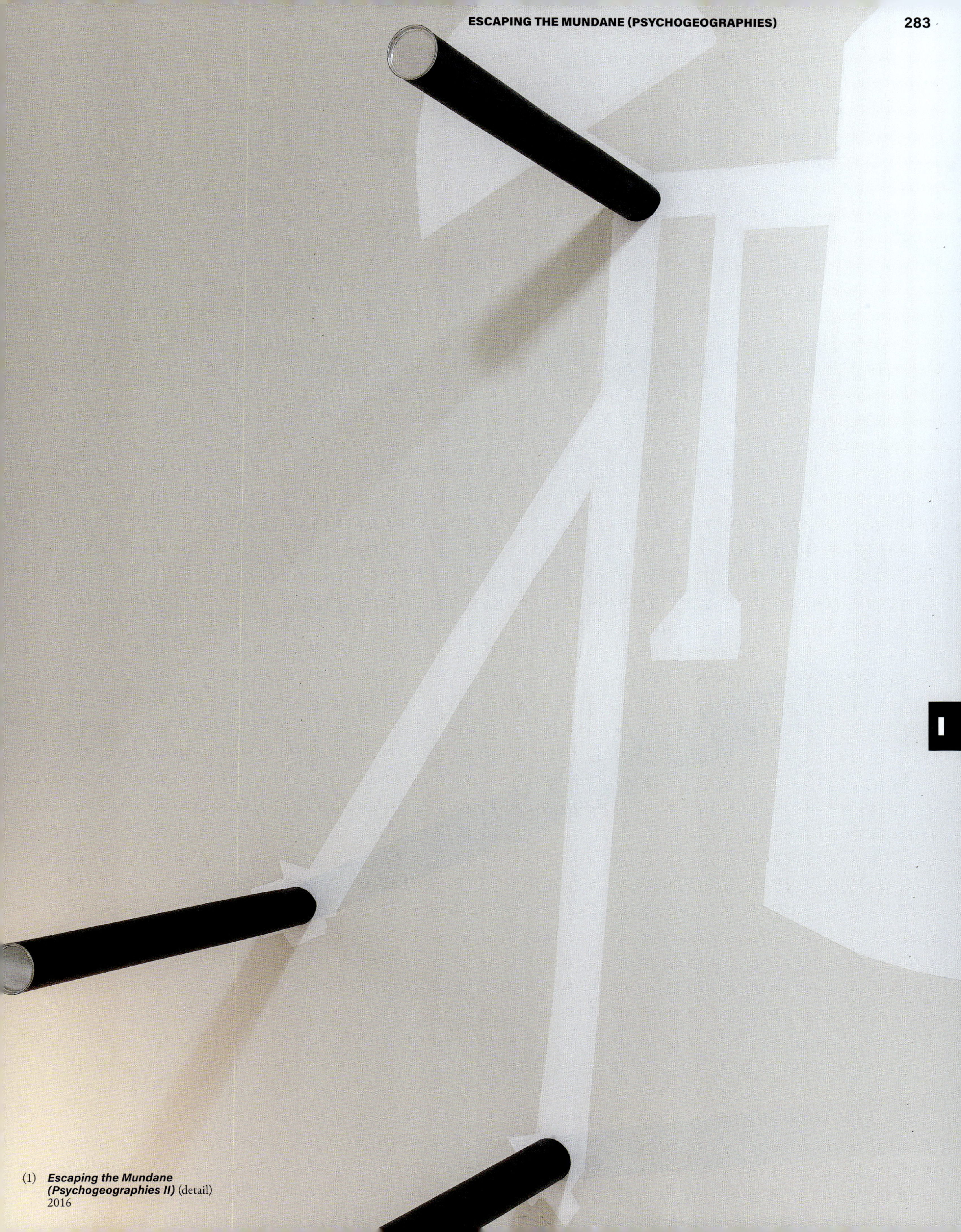

(1) ***Escaping the Mundane (Psychogeographies II)*** (detail)
2016

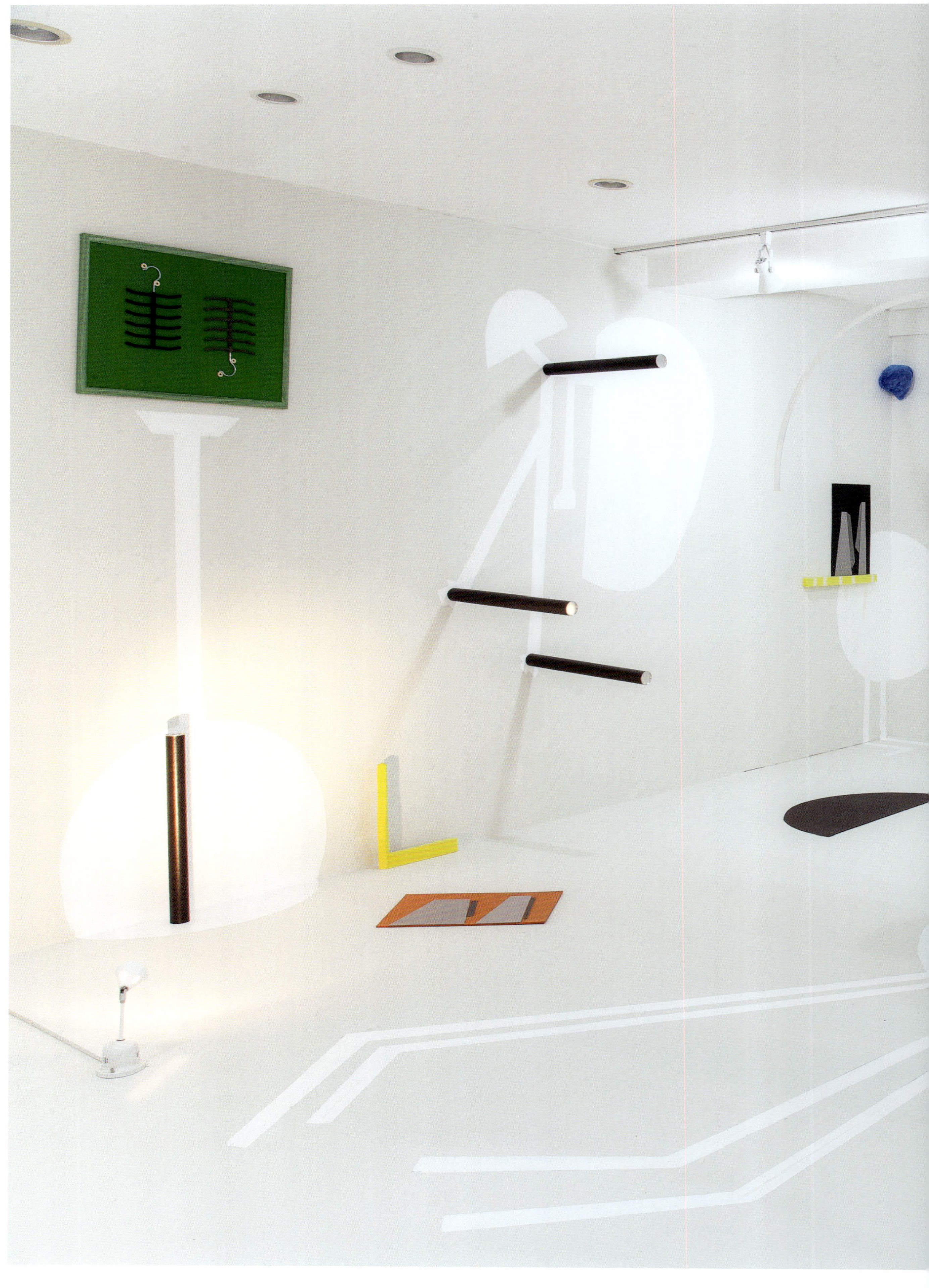

(2) ***Escaping the Mundane (Psychogeographies II)***
2016, various objects and materials, room: 6 × 5 m, Installation view GALLERY UNOFFICIAL PREVIEW, Seoul, South Korea

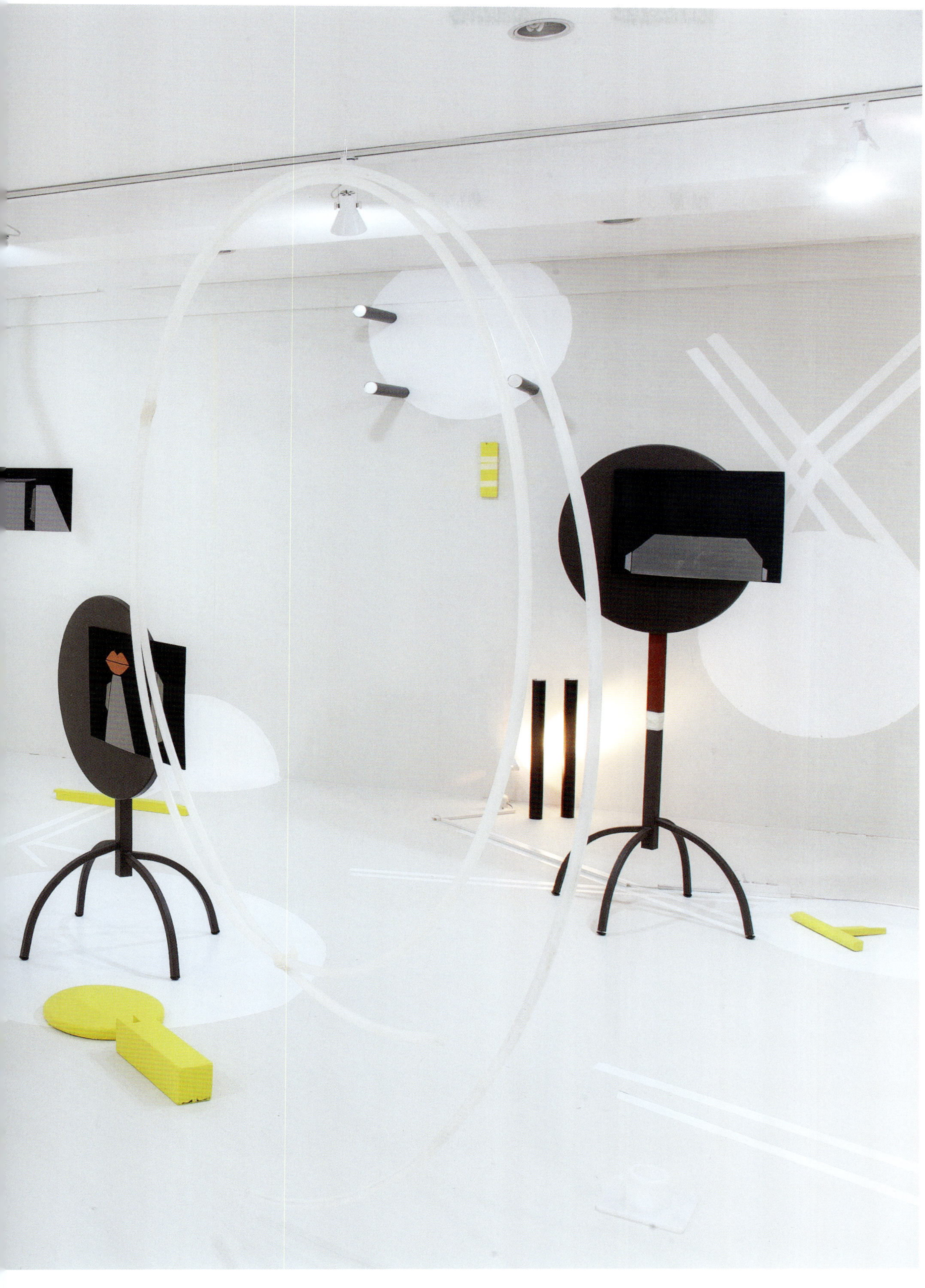

(3) ***Escaping the Mundane (Psychogeographies II)***
2016, various objects and materials, room: 6 × 5 m, Installation view GALLERY UNOFFICIAL PREVIEW, Seoul, South Korea

(4) ***Hi***
2016, foam and plastic, 120 × 80 cm

(5) ***Fight***
2016, foam and plastic, 120 × 80 cm

(6) ***Touch***
2016, cardboard, acrylic paint, foam, 120 × 120 cm

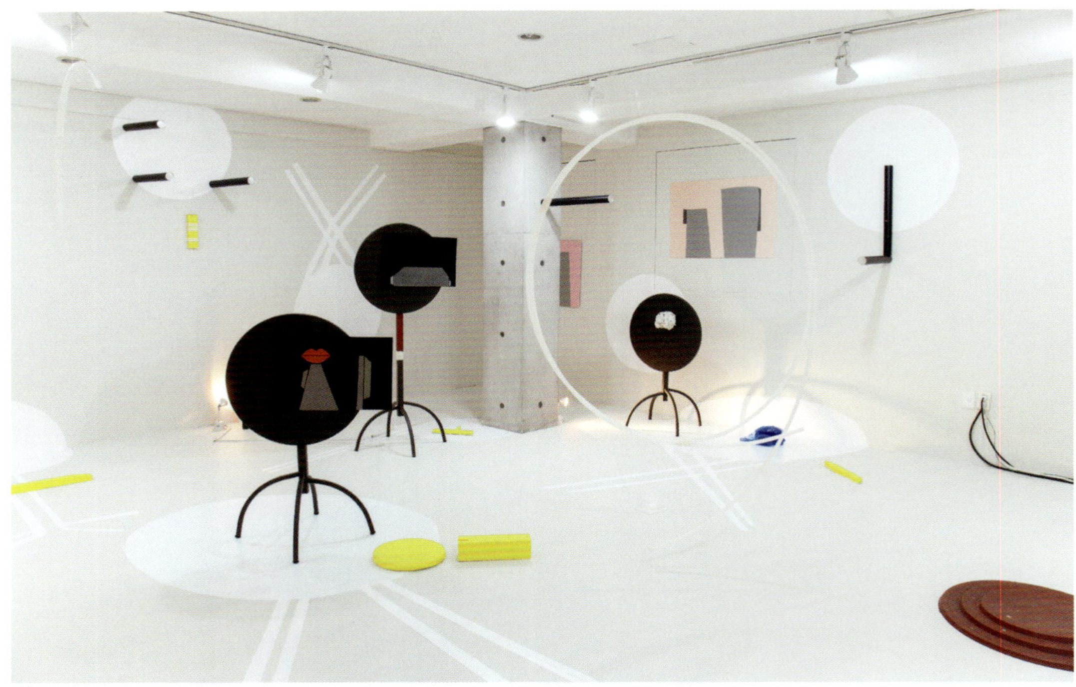
(3)

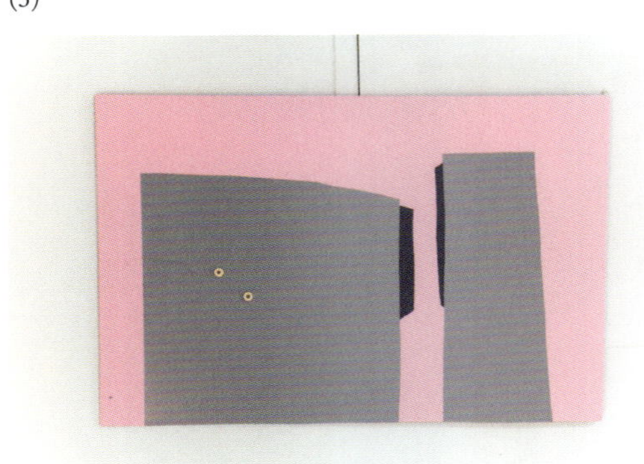
(4)

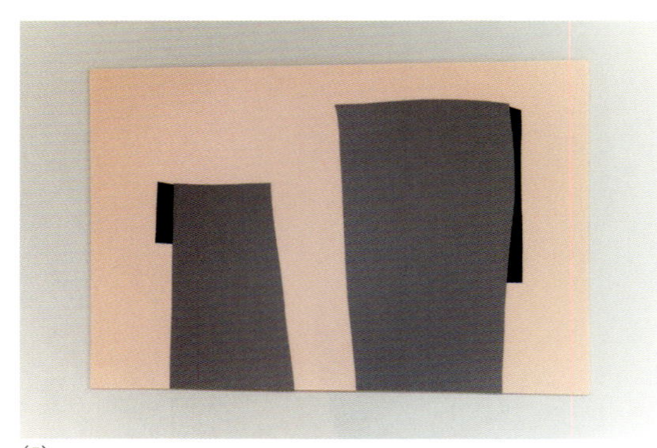
(5)

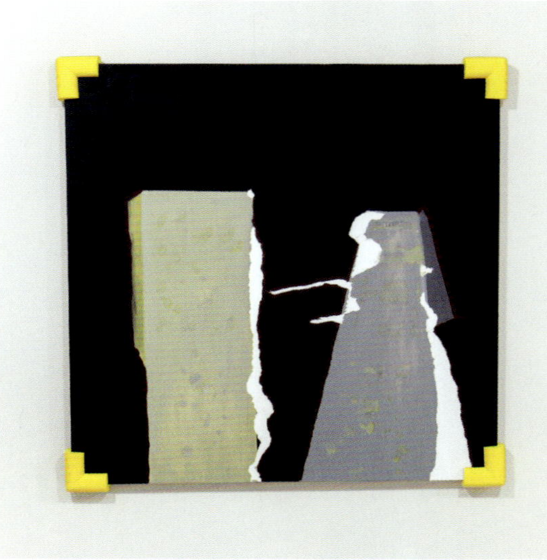
(6)

AUTOSCOOTER

V

INGREDIENTS
Twister ①
Scooter V ①
Twister II ③
Spinball ④
Flying Star ⑤
Spin Ball II ⑥
Shaker ⑨
Headspin ⑦
Flying Star II ⑧
Scooter ②
Scooter II ②

V

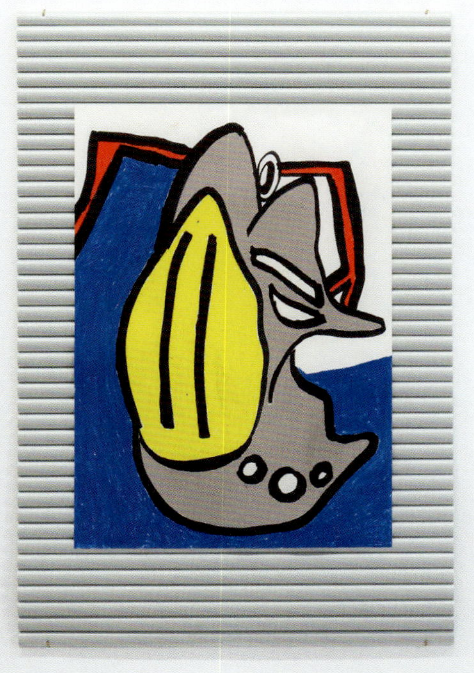

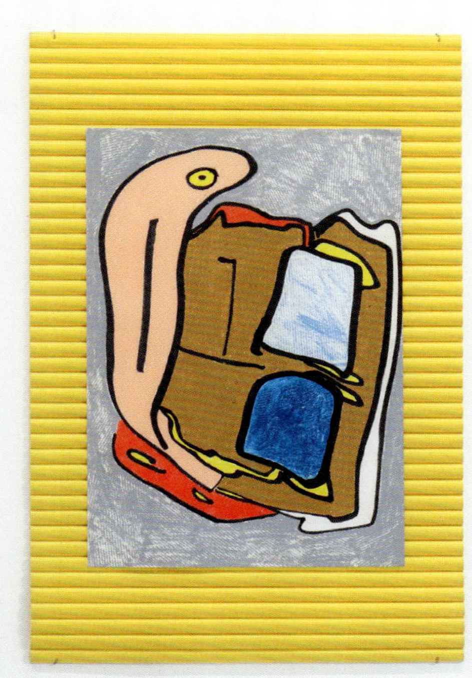

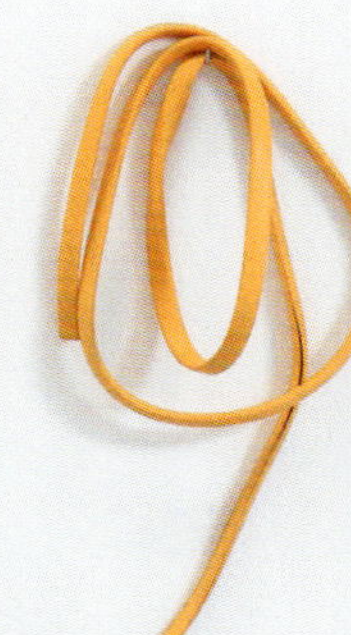

V

(1) ***AUTOSCOOTER***
2019, various works, wall painting, foam and Styrofoam, dimensions variable,
(left) ***TWISTER II***
2019, wax crayons and oil pastels on paper,
Japanese shock absorber mat, 42 × 63 cm,
(right) ***SCOOTER V***
2019, wax crayons and oil pastels on paper, Japanese shock absorber mat, 42 × 63 cm,
Installation view Gallery K'

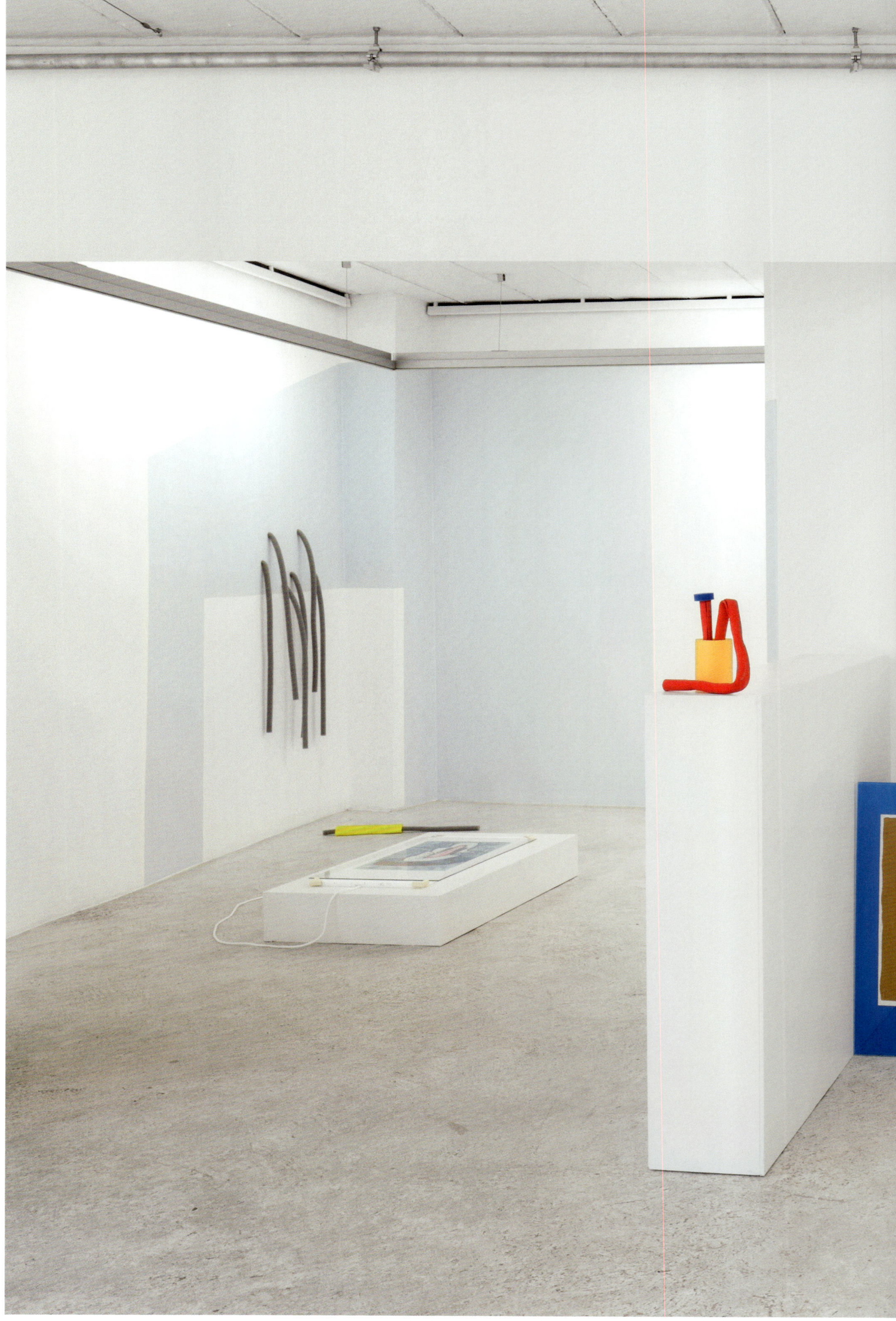

V

(2) ***AUTOSCOOTER***
2019, various works, wall painting, foam and Styrofoam, dimensions variable, Installation view Gallery K'

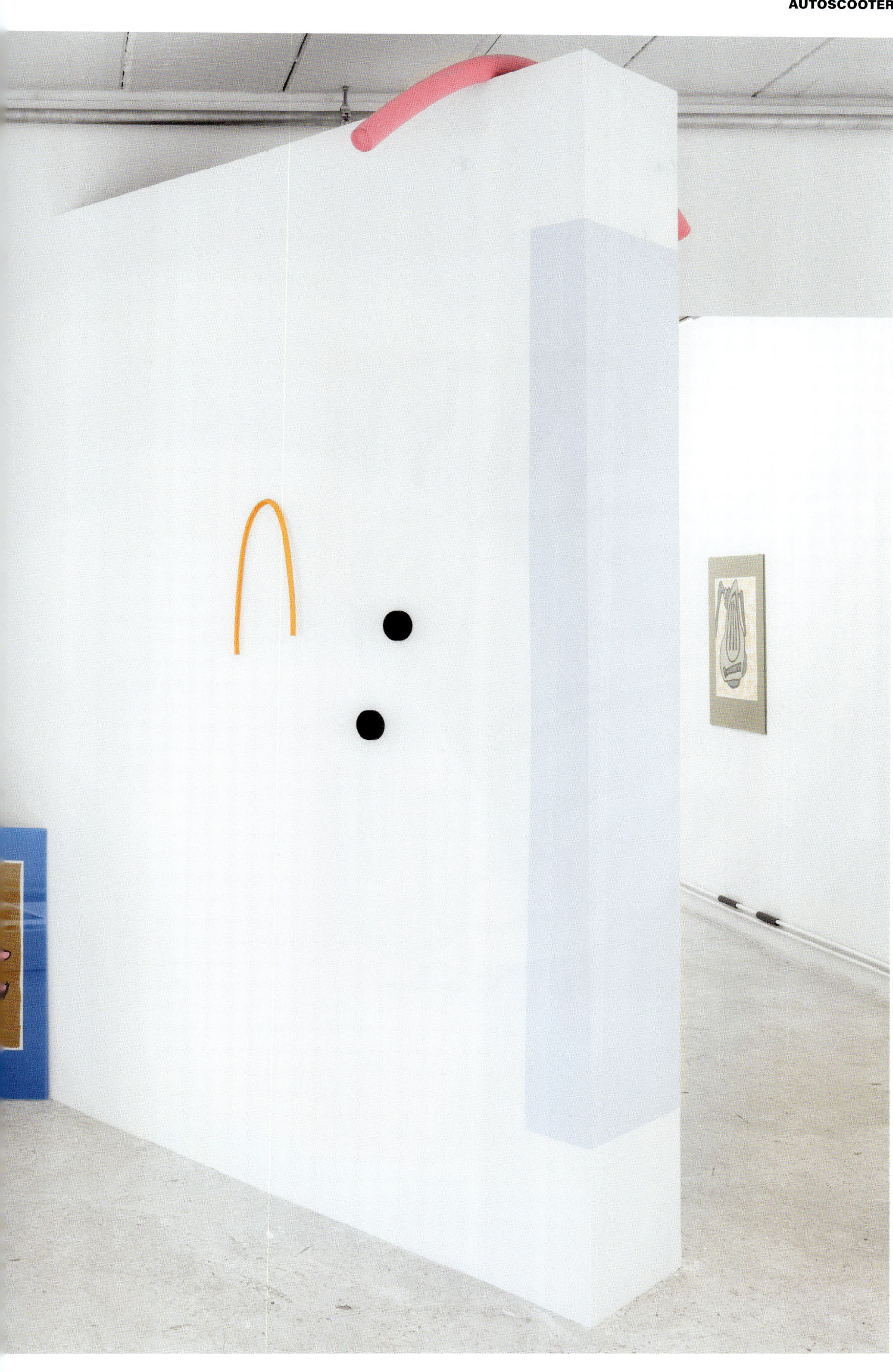

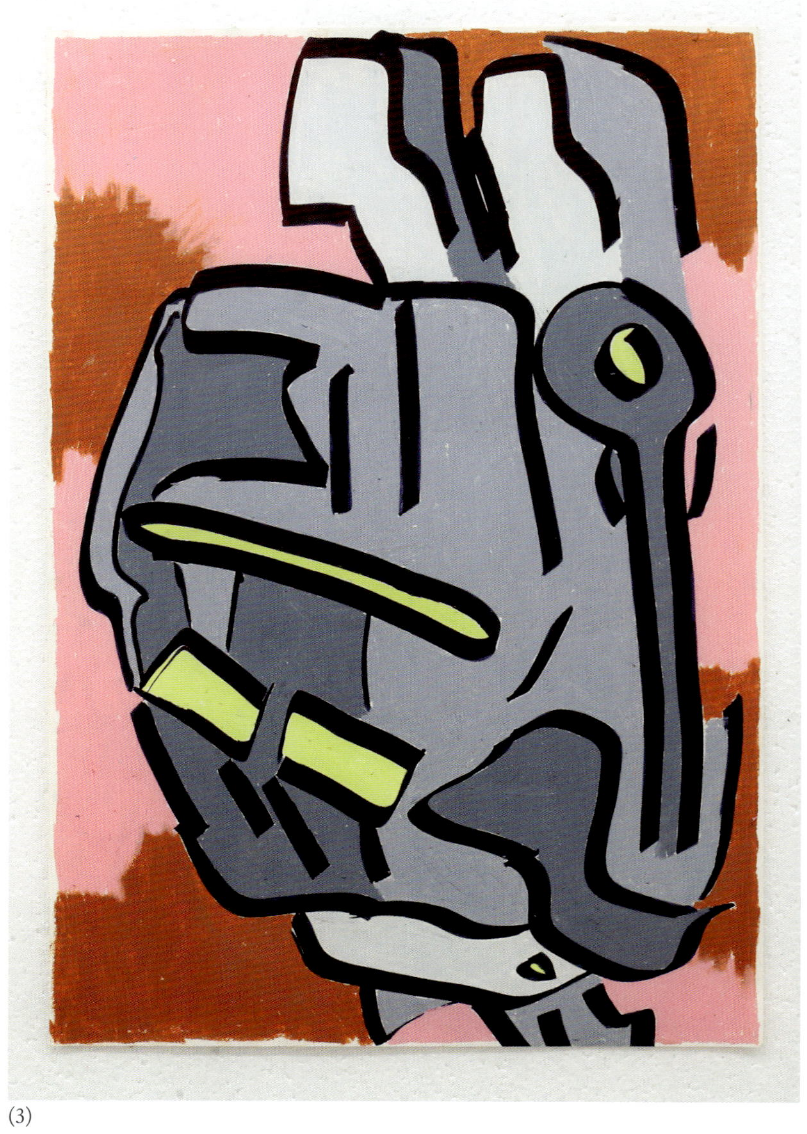

(3)

V

(3) ***TWISTER***
2019, wax crayons and oil pastels on paper, Styrofoam with acrylics, sealing material, Japanese bouncer, 42 × 63 cm

(4) ***SPINBALL***
2019, wax crayons and oil pastels on paper, Styrofoam, Japanese bouncer, glass, 42 × 63 cm

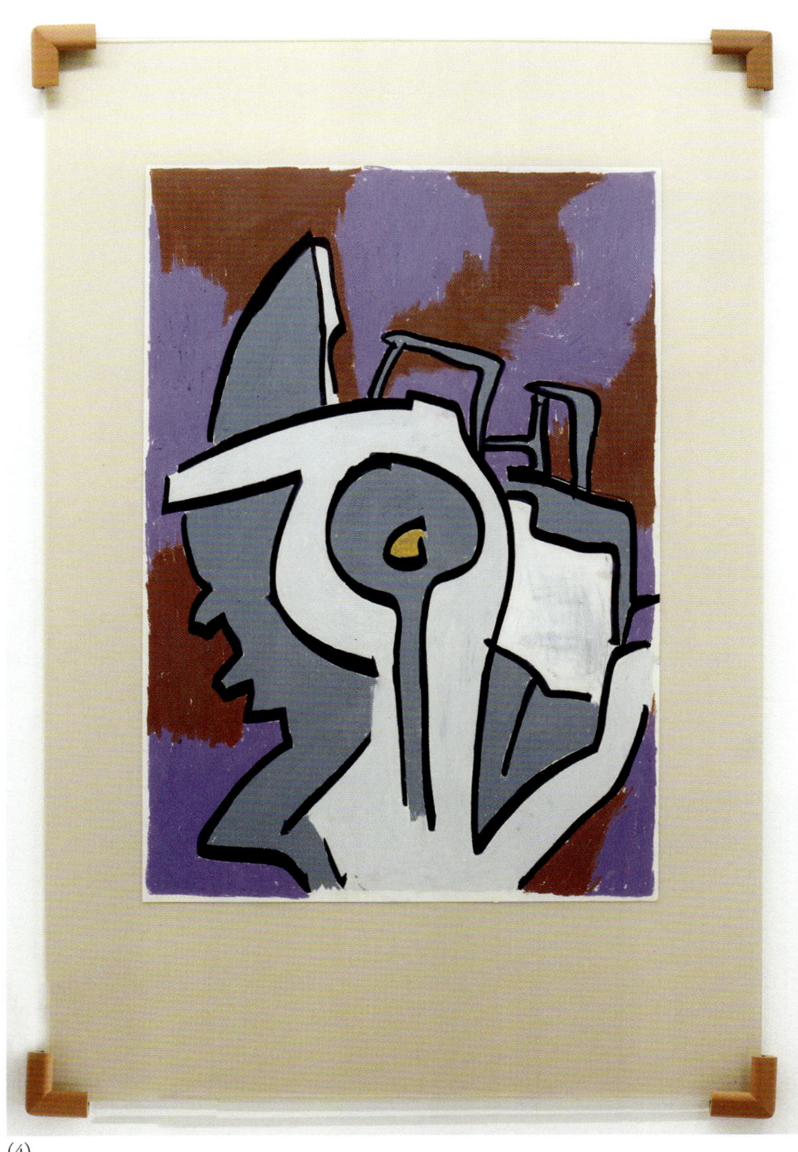

(4)

V

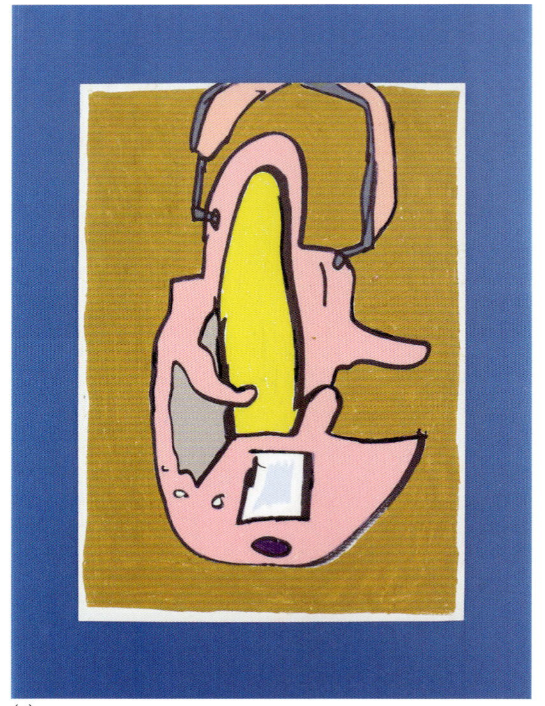

(5)

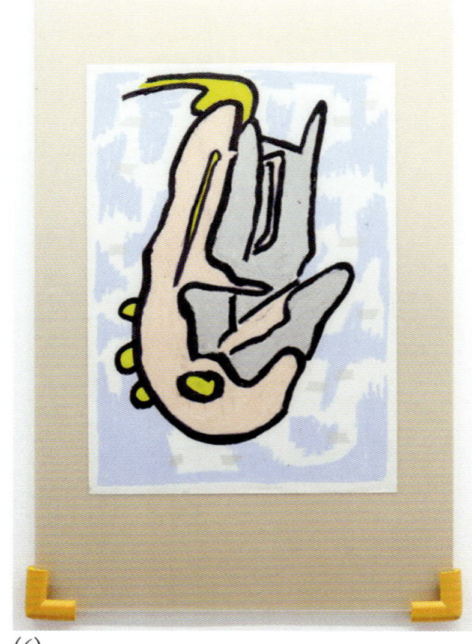

(6)

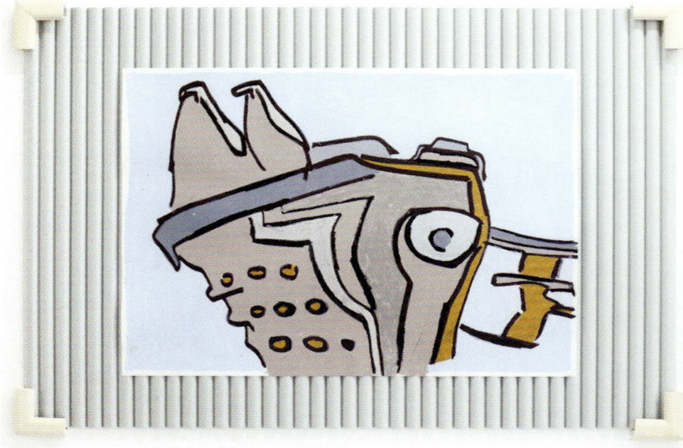

(7)

(9)

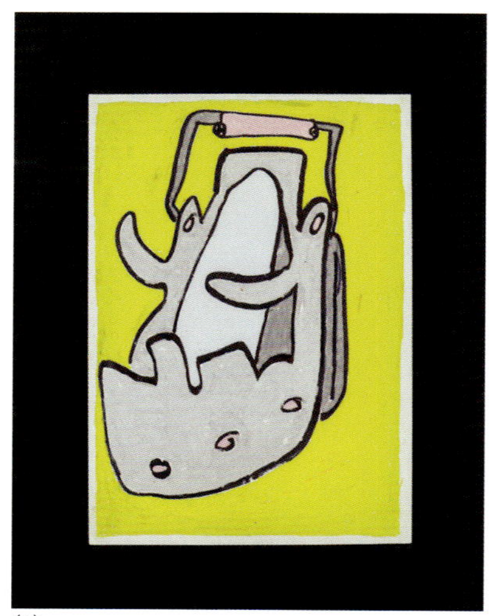

(8)

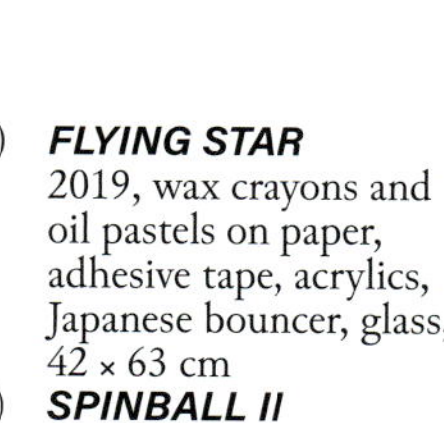

(5) ***FLYING STAR***
2019, wax crayons and oil pastels on paper, adhesive tape, acrylics, Japanese bouncer, glass, 42 × 63 cm

(6) ***SPINBALL II***
2019, wax crayons and oil pastels on paper, Styrofoam, Japanese bouncer, 42 × 63 cm

(7) ***HEADSPIN***
2019, wax crayons and oil pastels on paper, shock absorber mat, Japanese bouncer, 42 × 63 cm

(8) ***FLYING STAR II***
2019, wax crayons and oil pastels on paper, foam rubber, 42 × 63 cm

(9) ***SHAKER***
2019, wax painter and oil pastel on paper, acrylics, glass, 42 × 63 cm

FITNESS. KRAFT UND SCHÖNHEIT

V

INGREDIENTS
Stair Master ②
Stepper ②
Spinning Bike ⑥
Ideologischer Boden ⑦
Kraft und Schönheit ⑩
Grassroots movement ⑪
Kraft und Schönheit, Zeitschr. für vernünft. Leibeszucht ⑫

EN In her exhibition at the Kunstverein Jesteburg, Verena Issel focuses on the possibilities of ideological implementation in the context of practices of self-discovery and self-optimization. The exhibition is given a special local reference through the critical inclusion of questions of reception theory in the context of the neighboring Kunststätte Bossard. This is also reflected in the title of the exhibition—*Kraft und Schönheit* (Strength and Beauty), which quotes the title of a Lebensreform magazine of the same name (*Kraft und Schönheit: Zeitschrift für vernünftige Leibeszucht* [1901–1927], the monthly journal of the Verein für vernünftige Leibeszucht [Association for Responsible Physical Discipline]). Acceleration, growth, and the intensification of innovation are among the fundamental, structuring qualities of our contemporary Western society. As members of such a society, we are all subject to systemic imperatives that demand constant activity, flexibility, and self-optimization, as well as the constant accumulation of capital—be it economic, cultural, social, or physical. The so-called "elevator effect" attested to in the 1980s is increasingly absent in neoliberalism, giving way to multiple "slippery slopes" and everyday competition. In order to maintain the position we have achieved, we must now constantly improve, be even more innovative and creative, always remain flexible and agile. In response, terms like deceleration, resilience, and serenity are booming, along with yoga and mindfulness classes. The esoteric industry also owes its success to the situation described here. The concepts offered are often based on a longing for a different way of "being in the world." But this also gives rise to various beliefs, such as: If you can adopt the right attitude, the world cannot harm you. Precisely because many of these practices promise a "better" life and are designed to help us become more resilient, they all too often conform to the imperatives of optimization and reproduce or manifest—only in a more mindful and pliable guise—the demands placed on the individual. From the past to the present, we can observe time and again how good intentions can also give rise to dangerous ideological potential—how esoteric life support and conspiracy theories, hippiesque and right-wing nationalist ideas can merge.

In her exhibition, Verena Issel also traces these dynamics in the context of Johann Michael Bossard's connection to the Lebensreform movement, his own ideological ideas, and especially with regard to the concepts of mediation theory currently prevalent in the neighboring Kunststätte. The Kunststätte Bossard has been in the news recently because a new museum building is being planned as part of a large federal grant. In the context of the debate about the co-financing from district funds, some voices have been raised criticizing the institution's handling of Johann Michael Bossard's National Socialist past. In particular, a swastika that Johann Michael Bossard had integrated into the floor mosaic directly at the entrance to the so-called "Edda Hall" in 1934 was widely discussed in the media. Although the symbol was clearly visible at the entrance to the room, it was only recently discovered by museum staff. In Germany, there are good reasons why it is forbidden to display a swastika in public without contextualizing it in terms of political education. Symbols like the swastika have to be explained, they have to be clarified, they have to be put into a context. However, when the swastika in the floor mosaic of the Edda Hall was brought to public attention, the Kunststätte Bossard decided to lay a carpet over the symbol. Once again, without leaving any written commentary accessible to everyone. Verena Issel's exhibitions very often respond specifically to the exhibition venue, its surroundings, its perception, its architecture, or its history. For this reason, in the run-up to her exhibition at the KVJ, the artist also visited the Kunststätte, where she also booked a public tour in order to get a more detailed picture of the situation. Unfortunately, it quickly became clear that the Kunststätte Bossard is a classic example of how a backward-looking, obfuscating, whitewashing discourse that avoids confrontation with Nazi crimes has come to dominate the debate on National Socialism.

This practice of dealing with the past is unfortunately far from new in Germany, as in other parts of the world, and is currently reflected in the debate on colonialism. In her exhibition *Fitness. Kraft und Schönheit*, Verena Issel makes clear reference to the mediation practice of the Kunststätte Bossard, which can be seen as exemplary for the way many people deal with the past, and translates her observations and critical, questioning thoughts into multifaceted art: An elaborate floor piece in contemporary garb creates a direct link to Bossard's mosaic in the Edda Hall, while the video work produced especially for the exhibition—in which the costumes of the performers also refer specifically to the Kunststätte—can be read as a translation of how willing society is to sweep things under the rug or not question them closely as long as they appear to us at first glance to be pleasant, pleasing, and harmless in their decorative quality. In Verena Issel's exhibition, the classic instruments of art mediation remain what they are, but in the context described here, they also become exhibits themselves. The reader compiled for the exhibition, which enables visitors to delve deeper into the public debate surrounding the Kunststätte Bossard, the museum-didactic publication *Kraft und Schönheit*, and the detailed text explaining the origin and use of the swastika retain their function as museum educational tools, but at the same time also become part of Verena Issel's installation work: It is exhibited as it should actually be exhibited. Although the local relevance of the exhibition is more than clear, especially in Jesteburg, the theme of the exhibition is unfortunately a general and highly topical one: As a publicly funded institution, it is our duty to inform all visitors transparently and comprehensively, and as vigilant democratic citizens, we must help to ensure that history is critically scrutinized everywhere, especially in public spaces.

☐ ***Isa Hänsel, exhibition text***

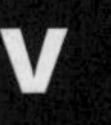

V

DE In ihrer Ausstellung im Kunstverein Jesteburg widmet sich Verena Issel den Möglichkeiten von ideologischen Implementationen im Kontext von Selbstfindungs- und Selbstoptimierungspraktiken. Die Ausstellung erhält einen besonderen Ortsbezug, indem sie rezeptionstheoretische Fragestellungen im Kontext der benachbarten „Kunststätte Bossard" kritisch mit einbezieht. Dies bildet sich auch im Ausstellungstitel ab –„Kraft und Schönheit" zitiert den Titel einer gleichnamigen lebensreformerischen Zeitschrift (*Kraft und Schönheit. Zeitschrift für vernünftige Leibeszucht* [*Monatsschrift des Vereins für vernünftige Leibeszucht*] 1901–1927). Beschleunigung, Wachstum und Innovationsverdichtung gehören zu den grundlegenden, strukturbildenden Qualitäten unserer zeitgenössischen Gesellschaft westlicher Prägung. Als Mitglieder einer solchen Gesellschaft unterliegen wir alle systemimmanenten Imperativen, die von uns permanente Aktivität, Flexibilität und Selbstoptimierung sowie die stetige Anhäufung unseres Kapitals fordern – sei es ökonomisch, kulturell, sozial oder körperlich. Der in den 1980er-Jahren attestierte „Fahrstuhleffekt" kann im Neoliberalismus immer seltener beobachtet werden, ist vielgestaltigen „slippery slopes", dem alltäglichen Wettbewerb gewichen. Um die Position, die wir erreicht haben, zu halten, müssen wir uns heute fortwährend verbessern, noch innovativer und kreativer sein, stets beweglich und agil bleiben. Als Reaktion darauf haben Begriffe wie Entschleunigung, Resilienz und Gelassenheit gemeinsam mit Yoga- und Achtsamkeitskursen Hochkonjunktur. Auch die Esoterikindustrie verdankt ihre Erfolge der beschriebenen Situation. Hinter den angebotenen Konzepten steht nicht selten eine Sehnsucht nach einer anderen Form des „In-der-Welt-Seins". Dabei werden allerdings auch unterschiedliche Glaubenssätze produziert wie: Wenn es dir gelingt, die richtige Haltung einzunehmen, kann dir die Welt nichts mehr anhaben. Gerade weil viele solcher Praktiken ein „besseres" Leben versprechen und uns helfen sollen, resilienter zu werden, fügen sie sich erstaunlich häufig allzu leicht in die Imperative der Optimierung ein und reproduzieren bzw. manifestieren – nur in einem achtsamgeschmeidigeren Gewand – die Anforderungen an die Individuen. Von der Vergangenheit bis heute lässt sich immer wieder beobachten, wie aus den guten Vorsätzen auch ein gefährliches ideologisches Potenzial erwachsen kann – wie es zu einer Vermischung von esoterischer Lebenshilfe und Verschwörungstheorien, von hippieskem und rechtsnationalem Gedankengut kommen kann. Diesen Dynamiken spürt Verena Issel in ihrer Ausstellung auch im Kontext von Johann Michael Bossards Verbindung zur Lebensreformbewegung, seinen eigenen ideologischen Ideen und insbesondere im Hinblick auf die in der benachbarten Kunststätte aktuell vorherrschenden vermittlungstheoretischen Konzepte nach. Jüngst war die Kunststätte Bossard in die Medien geraten, weil im Zuge eines großen Zuschusses aus Bundesmitteln ein musealer Neubau geplant werden soll. Im Kontext der Debatte um die Co-Finanzierung aus Mitteln des Landkreises wurden auch einige Stimmen laut, die den Umgang der Institution mit der nationalsozialistischen Vergangenheit Johann Michael Bossards in den Mittelpunkt der Kritik zogen. Insbesondere ein Hakenkreuz, welches Johann Michael Bossard 1934 in das Bodenmosaik direkt am Eingang des sogenannten Edda-Saals eingearbeitet hatte, wurde medial breit diskutiert. Wenngleich das Symbol deutlich am Eingang des Raumes zu sehen war, sei es von Angestellten des Museums erst jüngst entdeckt worden. In Deutschland ist es aus guten Gründen verboten, ein Hakenkreuz öffentlich zu zeigen, ohne es im Sinne der politischen Bildung zu kontextualisieren. Symbole wie das Hakenkreuz müssen erklärt werden, sie müssen erläutert werden, sie müssen in einen Zusammenhang gestellt werden. Als das Hakenkreuz im Bodenmosaik des Edda-Saals in den öffentlichen Fokus gerückt wurde, entschied man sich bei der Kunststätte Bossard allerdings dafür, einen Teppich über das Symbol zu legen. Erneut, ohne einen erläuternden Kommentar schriftlich und für jedermann zugänglich zu hinterlassen.
Mit ihren Ausstellungen reagiert Verena Issel sehr oft spezifisch auf den Ausstellungsort, sein Umfeld, seine Wahrnehmung, seine Architektur oder seine Geschichte. Aus diesem Grund stattete die Künstlerin im Vorfeld ihrer Ausstellung im KVJ auch der Kunststätte einen Besuch ab, bei dem sie auch eine öffentliche Führung buchte, um sich ein genaueres Bild der Situation zu verschaffen. Leider wurde sehr schnell deutlich, dass die Kunststätte Bossard als ein klassisches Beispiel dient – dafür, wie sich ein rückwärtsgewandter, verschweigender, schönfärberischer und einer Auseinandersetzung mit den NS-Verbrechen aus dem Weg gehender Diskurs über die Auseinandersetzung mit dem Nationalsozialismus gelegt hat. Diese Praxis im Umgang mit der Vergangenheit ist in Deutschland, wie auch in anderen Teilen der Welt, leider alles andere als neu, was sich aktuell auch in der Kolonialismusdebatte abbildet.
In ihrer Ausstellung *Fitness. Kraft und Schönheit* nimmt Verena Issel deutlich Bezug auf die Vermittlungspraxis der Kunststätte Bossard, die als exemplarisch für den Umgang vieler Menschen mit der Vergangenheit gesehen werden kann, und übersetzt ihre Beobachtungen sowie kritische, hinterfragende Gedanken in vielgestaltige Kunst: Eine aufwendige Bodenarbeit stellt in zeitgenössischer Gewandung einen direkten Zusammenhang zu Bossards Mosaik im Edda-Saal her, die extra für die Ausstellung produzierte Videoarbeit – in welcher die Kostüme der Darsteller*innen ebenfalls konkret auf die Kunststätte verweisen – kann als Übersetzung dafür gelesen werden, wie bereit die Gesellschaft ist, Dinge unter den Teppich zu kehren oder nicht genau zu hinterfragen, solange sie uns auf den ersten Blick gefällig, angenehm und in ihrer dekorativen Qualität auch harmlos erscheinen. Klassische Instrumente der Kunstvermittlung bleiben in Verena Issels Ausstellung zwar, was sie sind, werden aber gerade im geschilderten Kontext auch selbst zu Ausstellungsstücken: Der für die Ausstellung zusammengestellte Reader, welcher Besucher*innen ermöglicht, sich tiefergehend mit der öffentlichen Debatte um die Kunststätte Bossard auseinanderzusetzen, die museumsdidaktisch aufgearbeitete Publikation *Kraft und Schönheit* sowie auch der ausführliche Text, welcher die Herkunft und Verwendung des Hakenkreuzes erklärt, behalten zwar ihre Funktion als museumspädagogische Instrumente, werden aber zeitgleich auch zum Teil von Verena Issels installativer Arbeit: Es wird ausgestellt, wie eigentlich ausgestellt werden sollte. Wenngleich der Ortsbezug der Ausstellung gerade in Jesteburg mehr als deutlich wird, ist das Thema der Ausstellung leider ein allgemeines und hochaktuelles: Als öffentlich finanzierte Institution ist es Pflicht, alle Besucher*innen transparent und umfassend zu informieren, als wache demokratische Staatsbürger müssen wir dazu beitragen, dass Geschichte überall und auch insbesondere im öffentlichen Raum kritisch hinterfragt wird.

□ ***Isa Hänsel, Ausstellungstext***

V

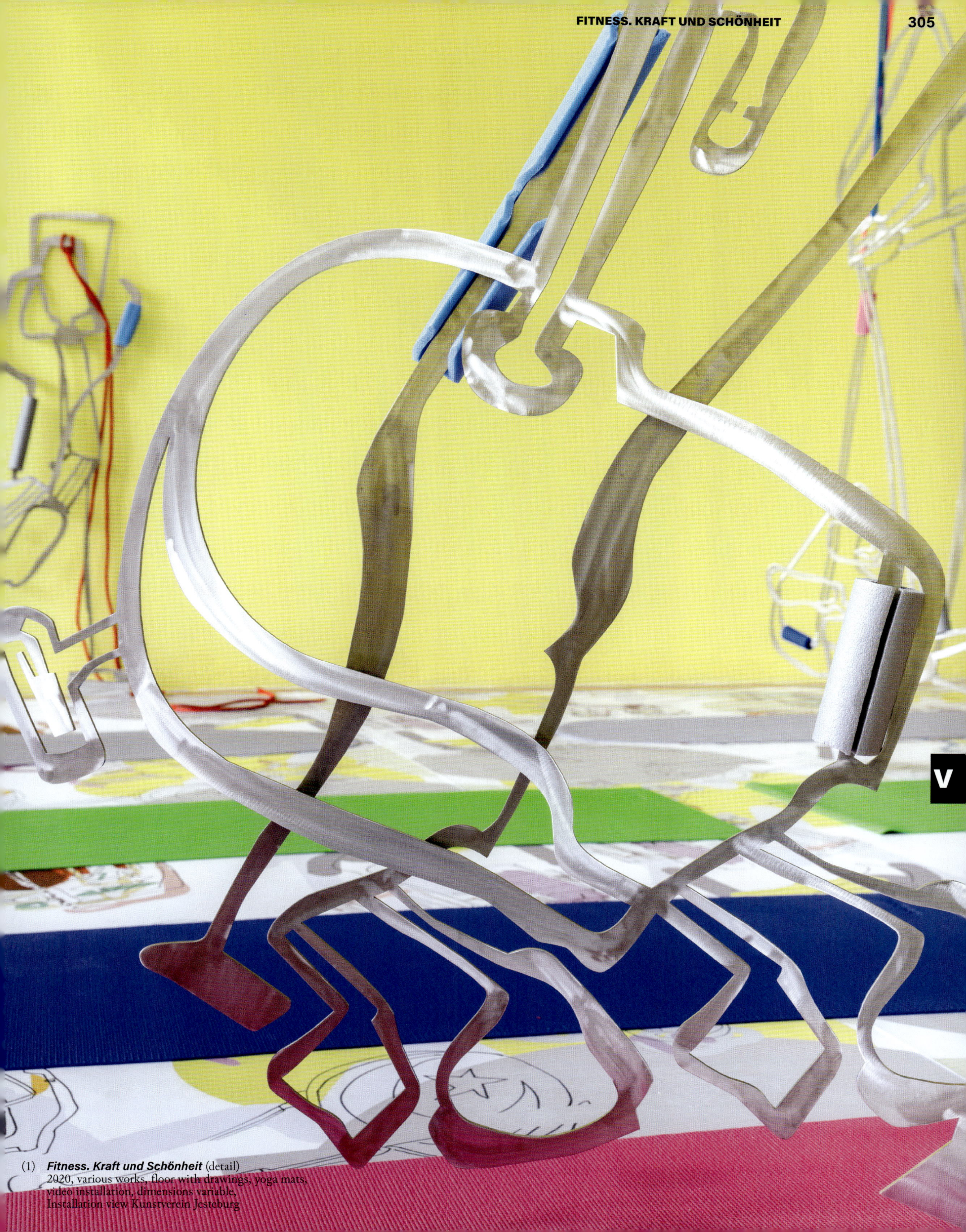

(1) ***Fitness. Kraft und Schönheit*** (detail)
2020, various works, floor with drawings, yoga mats, video installation, dimensions variable, Installation view Kunstverein Jesteburg

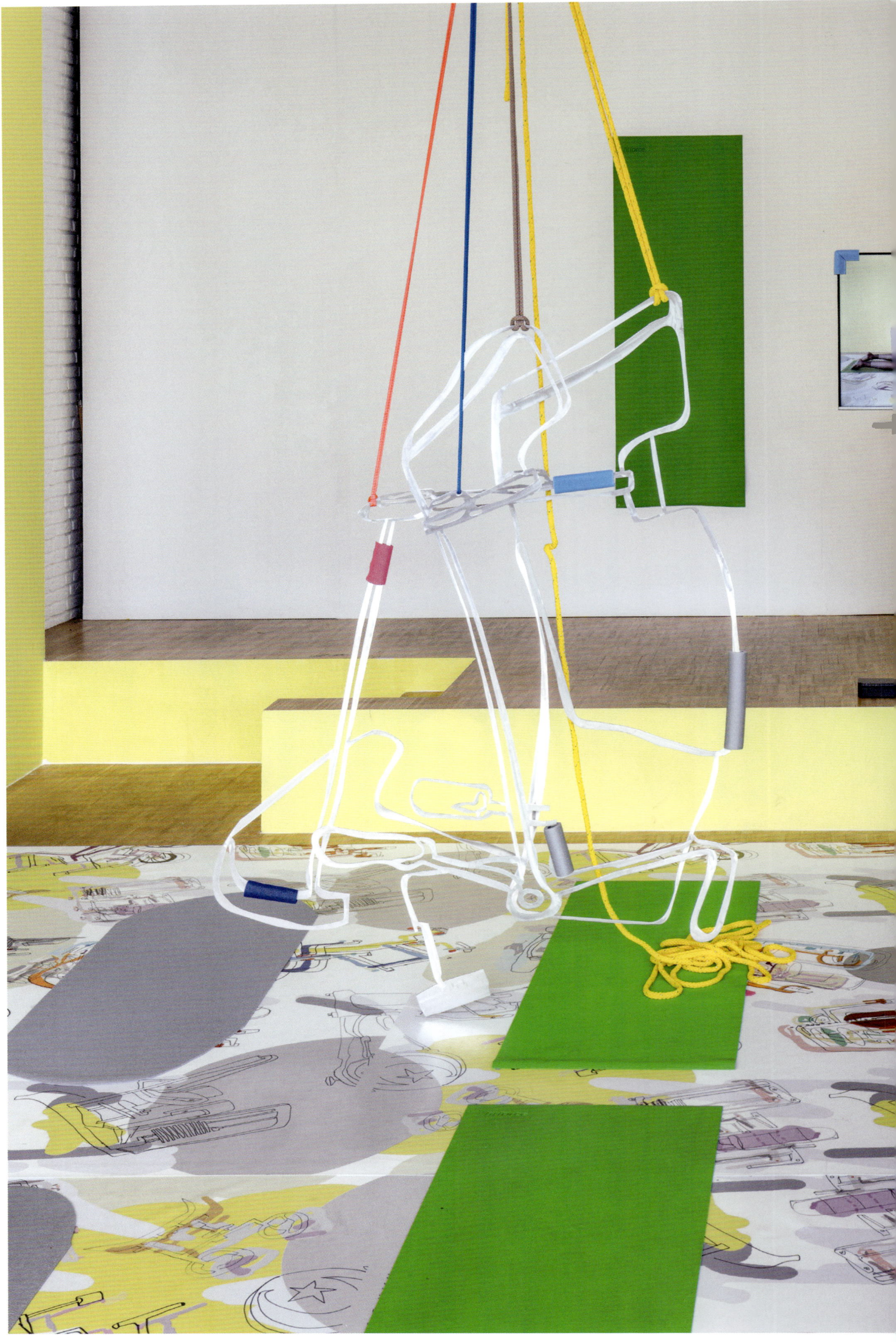

V

(2) ***Fitness. Kraft und Schönheit***
2020, various works, floor with drawings, yoga mats, video installation, dimensions variable,
(Hanging object on the left) ***Stair Master***
2021, ropes, stainless steel with ship ropes and foam, 186 × 150 cm,
(Object on the right) ***Stepper***
2020, ropes, stainless steel with ship ropes and foam, 186 × 150 cm,
Installation view Kunstverein Jesteburg

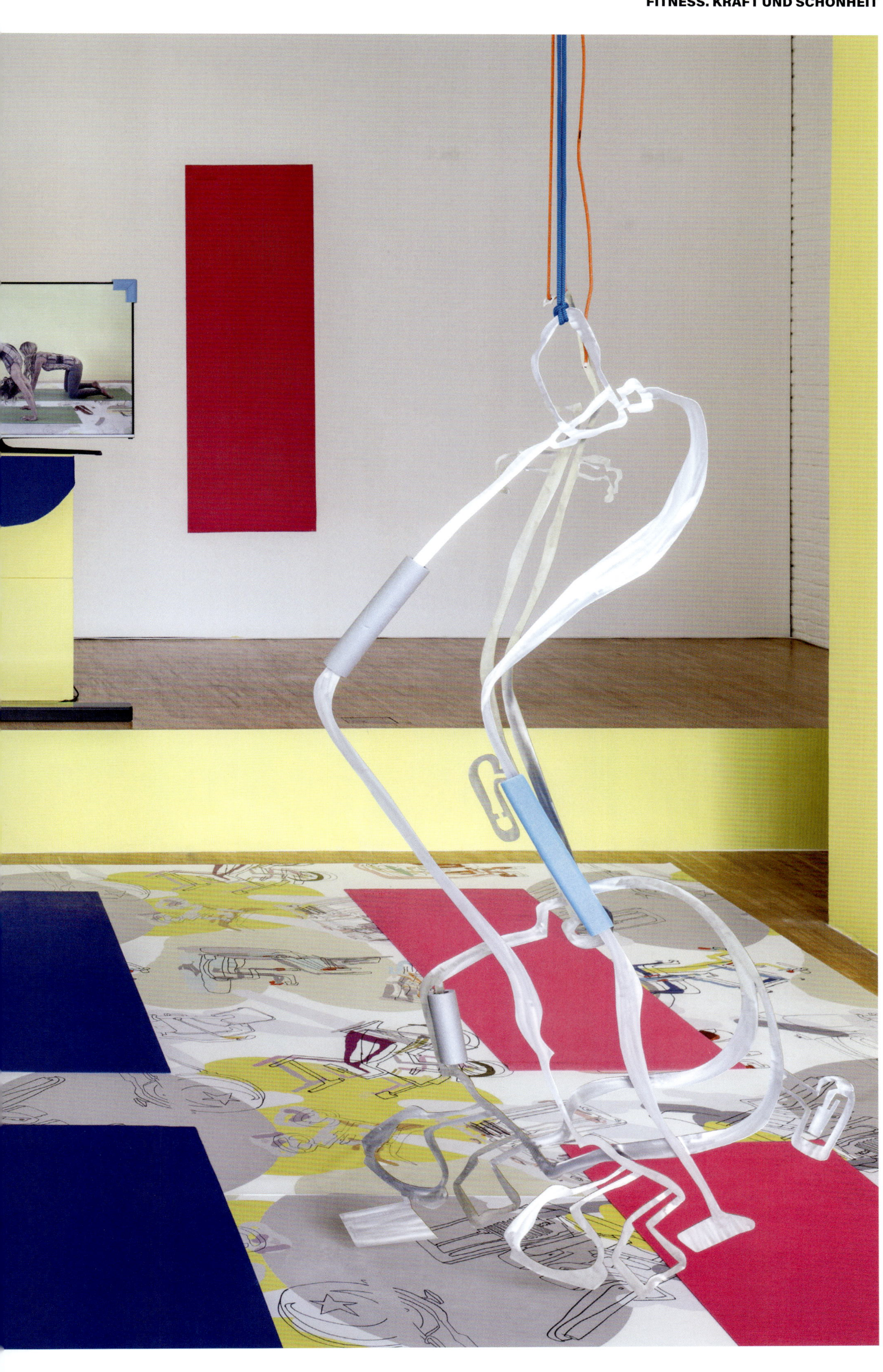

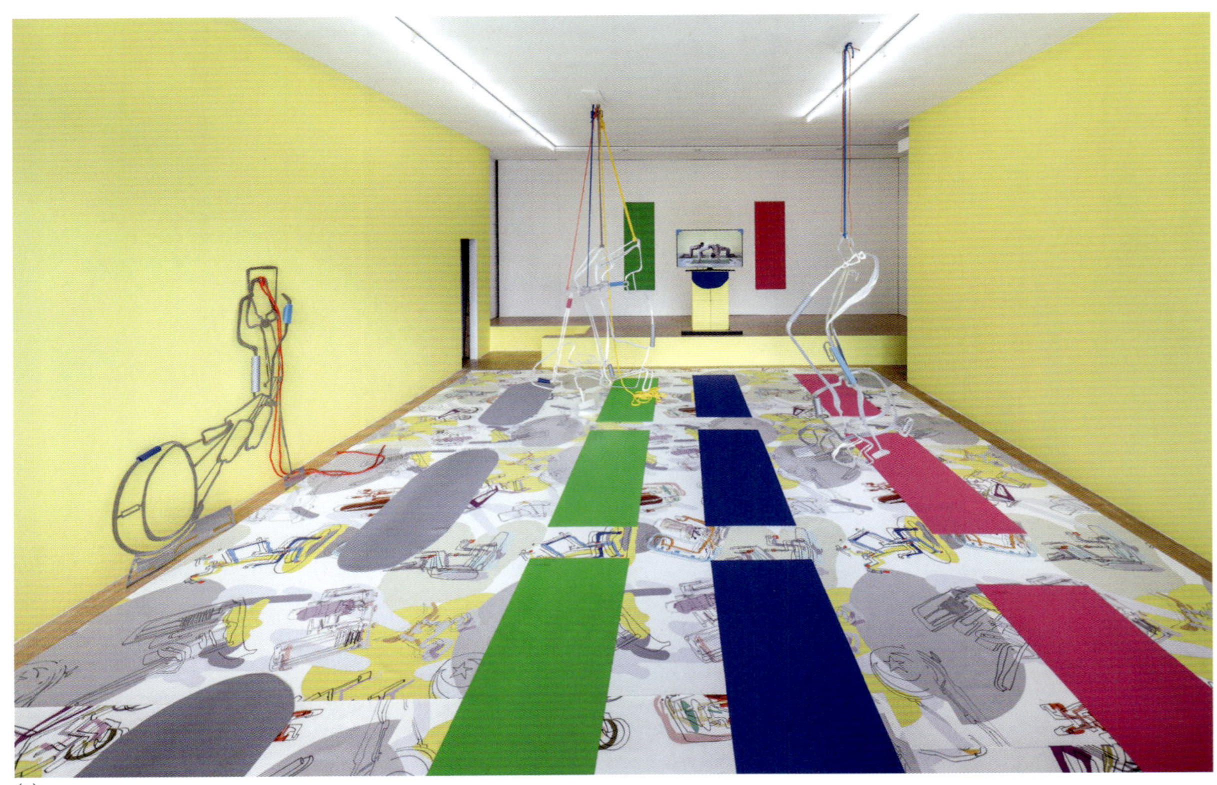
(3)

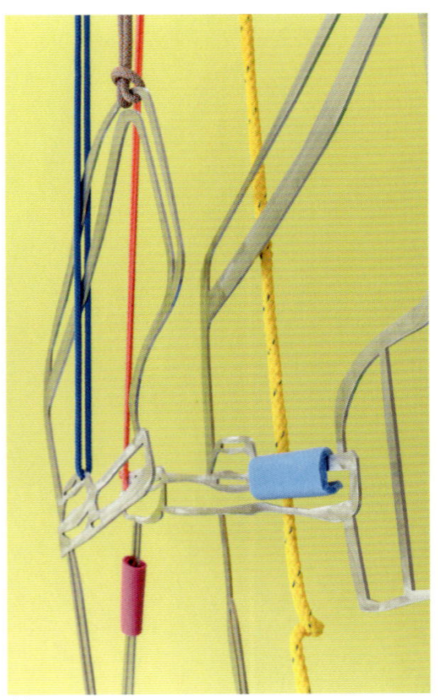
(4)

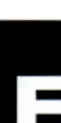
E

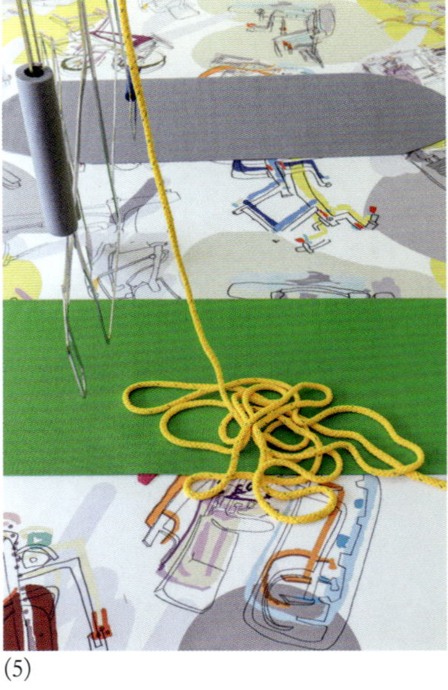
(5)

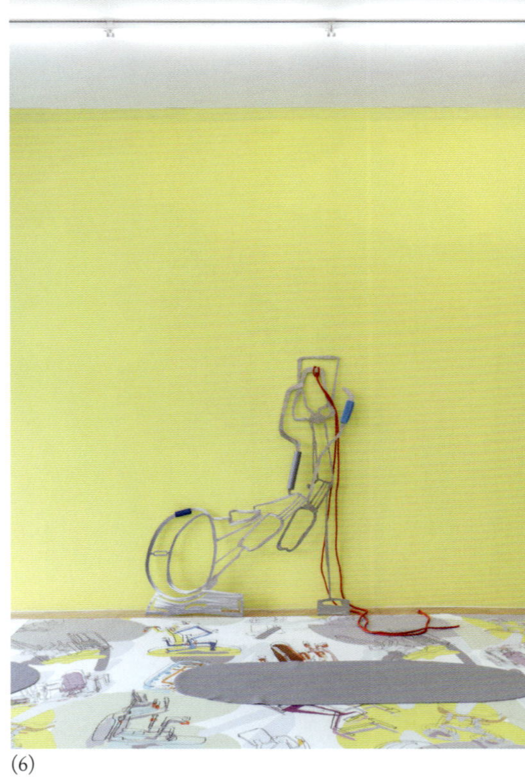
(6)

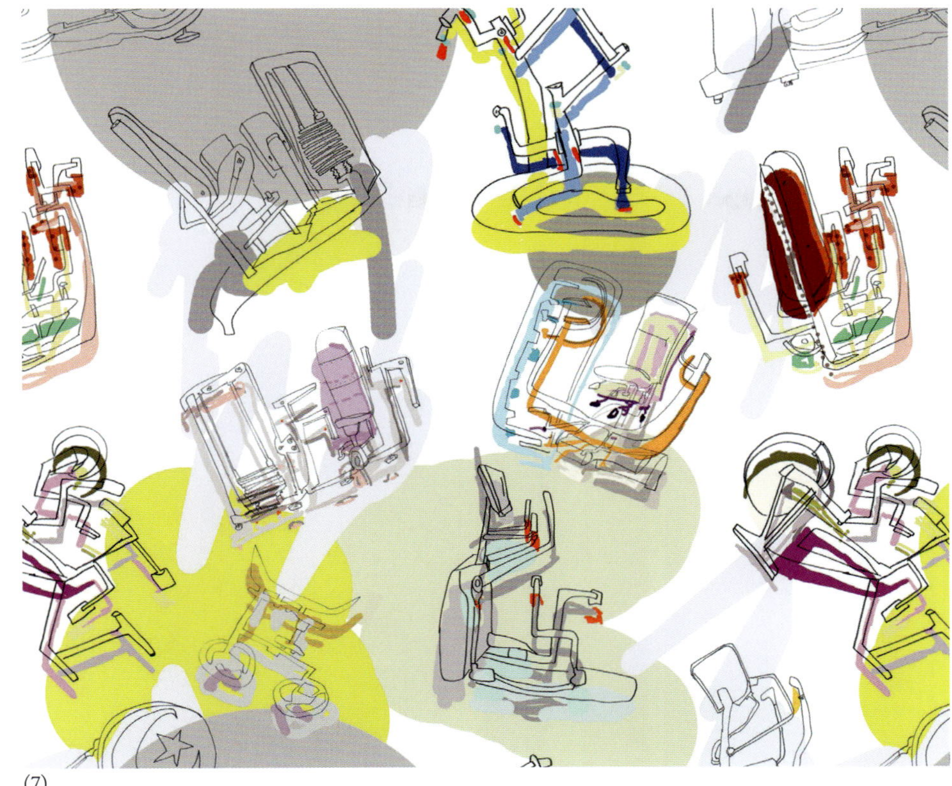

(7)

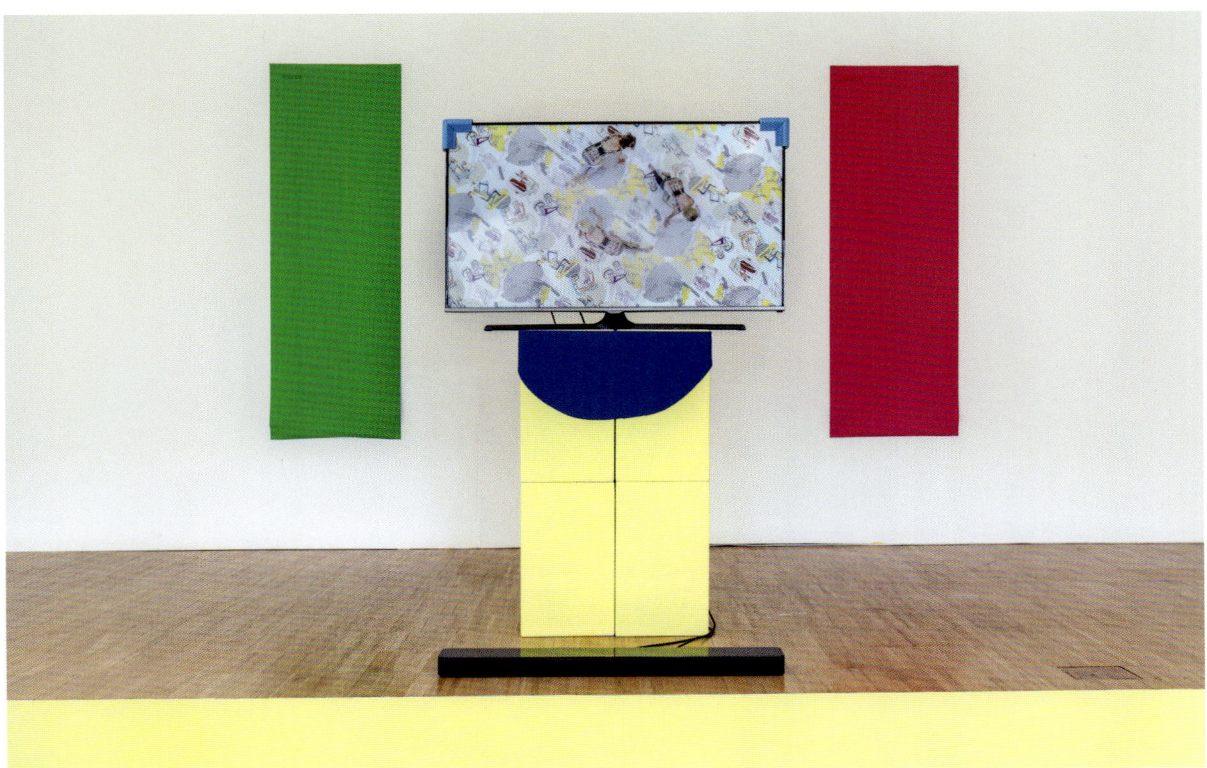

(8)

(3) ***Fitness. Kraft und Schönheit*** 2020, various works, floor with drawings, yoga mats, video installation, dimensions variable, Installation view Kunstverein Jesteburg

(4) ***Fitness. Kraft und Schönheit*** (detail) 2020, Installation view Kunstverein Jesteburg

(5) ***Fitness. Kraft und Schönheit*** (detail) 2020, Installation view Kunstverein Jesteburg

(6) ***Spinning Bike*** 2020, ropes, stainless steel with ship ropes and foam, 186 × 150 cm, Installation view Kunstverein Jesteburg

(7) ***Fitness. Kraft und Schönheit*** (detail) 2020, drawings on the floor in reaction to the local Kunststätte Bossard, a museum in which a swastika is still found on the floor mosaic. At the time of this exhibition, the government funded museum merely covered the nazi symbol with a carpet, without any further comments, Installation view Kunstverein Jesteburg

(8) ***Fitness. Kraft und Schönheit*** (detail) 2020, Video installation, Installation view Kunstverein Jesteburg

(9) ***Costume from video "Kraft und Schönheit"***
gymnast body suit with a printed photo of Kunststätte Bossard, a local museum in which a swastika is still found on the floor mosaic. At the time of this exhibition, the government funded museum merely covered the nazi symbol with a carpet, without any further comments

(10) ***Film stills from "Kraft und Schönheit"***
24:43 min, digital video, 2020, Concept, direction, editing, stage design and casting: Verena Issel, Concept, costume design, speaker, casting and production: Isa Maschewski, Camera, editing, image editing, animation, title design and color correction: David Schultz, Assistant director and Mask: Carmen Scholle Actors: Verena Issel, Ray Juster, Ronny M., Elmas Şenol, Rosa Thiemer, Texts: MANIFESTO OF POST-FUTURISM, Franco Berardi aka Bifo. Translation: Gerald Raunig, Verena Issel: Meditation collage, Music: Creative Commons Music: Yoga Relaxation Meditation Athmosphere Background Music 025 Created as part of the exhibition *Verena Issel: Fitness. Kraft und Schönheit* at the Kunstverein Jesteburg e.V., 2020, Funded by the MWK Niedersachsen

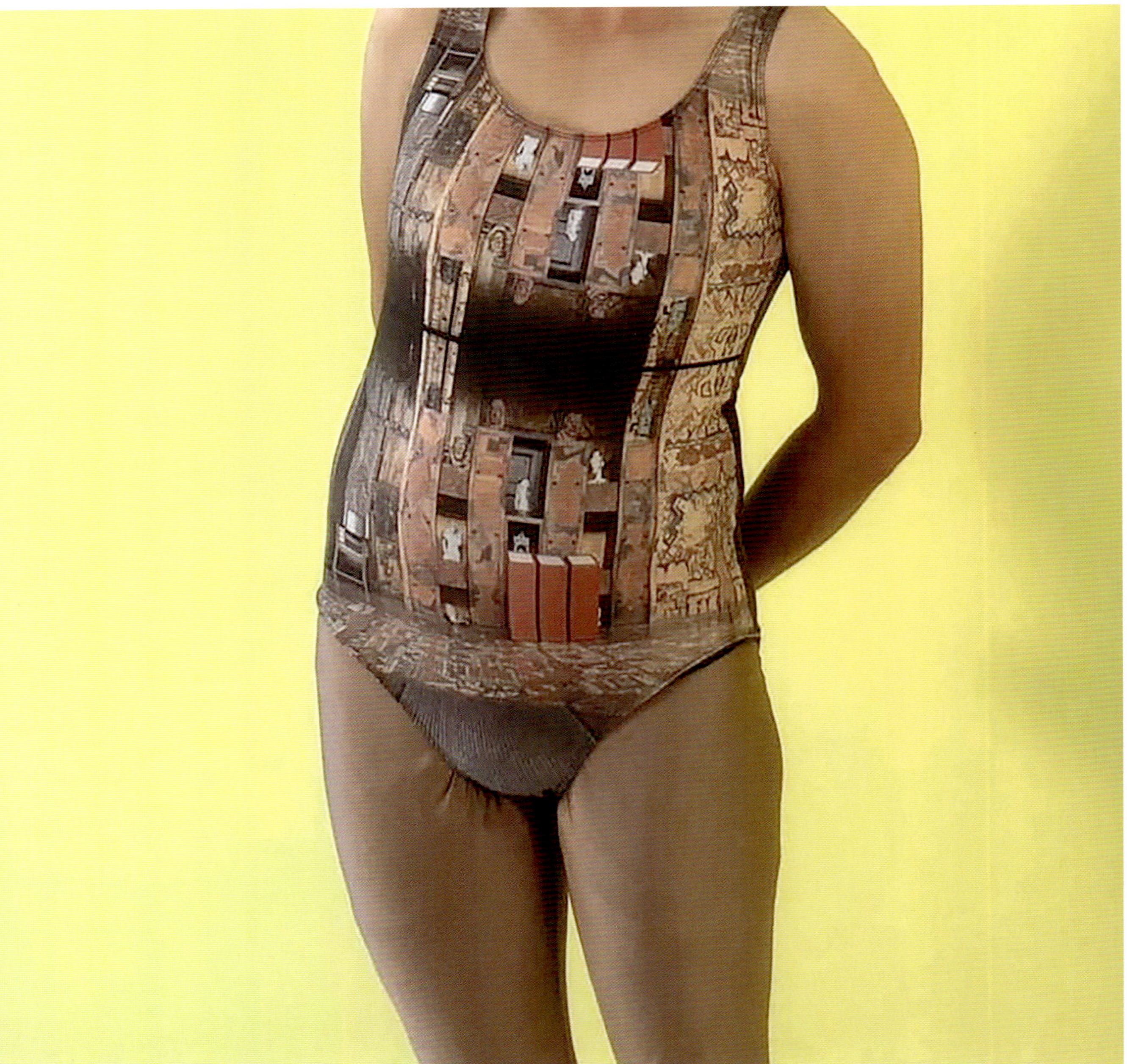

(9)

E

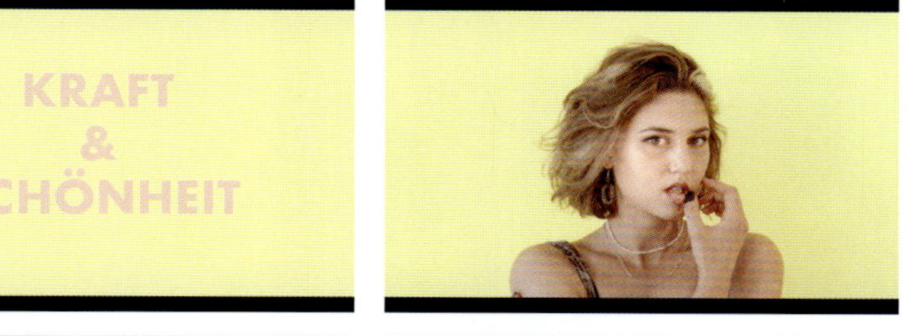

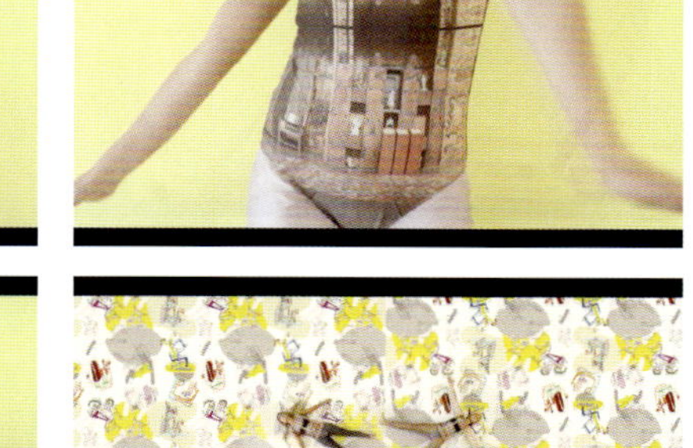

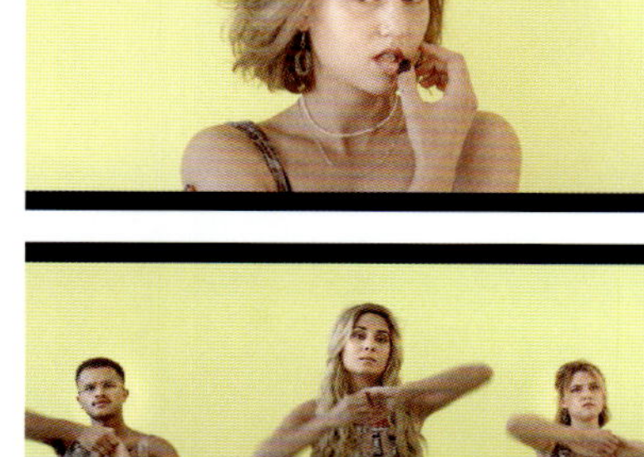

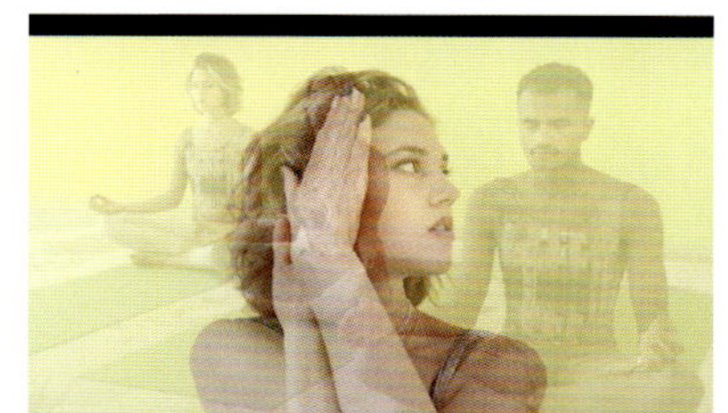

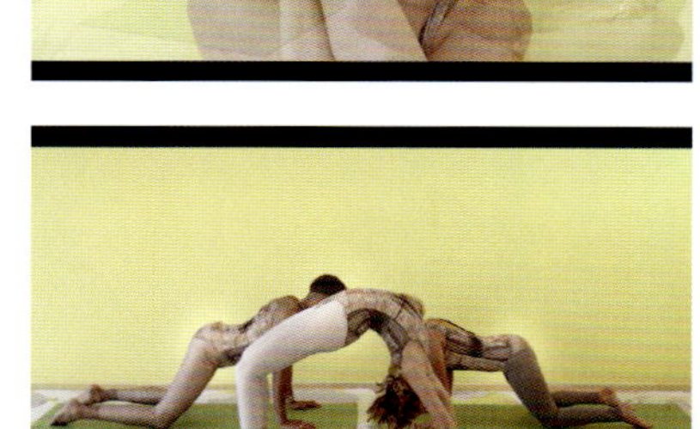

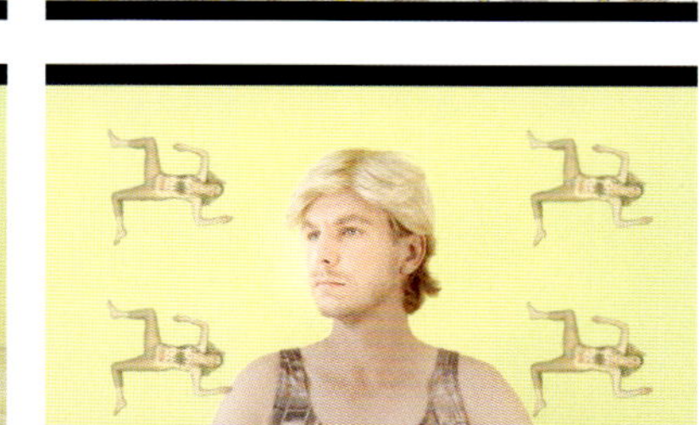

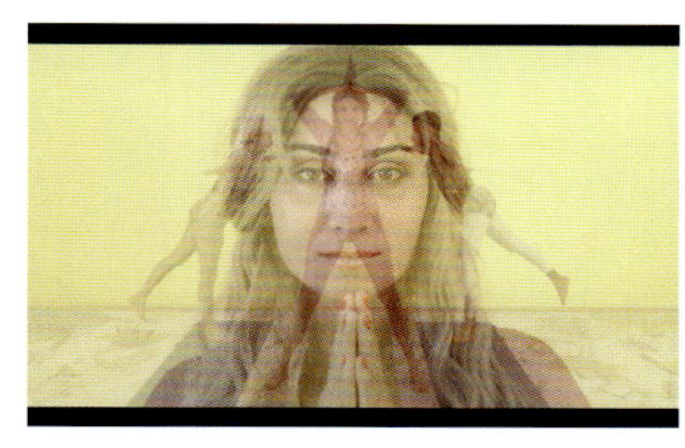

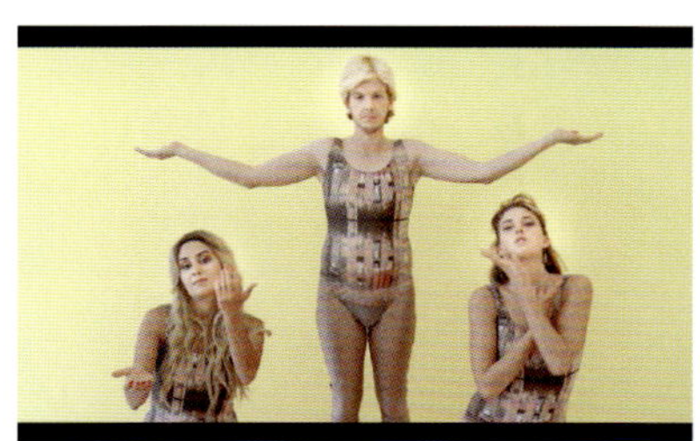

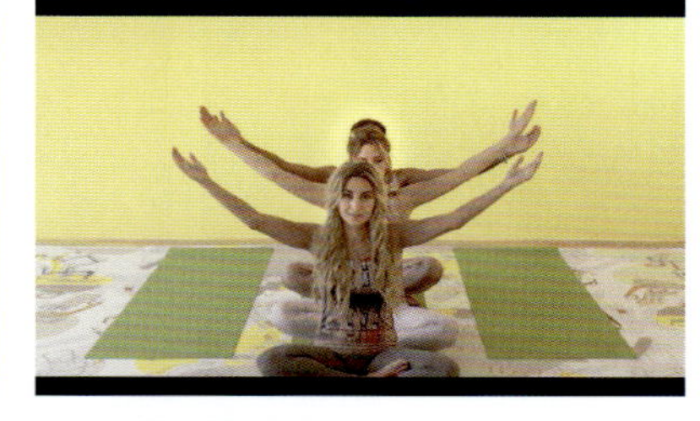

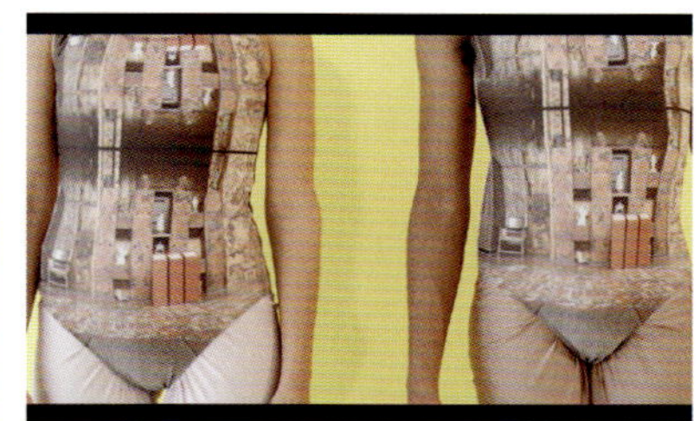

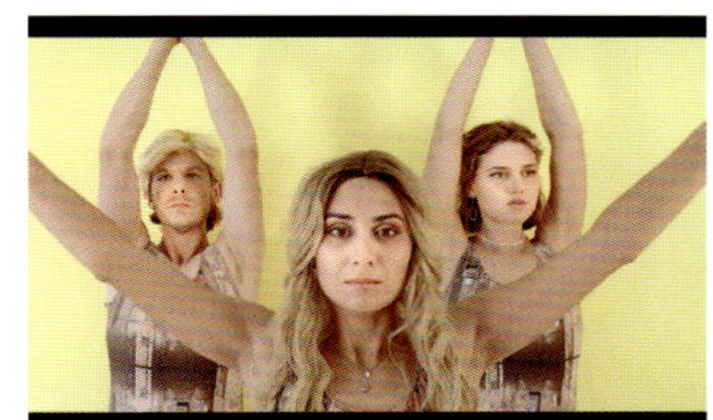

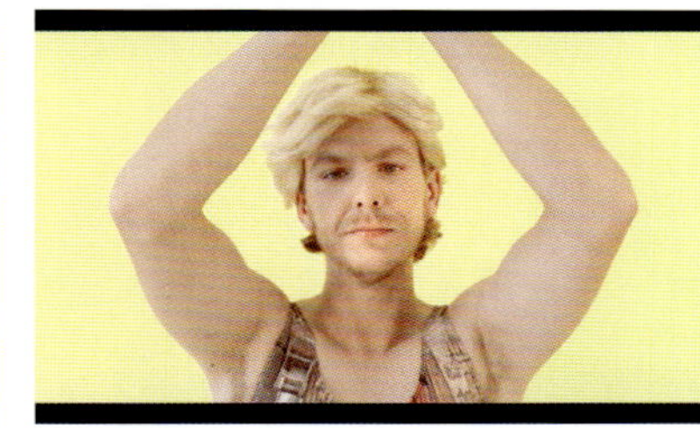

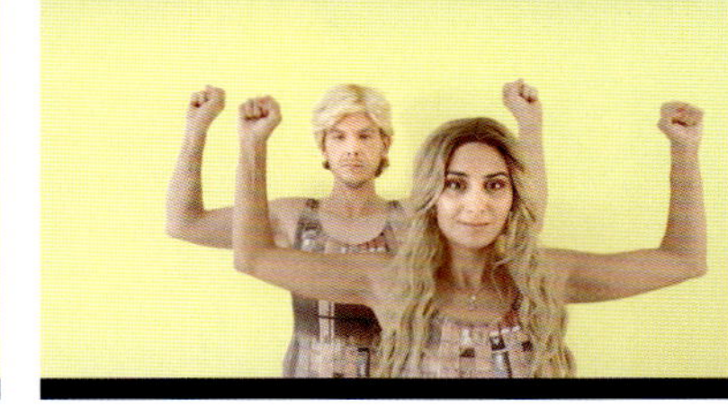

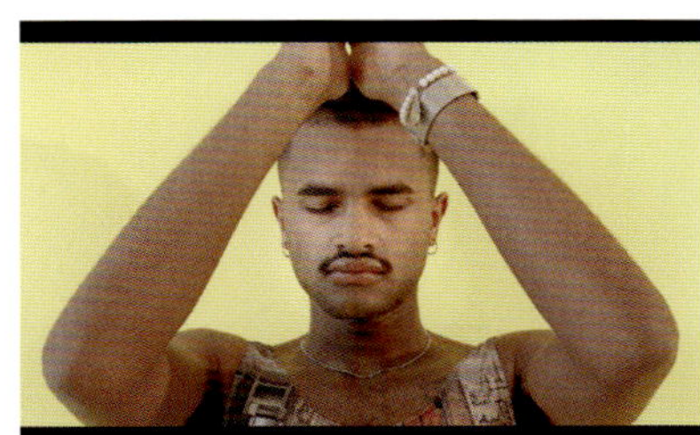

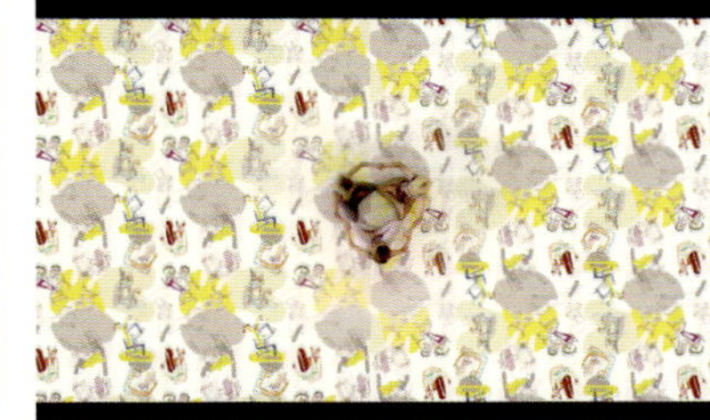

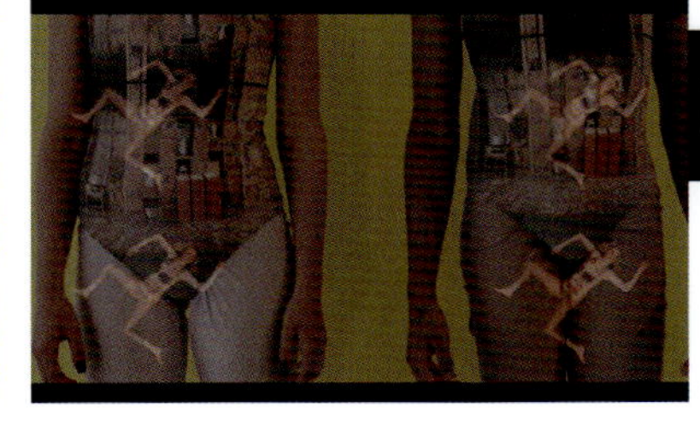

(10)

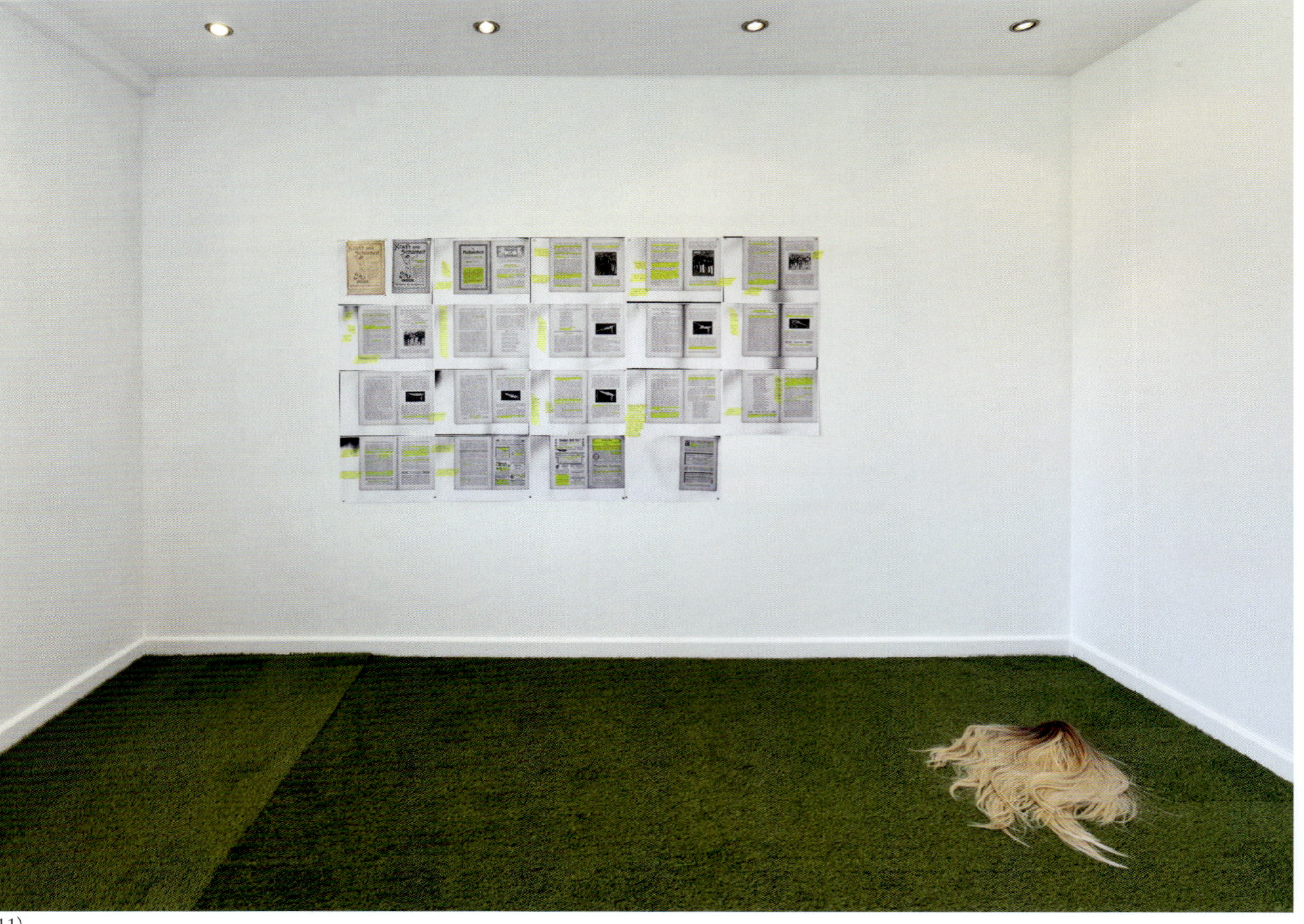

(11)

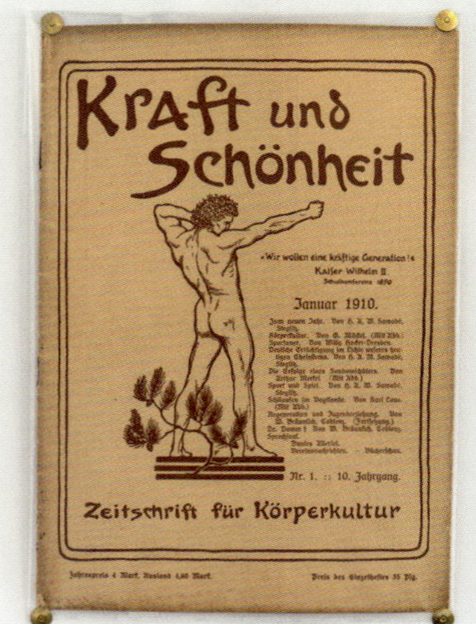

(12)

(11) ***Grassroots movement***
2020, artificial turf, blonde wig, original editions of the proto-fascist life reform magazine “Kraft und Schönheit” from 1909/10 including reading copies and newspaper articles on the Bossard art site and information texts on political symbols

(12) ***Kraft und Schönheit: Zeitschr. für vernünft. Leibeszucht***
Hier präsentierte Ausgaben erschienen Dez. 1909/Januar 1910 [1. Ausgabe]1901/02; 2.1902/03; 3.1903 – 26.1927; damit Ersch. eingest. Berlin: Kraft und Schönheit, Installation view Kunstverein Jesteburg, 2020

LOB DES LERNENS

E

INGREDIENTS
Dictator's eye ①②
Dictator's eye 2 ①②
Dictator's nose ①②
Dictator's mouth ①②
Dictator's ear ①②
Political cleansing ①②

EN During a residency at ZARYA Center for Contemporary Art in Vladivostok, Russia, Verena Issel observed the disappearance of numerous Soviet-era murals, reliefs, and mosaics that once adorned buildings in the city. Symbols of outdated ideology, these artworks are either covered with concrete, chipped off walls, or replaced by new images, often from commercial advertising contexts. For many Russians, especially in Vladivostok, the Soviet-era murals symbolize a dreadful time, evoking memories of harsh experiences such as labor camps, repression, and deprivation.

Attempting to consider these murals as artworks detached from propaganda and politics raises intriguing questions: To what extent is art ever detached from political interests? Is it "allowed" to appreciate such art? What about the autonomy of art today? Wasn't abstract expressionism also entirely funded as a propaganda tool by the USA, and how do we perceive it nowadays? Is art merely a trend that can be reinterpreted, forgotten, or destroyed based on the spirit of the times?

For her exhibition *Lob des Lernens* at the Oel-Früh Gallery, borrowing the title from Bertolt Brecht's worker poem of the same name, Verena Issel molded plaster parts from Soviet wall reliefs in Vladivostok. She combined these with mosaic-like elements crafted from Chinese foam rubber, a very contemporary and short-lived material. A Soviet mural is abstractly recreated and inserted into a diorama-like glass case, resembling a plastic mammoth from a bygone era, now preserved behind glass. Or is it more of a storefront display for a luxury boutique? Is everything now just decoration and shopping? However, from the front, the installation appears to be bricked up again, this time with cleaning sponges. New times are coming, and humans need new images.

The artist is currently grappling with a significant internal struggle, contemplating whether to accept a well-funded fellowship from a privately funded foundation with strong neoliberal connotations, despite financial concerns. Where does freedom begin, and where does it end?

☐ ***Frank Breker, 2018***

E

DE Während eines Arbeitsstipendiums bei ZARYA Center for Contemporary Art in Vladivostok, Russland, stellte Verena Issel fest, dass derzeit extrem viele der bislang die Gebäude dort zierenden Wandbilder, Reliefs und Mosaike aus der Sowjetzeit verschwinden. Als Propagandamittel einer überholten Ideologie werden sie mit Beton überdeckt, von den Wänden abgeschlagen oder aber durch neue Bilder, häufig aus dem kommerziellen Werbekontext, ersetzt.
Die Wandbilder aus der Sowjetzeit sind für nicht wenige Menschen in Russland Symbole für eine schreckliche Zeit, sie wecken teilweise Erinnerungen an grausame Erfahrungen wie Straflager, Unterdrückungen und Entbehrungen.
Beim Versuch, die Wandbilder losgelöst von Propaganda und Politik als Kunstwerke zu betrachten, stellen sich hier eine Reihe interessanter Fragen: Inwieweit ist Kunst jemals losgelöst von politischen Interessen? Darf man „so was" gut finden? Was ist heutzutage mit der Autonomie der Kunst? War der abstrakte Expressionismus nicht auch komplett als Propagandainstrument finanziert von den USA – und was hält man jetzt aktuell davon? Ist Kunst lediglich eine Mode und kann je nach Zeitgeist einfach anders gedeutet, vergessen oder vernichtet werden?
Für ihre Ausstellung *Lob des Lernens* in der Galerie Oehl-Früh, deren Titel dem gleichnamigen Arbeitergedicht Bertolt Brechts entlehnt ist, formte Verena Issel Gipsteile von Sowjetwandreliefs in Vladivostok ab und kombinierte diese mit mosaikhaften Versatzstücken, gefertigt aus chinesischem Schaumgummi, einem sehr zeitgenössischen und kurzlebigen Material. Ein Sowjetwandbild wird abstrakt nachempfunden und in einen dioramenähnlichen Glaskasten eingefügt; gleich einem ausgestorbenen Mammut aus Plastik ist es nun als Zeuge einer vergangenen Zeit hinter Glas zu betrachten. Oder geht es hier eher um eine Schaufenstergestaltung für eine Luxusboutique? Ist alles nur noch Dekoration und Shopping? Von vorne scheint die Installation jedoch schon wieder zugemauert zu werden, und zwar von Reinigungsschwämmen ... Neue Zeiten brechen an, neue Bilder braucht der Mensch?
Die Künstlerin muss derzeit stark mit sich selbst kämpfen, ob sie ein gut dotiertes Stipendium von einer als sehr neoliberal konnotierten privaten Stiftung trotz Geldsorgen ablehnt oder doch annimmt.
Wo fängt Freiheit an, und wo hört sie auf?

□ ***Frank Breker, 2018***

E

E

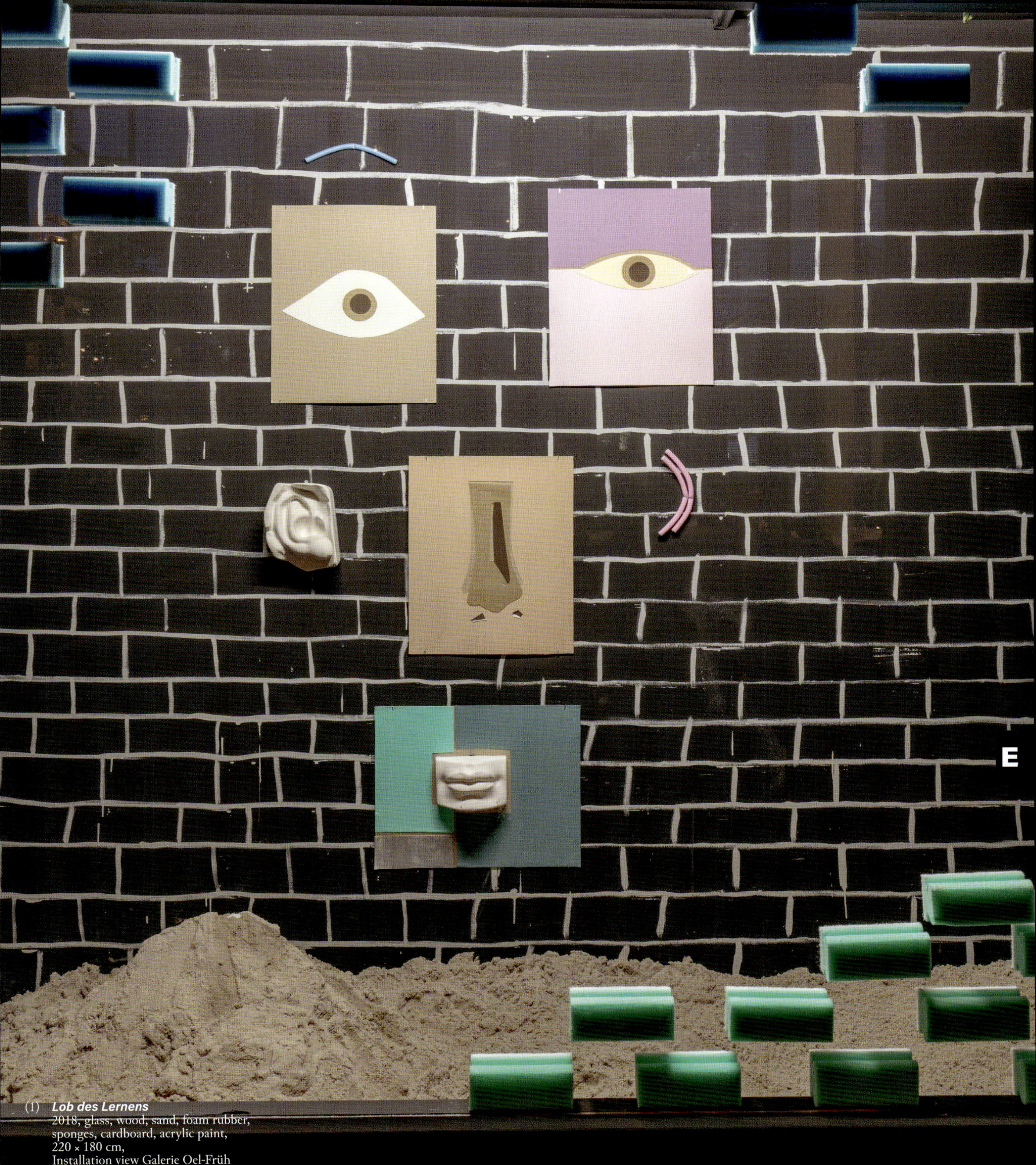

E

(1) ***Lob des Lernens***
2018, glass, wood, sand, foam rubber, sponges, cardboard, acrylic paint, 220 × 180 cm,
Installation view Galerie Oel-Früh

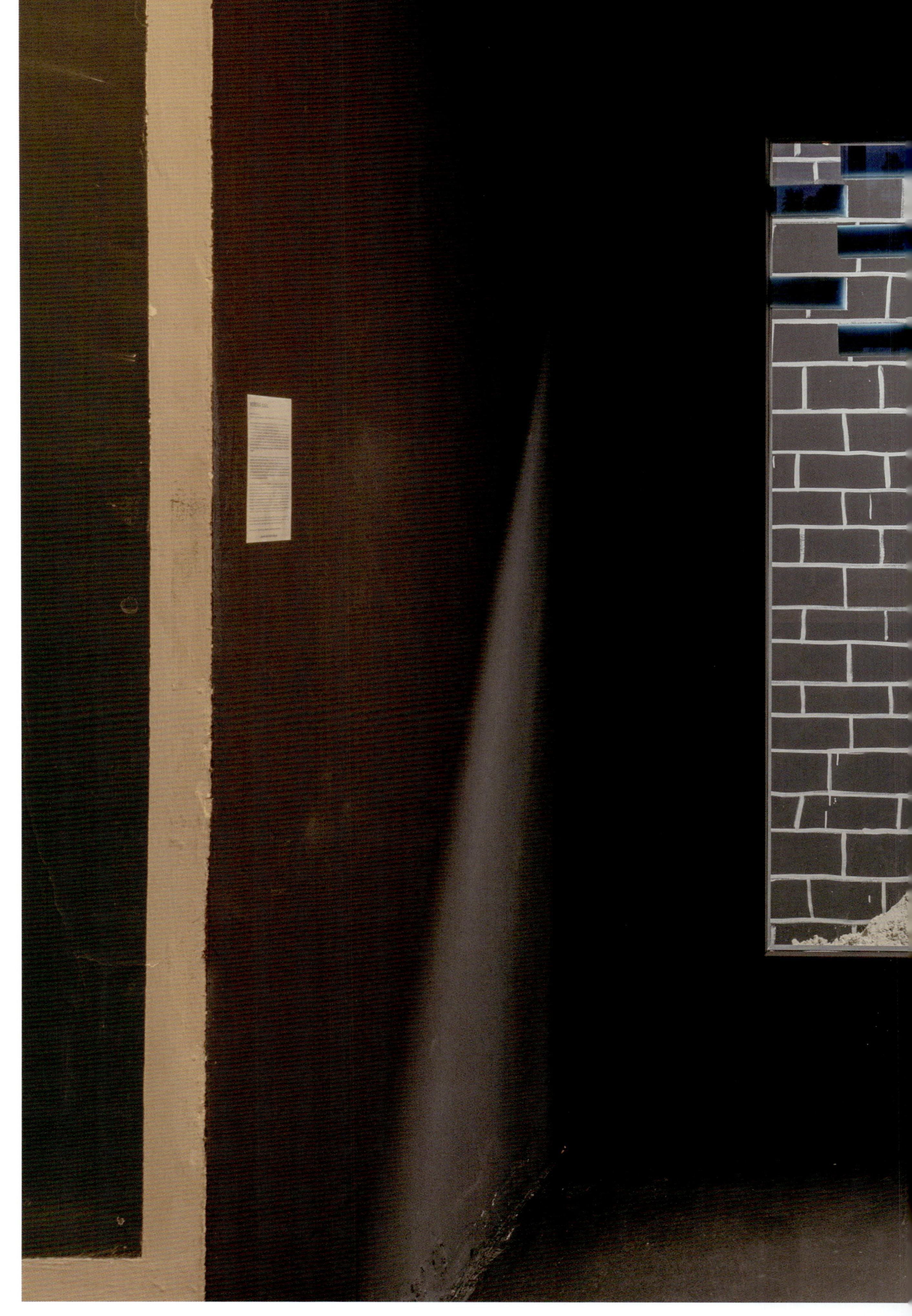

E

(2) ***Lob des Lernens***
2018, glass, wood, sand, foam rubber, sponges, cardboard, acrylic paint, 220 × 180 cm, Installation view Galerie Oel-Früh

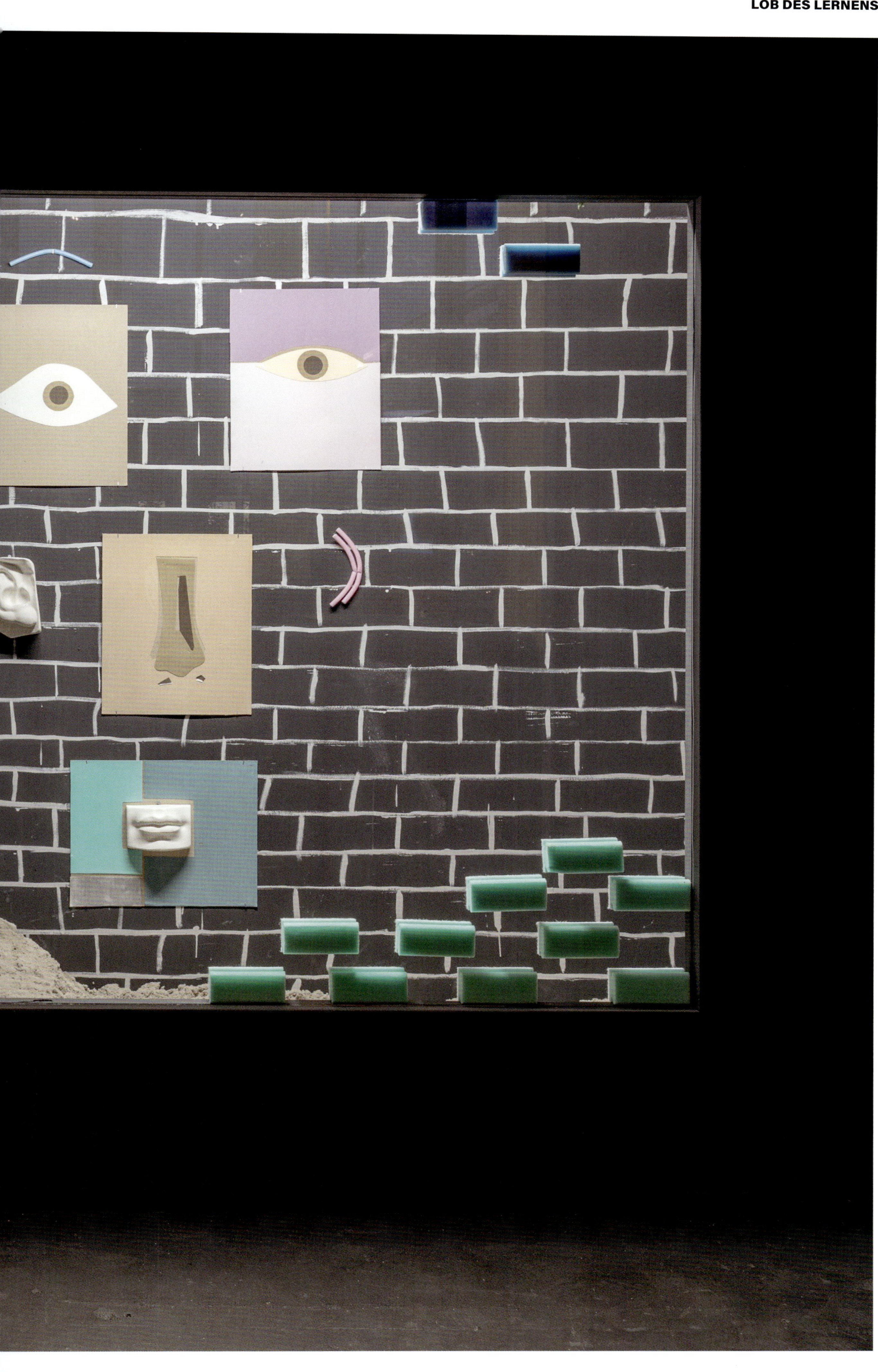

E

SILENT UTOPIA (MURALS OF A TOURIST)

E

INGREDIENTS
Forgotten Soviet Emperors I ②③
Nazca Lines I ②
Nazca Lines II ②
Forgotten Soviet Emperors II ①
Forgotten Soviet Emperors III ②
Nazca Lines III ②
Door Spy ②
Window Spy ②

/

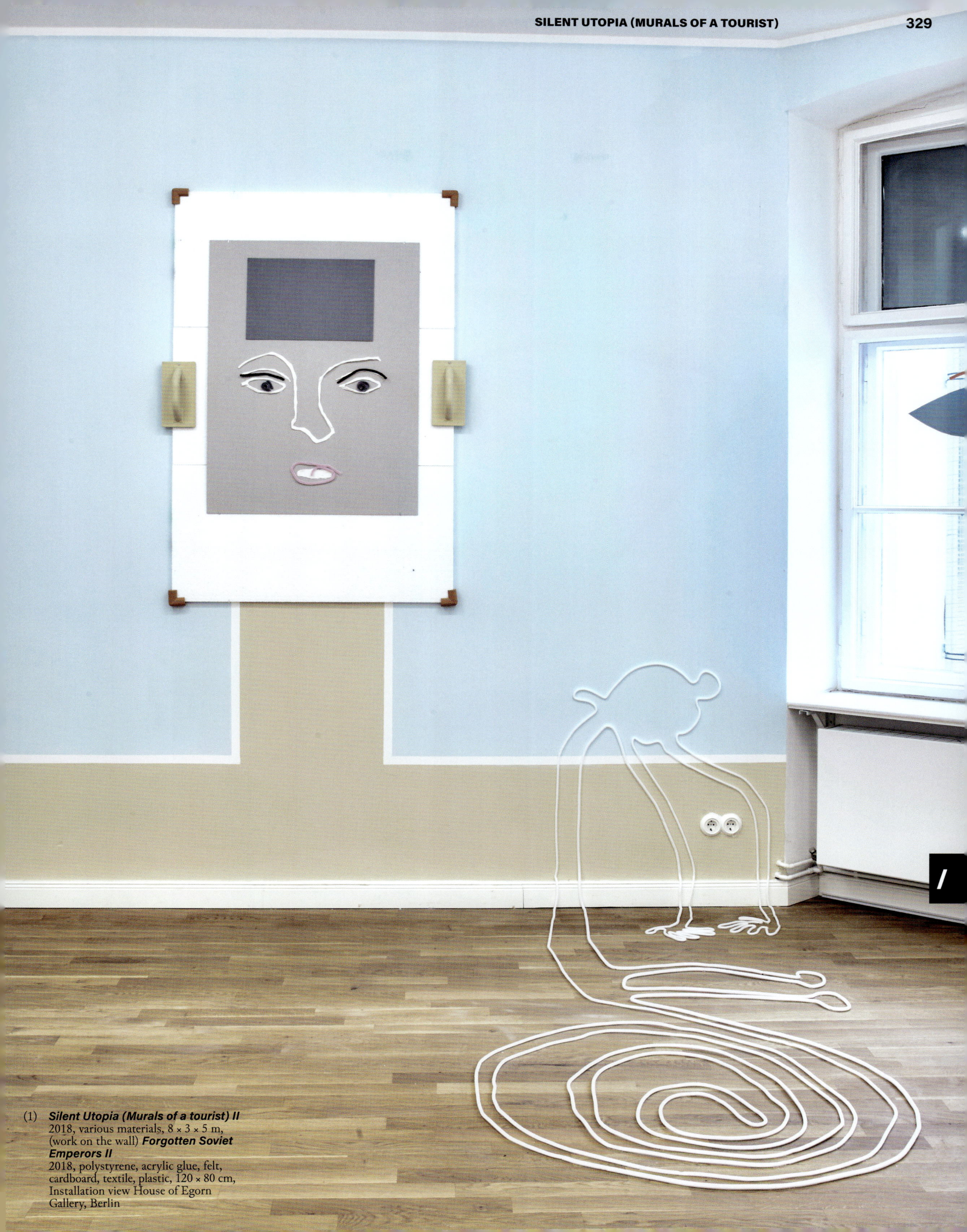

(1) ***Silent Utopia (Murals of a tourist) II*** 2018, various materials, 8 × 3 × 5 m, (work on the wall) ***Forgotten Soviet Emperors II*** 2018, polystyrene, acrylic glue, felt, cardboard, textile, plastic, 120 × 80 cm, Installation view House of Egorn Gallery, Berlin

I

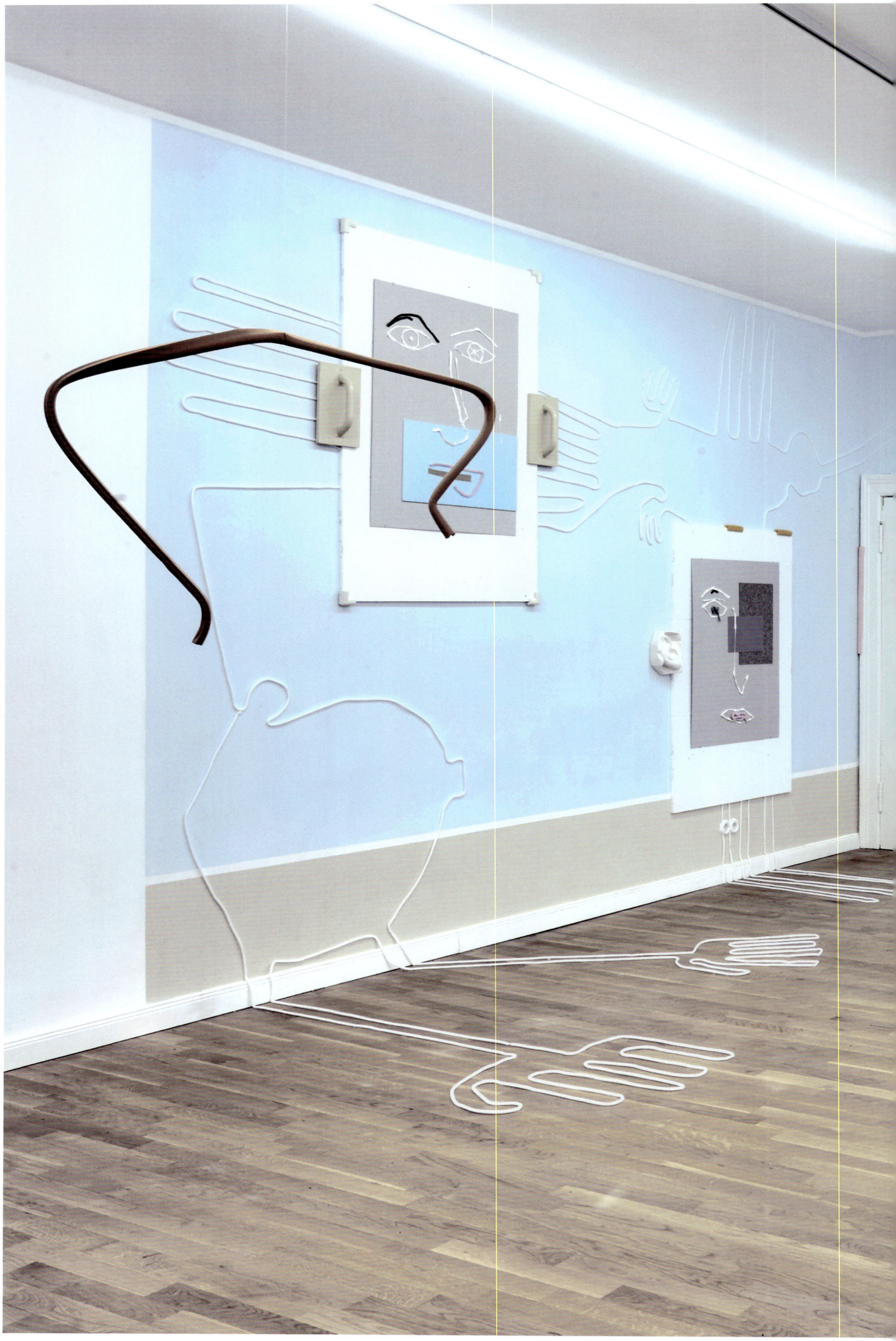

I

(2) ***Silent Utopia (Murals of a tourist) II***
2018, various materials,
8 × 3 × 5 m,
(works on the wall)
Forgotten Soviet Emperors I-III
2018, polystyrene, acrylic glue, felt, cardboard, textile, plastic,
120 × 80 cm,
Installation view
House of Egorn Gallery, Berlin

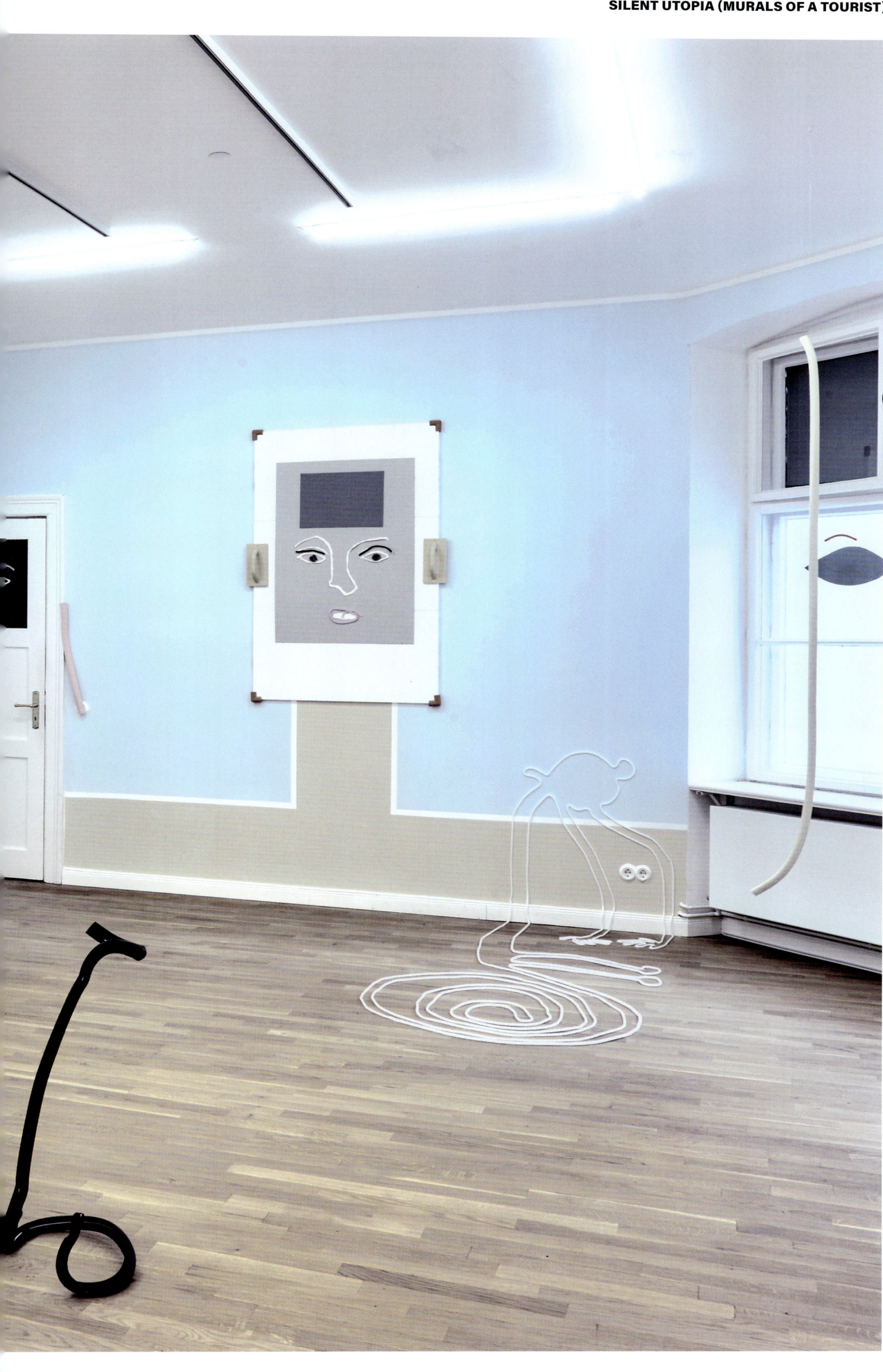

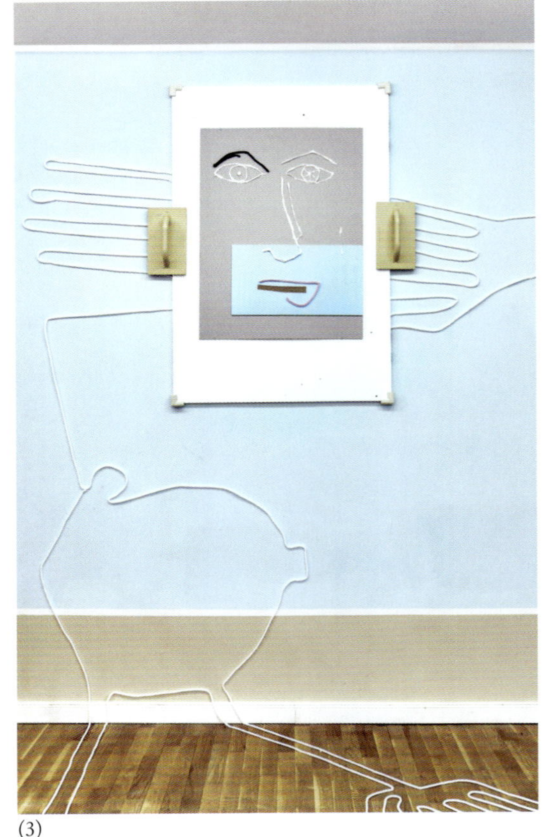
(3)

(3) ***Forgotten Soviet Emperors I***
2018, polystyrene, acrylic glue, felt, cardboard, textile, plastic, 120 × 80 cm, Installation view House of Egorn Gallery, Berlin

/

WURZELPOST (ECOSYSTEM M)

/

INGREDIENTS
Socks with Holes ①
Hairy legs, socks with holes ②

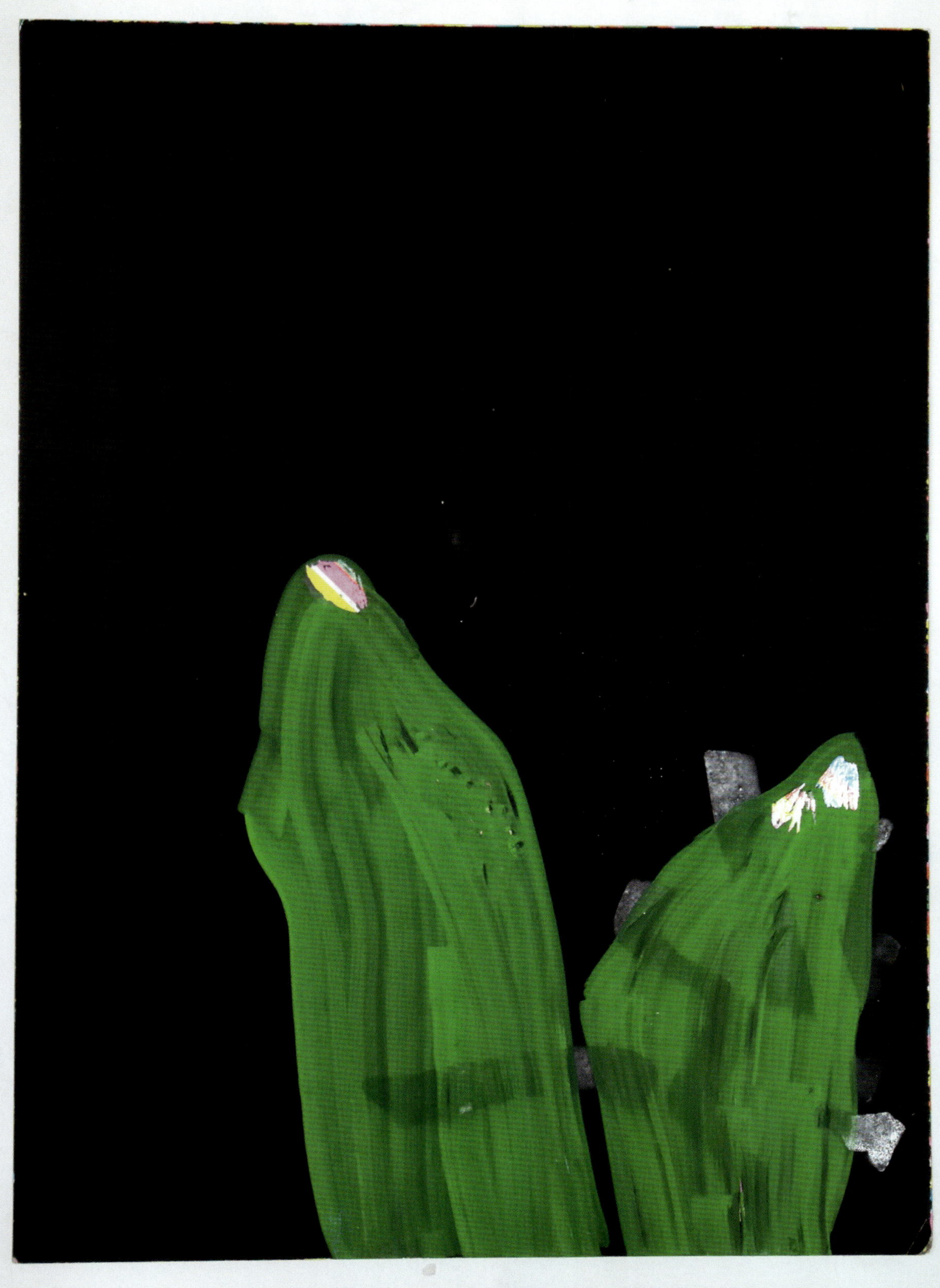

(1) ***Socks with holes***
2020, acrylic paint on scratch off paper, 20 × 31 cm

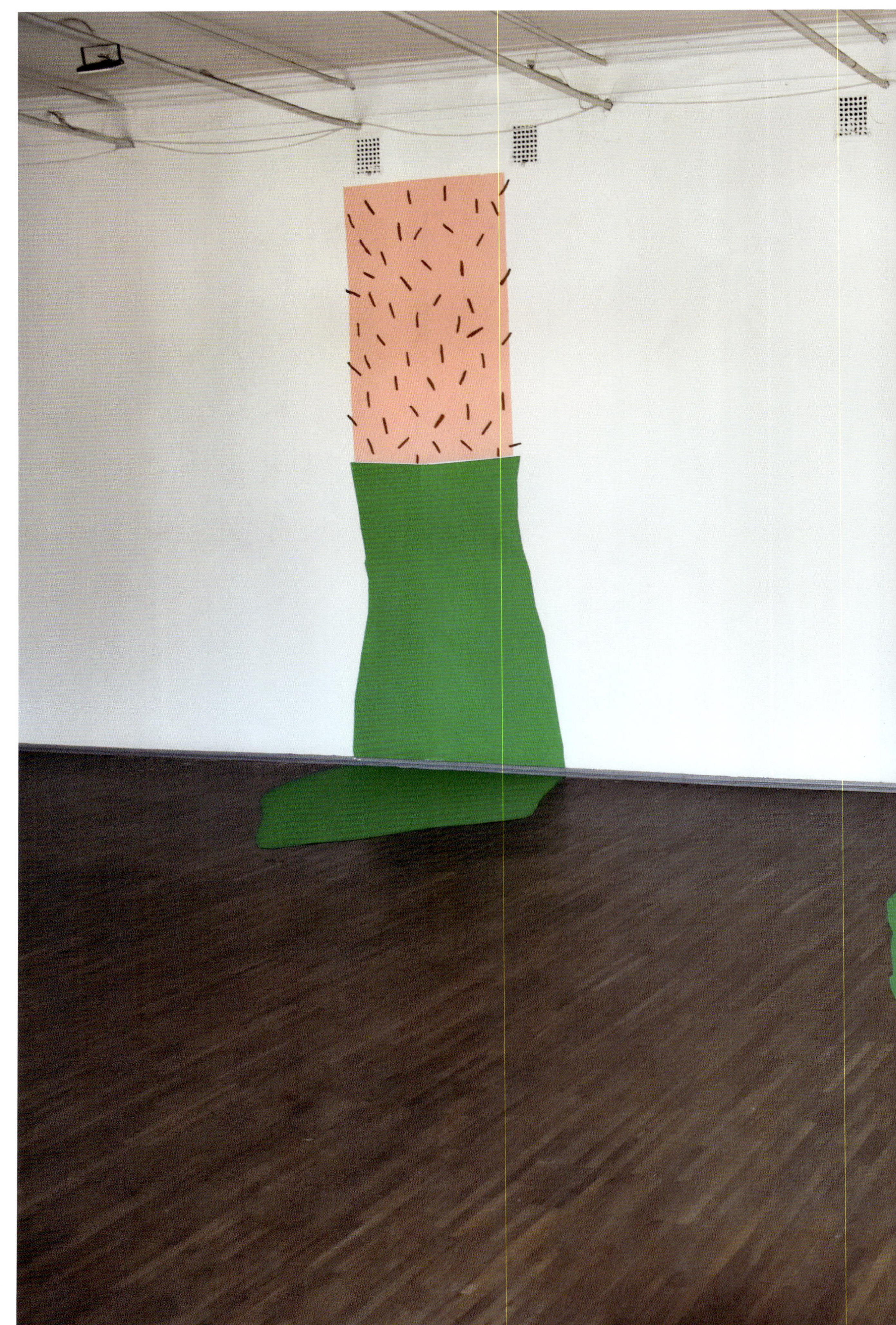

(2) ***Hairy legs, socks with holes***
2020, mural and painting, 400 × 280 cm, Installation view [si:said] gallery, Klaipeda, Lithuania

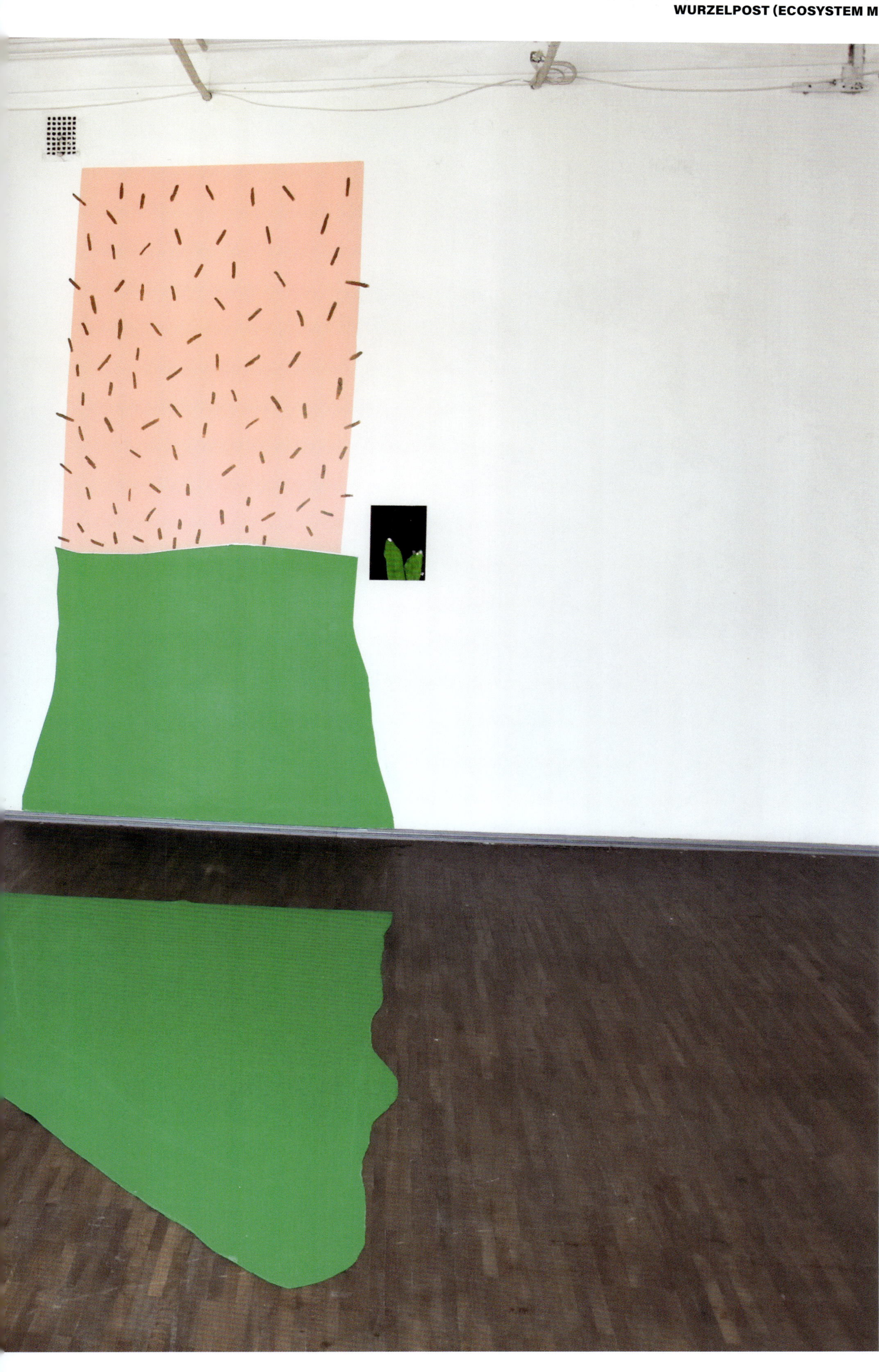

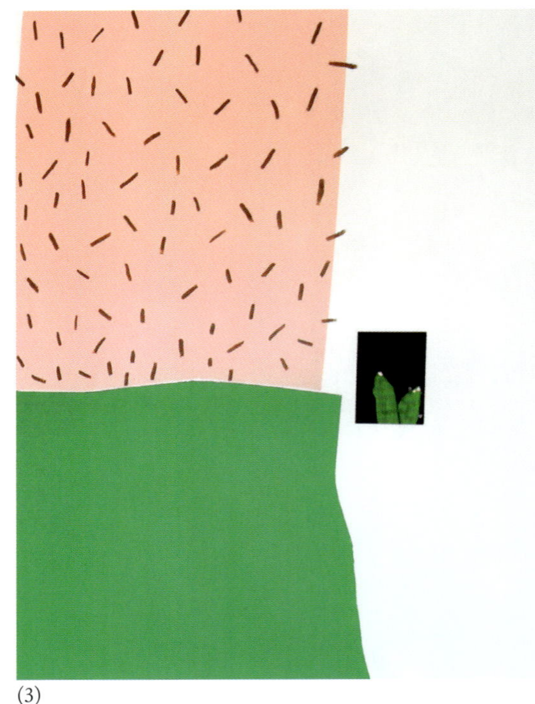

(3)

/

(3) ***Hairy legs, socks with holes***
2020, mural and painting, 400 × 280 cm, Installation view [si:said] gallery, Klaipeda, Lithuania

ARGO (WABI SABI)

INGREDIENTS
Untitled I ②
Untitled II ②
Untitled III ②
Untitled IV ②
Untitled V ②
Untitled VI ②
Untitled VII ②
Untitled VIII ②
Untitled IX ②
Untitled X ②
Untitled XI ②
Untitled XII ②
Untitled XIII ②
Untitled XIV ②
Untitled XV ②
Untitled XVI ②
Untitled XVII ②
Untitled XVIII ②
Untitled XIX ②
Untitled XX ②
Untitled XXI ②
Untitled XXII ②
Untitled XXIII ②
Untitled XXIV ②
Untitled XXV ②
Untitled XXVI ②

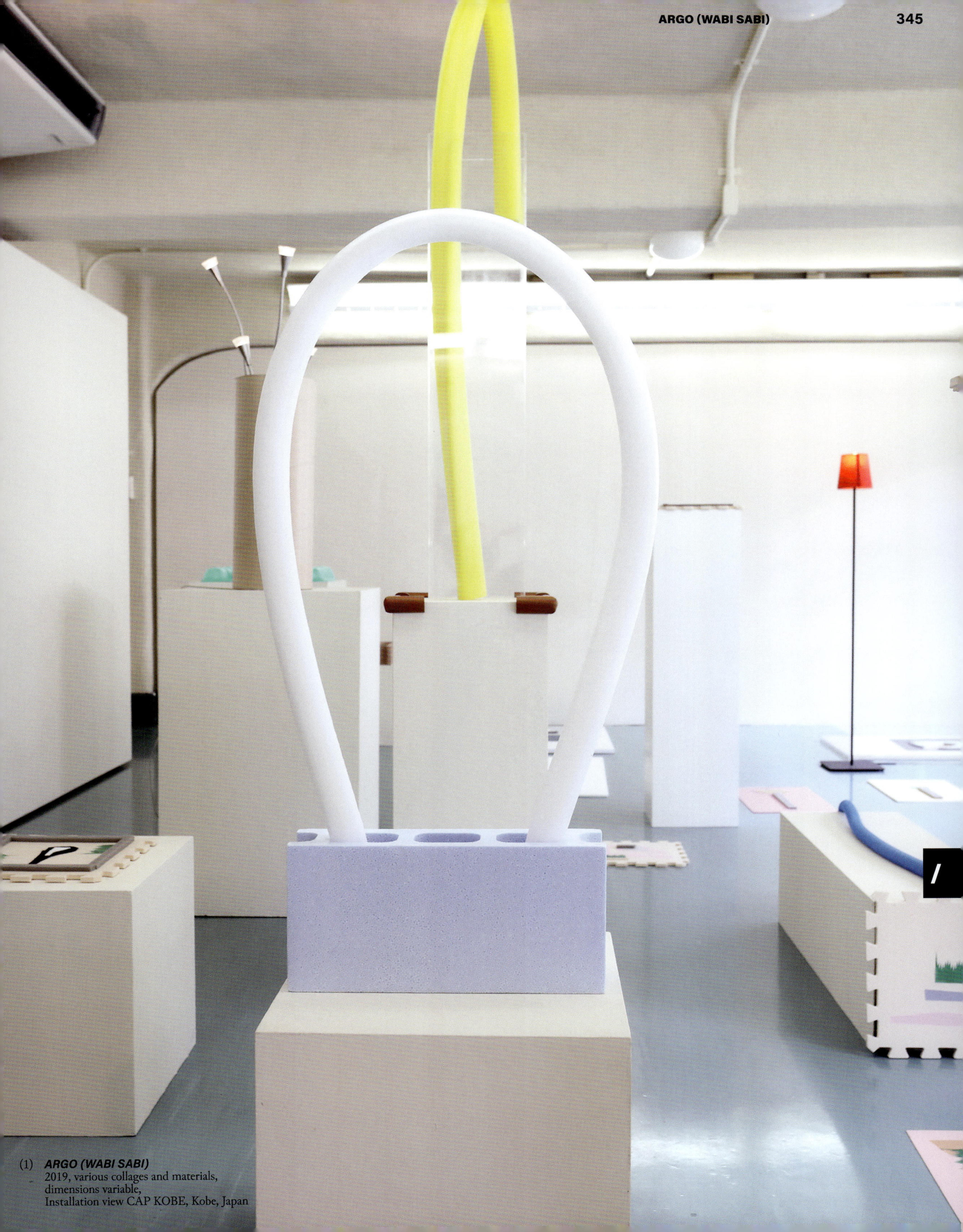

(1) ***ARGO (WABI SABI)***
2019, various collages and materials,
dimensions variable,
Installation view CAP KOBE, Kobe, Japan

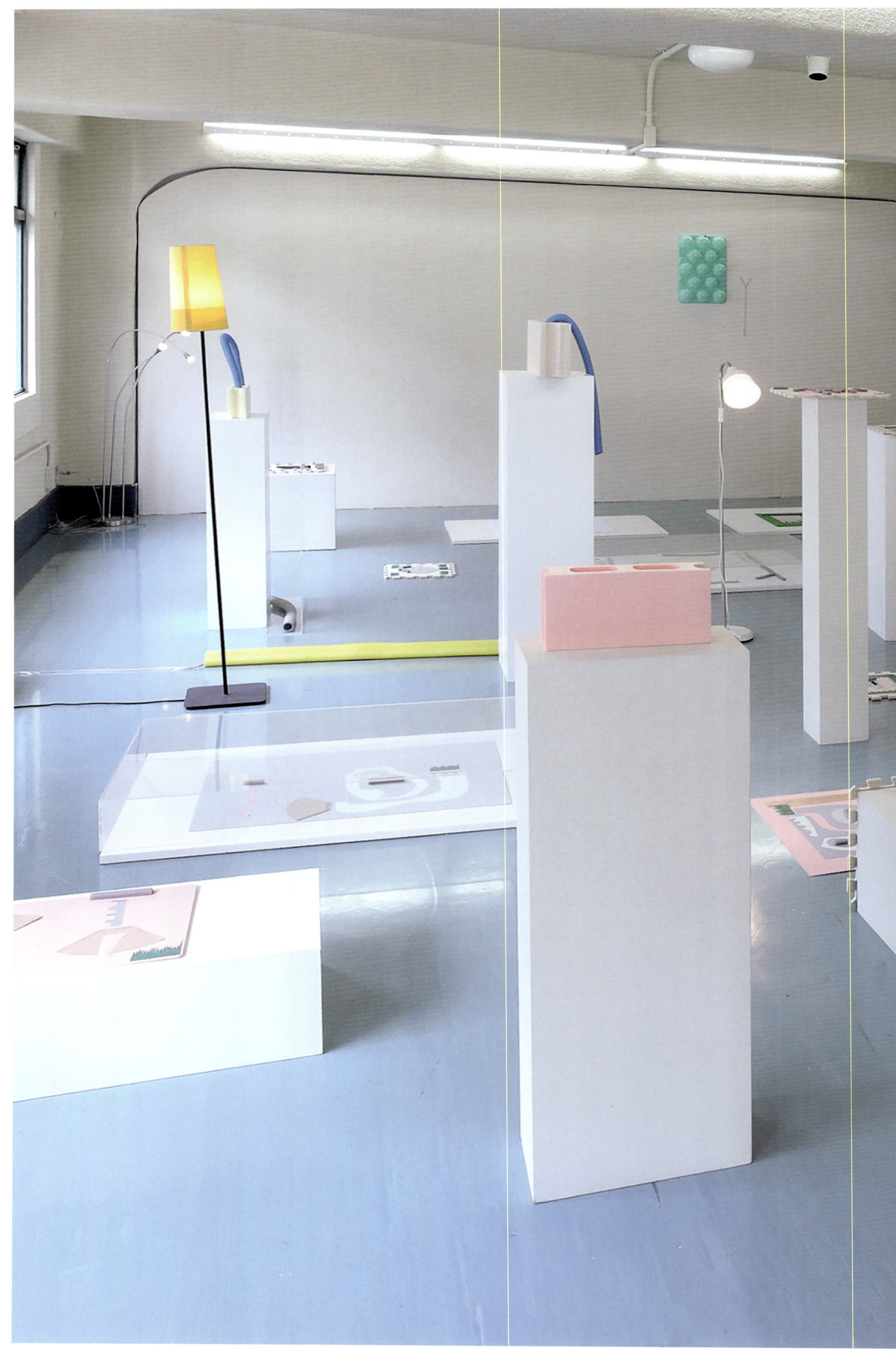

(2) ***ARGO (WABI SABI)***
2019, various collages and materials, dimensions variable, Installation view CAP KOBE, Kobe, Japan

I

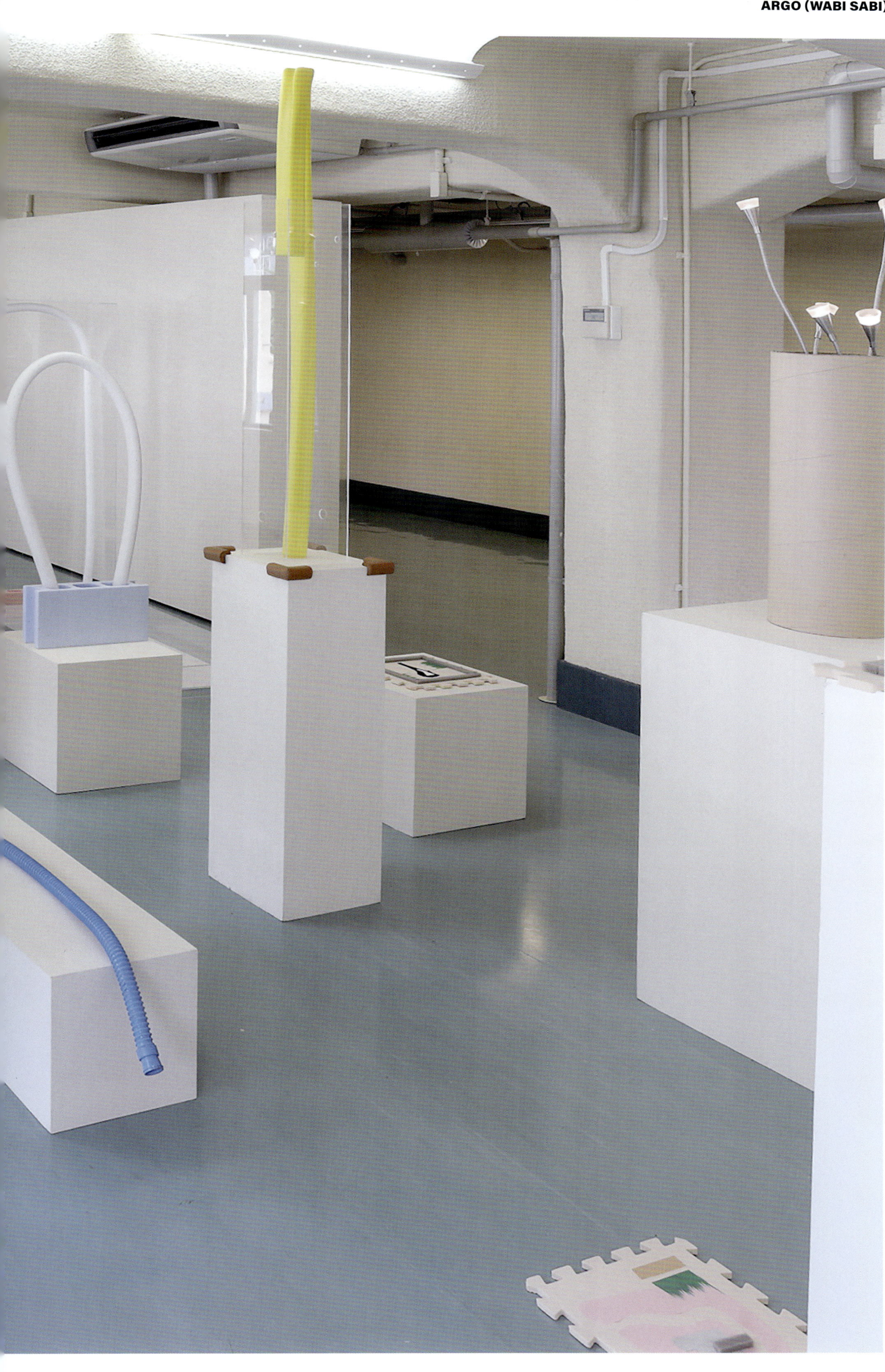

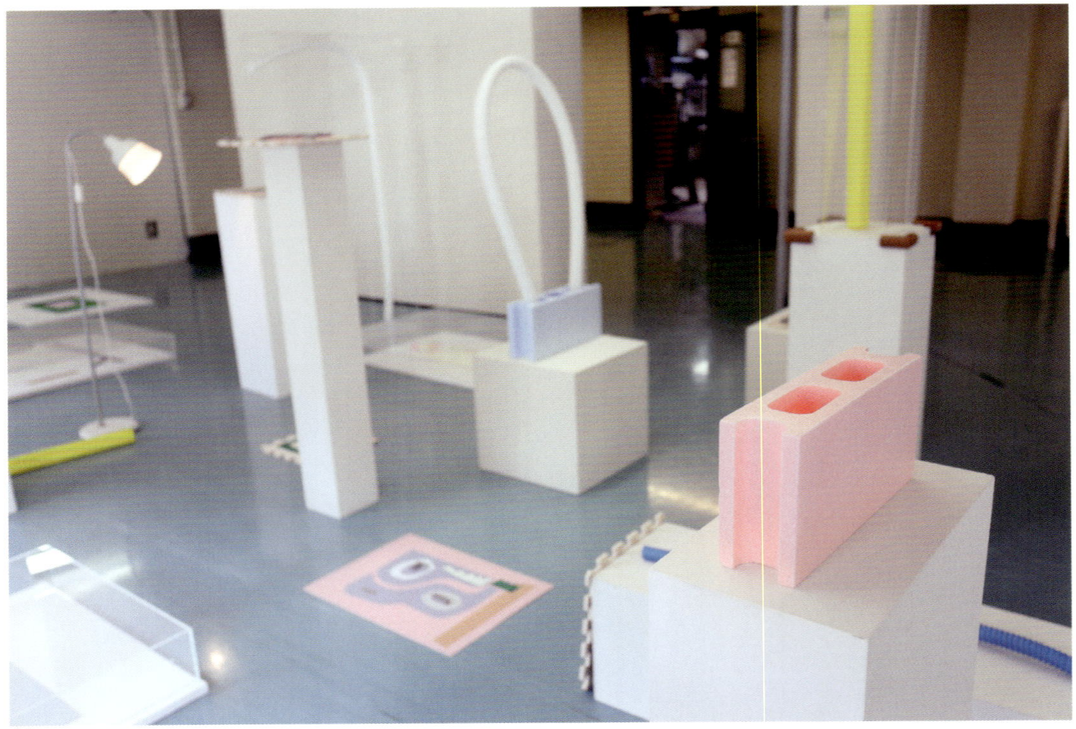

(3)

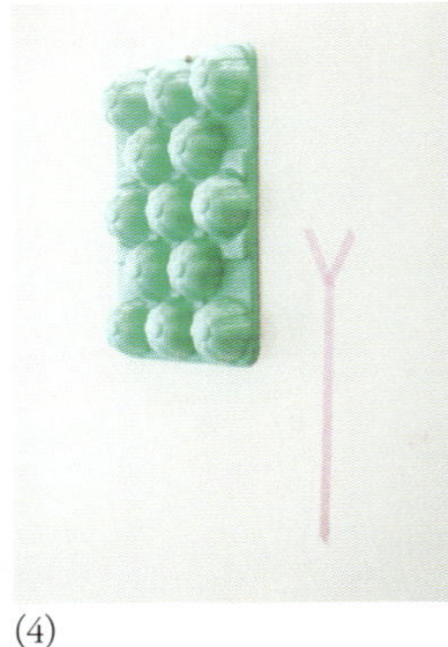

(4)

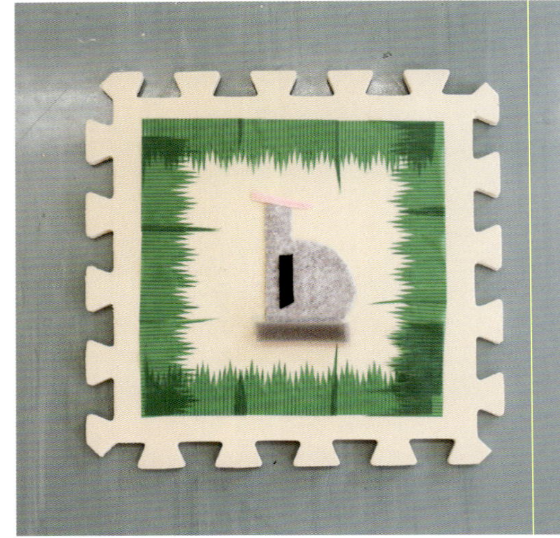

(5)

R

(3) ***ARGO (WABI SABI)***
2019, various collages and materials, dimensions variable, Installation view CAP KOBE, Kobe, Japan

(4) ***ARGO (WABI SABI)***
(detail)

(5) ***untitled***
2019, plastic, rubber, felt, 30 × 30 cm

HIDDEN AGENDA

R

INGREDIENTS
Male Gaze ①
Pervy Fuji ①
Unterbüxe ①
Legs①
Pants Down ①
Boobs ①
House of the rising sun I ①
House of the rising sun II ①
Sperminator ①
Grab Grab ①
Sunglasses At Night ①
Pimmeli ①
Yoko①
Ballz ①
Moriko ①
Hai Hai ①
Male Fuji ①
Sunglasses At Night II ①
False Affection (Pink Cube) ⑥⑦
Sad Madonna ⑤
13 Life stories ⑧⑨⑩

EN *Hidden Agenda* was an exhibition project in a former Japanese red-light district that has been transformed into a government-funded urban development project: Koganecho Bazaar in Yokohama, Japan. International artists were invited to develop installations in former brothels in order to revitalise the abandoned, partially stigmatised area. These former brothels are very distinctive buildings, built specifically for their purpose: small houses with a large window in the front to showcase the women who work there.
The rooms of the houses are very small to accommodate as many sex workers as possible.
These special buildings have now been entrusted to artists who have been commissioned to create installations there.
Verena Issel's installation dealt with the history of the place.
On the prominent entrance door was a text by British film theorist Laura Mulvey:
"The cinematic apparatus of classical Hollywood cinema inevitably puts the spectator in a masculine subject position, with the figure of the woman on screen as the object of desire and the 'male gaze.' Viewers are encouraged to identify with the protagonists, who were and still are overwhelmingly male. Meanwhile, Hollywood women characters are often coded with 'to-be-looked-at-ness' while the camera positioning and the male viewer constitutes the 'bearer of the look.' This look is adapted by females to judge both other females and themselves with male measuring rods."

Visitors entered a very bright entrance room, lightly painted and with a friendly atmosphere created by many small playful light sources. Here they were greeted by an installation consisting of many playful small objects spread across the walls, floor and ceiling.
The objects were all painted in bright pastel colors, making them seem small and harmless. This could be seen as a reference to the schoolgirl aesthetic of the neighbouring sex workers.

It took a second look to discover sexual allusions in almost all of the objects.

A third look revealed a tiny door hidden in the wall, which the artist had specially installed. Entering through this door, the visitor was greeted by a collage by Issel depicting a sad woman. Behind this small door, the former brothel was no longer renovated and brightly painted like the front area, but visitors were suddenly standing on the original tatami mats on which the sex workers used to work; the walls were worn and showed various traces of what had been there before.
In the back workrooms were small sculptures by Verena Issel. A reading room was set up in the last room. Verena Issel had spent several months collecting and transcribing the life stories of local sex workers.
In order to prevent these personal, explicit texts from being photographed and distributed without permission, the room was lit with blue-black light, making it very difficult to photograph the texts with mobile phones.
Visitors to the exhibition were invited to engage with the history of the place and the fate of the people who lived and worked there.

Issel tries to walk a tightrope here: to show the true face of the place, with all its sad facets, but also to allow for beauty in this rather dark place.
☐ ***Uwe Carlson***

R

DE *Hidden Agenda* war ein Ausstellungsprojekt in einem ehemaligen japanischen Rotlichtviertel, das in ein von der Regierung finanziertes Stadtentwicklungsprojekt umgewandelt wurde: Koganecho Bazaar in Yokohama, Japan. Internationale Künstler wurden eingeladen, Installationen in ehemaligen Bordellen zu entwickeln, um das verlassene, teilweise stigmatisierte Viertel wiederzubeleben. Diese ehemaligen Bordelle sind sehr charakteristische Gebäude, die speziell für ihren Zweck gebaut wurden: kleine Häuser mit einem großen Fenster an der Vorderseite, um die Frauen, die dort arbeiten, zu präsentieren.
Die Räume der Häuser sind sehr klein, um so viele Sexarbeiterinnen wie möglich unterzubringen. Diese besonderen Gebäude waren nun Künstler*innen anvertraut worden, die beauftragt wurden, dort Installationen zu schaffen. Die Installation von Verena Issel befasste sich mit der Geschichte des Ortes.
Die markanten Eingangstür zierte ein Text der britischen Filmtheoretikerin Laura Mulvey: "The cinematic apparatus of classical Hollywood cinema inevitably puts the spectator in a masculine subject position, with the figure of the woman on screen as the object of desire and the 'male gaze.' Viewers are encouraged to identify with the protagonists, who were and still are overwhelmingly male. Meanwhile, Hollywood women characters are often coded with 'to-be-looked-at-ness' while the camera positioning and the male viewer constitutes the 'bearer of the look.' This look is adapted by females to judge both other females and themselves with male measuring rods."

Die Besucher betraten einen sehr hellen und durch viele verspielte Lichtquellen freundlich wirkenden Eingangsraum, in dem sie von einer Installation aus vielen kleinen verspielten Objekten begrüßt wurden, die sich über Wände, Boden und Decke erstreckten.
Die Objekte waren in Anlehnung an die in Yokohama prominente Schulmädchen-Sexarbeiterinnen-Ästhetik sehr pastellfarben, klein und harmlos gestaltet. Erst auf den zweiten Blick entdeckte man in fast allen Objekten sexuelle Anspielungen.
Ein dritter Blick offenbarte eine winzige, von der Künstlerin eigens in die Wand eingelassene Tür. Trat der Besucher durch diese Tür, gelangte er in einen Rotlichtbereich, wo ihn eine Collage Issels mit einer traurigen Frau empfing.
Hinter der kleinen Tür war das ehemalige Bordell nicht mehr hell renoviert und freundlich gestrichen wie der vordere Teil, sondern die Besucherinnen und Besucher standen plötzlich auf den originalen Tatami-Matten, auf denen die Sexarbeiterinnen früher gearbeitet hatten, die Wände waren abgenutzt und zeigten vielfältige Spuren dessen, was sich vorher dort befunden hatte.
In den hinteren Arbeitsräumen fanden sich kleine Skulpturen von Verena Issel.
Im letzten Raum befand sich ein Lesezimmer. Verena Issel hatte über mehrere Monate hinweg Lebensgeschichten von Sexarbeiterinnen aus der Region gesammelt und transkribiert. Damit diese persönlichen und zum Teil sehr expliziten Texte nicht einfach fotografiert und unerlaubt weiterverbreitet werden konnten, war der Raum mit blauschwarzem Licht ausgeleuchtet, was das Fotografieren der Texte mit Mobiltelefonen sehr erschwerte.

Die Installation lud die Ausstellungsbesucher dazu ein, sich mit der Geschichte des Ortes und dem Schicksal der Menschen, die hier lebten und arbeiteten, auseinanderzusetzen.
Issel versucht hier den Spagat, das wahre Gesicht des Ortes mit all seinen traurigen Facetten zu zeigen, aber auch die Schönheit dieses eher dunklen Ortes zuzulassen.

☐ ***Uwe Carlson***

R

R

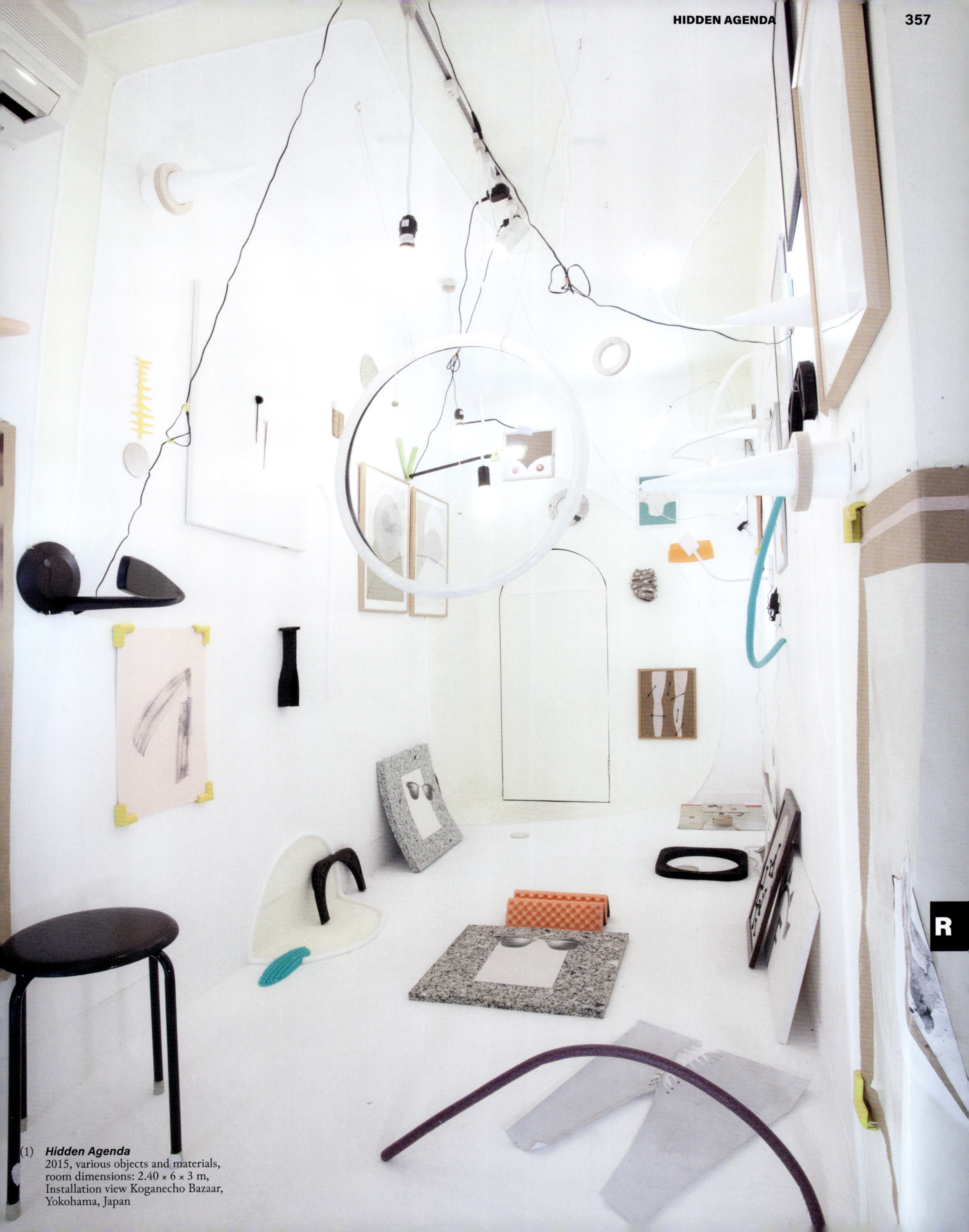

(1) ***Hidden Agenda***
2015, various objects and materials, room dimensions: 2.40 × 6 × 3 m, Installation view Koganecho Bazaar, Yokohama, Japan

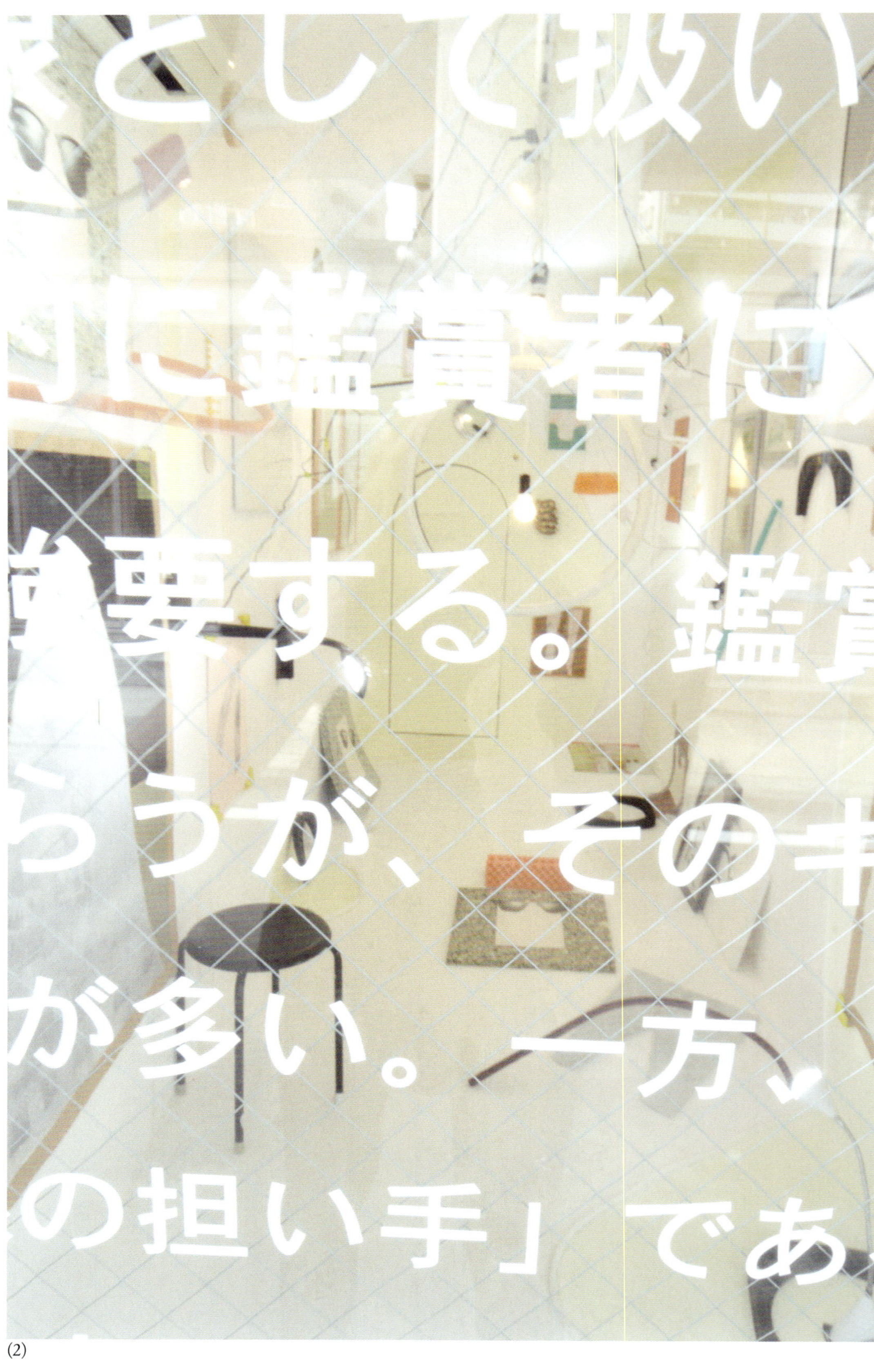

(2)

(2) ***Hidden Agenda***
Entrance door with text

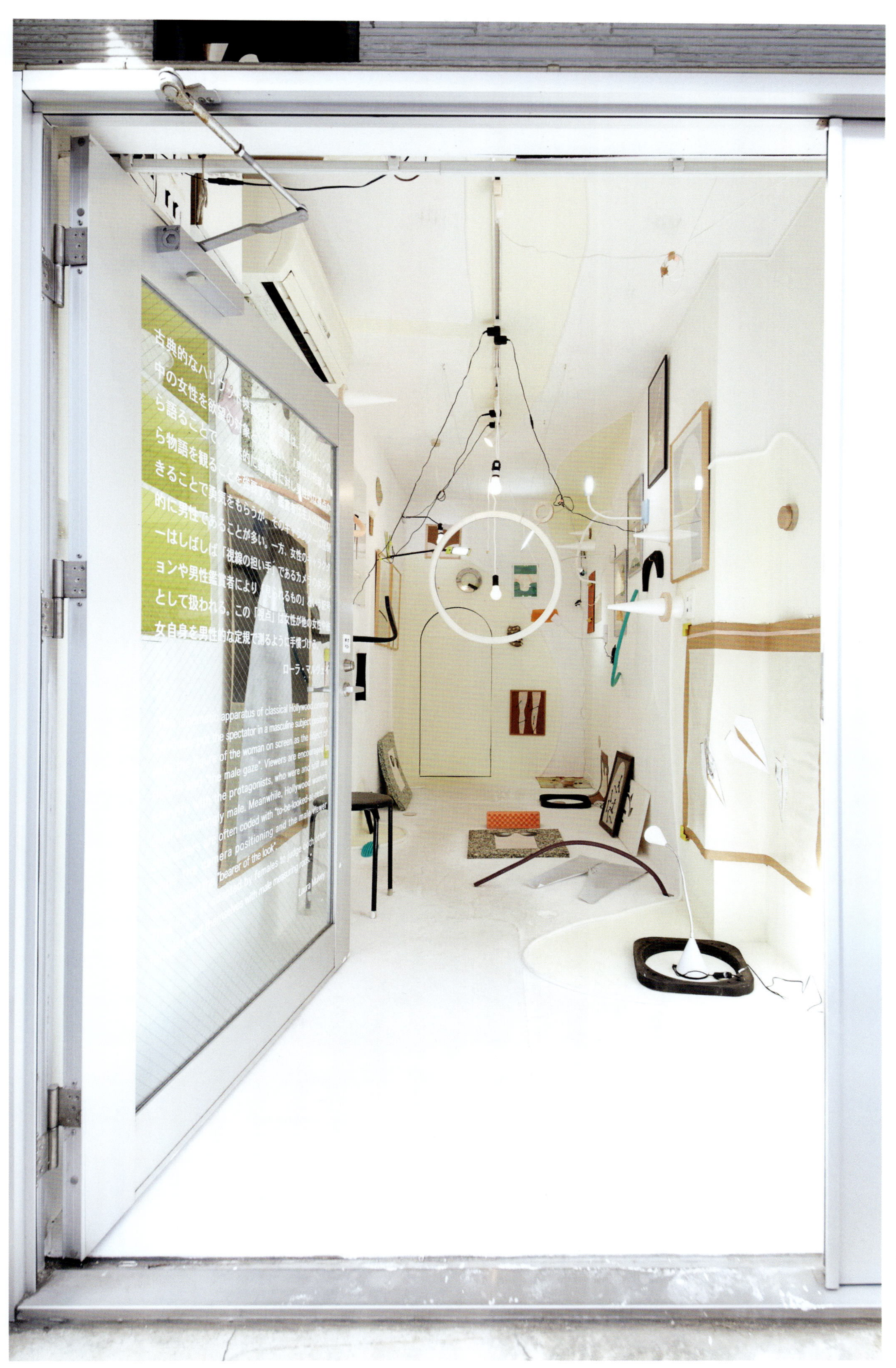

(3) ***Hidden Agenda***
2015, various objects and materials, room dimensions: 2.40 × 6 × 3 m, Installation view Koganecho Bazaar, Yokohama, Japan

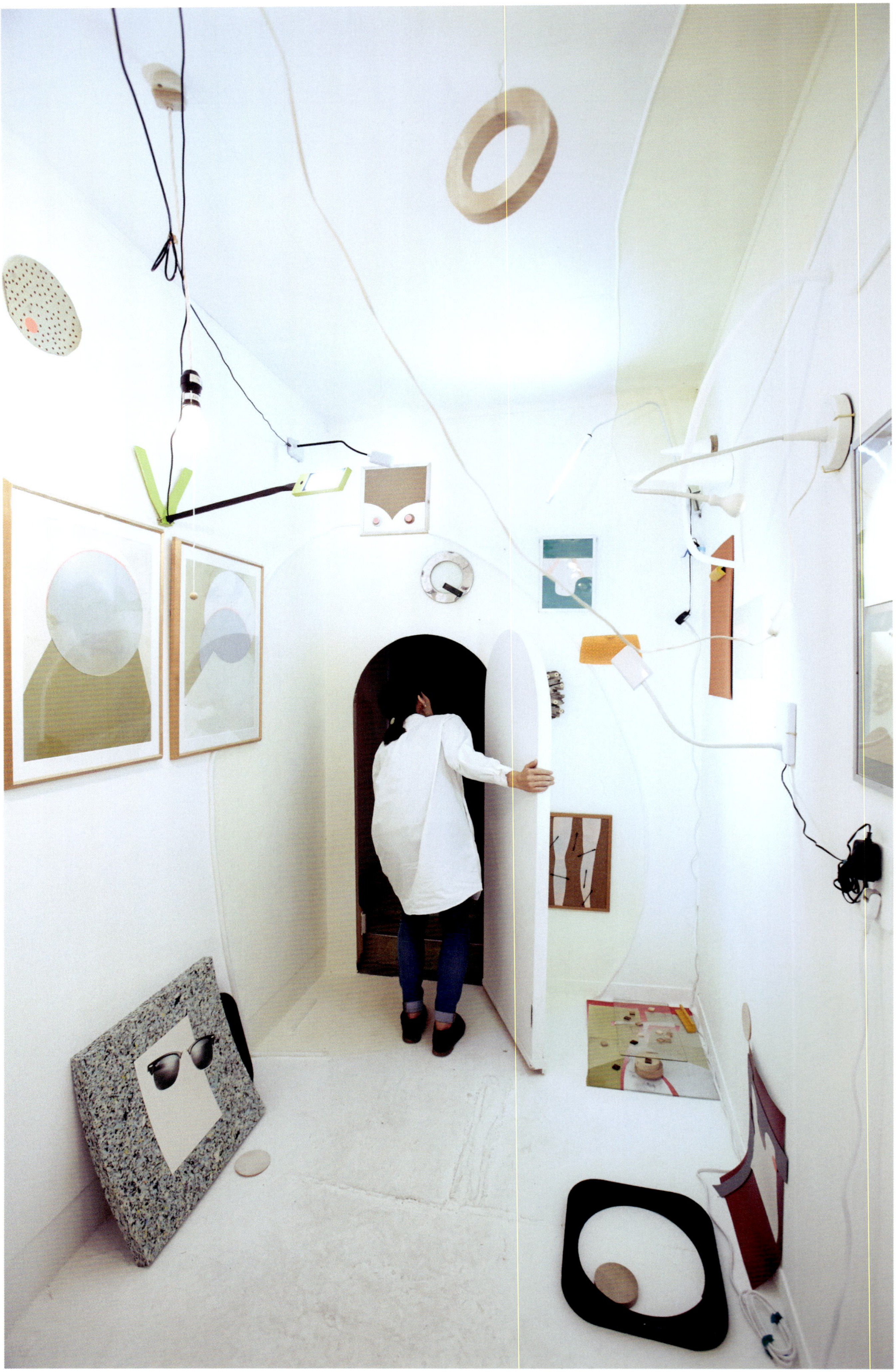

R

(4) ***Hidden Agenda***
2015, various objects and materials, room dimensions: 2.40 × 6 × 3 m, Exhibition in a former Japanese brothel, state-financed urban development project, Koganecho Bazaar, Yokohama, Japan —This page: Entrance to the hidden back room through a "secret" door specially built into the installation

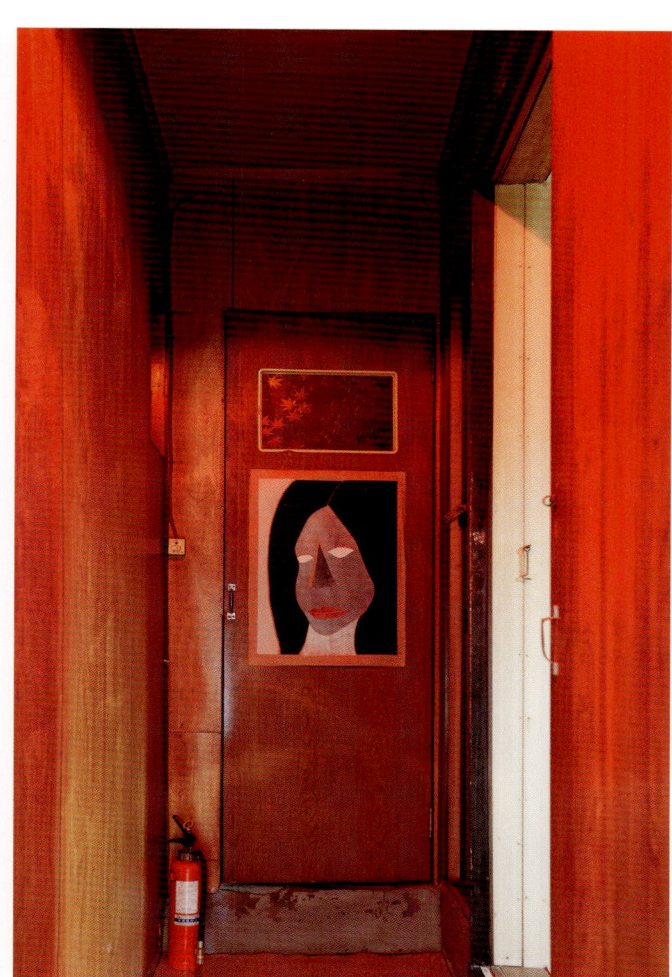

(5)

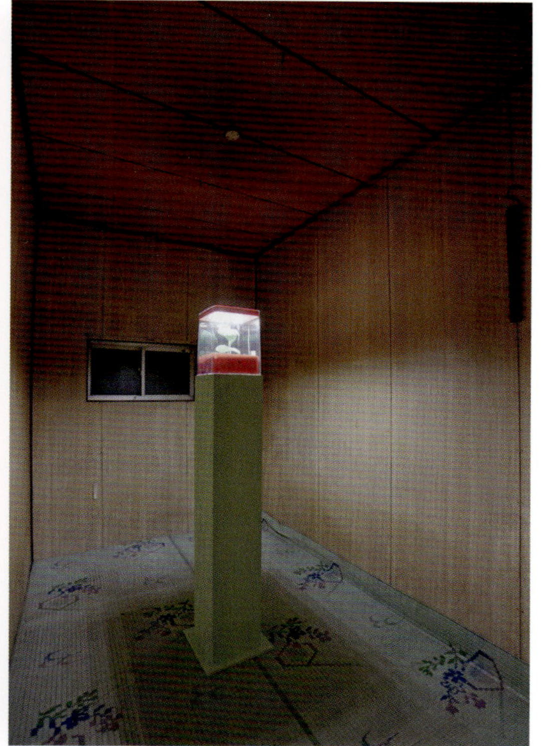

(6)

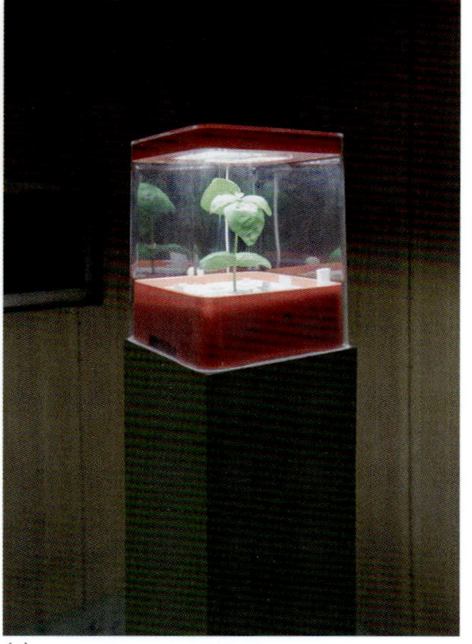

(7)

(5) ***Hidden Agenda***
2015, various objects and materials, room dimensions 2.40 × 6 × 3 m, Installation view Koganecho Bazaar, Yokohama, Japan, Here: The hallway behind the hidden door

(6) ***Hidden Agenda***
2015, first of two hidden back rooms: ***False affection (pink cube)***, 2015, original tatami mats, left behind by the sex workers, wooden base, with plant incubator, plastic, lighting, plastic basil, 160 × 24 × 24 cm

(7) ***Hidden Agenda***
2015, first of two hidden back rooms: ***False affection (pink cube)***, 2015 Original tatami mats, left behind by the sex workers, wooden base, with plant incubator, plastic, lighting, plastic basil, 160 × 24 × 24 cm

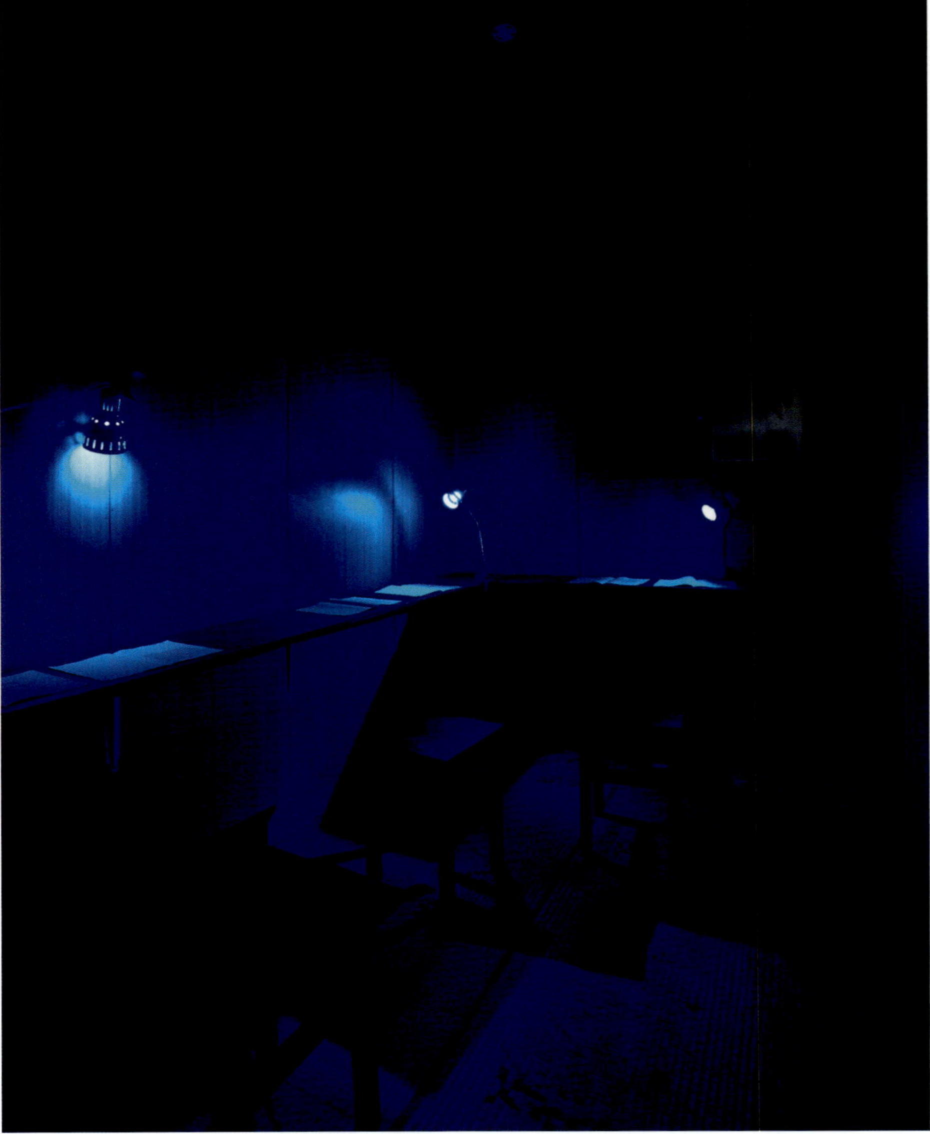
(8)

(10)

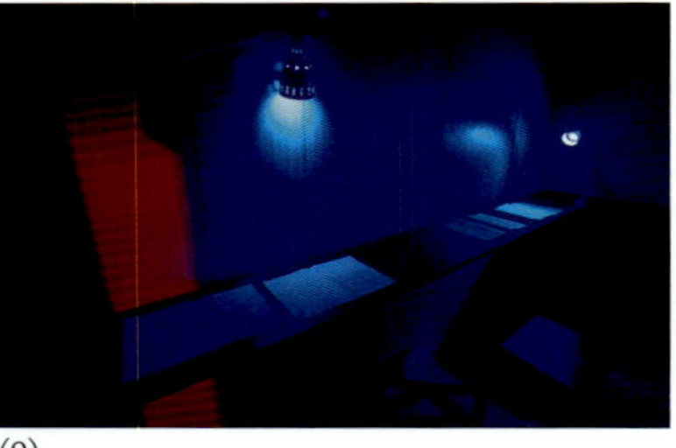
(9)

R

(8)
(9)
(10) ***Hidden Agenda***
2015, Second of two hidden back rooms: ***Living/Living room***, 2015, original tatami mats left behind by the sex workers who worked in this room before, wooden desk and chairs, photo inhibiting blue light and textbooks with the collected life stories of sex workers from Yokohama

WECHAT

INGREDIENTS
WeChat IIa ①
WeChat IIb ①
WeChat IIc ①
WeChat IId ①
Tell me, tell me – what will the future be like ④
Artphone I ②
Artphone II ⑤
Artphone III ②
Artphone IV ③
Artphone V
Tube I 7
Tube II 2
Tube III 8
Tube IV ③
Tube V ③
Tube VI 2
Tube VII ③
Tube VIII ③
Facebook ①
Facebook II 6
Untitled ②
Untitled II ③
Untitled III
Untitled IV
Spy tube ①
Spy tube ③⑥
In the name of safety ③
in the name of humanism
In the name of tradition I
In the name of tradition II
Big Spy Tube
Middle Spy Tube

EN WeChat (Chinese for "small message") was originally a Chinese chat service for smartphones, which has since expanded with many features. Users can not only engage in instant messaging but also send audio messages, make video calls, share photos, videos, and their location, order taxis, groceries, or food, pay restaurant or utility bills, purchase stickers, search for jobs or people nearby, book doctor appointments, apply for US visas, play games, and operate their own mobile stores.
The app has its own app store and a news feed called "Moments." Almost no one in China uses cash anymore; instead, they utilize the mobile payment system "WeChat Pay."

Since September 2017, the disclosure of almost all information to Chinese authorities has been part of WeChat's official privacy policy. As WeChat is a comprehensive system, the government knows almost everything about its citizens: how they live, who they talk to, what they eat, what they buy, what they think...

The Chinese ID card will be linked to the WeChat account in the future. Starting in 2020, Chinese citizens are expected to be monitored entirely through WeChat, receiving so-called social credit points. All citizens begin with a good social credit score, and "bad" behavior, traffic violations, inappropriate images, or critical statements will result in point deductions. It is still under discussion whether a low score might lead to exclusion from social insurance or if children of parents with a low score will still be admitted to state schools. As a first step toward the Social Credit System, the use of VPNs (programs that help evade internet surveillance) was penalized with imprisonment in February 2018.

The artist has been involved in exchange projects and received scholarships for multiple visits to China, most recently from July to December 2017 at the Swatch Art Peace Hotel Residency in Shanghai.
In her specially developed installation for the Oechsner Gallery, Verena Issel creates a self-contained system where standalone images are interconnected through wall paintings, plastic pipes, and chat symbols. The extensive control imposed by the WeChat program is satirized through its seemingly friendly demeanor. The apparently naive access to and through the app is brought back into the tangible world by magnifying other systemic parts of the surveillance company. The "Tubes" depicted in the paintings are tubular handles taken from Shanghai's subway (also known as "Tube" in English), pointing to the data network and simultaneously satirizing it.

As an artist whose interest lies in painting, Verena Issel explores the boundaries of two- and three-dimensional pictorial space through sculptural and installation approaches. She succeeds in eliminating or making invisible these interfaces.

☐ ***Annette Oechsner, exhibition text, 2018***

R

DE WeChat (chin.: kleine Nachricht) war ursprünglich ein chinesischer Chatdienst für Smartphones, der inzwischen um viele Funktionen erweitert wurde. Nutzer können neben dem reinen Instant-Messaging mit der App Audionachrichten versenden, Videotelefonate durchführen, Fotos, Videos und ihren Aufenthaltsort teilen, Taxis, Lebensmittel oder Essen bestellen, Restaurant- oder Stromrechnungen bezahlen, Sticker kaufen, Jobs oder Leute in der Nähe suchen, Arzttermine buchen, Visa für die USA beantragen, Spiele spielen und eigene Mobile-Stores betreiben.
Die App hat einen eigenen App-Store sowie einen Nachrichtenstream namens „Moments". Fast niemand mehr in China bezahlt mit Bargeld, alle nutzen das Mobile-Payment-System „WeChat Pay".
Seit September 2017 ist die Weitergabe nahezu aller Informationen an die chinesischen Behörden Teil der offiziellen Datenschutzerklärung von WeChat. Da WeChat ein umfassendes System ist, weiß der Staat fast alles über seine Bürger: wie sie leben, mit wem sie sprechen, was sie essen, was sie kaufen, was sie denken…
Die chinesische ID-Karte wird künftig mit dem WeChat-Konto verknüpft werden. Ab 2020 sollen die chinesischen Bürger mithilfe von WeChat gänzlich überwacht werden und sogenannte Social Credit Points erhalten. Alle Bürger starten mit einem guten Sozialpunktestand, bei einem „schlechten" Kaufverhalten, Verkehrsregelübertretungen, anstößigen Bildern, systemkritischen Äußerungen etc. gibt es jeweils Punktabzug. Es ist noch in der Diskussion, ob ein geringer Punktestand zum Beispiel zum Ausschluss aus der Sozialversicherung führt und ob womöglich Kinder von Eltern mit geringem Punktestand noch auf die staatliche Schule zugelassen werden. Als erster Schritt zu dem Social-Credit-System wurde nun im Februar 2018 die Nutzung von VPNs-Programmen, mit deren Hilfe man sich der Überwachung durch das Internet entziehen kann, mit Gefängnisstrafen belegt.
Die Künstlerin war mit Austauschprojekten und Stipendien wiederholt in China unterwegs, zuletzt von Juli bis Dezember 2017 in der Swatch Art Peace Hotel Residency, Schanghai.
In ihrer eigens für die Oechsner Galerie entwickelten Rauminstallation erschafft Verena Issel ein in sich geschlossenes System, in dem einzeln stehende Bilder miteinander verbunden sind durch Wandmalerei, Plastikrohre und Chatsymbole.
Die umfassende Kontrolle durch das Programm WeChat wird in seiner positiven Freundlichkeit karikiert, der scheinbar naive Zugriff auf und durch die App wird durch die Vergrößerungen anderer systemischer Teile des überwachenden Unternehmens zurückgeholt in die dingliche Welt: Die auf den Malereien abgebildeten „Tubes" (dt.: Rohre) sind der U-Bahn (auf engl. auch: *tube*) Schanghais entnommene röhrenförmige Haltegriffe (man verbringt durchschnittlich zwei Stunden pro Tag in der U-Bahn in Schanghai – und man wird dabei selbstverständlich gefilmt). Diese verweisen auf das Datennetz und persiflieren es gleichzeitig.
Die Künstlerin, deren Interesse der Malerei gilt, lotet im skulpturalen und installativen Umgang die Grenzen des zwei- und dreidimensionalen Bildraums aus. Ihr gelingt es, Schnittstellen aufzuheben bzw. unsichtbar zu machen.

☐ ***Annette Oechsner, Ausstellungstext, 2018***

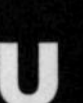

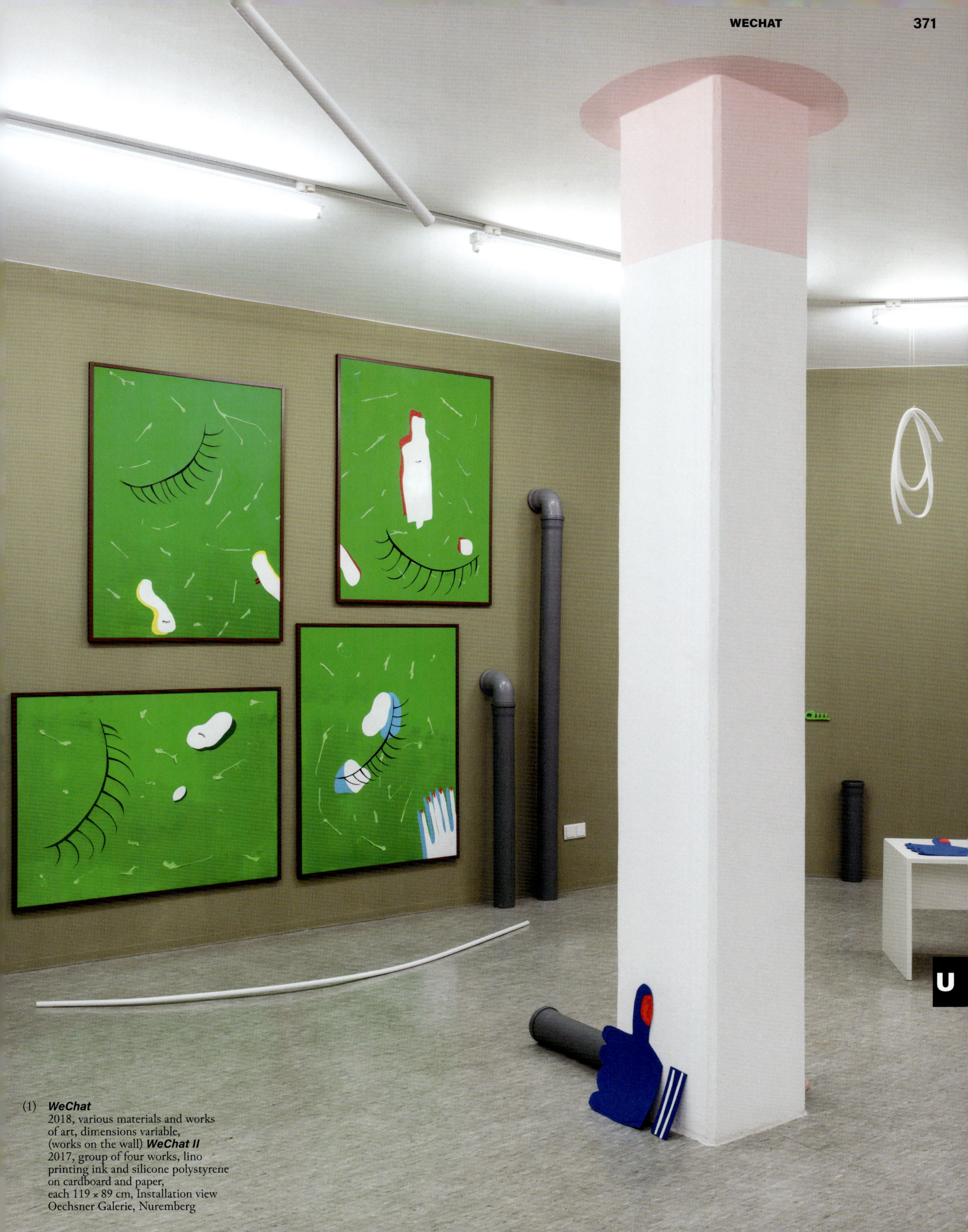

(1) ***WeChat***
2018, various materials and works of art, dimensions variable, (works on the wall) ***WeChat II*** 2017, group of four works, lino printing ink and silicone polystyrene on cardboard and paper, each 119 × 89 cm, Installation view Oechsner Galerie, Nuremberg

U

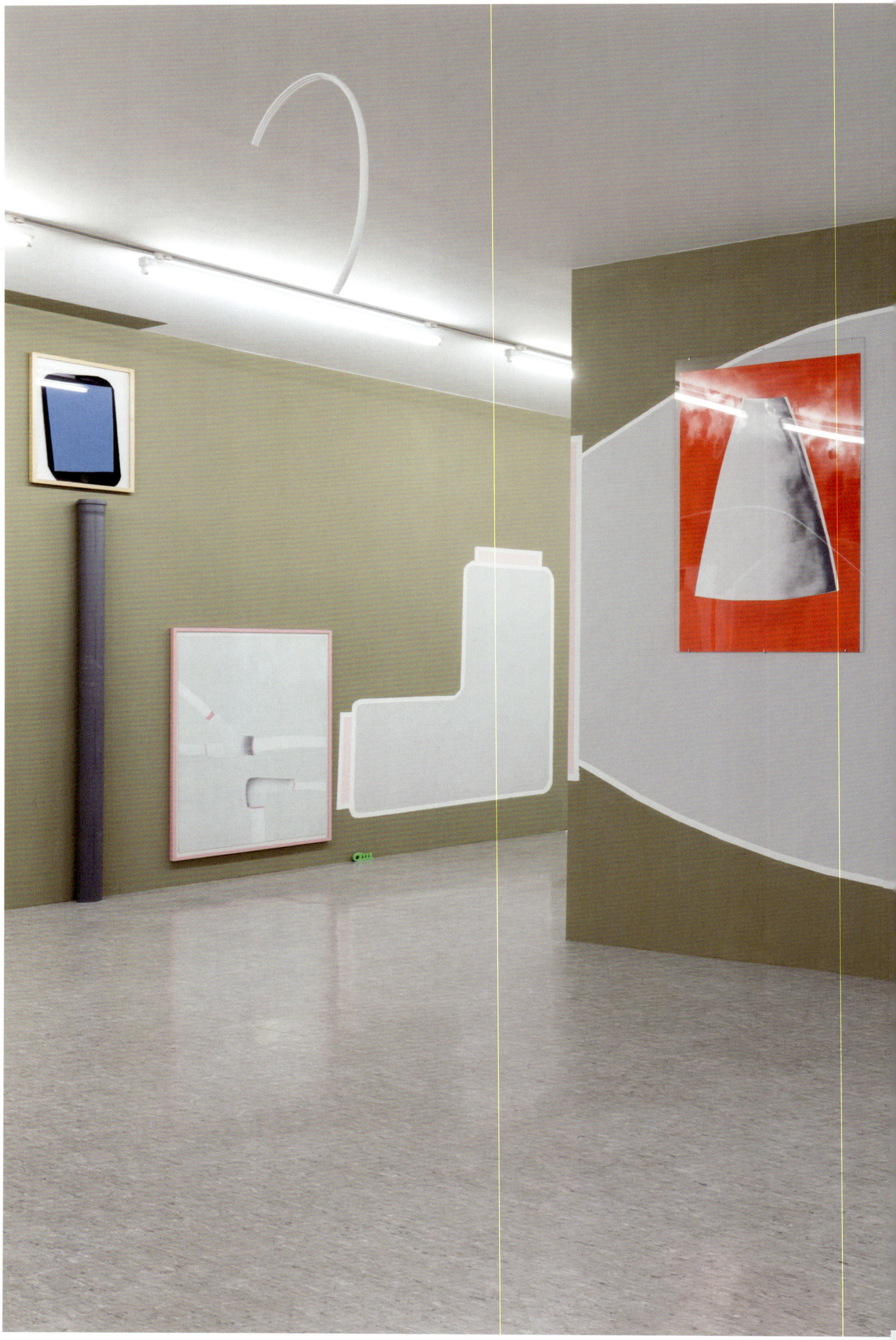

U

(2) ***WeChat***
2018, various materials and works of art, dimensions variable, Installation view Oechsner Galerie, Nuremberg

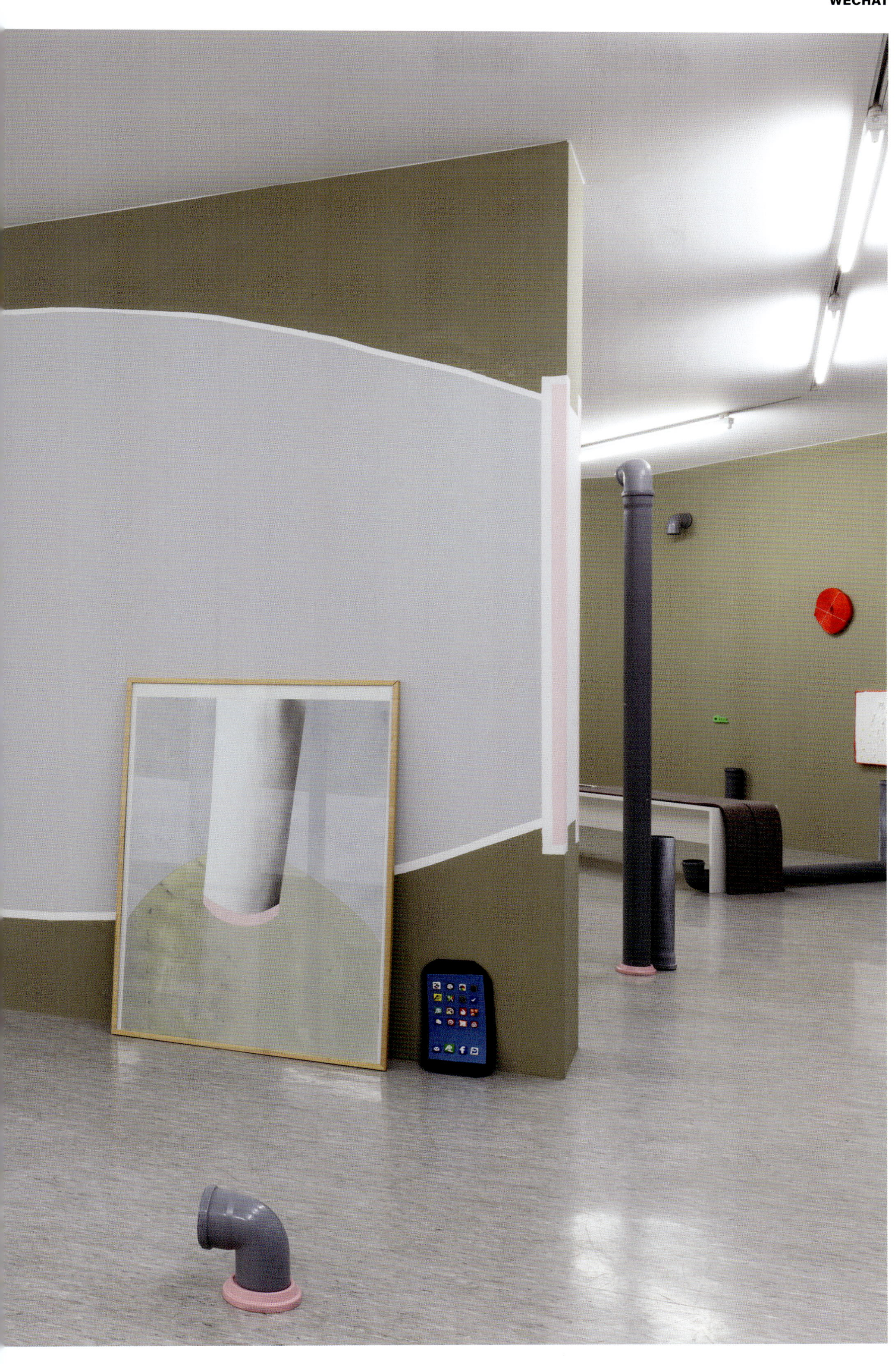

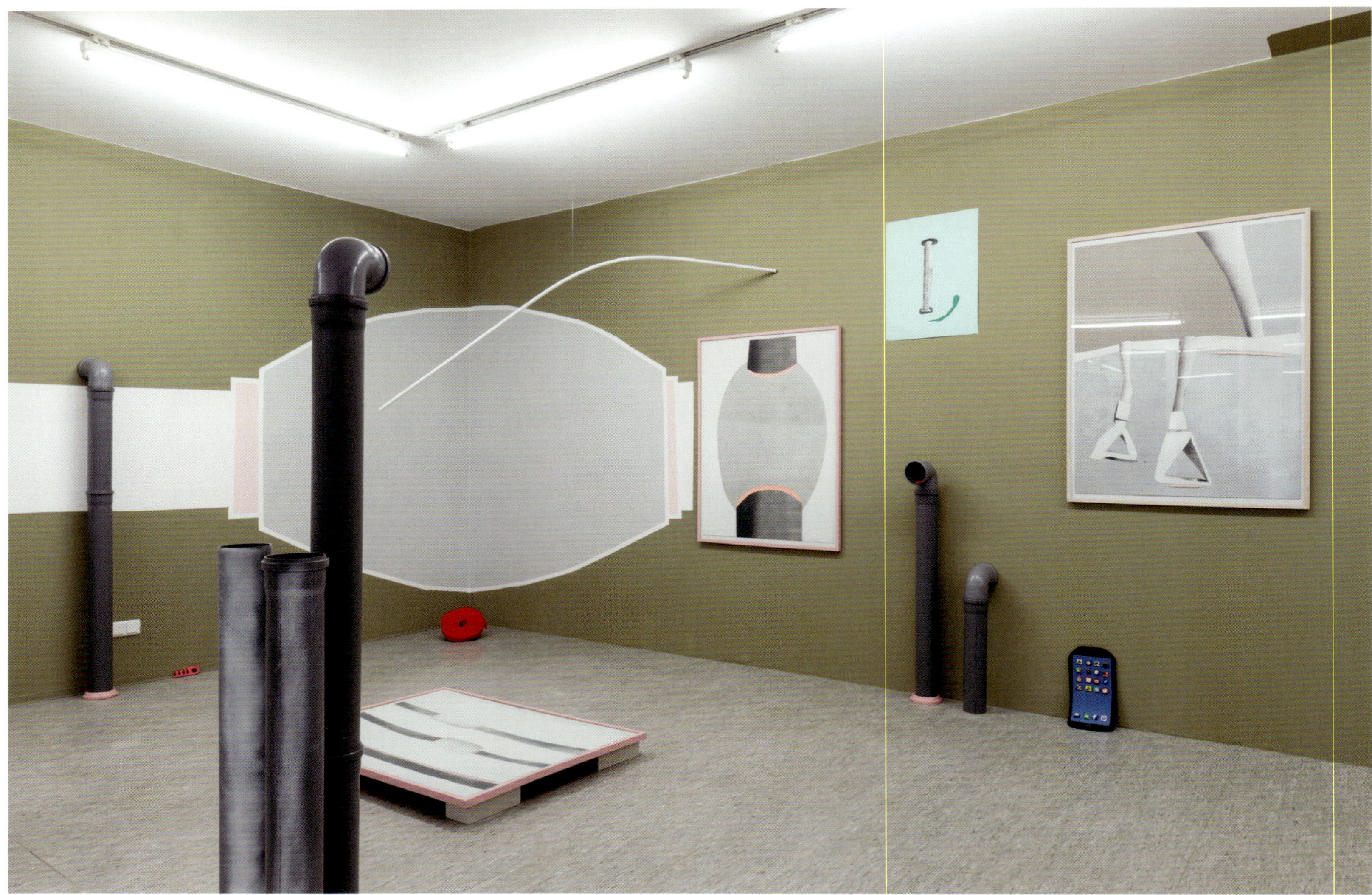
(3)

U

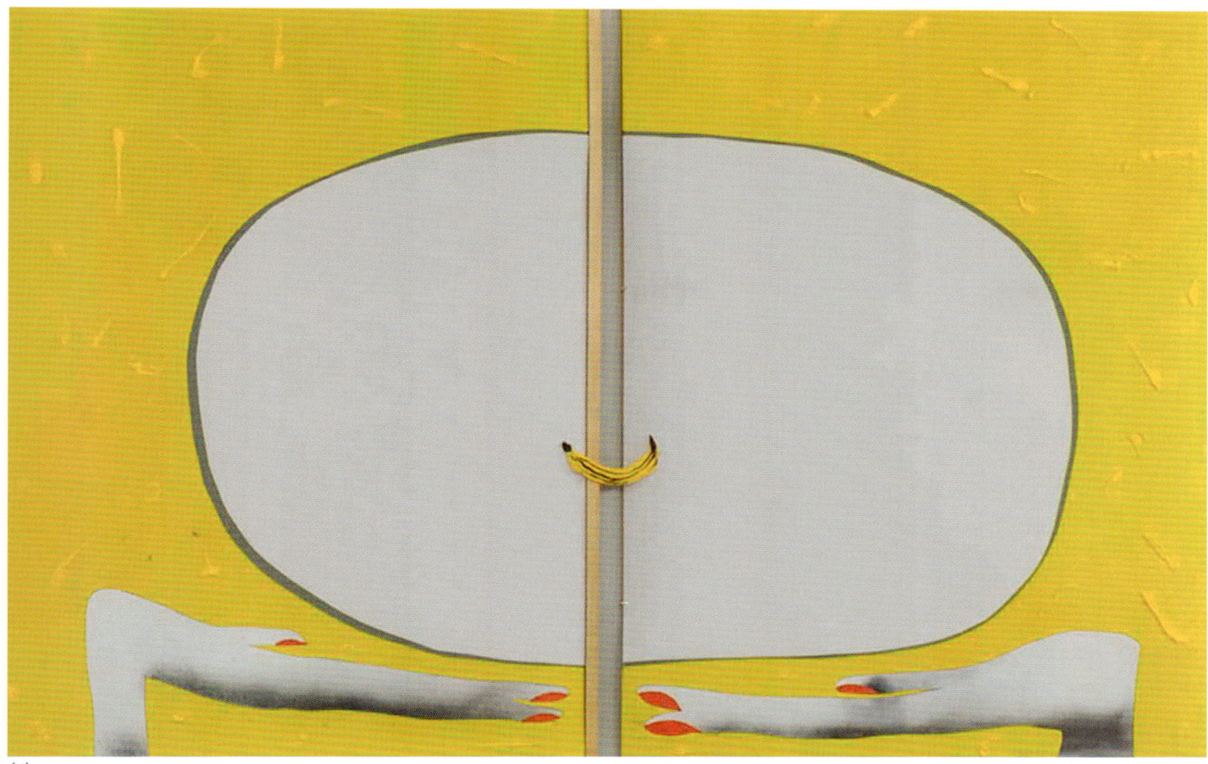

(4)

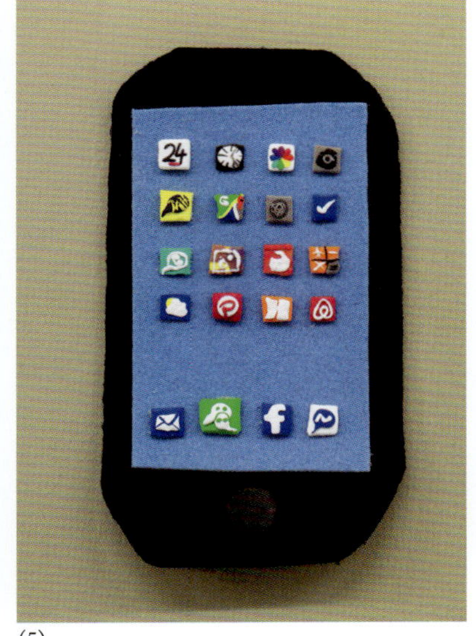

(5)

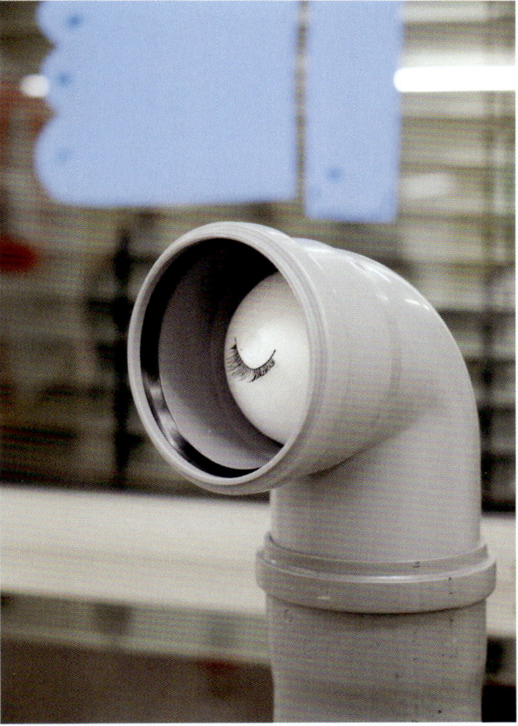

(6)

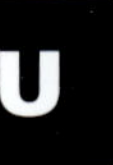

(3) ***WeChat***
2018, various materials and works of art, dimensions variable, Installation view Oechsner Galerie, Nuremberg

(4) ***Tell me, tell me – what will the future be like***
2017, printing ink, silk polyester cardboard and paper, 2-part installation, each 119 × 89 cm

(5) ***Artphone***
2018, felt, silicone polysterene, 39 × 32 cm

(6) ***WeChat*** (detail)
2018, Installation view Oechsner Galerie, Nuremberg

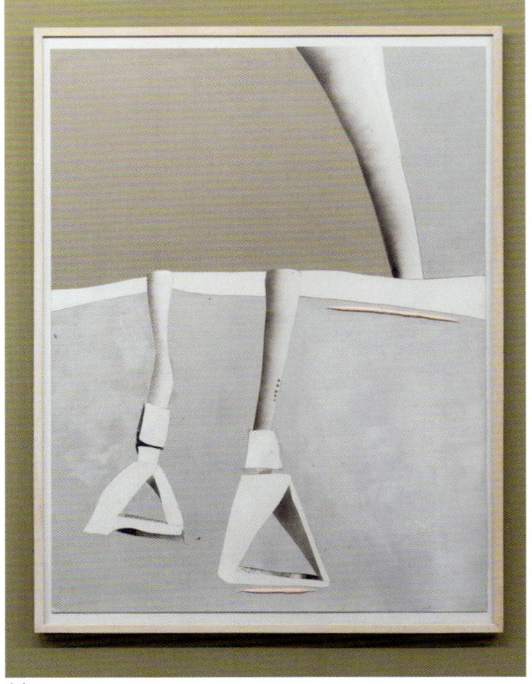
(7)

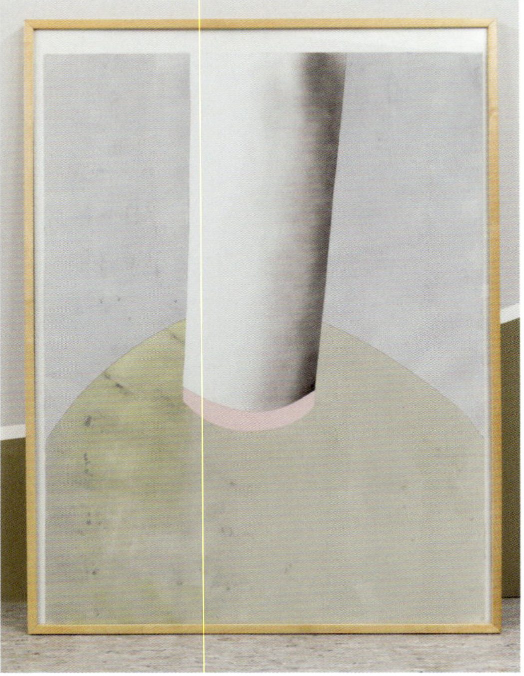
(8)

U

(7) ***Tube I***
2017, Linoprint ink on cardboard and paper, 119 × 89 cm

(8) ***Tube III***
2017, Linoprint ink on cardboard and paper, 119 × 89 cm

ON DISPLAY (ABORIGINALITY)

U

INGREDIENTS
Shell belt (Tao tribe) ②
Men's chains (Tao tribe) ②
Hunters skin ②
Classic vessel ②
Lanyu people (copy) ②
Han Chinese ①
Empty museum information stand I ③
Empty museum information stand II ④
Empty museum information stand III ⑤
Empty museum information stand IV ⑥
Empty museum information stand V ②
Shards ①

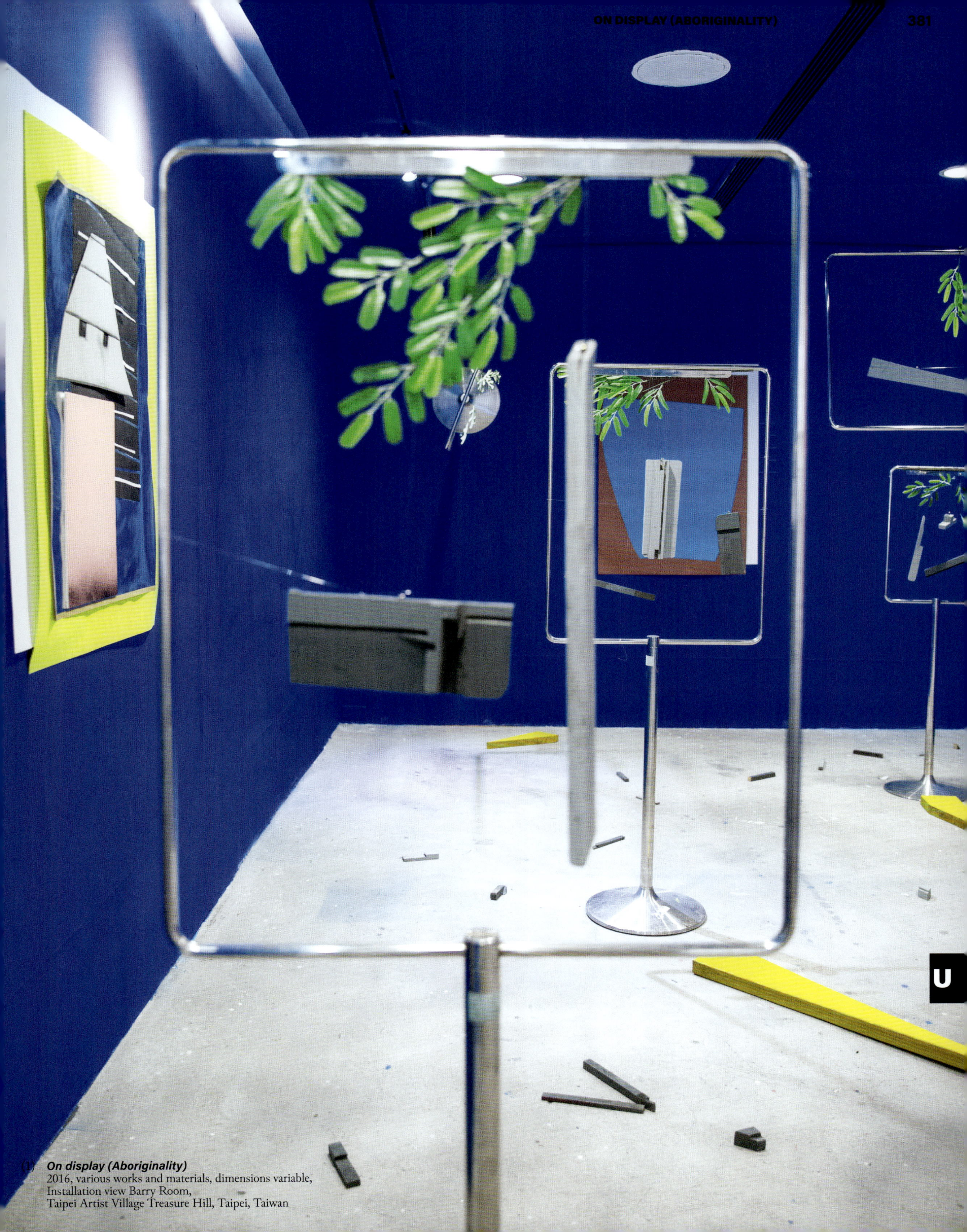

(1) ***On display (Aboriginality)***
2016, various works and materials, dimensions variable,
Installation view Barry Room,
Taipei Artist Village Treasure Hill, Taipei, Taiwan

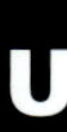

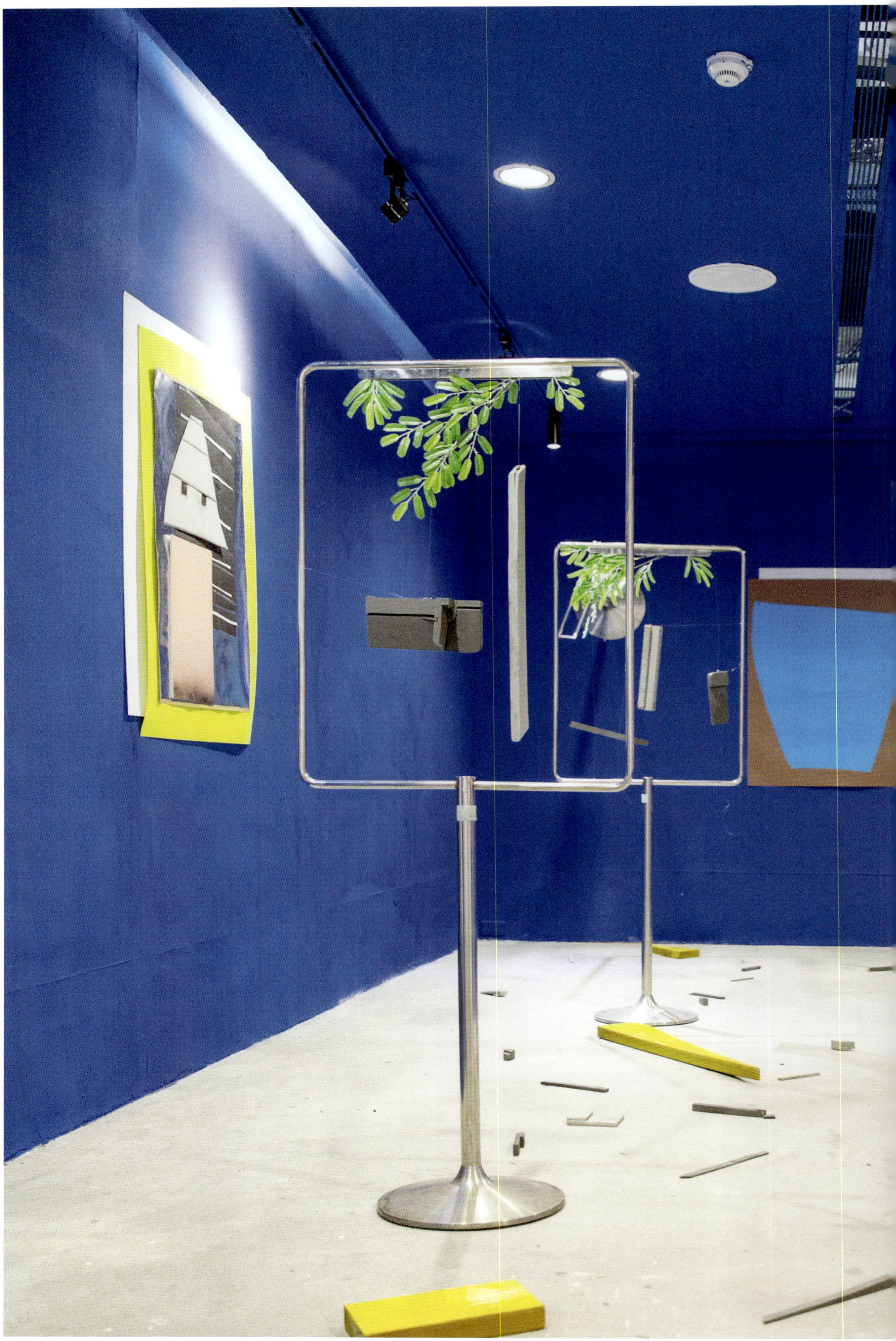

(2) ***On display (Aboriginality)***
2016, various works and materials, dimensions variable, Installation view Barry Room, Taipei Artist Village Treasure Hill, Taipei, Taiwan

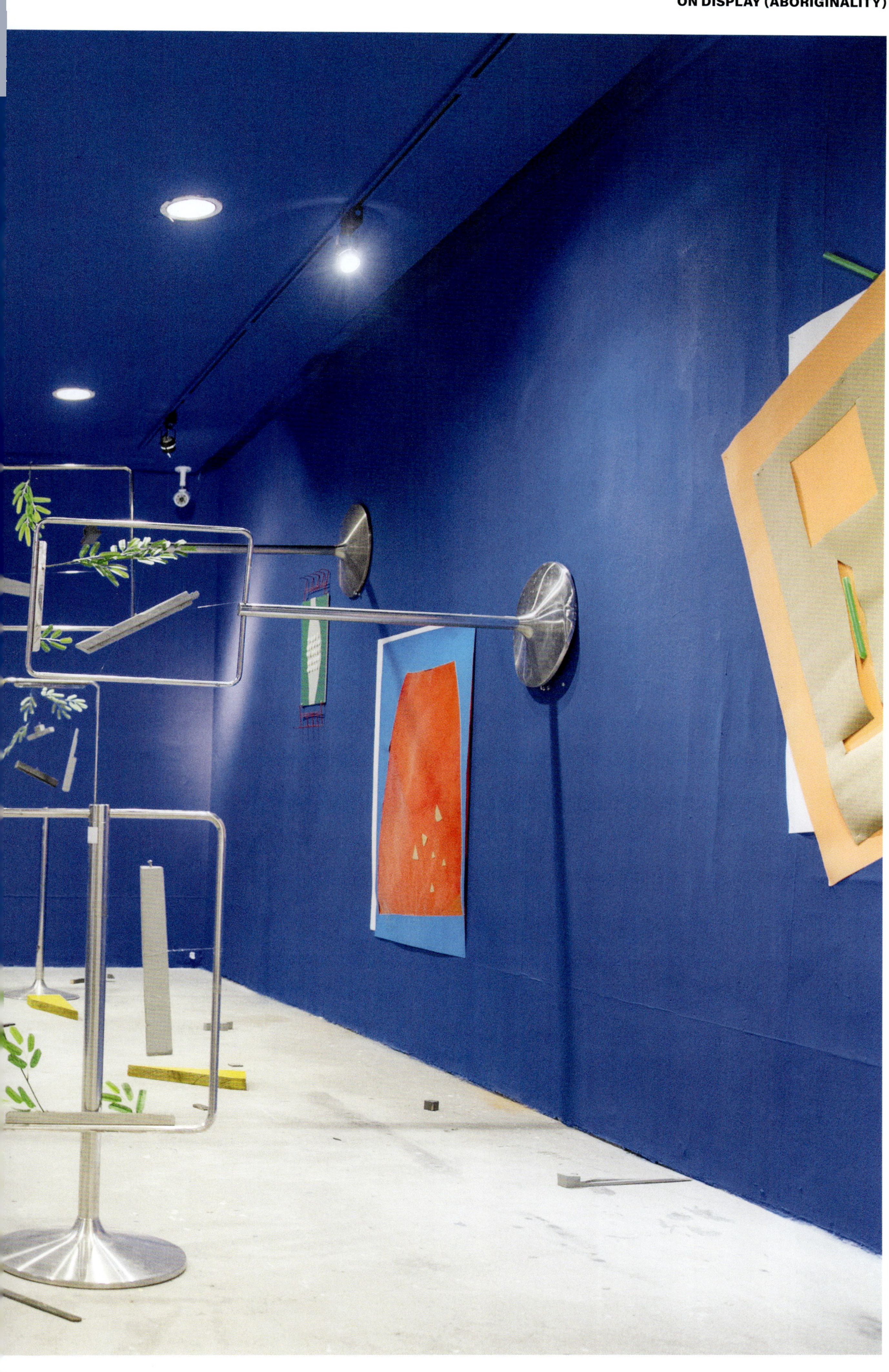

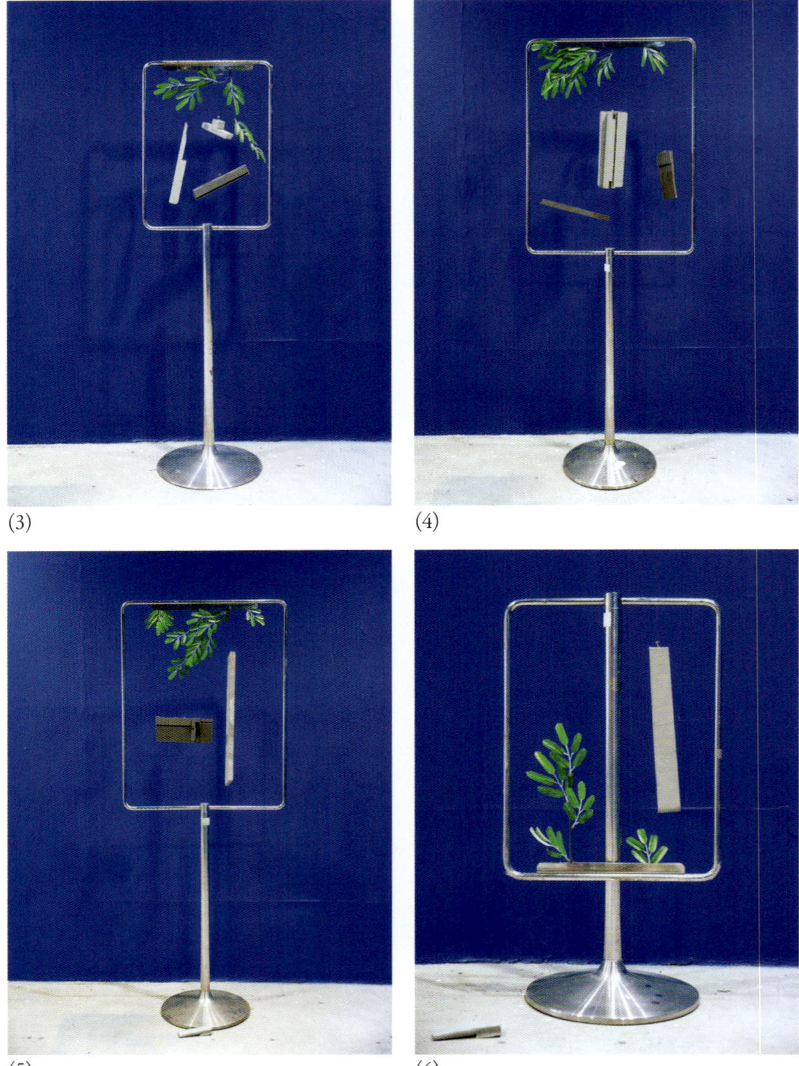

(3) (4) (5) (6)

U

(3)
(4)
(5)
(6) ***On display (Aboriginality)***
2016, various works and materials, dimensions variable, Detail: empty information stands of the National Museum of Taiwan, plastic bamboo leaves with the tips removed, wood, various sizes
Installation view
Barry Room,
Taipei Artist Village
Treasure Hill,
Taipei, Taiwan

STRIKES BACK – SOLAR RADIATION MANAGEMENT, CARBON DIOXIDE REMOVAL, THE JUNGLE AND MY GRANDMOTHER

INGREDIENTS
The New Mountains
The Sun Reflector

L

L

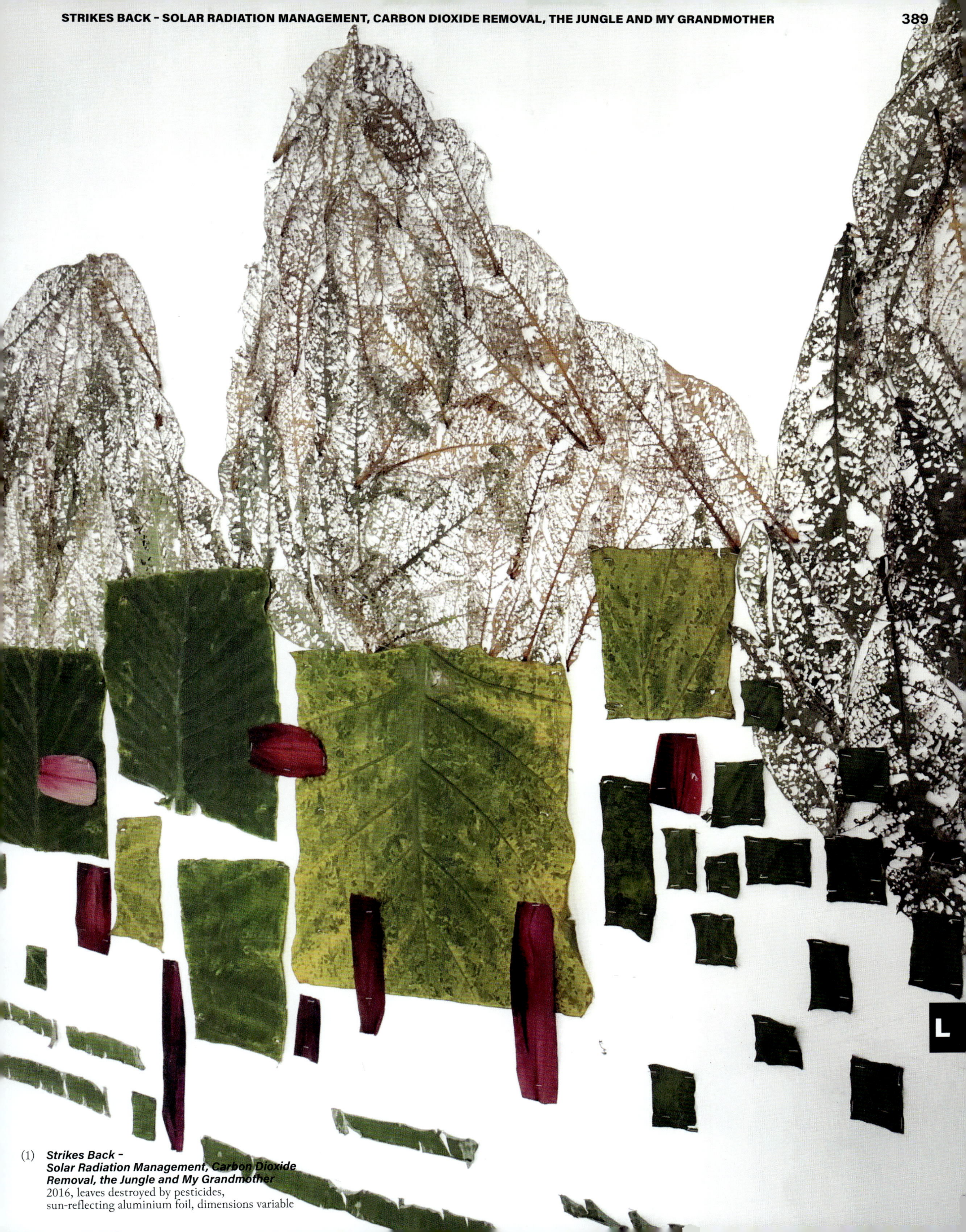

(1) ***Strikes Back –***
Solar Radiation Management, Carbon Dioxide Removal, the Jungle and My Grandmother
2016, leaves destroyed by pesticides,
sun-reflecting aluminium foil, dimensions variable

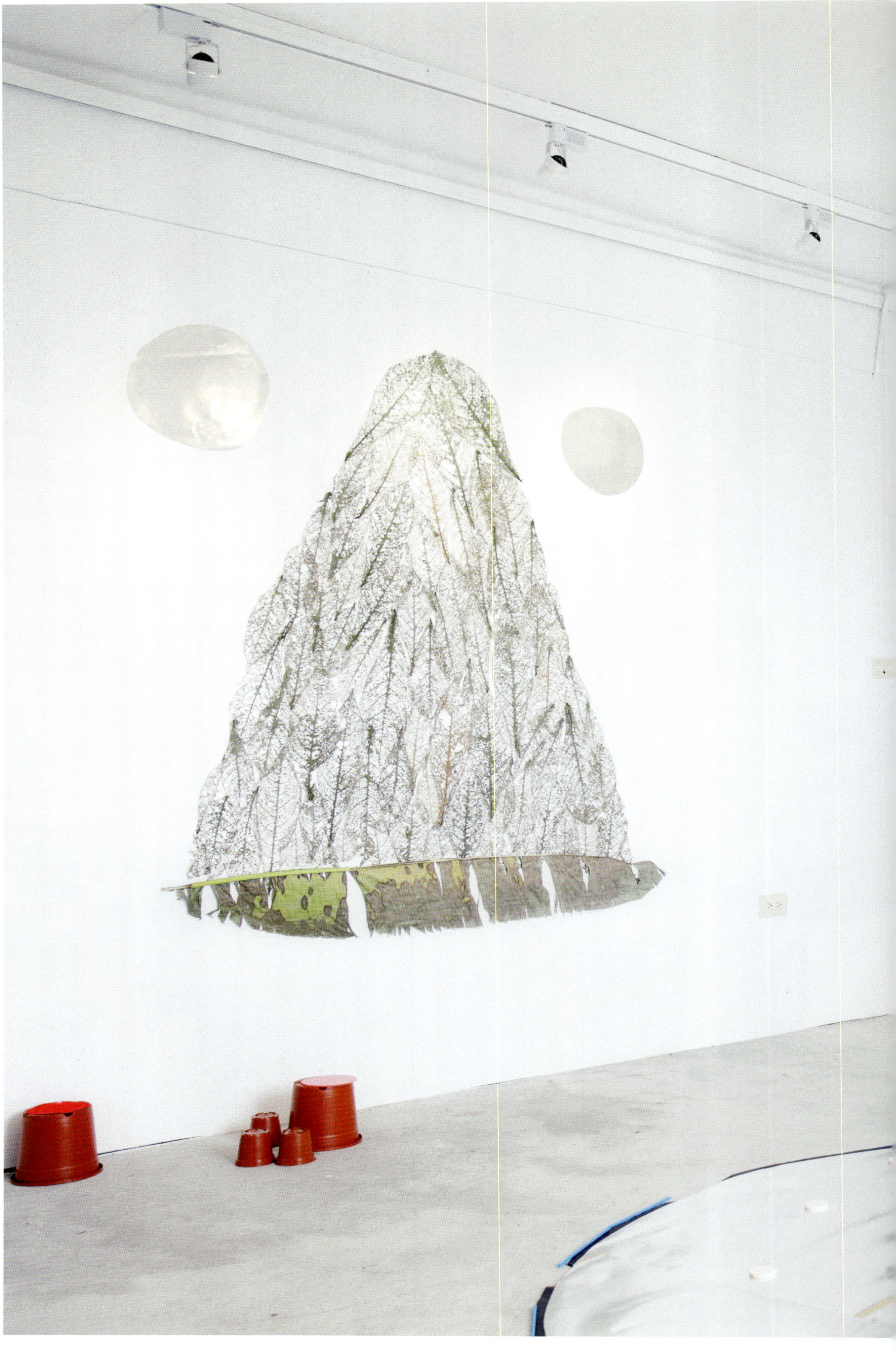

L

(2) ***Strikes Back – Solar Radiation Management, Carbon Dioxide Removal, the Jungle and My Grandmother***
2016, leaves destroyed by pesticides, sun-reflecting aluminium foil, dimensions variable

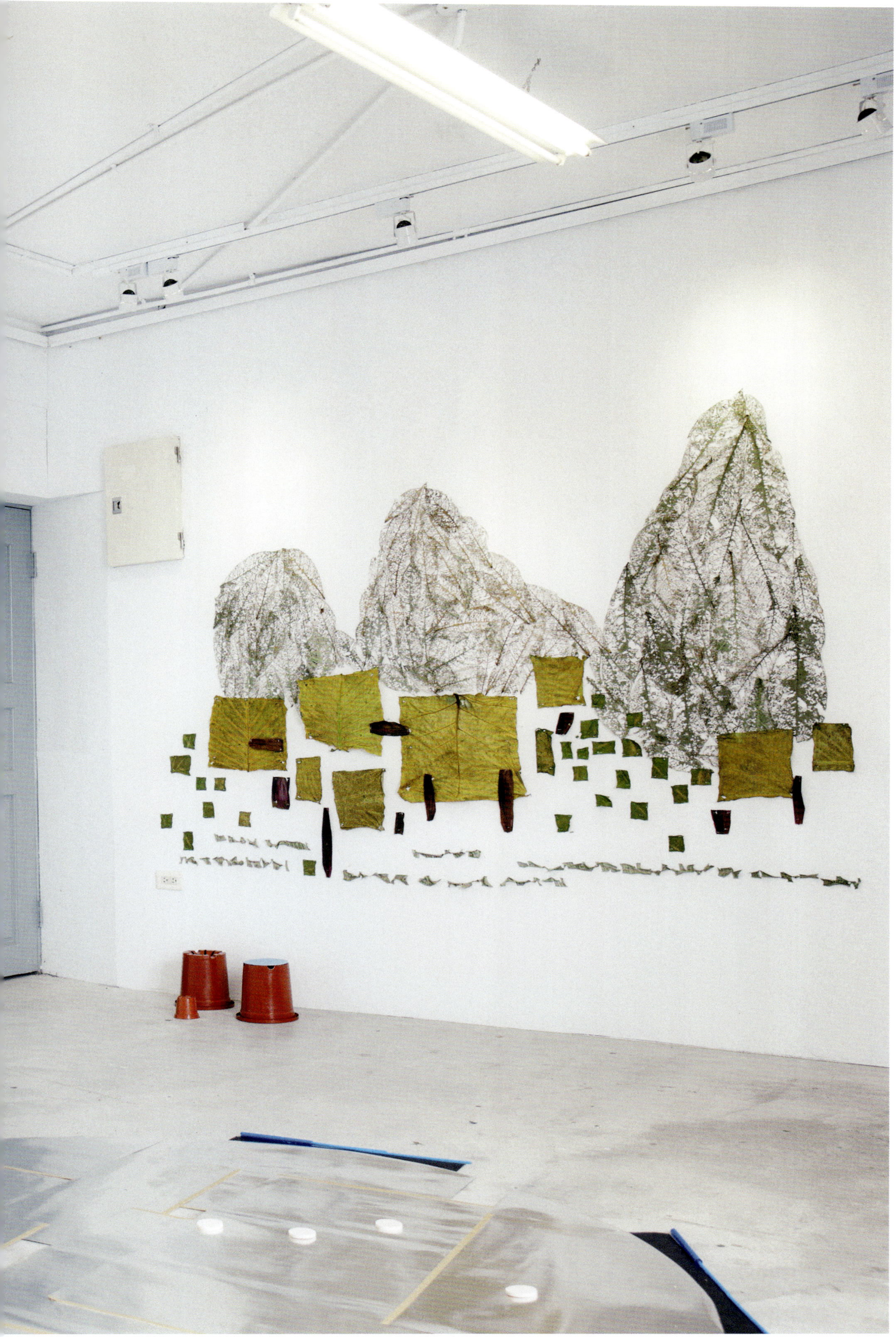

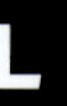
L

NUGAE

INGREDIENTS

Drunk Argos ①
Sowing Dragon Teeth (Hercules Superboy) ③
Rod of Asclepius 4
Adilette ⑤
Untote ⑥
Das Ri ⑦
Phaeton's chariot ⑧
Plate ⑨
Sword ⑩
Und darum hängen die Sternzeichen schief ⑪
Untitled ⑫
These Kids Are Not Okay/ Design solves problems (shards) ⑬
Buchdruck ⑭
Das Urteil des Paris ⑮
Untitled ⑯
Fitnessklotz ⑰
Untote II ⑱
Pulen ⑲
Brunnen (für F.) ⑳
o. T. (Platzdeckchen) ㉑
o. T. 1 ㉒
o. T. 2 ㉓
Garage ㉔
Sonnenuhr ㉕
Käsebrot ㉖
Sonnenuhr ㉗
Käsebrot II ②
Facebook- Schal ②
Scherben ②
Westlake (Reissack) ②

L

EN "Nugae" is a term by Gaius Valerius Catullus (c. 84 BC–c. 54 BC), a latin poet of the Republican period. He was a spoiled rich hipster kid coming from a leading equestrian family of Verona. He lived a lazy, sumptuous life in the luxury of inherited money, enjoying all kinds of men, women, and drugs. He was not a zoon politicon at all, following the philosophy of Epicurus.
The purpose of philosophy (and life) to Catullus was to attain the happy, tranquil life, characterized by *ataraxia*—peace and freedom from fear—and *aponia*—the absence of pain—and by living a self-sufficient life surrounded by friends. So Catullus happily doped around in his luxury villa, hanging out with his hipster entourage. Cicero hatefully called them the *neoteroi*—the new poets. Indeed, they did some new stuff. Catullus, for his part, hated the big epics and called his little poems *nugae.* Nugae are small honed, often funny poems on both mythological events and private interests and stories. Like Láthe biósas: "Live hidden/Live secretely. Back to privacy, I'd say."

☐ ***Nugae/back to privacy, 2013, excerpt from catalogue***

DE „Nugae" ist ein Begriff von Gaius Valerius Catullus (ca. 84 v. Chr.–ca. 54 v. Chr.), einem lateinischen Dichter der republikanischen Zeit. Er war ein verwöhntes, reiches Hipster-Kid, das aus einer führenden Ritterfamilie in Verona stammte. Er lebte ein faules, üppiges Leben im Luxus seines geerbten Geldes und genoss alle Arten von Männern, Frauen und Drogen. Er war ganz und gar kein Zoon-Politiker und folgte der Philosophie des Epikur. Der Sinn der Philosophie (und des Lebens) bestand für Catull darin, ein glückliches, ruhiges Leben zu führen, das durch *ataraxia* – Frieden und Freiheit von Angst – und *aponia* – die Abwesenheit von Schmerz – gekennzeichnet ist, und ein autarkes Leben umgeben von Freunden zu führen. So dopte Catullus fröhlich in seiner Luxusvilla herum und hing mit seiner Hipster-Entourage ab. Cicero nannte sie hasserfüllt die *neoteroi* – die neuen Dichter.
In der Tat, sie machten einige neue Sachen. Catull seinerseits hasste die großen Epen und nannte seine kleinen Gedichte *nugae*. Nugae sind kleine geschliffene, oft witzige Gedichte, die sowohl mythologische Ereignisse als auch private Interessen und Geschichten behandeln. Láthe biósas: „Lebe verborgen/Lebe heimlich. Back to privacy, I'd say."

☐ ***Nugae/back to privacy, 2013, Auzug aus dem Katalog***

L

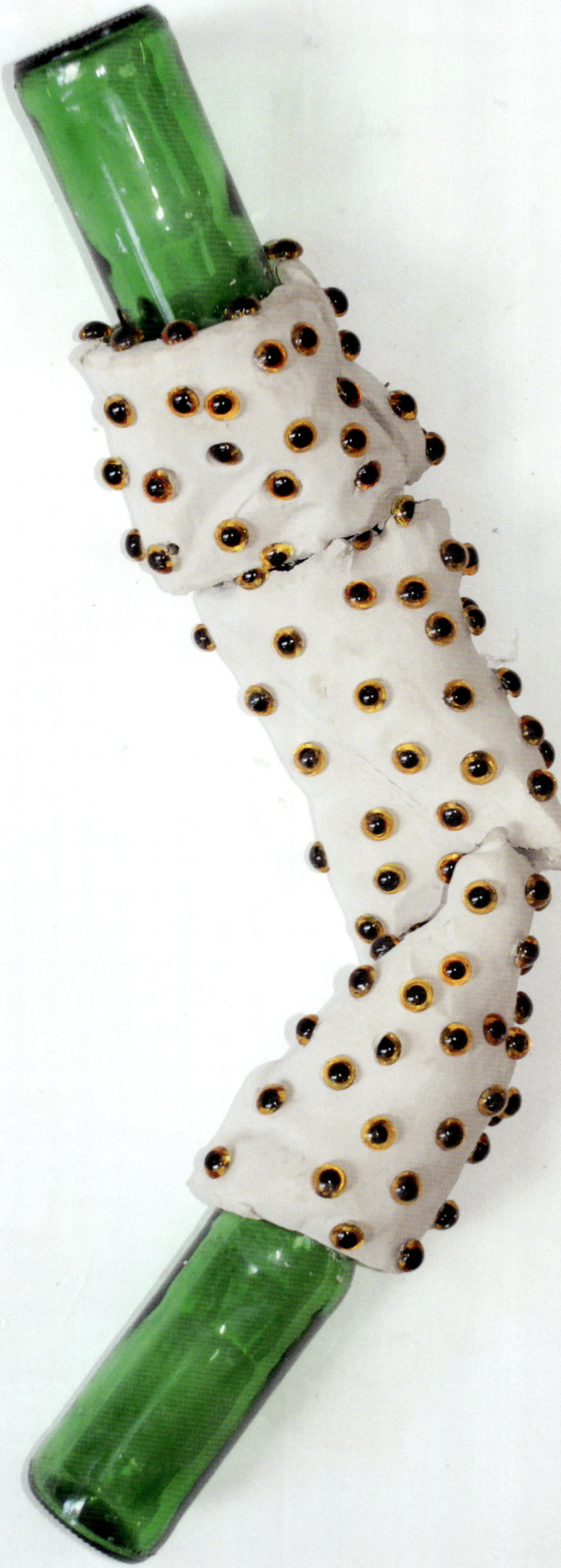

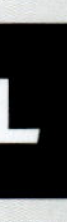

(1) ***Drunk Argos***
2009, ceramics, teddy bear eyes, glass,
60 × 15 cm

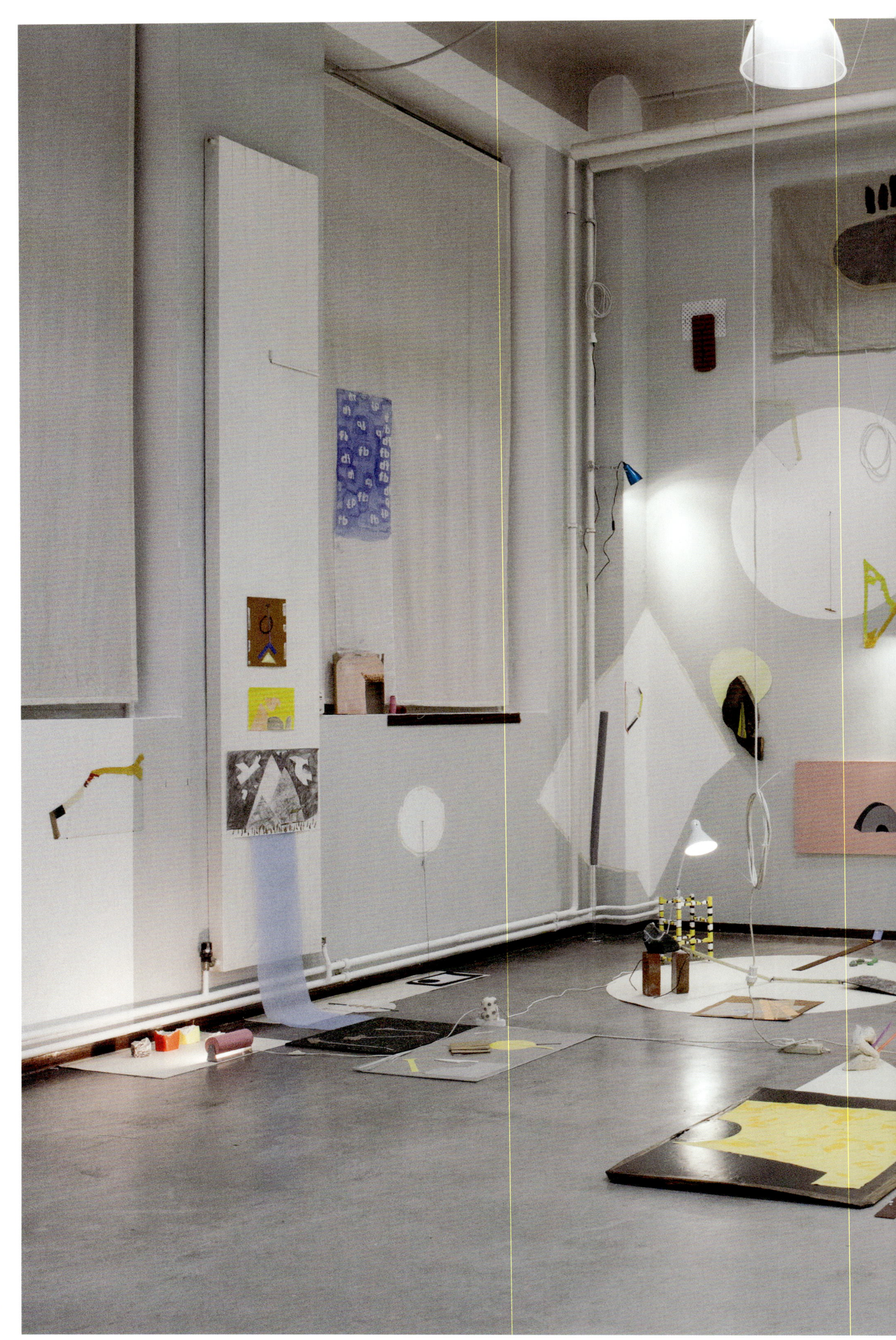

(2) ***NUGAE***
2012/13, various individual works and materials, 5 × 6 × 7 m, Installation view Kunsthaus Hamburg

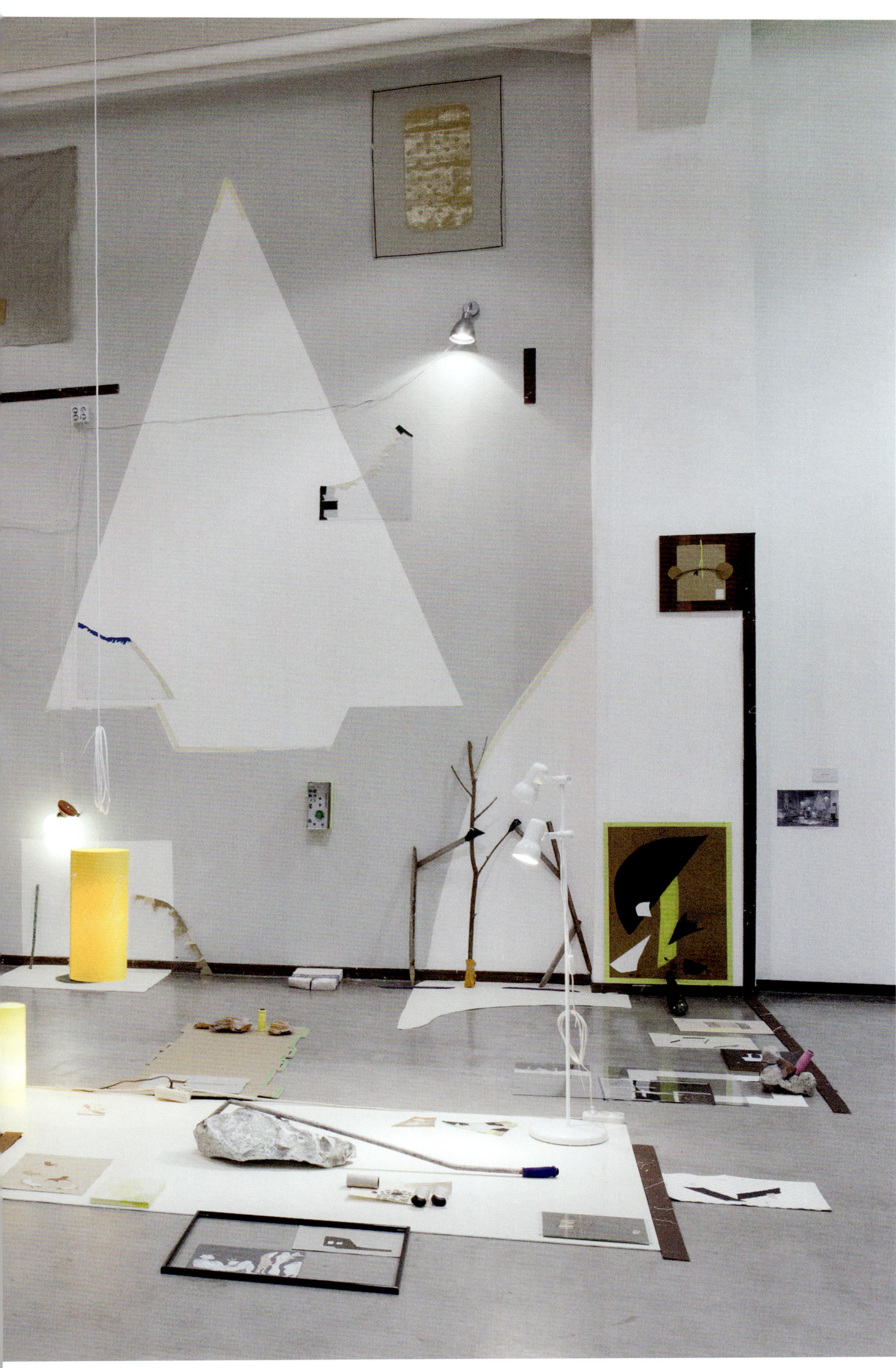

(3) ***Sowing Dragon Teeth (Hercules Superboy)***
2012, stones, color, dimensions variable

(4) ***Rod of Asclepius***
2012, pipe cleaner and metal, length 20 cm

(5) ***Adilette***
2012, stone, acrylics, plaster, tape, 20 × 38 cm

(6) ***Untote***
2012, watercolor, felt and adhesive tape on paper, 29 × 21 cm

(7) ***Das Ri***
2010/12, plastic and acrylics on wood, 10 × 15 cm

(8) ***Phaeton's chariot***
2012, stone, metal, mirror, wire, 40 × 160 × 45 cm

(9) ***Plate***
2012, acrylics and wood on ceramics, 12 cm diameter

(10) ***Sword***
2012, marble and cardboard on foam rubber, 20 × 30 cm

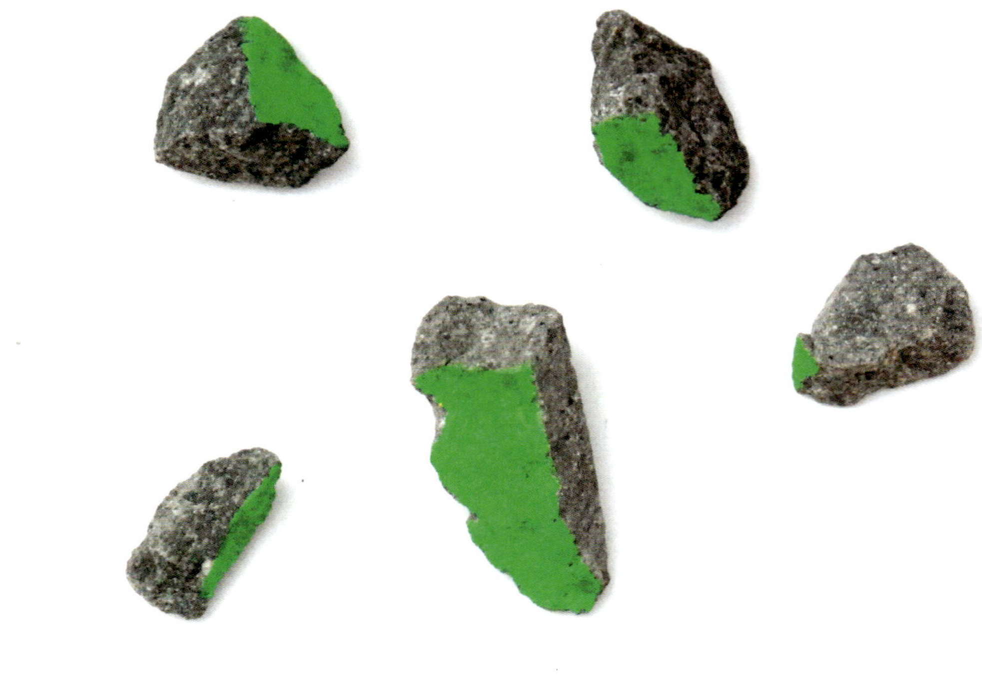
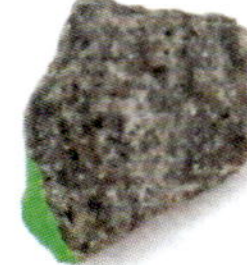
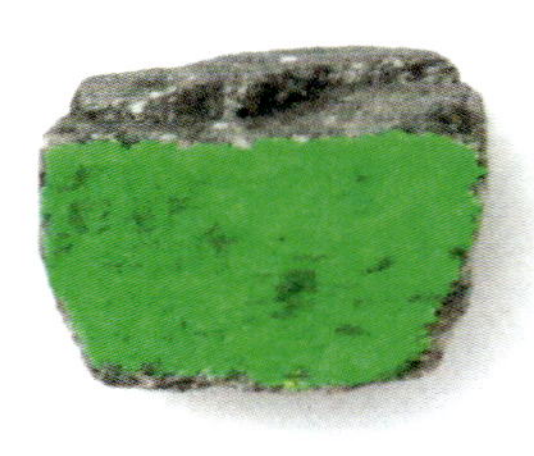
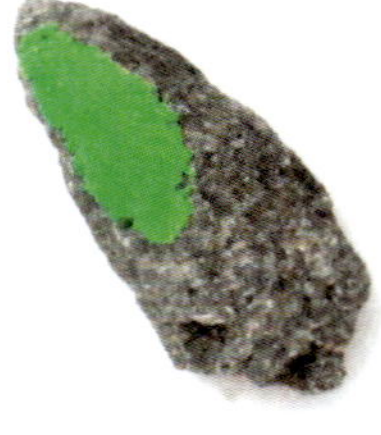

(3)

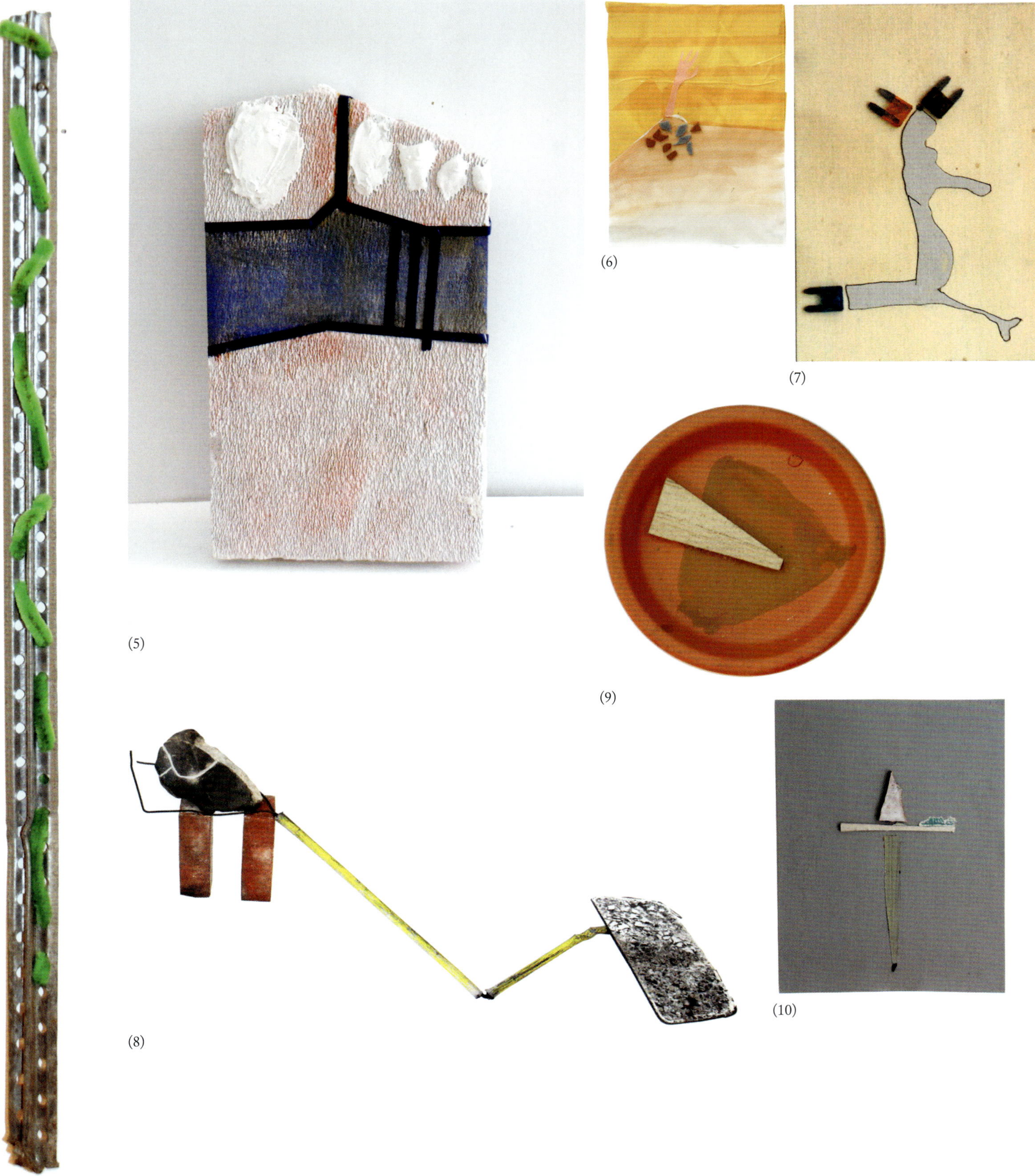

(4)

(5)

(6)

(7)

(8)

(9)

(10)

L

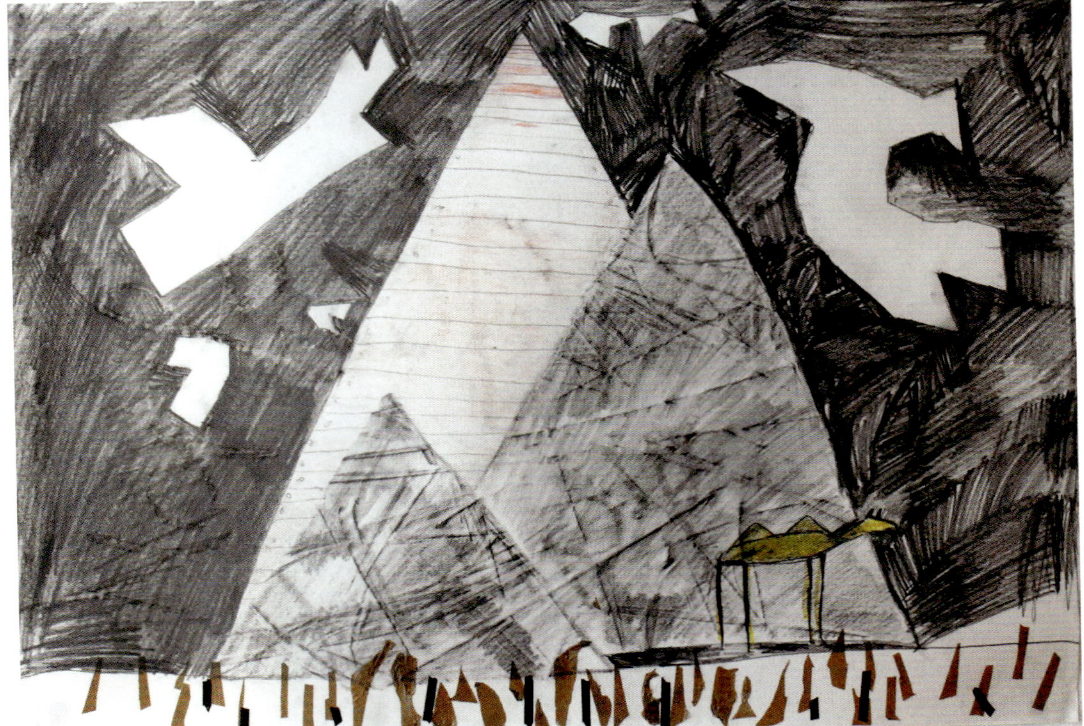

(11)

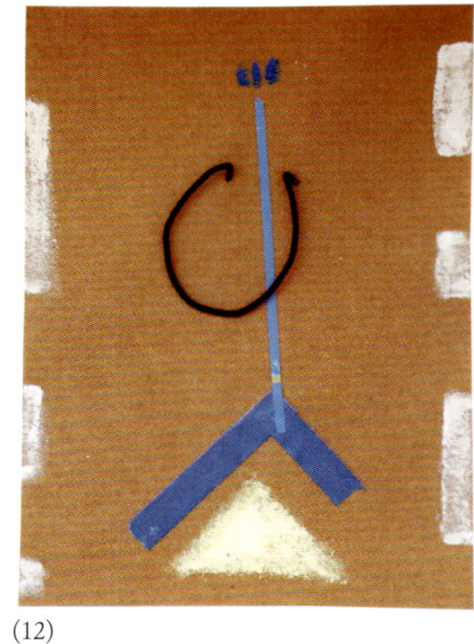

(12)

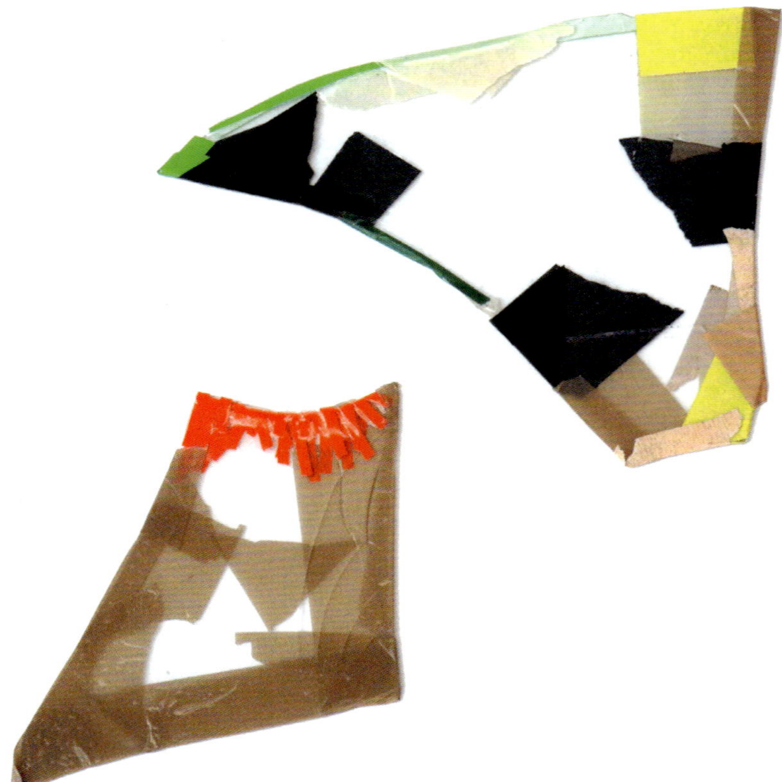

(13)

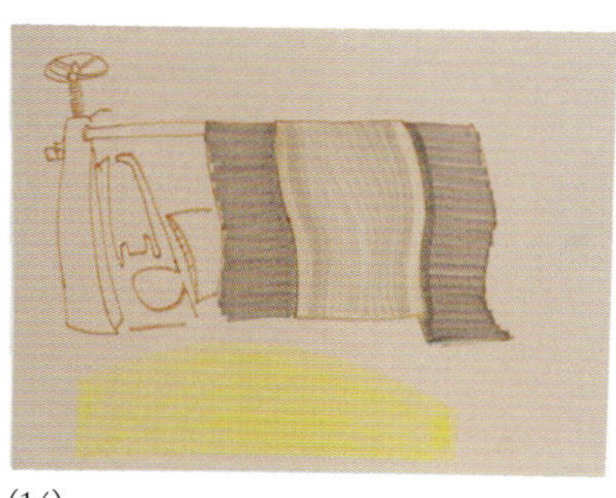
(14)

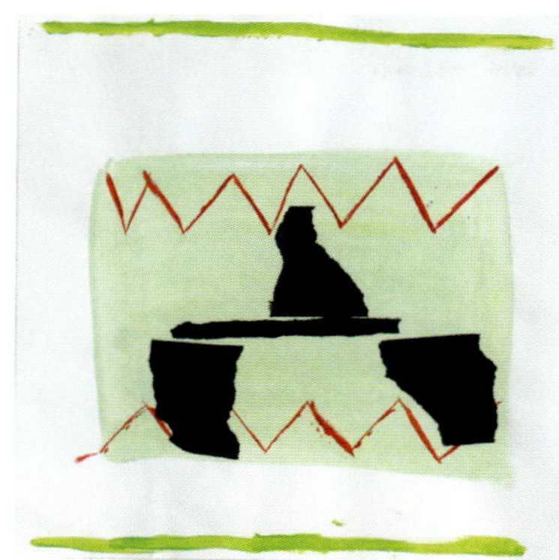
(15)

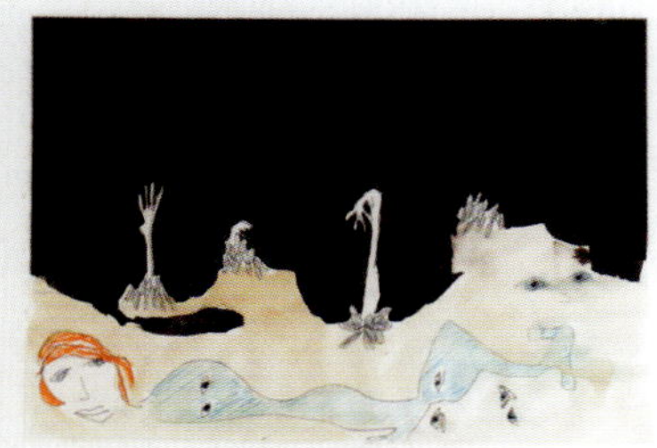
(16)

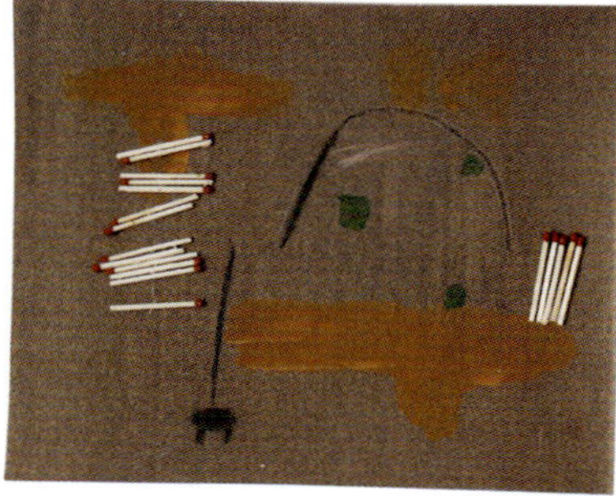
(18)

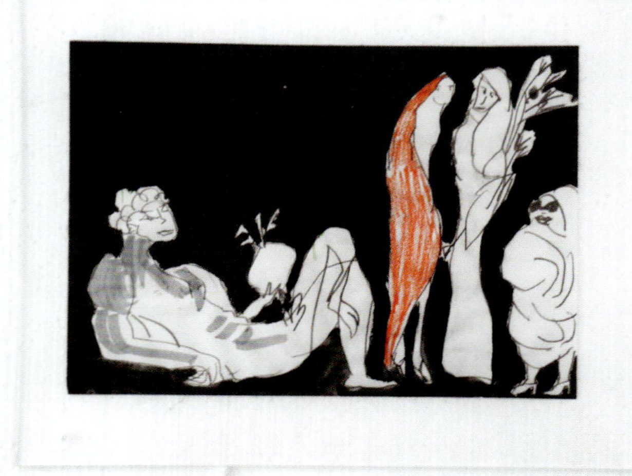
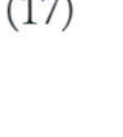
(17)

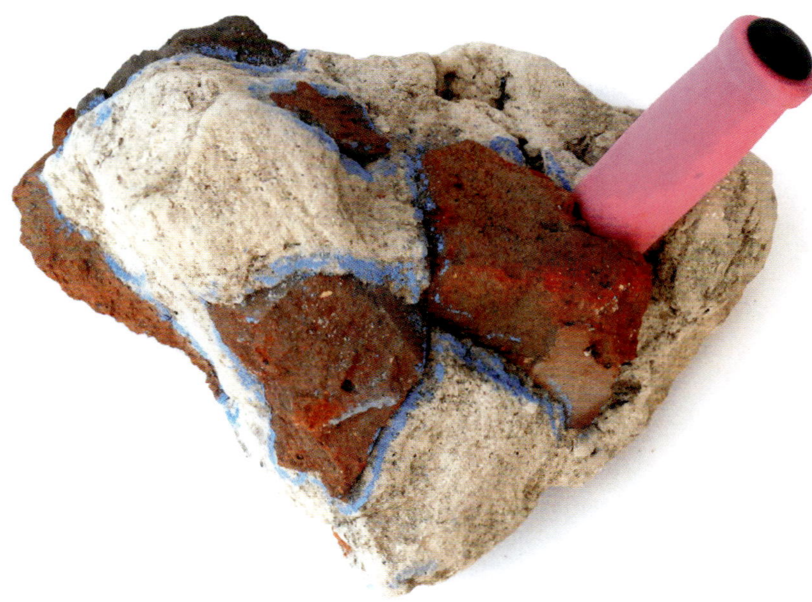
(19)

(11) ***Und darum hängen die Sternzeichen schief***
2012, graphite, adhesive tape and colored pencil on paper with plastic, 59.5 × 146 cm
(12) ***Untitled***
2012, acrylics, pipe cleaners and tape on felt, 24.5 × 33.5 cm
(13) ***These Kids Are Not Okay/Design solves problems (shards)***
2012, adhesive tape on glass, 20 cm × 26 cm
(14) ***Buchdruck***
2012, felt pen on foam, 20 × 30 cm
(15) ***Untitled***
2012, tape on felt, 20 × 30 cm
(16) **Untote II**
2012, watercolor on paper, 29 × 21 cm
(17) ***Das Urteil des Paris***
2012, ink, pencil and colored pencil on paper, 20 × 30 cm
(18) ***Untitled***
2012, matches and acrylics on sanding paper, 25 × 30 cm,
(19) ***Fitnessklotz 2***
012, stone, graphite, foam, diameter 20 cm

E

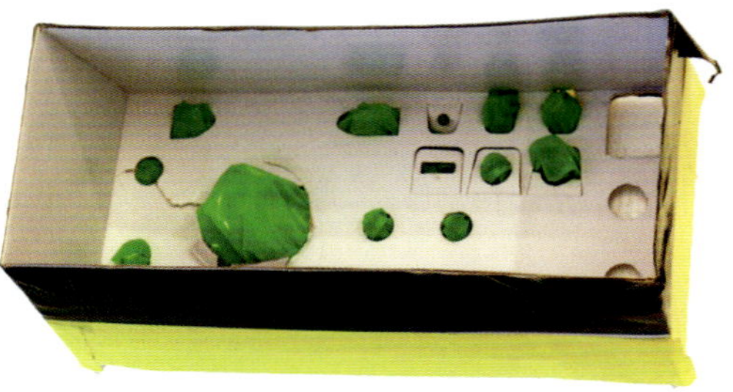
(20)

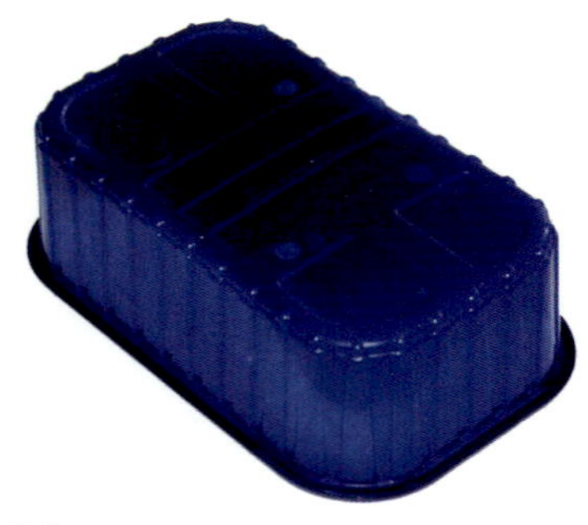
(21)

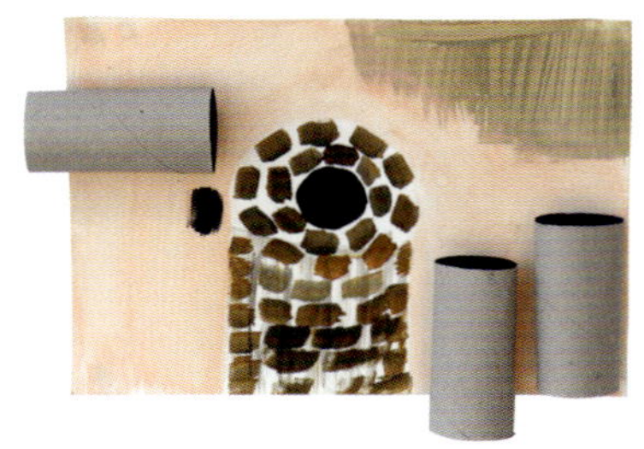
(22)

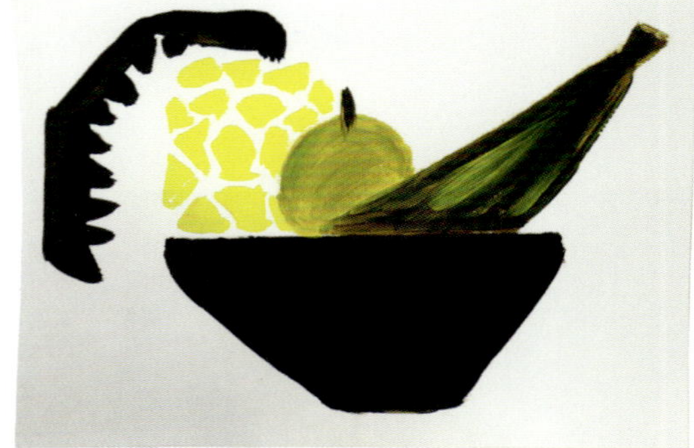
(23)

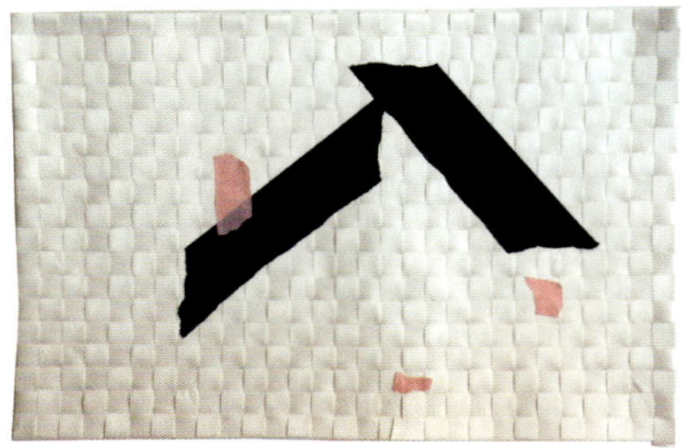
(24)

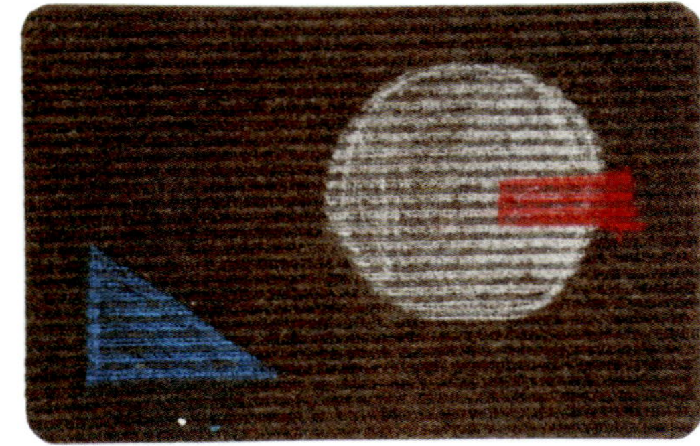
(25)

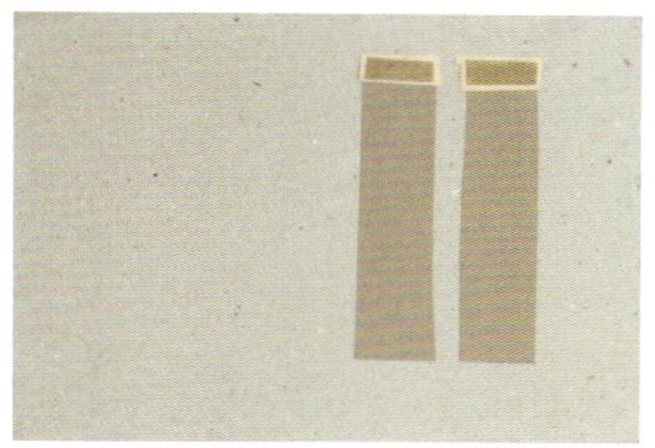
(26)

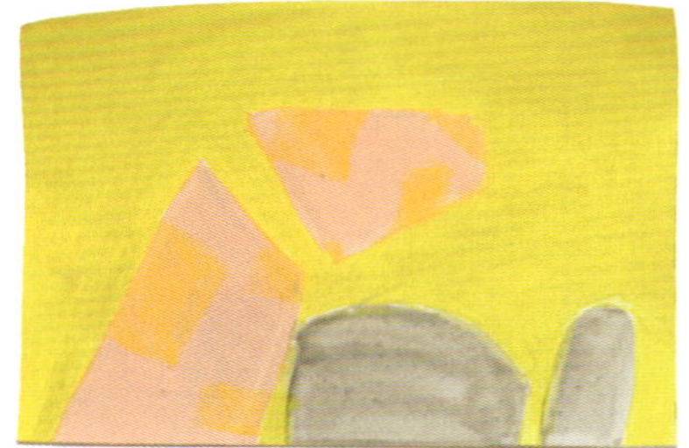
(27)

(20) ***Pulen***
2012, tape and plastic on cardboard, 20 × 24.5 × 12 cm
(21) ***o. T.***
2011, ready made plastic box, 15 × 18 × 8cm
(22) ***Brunnen (für F.)***
2012, acrylic paint on cardboard, 62 × 24.5 cm
(23) ***Obstkorb***
2013, acrylic paint and cardboard on paper, 20 × 30 cm
(24) ***o. T. (Platzdeckchen)***
2013, acrylic paint and cardboard on paper, 20 × 30 cm
(25) ***o. T. 1***
2013, chalk on doormat, 30 × 40 cm
(26) ***Garage***
2011, cardboard on paper, 62 × 24.5 cm
(27) ***o. T. 2***
2013, watercolor on paper, 20 × 30 cm

E

DUMMHEIT VON 1000 TÖPFE (DAS MOOR: ÜBERWACHUNGS-STAAT)

INGREDIENTS
Überwachungswohnung I ①
Überwachungswohnung II ①
Überwachungswohnung III ①
Überwachungswohnung IV ①
Überwachungswohnung V ①
Organik vs. Anorganik I ①
Organik vs. Anorganik II ①
Organik vs. Anorganik III ①
Organik vs. Anorganik IV ①
Organik vs. Anorganik V ①
Schrankbett ①
Dürers Mutter in der Schublade ①
Teekran ①
Superrechner ①
Superrechner II ①
Polizei ①
Fabrik ①
Moorgarten II ①
Mikroskophasi I ①
Mikroskophasi II ①
Teigschrank ①
Teigschrank II ①

EN Verena Issel has a lively, almost libidinous relationship with the material world, with the unique characteristics of its materialities, surfaces, structures, forms and colors, self-organizations, and other qualities, and especially with how these are present in the utilitarian and other objects of northern and central European culture with which she is familiar.
It would be wrong, however, to associate her material world with that of Arte Povera, since it is far removed from any dualistic pathos, but rather, in the broadest sense, with the world of objects of Nouveau Réalisme, and then (also in terms of the abundance of her activities) much closer to Dieter Roth than to Jason Rhoades, for example. She prosaically sets in motion an unpuristically complex, playful arte povera ricca that robs the abundance of the representational world, which is inevitably material in many ways, of all pre-coding and thus of its triviality, in order ultimately to gain knowledge from this liberation through enchantment.

In her choice of materials and objects, as well as in her choice of dimensions, combinations, origin, appearance, age, and even genre, there are hardly any clear preferences; she draws with great ease from unlimited resources. And she can justifiably rely on her almost somnambulistic aesthetic certainty of purpose, which is nourished by the independence of her mind, her love of experimentation, and her wide-ranging interests.

As a result, her work to date is already characterized by a remarkably multi-layered corpus, which can be seen in a general and genre-separating way, including drawing, photography, albums and notebooks (printing techniques of all kinds, batik), painting, flat and spatial multi-material and multi-media collages, wall and floor reliefs, murals, objets trouvés, sculpture (wood, plastic, ceramic, metal, plaster, papier-mâché), mosaic, installation, staged natural and artificial light, sound, kinetics, performance, and video.

However, a basic principle of her three-dimensional works, as well as her notebooks, books, and albums, which are always also reliefs, is that the above-mentioned genres do not appear separately as individual pieces, but rather manifest themselves simultaneously in a variety of ways, overlapping one another, emerging from one another, breaking apart, or dimensionally intensifying in the respective structure. In this way, highly complex material, medial, and dimensional systems are created, which are realized in small to very large dimensions and are of surprisingly peculiar and yet different beauty on all individual levels and as a whole.

These ordered conglomerates also stand in different and varying relationships to space; they not only stand, hang, or lie, but can also form themselves as lying objects from lying and/or standing objects, or as lying objects merging into hanging objects or vice versa, and so on.
In addition, the large units are composed of many different smaller and autonomous subunits, which in turn can be composed of even smaller subunits, and thus represent the basic material structure of all matter. This applies in particular to the two large polymorphic installations: *Dummheit von 1000 Töpfe (Das Moor: Überwachungsstaat)* and a large, untitled double-walled piece, which, despite its many differences from the installation, will not be described further here.

She is not concerned a priori with the principle of the Gesamtkunstwerk, but rather with illustrating her interest in systems and structures, their connections and overlaps, their interleavings and breaks both in languages and in the spaces of living, architecture, cities, etc.—that is, in systems of civilization as forms of human organization and communication. And she makes a point of entering these spaces in her own particular way, which she describes as "empathy versus abstraction."
[...]
It would probably be going too far to go into other levels of Verena Issel's work here, although its differentiated complexity would certainly demand it.
I have therefore tried to limit myself to the most important aspects.

☐ ***Andrea Tippel, expert recommendation for a scholarship***

E

DE Verena Issel verbindet ein quicklebendiges, geradezu libidinöses Verhältnis mit der materialen Welt, deren Eigenarten der Stofflichkeiten, Oberflächen, Strukturen, Formen und Farben, Selbstorganisationen und sonstigen Beschaffenheiten und darin besonders damit, wie diese in den Gebrauchs- und anderen Gegenständen der nord- und mitteleuropäischen Kultur, der ihr vertrauten, vorhanden sind. Es wäre allerdings falsch, ihre Materialwelt mit der der Arte povera in Verbindung zu bringen, weil sie von jedem dualistischen Pathos weit entfernt ist, sondern eher, im weitesten Sinn, mit der Gegenstandswelt des Nouveaux Réalisme und dann (auch was im Ansatz die Fülle ihrer Aktivitäten betrifft) deutlich näher mit Dieter Roth als z. B. Jason Rhoades verwandt, setzt sie prosaisch eine unpuristisch komplexe, spielerische Arte povera ricca in Gang, die die Fülle der gegenständlichen Welt, die zwangsläufig vielfältig materiell ist, aller Prae-Codierungen und damit ihrer Trivialität beraubt, um aus dieser Freisetzung durch Verzauberung letztlich Erkenntnis zu schlagen.

Es lassen sich in der Wahl ihrer Materialien und Gegenstände, aber ebenso in der Wahl der Dimensionen, der Kombinatorik, der Herkunft, der Anmutung oder des Alters und sogar des Genres kaum eindeutige Präferenzen ausmachen; sie schöpft mit großer Leichtigkeit aus dem Vollen. Und sie kann sich dabei zu Recht auf ihre fast schlafwandlerische ästhetische Treffsicherheit verlassen, die aus der Unabhängigkeit ihres Geistes, ihrer Experimentierlust und aus ihrer weitverzweigten Aufmerksamkeit gespeist wird.

Infolgedessen zeigt ihr bisheriges Werk schon einen beachtlich vielschichtigen Corpus, der sich, allgemein und gattungssepariierend betrachtet, aus Zeichnung, Fotografie, Alben und Heften (Drucktechniken aller Art, Batik), Malerei, flachen und räumlichen multimaterialen und -medialen Collagen, Wand- und Bodenreliefs, Wandbild, Objet trouvé, Skulptur (Holz, Kunststoff, Keramik, Metall, Gips, Pappmaschee,) Mosaik, Installation, inszeniertem natürlichen und künstlichen Licht, Sound, Kinetik, Performance und Video zusammensetzt.

Es ist aber ein Grundprinzip ihrer dreidimensionalen Stücke und auch der Hefte, Bücher und Alben, die stets auch Relief sind, dass die genannten Gattungen nicht voneinander getrennt als Einzelstücke erscheinen, sondern sich vielfältig ineinander übergreifend, auseinander entstehend oder sich dimensional brechend oder potenzierend im jeweiligen Gebilde gleichzeitig manifestieren und so material, medial und dimensional hochgradig komplexe Systeme entstehen, die in kleinen bis kleinsten bis zu sehr großen Ausdehnungen verwirklicht werden und auf all ihren einzelnen Ebenen sowie im Ganzen von überraschend eigenartiger und doch unterschiedlicher Schönheit sind.

Diese geordneten Konglomerate stehen außerdem in unterschiedlichen und dazu noch in sich variierenden Beziehungen zum Raum, sie können nicht nur stehen, hängen oder liegen sondern sich auch als Liegende aus Liegendem und/oder Stehendem bilden oder als Liegende in Hängendes übergehen oder umgekehrt usw.
Außerdem bilden sich die großen Einheiten aus einer großen Anzahl verschiedener kleinerer und autonomer Untereinheiten, die sich ihrerseits aus noch kleineren Untereinheiten zusammensetzen können, und bilden damit die stoffliche Grundstruktur aller Materie ab.
Dies gilt besonders für die zwei großen polymorphen Installationen: *Dummheit von 1000 Töpfe (Das Moor: Überwachungsstaat)* und ein, trotz seiner mehrfachen Verschiedenheit davon, hier nicht weiter beschriebenes, unbetiteltes großes Doppelwandstück.

Dabei geht es ihr nicht a priori um das Prinzip Gesamtkunstwerk sondern ist die Veranschaulichung ihres Interesses an Systemen und Strukturen, deren Verbindungen und Überlagerungen, Verschachtelungen und Brüchen sowohl in den Sprachen als auch in den Räumen des Wohnens, der Architektur, der Städte usw., also an Systemen der Zivilisation als Organisations- und Kommunikationsformen des Menschen. Und sie legt Wert darauf, sich in diese Bereiche auf ihre spezielle Weise zu begeben, die sie „Einfühlung versus Abstraktion“ nennt.
[...]
Es würde wohl zu weit führen, hier auf weitere Ebenen in Verena Issels Werk einzugehen, obwohl seine differenzierte Komplexität es durchaus verlangen würde. Ich habe mich deshalb auf die Hauptaspekte zu beschränken versucht.

☐ ***Andrea Tippel, gutachterliche Empfehlung für ein Stipendium***

E

E

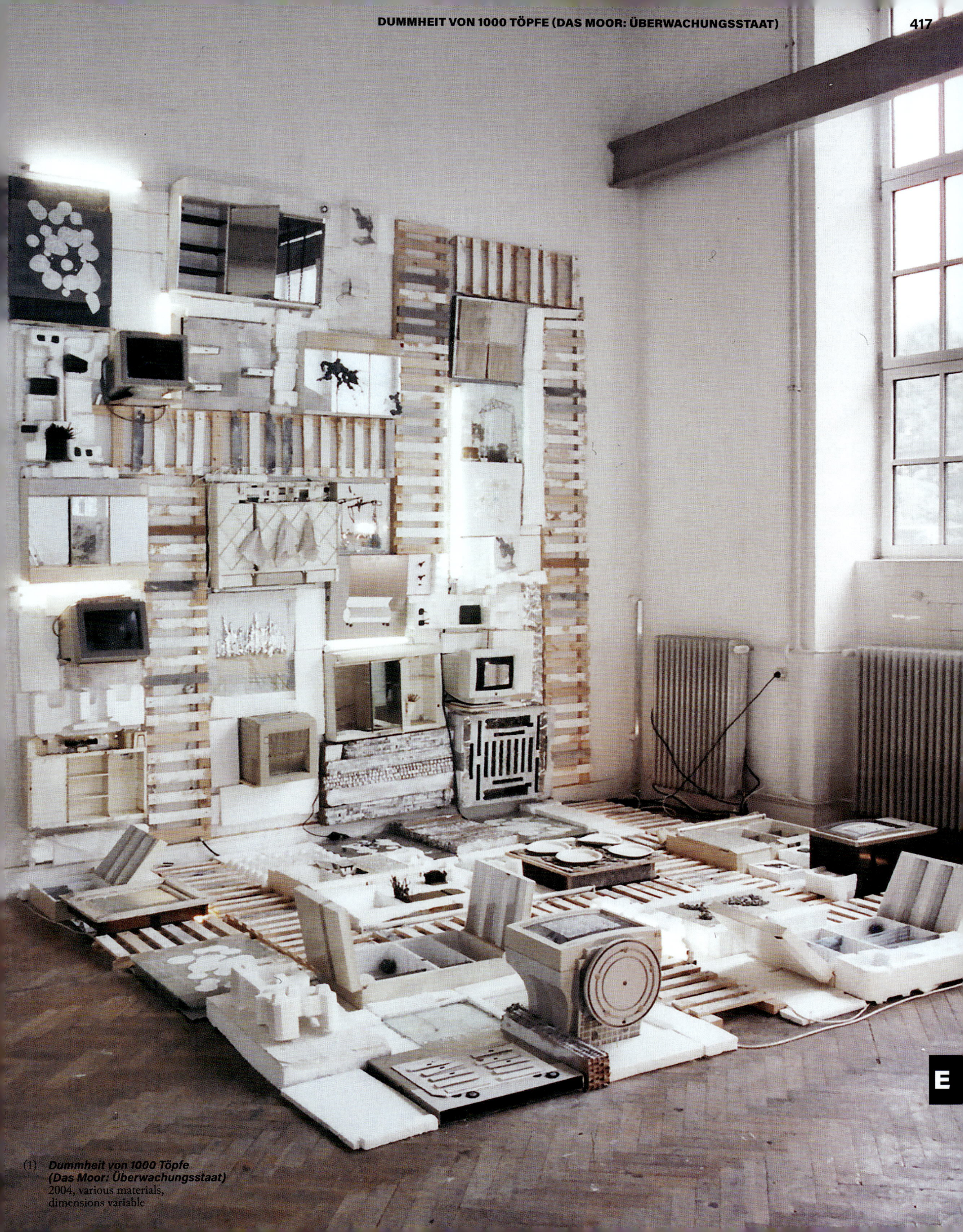

E

(1) ***Dummheit von 1000 Töpfe***
(Das Moor: Überwachungsstaat)
2004, various materials,
dimensions variable

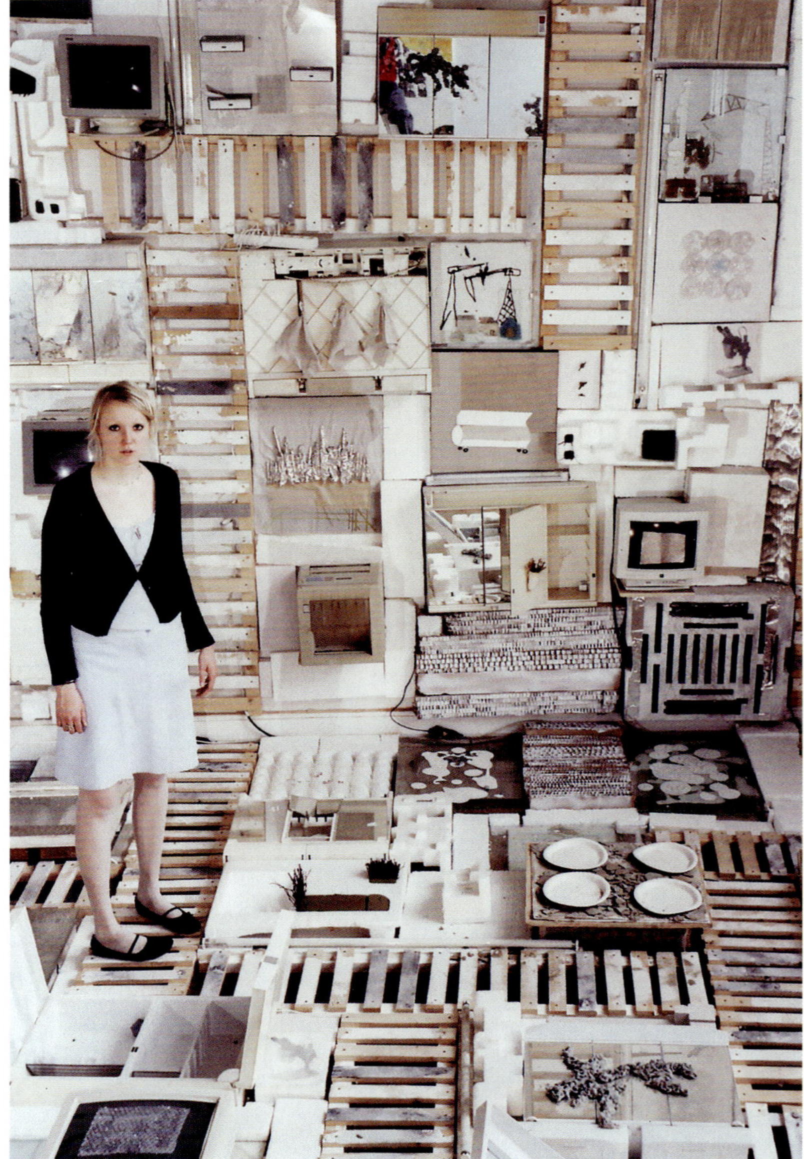

(2)

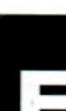

(2) ***Dummheit von 1000 Töpfe (Das Moor: Überwachungsstaat)***
2004, various materials, dimensions variable

PAINTINGS AND OBJECTS

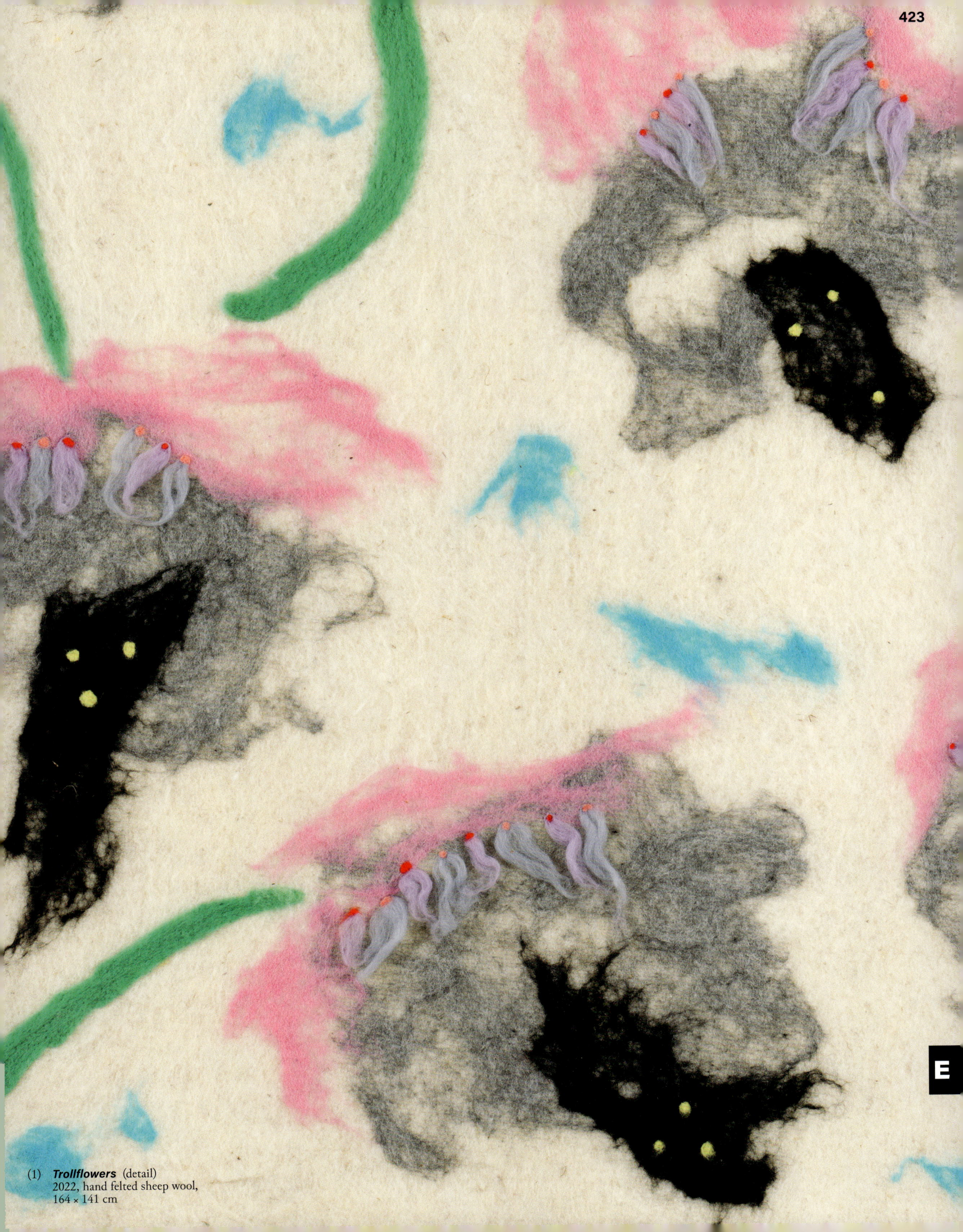

(1) ***Trollflowers*** (detail)
2022, hand felted sheep wool,
164 × 141 cm

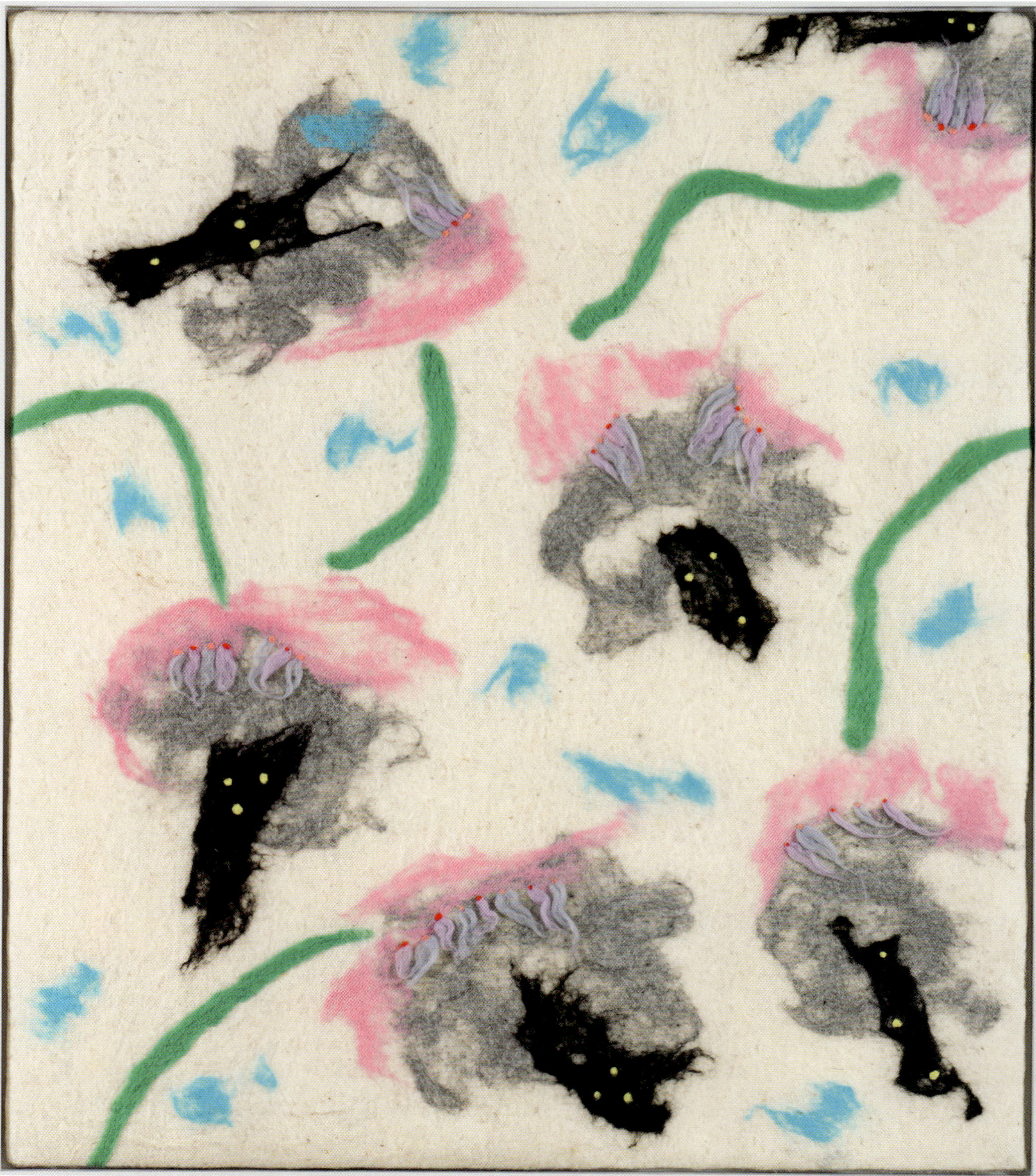

(2)

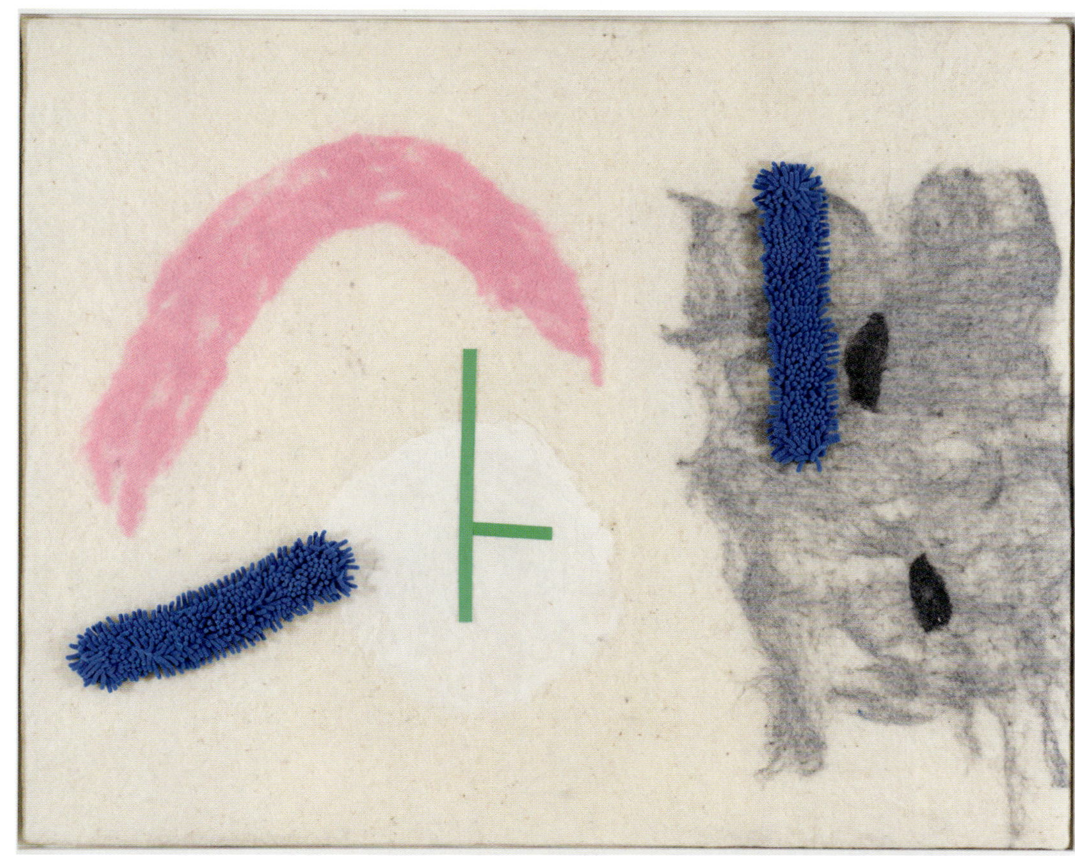

(3)

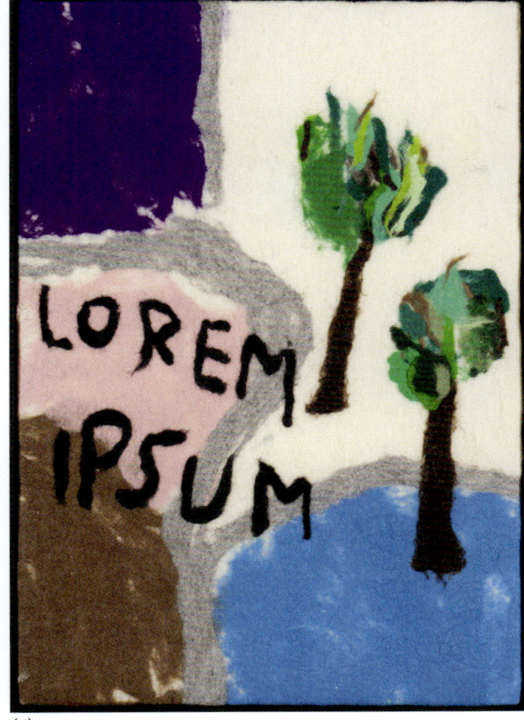

(4)

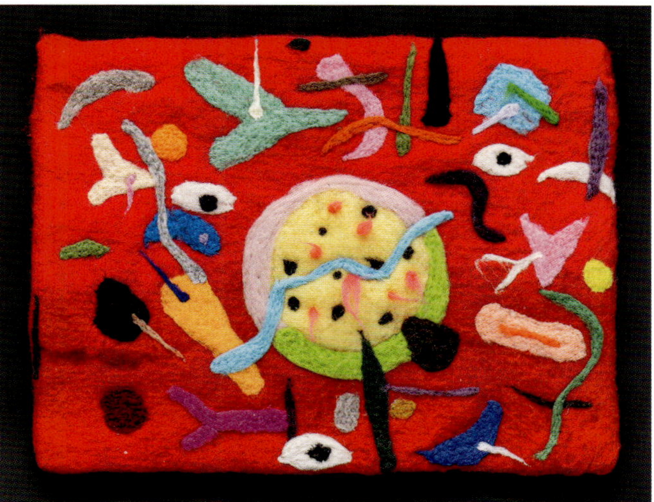

(5)

(2) ***Trollflowers***
2022, hand felted sheep wool, 164 × 141 cm

(3) ***Untitled***
2022, hand felted sheep wool with velcro and mop, 126.5 × 155.5 cm

(4) ***Lorem Ipsum***
2022, hand felted sheep wool, 135.5 × 95.5 cm

(5) ***Untitled***
2022, hand felted sheep wool, 56 × 40 cm

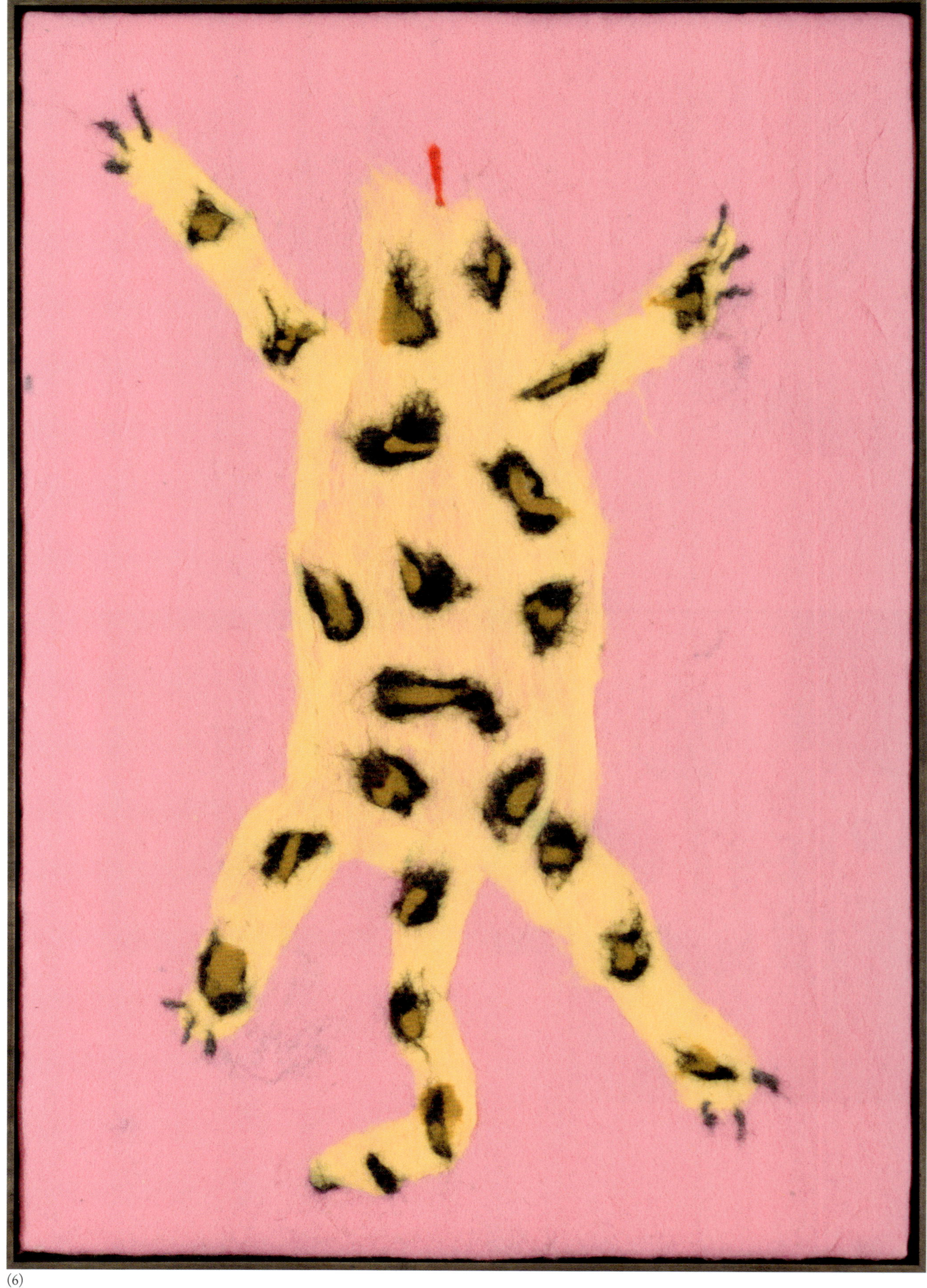

(6)

S

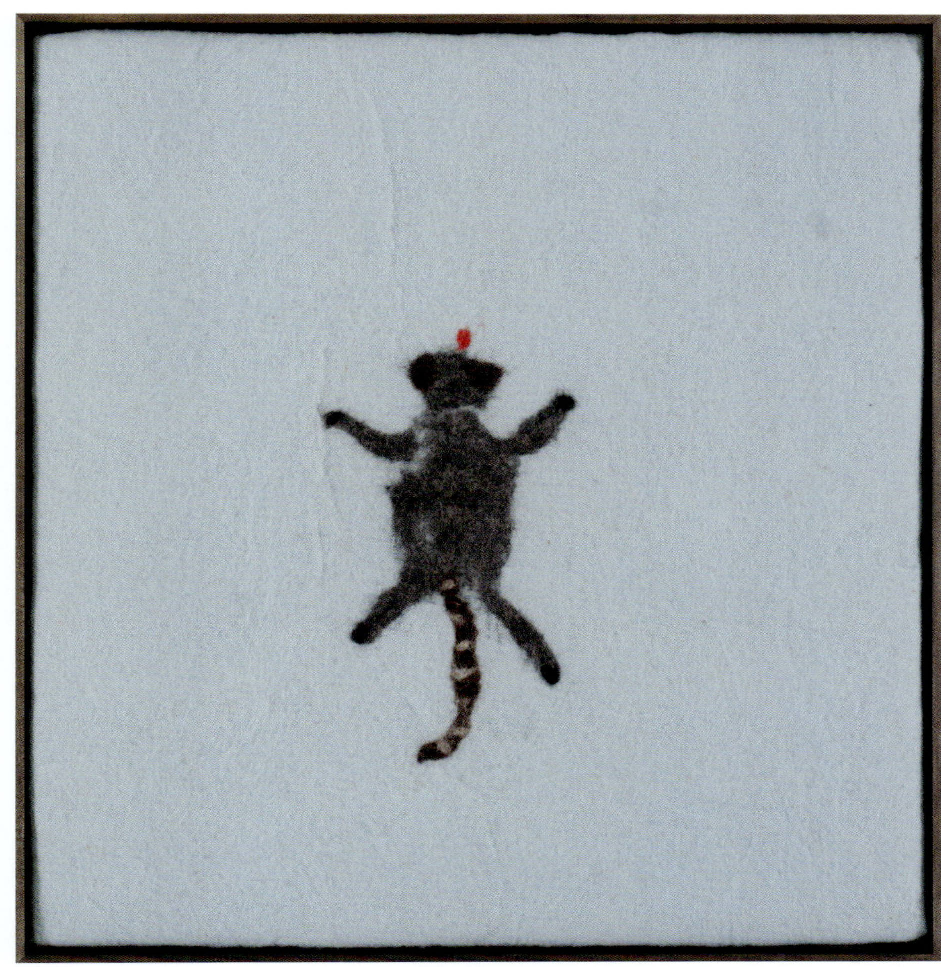
(7)

(6) ***Beute (Jaguar)***
2022, hand felted sheep wool, 118.5 × 83.5 cm
(7) ***Beute (Maus)***
2022, hand felted sheep wool, 78.5 × 74.5 cm

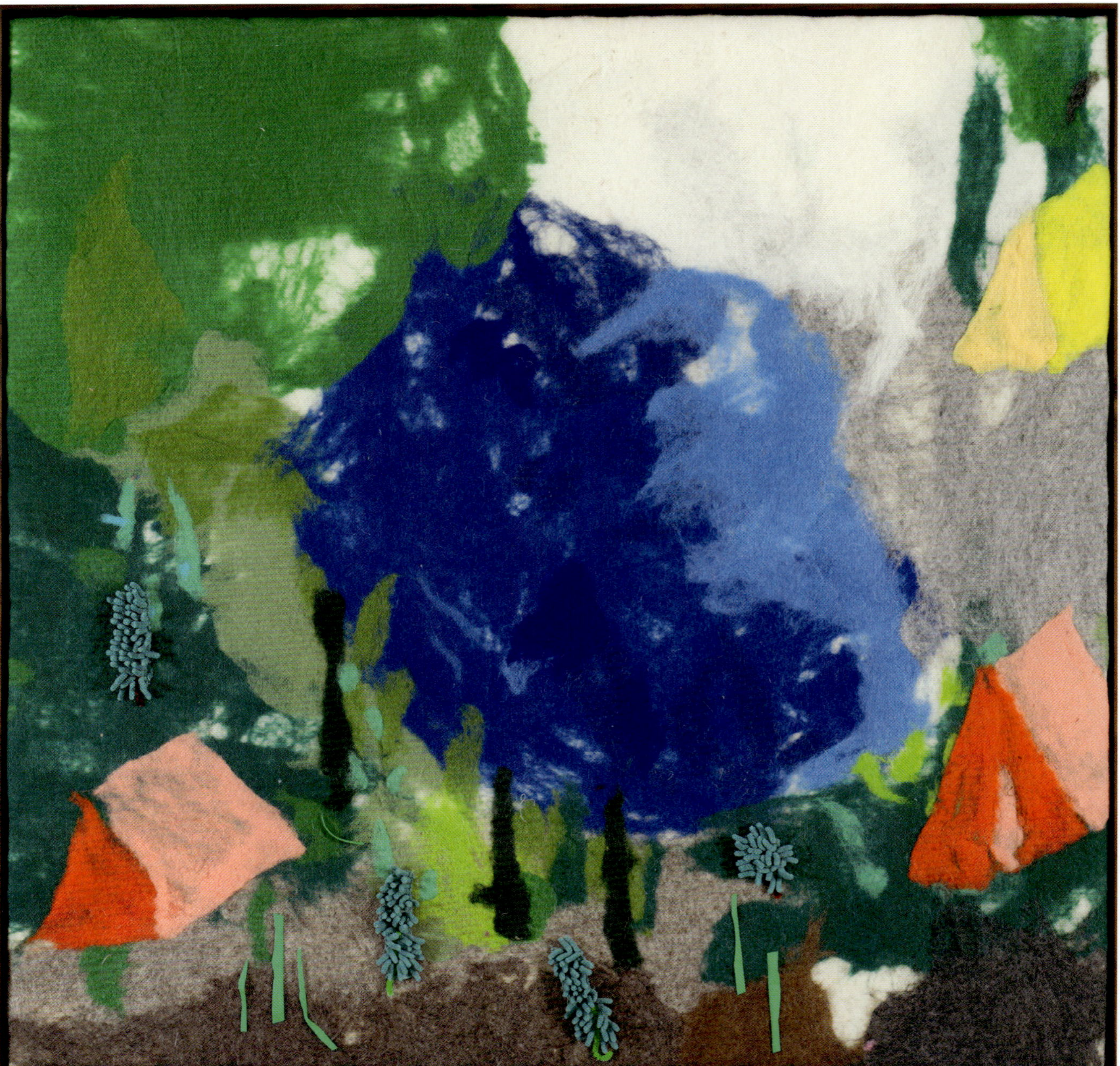
(8)

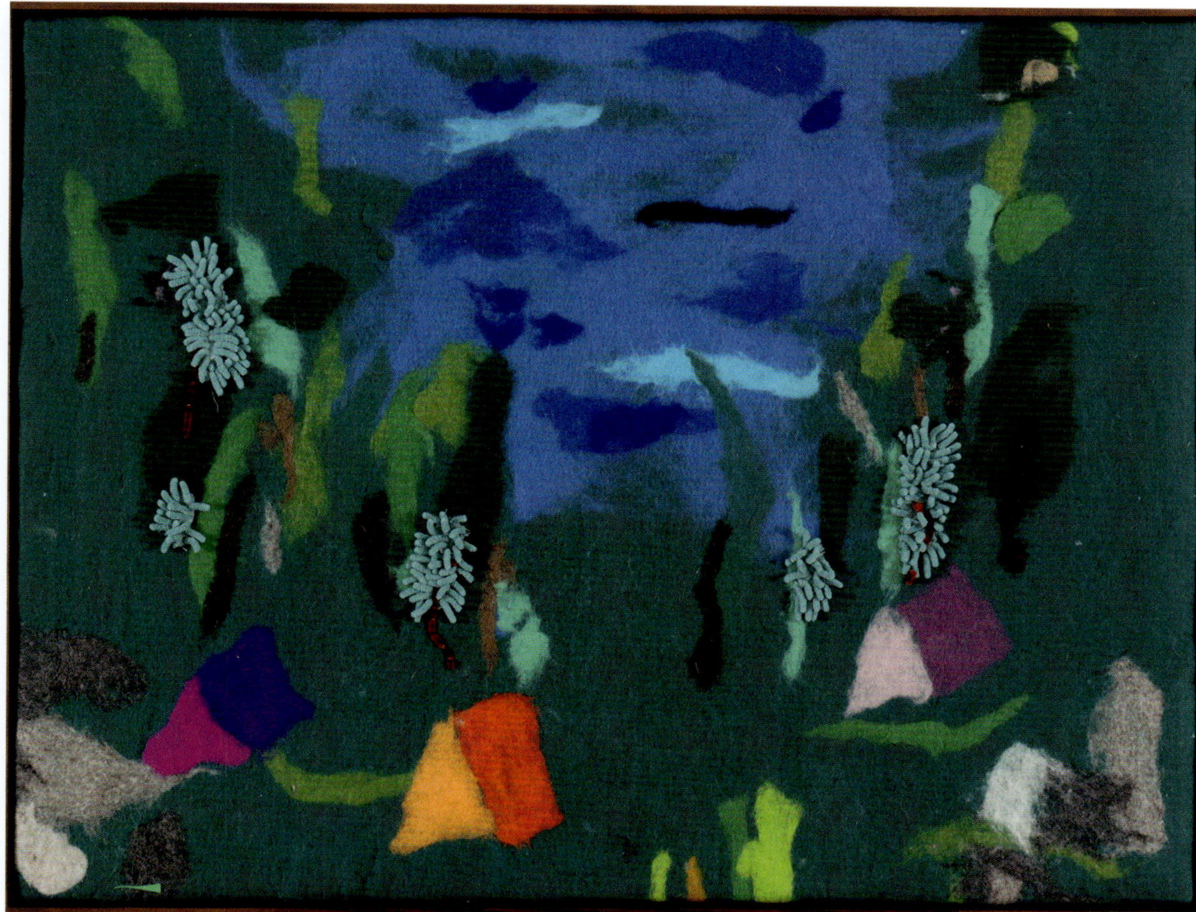
(9)

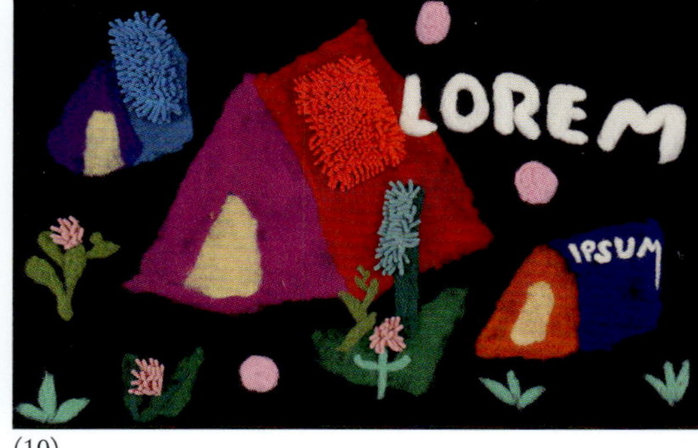

(10)

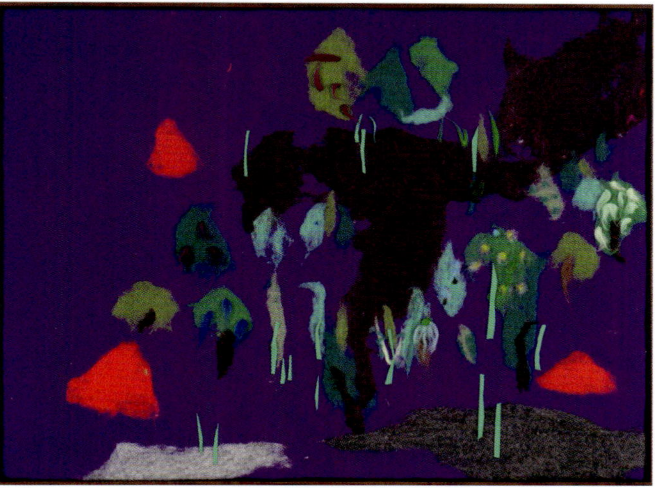
(11)

(8) ***Heimat, trotz euch III***
2022, hand felted sheep wool with velcro and mop, 138 × 140 cm

(9) ***Heimat, trotz euch***
2022, hand felted sheep wool with velcro and mop, 93.5 × 120.5 cm

(10) ***Heimat, trotz euch II***
2022, hand felted sheep wool with velcro, 93.5 × 120.5 cm

(11) ***Why***
2022, hand felted sheep wool with velcro and mop, 73.5 × 120.5 cm

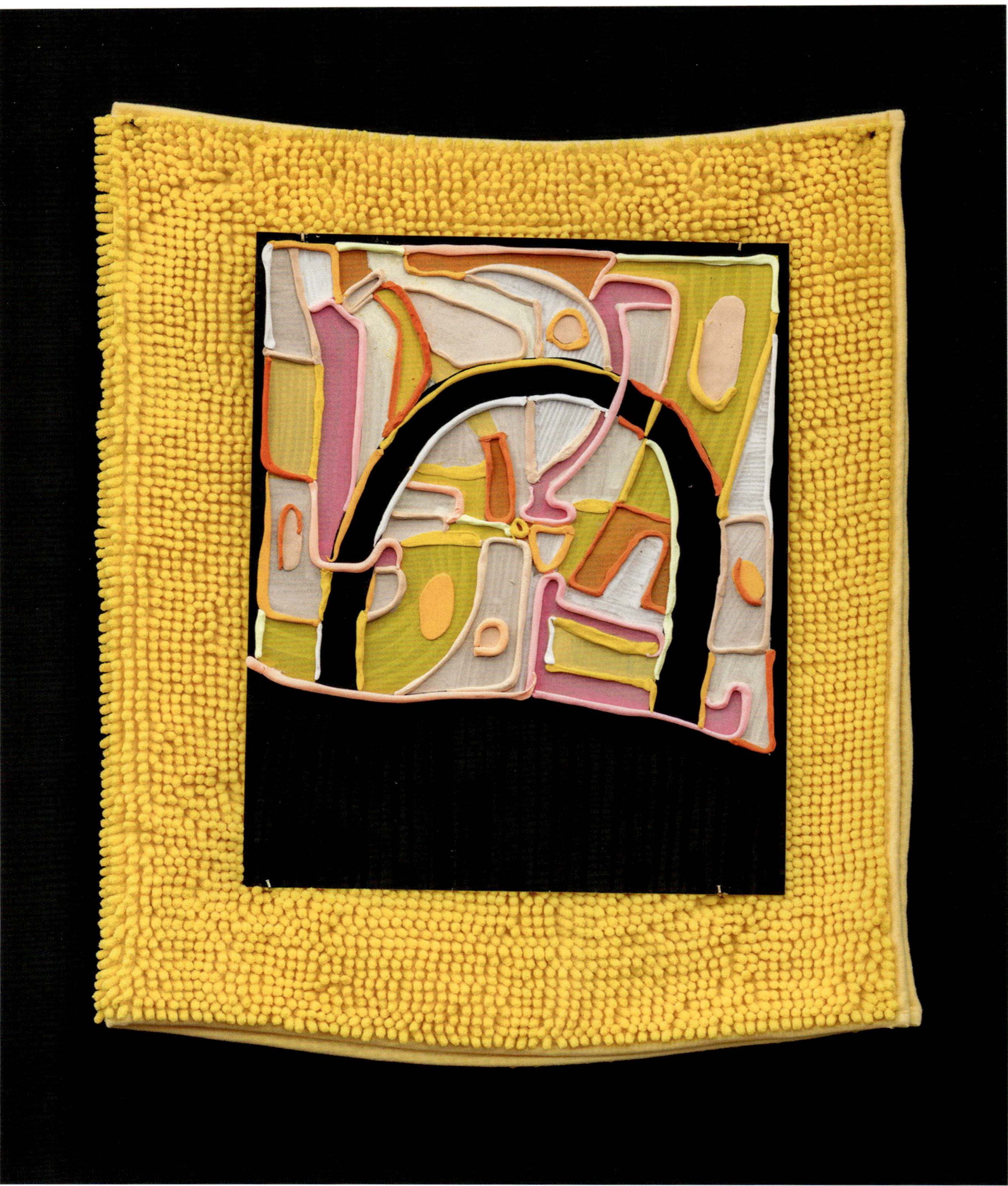

(12)

(12) ***o. T.***
2021, lacquer and Styrofoam Clay on cardboard with doormat,
55 × 70 cm

(13) ***Skandalöse Flora III***
2021, lacquer and Styrofoam Clay on cardboard with doormat,
55 × 70 cm

(14) ***Skandalöse Flora II***
2021, lacquer and Styrofoam Clay on cardboard with doormat,
55 × 70 cm

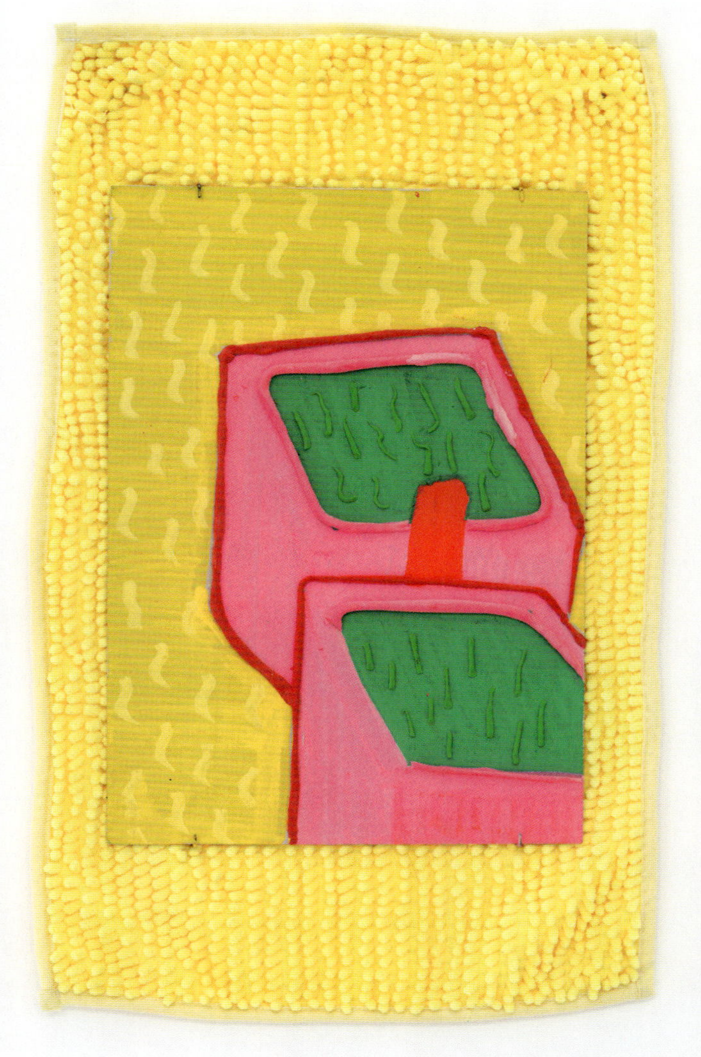

(13)

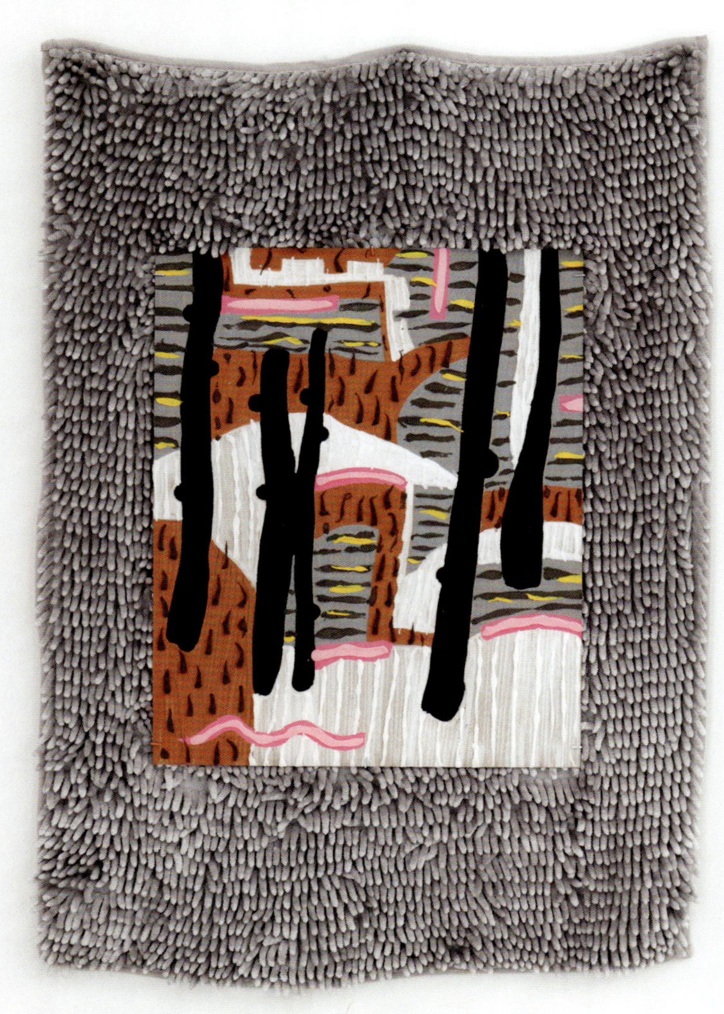

(14)

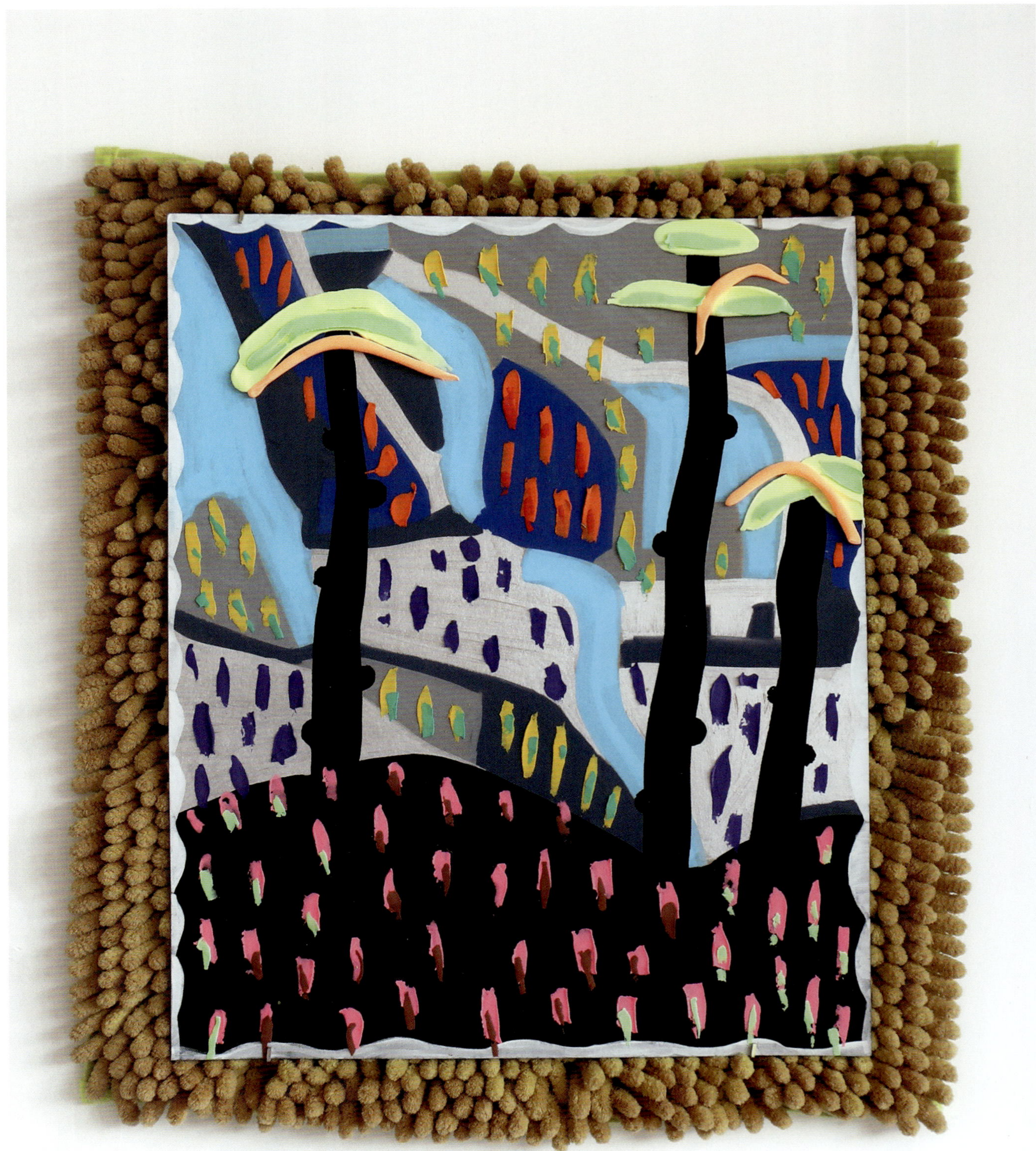

(15)

S

(15) ***Skandalöse Flora IV***
2021, lacquer and Styrofoam Clay on cardboard with doormat, 55 × 70 cm

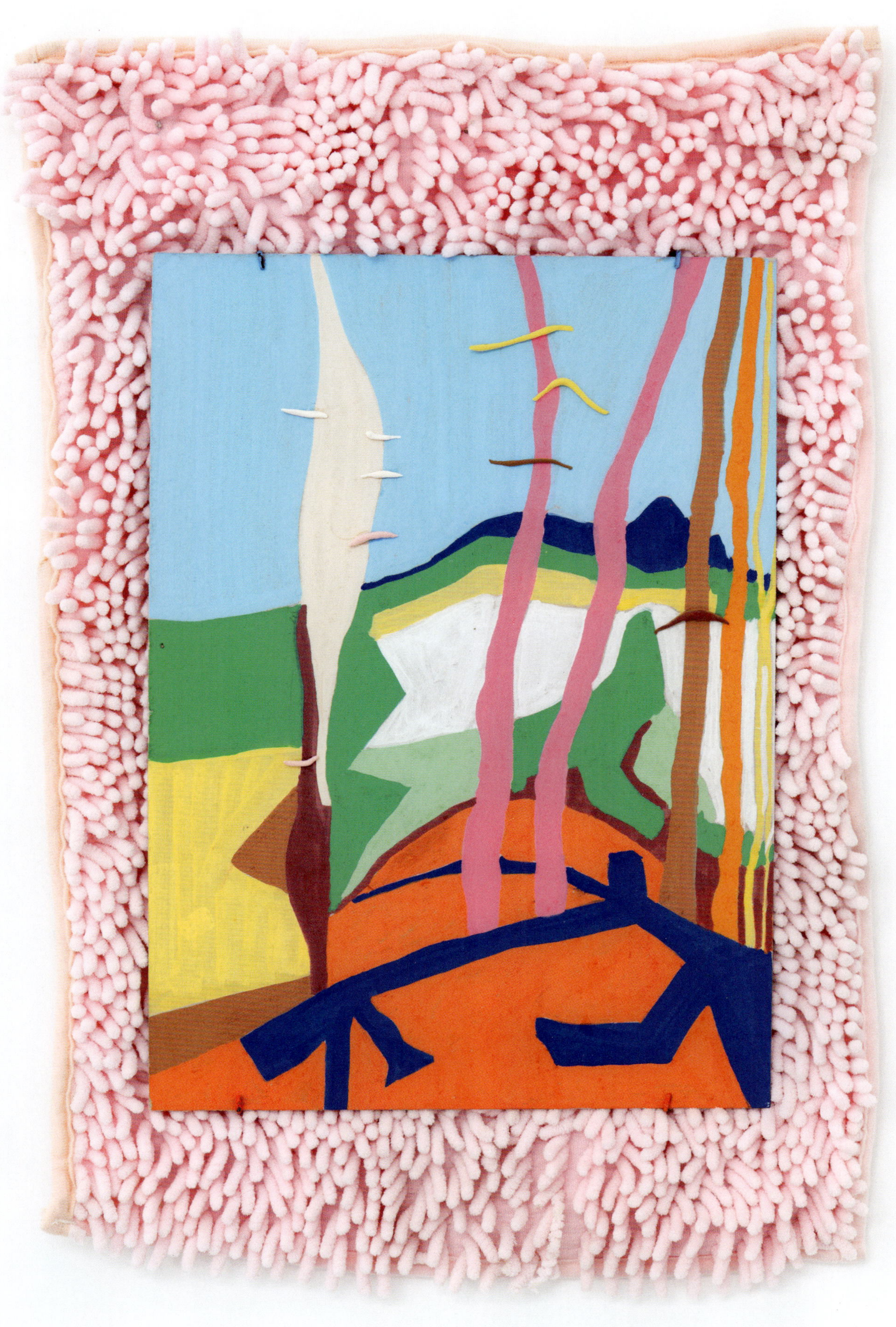

(16) ***Skandalöse Flora***
2021, lacquer and
Styrofoam Clay
on cardboard with
doormat, 55 × 70 cm

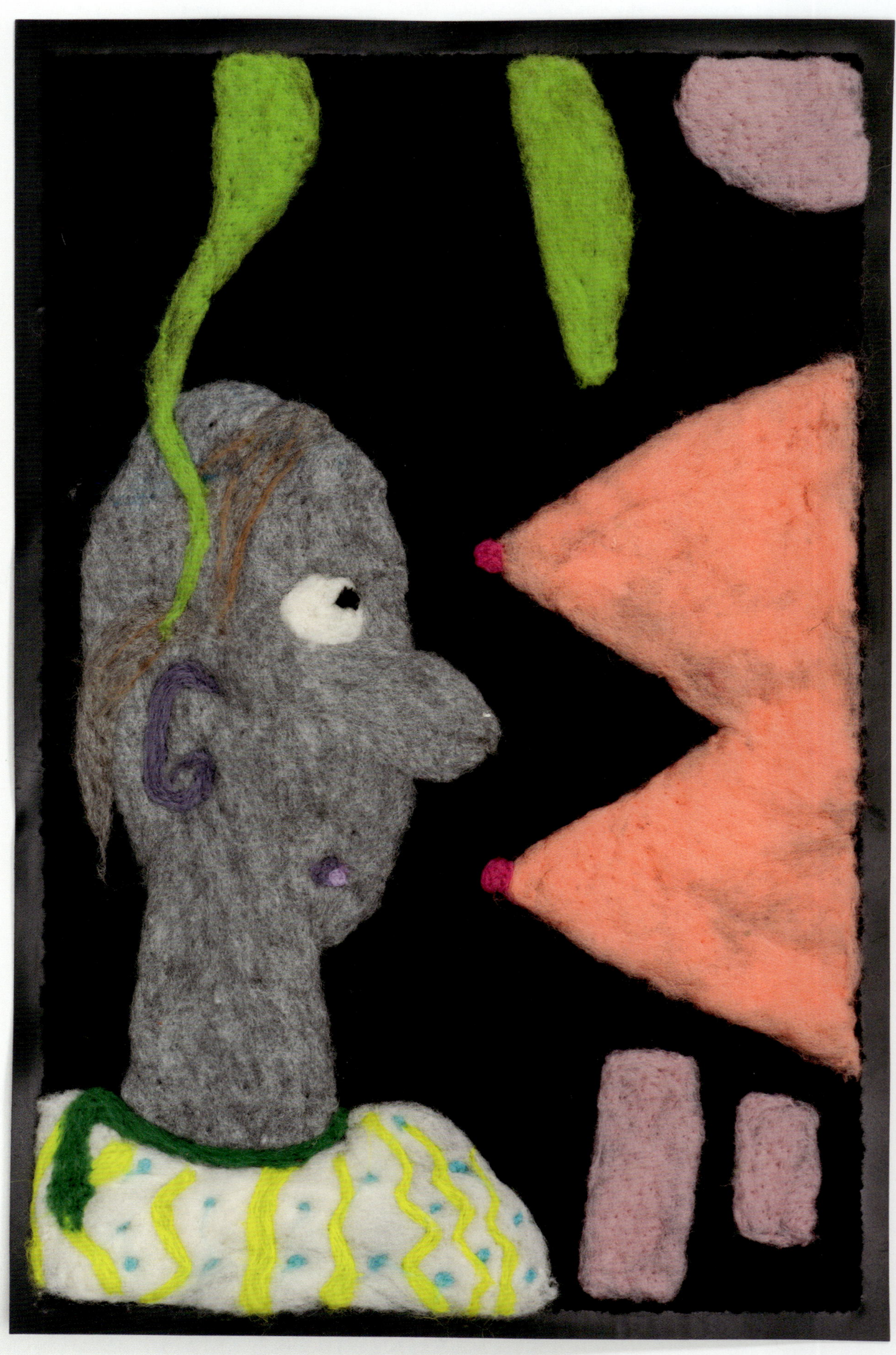

S

(17) ***Wow Frau***
2022, hand felted sheep wool on a doormat, 60 × 40 cm

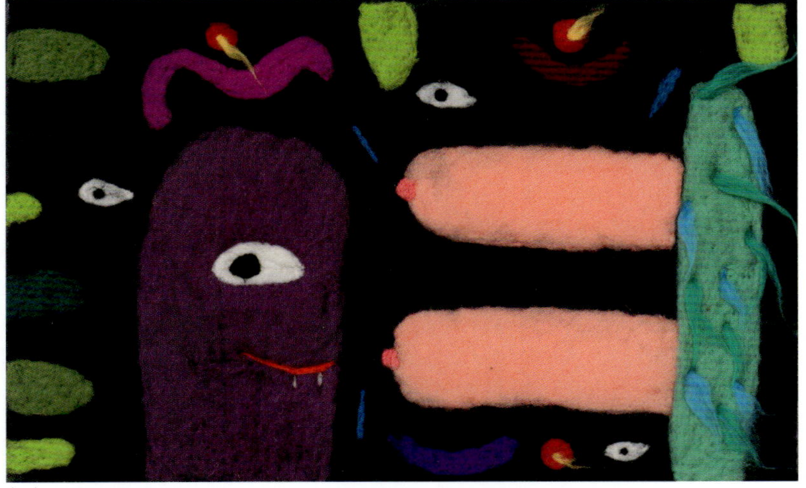
(18)

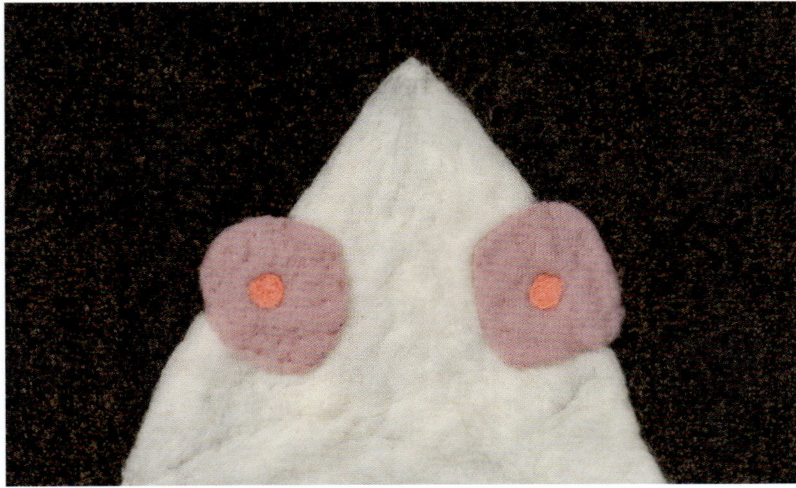
(19)

(18) ***YUM***
2022, hand felted sheep wool on doormat, 60 × 40 cm

(19) ***Fata Morgana im Eis***
2022, hand felted sheep wool on doormat, 60 × 40 cm

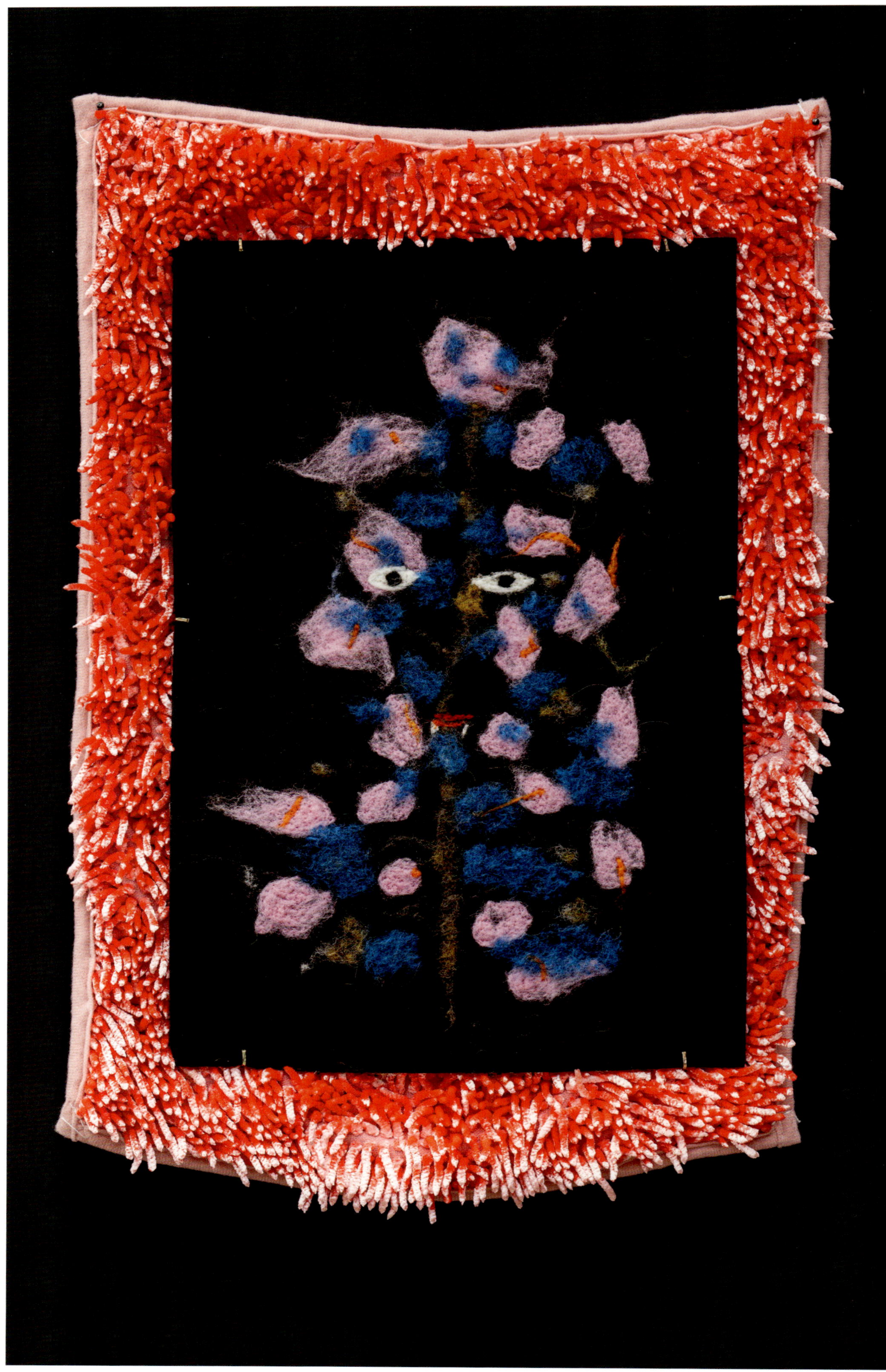

S

(20) ***Waldgeist, 2022***
hand felted sheep wool
on felt with doormat,
60 × 40 cm

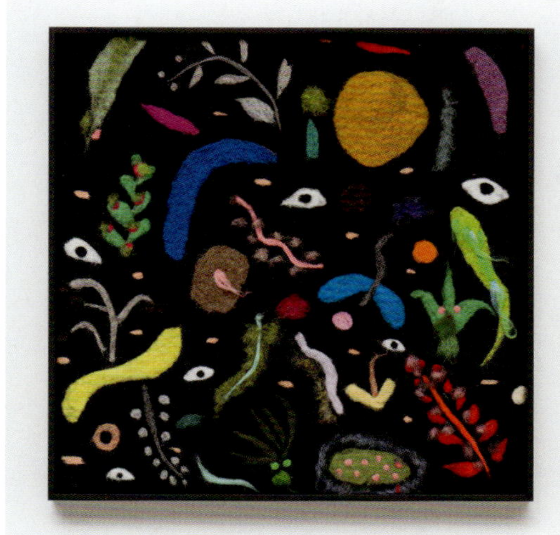
(21)

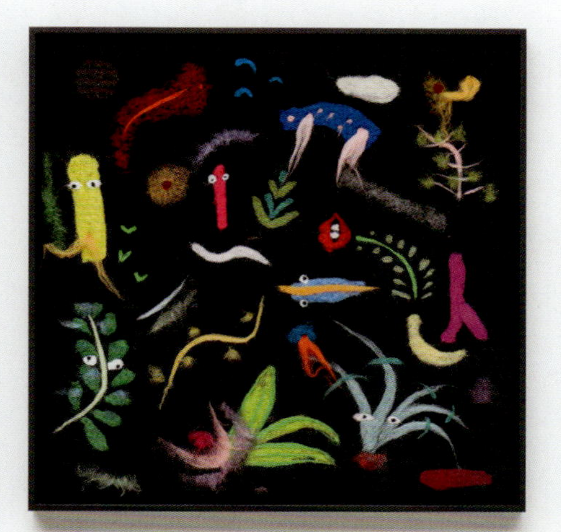
(22)

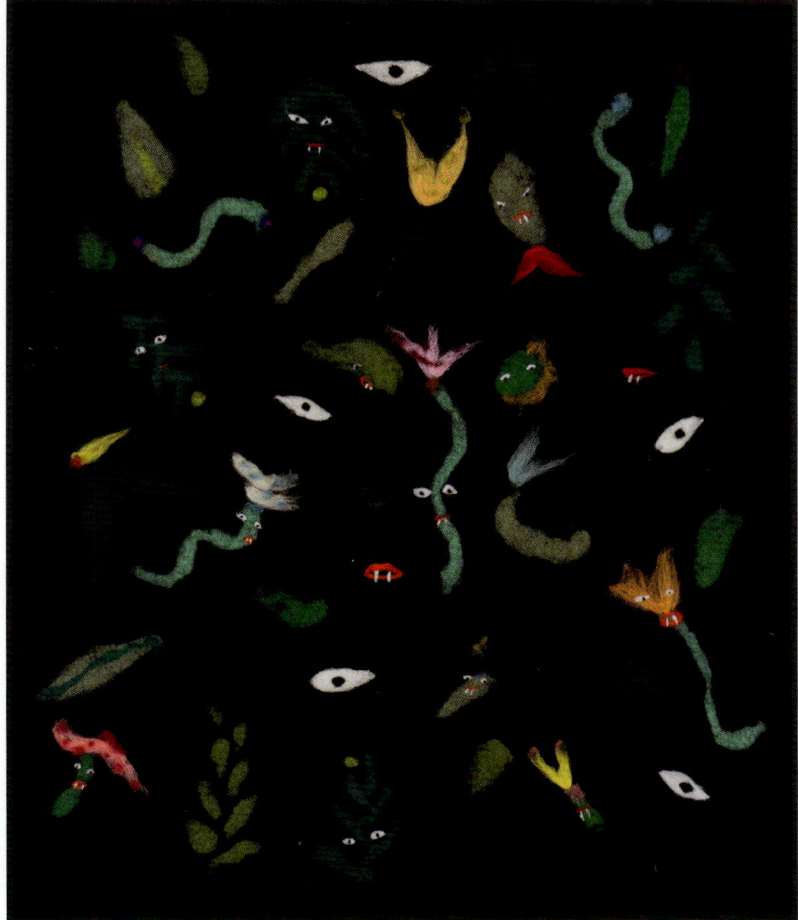
(23)

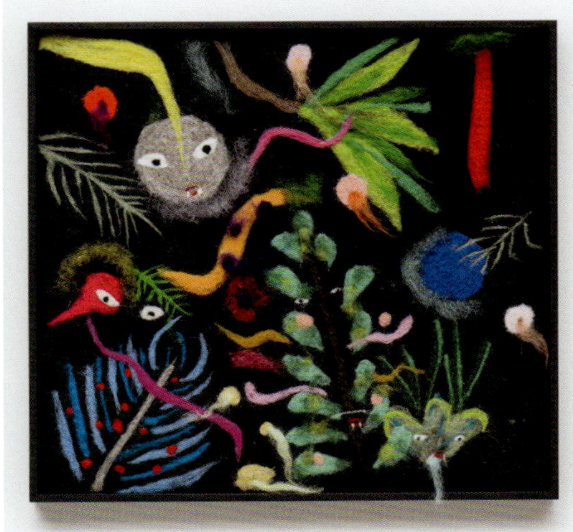
(24)

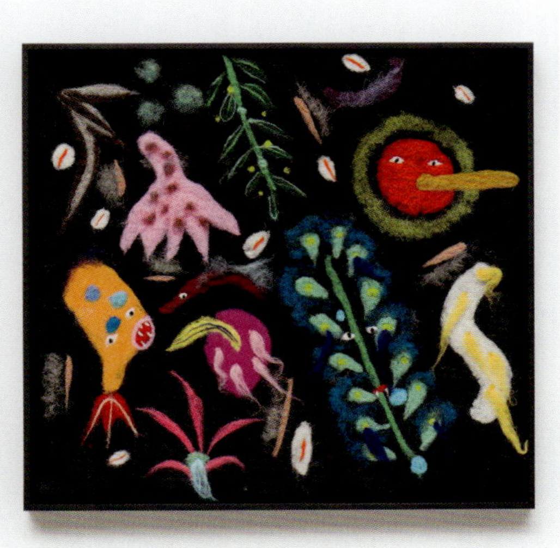
(25)

(21) ***Urwald IV***
2022, felt on wood,
58 × 57.5 cm

(22) ***Urwald II***
2022, felt on wood,
58 × 57.5 cm

(23) ***Urwald V***
2022, felt on wood,
65 × 60 cm

(24) ***Urwald III***
2022, felt on wood,
56.6 × 60 cm

(25) ***Urwald I***
2022, felt on wood,
49 × 52.5 cm

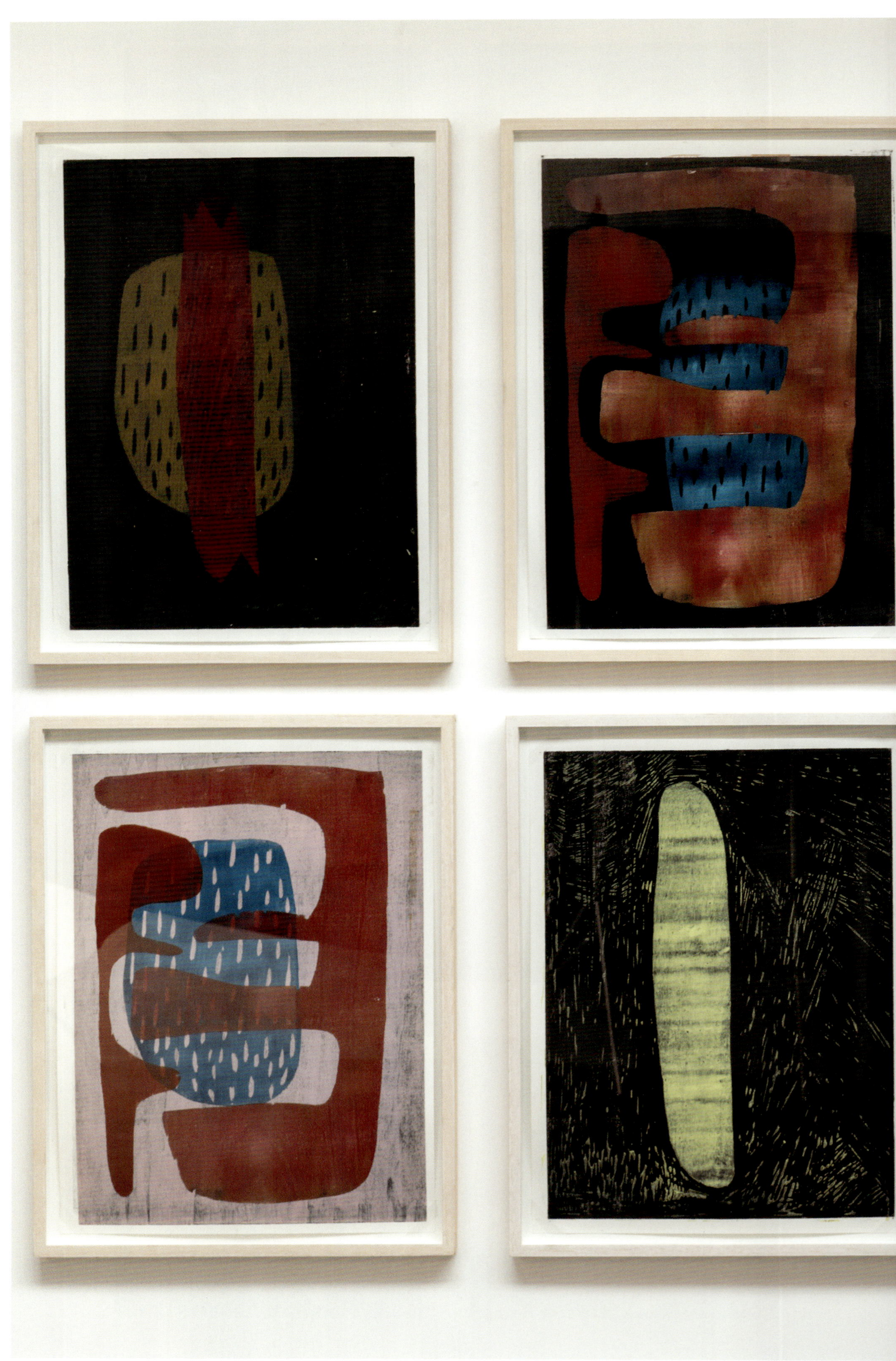

S

(26) ***Shapeset***
2022, wood block
print on paper,
each 80 × 60 cm

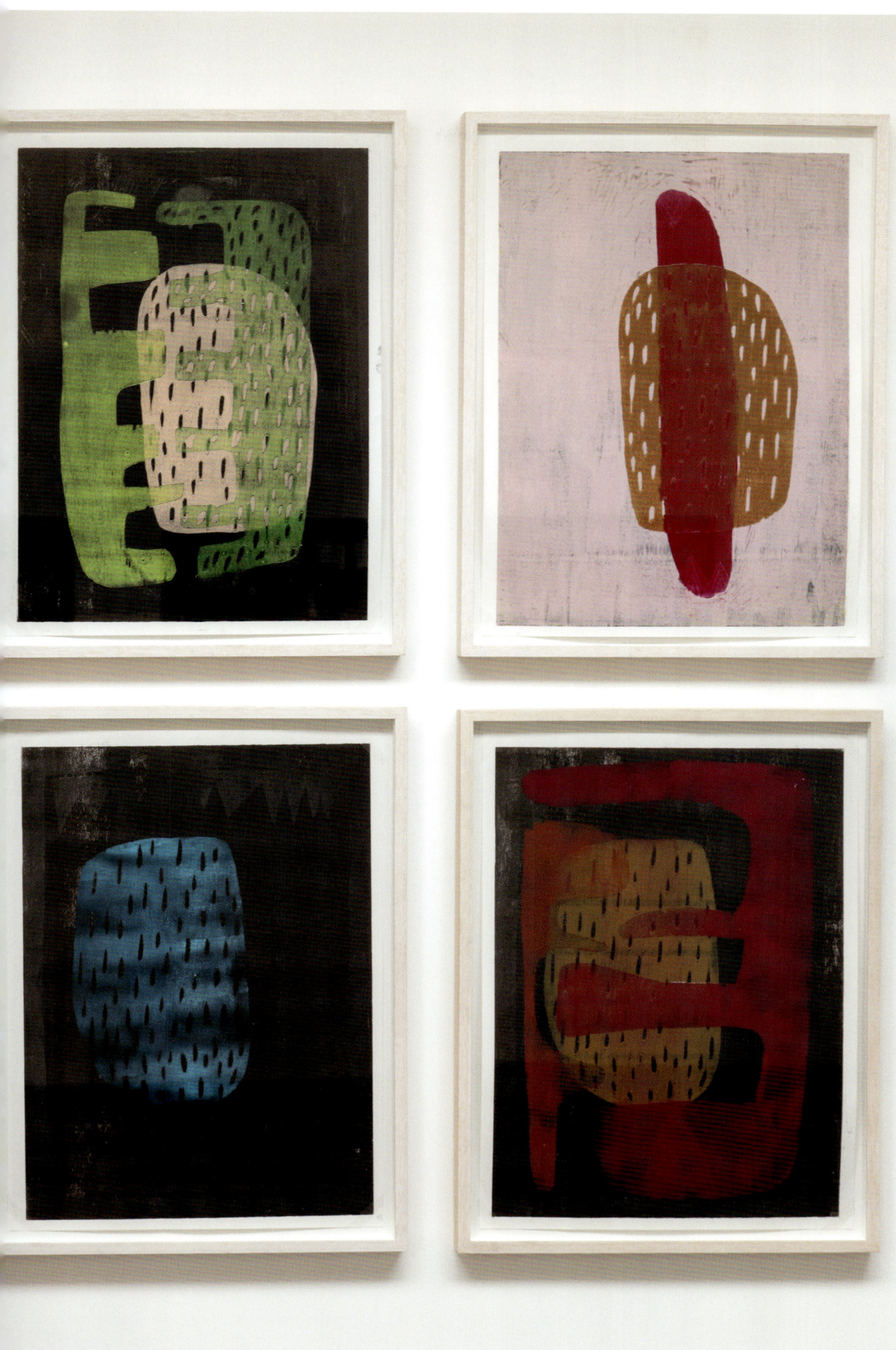

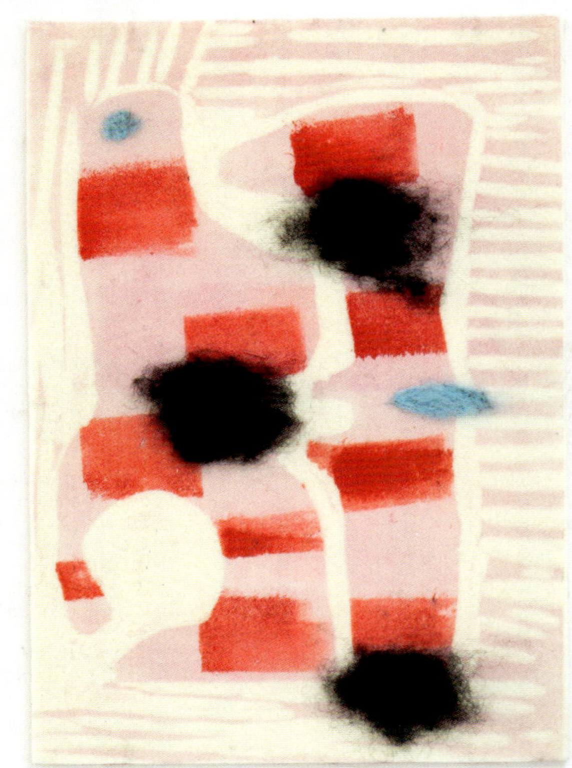

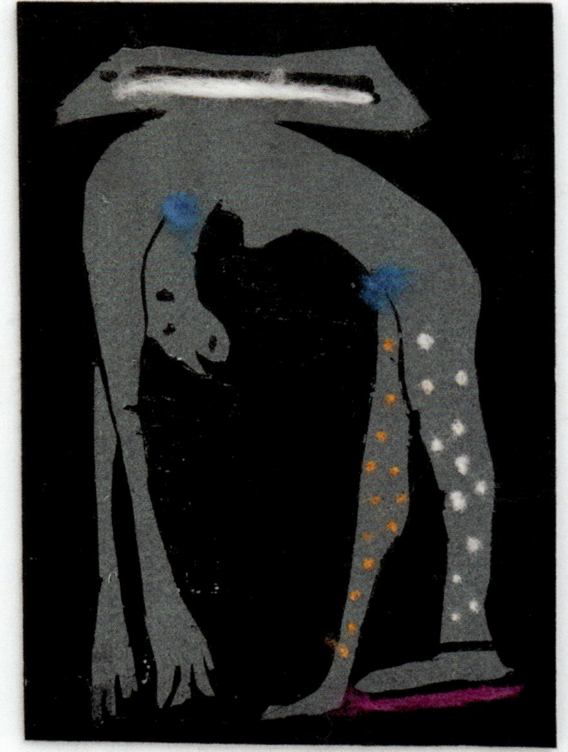

(27)

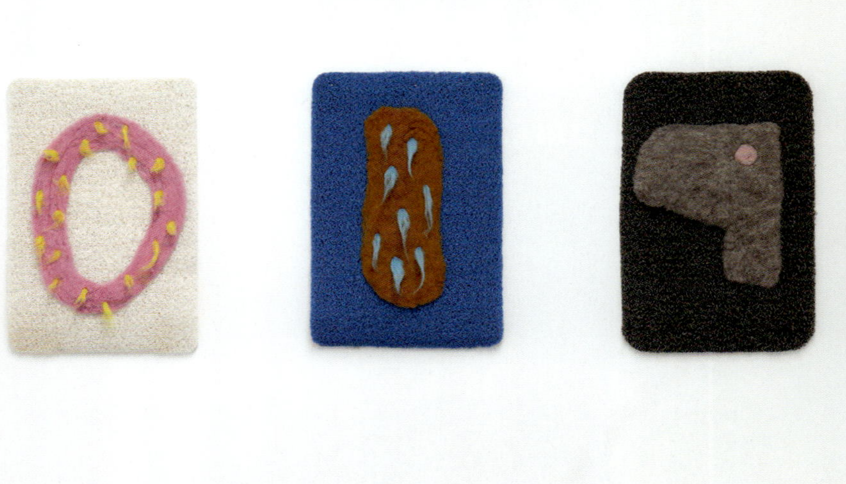

(28)

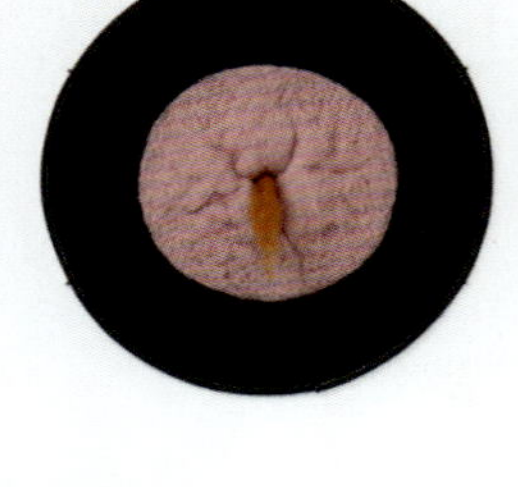

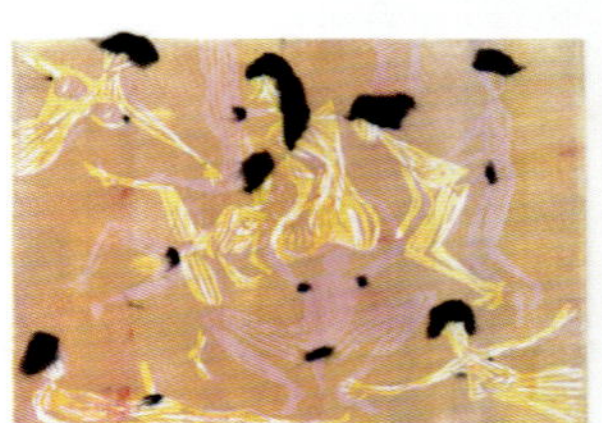

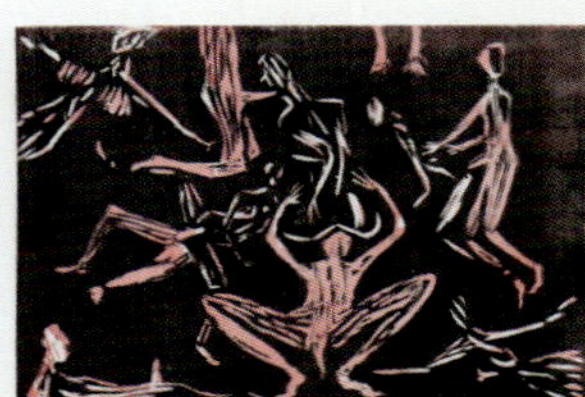

(29)

!

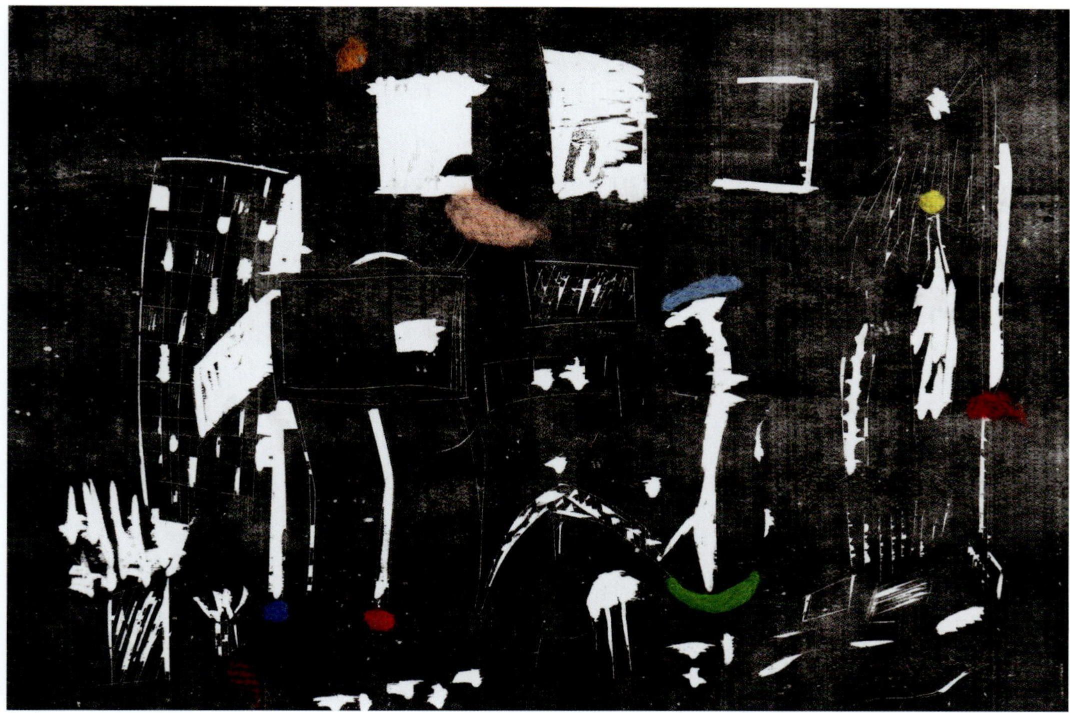
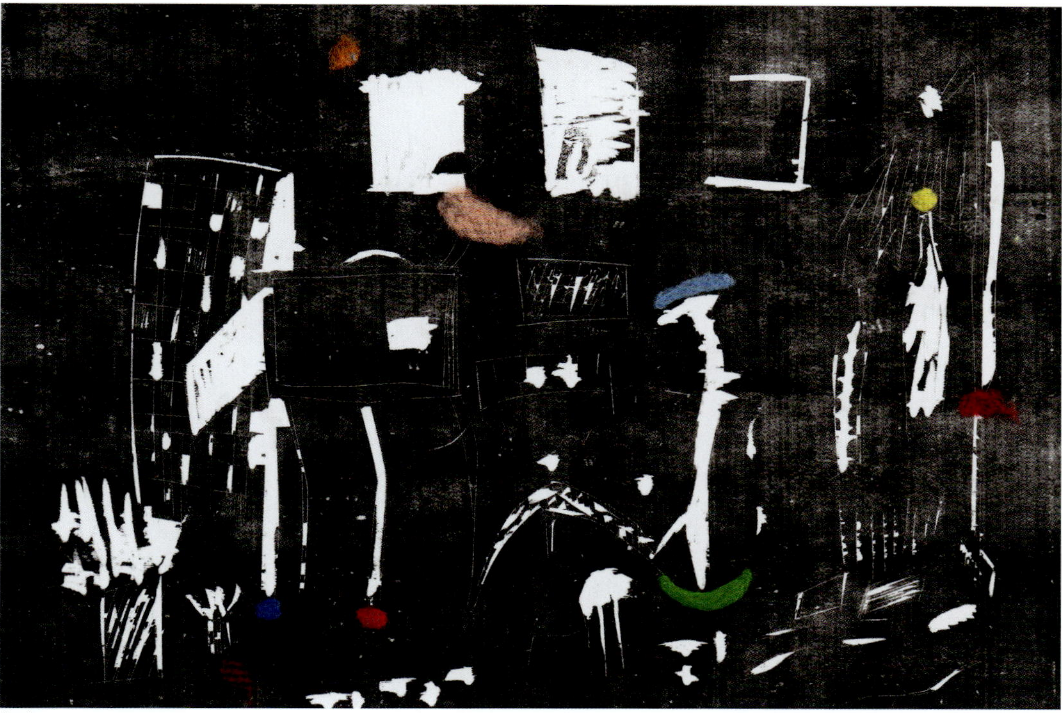

(30)

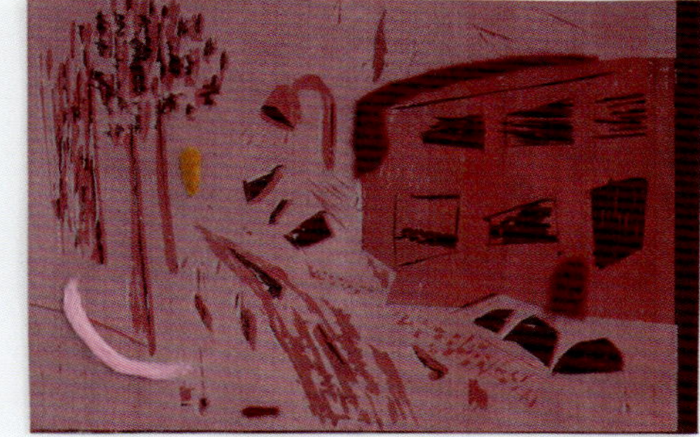

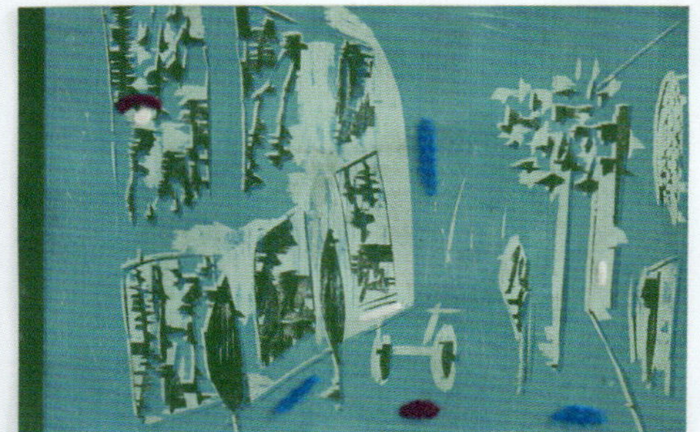

(31)

(32)

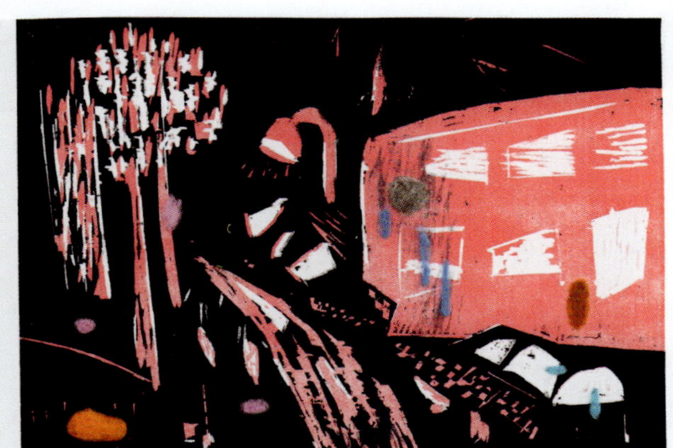

(33)

(27) (Above) ***Untitles***
2022, wood print on felt with hand felting, 30 × 20 cm
(Below) ***Tempelhüter***
2022, wood print on felt with hand felting, 30 × 20 cm

(28) ***Untitled***
2022, felt on doormat, each 40 × 60 cm

(29) (Above) ***Boob***
2022, felt on doormat, diameter 50 cm,
(Below) ***Hamburger Filz***
2022, wood print on felt with hand felting, each 60 × 80 cm

(30) ***Cityscapes I***
2022, wood print on felt with hand felting, 80 × 60 cm

(31) ***Cityscapes II and III***
2022, wood print on felt with hand felting, each 80 × 60 cm

(32) ***Cityscapes IV***
2022, wood print on felt with hand felting, 80 × 60 cm

(33) ***Cityscapes V***
2022, wood print on felt with hand felting, 80 × 60 cm

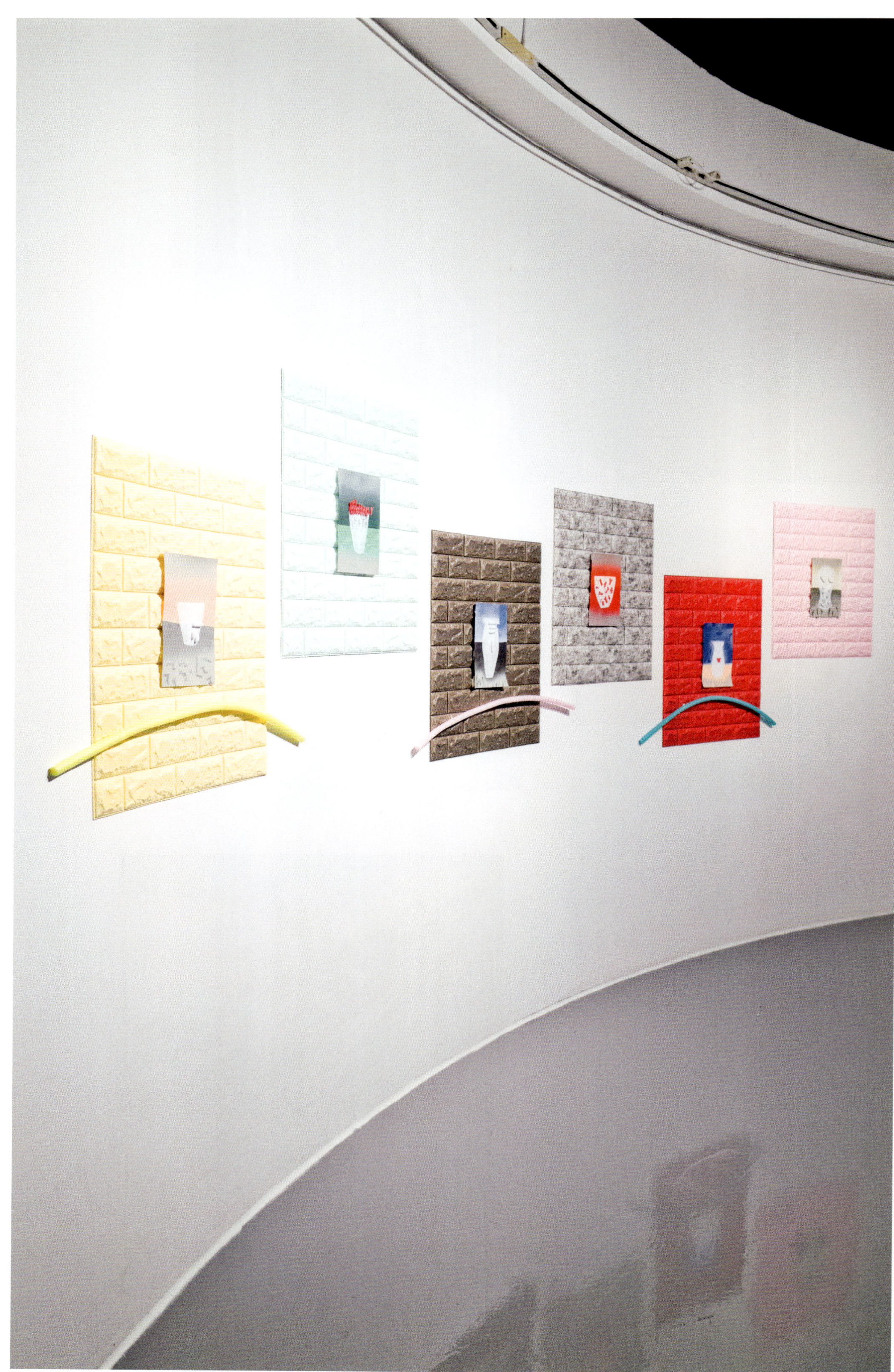

(34) ***Shanzai (Truth, Origin and Heritage) I-V***
2018, acrylic paint, plastic, foam, each 120 × 120 cm, Installation view SeMA NANJI, Seoul, South Korea

!

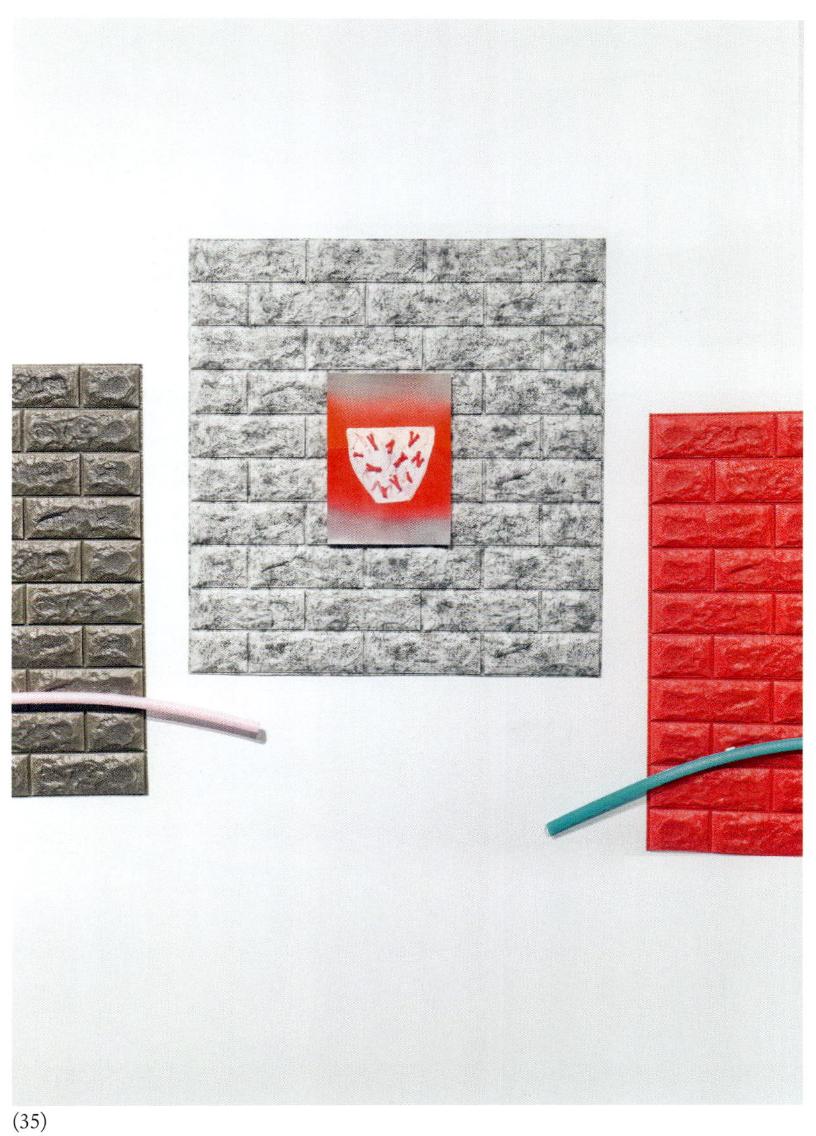
(35)

(35) ***Shanzai (Truth, Origin and Heritage) I-V***
2018, acrylic paint, plastic, foam, each 120 × 120 cm, Installation view SeMA NANJI, Seoul, South Korea

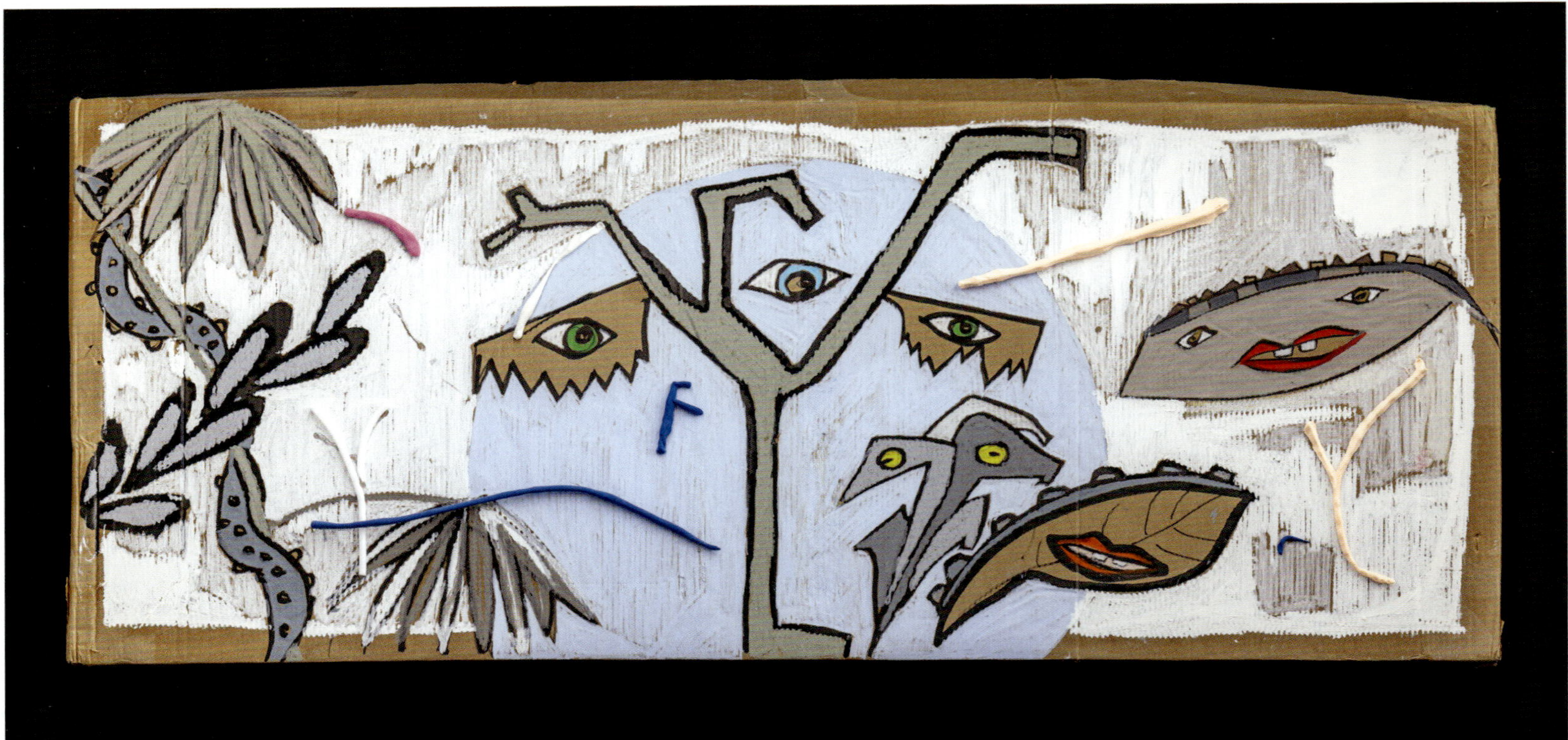

(36)

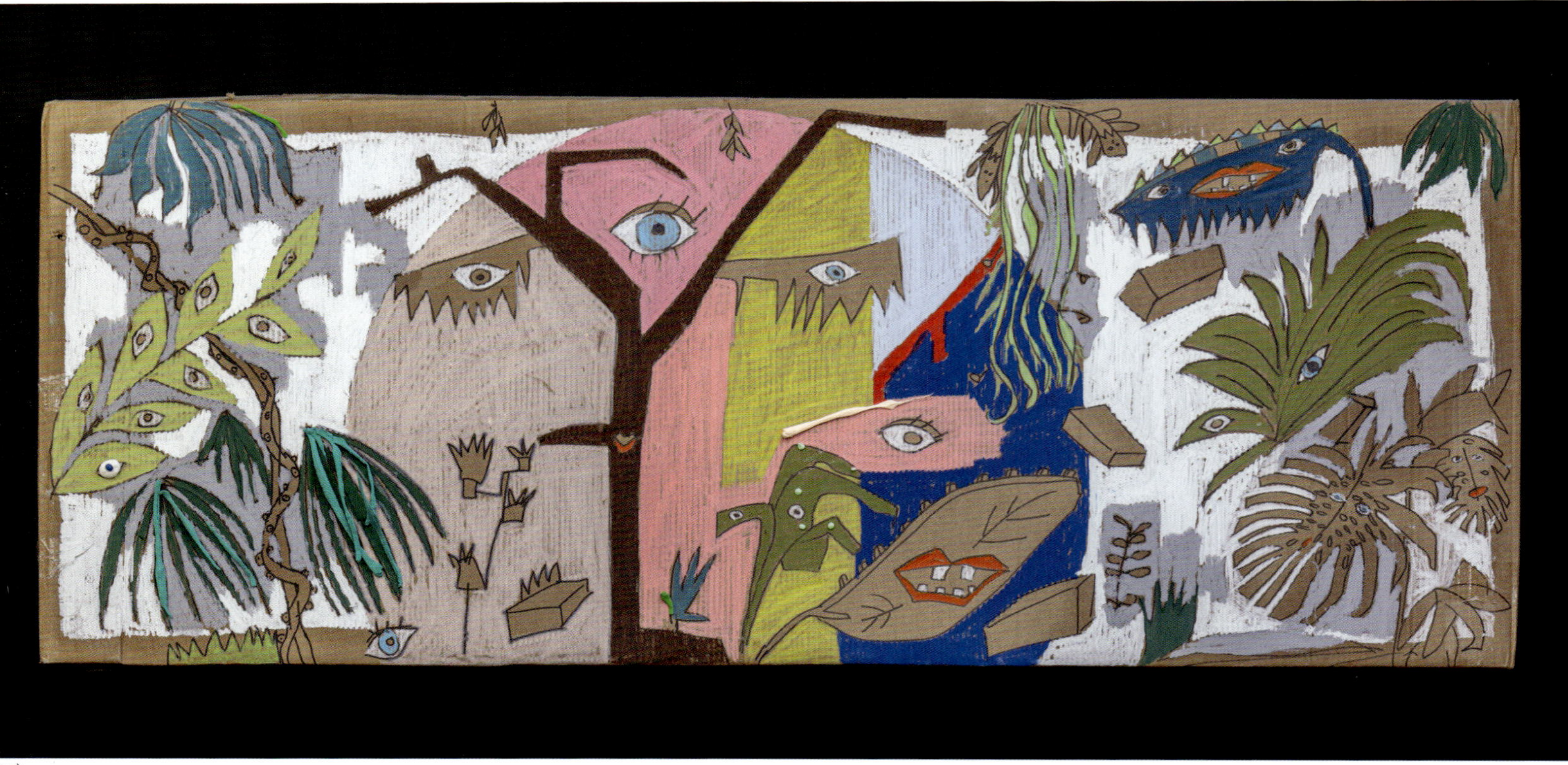

(37)

(36) ***Am Krautgarten***
2019, oil pastels with acrylic, Styrofoam on cardboard,
280 × 100 cm

(37) ***Am Krautgarten II***
2019, oil pastels with acrylic Styrofoam on cardboard,
280 × 100 cm

(38) ***Psychogeographies***
2016, foam and colored foam on foam,
each 30 × 40 cm

(39) ***Untitled***
2015, adhesive tape on linen, 40 × 25 cm

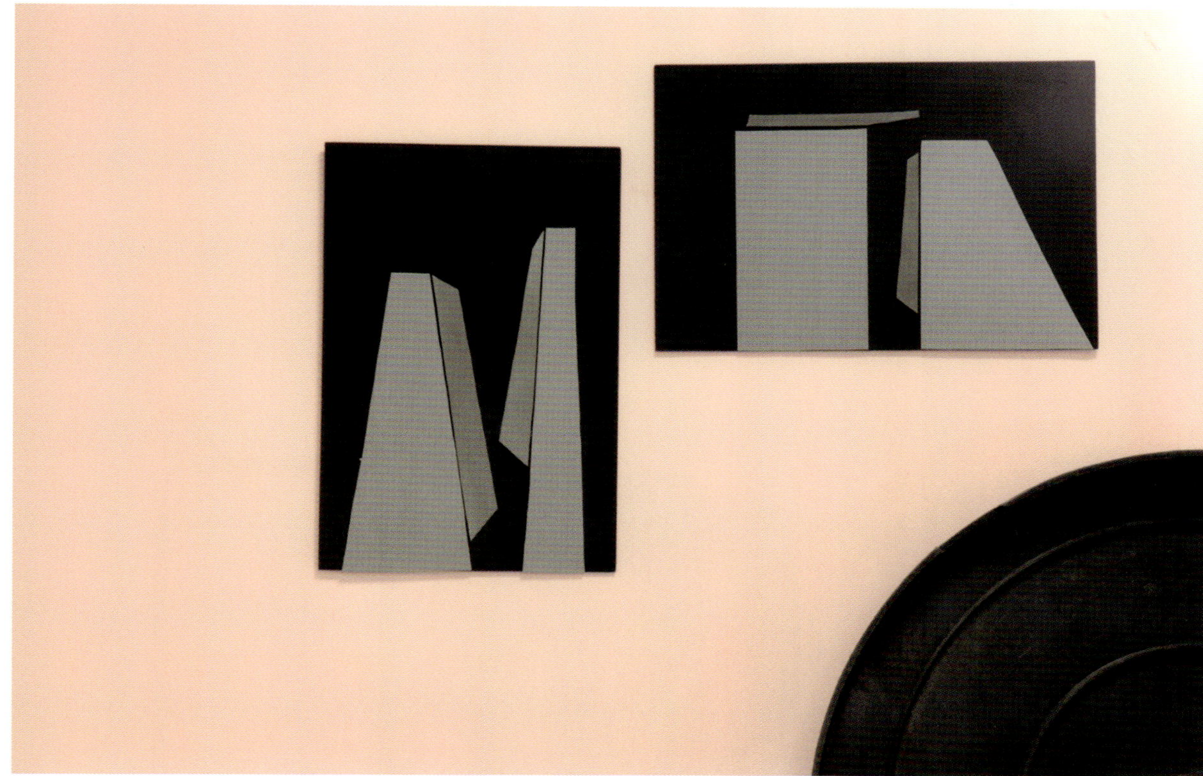

(38)

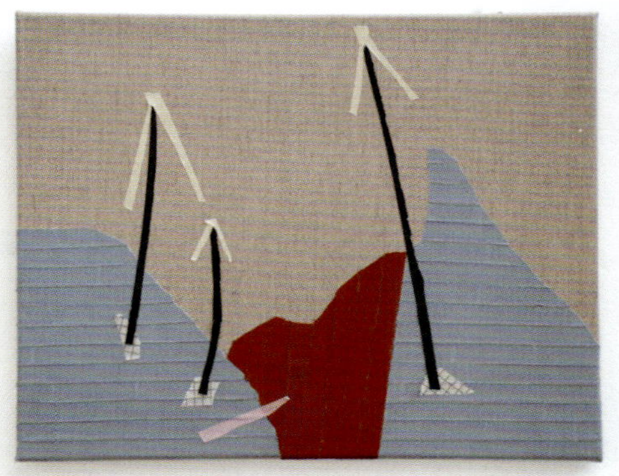

(39)

(40) ***Y***
2013, adhesive tape on cardboard, 62 × 24.5 cm
(41) ***Grüne Sonne***
2009, lacquer on wood, 60 × 40 cm
(42) ***Sol (kleiner Sonnengott, männlich)***
2010, picture frame, plastic film, pastels, diameter 20 cm
(43) ***Doormat (Darth Vader)***
2010, lacquer paint on rubber, 40 × 30 cm
(44) ***XY***
2009, various materials, 15 × 45 cm
(45) ***Kleines Bild, weiblich (prêt-à-porter)***
2009, dowels, cotton swabs and nail polish on plastic, 10 × 15 cm
(46) ***Astrastube (Horst)***
2009, beer wrapping cardboard and pastels on paper, 50 × 50 cm
(47) ***Minimalmarmeladenbrot***
2008, wood, acrylic resin, paper plate, 17 cm diameter
(48) ***Boot (die Yacht meines Vaters)***
2009, Keramiplast, 23 x 16 cm

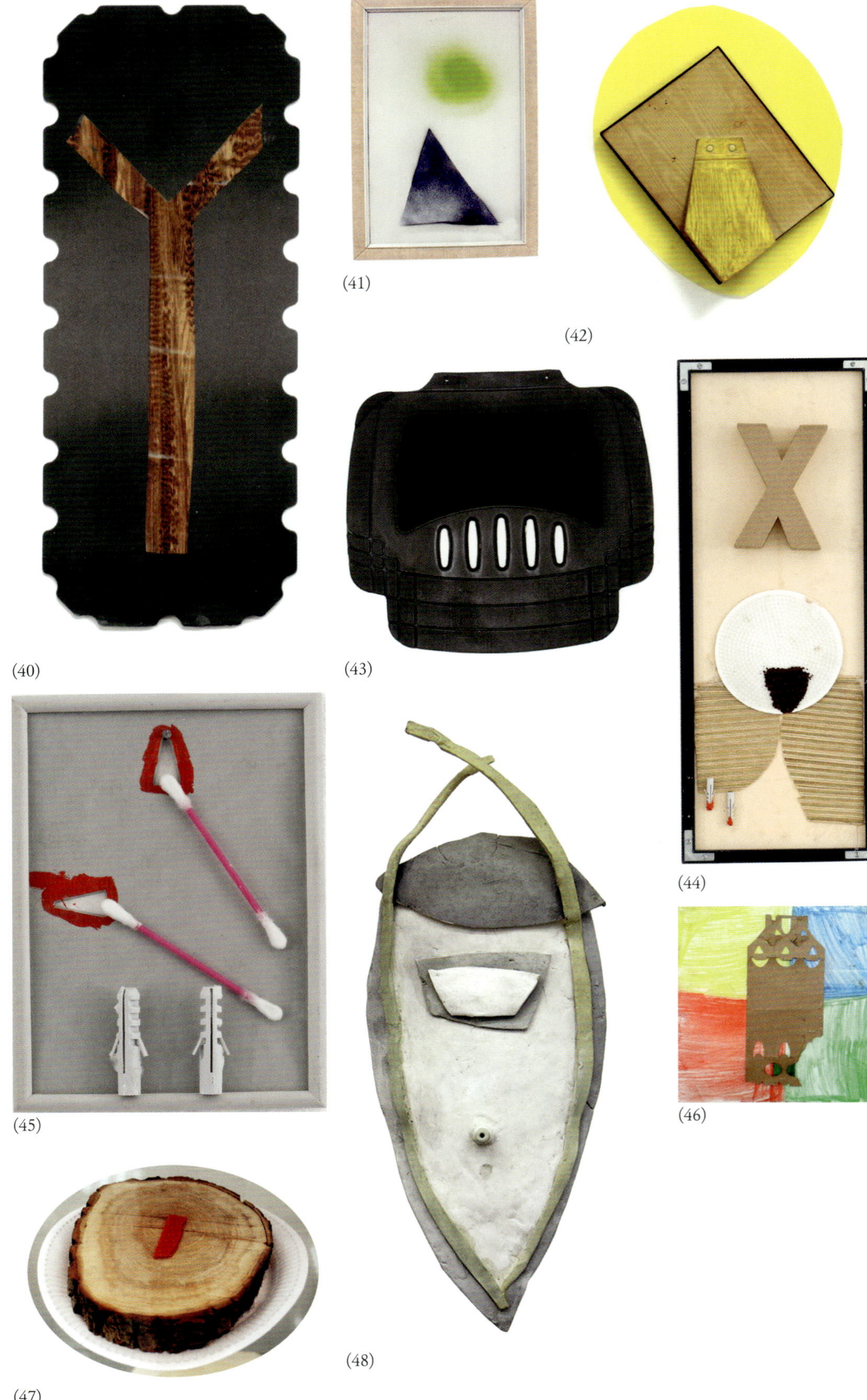

(40) (41) (42) (43) (44) (45) (46) (47) (48)

APPENDIX

ABOUT THE ARTIST

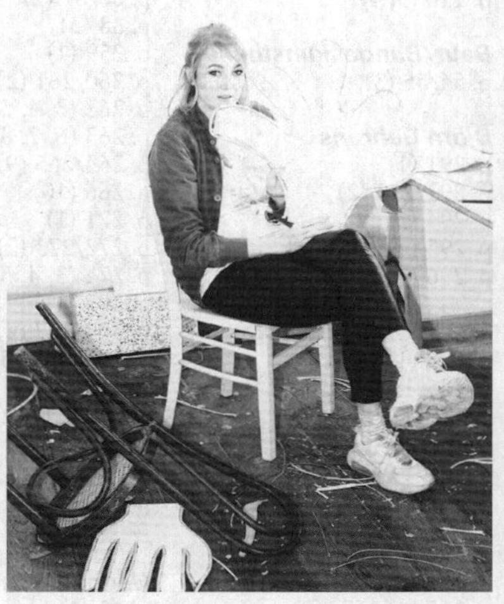

EN Verena Issel was born in Munich in 1982 as the daughter of a German father and a Norwegian mother. After years in Bergen, Norway, Issel studied fine arts with a focus on installation and sculpture at the Hochschule für Bildende Künste Hamburg, the China Academy of Art Hangzhou (China) and the Faculdade de Belas-Artes Lisboa (Portugal) as well as classical philology (Latin and Ancient Greek) at the University of Hamburg. Numerous travel grants and artist-in-residence programs have taken her to Russia, Taiwan, South Korea, Japan, Zambia, Mexico, Iran, Lithuania, and Papua New Guinea. In recent years, Kunsthalle Mannheim (DE), Volksbühne Berlin (DE), ZARYA Center for Contemporary Art (RU), Trafo Kunsthall (NOR), Museum Lothar Fischer (DE) and Westfälischer Kunstverein/LWL Museum Münster, among others, have dedicated solo exhibitions to her. Between 2019-2021, Verena Issel was a visiting professor at the Hochschule für bildende Künste Hamburg. Since October 2023, Verena Issel is a professor of Fine Arts at the BTU (Brandenburgische Technische Universität) Cottbus-Senftenberg. Verena Issel creates installations, sculptures, films, drawings, collages and wall objects. The artist creates sometimes strange, comic, dangerous or humorous-looking, expansive scenarios whose sociopolitical references can develop a haunting seriousness at second glance.
The content of Verena Issel's works varies, but always takes place in the context of relevant contemporary discourses. Her themes, as well as the form and material of her installations, respond precisely to the exhibition environment.

□ *Isa Hänsel*

DE Verena Issel wurde 1982 in München geboren als Tochter eines deutschen Vaters und einer norwegischen Mutter. Nach Jahren in Bergen, Norwegen, studierte Issel Freie Kunst mit Schwerpunkt Rauminstallation und Bildhauerei an der Hochschule für Bildende Künste Hamburg, der China Academy of Art Hangzhou (China) und Faculdade de Belas-Artes Lisboa (Portugal) sowie klassische Philologie (Latein und Altgriechisch) an der Universität Hamburg.
Zahlreiche Reisestipendien und Artist-in-Residence-Programme führten sie unter anderem nach Russland, Taiwan, Südkorea, Japan, Sambia, Mexiko, Iran, Litauen und Papua-Neuguinea. In den letzten Jahren widmeten ihr u. a. die Kunsthalle Mannheim (DE), die Volksbühne Berlin (DE), das ZARYA Center for Contemporary Art (RU), die Trafo Kunsthall (NOR), das Museum Lothar Fischer (DE) sowie der Westfälische Kunstverein/LWL-Museum Münster Einzelpräsentationen.
2019–2021 war Verena Issel Gastprofessorin an der Hochschule für Bildende Künste Hamburg.
Seit Oktober 2023 ist Verena Issel Professorin für Bildende Kunst an der BTU (Brandenburgische Technische Universität) Cottbus-Senftenberg.
Verena Issel schafft Rauminstallationen, Skulpturen, Filme, Zeichnungen, Collagen und Wandobjekte. Die Künstlerin lässt mitunter sonderbar, possierlich, gefährlich oder humorvoll anmutende, raumgreifende Szenarien entstehen, deren gesellschaftspolitische Bezüge auf den zweiten Blick eine eindringliche Ernsthaftigkeit entfalten können.
Die Inhalte von Verena Issels Arbeiten variieren, versammeln sich aber stets im Umfeld relevanter Gegenwartsdiskurse. Ihre Themen, ebenso wie Gestalt und Material ihrer Rauminstallationen, reagieren präzise auf das jeweilige Ausstellungsumfeld.

□ *Isa Hänsel*

Renan Asadov
p. 113 (1)
p. 114/115 (2)
p. 116 (3, 4)

Baur/Bundeskunsthalle
p. 54/55 (3)

Björn Behrens
p. 291 (1)
p. 292/293 (2)
p. 294 (3)
p. 295 (4)
p. 296 (5, 6, 7, 8, 9)

Fred Dott, Hamburg
p. 125 (1)
p. 126/127 (2, 3, 4, 5)
p. 128/129 (6)
p. 147 (1)
p. 148/149 (2)
p. 152 (31, 32, 33, 34, 35, 36, 37, 38, 39, 40, 41, 42, 43, 44)
p. 154 (45)
p. 155 (46, 47, 48)
p. 156 (49)
p. 157 (50, 51, 52, 53, 54)
p. 158 (55)
p. 175 (1)
p. 176/177 (2)
p. 178 (3, 4)
p. 187 (1)
p. 188/189 (2)
p. 190 (3)
p. 191 (4, 5, 6, 7)
p. 192/193 (8, 9, 10, 11, 12, 13, 14, 15, 16, 17, 18, 19, 20, 21, 22, 23, 24, 25, 26, 27, 28, 29, 30, 31)
p. 194/195 (32)
p. 196 (33)
p. 197 (34)
p. 198 (35, 36, 37, 38)
p. 203 (1)
p. 223 (1)
p. 224/225 (2)
p. 226 (3, 4)
p. 231 (1)
p. 232/233 (2)
p. 234 (3, 4, 5, 6)

Carl Gross
p. 401 (1)

Jack Hare
p.137 (1)
p.138 (2)

Yasuyuki Kagi
p. 357 (1)
p. 358 (2)
p. 359 (3)
p. 360 (4)
p. 361 (5, 6, 7)
p. 362 (8, 9, 10)

Jung Hyun Kim
p. 283 (1)
p. 284/285 (2)
p. 286 (3, 4, 5, 6)

Annette Kradisch
p. 371 (1)
p. 372/373 (2)
p. 374 (3)
p. 375 (4, 5, 6)
p. 376 (7, 8)

Marcel Kummrich
p. 34 (15, 16)

Kairon Liu
p. 381 (1)
p. 382/383 (2)
p. 384 (3, 4, 5, 6)
p. 389 (1)
p. 390/391 (2)

Isabel Mahns-Techau
p. 417 (1)
p. 418 (2)

Helge Mundt
p. 52/53 (2)
p. 65 (1)
p. 66/67 (2)
p. 68 (3)
p. 259 (1)
p. 260/261 (2)
p. 262 (3, 4, 5)
p. 263 (6, 7, 8)
p. 264/265 (9)
p. 266 (10)
p. 271 (1)
p. 272/273 (2)
p. 274 (3, 4, 5, 6, 7, 8)
p. 305 (1)
p. 306/307 (2)
p. 308 (3, 4, 5, 6)
p. 309 (7, 8)
p. 312 (11, 12)
p. 321 (1)
p. 322/323 (2)
p. 436 (20)
p. 444 (36, 37)

Hanna Neander
p. 43 (1)
p. 44/45 (2)
p. 46 (3, 4)

Stephanie Neumann
p. 451

Timo Oehlert
p. 204/205 (2)

Andreas Pauly
p. 77 (1)
p. 78/79 (2)
p. 80 (3, 4, 5, 6)
p. 81 (7)
p. 82/83 (8)
p. 84 (9)
p. 85 (10)
p. 86/87 (11)
p. 88 (12, 13, 14, 15)
p. 89 (16)
p. 90 (17)
p. 99 (1)
p. 100/101 (2)
p. 102 (3)
p. 103 (4)
p. 104 (5)
p. 163 (1)
p. 164/165 (2)
p. 166 (3, 4, 5)
p. 430 (12)
p. 431 (13, 14)
p. 432 (15)
p. 433 (16)
p. 438/439 (26)
p. 440 (27, 28, 29)
p. 441 (30, 31, 32, 33)

Andrew Phelps
p. 243 (1)
p. 244/245 (2)
p. 246 (3)
p. 247 (6, 7, 8, 9, 10, 11)

Lukas Pürmayr
p. 211 (1)
p. 212/213 (2)
p. 214 (3, 4, 5)
p. 215 (6, 7, 8)
p. 216/217 (9)
p. 218 (10, 11)
p. 248/249 (13)

LM Rath
p. 51 (1)

Sebastian Reuss
p. 130/131 (7, 8, 9, 10, 11, 12, 13, 14, 15, 16, 17, 18, 19, 20, 21, 22, 23)
p. 132 (24, 25, 26, 27, 28, 29)
p. 402/403 (2)
p. 404 (3)
p. 405 (4, 5, 6, 7, 8, 9, 10)

Marcus Schneider
p. 150/151 (3, 4, 5, 6, 7, 8, 9, 10, 11, 12, 13, 14, 15, 16, 17, 18, 19, 20, 21, 22, 23, 24, 25, 26, 27, 28, 29, 30)
p. 158 (56, 57, 58, 59, 60, 61, 62, 63, 64, 65)
p. 247 (4, 5, 12)
p. 250 (14)
p. 423 (1)
p. 424 (2)
p. 425 (3, 4, 5)
p. 426 (6)
p. 427 (7)
p. 428 (8)
p. 429 (9, 10, 11)
p. 434 (17)
p. 435 (18, 19)
p. 437 (21, 22, 23, 24, 25)

ACKNOWLEDGMENTS

First and foremost

First and foremost, I would like to thank all the people around me who put up with me.

I would like to thank everyone who made this book possible: All the great writers and photographers involved. The fantastic Stiftung Kunstfonds, without whose support this book wouldn't have been possible. Special thanks to my girl, Laura Helena Wurth, for helping me come up with the concept of this colorful thing and finally for the great text that ties it all together!

I can't say thank you enough to all the people who contributed texts and photos to this book. Without your work, no book would have been possible! Please check the imprint to find all the names and links. Each of you is amazing. Thanks so much!

Nothing would look this good without Catrin Roher, who immediately understood the loose sketch of my vision and translated it into graphics, taking it all to another level with her elegance and charm. Nothing would shine like this without Tim Albrecht, who did the lithography as well as some fantastic photography in this book.

I would also like to thank everyone who supports me in my work: Thank you, dear Jan-Philipp Sexauer, for your great faith in my work! It's so cool that you just let me get on with it!

Thanks to the fantastic BTU Cottbus-Senftenberg and the great people there who support me, who let me run around and make art possible, thinkable and learnable. To all of you who are open to new ideas and concepts and who asked for this book: Here it is! Thank you!!!
Thank you for trusting me to be with you! I am looking forward to many colorful years! Special thanks to Gesine Grande, Jo Achermann, Daniela Ehemann, Karen Eisenloffel, Stephan Kaiser, Marko Kliem, Per Pedersen, Bernhard Weyrauch, Volker Wetzk, Diana Zeitschel and of course Marianne Köhler and Marleen Minde!

the biggest thanks go to all the people who accompanied me from an early age and believed that there could be something to this strange tinkering

But perhaps the biggest thanks go to all the people who accompanied me from an early age and believed that there could be something to this strange tinkering:

Andrea Tippel, my first professor: I don't have the right words. Without you, everything would be different. May you rest in peace.

Franz Erhard Walther, who invited me from the hallway of the HFBK, where I always worked because of my smelly art and smelly dog, into his class where I learned art theory and art history like never before. It changed my way of thinking forever.

Pia Stadtbäumer, who finally inspired me formally and aesthetically to new heights: "You can be bolder and more colourful! Don't be afraid!" Thank you, dear Pia!

Big thanks to Michaela Mélian, Fritz Kramer, Gerd Roscher: I enjoyed your classes!

I've had a great friendship since the second semester with Ludwig Seyfarth, who stoically continued to read *Texte zur Kunst* to me on an excursion to St. Petersburg while I was throwing up out of the window after drinking far too much vodka and said, "That's it, let it out, that's how I think about this text as well!" Thanks for all the texts (and drinks) ever since.

Equally important are all the people who have supported me outside of this academy:
I would like to thank all the curators who ever invited me, recommended me, believed in my work and gave me advice. You are the greatest. I won't mention names because it would be too long, but I have you all in my heart and thank you for the trust, the conversations, the advice, the support.

There is one thing I would like to say, not just for myself, but for society in general and on behalf of other artists: One can't say thank you enough to those who are patrons of the arts and who support the making of the art. I'm thinking of all the fantastic institutions that have given me grants, residencies, and scholarships that keep me working.

One can't say thank you enough to those who are patrons of the arts and who support the making of the art.

For me, who does not come from any sort of monetary wealth, this would not have been possible without so much support. I probably wouldn't be an artist, because I couldn't have afforded it.

I would like to thank:

- ☐ Museum Lothar Fischer
- ☐ Stiftung Kunstfonds
- ☐ Pocoapoco, Oaxaca, Mexiko
- ☐ MODZI AIR, Lusaka, Zambia
- ☐ Land Schleswig-Holstein
- ☐ Land Niedersachsen
- ☐ Oslo Kommune
- ☐ The Arctic Circle, Svalbard, Norwegen
- ☐ Senatsverwaltung für Kultur und Europa, Berlin
- ☐ VYKSA AiR, Wyksa, Russland
- ☐ Griffelkunst, Hamburg
- ☐ C.A.P., Kobe, Japan
- ☐ ZARYA, Vladivostok, Russland
- ☐ SeMA NANJI, Seoul, Südkorea
- ☐ Goethe Institut Teheran/Kooshk Teheran, Iran
- ☐ Swatch Art Peace Hotel, Shanghai, China
- ☐ Taipei Artist Village, Taipeh, Taiwan
- ☐ Kulturbehörde der Freien und Hansestadt Hamburg
- ☐ Geumcheon Art Space, Seoul, Südkorea
- ☐ Koganecho Bazaar, Yokohama, Japan
- ☐ KKKC, Klaipeda, Litauen
- ☐ Arthur Boskamp Stiftung M.1., Hohenlockstedt
- ☐ Hamburgische Kulturstiftung
- ☐ DAAD
- ☐ Arbeitsstipendium GSM, Hamburg
- ☐ Künstlerhaus Lauenburg des Landes Schleswig-Holstein
- ☐ Berenberg Bank (Berenberg Preis)
- ☐ Klaus-Kröger-Atelierstipendium, Hamburg
- ☐ Karl H. Dietze-Stiftung, Hamburg
- ☐ Freundeskreis der HFBK Hamburg

Last but not least: Thanks to all my friends, you know who you are anyway.
Without you I would be nothing.

But friends of my art AND me get special thanks:
Carl G., for all the loving, intelligent, critical thinking over so many years.
Thank you. Always in my heart, your voice is often in my ear when I work.

Frankie B., thanks for the best mood, great exhibitions, sculptures, walls, everything.

hahahah!

Carmen S., all those visions and pantaloons and paper experiments: hahahah!
What a pleasure to have you in my life.

!

Simon H., all this thinking about sense and nonsense: MERCI.

Anna R.: Nobody understands my work as well as you do and advises me so well.
You are an elegant witch!
Monique, Dirk, Bettina, Anja: see above, but nevertheless.
Thank you for so many great times.

Juliet K.: So many nice shows because of you and your smart eye and mind.
Can't thank you enough!

Hagen S.: always there and always smart all these years, be it in the hospital or in the galleries.
Thank you.

Helge Mundt: thank you for all the great pictures and the good times!

Siri S.: Du er min beste venn og favoritt kunstner. Selv om du ikke liker det. Hahah.
Gleder meg til homosenteret i Brekke! Ditt største prosjekt. Hehe.

BF: Youuuuuuuuuu! ...

Tusen takk!

MERCI.
Thank
Youuuuuuu!
Tusen takk!

!

Concept/Konzeption .... Verena Issel
Design/Gestaltung .... Catrin Roher
Texts/Texte .... Frank Breker, Uwe Carlson, Bettina von Dziembowski, Tanja Gorges, Isa Hänsel, Anja Heitzer, Alfons Hug, Lee Dong-Uk, Stefanie Sembill, Andrea Tippel, Annette Oechsner, Marianne Wagner, Marc Wellmann, Silvan Wilms, Laura Helena Wurth
Translation/Übersetzung .... Tristan Wheeler, Gérard Goodrow
Copy editing/Lektorat .... Lotta Bartoschewski
Image editing/Lithografie .... Tim Albrecht
Production management/Produktion .... Vinzenz Geppert, DCV
Printing and binding/Gesamtherstellung .... F&W Druck- und Mediencenter GmbH, Kienberg

This publication is listed in the German National Bibliography by the German National Library. Detailed bibliographic data are available at http://dnb.d-nb.de./
Die Deutsche Nationalbibliothek verzeichnet diese Publikation in der Deutschen Nationalbibliografie; detaillierte bibliografische Daten sind im Internet über http://dnb.dnb.de abrufbar.

Distribution and marketing/Vertrieb und Marketing
DCV
sales@dcv-books.com

ISBN 978-3-96912-188-7
Printed in Germany

DCV

Published by/Erschienen bei DCV
www.dcv-books.com

Gefördert von

STIFTUNGKUNSTFONDS

Die Beauftragte der Bundesregierung für Kultur und Medien